Immigration, Integration, and Security

The Security Continuum:
Global Politics in the Modern Age
SERIES EDITORS: *William W. Keller and Simon Reich*
A series published in association with
the Matthew B. Ridgway Center for International Security Studies
and the Ford Institute for Human Security

Immigration, Integration, *and* Security

AMERICA
AND EUROPE IN
COMPARATIVE
PERSPECTIVE

EDITED BY

Ariane Chebel d'Appollonia

AND

Simon Reich

UNIVERSITY OF PITTSBURGH PRESS

Published by the University of Pittsburgh Press, Pittsburgh PA 15260
Copyright © 2008, University of Pittsburgh Press
All rights reserved
Manufactured in the United States of America
Printed on acid-free paper
10 9 8 7 6 5 4 3 2 1
ISBN 13: 978-0-8229-4344-0 (cloth)
ISBN 10: 0-8229-4344-1 (cloth)
ISBN 13: 978-0-8229-5984-7 (paper)
ISBN 10: 0-8229-5984-4 (paper)

Library of Congress Cataloging-in-Publication Data

Immigration, integration, and security : America and Europe in comparative perspective /
edited by Ariane Chebel d'Appollonia and Simon Reich.
        p. cm. — (The security continuum : global politics in the modern age)
    Includes bibliographical references and index.
    ISBN-13: 978-0-8229-4344-0 (cloth : alk. paper)
    ISBN-10: 0-8229-4344-1 (cloth : alk. paper)
    ISBN-13: 978-0-8229-5984-7 (pbk. : alk. paper)
    ISBN-10: 0-8229-5984-4 (pbk. : alk. paper)
    1. European Union countries—Emigration and immigration—Government policy. 2.
United States—Emigration and immigration—Government policy. 3. European Union
countries—Emigration and immigration—Social aspects. 4. United States—Emigration
and immigration—Social aspects. 5. National security—European Union countries. 6.
National security—United States. 7. Terrorism—European Union countries. 8.
Terrorism—United States. I. Chebel d'Appollonia, Ariane. II. Reich, Simon, 1959-
    JV7590.I4866 2008
    325.4—dc22

                                2007049533

Contents

List of Tables and Figures   vii

Preface and Acknowledgments   ix

1. The Securitization of Immigration: Multiple Countries,
    Multiple Dimensions   1
        Ariane Chebel d'Appollonia and Simon Reich

2. Identity Discourse in Western Europe and the United States
    in the Aftermath of 9/11   23
        Ilya Prizel

3. Religious Legacies and the Politics of Multiculturalism:
    A Comparative Analysis of Integration Policies in Western
    Democracies   44
        Michael Minkenberg

4. The Emergence of a Consensus: Global Terrorism, Global
    Insecurity, and Global Security   67
        Didier Bigo

5. European Security and Counter-Terrorism   95
        Jolyon Howorth

6. Immigration Policy and Reactions to Terrorism after
    September 11   111
        Martin Schain

7. Migration and Security: Crime, Terror, and the Politics
    of Order   130
        H. Richard Friman

8.   The Security Myth: Punishing Immigrants in the Name of
     National Security   145
     Jennifer M. Chacón

9.   National Security and Political Asylum   164
     Elena A. Baylis

10. Immigration Enforcement and Federalism after September 11,
     2001   181
     Anil Kalhan

11. Immigration, Security, and Integration in the European Union   203
     Ariane Chebel d'Appollonia

12. Muslims and the State in Western Europe   229
     Jonathan Laurence

13. Dissonance between Discourse and Practice in EU Border
     Control Enforcement: The Spanish Case   254
     Francisco Javier Moreno Fuentes

14. The Challenge to Integration in France   283
     Sylvain Brouard and Vincent Tiberj

15. "Weak Immigrants" in Britain and Italy: Balancing Demands
     for Better Support versus Tougher Constraints   300
     Manlio Cinalli

16. Immigration: Tensions, Dilemmas, and Unresolved Questions   321
     Ariane Chebel d'Appollonia and Simon Reich

     Notes   341
     Bibliography   417
     List of Contributors   461
     Index   465

Tables and Figures

Tables

3.1. Religious diversity in nineteen Western democracies 48
3.2. Levels of cultural integration in Western democracies (1990s) 52
3.3. A typology of immigration and cultural integration policies (1990s) 53
3.4. Religious legacies: Confessions, religiosity, state-church relations, and cultural integration policies 56
3.5. The effects of religious partisanship on cultural integration 59
3.6. The effects of type of democracy and religiosity on cultural integration 60
3.7. Cultural group rights in nineteen democratic nations 65
3.8. Summary of cultural integration and religious and cultural group rights in Western democracies 66
6.1. The perception of immigration from the third world as "good" or "bad," 2002 versus 2005 126
6.2. Responses to the question of whether immigrants are having a good or bad influence on the nation overall 126
6.3. Percentage of French voters motivated by particular issues, by party affiliation, 1984–2004 127
6.4. MORI Political Monitor: The three most important issues facing Britain (2001–2005) 128
6.5. American responses to survey questions about the most important problem currently facing the United States 128
11.1. Population by citizenship groups in the EU 15 209
11.2. Asylum applicants in the EU 15 211
11.3. Net migration in the EU 15 212
11.4. Attitudes toward minorities in Western and Eastern European societies 220

11.5. Attitudes of majorities versus minorities regarding
       immigrants and the law   221
13.1. Foreigners living in Spain by region of origin   257
13.2. Participation in different economic sectors by origin   258
13.3. Evolution of political asylum in Spain, 1986–2006   264
13.4. Political asylum cumulative statistics, 1989–1998   265
13.5. Regularization processes implemented in Spain, 1986–2006   268
13.6. Evolution of attitudes toward migrants in Spain,
       2000–2004   278
14.1. Opinions about integration   287
14.2. Issues selected as being of primary importance by survey
       respondents   288
14.3. Religious affiliations of survey respondents   292
14.4. A comparison of the importance of religion among
       Catholics and Muslims   292
14.5. Typology of French Muslims' involvement in Islam   294
14.6. Religious issues and religious affiliation   296
14.7. Inter-sample comparison of reported feelings of closeness to
       several groups   298

Figures
3.1.   Resistance to multicultural society in the EU 15   62
15.1. Interorganizational cooperation among British pro-
       immigrant groups   310
15.2. Interorganizational disagreement among British pro-
       immigrant groups   311
15.3. Interorganizational cooperation among Italian pro-
       immigrant groups   312
15.4. Interorganizational disagreement among Italian pro-
       immigrant groups   313
15.5. Interorganizational cooperation between British pro-
       immigrant groups and civil society   314
15.6. Interorganizational cooperation between Italian pro-
       immigrant groups and civil society   314
15.7. Vertical links between British pro-immigrant groups and
       policy actors   317
15.8. Vertical links between Italian pro-immigrant groups and
       policy actors   317

Preface and Acknowledgments

The issue of the linkage between immigration, integration, and security has never been more pressing. The authors of this book were asked to address a set of central questions about those links. These questions concerned the sources of policy; the forms of policy; their degree of convergence; and their consequences for both national security and the civil liberties of potential migrants, asylum seekers, and minority populations living in host countries. Coming from a variety of disciplines, perspectives, and countries, the authors often drew starkly contrasting conclusions—outlined in the following pages.

Perhaps predictably, the American debate has had its own peculiar character, even if the policy prescriptions followed were not as unique as Americans often assume. As we compose this preface, the U.S. Senate has just inconclusively debated the greatest reform to American immigration law in the last two decades. Interestingly, while political debate furiously focused on the issues of an amnesty for illegal immigrants and the terms of future migration, the question of security was narrowly defined. The prescription consistently offered was high fences coupled with a scrupulous and avid study of applications from foreigners seeking visas and political asylum. On talk shows and the nightly news, political pundits collectively described these measures in shorthand as "border control." Proponents of this position assume that Americans can be effectively protected in their homeland.

Yet, concurrent with this debate, a man who had contracted a virulent and deadly form of tuberculosis and whom U.S. authorities identified by both name and passport number was able to board two airplanes that took him across Europe and then the Atlantic Ocean. He was then able to rent a car and drive across the U.S. border from Canada without being challenged. Neither American nor European authorities could thwart the movement of a single, identified individual who traveled under his real name and passport and was determined to gain entry into the United States.

While the implications of this episode for the fight against terrorism were noted by some commentators, they did not seem to have much of an impact on the congressional debate about the utility of border controls. Indeed, there seemed relatively little pause for thought about the inadequacy of these security safeguards. The majority of politicians, pundits, and the public apparently maintains faith in the idea that the United States can insulate itself from infiltration by terrorists, despite the failure of this presumptive test of the homeland security system.

European policymakers have certainly been less optimistic about the effectiveness of border control. The expanding and thus ever more porous borders of the European Union have all but the most blinkered of policymakers convinced that patrolling the boundaries of the EU is of symbolic political importance but may ultimately be ineffective. Thousands of illegal immigrants have been intercepted in the Atlantic Ocean and the Mediterranean and Adriatic Seas since 2000. Indeed, sources suggest that more than three thousand people have died at sea in the last several years when EU authorities encountered them trying to enter Spain from North Africa. Even such staggering numbers fail to deter prospective illegal immigrants, let alone terrorists.

In contrast, individual European nations have focused their security efforts primarily on policing at home, based on the fact that "home-grown" terrorists carried out the Madrid and London transit bombings in 2004 and 2005. Using legislation that often dates back to prior encounters with domestic terrorist groups such as the IRA or ETA, European governments have emphasized the importance of domestic intelligence and surveillance. The social control of the radical fringe, coupled with varied efforts by national governments to co-opt the mainstream of Muslim migrant communities, has met with uneven results.

The implications for the civil liberties of prospective migrants and asylum seekers have been significant in both Europe and the United States. While the exigencies of national security and individual rights may be inherently problematic in wartime, the new "war on terror" offers degrees of complexity and nuance that may be historically unparalleled in balancing the relationship between the two. That challenge, however, is further complicated by the presence of large numbers of immigrants from outside "the West" who are already domiciled in these host countries. Does any policy designed to encourage their assimilation engender a greater degree of security? Or do such policies, in fact, create more insecurity because they potentially radicalize a fringe vulnerable to violent prescriptions? Again, the contributors to this volume have explored the problem from differing perspectives and with contrasting conclusions. Predictably, however, one consensus was clear: that the challenges of maintaining the safety of populations and the integrity of borders are not amenable to simple solutions. The need to integrate minority populations is evident; the means and capacity of the United States, the EU, and the national governments of Europe to do so are not.

While the governments of European nations and the United States have failed to coordinate their activities effectively since 2004, this project has been a successful joint transatlantic endeavor in every sense of the word—and for nearly as long. The project was originally conceived as a collaboration between the Ford Institute for Human Security, located at the University of Pittsburgh, and the Center for Political Research (CEVIPOF), located at the Fondation Nationale des Sciences Politiques (Sciences Po) in Paris. As part of the project, two workshops were held at these locations, one in the fall of 2005 and one in the spring of 2006. But, in the course of its duration, the project became a far broader collaboration on both sides of the Atlantic involving more than fifty academics, policymakers, and civil society representatives who engaged in a rich and vigorous debate that can only be partially captured in this volume.

This volume and the working group that produced it were made possible by a generous grant from the Ford Foundation for "The Determinants of Security Policy in the 21st Century" (Grant no. 1050-1036.). We would also like to thank the following institutions for their financial and logistical support: the Graduate School of Public and International Affairs, the University Center for International Studies and the Matthew B. Ridgway Center for International Security Studies at the University of Pittsburgh; and the Center for Political Research (CEVIPOF) and the president's office of Sciences Po in Paris. Individually, we would like to acknowledge the following people for their logistical support and their intellectual contribution to this project from each side of the Atlantic: from Sciences Po we thank its president, Richard Descoings, as well as Didier Bigo, Pascal Perrineau, Philippe Bonditti, and Marcelle Bourbier. From the University of Pittsburgh we thank Provost James Maher, William Keller, and Alberta Sbragia.

A. S. M. Ali Ashraf, Patricia Hermenault, and Sandra Monteverde all played invaluable roles in the preparation of the manuscript, as did Peter Kracht, editor at the University of Pittsburgh Press, as we moved through the process of production.

Finally, this book is dedicated to migrants across the globe—of which the editors of this volume count themselves among the luckier ones.

ARIANE CHEBEL D'APPOLLONIA and SIMON REICH
September 2007

Immigration, Integration, and Security

1

The Securitization of Immigration

Multiple Countries, Multiple Dimensions

ARIANE CHEBEL D'APPOLLONIA AND SIMON REICH

Immigration policy has become a template for some of the key issues facing the West today. It links together what are conventionally regarded as diverse areas of public policy. These areas include national security policies concerning border controls; integration policies regarding assimilation and reciprocal acceptance of cultural rights; urban policies relating to housing and unemployment; and internal security policies linking the safety of societies with the equitable application of political liberties and civil justice. The definition of who constitutes an immigrant and the measures by which citizenship is attained have varied across time and now vary across space—in this case, the countries of the European Union (EU) and the United States.[1] These questions obviously pre-dated 9/11 but have become increasingly complex in the aftermath of the terrorist attacks in the United States and Europe. These attacks re-ignited concerns about the failure of border controls and the need to improve immigrant integration in a context characterized by the blurring of external and internal security. The clustering of these issues means that these countries all face a new challenge in reconciling the requisites of public safety with the foundations of the "open society" upon which political and social relations have been constructed.

While some aspects of the problems highlighted in this book have been more widely studied, including the tension between public safety and the adjudication of civil rights, some aspects are indeed novel and their coalescence is quite original. Countries in a state of war have often resorted to limiting immigration and have suspended or constricted the legal rights of select members of the population (including Japanese Americans and European refugees in the United Kingdom during World War II). Anti-terrorist measures were also adopted before 9/11 in the United States as well as in Europe (at the EU and national levels).[2] But jihadist terrorism threatens public safety in novel ways, particularly because of its nongeographically based membership and operational base, strategy of attacking targets on a global basis, and expressed primary intent to inflict injury to civilians. The novel dimensions of jihadist terrorism coupled with the significant Muslim and Arab populations in the EU and United States have created a series of threats that have rarely, if ever, been aligned. The contributors to this book identify at least four such threats: (1) the threat to national security posed by enlarged borders; (2) the threat to political and civil rights posed by an unprecedented number of noncitizen residents; (3) the threat to racial, ethnic, and religious tolerance in civil societies posed by a potential "enemy inside"; and (4) the threat to the capacities of these countries' economies to generate wealth and redistribute it through effective social policies for second- and third-generation immigrants. These successive generations often remain economically excluded, if not destitute, and are potentially amenable to recruitment by foreign terrorist groups.

The net effect is that while policymakers often resort to rhetoric that labels the enemy as an outsider (such as George W. Bush's preferred label, "Islamic fascists"), we are reminded of the cartoon character Pogo's famous aphorism, "I have seen the enemy, and it is us." In democratic societies, it is only "us" who can constrain our civil liberties and generate both policies and prejudices that can feed the intolerance upon which political extremism grows. Furthermore, it is members of those same polities who have often been recruited to carry out terrorist attacks. They may be doing so for the foreseeable future, if the revelations—and prognosis—of Eliza Manningham-Buller, former head of Britain's MI5, about the growing threat of domestically organized and implemented terrorist attacks in Britain are correct.[3] The consequence of this twofold, interrelated problem—the external threat to security and the simultaneous internal threat to democracy and civil order—is a formidable challenge to the stability of Western states. No book can comprehensively address the multiple dimensions of this issue because the threads are too numerous. But the contributors to this book explore three aspects of this problem, highlighting the policy challenges posed by immigration to border control and public safety, to racial and ethnic relations, and to civil liberties.

In piecing together these issues and contemplating some of the major linkages, the central questions that the contributors were asked to consider were also threefold. The first concerns the historical antecedents of the dilemma posed by terrorism and immigration. For an American audience, the temptation is to assume that the events of 9/11 provided a demarcation point between old and new policy problems. One set of authors attempts to trace trends to before 9/11 in both the United States and Europe in order to assess elements of both continuity and change in the early years of the twenty-first century.

The second question the authors address is the tensions generated by the new constellation of security issues both between and within Western states. In the interregnum period following the demise of the Cold War system, scholars and policymakers searched for an adequate, if temptingly oversimplified, formulation of "the enemy." American policymakers have clung to a traditional conception, attempting to crystallize the new enemy as foreign and geographically situated, in terms of both their rhetoric and their security strategies (e.g., "Islamic fascists" based in Afghanistan, Iraq, Iran, and Lebanon). But the transit bombings in London and Madrid have made it increasingly evident to European policymakers, analysts, and academics that the source of the threat is both transnational and domestic in character. It is diffuse globally, but it also exists within the borders of the EU nations and is growing. This view has often led to differences in policies, with an American focus on the use of military forces and a European emphasis on a mixture of internal policing and co-optation strategies, with the result being a well-documented friction between Europeans and Americans.[4]

The third question inquires about the consequences of the "securitization of immigration policy." Not surprisingly, the answers provided by the authors vary. But the implications are evident. Essentially, if governments choose not to recognize critical situations or fail to rectify them, the current version of the problem poses a historic challenge to both the safety and the liberty of civil society in the EU and the United States. Despite the different policy approaches employed in Europe and the United States, carrying out policies designed to stymie the threat to public safety often involves a selectively targeted erosion of long-standing civil liberties against migrants on both continents. The results are harmful for both legal and illegal migrants, as well as those seeking asylum. In the final chapter of this volume, we attempt to highlight for both scholars and policymakers the lessons derived from the preceding chapters.

Common Issues, Different Policies

While facing similar issues, American and European policymakers have differed in their worldviews over the course of the last decade. Robert Kagan, author of the book *Of Paradise and Power,* is only the most notable among those who criticized European policymakers as being overly reliant on diplomacy rather than material power.[5] Kagan buttressed the view expressed by former U.S. Defense Secretary Donald Rumsfeld that "Old Europe" pursued policies distinct from those of the "New United States" because they no longer shared common interests. Rumsfeld's view was epitomized by the statement that "it is time to stop pretending that Europeans and Americans share a common view of the world, or even that they occupy the same world."[6] According to Kagan, these differences are fundamental: "When it comes to setting national priorities, determining threats, defining challenges, and fashioning and implementing foreign and defense policies, the United States and Europe have parted ways."[7] Timothy Garton Ash, the British historian, gave a vivid summary of this common variant of American anti-Europeanism: "if anti-American Europeans see 'the Americans' as bullying cowboys, anti-European Americans see 'the Europeans' as limp-wristed pansies. The American is a virile, heterosexual male; the European is female, impotent or castrated. . . . The word 'eunuchs' is, I discovered, used in the form 'EUnuchs.'"[8] Tony Judt presents an alternative caricature of European anti-Americanism: "The U.S. is a selfish, individualistic society devoted to commerce, profit, and the despoliation of the planet. . . . The U.S. rides roughshod over laws and treaties and threatens the moral, environmental and physical future of humanity. It is inconsistent and hypocritical in its foreign dealings, and it wields unparalleled military clout. It is, in short, a bull in the global china shop."[9] Rather than simply attacking the United States, responses defending Europe's policies have varied. They range from Jeremy Rifkin's denial of the normative values espoused by people such as Kagan to T. R. Reid's provocative suggestion that "the United States of Europe" will grow to rival the United States of America as a superpower.[10]

It would be easy to view the immigration debate through the same lenses, implying that contrasting policies are based on differing perspectives, but it would be a mistake. The purported transatlantic divide shrinks if we examine the commonalities on this issue. Politicians on both sides of the Atlantic seize upon the images of rioting youths, human and drug traffickers, and terrorists. They do this to generate domestic political support for the securitization of immigration policies, intent as they are on patching holes in the fabric of their civil societies. Their policy prescriptions are somewhat varied but nevertheless predictable: the consistent coercive themes invoked are to secure the borders and to expel or incarcerate illegal, criminal, or suspect migrants. This coercive response is coupled with the demand that those in residence throw off their headscarves, swear allegiance to the governing authority, and accept the values of the postmodern societies in which they now live.

The evidence drawn from this book, however, offers some surprising findings. The first surprise is that the historical origins of the current measures debated and invoked in both Europe and the United States often pre-date the events of 9/11. Commentators and policymakers frequently claim that these measures were a watershed in the treatment of migrants. As contributor Martin Schain's comparative chapter on France, the United Kingdom, and the United States demonstrates, many of the shifts toward securitization were accelerated by these events rather than initiated by them. At the EU level, as demonstrated by Ariane Chebel d'Appollonia's chapter on the EU, the shift to these more security-conscious policies began in the mid-1990s, with the adoption of a series of counter-terrorism measures by the EU's Justice and Home Affairs (JHA) Council.

The second surprising finding is that there is neither an overall pattern of policy convergence nor diffusion in Western countries. The variants are more subtle, the areas of respective convergence or diffusion more compelling. While there is evidence of the divergence in both immigration and integration policies between Europe and the United States that commentators such as Kagan would anticipate, there is both a notable degree of policy convergence between some European states and the United States. There is also an unanticipated degree of divergence among the countries of Europe despite the adoption of common EU regulations. The convergence is most evident in the largely uniform process of the securitization of immigration. However, in contrast to conventional notions about a "clash of civilizations," Michael Minkenberg's findings suggest that there is no coherent "West," based on religious doctrine, when it comes to immigration policy. Catholic countries have some proclivities, Protestant countries have others. But there are no discernible common patterns. Yet this finding of policy divergence is challenged elsewhere in the volume. Schain's chapter, for example, provides evidence that the security measures invoked as new and original by the United States after 9/11 owe much to the experience of their European counterparts.

The third point is perhaps the most disconcerting: immigration policies often produce paradoxical and unforeseen consequences on both sides of the Atlantic. Although the possible combinations of rules in immigration, integration, and security policies seem unlimited, some results seem common—and counterproductive. Migrant populations feel themselves to be under siege. They remain abject about what they perceive as racial profiling and are often subject to a xenophobic and racist backlash as they struggle to reconcile their traditions with the expectations of their host societies.[11] They frequently suffer a loss of civil and political rights as well as increased alienation, even as they demand greater sensitivity and tolerance toward their cultural and religious differences. The product of this process is often the heightening of racial and religious tensions, unmet demands for greater participation in governmental processes and economic opportunities available to other citizens and residents, and a greater susceptibility to the radicalism that these governments claim to oppose.[12] For example, Jack Straw, then leader of the House of Commons, called for Muslim women in Britain to discard their niqabs (the veils they wear to cover their faces) in October 2006. The public debate that followed "unleashed a storm of prejudice and intensified division," according to one commentator.[13] His call for assimilation therefore had quite the opposite effect. In sum, the history, diversity, and unforeseen consequences of choices play a far greater role in the current dominant policy than political rhetoric might suggest.

Areas of Debate

The contributors to this book, drawn from both sides of the Atlantic and across multiple disciplines, find much to agree about and just as much to disagree about. Essentially, they collectively identify four key areas of debate.

The first concerns the different character of the narrative adopted both on the western side of the Atlantic and within Europe. The authors address the issue of whether responses to the immigration/security debate are functional and proportionate as well as if they are consistent with traditions of human rights and civil liberties. The authors find much to debate about these normative issues. Although this debate extends throughout the book, we point to one notable voice. Ilya Prizel highlights the differing metanarratives between Europe and the United States. He contrasts a more functional and coherent American sense of identity with a European moral relativism that has been thrown into crisis by the debate on immigration and security. Prizel's relatively benign interpretation of the American position contrasts, however, with that offered by Didier Bigo. Bigo contrasts the American narrative that characterized 9/11 as an act of war with the European one that treated the bombings in much of Europe as criminal acts. This difference in framing, he suggests, had startlingly different results. The product of the former was war in Afghanistan and Iraq; the product of the latter was greater policing and tighter surveillance. Similarly, the chapter by Jennifer Chacón demonstrates how the framing of the new "national security myth" has linked terrorism and security in a new method of law enforcement.

The second thematic debate that runs through the book concerns reliance on the policies of border control and the filtering and surveillance of immigrants as security techniques. Clearly, the United States has opted for a greater reliance on border control than have its European counterparts, who have invested more in filtering and surveillance. While the overall propensities might be clear, however, the balance is contested. Some authors, for example, point to greater U.S. efforts at internal surveillance (Anil Kalhan) while others point to the EU's efforts to stop potential immigrants at the border (Francisco Javier Moreno Fuentes).

A third area of disagreement concerns the likelihood of cooperation across and within states. While it is tempting to assume a greater degree of cooperation among the governments of the EU, for example, some authors point to the problematic normative and structural constraints of various countries' efforts to do so. Jolyon Howorth is notable for sketching out such limitations in the context of EU security policy. Yet Kalhan points to the tensions that exist regarding such efforts within the United States between various levels of government.

The fourth and final area of debate reveals no common position on the prospects for the successful integration of new immigrants. The prototypical view is that the American "melting pot" model more readily accommodates new immigrants than the variety of European models (such as assimilation or multiculturalism) that have been characterized as failures for leaving an alienated migrant population with a potentially radicalized fringe. Yet the contributors' case studies of Europe paint quite a varied picture. Jonathan Laurence's discussion of the integration of Muslims in France suggests active measures to create new institutions of representation that offer grounds for optimism. Likewise, Moreno Fuentes's chapter on Spain depicts a responsive state apparatus— all the more unanticipated in the aftermath of the Madrid transit bombings. Yet this relatively "optimistic" characterization contrasts with other chapters that offer a less than sanguine view of the prospects for immigrant integration. Sylvain Brouard and Vincent Tiberj, for example, note the high degree of suspicion felt by large sections of the French population toward Muslim immigrants and their native-born children. This discomfort has, ironically, reached the point where the immigrant community is more optimistic about its capacity to integrate than is the general population. Correspondingly, Manlio Cinalli's chapter comparing Britain and Italy portrays two countries where, in both cases, governments have proven reluctant to recognize claims made by weak elements in the pool of immigrants and asylum seekers.

Major Findings

The contested areas are therefore both theoretical and empirical in character. Yet there are, nonetheless, five major identifiable findings in the project that formed the basis for this book.

The first finding of this study is that both the EU and the United States introduced measures in the policy areas of counter-terrorism, immigration, and asylum seekers well before the events of 9/11. The implications of this finding may be more meaningful for an American audience, fed on a daily dose of news that suggests that the "world turned" on that date. The rhetoric of the war on terror sparked new military offensives in Afghanistan and Iraq. But understanding that the 9/11 attacks, together with the London and Madrid transit bombings, increased the momentum of provisions in these other areas, rather than marking a shift in direction, may be a key component in assessing the motives behind these measures as well as their consequences. Arguably, these sad events may have helped consolidate changes sought by policymakers on both continents rather than requiring them to embark on a wrenching shift in policy.

The second finding is related: measures to tighten border controls on both sides of the Atlantic clearly pre-dated the same series of events. American concern about illegal migrants and the "war on drugs"—in the context of the growing trade engendered by the North American Free Trade Agreement (NAFTA)—had already generated the political pressures needed to lobby effectively for a shift in resources. Governmental concerns about criminality and population flows, often fomented by the media and growing disquiet in public opinion surveys, led to the same in Europe. On both continents, however, this shift in policy focus (and the accompanying resources) was to the detriment of efforts to integrate already domiciled immigrants through economic and social policies. Keeping more immigrants out therefore took precedence over effectively incorporating those who had arrived (in the context of scarce resources) on both continents.

Third, we have previously noted that the shift toward initiatives regarding terrorism, immigration, and asylum seekers pre-dated the terrorist attacks of 9/11. Yet these attacks had a similar impact on both sides of the Atlantic in terms of consolidating the shift toward linking immigration with security. Immigration became part of a war in the United States, just as poverty and drugs had under prior presidential administrations. In Europe and the United States, immigration was no longer primarily an economic or cultural issue about the safety of vulnerable domestic populations. The immigration issue now had long tentacles that reached into a variety of policy domains.

We have identified two areas of divergence that are just as worthy of note. The first was the most obvious: the American focus on the external enemy—through wars in Afghanistan and Iraq and the support of regimes, such as Pakistan's, that are engaged in the conflict with Al Qaeda—justified by the U.S. claim that it preferred to fight the enemy abroad rather than at home. This focus is in direct contrast to the European preference for focusing on the "enemy within," in which the EU did not view limiting immigration as a means of preventing terrorism at home. One of the attendant consequences of this approach, however, may have been both a heightened xenophobia among the general population as well as the further alienation and isolation of the minority populations within these countries.

The second area of divergence was in the substance and process of counter-terrorism policies. Indeed, the differences were clear early on but may have proliferated after 9/11, both between the EU and the United States and among the EU member nations. European national governments, in differing national contexts, pursued contrasting policies with regard to their use of sur-veillance techniques to collect data, conduct espionage, and infiltrate groups in their own societies. European governments disagree with U.S. authorities on several issues, such as the death penalty (which limits the enforcement of the agreement on extradition concluded in 2003 between the EU and the United States), the protection of fair trial rights in criminal proceedings, and the jurisdiction and role of international courts.

Connecting the Dots and Analyzing the Arguments

Arguably, the relationship between immigration, integration, and security has never been so complex nor its linkages as poorly understood. It connects the issues of terrorism, rendition, and torture to that of human rights. It associ-ates security policies with policies dealing with urban issues and against dis-crimination. It links the governments of countries spanning Europe with the U.S. government as they face both common and disparate challenges. If un-addressed, this conundrum forms the basis for the shredding of the cloth that weaves societies together, resulting in urban violence and terrorist attacks. It is not preposterous to suggest that governments have never faced the type of challenge posed by the novel relationship between human flows, demograph-ic aging, domestic stability, economic abundance, external and internal secu-rity, and civil rights. The dynamics of these relationships, and the consequences of the policy choices made in the aftermath of 9/11, are ex-plored in the pages that follow.

The book is conceptually organized to cover four areas of interest, proceeding from more conceptual questions about coherence and fissure in the West to the concrete policy challenges that the securitization of immigration poses for governments, individuals, and the societies in which they live. The first two chapters consider the cultural, intellectual, and religious foundations of the EU and the United States. The next three chapters are devoted to the evolution of emergent security frameworks and their implications for regional and national policymakers. Four chapters then examine questions about the regional and national administration of immigration policies, and their implications for the integration of migrants, in the United States. Five chapters then do the same for migrants in the European Union.

The authors of the first two chapters—Ilya Prizel and Michael Minkenberg—consider the question of whether there is a "West" from two perspectives. Prizel writes from a philosophical perspective, whereas Minkenberg examines empirically whether there is a homogeneous view reflected in the relationship between the dominant religious practices in a country and policies regarding immigration and integration. The former suggests a clear transatlantic divide and the latter, a far greater degree of fragmentation.

Prizel examines how the constitution of identity unites and divides the countries of the EU from the United States. Tracing their differing historical lineages, Prizel focuses on how a European conception of identity was formulated and reconstituted in the second half of the twentieth century. He sees three stages in that process: postwar amnesia, thus avoiding the guilt for having collaborated with Nazi Germany; a post-1968 rejection of identity politics and the concept of a metanarrative; and a subsequent guilt-ridden response to the trauma of imperialism. The aggregate intellectual effect of all three was to exclude notions of both ethnicity and religion from public discourses about identity. The practical effect was either to welcome immigrants, even if their cultural proclivities and economic interests could not be accommodated, or to ignore their presence on the pretext that their stay would be temporary.

Prizel suggests that the ambivalence of that process, coupled with the terrorist attacks in London, New York, and Madrid (and with the murder of Theo van Gogh in the Netherlands), has left European policymakers and scholars with a quandary. It forces them to figure out how to accommodate the demands of immigrants and new citizens while mounting an effective resistance to external security challenges posed by jihadists. The political left, in crisis, has—Prizel contends—responded in multiple ways but notably often by retreating from notions of multiculturalism and "moral relativism." The right has withdrawn from a pan-Europeanism to a decidedly "Christian" definition of Europe.

Prizel is more optimistic about both the durability and the efficacy of America's "metanarrative." While there have been several stages of evolution, its Anglo-Saxon Protestant creed has endured. Paradoxically, this creed has historically made it not only more accommodating to immigration, because of its multicultural proclivities (at least in terms of a variety of European cultures) but also currently more responsive to and better placed to now accommodate immigrants, many of whom may no longer originate from Europe. But these immigrants are overwhelmingly Christians (predominantly from Central and Latin America). Indeed, the current messianic and evangelical character of American Christianity means that migrants are not only accepted but also aggressively sought in order to bolster the membership of religious communities. While the events of 9/11 created a fissure between American and European practice, they did little to interrupt (and indeed Prizel claims they may have galvanized) that spirit in regard to the export of capitalism and democracy and the import of immigrants receptive to the "Word." Although this reading supports the notion that there is a "right" immigrant and a "wrong" one, Prizel's conclusion is that the overall environment for immigration is far more hospitable in the United States than in the EU.

If Prizel finds a transatlantic fissure that confounds notions of a Western civilization, Minkenberg's assessment in his chapter on the relationship between religion and both integration and immigration policies suggests both fracture and fragmentation. Examining nineteen Christian, democratic European, and "settler" countries (such as Canada, Australia, and New Zealand), Minkenberg examines how religion has shaped integration policies in Western democracies. He does so with regard to both the religious legacies of the host countries and the (predominantly Muslim) religion of immigrant groups. Dating his analysis from the early 1990s, Minkenberg demonstrates that cultural legacies such as Christian denominations, in combination with more political factors such as the role of religious parties, play an important role in shaping a country's readiness to accommodate non-Christian immigrant groups. He demonstrates three important findings: that there is enormous variation in policies across what might appear superficially similar cases; that these variations are steeped in long-term historical choices; and that therefore the effects of 9/11 can be demonstrated only at the level of the mass public rather than at the policy level—with few signs, therefore, of policy convergence.

The next group of chapters examines the historical, conceptual, and policy dimensions and dynamics of the new security environment as well as its impact on migrants in the light of recent changes. Didier Bigo lays out the shifting contours of the new security environment, how it has been defined, by whom, and for what purpose. Jolyon Howorth outlines the problems besetting the EU and United States as they attempt to share intelligence in a context where their understandings of the problem are fundamentally different. Martin Schain evaluates the regulation of the changing security environment by comparing national policies regarding terrorism in the United States and Europe, both synchronically and diachronically.

Bigo's chapter opens this section by examining changes in the definition of security after September 11 and the subsequent transit bombings in Madrid and London. He explains how these shifts have helped frame the debates about the primary form of the new threat, who constitutes the enemy, which forms of violence are considered legitimate, and what the most appropriate policy responses might be. He demonstrates that the scope, domain, and primacy of the new war on terror have been contested. Ultimately, however, the paramount political needs of the most powerful states are to show that they can respond effectively in a "crisis" and that they can assert a continued element of sovereignty.

Bigo's analysis identifies three key components in the emergence of a new security framework designed to achieve these goals. One is the claim that terrorism is the primary threat and that it has redefined the scope and domain of conflict. Simultaneously, the proponents of the new security framework have modified the geographic frame of reference for violence from the national or regional to the global or transnational—necessitating a global response. The threat of a terrorist attack exists everywhere, but tighter and more numerous border controls coupled with global preventative measures are a means to enhance domestic security.

According to Bigo, new threats also require a new, broader definition of the enemy in order to generate a shared interest—and subsequently a new security order. Global terrorism is carried out not only by Al Qaeda but also by a variety of associated groups and sympathizers. The new enemy thus extends beyond rogue states to include individuals. Everyone is potentially suspect, although profiling narrows the pool. While the new terrorism is therefore global, the enemy may be local. The lines between external and internal security have thus been obliterated.

Finally, Bigo argues, the new dynamics require an attendant new linkage between security and freedom. Instead of defining freedom conventionally in terms of civil and political liberties, which conflict with new security measures that extend to surveillance and regulation at the local level, Bigo suggests that freedom has been redefined by some proponents as "safety." He thus implies that the two concepts of freedom are not only reconcilable but, indeed, complementary.

Having successfully framed the new security conundrum in this manner is key to understanding the dilemmas faced by immigrant populations. The U.S. and EU member governments portray these populations to an increasingly receptive domestic audience as pools from which are likely drawn potential perpetrators of illegitimate violence. Recognizing the "new reality" created by this depiction, the remainder of this chapter examines the varied dynamics created for the processes of both immigration and integration in America and Europe, respectively.

Rather than emphasizing the overall trends, Jolyon Howorth examines specific areas of security policy and highlights the areas of disagreement between the EU and the United States and their policy implications for effective cooperation and burden-sharing in the realm of intelligence. America and Europe, he argues, adopted different strategic approaches in attempting to find both a suitable response to the short-term threat of terrorist attacks and a long-term set of policies designed to address the causes of terrorism. The United States made the short-term threat its policy priority, while European policymakers emphasized a long-term focus on the latter.

Howorth argues that the two sides differ over both their assessment of the threat posed by modern terrorism and its differences from earlier forms of terrorism. Europeans see the modern threat as a continuation of the more traditional nationalist threats (at least operationally) while their American counterparts consider it a "global war" involving states as well as transnational movements. The United States has centralized its anti-terrorist operations while the structure of the EU constrains such activities. Perhaps not surprisingly, the United States has focused on measures involving the use of military hardware while their European counterparts have tended to invoke "softer" approaches, with a special concern for the importance of international law. The American debate over the use of torture only serves to highlight Howorth's point in that regard. Despite the array of cooperative security agreements instituted between the United States and EU since 9/11, Howorth concludes that serious structural and normative differences still exist, undermining the ability of the two sides to cooperate effectively.

Martin Schain's chapter focuses on the linkage between anti-terrorism policy (both the legislative creation and administrative application of extralegal powers) and immigration at the level of national governments in Britain, France, and the United States. Examining the legislative process in all three nations both before and after 9/11, Schain argues that the more recent reactions to terrorism have been shaped by long-term historical responses and the comparable historical relationships between terrorism and immigration policy.

Schain notes that the effect of policy in all three countries post-9/11 has been to compromise civil liberties through the expansion of security measures. Furthermore, in all three countries, despite these measures, immigration policy has become more expansive even as the security focus on immigrant populations has grown. "Thus, increasingly," Schain suggests, "anti-terrorism actions are also actions that inevitably implicate immigrant populations." He concludes that the European countries have converged in their concerns about terrorism, while the United States has changed the most in this regard through the use of executive powers. The greatest areas of convergence have been the surveillance of and actions taken against immigrant populations. In Europe, immigration has thus perhaps been replaced by integration as a central security issue.

Subsequent chapters of the book are area specific, examining aspects of immigration and integration in the United States and Europe, respectively. Four chapters are devoted to the United States. One focuses on the linkage between criminality, terrorism, and migration, and three examine aspects of the legal and administrative consequences of linking security and immigration within the context of the United States' federalized democratic polity.

H. Richard Friman's chapter focuses on how immigration policy has intersected with security policy in the United States since 9/11. He scrutinizes changes in the rules of entry and in the operation of administrative regulations as applied to immigrants regarding arrest and deportation. Importantly, Friman points out that "immigration" as a term has been used loosely, having been linked to legal permanent residents and individuals in a variety of situations, including persons who overstay their visas or gain entry illegally. In discussing the linkage between security and immigration, he notes that there is a similar lack of distinction between criminals and terrorists.

Friman identifies two long-term trends in American policy. The first is that the effort to make immigration a security issue is not a new phenomenon in the United States. He employs Barry Buzan, Ole Wæver, and Jaap de Wilde's definition of securitization as something that constitutes "an existential threat requiring emergency measures and justifying actions outside the normal bounds of political procedure."[14] American policymakers employed rhetoric positing such "existential" threats two centuries ago. Friman notes, however, that the debate over the rights of migrants has a more recent vintage, originating with the wave of new arrivals that occurred in the 1960s, and has resulted in lobbying, legislative initiatives, and judicial rulings.

Yet it was not until the 1980s, Friman suggests, that a watershed event occurred: the Immigration and Nationality Act was rewritten to incorporate a slew of amendments. These new features resulted from an expansion of justifications for state preventative measures to incorporate a new class of aggravated felony offenses. Detailing the ways in which this process continued through the 1990s, he outlines ways by which the categories and processes have expanded in the aftermath of 9/11. Friman remains agnostic about the security benefits derived from a subsequent expansion of the categories.

The three chapters following Friman's examine the consequences of post-9/11 changes in the security environment for immigrants to the United States. They analyze these consequences in terms of the rights and responsibilities of states and municipalities in the United States' federalized system; the civil and political rights of migrants both as entrants and in domicile; and the identification of refugees or asylum seekers as a distinct subgroup of migrants.

Jennifer Chacón's chapter both mirrors and complements Friman's. Friman examines how the external environment has shaped the substance of regulations regarding the entry and domicile of migrants. Chacón focuses on how the new "national security myth" has added terrorism to the traditional concern about crime control in regard to immigrants, leading to "more vigorous law enforcement." Potentially effective options for reform were passed over in favor of consolidating many of the immigration administrative institutions within the Department of Homeland Security.

These measures, Chacón argues, were buttressed by a rhetoric that emphasized the importance of national security and thus insulated the department from the constitutional constraints that would have applied had these measures been considered part of the criminal justice system. She then details how recent legislative changes have converted aspects of immigration enforcement into parts of crime control and how the bureaucracy charged with immigration enforcement has assumed newly expanded powers since 2001. The legal implications that these enhanced powers have for the civil and political rights of migrants, she argues, are both significant and deleterious for a large and growing section of the American population.

In her chapter on asylum policy in the United States and Europe, Elena A. Baylis points out that the United States has had a historic commitment to honoring the legitimate applications of asylum seekers as an instrument of foreign policy. This obligation was, prior to 9/11, consistent in substance with the principles of international law, the United States having generally been responsive to the needs of political refugees.

This long tradition of accepting refugees from hostile countries changed in the aftermath of 9/11, as the primary source of asylum seekers has shifted from the communist bloc to failed states with large Muslim populations. Instead of accepting them because it served the United States' geostrategic interests, the United States has adopted a new position. This new stance prioritizes a vision of national security built on the notion that the nation needs to insulate itself against the possibility that a terrorist posing as an asylum seeker may apply for entrance to the United States. The new American vision of national security is therefore buttressed by anecdotes claiming that the asylum system is a means by which terrorists enter the United States. This vision persists even though, as Baylis notes, none of the September 11 attackers, all of whom had entered the United States legally, arrived through the asylum system.

In practice, Baylis argues, these new limitations on asylum were introduced in 1993 and thus pre-dated the events of 9/11. They have been generated and implemented incrementally, often spurred by unrelated domestic events (such as the Oklahoma City bombing) rather than by jihadism. These measures now allow the United States to refuse asylum to those who have unwittingly assisted terrorist groups or did so only as a result of coercion. Furthermore, it raises the standard of proof required of applicants, including the need to provide more exacting corroborating evidence. Baylis contends that the effects of the additional "sweeping breadth" of the provisions introduced since 2001—notably the PATRIOT Act of 2001 and REAL ID Act of 2005—have been extensive and severe. Baylis notes that this development is in sharp contrast, explicitly and empirically, to measures applied to those seeking asylum in the EU.

Furthermore, Baylis concludes that the new rules governing asylum applications now place the United States in conflict with its own international legal obligations; with the rationale for, and practice of, asylum law by the EU itself and in (at least part of) Europe by national governments; and with the institutional precedent of evidence and the principles of administrative law on which the United States' own asylum system was historically built. Baylis argues that all of these new security-conscious rules do little to enhance American security.

Anil Kalhan's chapter addresses a further dimension of the legal and political conundrum generated by the new security threat. The tension within Europe over immigration and internal security generally plays itself out between the governance structures of the EU and national governments. National policies often contradict EU directives. In the American federalized system, this problem is most evident in the federal government's attempts to employ the apparatus of state and local government in the enforcement of new security measures because of the constitutional division of powers.

The integration of the Immigration and Naturalization Service (INS) into the Department of Homeland Security has been accompanied by the federal government's attempt to expand its regulatory powers. These initiatives include efforts to mandate that states (on an unfunded basis) monitor the activities of immigrants and report them to federal agencies and that they enforce federal laws. The police, highway patrol, corrections officials, and even welfare agencies, educational institutions, and hospitals have been asked to collect data on immigrants, deny services, or report suspected illegal or suspicious immigrants to federal agencies. Such activities may potentially usurp the legal powers of subnational authorities or even contradict state and local laws regarding civil liberties, the right to privacy, or the jurisdictional authority of state and local governments.

Kalhan's examination points to the clear dangers in the expansion of federal powers to make immigration status and unlawful presence a routine issue. These dangers include the legal and illegal migrant communities' increased distrust of and alienation from all levels of government; their concomitant reluctance to engage those authorities by reporting illicit or suspicious behavior; the enhancement of racial and national profiling; and an abrogation of both civil liberties and jurisdictional authority—all without a demonstrable enhancement of security.

Five contributors examine comparable problems of security, immigration, and integration in Western Europe. Their approaches range from a cross-national analysis of the linkage between migration and security in several European countries to a detailed analysis of the attitudes of both the general public and the immigrant community in the aftermath of the French riots of November 2005.

Ariane Chebel d'Appollonia scrutinizes both the way in which the EU has linked immigration and security and the discriminatory impact of EU policies. Analyzing the shift toward the "Europeanization" of national policies through the mechanisms of the EU, she suggests that the construction of immigration as a security issue took place in three stages. Each stage contributed to the developing notion of immigration as a security threat. From the mid-1970s to the mid-1980s, immigrants were both depicted and perceived as posing a threat to the job security of natives. As a result, the main objective was to limit the number of "newcomers," even among countries with differing immigration histories. Unable to curb illegal immigration and asylum applications, EU member states gradually moved away from unilateral national policies toward intergovernmental cooperation. This second stage, dating from the mid-1980s, was marked by a growth in prejudicial attitudes and discriminatory practices by anti-migrant groups who accused them of perverting national identity and threatening social cohesion. This period was notable for the signing of the Schengen Agreement and the introduction of new restrictive immigration measures designed to support the development of a single EU market.

Since the mid-1990s, the situation has become more complex. The Area of Freedom, Security, and Justice (AFSJ) under EU law has combined the former immigration and asylum policies with both the old security issues and the new humanitarian measures; these measures were intended to balance the exclusionary effects of the so-called "Fortress Europe." As a result, a long-standing commitment of the EU to support the equal treatment of all residents was strengthened by the adoption of two major anti-discrimination directives in 2000. However, the success of the EU's fight against discrimination and xenophobia has been limited, largely by the reluctance of its members to implement the provisions that were intended to assist in the integration of minority groups.

Furthermore, both the EU and its member states adopted additional counter-terrorism measures in the aftermath of the terrorist attacks in New York, London, and Madrid. Chebel d'Appollonia argues that these security measures not only fail to address the issue of internal security but also threaten human rights and civil liberties in Europe. European countries are so obsessed with border controls that they neglect to address critical issues designed to assist in the social integration of immigrants and minority groups. European governments still emphasize the external dimension of terrorism by using border controls and restrictive asylum policies as a way to improve their internal security. They continue on this path despite strong evidence—those who committed the London and Madrid transit bombings were mainly nationals—that the failure of integration is the main root of political radicalization and terrorist violence. As a result, there is a gap between rhetoric and action in both EU and national policies in this area. Governments argue against prejudice and discrimination but, through their security policies, encourage both. This gap is expected to last as long as European governments refuse to acknowledge past policy failures and remain reluctant to address the deep-seated social malaise from which their nations suffer.

Among the authors of these chapters on Europe, Jonathan Laurence perhaps strikes the most optimistic note. He rejects the proposition that authority for integration policy has moved either up to the EU or down to subnational actors. On that basis, Laurence compares and contrasts the efforts of a number of European states—including Belgium, France, Germany, Italy, and the United Kingdom—to incorporate the official religious organs of the Muslim religion into the broader state apparatus. The goals, he suggests, are to achieve interreligious dialogue, some degree of representation for the Muslim community within the democratic process, and integration of Muslims into a broader political and social milieu.

Laurence's chapter therefore examines how different national interior ministers have sought to manage the "transnational threat" posed by Muslim extremism, given the incapacity of political parties and the apparent inability of the education system in these countries to do so. He contends that states in these countries are engaged in a process of effectively incorporating Islam into pre-existing institutional state-church relations. This process, he suggests, has involved the prioritization of national law over religious texts and the separation of church and state. The effects have been to guarantee equal access to the exercise of religion, to establish principles of transparency, and to integrate religious representatives through the establishment of councils.

While these bodies cannot legitimately claim to represent each Muslim, they have assisted in a steady movement toward molding these communities into coherent, homogeneously organized units—comparable to the process successfully undertaken by other religions. The benefits of such efforts are tangible, claims Laurence. This process constitutes, he says, an important step toward both the construction of "political opportunity structures" and the reconciliation of Islam with the values of liberal democracy. The result has been a measure of success, with disputes such as those over the Danish cartoons of the prophet Mohammed being handled lawfully and peaceably where national religious organs have been more fully developed in Europe.

Francisco Javier Moreno Fuentes examines the case of Spain. Spanish authorities have been confronted with a series of major challenges as the country shifted from being a traditional country of emigration to one of immigration. Indeed, the influx of foreigners, notably from Eastern Europe, Latin America, and North Africa, has been unprecedented in scale, particularly since the turn of the twenty-first century, with census data suggesting the number has more than doubled in that period to more than four million.

At its closest border point, Spain is only a few miles from Morocco, constituting the world's two most proximate countries with the biggest disparity in wealth. Added to the problem of this influx is the tension created between the relatively liberal immigration policies that have been instituted by successive Spanish governments since the 1990s and the impetus of the EU's policy directives. Spanish governments have implemented measures designed to legitimate undocumented immigrants, signed bilateral agreements with many sending countries, and extended economic and social rights to new immigrants. EU directives, meanwhile, have moved in the opposite direction, with measures designed to provide disincentives for migrants, regulate immigration flows, harmonize policies on asylum and family reunification, and introduce stricter border controls. Most Spanish policy since 1991 has therefore stood in contrast to the thrust of the EU's efforts, and Spain has had to adapt to these new initiatives. The result has been a steadily shrinking sphere of autonomy and flexibility for Spanish authorities as they attempt to comply with an increasing number of EU rules and to address other member states' concerns that Spain is a gateway for entry into "Schengenland." Moreno Fuentes contends that Spain has been forced to become "the guardian of the EU's southern border."

Complicating the Spanish position further are the multiple security complexities engendered by the Madrid transit bombings of March 2004. The attack served to enhance the anxieties of a domestic population already alarmed by the large and growing North African population living in the ostensibly Catholic country. As Moreno Fuentes points out, in the aftermath of the Madrid bombings, opportunistic right-wing politicians amplified xenophobic prejudices among nationals who already feared that these foreigners were the source of increased criminality. Yet opinion surveys suggest that the Spanish public was able to dissociate immigrants from militants, even as they expressed their dislike of—and cultural distance from—North Africans. Nonetheless, individual racist incidents, coupled with a greater focus on vigilance against a recurrence of any terrorist attacks, have left the Spanish government with a major task. While staying focused on security, it must integrate a segment of the migrant population that is both culturally isolated and remains heavily concentrated in low-paying jobs in the agricultural, construction, and service sectors of the "gray" economy.

Sylvain Brouard and Vincent Tiberj consider how the French urban riots of 2005 tested the French integrationist model. Their central question is whether Islam, French identity, and the French mainstream can be reconciled. After conducting an unprecedented survey of public opinion in both the immigrant community and among the broader French public, Brouard and Tiberj offer interesting findings that both confirm and confound conventions.

Predictably, their work reveals that immigrants and the general French population are divided on the issue of responsibility for the failure of integration. A significant majority of immigrants focus on general conditions in explaining the problems they encounter with integration, while nearly half (48 percent) of the French population blames the migrants themselves for their lack of integration. About the same number, drawn from the general population, states that there are too many immigrants in France.

Approximately half of immigrants (49 percent) believe that anyone can succeed in France, regardless of their skin color. Forty-one percent think that they can easily integrate—a significantly higher proportion than the general population (33 percent). It is clearly disturbing to find that the majority of the immigrant population are so disillusioned that they think that they can neither integrate nor achieve success in their adopted country. It is perhaps worse to

discover that the general population is even less sanguine. Yet, more optimisti-
cally, only approximately one in four of both the migrant community *and* the
general community believes that the problem of integration of the immigrants
will worsen in the next few years. In addition, the majority feel that sustaining
cultural identity and French national identity is complementary.

In analyzing the results, Brouard and Tiberj classify the French respondents as being part of three groups: a plurality who are the more conservative-
minded assimilationists (46 percent), a minority (36 percent) they characterize
as Republicans, and a single-digit group comprising the more liberal multiculturalists (8 percent).

Their findings provide a disturbing picture of a French electorate that is
intransigent and relatively intolerant on issues of integration toward the most
populous Muslim immigrant community in Europe (although they note that
many of these Muslims do not practice their religion).

Finally, Manlio Cinalli considers the question of what marginalized immigrant populations, with few rights, can do to help themselves. Employing a
network analysis, Cinalli examines the cases of asylum seekers in Britain and
undocumented illegal workers in Italy. He documents how pro-immigrant
movements and formal organizations have pursued campaigns through legitimate channels on behalf of those themselves excluded, in both countries,
from the political process. He suggests that the different network patterns in
the two countries account for the main differences in their success in having
their demands incorporated into the political agenda.

Aspects of immigration and security have become synonymous in Europe and
the United States since 2001. There is a temptation to link them through the
singular dimension of border control. This book seeks to expand our understanding of the problem in the search for a better comprehension of causative
linkages and for possible policy solutions. It therefore connects security policy to many facets of domestic policy—which are often not thought of or characterized as being in the same realm—by incorporating the concept of
integration as a third component in the analysis. The London and Madrid
transit bombings provide strong evidence that while border control may be
indispensable as a policy tool, finding ways to reconcile differing communities complements these efforts in the battle against transnational terrorism.

American policymakers have ignored this dimension of the problem, assuming that the historic capacity of the United States to integrate waves of
immigrants will address the problem and that enhanced policing will take care
of those external enemies who slip through the net designed to catch them
prior to entry. The very possibility of second- or third-generation immigrants

joining the jihadist ranks is an anathema to their way of thinking. Individuals such as John Walker Lindh, who fought on behalf of the Taliban, Nareed Afzalltaq, who attacked an office of the United Jewish Federation in Seattle (killing one woman and wounding five), or the foiled plot by inmates in a Southern California prison to conduct a bombing campaign are all regarded as outliers rather than as individuals symptomatic of a broader concern.

European policymakers are far more cognizant of the problem but have focused on its cultural dimension as their communities have become increasingly segmented. They have done little to publicize the fact that integration policy has become an integral component in establishing domestic security. Indeed, a growing intolerance toward North African and Middle Eastern immigrants and their descendants in many European countries, from the UK to France, the Netherlands, and Germany, suggests that the problem of integration is worsening rather than improving. This may, in itself, present an emergent series of dilemmas on both sides of the Atlantic as policymakers seek to balance the demands of minority populations with the fears of the middle class, who have historically provided the foundation for democratic systems, and tolerance, in liberal democracies.

2

Identity Discourse
in Western Europe and the United States
in the Aftermath of 9/11

ILYA PRIZEL

In the presence of [ethnic] diversity, we hunker down.
We act like turtles. The effect of diversity is worse than had been imagined.
And it is not just that we do not trust people who are not like us.
In diverse communities, we don't trust people who do look like us.

ROBERT PUTNAM, *Harvard University*

The attacks of September 11, 2001, ended the post–World War II understanding of both international and domestic politics in the United States and Europe as well as in the Muslim world. The utilitarian notion of states and polities pursuing "rational" policies driven by the desire to maximize well-being and avoid another cataclysm as well as the belief in an ever-greater cultural convergence were both buried in the debris of the Twin Towers in New York City.

In many ways the years from 1945 to 1991, shaped by post–World War II bipolarity, were a historical anomaly. One of the strangest features of the Cold War period was the virtual disappearance of an overt identity discourse in much of the world. The intellectual climate of the era was shaped by an acceptance of a Hegelian teleology, which argued that humanity was on a linear march toward a rational end goal and that such irrational relics as nationalism and religion would shrink in importance when confronted with the forces of reason and progress. The Cold War period was dominated by two superpowers, each of which, for its own reasons, thrived on the concept of identity-free politics with a deliberately induced amnesia. The bolshevik ideology of the Soviet Union was based on the denial of distinct ethnic or cultural identity, instead ascribing historic developments to the dynamics of economic class struggle. Following World War II, the United States adopted an extreme version of Wilsonian internationalism in which, again, the concept of ethnic and cultural identity clashed with the notion of the "rational actor." This concept became the centerpiece of American ideology, sidelining the entire notion of the politics of cultural identity in favor of a vague notion of common human values.

Paradoxically, if the first half of the twentieth century was dominated by struggles between the social and philosophical constructs of Marx and the European right, the post–World War II era was dominated by the social and philosophical constructs of Adam Smith. It was Smith who argued that economic performance was the key tool needed to "domesticate" human passion and spread civilization around the world. All three major polities of the post–World War II order (the United States, the Soviet Union, and the nascent European Union) therefore saw economic performance as the key pillar legitimating their particular political structures, while relegating national identity to the background.

The process of delimiting the identity discourse was further accelerated by the upheavals of 1968. In France, Germany, and, to a lesser degree, Italy, the revolt of the youth was very much a reaction against the past. Europe's young perceived this past, with its emphasis on identity, as the culprit responsible for fascism, colonialism, and Europe's genocidal politics in the nineteenth and first half of the twentieth century. In the United States, comparably, the double crisis of the war in Vietnam and the struggle for civil rights stirred American thinkers. Figures such as Susan Sontag, Herbert Marcuse, and Philip Foner contended that American obsession with national identity, which they termed "exceptionalism," was the root cause of U.S. imperialism, its rapacious capitalism, and the exploitation of the emerging "third world."[1] In short, America's leftists, much like their European counterparts, considered the notion of national grand-narratives as merely a tool to legitimate American hegemony and repression. The disappointments of the late 1960s have resulted in the prevalence of a "post-historical" mindset among many leftist intellectuals in Europe and the United States. These leftists argued that any attempt to build identity on the basis of a unifying grand-narrative was an elite tool intended to create "a standardized humanity [that] would now treat otherness as a pure deviation and place it in the hands of doctors or the police."[2]

It is noteworthy that the rejection of the discourse of identity as a legitimate basis of political discourse spilled over into much of the third world, with most regimes claiming non-national attributes such as socialism or anti-imperialism in order to legitimate themselves. Thus, when the Soviet Union collapsed and the Cold War ended, the general consensus was that the Soviet Union had faltered precisely because it had failed, by Adam Smith's criterion of "pacifying prosperity," to compete with the liberal capitalist model. This, in turn, would lead to the "end of history," a situation in which all polities would pursue the holy grail of economic growth, resulting in a Hegelian "perpetual peace." Dankwart Rustow's argument that identity consensus was a pre-condition for a successful democratic transformation was rejected as old-fashioned if not outright racist.[3]

Few realized at the time that the end of the Cold War marked the end of the struggle between two universalist utopian ideologies, each relying on its version of *Homo economicus.* Yet irrational politics, which had been relegated to the trash heap of history, suddenly made a startling comeback with the emergence of the Islamic Republic of Iran (1979), the breakup of both the Soviet Union (1991) and Czechoslovakia (1993), and, finally, the violent disintegration of Yugoslavia. These events destroyed the consensus in both Western academia and the halls of power that identity politics were a relic of the fascist past and thus pertained only to the periphery of the international system.

The academic response to the rebirth of identity politics was wide ranging. At one end was Francis Fukuyama's "end of history," which claimed that with the collapse of communism we had reached the end of the politics of ideology and were now marching in lockstep toward a global "neoliberal peace." At the other end was Samuel Huntington. In his book on the clash of civilizations he argued that with the end of the Cold War we were bound to see violent confrontation among the larger religious groupings—a situation where the mere presence of multiple "civilizations" would cause conflict.[4] The reality of ethnic violence was becoming all the more apparent. Still, Amartya Sen, in his book *Identity and Violence,* argued implausibly that the root cause of intercommunal violence is our "miniaturization of the human beings." This "miniaturization" amounted to internalizing all human interactions on the basis of race, religion, ethnicity, and so forth. According to Sen, had we been able to view a person's multiple identities rather than insist on a narrow characterization, the clashes would have been averted.[5] Kwame Anthony Appiah, rehashing the liberal "multi-identities" position in his book *Cosmopolitanism: Ethics in a World of Strangers,* argued that conflict arises when we forget that "all humanity is valid." Hence, we must focus on intercommunal (civilizational) dialogue even if we never arrive at consensus.[6]

While all these positions offer interesting conceptions of post–Cold War reality, they ignore three major changes that have taken place in the international body politic, each of which has had a long-term impact on the politics of identity.

One systemic change is that Islam is in its early phases of reformation and counter-reformation. Islam's main clash is not with the West but is instead an internal one between the elite-driven caliphate, derived from Sunni Islam, and its populist rival, Shia Islam.[7] If the experience of reformation and counter-reformation in Christianity in the sixteenth and seventeenth centuries is any indicator, an intrareligious clash is prone to radicalize rather than moderate the fundamentalist discourse within that religion.[8] Since it is the Islamic world that is the largest exporter of immigrants to Western Europe, Oceania, and, to a lesser degree, the United States, it stands to reason that the strife within the Islamic communities will ricochet in the host countries.

Another change is that the last quarter of a century has witnessed a radical political and identity realignment in the United States. America's traditionally nativist evangelical Christians shed their historic isolationist stance and adopted a global messianic position. Domestically, America's evangelicals joined with their historic nemesis, the Catholic Church, in support of an array of domestic issues, including immigration and a universal messianic posture for the United States.

A third change is that the demise of communism fundamentally undermined the left-right divide, which had underpinned European politics since the end of the nineteenth century. Furthermore, Europe demographically mutated from the world's largest exporter of people to a continent with a rapidly shrinking population, making it increasingly dependent on immigrants, who have experienced far greater difficulty finding a cultural symbiosis with the host culture than have immigrants to the United States.

These changes have had a notable effect on attitudes toward migrants in Europe and the United States. The mass migration to Europe since 1960 and to the United States following the reforms of 1965 has resulted in huge demographic shifts that have further complicated the accommodation of immigrants by the host culture. The responses of Europe and the United States have differed significantly. The result is a fundamental division between the two continents in terms of both attitudes and politics.

New Immigration Challenges

Although the scale of migration between 1970 and 2000 was smaller, in relative terms, than that of 1860–1914, the current migrations present problems on both continents that the previous mass migrations did not. While the prior immigration was huge in size and proportion, it occurred in an overwhelmingly European Christian context. Hence, although there was a cultural gap between immigrants and host populations, the two shared many basic common parameters, which the current immigrants and hosts often do not. The composition of new migrants is far more heterogeneous than in the previous wave.

Furthermore, nineteenth- and early twentieth-century immigrants assumed that they were moving to a more "advanced" country and accepted—in fact welcomed—assimilation into the host culture. Migration from *Dar al-Islam* (House of Islam) to *Dar al-Harb* (House of War, House of the Infidel) rarely creates a set of attitudes similar to that of the European or Asian immigrants who flooded North America between 1860 and 1914. The children of early twentieth-century immigrants generally perceived their parents' heritage as either a nostalgic relic or a source of embarrassment. In contrast, in the case of late twentieth-century immigrants, members of the second generation are often more alienated from their host culture than are their immigrant parents.[9]

Even in the nineteenth century, immigrants did bring political issues from their native countries that they tried to transplant into the host country's soil. Examples can be found in the Fenian Raids, in which Irish Americans attacked British installations in Canada to push their demand for a free Ireland, or in the assassinations of American politicians by European anarchists hoping to undermine the existing order in Europe. However, the cases of such violence were rare and seldom extended to second- or third-generation immigrants. Late twentieth-century immigration presents a far more serious security challenge in the form of clashes between various immigrant groups domiciled in the host country, such as Singhalese and Tamils in Germany, Sikhs and Muslim Kashmiris in Canada, Serbs and Croats in Australia, and North African Arabs and Jews in France. This new phenomenon often has a deadly impact on the host population. Furthermore, the inability of host countries to absorb second-generation Muslims into the host community effectively has led to a spillover of Islamic internal strife in the host countries, creating a security challenge unknown in previous immigrations.

Another new immigration challenge is that criminality among immigrants has taken on previously unknown proportions. It is true that there was always a link between immigration and criminal activity, derived from the closed community of immigrants and their connection with syndicates in their native countries. It was these twin pillars that enabled the Sicilian mafia to present a security challenge to the host societies. Similar structures enabled Jewish "Odessa" syndicates to promote white slavery in Latin America, Chinese criminal gangs to terrorize fellow Chinese immigrants in Hawaii and on the West Coast of the United States, and Irish immigrant groups to control trade in illicit alcohol. However, immigrant criminality historically operated on the edge of society, with little challenge to the legal structure of the host culture. While the pillars of immigrant criminality have not changed, the volume has increased to a point where it often threatens the host's political establishment. According to the United Nations, the Russian, Nigerian, Colombian, Albanian, Italian, Chinese, and Arab mafias generate revenues of between $1 trillion and $1.5 trillion a year. They have created "off-limits" areas in North America and Europe where the presence of the host state's authority has all but vanished. The potential collaboration of political radicals and criminal elements within the immigrant community has created a serious security challenge to host polities, particularly in Europe.[10] It is these drastic changes in the nature of the immigrant populations that have had such a dramatic collective impact on identity discourse within the host polities after the attacks in New York, Madrid, and London.

From Postmodernity to a New Search for a Metanarrative in Europe

Perhaps the most profound repression of the discourse of identity took place in Western Europe, where the politics of amnesia and identity denial were essential tools for putting public discourse beyond the bitter legacy of World War II. It may well be that Europe's legacy of industrial genocide and brutal colonization and the worship of the Moloch of Stalinism by European intellectuals created a strange brew of amnesia and nihilism. Since World War II, Europe's ethnic discourse has undergone three dramatic shifts. For the first fifteen years after World War II, the discourse of identity was characterized by deliberate amnesia. While no European polity denied its grand "metanarrative," it was presented in a sanitized, selective, and often dishonest fashion. In France, for example, General de Gaulle created the myth of virtually universal French resistance to Nazism and, following the defeats in Vietnam and Algeria, obfuscated the details of France's colonial legacy. In Germany, Konrad Adenauer spoke of "good Germans" versus "bad Nazis," thus exonerating (deceptively) the Wehrmacht from the atrocities of the Holocaust and laying the blame solely on "Nazis." In Austria, the myth of its being the "first victim" of Nazism was perpetuated, creating a new identity under the cover of "neutrality." The Dutch government clung to the "icon" of Anne Frank, while conveniently ignoring the fact that the Dutch level of collaboration with Nazism was the highest in occupied Europe. Sweden focused on the courage of Raoul Wallenberg and conveniently forgot that, without outside pressure, it instituted Nuremberg-style racial laws in 1937.[11] Simultaneously, the European left attempted to defuse its complicity in Stalinist genocide under the guise of its struggle with Fascism. It made events such as the Spanish Civil War and Soviet losses in World War II into their new icons of leftist martyrdom. Somehow, in the mythology of the left, the struggle with Fascism exonerated the left from responsibility for Bolshevik mass murder.

This amnesia was confronted by the youth uprisings of the spring and autumn of 1968. Reacting to the deceptive "grand-narrative" of elites in each European polity, the "Generation of 1968" rejected the entire notion of a discourse of identity, particularly as it pertained to their own identities. In France, for example, intellectuals such as Claude Levi-Strauss, Jean Baudrillard, Jacques Derrida, Michel Foucault, and Jean François Lyotard focused on the absence of a "metanarrative." They argued that standard histories are little more than a legitimating tool of the hegemonic elite. In Germany, there were the adherents of the "Frankfurt School," including Herbert Marcuse, Max Horkheimer, Erich Fromm, and, a generation later, Jürgen Habermas. While remaining committed to the notions of enlightenment, "democracy," and freedom, they left little room for the politics of identity and grand-narratives. As Pierre Nora observed, "memory has replaced history."[12] Some European thinkers went even further, asserting that the natural outgrowth of democracy is a teleological disappearance of collective values and identities in favor of postmodernism.[13]

Perhaps the trauma of guilt resulting from the colonial legacy of Europe had the most enduring impact on the discourse of identity. Regardless of whether the de-colonization process was brutal (as in the case of France, the Netherlands, and Portugal) or relatively peaceful (as in the case of Britain), the politics of identity across Europe was driven by a profound sense of shame and guilt. Any questions about whether European host societies had a right to demand that immigrant populations adapt to the value systems of the host society were adjusted to be beyond the realm of politically acceptable discourse. In fact, multiculturalism was interpreted by many European polities not simply as toleration of differences but rather as legal recognition of different groups, each entitled to have its own dedicated educational systems and to follow its own social mores. Thus, the British politician Enoch Powell was quickly dismissed as a fascist and was effectively confined to the political wilderness when he warned that uncontrolled immigration across cultural lines would result in "rivers of blood." The French explorer and novelist Jean Raspail was dismissed as a racist and a bigot when he predicted a major culture clash between West European natives and third world immigrants in his novel *The Camp of the Saints* (1973). The obsession with the "authenticity" of the third world, and the sense of guilt toward it, made any critique of the third world or its thinkers beyond the accepted norms. Thus, when Albert Camus, despite his commitment to Algeria's independence, questioned its democratic future, he was effectively banished by the French intellectual left. On the other hand, when Franz Fanon suggested that violence was a catharsis of spiritual liberation for Africans, this view was enthusiastically endorsed by Jean-Paul Sartre (who wrote the introduction to Fanon's book, *The Wretched of the Earth*). Similarly, Edward Said's thesis of "Orientalism"—that Europe's quest was to degrade, dehumanize, and hence exploit the Muslim world—has overnight become the accepted dogma of Europe's left-leaning intellectuals. This acceptance further institutionalized the morally relativist world view of the Generation of 1968.[14] The intellectual atmosphere of the last quarter of the twentieth century has therefore been one that has questioned Europe's moral zeitgeist *in contrast to* the value system of the Islamic world. Thus, as Muslim immigration from North Africa, Turkey, and the subcontinent accelerated rapidly, no debate on the impact of the rapid demographic change was tolerated, and concerns were therefore rarely articulated.

The leftist intellectual hegemony within the Generation of 1968 had undergone a major reorientation among traditional European leftists. Khrushchev's exposure of the crimes of Stalinism (in 1956), coupled with the thwarting of the "Prague Spring" in 1968, exhausted the ability of the European Left to obfuscate the reality that lay behind the "Soviet Utopia." The "New Jerusalem" of the Generation of 1968 thus became the third world.[15] The new European identity was based on opposition to two "others"—the United States and Israel—whose presence symbolized the unreformed "fascist" West. It was not long before criticism of specific policies of the United States and Israel deteriorated into an attack on the legitimacy of the polities themselves and, ultimately, into overt anti-Semitism. Social class, which had been the shibboleth of the traditional European Left, was virtually subsumed by the "anti-imperial obsession" of the new European Left. This issue came to dominate the discourse after 1968.[16] America's traditional notion of national citizenship, sovereignty, and the perpetuation of a grand-narrative was increasingly perceived by Europe's intellectual elite as a dangerous anachronism. Accordingly, the United States was increasingly characterized as Europe's moral "other."[17] Emblematic of the Western European intellectual climate in the first years of the twenty-first century were its two most prominent intellectuals: Derrida and Habermas. In a joint publication entitled *Philosophy in the Time of Terror,* they stated that Europe's identity is a postnational one based on a welfare state social contract, with the United States forming a natural contrast. In fact, the authors called for the designation of February 5, a day marked by anti–United States demonstrations, as an official holiday known as "Europe Day."[18] The shrillness of the anti-American discourse in Europe is reflected in Pascal Bruckner's description: "America is the bad Europe, colonizing and arrogant; the dissolute, illegitimate daughter who brings together all the negative traits of her parent countries."[19]

Indeed, the dominant West European identity discourse from 1968 onward has been centered almost exclusively on the intellectual concept of "transnational progressivism." It consists of several fundamental precepts. One precept is that the political unit is not the individual but rather the group into which one is born (race, gender, sexual orientation, etc.). Another is that politics is characterized by the dichotomy between oppressors and oppressed. Immigrants, women, citizens of former colonies, gays, and others are by definition oppressed. Also, multiculturalism is considered a binary adversarial relationship between the "privileged" and "marginalized," between the "oppressive hegemon" and the oppressed "other." A further precept is that institutions should reflect the agenda of the "oppressed" groups and should proportionally represent them. The national narrative should reflect this new reality (for example, the UK state commission known as Multi-Ethnic Britain noted in its report that the concept of "Britishness" has "systemic racial connotations" and thus needs to be revised, rethought, or jettisoned). A final precept is that citizenship should be reconstituted to reflect a new transnational character as a new form of belonging.[20]

A key determinant of the impact of transnational progressivism in Western Europe is that it has taken place against the backdrop of massive immigration to Europe from North Africa, the Levant, and the Indian subcontinent.[21] Discussion of immigration to Europe, which accelerated in the 1960s, became essentially taboo within Europe's traditional discourse. Political elites minimized the significance of the migrant inflows. In France, elites argued that immigrants would adopt the "republican tradition" and become French; Germany's elite perpetuated the myth that the immigrants were "guests" who would go home; early immigrants to Britain were treated as part of the "Commonwealth" project.

Given the new discourse of identity promulgated by the Generation of 1968, the dominant position adopted in most European countries was a relativist policy of "multicultural" social structure, often perceiving the notion of "functional assimilation" as a form of cultural oppression. This attitude was reflected in a comment by English novelist A. S. Byatt: "[I see] our nation as a bright mosaic of unrelated polities." The London-based feminist Germaine Greer defended female circumcision within the Muslim immigrant community, decrying efforts to stop the practice in England as "an attack on cultural identity" and adding, "One man's beautification is another man's mutilation." Michel Foucault found in the violence and the degradation of the Iranian Revolution a "new spirituality."[22]

Notably, the cultural relativism accepted by the political class of the Generation of 1968 was not fully accepted by either the host population or by some of the immigrant groups. Wolf Birmann, the German poet and dissident, charged that by accepting the concept of cultural relativism, the European political class hoped to make the immigrants the "invisible people" whose unappealing practices could comfortably be ignored. Ayaan Hirsi Ali, the Somalian refugee, feminist, and member of the Dutch parliament, observed that "colonialism and slavery have created a sentiment of culpability in the West that leads people to adulate foreign tradition. This is a lazy and even racist attitude."[23] It is interesting to note that Murina Mirza, author of the survey *Living Together Apart: British Muslims and the Paradox of Multiculturalism,* observed that while 84 percent of Britain's Muslims believed that they were treated "fairly" by British society, a majority of those below twenty-four years of age felt hostile to Britain and its culture. When asked to explain the paradox, Mirza stated that "the emergence of a strong Muslim identity in Britain is, in part, a result of multi-cultural policies implemented since the 1980s which have emphasized difference at the expense of shared national identity and divided people along ethnic, religious and cultural lines."[24]

The transnational progressivism which has gained great popularity among the political class has not attained grassroots acceptance either. The recent success of Michael Collins's book *The Likes of Us: A Biography of the White Working Class,* which decries the elite notion of multiculturalism, was awarded the George Orwell Prize and became a successful BBC series. Similarly, Oriana Fallaci's pamphlet "Rage and Pride" was dismissed by Europe's intellectuals as a "retrograde tirade." It soon became, however, one of the most read tracts across the continent. The success of these publications is indicative of a growing gap between Europe's elites and its general populace.[25]

By 2001, the paradigm of the Generation of 1968 was, indeed, in retreat. On the emotional level, the concept of a "civil society" has proved to be highly utilitarian but incapable of sustaining the long-term commitment of a population. Habermas's concept of "constitutional patriotism," based on the notion of "common sense" and on the values of "reason and enlightenment"—with no historic memory or cultural attachment—proved to be feeble.

Another contributing factor in the demise of the Generation of 1968's paradigm and its ideas about identity was the collapse of the left as a viable political force in European politics. In Britain, the "Old Labour" Party, wedded to the ideas of transnational progressivism and unilateral disarmament, metamorphosed into a "New Labour" Party after losing four consecutive elections. They adopted many of Margaret Thatcher's dogmas, albeit without her shrill rhetoric. In France, the legacy of François Mitterrand was the rejection of the leftist idea, best symbolized by the racist Jean-Marie Le Pen's defeat of the socialist presidential candidate Lionel Jospin.

In Germany, reunification finally allowed a "return to normalcy." This meant that, after forty years of near silence about German identity and cultural space, German intellectuals from across the political spectrum (Martin Walser, Günter Grass, Rolf Hochhuth, W. G. Seabald, et al.) refocused Germany's postwar political discourse from Nazi atrocities to German victimhood. While German intellectuals now do not deny German atrocities in the Holocaust, this tragedy is treated as a "pan-European phenomenon."[26] By doing so, they transferred culpability from Germany to all of Europe. Leftwing intellectuals in Germany have rediscovered the German grand-narrative and have refused to reduce that narrative to the twelve-year experience of the Third Reich. They often argue that the left must regain the grand-narrative to prevent its becoming the exclusive domain of the political right. The left, which was at the forefront of the "postnational discourse," has been stunned by its inability to stem the tide of globalization and has rediscovered nationalism in a last-ditch effort to resist the forces of globalization in Western Europe.[27] It is noteworthy that a key element in defeating the EU constitution in both France and the Netherlands was the left's opposition to globalization and its assault on "native culture." The gap between leftist elites and their constituencies has increased dramatically since the mid-1980s, when France's Mitterrand abandoned all pretense of creating a socialist economy and embraced the inevitability of globalization. Having lost much of their distinctiveness from the right in terms of economic policy, the left's self-definition increasingly depended on the commitment to multiculturalism, cultural relativism, and "solidarity with the enemies of imperialism."

The New Discourse of Immigration in Europe

Both immigration and the terrorist attacks in New York, Madrid, and London have accelerated the intellectual demise of the Generation of 1968. Initially, some of the scions of this generation justified terrorism and explained its origin as being rooted in imperialism, humiliation, and exploitation. Some, such as Noam Chomsky and Jose Saramago, retain this position. Increasingly, however, these thinkers have been on the defensive. Multiculturalism, which was previously the sacred cow of Europe's political discourse, is now increasingly perceived as a failed policy that poses a long-term danger to Europe's culture and values. Vehement public debate about issues such as the "honor killings" of women (whose behavior often consists of a romance with a non-Muslin) and the controversy over the cartoon depiction of Mohammed in the Danish press have raised a fundamental question: does the European left support the universalist values of liberalism, freedom of expression, and human rights, or does it embrace a form of moral relativism that sometimes conflicts with these values?

Even the literary world debates the challenge posed by Islam in Europe. In France, reflecting the new mood among post-1968 intellectuals, best-selling novelist Michel Houellebecq called for the trial of the "sadistic hedonists" of the Generation of 1968 who imported and tolerated the "stupid" religion (Islam). In Britain, Martin Amis published a three-part essay entitled "The Age of Horrorism" in which the author depicts Islam as incompatible with democracy and enlightenment. In Germany, Henryk M. Broder wrote the best-selling *Hurra, Wir Kapitulieren (Hurray! We're Capitulating),* which argues that Europe's policies of multiculturalism are leading to the demise of Europe's values and heritage.[28] Yet perhaps the greatest indication of the shift in the European attitude toward Islam and multiculturalism is the glaring contrast between the positions of the last two popes. Whereas John Paul II tirelessly campaigned for a dialogue between Christianity and Islam, focusing on communism as the existential threat to Western civilization, Benedict XVI did not hesitate to describe Islam as a culture of violence and intolerance, in quoting a Byzantine emperor, Manuel II.[29]

The collapse of the long dominant multicultural, relativist paradigm of identity has had a profound effect on both Europe's left and right. The European left has split into three groups, each heralding its own preferred version of identity. The extreme left has continued to argue that Europe's future lies in an ever closer alliance with Islam and the third world in its confrontation with capitalist globalization.

Oskar Lafontaine, the former chairman of the German Social Democrats, in analyzing the state of Europe's social challenges, called for a "change through ingratiation [stressing] commonalities between leftist policies and the Islamic religion." First, in an interview with *Neues Deutschland,* Lafontaine asserted, "Islam depends on community, which places it in opposition to extreme individualism, which threatens to fail in the West. The second similarity is that the devout Muslim is required to share his wealth with others. The leftist also wants to see the strong help the weak. Finally, the prohibition of interest still plays a role in Islam, much as it once did in Christianity. At a time when entire economies are plunging into crisis because their expectations of returns on investment have become totally absurd, there is a basis for a dialogue to be conducted between the left and the Islamic world. . . . We must constantly ask ourselves through which eyes the Muslims see us." Lafontaine expressed sympathy for the indignation of Muslims. He suggested that "people in Muslim countries have experienced many indignities, one of the most recent being the Iraq war. What we are seeing here is resource imperialism."[30] London's mayor, Ken Livingston, commenting on the London transit bombings, suggested that "they [Islamist terrorists] do not have jet planes, do not have tanks; they only have their bodies to use as weapons. In an unfair balance [*sic*], that's what people use."[31]

Another group of former supporters of the doctrines of the Generation of 1968, however, has moved dramatically to the right. Paul Berman, in his book *Terror and Liberalism,* argues that many "68ers" not only reject the root cause argument but also recognize that if the left is to retain its moral credibility, it must take part in confronting "new totalitarianism" in the guise of fundamentalist Islam.[32] Joschka Fischer has depicted fundamentalist Islam as the new totalitarianism, while strikingly similar views have been articulated by Filip Dewinter, the leader of the right-wing, xenophobic Vlaams Blok in Belgium. Helmut Schmidt, a Social Democrat who was once West Germany's chancellor, has ruefully acknowledged that "to convert them [Muslims] to democracy will take generations." The *Berlin Tageszeitung,* long an icon of the 68ers, openly called for confronting the depravity and misogyny of fundamentalist Islam.[33] The mainstream of the European left, however, while recognizing that the traditional paradigm of the Generation of 1968 is no longer sustainable, have attempted to find a compromise position between the unrepentant multiculturalism of Oskar Lafontaine and Ken Livingston on the one hand and Joschka Fischer and Helmut Schmidt's revisionism on the other. Politicians such as Tony Blair and the Dutch and Danish socialists have tried to delineate a middle ground, separating multiculturalism from moral relativism. They have attempted to create "national values" by retooling the educational system to stress "Britishness" or "Dutchness." At the same time they have tried to incorporate Islamism by assuming greater control over the curriculum of Islamic schools, adding compulsory civics education for immigrants, and creating native schools for Islamic preachers. In sum, they are attempting to build an identity on the basis of what Yael Tamir referred to as "deep civic nationalism" by reconciling liberalism with nationalism.[34]

If the collapse of the multicultural relativist paradigm has disoriented Europe's left, it has energized its right. The European right has been galvanized by the events of 9/11, the murder of the Dutch filmmaker Theo van Gogh, the transit bombings in Madrid and London, and the suburban riots in Paris. The apparent radicalization of groups of Muslim youth across Europe, along with the potential membership of Turkey in the EU, has further fueled this rightist fire. Habermas's view of democracy as "constitutionalism in a postnational context" has been replaced by George Schopflin's: that democracy rests on the cohesion provided by "nationhood" and shared identity. The right, however, has not presented a unified vision for a new European identity. A small "nativist" group, hostile to globalization, multiculturalism, and the European Union, as well as the pernicious Americanization of their societies, has re-embraced the concept of a "pure" nation-state. Trading in "fantasies of salvation," this group has proposed a return to the purity and democracy of an ethnic nation-state, free of the intrusion of "alien" cultures or interference from Brussels.[35] They argue that the state is the key to identity. Any supranational arrangement such as the EU is, therefore, the harbinger of the death of identity. While they remain electorally weak, they have managed to establish a parliamentary presence in most European assemblies (national or local) and to form a vocal presence within the European Parliament in Strasbourg.[36]

Another group on the right that emerged after the collapse of Europe's multicultural, relativist paradigm is what the Hungarian, Gaspar Tamas, defined as the "post-fascist" right. "Post-fascism" differs from traditional fascism in the sense that it rejects narrow nationalism in favor of "pan-Europeanism" and accepts liberalism in the form that Roger Griffin defines as "ethnocratic liberalism," a liberal paradigm limited to "European civilization."[37] This notion of Europe as a civilizational space that must be shielded from destruction by multiculturalism has been embraced by a number of prominent public figures. They include Vaclav Klaus (who referred to multiculturalism as a brothel), Jose Maria Ansar, Valery Giscard-d'Estaing, Victor Orban, Edmund Stoiber, Wolfgang Schussel, and, lately, Pope Benedict XVI, who declared that "what Europe needs is a new self acceptance as a civilization."[38] Accordingly, it is commonly suggested that one of the first demonstrations of Europe's "self-acceptance" should be the blocking of Turkish entry into the EU, as a means by which to slow the Islamization of the continent.

A third new grouping on the right to emerge in the twenty-first century mainly clusters around the German Christian Democratic Union Party. They attempt to reconcile the concept of multiculturalism with that of *Leitkultur* (leading culture). According to advocates, while European polities must accept the heterogeneous nature of their populations and be tolerant of immigrants, minority cultures must conform to basic native cultural mores. From this perspective came Jacques Chirac's move to ban head scarves in French schools and David Cameron's statement that British society cannot tolerate the oppression of Muslim women "behind a screen of cultural sensitivity."[39] In Bavaria, following the notions of *Leitkultur*, the state insisted that in deference to Bavarian cultural heritage crucifixes would continue to hang in every classroom, even if much of the student body is not Christian. Furthermore, overt Islamic clothing such as the hijab would be banned in state schools.

Post–Cold War Europe, traumatized by its impotency in the face of the war in the Balkans, by terrorist attacks in Madrid and London, and by the seemingly irrepressible flow of migrants, is a continent intellectually and politically adrift. It is the identity of the West European center that is at its most vulnerable since the late 1940s.[40] Given the emergent paradigms of unassimilated non-European immigrants across Europe's political spectrum, these populations are often depicted as both a security threat and a challenge to the idea of post-enlightenment Europe. While there appears to be a consensus that Europe's experiments with multiculturalism have failed, there is no new model in sight, leading politicians across the continent to resort to police action as a substitute for an immigration policy. Clearly, while there are trends, there is no "European" position on the great debates about how to deal with migrants, Islam, or the brave new world of identity politics.

The American Paradox

Almost a century has passed since Israel Zangwill famously observed in his 1909 play, *The Melting Pot,* that "America is God's Crucible, the great Melting-Pot where all the races of Europe are melting and reforming! . . . No, . . . the real American has not yet arrived. He is only in the Crucible; I tell you—he will be the fusion of all races, perhaps the coming superman." Even at the time these words were written, they did not reflect the American reality, which was ambivalent toward both immigration and the concept of the melting pot. The history of the United States is one of massive, extended, and disruptive waves of immigration (1830s–1850s, 1880s–1920s, 1968–present). Each wave was met with a nativist backlash, ranging from the Alien and Sedition Acts of 1798 and the Chinese Exclusion Act of 1882 to the Literacy Act of 1917 and the Immigration Restriction Act of 1924.[41] Each wave produced a new reactive cohort of nativists who argued that immigration would destroy the identity of America. The Know-Nothing Party claimed that the Irish Catholics were a threat to "Americanism." Some sounded a shrill alarm about the "Chinese Peril" that would overwhelm the American West. Madison Grant was known for his ravings that Jewish immigrants would diminish the overall intelligence of the American population. Samuel Huntington expressed fear that Latino immigrants would reshape America's political and moral posture, pulling it from its original roots.[42] Those who favored immigration always defended the phenomenon as an economic necessity and claimed that the immigrants would eventually "melt" into the general society. Despite clear evidence since the massive Irish immigration of the mid-nineteenth century that not all groups would "melt," the myth of the "melting pot" endured until World War II, deflecting the question of whether immigration posed a challenge to an American identity.[43]

In terms of identity politics, the United States may well be the most conservative industrialized democracy in the world. Despite this ebb and flow of attitudes toward specific immigrations and despite the repeated conviction of some that the latest wave of immigrants would undermine America's moral and cultural fiber, immigration to the United States has continued essentially unabated since its inception. At the same time, the basic value system of the United States has undergone fewer changes than those of the more homogeneous societies of Europe.

So, did the American "melting pot" disappear or did it re-invent itself? By the 1960s the myth of the "melting pot" had all but vanished, replaced by the new dogma of permanent retention of a specific ethnic identify and multiculturalism.[44] Prominent mainstream American thinkers such as Arthur Schlesinger Jr., Nathan Glazer, and Samuel Huntington have all proclaimed the erosion of American identity under the pressure of multiculturalism, because multiculturalism in the American context differed fundamentally from both its European and Canadian counterparts.[45] While the nineteenth-century notion of acculturation into an Anglo-Saxon milieu was rejected in favor of ethnicity, American multiculturalism never tolerated a legal recognition of any specific group other than Native Americans. Attempts to establish German language education in the eighteenth century, affirmative action for disadvantaged groups, or specific constitutional amendments for women ran into powerful cultural resistance and thus largely failed to become institutionalized. Support for multiculturalism in the United States has always emphasized tolerance rather than the legalization of group rights.

Paradoxically, although the ethnic and cultural makeup of the United States has undergone a dramatic change since the late nineteenth century, the creed of the United States has remained a rather constant form of Anglo-Saxon Protestantism. It has relied on a synthesis of "evangelical Protestantism, republicanism, and commonsense [utilitarian] moral reasoning."[46] Seymour Martin Lipset argues that the "exceptionalism" that has enabled the American polity to absorb such diverse groups of immigrants, while retaining its distinct identity, rests on five pillars: equality of opportunity; anti-statism (embracing what Isaiah Berlin called negative freedom, rather than Europe's notion of positive freedoms); individualism; cultural populism; and laissez-faire economics.[47] In other words, America embraced a minimalist construction of identity open to all. Harold Bloom posits that the plethora of native-grown splinter versions of Calvinism is the essence of America's cultural expression: "If we are Americans, then to some degree we share in the American religion, however unknowingly or unwillingly."[48] Consistent with this theme, Laurence Moore notes that America's native Christianities shaped America's common national creed, not only through direct religious activity but also and primarily through their penetration of America's popular culture. Eldon Eisenach goes even further, arguing that it is this ubiquitous religion-inspired creed that kept American multiculturalism in check, preventing the kind of identity atrophy of the host culture that we now witness in Europe.[49]

The foundations of American discourse have remained broadly constant since the eighteenth century. Yet the notion of America's identity did produce three distinct strands: a nativist populism, a Wilsonian internationalism or liberalism, and a populist messianism. The common denominator of these three strands of American identity was a powerful subtext of "conservative optimism." Unlike its pessimistic European counterpart, it promotes the Calvinist notion of the human ability and, in fact, the duty to create heaven on earth. It is noteworthy that in Allan Bloom's bestseller, *The Closing of the American Mind*, the author sees the invasion of European gloominess and nihilist pessimism as one of the key moral threats to America.[50]

Nativist populism is often associated with movements such as the Know-Nothing Party of the mid-nineteenth century. Proponents included Andrew Jackson, William Jennings Bryan, and Warren Harding, as well as the various anti-immigration movements of the nineteenth and twentieth centuries. Relying on the principles of insularity and isolation, they viewed America as an arcadian "New Jerusalem." They believed that the only way to preserve America's virtue was to insulate it from unhealthy influences across the Atlantic and the Pacific. The purpose of American foreign policy was to keep Europe's "seditious" influence from affecting the Western hemisphere (hence the Monroe Doctrine) and to prevent immigration of non-northwestern European immigrants. Advocates of this view of Americanism engineered the various efforts to limit Irish, Asian, and later Eastern and Southern European immigration to the United States. This view of American identity was a constant presence in American politics. It underpinned much of the anti-Catholicism of U.S. politics in the late nineteenth century and succeeded in limiting Asian immigration in the late nineteenth and early twentieth centuries. The electoral peak of this perspective was reached in the 1920s when Warren G. Harding was elected on the platform of "normalcy." This platform consisted of virtually eliminating immigration from areas outside northwestern Europe (in fact, converting the racist diatribes of Madison Grant into national dogma), disengaging from "foreign entanglements," and attempting to censor and limit the flow of ideas from "decadent Europe." The Great Depression and World War II, however, politically marginalized this strand of American identity, and the selection of Dwight Eisenhower over Robert Taft as the Republican standard-bearer marked the final demise of the nativist paradigm of American identity.

With the collapse of the nativist paradigm, a new consensus emerged following World War II, which institutionalized the Wilsonian liberal internationalist paradigm (1945–1976). It too still insisted on the idea of American exceptionalism but offered two key innovations. It accepted the notion that America had a permanent role to play in the international system. Indeed, it asserted that the only way the United States could preserve its ideals at home was to spread them abroad through its participation in the international system. In addition, the concept of Americanism moved away from Protestantism or Christianity toward a generic deism. It was during this period that public references to Christianity were curtailed, often by acts of the U.S. Supreme Court, while references to God became more ubiquitous. As a result of this new definition of Americanism, the St. Patrick's Day parade was joined by a plethora of other ethnic parades, legitimating the notion of multiculturalism as an acceptable form of American identity. It was this shift in America's concept of its own identity that made it possible to abolish the ethnoreligious immigration legislation of the 1920s and replace it with the 1968 Immigration and Nationality Act. This legislation removed ethnicity as a criterion in selecting candidates for immigration. The effect was a sharp decline in immigrants from northwestern Europe and a massive increase in immigration from Asia and Latin America.[51]

The hegemony of the Wilsonian liberal paradigm began to disintegrate in the 1970s and collapsed with the election of Ronald Reagan in 1980. Several basic explanations are usually offered to explain the collapse of the liberal paradigm. Robert Putnam argues that the worship of mammon in the name of economic freedom is directly linked to the decline in the nation's "social capital" and "civil society" and the rise of crude consumerism and a society devoid of ideals.[52] John Kekes, among others, has argued that the cause of the collapse of the liberal paradigm of U.S. identity was disillusionment with the New Deal and the Great Society programs as well as a state-sponsored drive toward human perfectibility policy initiatives that clashed with the Calvinist creed of the country.[53] Others have blamed the demise of liberalism on an activist Supreme Court that was perceived as a liberal body deconstructing America's social creed. One final view is that the hyper-realistic foreign policy of President Nixon and Secretary of State Henry Kissinger constituted a betrayal of the foundations of the American moralist-evangelical creed, leading to the fourth revival of American evangelism.

This populist revolt of the late 1970s and 1980s was, in some ways, reminiscent of the prior nativist rejection of European social and cultural models and values. In fact, the American body politic entered what often is referred to as the "Fourth Great Revival," with the evangelical Protestant creed once again becoming the shibboleth of American political discourse. Despite the superficial similarities to the nativist discourse of the nineteenth century, this period is different in one key respect: unlike its predecessor, this evangelical revival is not insular but rather aggressively "messianic." In foreign policy, every president since Jimmy Carter has had to make "human rights" a component of U.S. foreign policy. The only portion of the Helsinki Agreements (1975) that was therefore important for the American public, for example, was "Basket III," which dealt with human rights. Accordingly, the world has been divided into "good" and "evil"—a fundamentalist paradigm containing no middle ground. In economic terms, "neoliberalism" and "globalization," with their strong element of the Calvinist creeds of competition, individual initiative, and self-reliance—have been accepted as cornerstones of "Americanism." Efforts by traditional nativist-populists such as Ross Perot, who ran for president on an anti-globalist, isolationist platform, have failed to gain a following large enough to make adherents to such a platform a permanent presence in American electoral politics. Whereas the earlier version of American nativism either ignored or sought to avoid the outside world, contemporary American populists take the view that success beyond the shores of America is an affirmation of their version of Americanism. The collapse of communism is therefore directly related to the pursuit of a "moral" policy vis-à-vis bolshevism. The spread of democracy is, likewise, directly tied to the success of the neoliberal model, one free of the "godless" etatism that created communitarians and a threat to democracy.[54] Finally, unlike the nineteenth-century populists who wished to limit America's immigrants to northwest Europeans, current American populists see the political and religious mission of the United States in relation to prospective immigrants rolled into one. It is in the third world that evangelical churches have grown the fastest. The success of American evangelicals in creating huge new memberships in Africa, Eastern Europe, Latin America, and Southeast Asia has created a latter-day version of "manifest destiny." The result of these efforts is the largest global revival of Christianity since the French Revolution.[55] One further point is crucial: unlike in the past, when nativists opposed "foreign" immigration, in contemporary America it is evangelical churches that actively sponsor immigrants to swell their religious ranks.

One of the most significant changes in American identity politics is the newly forged alliance between "nativist evangelicals" and their historic nemesis, the Catholic Church. Whereas the two institutions traditionally defined themselves in opposition to each other, these two institutions have increasingly found common ground in the last twenty years. Included among the issues upon which they have converged in opinion is immigration, the two institutions (both with a large and growing Latino constituency) sharing an identical view and thus creating a political bloc that has fundamentally altered America's political landscape.[56] Indeed, the success of the evangelicals in recruiting Latino immigrants has dramatically reduced the nativist opposition to immigration.

Opposing immigration has therefore ceased to be a mode of defending Americanism among broad swaths of the population. Given the re-orientation on the issue of immigration within elements of the Republican Party, George W. Bush and Arnold Schwarzenegger have done more to encourage Latino immigration than many liberal politicians of earlier generations. It was telling that Vicente Fox, Mexico's president, traveled to Utah (currently one of the most pro-immigration states in the Union and historically the heartland of isolationist nativism) when he sought to garner support for a nonrestrictive immigration policy to the United States.[57] Contemporary opposition to immigration in the United States is primarily voiced by African Americans and labor groups who perceive immigrants as economic competitors; the opposition, however, is economic rather than either security or identity driven. It is noteworthy that U.S. presidents, ranging from Franklin Delano Roosevelt to Jimmy Carter to George W. Bush, referred to themselves as "immigrants" and defined immigration as a pillar of Americanism.

The events of 9/11 only galvanized the messianic appeal of American populism. Concepts such as the "export of democracy" and "nation building" have become the new populist battle cry. As the conservative historian Paul Johnson asserted, the attack on the Twin Towers in New York propelled America to scuttle the security doctrine enshrined in a National Security Council report (NSC 68, released in 1949) whose aim was to contain evil. The new populist doctrine calls for America to instead embrace a proactive global policy intended to establish a new "empire of liberty."[58] Nineteenth-century American evangelical preacher Lyman Beecher's exhortation that "nation after nation, cheered by our example, will follow in our footsteps till the whole earth is free" echoes the mindset of the "nation-building," "democracy-exporting" United States in the early twenty-first century.[59]

Despite its messianic self-righteousness, the American right wing is pathologically optimistic in contrast to its European counterpart. It lacks the kind of xenophobic element that has typified many European right-wing movements.[60] That is not to say that this radical shift does not pose a threat both at home and abroad. On the domestic front, the religious messianic revival poses a threat to the "hybridity" of America's approach to immigration, which demands shared cultural values between host and immigrants in the public sphere, while accepting a separate value system in the private sphere.[61] The number of immigrants from the British Isles was therefore long ago eclipsed by Germans, South Europeans, and other groups. However, the social mores, the notions of civil society, and broad concepts of political "Americanism" penetrated most groups; even if dating from the mid-nineteenth century, the immigrants refused to "melt" or forget their old country, ethnic foods, and separate religious establishment.[62]

The debate over how to handle illegal immigration will continue to dog the Republican Party; the question of amnesty for the illegal immigrants already in the United States will remain a controversial issue for both parties. The concept of immigration, however, will not.

It is very likely that the public's association of Islam with terrorism may well lead to discriminatory immigration policies toward Arabs and Muslims, akin to the exclusion of Chinese immigrants in the nineteenth century or of East Europeans in the twentieth. However, the bulk of immigration to the United States, particularly from Latin America and East Asia, will continue to be generally viewed as an enduring part of the American ethos. In the case of the United States, immigration remains a legal rather than a security issue or a challenge to America's notions of its identity despite the events of 9/11. The mainstream of American politics within both political parties views immigration as an essential pillar of "Americanism." European incoherence regarding how to deal with immigrants therefore contrasts with both American coherence and stability. It is hard to argue there ever was a "West." On the issue of immigration, there certainly isn't one.

3

Religious Legacies and the Politics of Multiculturalism

A Comparative Analysis of Integration Policies in Western Democracies

MICHAEL MINKENBERG

Landmark events of global significance have repeatedly raised issues of policy convergence or divergence across nation-states, as well as issues of continuity or stability across time, or a combination of both. This is particularly true for events such as the end of the Cold War and 9/11, for the area of immigration and integration policies, and for the politics of citizenship and multicultural-ism. These issues are addressed here with respect to cultural path-dependency. The need to include religion and religious legacies in the analysis of these pol-icy areas is critical, underscored by the very fact that in many Western coun-tries, especially post-9/11, immigration and integration debates focus on the "religious" aspect of immigrants, that is, their non-Christian religion(s). More specifically, the Muslim backgrounds of immigrants contextualize the issue of immigrants' integration in light of a more fundamental debate on the com-patibility of modern democracy and Islam.[1] The renewed interest in religion as a political force in Western or largely secularized societies is not surprising.[2] What is surprising is the relative lack of effort to relate the religious legacies of the host societies (and not just the immigrants' religious backgrounds) with analysis of immigration and integration policies.

As Tomas Hammar reminds us, the very concept of citizenship in the pre-modern past was closely connected to religion, and modern citizenship can be seen as one of the results of secularization.[3] The well-known argument by Rogers Brubaker about the role of "cultural idioms" for citizenship can be linked to religious components of cultural and national identities.[4] Finally, the current debates regarding Muslim integration in Western democracies or Turkey's status as a candidate for EU membership vividly illustrate how religious arguments affect access and membership. Yet very few studies in the field of comparative politics ask what role religion plays in the functioning of multicultural societies. Moreover, there are surprisingly few systematic and empirical studies that investigate how national political—and politico-religious—contexts shape actions and claims made by groups with different ethnic and cultural backgrounds. The few studies that explicitly address the interplay of religion on both sides deal with only a few cases and their findings are limited in scope, especially with regard to the topics of convergence and continuity.[5]

A systematic analysis of the relationship between the religious legacies of countries receiving immigrants and the politics of multiculturalism (a term used synonymously with such terms as integration and incorporation) is offered here. The issues of continuity and change, and of convergence and divergences in these policy areas, are discussed in light of arguments about cultural path-dependency as they are used, for example, in secularization theory. Hence, the central question concerns whether variation in the politics of multiculturalism correlates with cultural and religious variations and to what extent it can be attributed to these differences within the Western democracies. Especially regarding the integration of religious "others" into a society shaped by Christianity, one might hypothesize that cultural heritage in Western democracies (Catholicism versus Protestantism) can account for variation in immigration and integration policies, as has been found for other policy areas.[6] This is the argument of divergence. Alternatively, one might predict that in the face of Muslim immigration, particularly after 9/11, these differences pale in light of a "Western" response to the perception of an "anti-Western threat." This is an argument in favor of convergence.

Religious legacies, however, should not be confined to the issue of denominations. Rather, other dimensions of the religious factor should be considered as well, in particular the institutional arrangement of church-state relations and the degree of official recognition of organized religion, the degree of secularization, and the existence and importance of religiously oriented political parties. For example, one might look to a recent study on state accommodation of Muslim religious practices in three Western European countries (the UK, France, and Germany). This study argues that the inherited particularities of church-state relations can better explain a nation's approach to Islam and the religious demands that Muslims have made than can the political resources of Muslim communities, the political opportunity structures available to them, or ideological factors such as attitudes about citizenship and nationality.[7] Other studies emphasize the importance of a Christian Democratic model of politics and policies, which, by implication, means that the vigorous role of Christian Democratic parties in a nation's politics should also affect the politics of multiculturalism.[8]

In light of this, I attempt in this chapter to "map" patterns of religion with regard to the politics of multiculturalism. Having established general patterns, I ask to what extent landmark events such as the end of the Cold War and 9/11 have affected these policies and, possibly, contributed to a policy convergence. The general argument of this chapter is that national legacies (or path-dependence) are still an important impediment for real convergence of policies across countries. Their importance persists despite the pluralization of the international order after 1989, globalization, EU integration, and 9/11. My arguments are built on a conceptual framework developed elsewhere with regard to nineteen Western democracies. These countries are characterized by their size, high levels of socioeconomic development, stable democratic systems, and a (Latin) Christian religious legacy.[9]

New Challenges to the Political Regulation of Religion and the Functioning of Democracies

For a long time, the so-called "Western world" has been interpreted as undergoing a long-term process of secularization or the decline of religion, in other words, the replacement of religious values by secular values. However, there is sufficient empirical evidence to demonstrate that even in the West, religion is a power that does not easily vanish.[10] Many religious traditions encourage the formation of conservative or fundamentalist religious movements, even in established democracies among non-Christian and Christian traditions alike, not to mention in developing countries.[11] Many Western countries experience an increasing public role of both established and non-mainline churches, a process that José Casanova calls the "deprivatization of religion."[12] As further evidence, one should include the multitude of new sects, religious cults, and small religious communities, although the spread of New Age, Buddhist, and other cults in the Western world is difficult to measure and interpret.[13] In addition, one of the effects of 9/11 was to bring back religion as a marker for violent global conflicts, almost a self-fulfilling prophecy of Samuel Huntington's scenario of civilizational clashes around the world in which "the West" is positioned against "the rest."[14]

In Europe, more than anywhere else, many signs have pointed toward the receding political influence of organized religion since the 1960s. These signs include church attendance rates, the number of priests, the participation of the young, and knowledge of the faith.[15] But even in Europe, the pluralization and increasing heterogeneity of the religious map lead to growth in both the number and intensity of conflicts at the intersection of politics and religion. One of the most visible examples is the increasing immigration of non-Christian minorities, particularly Muslims. They are at the center of current controversies about multiculturalism, the integration of ethnic and religious minorities, and transnational identities.[16] There are also those immigrant minorities that have a Christian background but are of a rather different theological fabric, such as the Orthodox churches of Eastern Europe or Christianity in the developing countries. Moreover, there are increasing numbers of atheists or persons unaffiliated with any religion. For example, in Germany, with the accession of the German Democratic Republic (GDR) in 1990, the percentage of officially counted nonreligious, or those not affiliated with any church, jumped from a few in the old Federal Republic to about 27 percent by 2000.[17] Finally, it is the European integration process itself that triggers new and heated discussions. Debate has arisen over religious references in the preamble of the future constitution of the EU and, even more vividly, about whether Turkey, for religious and cultural reasons, belongs to Europe and should be an EU member or not.[18] An overview of the current religious complexity of Western societies is given in table 3.1.

The data in table 3.1 show that in fourteen of nineteen Western democracies, Islam is the third- or even second-largest religious community. The five countries where Islam is second are, except for Denmark, all traditionally Catholic and located in the south and west of Europe. Somewhat mirroring this pattern, it is in particular the group of Protestant immigrant countries (Australia, Canada, and the United States, plus Finland) in which the Orthodox Church takes third or second place. Some argue that within Western democracies, religious traditions, especially Protestantism or Catholicism, assume a particular role in shaping politics and policies. Those policies deal with social programs or immigration and integration issues. The argument is, basically, that there are so-called "families of nations" shaped, in part, by particular Christian legacies.[19]

All these developments lead to the same conclusion. In effect, the long-established institutional and political arrangements to regulate the relationship between religion and politics in the framework of liberal democracies, are

Table 3.1
Religious diversity in nineteen Western democracies (mid-1990s or most proximate year, in percent of resident population)

	Protestant	Catholic	Jewish	Muslim[1]	Orthodox	Other
Austria (A)	5	78	0.1	2.6	—	0.2
Australia (AUS)	36.3	26.2	0.44	1.1	2.8	4.8
Belgium (B)	**0.4**	**88**	**0.35**	**3.8**	**—**	**n.d.**
Canada (CND)	30	40.3[2]	1.2	0.9	4.7[3]	8.8
Denmark (DK)	**89**	**0.62**	**0.06**	**2.8**	**—**	**n.d.**
Finland (FIN)	86.6	—	—	0.4	1.1	n.d.
France (F)	**1.6**	**81**	**1.2**	**7.0**	**0.2**	**n.d.**
Germany (D)	34.1	33.4	0.04	3.3	0.6	0.7
Great Britain (GB)	71.8	13.1	0.52	2.7	—	1.3
Ireland (IRE)	3.7	87.8	0.8	0.2	—	n.d.
Italy (I)	**0.09**	**90**	**0.05**	**1.0**	**—**	**n.d.**
Netherlands (NL)	26	36	0.19	4.6	—	n.d.
New Zealand (NZ)	38.5	13.8	—	0.4	—	13.4
Norway (N)	89	0.83	—	0.5	—	n.d.
Portugal (P)	0.5	93	0.02	0.3	0.2	1.3
Spain (SP)	**0.1**	**97.3**	**0.03**	**0.7**	**—**	**0.4**
Sweden (SW)	91.7	1.7	0.19	1.2	1.17	0.03
Switzerland (CH)	40.1	46.3	0.26	3.0	1.04	0.42
United States (USA)	52.6[2]	26	2.6	1.8	1.5	n.d.

Sources: Brigitte Maréchal and Felice Dassetto, introduction to *Muslims in the Enlarged Europe: Religion and Society*, edited by Brigitte Maréchal et al. (Leiden and Boston: Brill, 2003), tables 1 and 2; Mark Noll, *The Old Religion in a New World* (Grand Rapids, MI: Eerdmans, 2002), 282–83; *Der Fischer Weltalmanach 2000* (Frankfurt: Fischer Verlag, 1999), and various governmental sources and statistical yearbooks from the 1990s.

Notes: Countries in which Islam constitutes the third largest religious community are shaded gray; countries in which Islam constitutes the second largest religious community are shaded gray and in boldface type.

[1] Data for Muslims in Europe are estimates for the late 1990s by Maréchal and Dassetto, introduction to *Muslims in the Enlarged Europe*. In general, their estimates exceed those from other sourcebooks such as Fischer's *Weltalmanach* (e.g., here the percentages for Muslims in Belgium are 2.5 percent, in France 5.1 percent, in the UK 1.4 percent, in the Netherlands 3 percent, in Switzerland 2.2 percent). In a few countries, Maréchal and Dassetto's estimates are below those in other sources (Germany 3.7 percent, Italy 1.24 percent, Spain 0.75 percent).

[2] This figure includes 23 percent evangelical Christians as measured by survey data (Kenneth Wald, *Religion and Politics in the United States* [Lanham, MD: Rowman and Littlefield, 2003], 161).

[3] These figures are for 2000 and come from Noll, *The Old Religion in a New World*.

being challenged fundamentally and require new approaches. Even discounting the effects of 9/11, the multicultural facts of modern Western society raise new (and some very old) questions about the political regulation of religion. Accordingly, we see some major shifts in the debate in two groups of Western democracies: the ones with a more or less established church structure, and those with a more or less clear separation between church and state.[20]

In the first group (Great Britain, the Federal Republic of Germany, and the Scandinavian countries) we witness increasingly conflict-ridden processes of realigning religion in the public sphere. These conflicts can be seen in the area of religious education (an increasingly controversial topic in Germany). Another realm of conflict is religious symbolism in public, such as the wearing of head scarves or the presence of Christian symbols in official venues. There is also the fight for religious freedom for non-Christian congregations (e.g., the debate in Great Britain regarding the recognition of Muslim communities and the conflicted position of the established Church of England). A final example might be the steps toward disestablishment of the state church in Sweden in 2000.[21] But also in the "separationist group" (the United States and France, but also Turkey), the established role of religion is experiencing increasing pressures. These pressures come from actors who interpret the neutrality and indifference of the state in religious matters as an adoption of particular political positions at the expense of religion. Secularism is seen not as a guarantee of state neutrality and a balance between all religious forces but as a political program equivalent to a secularist state religion.[22]

Moreover, these developments in various parts of the world are accelerated by and interwoven with economic and cultural globalization processes.[23] The weakening of state institutions and national identities by these processes, which are even more dramatically highlighted by internal conflicts in the developing world, result in an ideological vacuum. This provides an opportunity for religious traditions, or their "re-inventions," to gel into cores of cultural identities and projects promoting transnational unities and loyalties. It is this scenario where Huntington's argument of a "clash of civilizations" finds its most persuasive power.[24]

It is against this backdrop that the specific effects of 9/11 on the current politics of immigration and integration in Western democracies need to be analyzed. But such an analysis can begin only if the developments and patterns that preceded September 2001 are well understood. A general overview of the various approaches toward multiculturalism in the Western world and their relationship to particular religious legacies will serve to enhance our understanding of the issue.

Conceptualizing the Comparative Politics of Multiculturalism

In order to situate comparative immigration and integration policy research within the larger field, it is worth remembering that Gabriel Almond and G. Bingham Powell distinguish four kinds of public policies: (1) policies of extraction, (2) policies of distribution, (3) policies of regulation, and (4) symbolic policies.[25] The former two largely involve money in terms of taxation and spending. It is the third type, "the exercise of control by a political system over the behavior of individuals and groups in the society," along with the fourth, which is of special interest here.[26] To a large extent, immigration and integration policies belong to this type, as does the politics of civil liberties, including human security. Many of the domains that Almond and Powell attribute to particular types of regulatory policies, such as family relations, personal conduct, protection of the person, and religious activities belonged historically, at least in Europe, to the domain of the churches instead of the state.[27] This mirrors the fact that historically, citizenship was based on membership in particular religious communities.[28]

An obvious problem for a cross-country comparative study of integration policies lies in the absence of any systematic and comparable data. Some might argue that on a global scale, differences in integration policies are fading, at least among Western democracies, due to processes of globalization and the emergence of transnational actors and approaches. This is particularly the case in the context of European integration and harmonization.[29] Such a comparative analysis should thus be obsolete. But I argue that nation-states remain the principal actors in establishing boundaries of territory and citizenship, and they control access and manage ethnic relations internally.[30] I believe this to be true despite some processes of convergence due to globalization and European integration and to similar reactions of Western nations to new waves of immigration. For the analysis at hand, the data collected in a five-country study by Ruud Koopmans et al. is very useful because it includes a variety of measures and indicators for the comparative analysis of the politics of citizenship and ethnic relations.[31] Koopmans et al. analyze France, Germany, the Netherlands, Switzerland, and the United Kingdom; for the remaining fourteen countries of interest in this study, data had to be collected case by case.

In order to manage the complexities of the issues at hand, several assumptions and qualifications are applied here. The analysis follows the fundamental distinction made by, among others, Hammar, who (in one of the first comparative studies of immigration policies) differentiates between the politics of immigration control and immigrant policy. The first term refers to "the rules and procedures governing the selection and admission of foreign citizens" and has been the subject of an earlier comparative analysis. The second term involves "the conditions provided to resident immigrants."[32] It includes aspects of integration and the management of cultural pluralism and shall be at the core of the analysis here. Another limitation concerns the concentration on policy output as opposed to policy outcomes.[33] While the former refers to official government policies and legislation, the latter includes the implementation of the policies and their societal consequences, such as changes in immigration rates or (xenophobic) reactions to certain laws or regulations. The relationship between outputs and outcomes is at the heart of many studies of immigration and one of the core issues in the question of whether politics matters. But here, it is of secondary importance, as is the political discourse on immigration and integration, which more often than not differs from official policies.

The concept of integration policies I employ borrows heavily from the work of other experts in the field.[34] In particular, the conceptual framework developed by Ruud Koopmans and Paul Statham seems fruitful for such a comparison.[35] In it, they distinguish two dimensions of integration, one based on individual rights, such as access to citizenship, benefits, and voting rights, and another based on cultural group rights such as the recognition of religious communities, education, and political representation.[36] Following this distinction, the comparison I make here addresses measures of cultural integration. These measures are analyzed in order to determine the policy approaches prevalent in each of the nineteen countries after migration began increasing in 1989 and to discuss various changes and the role of religious legacies and other (political) factors for these nations before and after 9/11.[37]

For a measure of cultural integration policies, the logic of Koopmans et al. is applied by considering cultural and religious rights outside of and inside public institutions.[38] The selection of criteria for group rights is guided by the reasoning that in many countries Muslims constitute the largest non-Christian religious minority (see table 3.1). Muslims are therefore not only more visible as a distinct cultural group but their distinctiveness as "cultural others" also provides a particular challenge to Western societies' integration policies. Hence there is a particular focus on Islamic practices in assessing cultural group rights, although in theory such rights would apply to other groups as well. These rights belong to two of the five dimensions analyzed by Koopmans et al.: religious rights outside of public institutions (e.g., ritual slaughter, Islamic calls to prayer, and provisions for Muslim burials) and cultural rights in public institutions (e.g., state recognition and funding of Islamic schools, the provision of Islamic religious classes in state schools, the right of female teachers to wear the Islamic head scarf, the provision of programs in immigrant languages in public broadcasting, Islamic religious programs in public broadcasting [for details see the appendix to this chapter]). The other three dimensions (political representation rights, affirmative action, and cultural requirements for naturalization) are not considered here because they touch upon other policy concerns, such as political integration and formal citizenship requirements. Table 3.2 shows these values for the five countries in Koopmans et al. and adds the other countries with the help of data on these indicators in the comparative literature and in primary sources. My primary focus here is on the overall cross-national patterns of policy approaches post-1989. For that reason, and to simplify the analyses that follow, the scores for the two time points of 1990 and 2002, where available, are averaged (for details, see the appendix to this chapter).

The distribution shown in table 3.2 summarizes a wide range of cultural integration policies with two distinct poles. At one end are found countries with a traditionally assimilationist and (with the exception of Switzerland) unitary approach to cultural difference. At the other end the "usual suspects" of multicultural democracies appear, that is, the classical "settler countries," along with the Netherlands and Sweden. Interestingly, the United States and Great Britain do not score as high as the other older immigration countries but are at the high end of the middle group.[39] Moreover, cultural integration policies do not match political integration policies as measured, for example, by voting rights for noncitizens.[40] There is very little overlap: only one country, Switzerland, is ranked low in both dimensions, and only two, New Zealand and Sweden, rank high in both. All other countries exhibit a mix of policies.[41]

A closer look at cultural group rights at separate data points in 1990 and 2002 reveals a general shift away from policies of "cultural monism" toward

Table 3.2
Levels of cultural integration in Western democracies (1990s)

Low (–1 to –0.34)	Medium (–0.33 to +0.33)		High (+0.34 to +1)
CH	A	FIN	AUS
F	B	I	CND
IRE	D	N	NL
P	DK	SP	NZ
	GB	USA	SW

Sources: See the appendix to this chapter.

those of "cultural pluralism" in most countries but with no signs of convergence.[42] The biggest shifts occurred in Portugal, Switzerland, Germany, and Denmark (starting at a lower level of −1.00, −0.90, −0.47, and 0.00, respectively, in 1990) and in Sweden and the Netherlands (at a higher level of 0.33 and 0.63, respectively). In contrast to this, Great Britain and France experienced little change, and Belgium and Italy experienced no change at all in this period, whereas in Australia a reverse shift away from cultural pluralism could be observed.

It could be argued that integration policies are a function of a country's immigration policy. After all, if a country pursues an open immigration policy it could be expected to make an effort to accommodate the various new migrant groups in its politics and culture. But this holds true only with a few qualifications. Table 3.3 demonstrates that there is a moderate relationship between a country's immigration policies and its cultural integration policies. While there is only one country with a "consistently" restrictive position on

Table 3.3
A typology of immigration and cultural integration policies (1990s)

Immigration policies	Cultural integration (religious and cultural group rights)		
	Low	Medium	High
Restrictive	Switzerland	Austria Denmark Germany Norway	
Moderate	France Ireland Portugal	Belgium Great Britain Finland Italy Spain	
Open		United States	Australia Canada New Zealand Netherlands Sweden

Sources: See the chapter appendix and Michael Minkenberg, "Religious Effects on the Shaping of Immigration Policies in Western Democracies," paper presented at the ECPR joint sessions workshops, Uppsala, Sweden, April 2004.

these two scales (Switzerland), the group with the high level of multicultural policies is also the group with a rather open immigration policy. It should not come as a surprise that those countries that experienced a long history of immigration and cultural diversity would match their immigration and integration policies (e.g., Australia, Canada, New Zealand, and—somewhat—the United States). But in the European context, Sweden and the Netherlands clearly stand out.[43] A particular discrepancy is found in the two Central European countries (Germany and Austria) where the growing acceptance of multicultural policies does not reflect a liberalization of immigration policies. Rather, multiculturalism appears to have been forced upon the political system by the growing pressures of cultural diversity from within rather than stemming from a political strategy to open up the borders to the outside.[44] This policy pattern dissolves, however, when cultural integration is replaced by political integration.[45] There is no clear relationship between these two policies, with only Switzerland being consistently restrictive in both regards whereas New Zealand and Sweden are consistently open.[46]

The Role of Religious Legacies in Church-State Relations

As I have shown in my earlier work, standard explanatory models of comparative policy research have not yielded clear results with regard to immigration policies, although some patterns could be identified.[47] I am introducing the religious dimension of immigration policy, discussing in particular the question of whether Francis Castles's "family of nations" model is appropriate in analyzing variations in immigration policy.[48] Unlike in Castles's studies, however, I do not reduce religion to the confessional heritage or role of Catholic parties. Instead, following earlier analyses, the religious factor is decomposed into a historic-cultural dimension (i.e., the role of confessional patterns) and a sociocultural dimension of religiosity (as measured in church-going rates, a further institutional dimension of patterns of church-state relations).[49] I also introduce a more political dimension by looking at religious parties and movements separately and at the type of democracy practiced.

In order to measure the cultural legacy of religion, two dimensions are considered. One is the confessional composition of a country that, if at all, is the standard variable of religion's input in comparative public policy research. The other is the level of religiosity as a measure of a country's "embeddedness" in religious practice.[50] In terms of the secularization argument, the first dimension might be seen as an indicator of a country's cultural differentiation, or cultural pluralism. The second dimension, however, points to the country's path of secularization as disenchantment. Most texts that emphasize the role of confessions in a nation's history classify countries as Catholic, Protestant, or confessionally mixed. Most of those texts also assert that these cultural patterns have a long-lasting influence on current policy and politics.[51] Following David Martin, I use three categories for the countries under consideration: (1) cultures with a Protestant dominance, resulting either from a lack of Catholics (the Scandinavian countries) or because Catholic minorities arrived after the pattern had been set (England, the United States); (2) cultures with a historical Protestant majority and substantial Catholic minorities (the Netherlands, Germany, Switzerland) where a cultural rather than a mere political bipolarity has emerged along with subcultural segregation; and (3) cultures with a Catholic dominance and democratic or democratizing regimes (France, Italy, Belgium, Austria, Ireland) that are characterized by large political and social fissures, organic opposition, and secularist dogmas.[52]

Another component of the cultural legacy is the actual degree of individual attachment to established religion. This is important because high levels of religiosity give churches greater legitimacy as political actors. Moreover, religiosity may be a better predictor for public policy than confessional composition alone. This is particularly so if the question of whether a country is Catholic or Protestant is considered less important than whether Catholics or Protestants actually attend church or believe in the teachings of the church. In this analysis, religiosity is measured by frequency of church-going rather than by religious beliefs because religiosity is thus tied to existing institutions rather than abstract religious concepts and values. Data on church-going in the nineteen countries analyzed here are taken from the 1980s and 1990s waves documented in the World Values Survey.[53] The data for the 1980s and 1990s are then averaged and the countries are grouped according to the frequency of church-going ranging from low (less than 20 percent who go at least once a month), to medium (20 to 40 percent), to high (above 40 percent).[54]

The relationship between the religious legacies of the nineteen countries and their integration policies is presented in table 3.4. The overall picture suggests a denominational effect on integration policies. Predominantly Protestant countries exhibit moderate to high levels of cultural group rights recognition whereas Catholic countries fall in the range of low to moderate levels. In this regard, it is noteworthy that the shifts toward cultural pluralism from 1990 to 2002 occurred mostly in Protestant countries—regardless of their "starting point"—whereas Catholic countries remained more static in this period (see the chapter's appendix).

The notion of clustering a unique Southern European or Mediterranean group of countries with regard to their policies is not supported by the distribution in table 3.4.[55] In part, this misconception results when one conflates immigration rates and immigration policies.[56] While Mediterranean countries share the common fate of being latecomers as receiving countries, their approach to integration is also shared by other, non-Mediterranean countries as well (Belgium, Austria). My analysis suggests that what this group has in common is their religiosity, not their geography. This is also true with regard to the growing proportion of Muslims in these countries. All four countries, all Catholic, where Islam is the second religion (see table 3.1), employ a low- to moderate-level integration policy. Secularization measured in church-going rates underscores this trend. With the exception of Canada, all countries with high church attendance show low to moderate recognition of cultural group rights. On the other hand, again with the notable exception of France, countries with low church-going rates are more ready for such an integration policy.

Finally, one must go beyond confessions and church-going rates when looking for a common religious denominator for the group with open immi-

Table 3.4
Religious legacies: Confessions, religiosity, state-church relations, and cultural integration policies

	Recognition of group rights		
	Low	Moderate	High
Predominantly Protestant		Great Britain *Denmark* *Finland* *Norway* **United States**	Australia New Zealand *Sweden*
Mixed Protestant	Switzerland	Germany	Netherlands **Canada**
Catholic	*France* **Ireland** **Portugal**	Austria Belgium **Italy** **Spain**	

Note: Countries in **bold** type are those with **high religiosity**; countries in *italics* are those with *low religiosity*. Countries that are underlined fall into the category of strict church-state separation.

gration policies. As I have demonstrated in prior analyses, the regime of church-state relations can also account for variations in particular public policies.[57]

This institutional dimension of religious legacies is measured by the degree of deregulation of churches in financial, political, and legal respects. This procedure applies a six-point scale developed by Mark Chaves and David E. Cann and adds two more criteria related to public support for religious education.[58] Chaves and Cann point out that regardless of the official relationship between church and state, by definition Catholic societies are much less pluralistic in religious terms than Protestant societies and that different dynamics are at work. But as the data in table 3.1 demonstrated, this historical disequilibrium is already in the process of revision. For the purpose of the analysis here, the church-state scale is summarized in a threefold typology: countries with full establishment of a national religion (such as the Scandinavian countries), countries with partial establishment (such as Germany but also Italy and Great Britain), and countries with a clear separation of church and state (such as the United States and France).[59]

The distributions summarized in table 3.4 show that there is hardly any overall effect of this particular institutional arrangement on the level of cultural integration offered.[60] This is in contrast to the relevance of church-state relations for immigration policies and contrary to the argument made by Joel Fetzer and J. Christopher Soper in *Muslims and the State in Britain, France, and Germany* (2005). There seems instead to be a polarization, with only the United States taking a middle position. A separationist regime per se does not lead to a low recognition of cultural group rights. On the basis of the data in this table, however, one can detect such an effect in combination with Catholicism. Among Protestant countries, there appears to be an effect in the opposite direction, with Sweden as a prominent outlier. I offer, based on table 3.4, the general argument that religious and cultural groups (in particular Muslims) get higher recognition in those Protestant countries where there is a clear separation of church and state. Protestant countries where church-state relations are less distinct are less accepting of such cultural group differences. That is, Fetzer and Soper's conclusion about the non-accommodating effects of separationist church-state regimes holds only for France and possibly Ireland but cannot be generalized. Moreover, as has been shown elsewhere, one has to distinguish the type of Muslim group organizations when analyzing the effects of state-church relations in Europe.[61] Until 1989, European states dealt with groups that they considered representatives of an "official Islam," but beginning in the 1990s, the focus shifted to "political Islam" (as discussed by Jonathan Laurence in chapter 12, this volume).

Political Parties, Regime Patterns, and Integration Policies

Having read the studies of strong left-wing parties and generous welfare states, one might expect a relationship between the presence of these parties and a restrictive output in integration policies. However, while the class cleavage has undergone a steady decline in significance, the religious cleavage in terms of the relationship between religiosity (as measured by church attendance) and left-right voting behavior has stayed rather stable. In the United States, there was even a slight but steady increase of religious voting attributable to the growing mobilization efforts of the new Christian right.[62]

In order to derive a measure that captures a broad Christian partisan impact instead of a merely Catholic partisan impact, the countries are classified in three ways. The first is according to the role of religion in the identity and program of particular parties and their relationship to religious groups. The second classification is in the salience of the religious cleavage in voting behavior. The third focuses on how long these parties have participated in national governments.[63] The resulting six-point scale is summarized in three categories, ranging from low to medium to high religious impact.

Table 3.5 depicts an interesting role that these parties play. It confirms what has been shown with regard to other social policies. A strong Christian Democratic presence corresponds not just with a moderate abortion ruling and family policies but also with moderate integration policies.[64] It thus reflects a particular policy profile of Christian Democracy in association with a larger and distinct vision of society.[65] This effect, while disappearing with regard to the relative openness of immigration policies (i.e., the question of how to control access to the country), is clearly reinforced with regard to the accommodation of non-Christian minorities. Only the Netherlands strays from the "centrist" Christian Democratic group.[66]

Overall, however, a comparison of tables 3.4 and 3.5 suggests that religious partisan effects are less significant than those of religious legacies.

The final issue I address is the role of the political system as a whole. One of the most influential lines of argument explaining divergence in policy output focuses on the type of democracy. A prominent model is Arend Lijphart's distinction between majoritarian and consensual democracies, distinguished by the degree to which political power is centralized and uninhibited by checks and balances.[67] In majoritarian democracies, the parliamentary majority and the executive that emerges from it encounter few constraints on their exercise of power. In consensus democracies, on the other hand, the power of the executive is mediated by a variety of other institutions, such as an independent parliament, coalition-building among parties, federalism, and an in-

Table 3.5
The effects of religious partisanship on cultural integration

	Recognition of group rights		
	Low	Moderate	High
Low religious partisan impact	*France*		**Canada** Australia New Zealand
Medium religious partisan impact	**Ireland** **Portugal** Switzerland	**Spain** **United States** Great Britain	*Sweden*
High religious partisan impact		**Italy** Austria Germany Belgium Denmark Finland Norway	Netherlands

Note: Countries in **bold** are those with a **high level of religiosity**; countries in *italics* are those with *low religiosity.* Countries that are <u>underlined</u> are those with <u>strong Christian Democratic</u> elements in the party system.

dependent judiciary. Lijphart summarizes these factors along two dimensions. The first is the party-executive dimension, which concerns mostly the relationship between political parties, the executive, and parliament. The second is the federalism-unitarism dimension, which is rather independent from the former and is constituted by factors such as a strong or weak judiciary, bicameralism versus a single parliamentary chamber, and a federalist rather than a unitary state. Lijphart's classification of countries diverges somewhat from the one applied here, however, because he decides to drop the federalism dimension and uses only the party-executive dimension to group the countries. However, I, in effect, take his classification more seriously than he does. I classify as consensus democracies only those countries that have positive values in both dimensions. I classify as majoritarian only those countries that have negative values in both dimensions. All other countries are classified here as mixed forms.

Lijphart argues that the character of democracies matters significantly for policy output and that consensus democracies are largely more inclusive and more adequately represent minority interests than do majoritarian democracies. Does this translate into a more inclusive integration policy? The summary in table 3.6 casts some doubt on this proposition. It seems that there is no relationship at all between the type of democracy and the level of acceptance of cultural group rights. While Lijphart demonstrated some relationship between consensus democracy and the responsiveness to minorities' and women's concerns, this correlation does not extend into the realm of multicultural politics. Here the combination of party politics and confessional legacies, for example, a "Catholic cultural effect" in the sense that Francis Castles uses it, seems the most important factor.

Convergent or Divergent Trends after 9/11 in Light of Cultural Legacies

In the 1980s, Tomas Hammar observed that among the nineteen democracies, the politics of multiculturalism seemed to diverge more than did their immigration policies.[68] The current post-9/11 debates about head scarves, the securitization of immigration, and immigrant policies indicate some convergence in Europe. Some authors argue that even prior to 9/11 there had been a trend of convergence in European countries with regard to control of immi-

Table 3.6
The effects of type of democracy and religiosity on cultural integration

	Recognition of group rights		
	Low	Moderate	High
Majoritarian democracies	France **Ireland**	Great Britain	New Zealand
Mixed types	**Portugal**	*Denmark* *Finland* *Norway* Italy Spain **United States**	*Sweden* **Canada** Australia **Canada**
Consensus democracies	Switzerland	Austria Germany Belgium	Netherlands

Note: Countries in **bold** are those with a **high level** of **religiosity**; countries in *italics* are those with *low levels*. Countries that are underlined are those with strong Christian Democratic elements in the party system.

gration and conceptions of citizenship.[69] However, assessments regarding convergence depend on the measurement and interpretation of magnitude and direction. Koopmans et al. evaluated their results for the five Western European countries in their study based on the three data points of 1980, 1990, and 2002. They claimed that there was "convergence in the sense that all five countries have—to smaller or greater extents—moved in the same direction. All countries—with the exception of the United Kingdom, which was already close to the civic pole—have shifted toward a more civic-territorial conception of citizenship, although the ranges have been quite marginal in the case of Switzerland. Similarly, all countries have moved away from the assimilationist pole toward a stronger recognition of cultural rights and differences. Again, the strength of this trend varies greatly among the countries; it is weak in France, and even more so in Switzerland."[70] This finding is even less uniform in the expanded sample examined in this chapter: some countries such as Belgium and Italy have not experienced any significant shifts while Australia has reversed some of its multicultural approaches.[71]

Viewed in terms of the range of variation between countries, however, there is no real apparent convergence. Instead, some signs of divergence can be observed, with the Netherlands, Britain, Sweden, and even Denmark (until recently) following the path of multiculturalism and Belgium, France, and Switzerland making only very modest progress. A particular shift occurred in Portugal. Despite the provisions of religious freedom and state neutrality enshrined in the 1976 constitution, non-Catholic minorities hardly had any group rights until the very end of the twentieth century. This changed only and rather abruptly with the passing of a new law on religious freedom, which took five years of preparation and was passed in the summer of 2001.[72] Hence, by the beginning of the new millennium the differences between cultural monist and cultural pluralist approaches to the integration of immigrants were more pronounced than at the end of the Cold War.[73] So, did any of this change after 9/11, and, if so, to what extent are these changes shaped by a country's religious legacies?

Koopmans et al. themselves claim that there has been a reversal in the trend toward differential citizenship in the wake of September 11, 2001.[74] Their data, however, which covers only the period up to 2002, do not provide empirical evidence for such a general claim. In fact, where such reversals can be substantiated, as in the case of Australia, they were initiated prior to 9/11 and can be explained by the rise of a religiously oriented conservative government. Notably, Australia's integration policies are still more pluralist than the average.[75] The slow implementation of the new Portuguese law on religious freedom after 2001 can be attributed in part to the effects of 9/11, but it was nonetheless fully completed by 2003—despite 9/11 and a modest increase in the Portuguese resistance to multiculturalism (see figure 3.1). Furthermore, in France the modest changes and the slowdown of reforms after 2002 may have more to do with the hegemonic political tradition of republicanism and the interplay between the Front National and the dominant political forces than with the effects of 9/11.[76] Chapter 6 in this volume, written by Martin Schain, underscores that point. Schain's findings suggest that there is less change in Europe than generally assumed, that convergence between the United States and Europe occurred mostly in the area of security measures such as surveillance and related actions directed against immigrant populations.

Moreover, there are discrepancies between Western public opinion and government policies. On the one hand, survey data demonstrate weakening public support for policies based on cultural pluralism. Fetzer and Soper analyzed public support for Islam in schools in three Western European countries. They show, for example, that after 9/11 there was a decline in support of state funding of Islamic schools (Britain), for providing Islamic instruction in public schools (Germany), and for allowing the hijab in public schools (France).[77] They argue that this shift, however, is not mirrored at the level of elites or, one could postulate, in public policies: "the Islam-related attitudes of European elites . . . are much more constrained by their country's particular church-state arrangement than are the views of ordinary citizens."[78] On the other hand, a survey analysis by the European Monitoring Centre on Racism and Xenophobia shows that, with the exception of Greece, resistance to multicultural society did not increase in EU member states between 2000 and

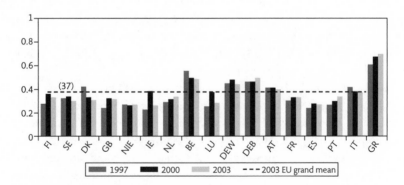

Fig. 3.1. Resistance to multicultural society in the EU 15 (longitudinal changes per country).
Source: European Union Monitoring Centre on Racism and Xenophobia (EUMC), *Report on Migrants, Minorities, and Employment* (2003), 42.

2003. Rather, it decreased in many countries during that period.[79] The levels were particularly low in the Nordic countries where, apparently, the Protestant legacies constrain such reversals. A modestly increasing resistance to multicultural policies could be observed in the Mediterranean countries and in those with high levels of, and long association with, multiculturalism (Great Britain, the Netherlands).

In a similar vein, the reactions to the London bomb attacks of July 2005 and their impact on Muslim communities in the EU triggered new or reinforced existing initiatives by the government to reach out to the Muslim community rather than a reversal of such policies.[80] This reaction was not limited to Europe. In July 2005, several mosques were attacked in New Zealand, but the government responded with its outreach program. These outreach efforts clash, however, with the growing securitization of immigration policies, and they affect civil liberties for both citizens and migrants alike (see chapter 4, by Didier Bigo, in this volume).

This chapter has addressed the question of how the growing complexity and the cultural diversity of Western countries in the face of new immigration waves affect the functioning of democracies and in particular the politics of multiculturalism. It demonstrated that there is a considerable diversity in such policies in the West, not just between the "settler countries" and the European countries but also within these categories. It also demonstrated that a modified "families of nations" concept may be a better frame of analysis than standard models. This concept should adjust for the interplay of nation-building, religious traditions, and institutional management of cultural diversity. It also needs to address the role of parties, in particular the policy characteristics of Christian Democracy.[81]

Moreover, the analysis suggests that the cultural integration of noncitizens does not neatly correspond with the openness of immigration policies. In a similar vein, the degree of social integration of "guest workers" in Germany clearly exceeds that of labor migrants in France.[82] I have attempted here to introduce a step toward more comparative research regarding group recognition and civil liberties of religious minorities, in particular the large and growing group of Muslims.[83] This research shows that cultural legacies such as Christian denominations, in combination with more political factors such as the role of religious parties, play an important role in shaping a country's readiness to accommodate non-Christian immigrant groups. The effects of 9/11 can so far be demonstrated only at the level of the mass public rather than in public policies.

Appendix
Scale of Cultural Group Rights in Nineteen Democracies (1990/2002)

Cultural group rights as defined by Koopmans et al. in *Contested Citizenship*
Allowances for religious practices outside of public institutions
• Ritual slaughtering according to Islamic rite
• Islamic call to prayer
• Provision for Muslim burials

Cultural rights and provisions in public institutions
• State recognition and funding of Islamic schools
• Islamic religious classes in state schools
• The right of female teachers to wear the Islamic head scarf
• Programs in immigrant languages in public broadcasting
• Islamic religious programs in public broadcasting

Table 3.7

Table 3.7
Cultural group rights in nineteen democratic nations

	Religious rights (RR)		Cultural rights (CR)		Average RR and CR		
	1990	2002	1990	2002	1990	2002	1990/ 2002
A	−0.66	0.33	0.50	1.00	−0.08	0.67	0.29
AUS	0.50	0.50	0.20	0.40	0.50	0.30	0.40
B	0.00	0.00	−0.20	−0.20	−0.10	−0.10	−0.10
CH	−1.00	−0.66	−0.80	−0.60	−0.90	−0.63	−0.76
CND	n.d	1.00	n.d.	0.40	n.d.	0.70	0.77
D	−0.33	0.00	−0.60	0.00	−0.47	0.00	−0.24
DK	0.00	0.00	0.00	0.66	0.00	0.33	0.17
F	−0.33	0.00	−0.60	−0.60	−0.47	−0.30	−0.39
FIN	n.d.	0.33	n.d.	−0.20	n.d.	0.13	0.13
GB	0.33	0.33	0.00	0.20	0.17	0.27	0.22
I	0.00	0.00	−0.33	−0.33	−0.17	−0.17	−0.17
IRE	0.00	0.33	−1.00	−0.60	−0.50	−0.27	−0.39
N	n.d.	0.33	n.d.	−0.40	n.d.	−0.03	−0.03
NL	0.66	1.00	0.60	0.80	0.63	0.90	0.77
NZ	1.00	1.00	0.00	0.60	0.50	0.80	0.67
P	−1.00	0.66	−1.00	−0.20	−1.00	0.23	−0.39
SP	n.d.	0.33	n.d.	0.00	n.d.	0.17	0.17
SW	n.d.	0.66	0.33	0.50	0.33	0.58	0.45
USA	n.d.	1.00	n.d.	−0.40	n.d.	0.30	0.30

Sources: John Anderson, *Religious Liberty in Transitional Societies: The Politics of Religion* (Cambridge: Cambridge University Press, 2003); Fahad Ansari and Uzma Karim, *Hijab and Democracy* (Wembley, England: Islamic Human Rights Commission, 2004); Mohamed El Battiui, Firouzeh Nahavandi, and Meryem Kanmaz, *Mosquées, imams et professeurs de religion islamique en Belgique: état de la question et enjeux* (Brussels: Fondation Roi Baudouin, 2004); Bernabé López Garcia and Ana Planet Contreras, "Islam in Spain," in *Islam, Europe's Second Religion*, ed. Shireen T. Hunter (Westport, CT: Praeger, 2002), 156–74; Ruud Koopmans et al., *Contested Citizenship: Immigration and Cultural Diversity in Europe* (Minneapolis: University of Minnesota Press, 2005); John Madeley and Zsolt Enyedi, eds., *Church and State in Contemporary Europe: The Chimera of Neutrality*, special issue of *West European Politics* (London: Frank Cass, 2003); Steven J. Monsma and J. Christopher Soper, *The Challenge of Pluralism: Church and State in Five Democracies* (Lanham, MD: Rowman and Littlefield, 1997); James T. Richardson, ed., *Regulating Religion: Case Studies from around the Globe* (New York: Kluwer Academic/Plenum Publishers, 2004); Ingvill Thorsen Plesner, "State Church and Autonomy in Norway," in *Church Autonomy: A Comparative Survey*, ed. Gerhard Robbers (Frankfurt: Peter Lang, 2001), 467–84; http://euro-islam.info.html; plus personal research and communication with country experts.

Table 3.8
Summary of cultural integration and religious and cultural group rights in Western democracies (averages, 1990 and 2002)

−1.00 to −0.34	−0.33 to +0.33	+0.34 to +1.00
CH	A	AUS
F	B	CND
IRE	D	NL
P	DK	NZ
	GB	SW
	FIN	
	I	
	N	
	SP	
	USA	

4

The Emergence of a Consensus

Global Terrorism, Global Insecurity, and Global Security

DIDIER BIGO

Since the 1990s, an increasing number of scholars studying security, as well as security professionals, have come to the same conclusion: that internal security and external security are merging under the pressure of globalization. Traditionally, these two separate domains have essentially been the concern of different institutions—the police internally and the armed forces externally—but their domains now seem close to overlapping as new circumstances present themselves. The missions of the police and the armed forces converge on issues such as terrorism, organized crime, surveillance of people, and possible threats to identity. Terrorists, suspected terrorists, and members of transnational crime organizations have changed fundamentally in character and, as such, demand that we develop new ways of thinking about security. Internal policing is insufficient. To fight against such varied threats as suicide bombers, operatives of clandestine political organizations, and even ordinary criminals coming from abroad, it is first of all necessary to identify them. This is done largely by expanding surveillance and police controls beyond the traditional list of habitual offenders. This expansion has resulted in intelligence being gathered on the flimsiest of presuppositions. The profiled migrants may belong to the "same" religion, have had chance encounters with members of clandestine organizations, be refugees of the same nationality, or even be tourists of whom police are vaguely suspicious. This beefed-up surveillance is conducted on an international basis, as government and law enforcement agencies seek information on selected suspects: if they have traveled, where they have been, with whom, and for what purpose. It is also crucial to "trace" them within borders. If the surveillance targets are connected with a hostile regime or a hostile minority group that could provide them with weapons and organizational or financial support, their criminal activities may well be considered acts of "war," in a newfangled sense.

Furthermore, in this new "global age," individual activities become connected in the public mind to a global state of undeclared war. From the narrative of today's security experts emerges a new consensus that is taken at face value. It describes the world as a more dangerous place than ever, with the rise in global insecurity characterized by a concomitant expansion of transnational organized crime and terrorism, which requires new measures heightening the level of security.[1] These experts have developed a mantra. It intones that, in order to combat new threats, we need new solutions, a new balance between freedom and security, a new equilibrium between the need for international cooperation and the requirements of national sovereignty, and, finally, a new acceptance of and submission to the providers of global security. What is more, we owe these providers our obeisance whether they are private or public and even if they operate at another level, in a netherworld beyond the reach of national institutions.

At some point after September 11, 2001, this discourse, already emerging in the 1990s, acquired the status of truth and was unchallenged by the media and some political elites.[2] It became the consensus and the foundation upon which other theories were built.

Grounding the Global Insecurity Thesis on the Events of 9/11

In the wake of 9/11, there has been unprecedented intensity in the discourses that the United States and its closest allies have put forward asserting the need to globalize security and promoting the wars in Afghanistan and Iraq. At the core of these discourses is the idea that terrorism now exists on a global scale.[3] Terrorism from below, as the discourse goes, is destroying sovereign states, even the most powerful of them. The danger is now coming from a handful of individuals, who may be religious fanatics and may gain access to unconventional weapons. This terrorism from below is now both global and hidden. International networks of terrorist cells render traditional territorial borders meaningless. The threat no longer originates from a specific place and from a specific enemy that can be watched. A fearful consensus has been reached: we have good reason to fear the future unless we create new means of deterrence to thwart the intentions of those who would use violence against civilians to promote political goals. "Global terrorism" has become the accepted term to describe the new paradigm for the post–September 11 world, even by critics of U.S. policy. But to analyze the attacks of 2001 in New York and Washington as acts of terror is in some ways misleading, at least as far as the formal definition of terror is concerned.[4]

The popular narrative about the attacks of September 11 is that they have spread terror all over the world, that they terrified the public, that the public was in need of immediate protection, and that the terrorists are powerful while governments are weak. Following this line of thinking, it becomes therefore important to fight back, to take emergency actions, and to use exceptional measures, even circumventing the established rule of law. However, if September 11, 2001, has changed anything in the world, it is not because the attacks "terrorized," that is, paralyzed the U.S. government with fear. One can say the same about the March 11, 2004, transit bombings in Madrid and those on July 7, 2005, in London. In those two cases, the population immediately demonstrated that if the plan was to intimidate them, then they would react by going about their everyday routines with a casual sort of courage. The effects of the transit bombings were not a "new wave of terror," of "panic," as the media stated again and again. The effect was instead a renewed will to resist terror, to find the criminals, and to understand their behavior. Life as usual was clearly the answer in London and Madrid, even if it was less the case in New York and Washington.

The Choice for "War"

The scale of the attacks on 9/11 and the surprise that New York and Washington were targeted created a different situation. It allowed the U.S. government to manipulate feelings of despair, encourage popular rage, and promote patriotism in order to create an atmosphere of war. Patriotism was soon converted into a thirst for revenge to erase the shame of having been attacked in the homeland. It also became a yen to spread this fight for revenge across the world and to make it seem not only understandable but also legitimate. The media argument that the bombings were not an odious crime but an act of war, comparable to the attack on Pearl Harbor, was incredibly powerful and

largely unanimous. The attacks were not interpreted as anything even remotely close to intimidation and paralysis; instead, they were framed with a military spirit, one that sought a target against which reciprocal violence would
be justified. As soon as Al Qaeda and Osama bin Laden were identified as the
perpetrators, their link with the Taliban made Afghanistan the most viable
target for such a decentralized organization whose bases were also in Sudan,
Ethiopia, Saudi Arabia, and many others countries, including Western ones.
The only possible response to such a violent deed was allegedly another act of
violence. This retaliatory act would appease the suffering of the victims, ex-
punge the shame of the government, and punish those who ordered and plot-
ted destruction on such a scale. The punishment would seem particularly
reciprocal in the case of New York, where the terrorists had clearly targeted
American civilians and other parties not remotely responsible for any crucial
U.S. foreign policy decisions.[5] Using "punishment abroad" as a form of undeclared war, one justified by an unprovoked attack and the right to preventive defense, was considered the answer to any objections. The line from
Washington was that no place on earth would be a safe haven for America's
enemies, who would be made to surrender unconditionally. Every foreigner
fighting in Afghanistan against the United States would be considered a terrorist, an unlawful combatant who is neither a criminal nor a soldier.

September 11, 2001, then, did not signal the birth of a new form of terror in the global age. It did not create waves of intimidation. It cannot be considered an "unprecedented event" that radically changed the face of the
modern world, even if it was a tragic moment. It did not mark the birth of a
new age of terrorism, or "hyperterrorism," or "megaterrorism," or some "third
type" of terrorism.[6] The development of transnational political violence targeting civilians of other countries in order to bend the policy of a government
has been a long process, dating as far back as the decolonization processes of
the 1950s. It can be observed in the hijacking of aircraft in the 1970s, the development of remote bombing technologies in the 1980s, and the radicalization of conflicts in Lebanon and Palestine. This stream of terrorist activity can
also be traced to suicide bombers using trucks against French and U.S. armies
in Beirut and to weaponry that the United States gave to the *mujahadeen* to
use in their struggle against the Soviet Union in Afghanistan.

It was definitely unusual for the U.S. mainland to be attacked. But to the
extent that such "novel" actions may be found within the repertoire of enemy
actions, they involved merely new combinations of traditional forms of action
(suicide bombing, plane hijacking, civilian targets for mass murder). They
were not, as so many official accounts have implied, some grand new force

combining weapons of mass destruction with fanatical and irrational clandestine organizations. Nevertheless, a powerful narrative of hyperterrorism has created this impression of novelty and offered justification for the exceptional measures taken in the name of the "survival of the nation" and the "protection of the population."[7]

Thus, September 11 does not signal the paralysis of the will of the United States. However, with so many victims killed in such a spectacular way and without any warning, many Western states became anxious that their long-standing monopoly of violence within a specific national territory was coming to an end. It is this anxiety that has promoted the idea of preventing such a danger by closing the borders, immediately launching a territorial war to demonstrate the strength of the country, and manipulating popular feelings to take revenge, to punish someone—anyone—even if it is not the guilty party.

But the rhetoric of global terrorism, while useful for creating a connection between an undetected agent and a territorial base, leaves a major problem unsolved. That dilemma is how to execute an efficient struggle against an enemy that is not territorially fixed. How does a nation prevent such an enemy from striking again? The old solutions do not work anymore, even if the Afghanistan invasion was launched with the hope of destroying all the infrastructures of the alleged center of Al Qaeda operations. The presentation of new solutions was thus a vital necessity for the politicians in power at that time. Conveniently, the "global insecurity" narrative was already well developed after the end of the Soviet-American bipolarity, especially in some neoconservative circles (but not only in these circles). It quickly became the main framework for a new paradigm of resistance and the basis for justifying increased surveillance and more oppressive laws.[8]

Because the U.S. government framed its response in the context of the future, that is, what the terrorists might do next, not all of the energies of the United States were directed at finding the perpetrators of September 11 (as in a criminal justice context). Instead, the primary focus was on the future: preventing a new and more dangerous attack (as would be the case in a military or intelligence context). The option to consider the attacks criminal acts instead of acts of war, to use the law enforcement and criminal justice systems instead of taking military action, was immediately dismissed, within a few hours after the attacks. No real alternative was ever discussed in policy circles after that.[9] And if we compare this reaction to that which occurred after the transit bombings in Madrid and London, we clearly see the difference that this framing makes. In the two European capitals the bombings were considered to be very serious crimes, but the major focus was on finding the bombers and their accomplices. In the United States, the reaction was to launch a territorial war abroad in order to apprehend those who had supported the perpetrators and to destroy their organizational base. This rationale immediately blended the two options and the two visions by merging them into a "war on terror." It has created a juridical nightmare at both the international and domestic levels by destroying the basic principles of the rule of law and trying to create "new" categories corresponding to the "new" situation. It became a "war against evil" that has merged internal and external security fears once and for all. It coalesced around one country: Taliban-ruled Afghanistan, for its support of Al Qaeda. (The United States neglected to consider making Saudi Arabia a target, despite the fact that most of the suicide bombers were from Saudi Arabia and were coming directly from there, not from Afghanistan.[10]) An enemy had to be given form and substance beyond the vaporized bodies of the suicide bombers. It took the form of a list of "rogue states" that sponsor terrorist networks and that are designated as enemies of the United States. This list was drawn up in forty-eight hours and included, for the first time, Taliban-ruled Afghanistan. In this discourse, war, invasion, and occupation are seen as solutions to terrorism. Legitimate violence (war), is thus presumed to be the only means of opposing illegitimate violence (terror).

Politicians made up their minds very quickly at a very difficult time. The violence, the number of casualties, and the spectacular images of the attacks were broadcast globally. U.S. leaders chose "war" instead of "crime." The general public was left to accept or reject this perception. Choosing "war" was a way to frame the political violence of the clandestine organization that had already attacked them (under the label of Al Qaeda). Politicians reacted to the scale of the violence by framing the response as a global war on terror. U.S. leaders desperately needed a narrative to avoid being perceived as powerless in the aftermath of the attacks.[11] This idea of the rise in global insecurity merging the internal and external threats, of the transversal risks and dangers, was still a subject of fierce debate among security professionals. Political necessity, however, converted it into the "consensus," the "explanation" for what had happened on September 11.[12]

The narrative of "global terrorism" was a way of ending the agonizing effort of trying to make sense of the attacks, of neutralizing the fear of whatever might have been the reason for the attacks. The idea of "global terrorism" incorporates the attacks into a metanarrative about globalization and its dangers, which had already become apparent. It was a way to discuss the attacks from the standpoint of "answers" instead of questions. Debate was then pos sible only inside this framework. This framework silenced any discussion about the origins of violence, its political element, its symmetry, and any questioning of the idea that violence is the only way to stop violence.[13]

Fear of the Future

The attacks and their framing as global terror have activated a different form of fear. This fear is not directly linked to Al Qaeda or other violent and clandestine political organizations but to the ontological fear of a chaotic world. In this nightmarish world, weapons of mass destruction are controlled not only by rational state actors but also by a handful of fanatics. The attacks have embodied a profound fear of the future driven by a worst-case scenario. It focuses on an image widely used in movies: a mushroom cloud rising over a U.S. city. Two phrases have been repeated over and over again: "the world is no longer safe, nor will it ever be again," and "the question is not if, but when."

From a U.S. perspective, September 11, 2001, has been seen as something radically new.[14] The "impression" is in itself an "event." Justified or not, the impression was "globalized," and the "impression" added affects, interpretations, images, and memories of what each of the "viewers" was doing at that moment as a confirmation of the intimate truth of the moment. And, as Derrida warned us, the first task of the analyst is to distinguish between the "brute fact," the "impression," and the "interpretations."[15] Here, the impression is that the "events of 9/11" are the prefiguration of future wars and the dangerous combination of clandestine organizations of fanatics with weapons of mass destruction provided by rogue governments. The fear is that this combination could lead to the Apocalypse, perhaps not today but possibly tomorrow. The "impression" is fed by the attacks and all the previous movies and novels dealing with this violation of the territorial political body of the United States. The "impression" compacts or concatenates in the facts, the individual memory, and the movies about massive destructions. Thus the analysis or interpretation is not oriented toward the past and present but toward the future. The newness of September 11 is situated in the idea that the attacks foreshadow the future of conflict and war, something that will happen again on an even larger scale. This is also why all the discourses in the United States are linked with the absolute necessity of seeing the September 11 events as related to "mass destruction."

The number of people killed in the World Trade Center towers immediately created an emotional link between two connotations of mass destruction: mass destruction by traditional means such as downing airplanes, and mass destruction by the use of new technologies such as nuclear, biological, or chemical (NBC) weapons. It is also important to remember the role that fear about the anthrax letters played in this discourse.[16] The anthrax threat has been a critical element in getting people to believe the narrative linking NBC weapons, indiscriminate targets, and the nefarious activities of clandestine organizations. It has given support to the idea that the hatred harbored by these shadowy organizations is expressed by massive attacks that could put the survival of the nation at stake. It created anxiety for weeks and further complicated the nation's post–September 11 "recovery" by perpetuating fear of the unknown. As George W. Bush said immediately after September 11, "It is my responsibility not to wait for the next bombing which could have the form of a mushroom cloud." Secretary of Defense Donald Rumsfeld added, "Next time it will not be 3,000 innocent civilians killed, but 30,000, 300,000, or even 3 million."[17]

The presence of angst about a doomed fate is understandable. The validation of the "impression" by the highest level of government officials, and its dissemination by the mass media, has saturated the sphere of communication at the interpersonal level, thereby blocking possible emergence of other narratives.

The reframing of security as "global" security was then presented as the only way to protect citizens against the risk of Armageddon. The traditional liberal idea that the government may be jeopardizing individual freedoms had to be discarded, at least for the duration of the emergency, due to the scope and imminence of the threat. The normal balance, analyzed in terms of costs and benefits or the probability of the threat and the drawbacks of surveillance and coercion, had to be changed dramatically in response to the worst-case scenario: the use of nuclear, biological, or chemical devices by a group of fanatics who consider their own deaths a contribution to their struggle and are thus willing to commit suicide to destroy major cities. If all state efforts and resources are directed at this worst-case scenario, for which there is only one solution—to act before violence happens—governments can no longer be criticized as in the past. Governments and leaders thus must act before they are in possession of full and accurate knowledge. They have to follow the crime-prevention methodology that involves looking for would-be criminals and detaining them in camps before they can commit violent acts.

Government policy is thus not driven by the present but instead by the prospect of a worst-case scenario in the future.[18] What is at stake is not only control of a global space but also timely anticipation intended to cope with the danger as it is now framed.

Coordinating Internal and External Security in the Context of Global "Insecurity"

The globalization of insecurity linked to the spread of terrorism supposedly has three consequences. It makes obsolete the conventional distinction between the two realms of war: defense, international order, and strategy on one hand; and crime, internal security, public order, and police investigations with the exposure of infiltrated enemies on the other. A second consequence is that this globalization simultaneously undermines traditional national sovereignty and obliges all state agents in the international arena to collaborate. Finally, it makes national borders effectively obsolete, as they no longer operate as effective barriers, fences, or fortresses behind which the population can feel safe.

Once it is accepted that the fight against threats to security, on a global scale, is a legitimate violent response designed to put an end to erratic violence, the response needs to be both internal (domestic) and external (global or international in scope). This means that the military, the intelligence services, and the police, irrespective of their traditional spheres of action and competence, must cooperate. Military intelligence must then operate inside the national territory but outside the reach of the judiciary to ensure faster and more efficient information gathering. Furthermore, to collect information in real time and to carry out acts of coercion, the police must go outside the country, analyze transnational crime networks, restore law and order, impose peace, and even build democracy. Employing the same logic, intelligence services must coordinate the activities of the military, police, customs, and border control agencies. They must do this in order to centralize information, make comparative analyses of previous actions through profiling, detect who may be dangerous, and anticipate the future, all with the capacity to preempt any potentially violent or subversive action, internal or external.

Further exacerbating this tendency is the fact that, since September 11, 2001, there has been frenzied speculation throughout the Western political world and among its security experts as to how the relationship between external defense and internal security should be handled. In the new context of global insecurity, both security professionals, especially the intelligence services, and politicians in government must make decisions based on intelligence reports asserting probability instead of certainty.[19] But how can the veracity of information be assessed in an emergency situation when the time needed to obtain evidence is considered a delay that jeopardizes security? Taking time to ascertain the validity of evidence is now regarded as dangerous inaction, and immediate coercive action is tantamount to enhanced security. The latter delegitimizes judges, democratic discussions in the legislative body, and even

criminal police investigations. It gives the advantage to prearranged emergency administrative procedures, high-technology profiling, and intelligence
service suspicions. It narrows the number of key political players but gives intelligence services newfound political influence that they have wielded by dar-
ing to compete with top political professionals in assessing the validity of the
supposed immediate threat. Due to these transformations in timeframe, de-
lays, and truth, the debate in all the countries that chose to go to war in Iraq
is now framed by whether the evidence presented is based on lies or truth—
and on who is responsible for truth. So the issue of who is in charge of pre-
dicting the future on the basis of assumptions instead of evidence has become
crucial. What responsibility do politicians and the bureaucracies have when
they decide to go to war in a context of ambiguous information and knowledge? How can these actors escape the teleological argument that the rise in
global insecurity due to the multiplication of potentially NBC-armed agents
at the subnational level leads inevitably to apocalypse? The answer, for lack of
a better one, is that it is possible to preempt the global disorder and to impose
a new world order.

Emergency as the Justification for a Unique or Coordinated Thread of Information

Strong leadership and the claim of acting with respect to the future drove the
interpretation of all the events following the 9/11 attacks. It was essential "not
to wait" but to act under the pressure of emergency. It was crucial to strike
and to deter any new attempts. Arguments in favor of waiting until data collection was more complete and accurate were dismissed as a waste of critical
time. In this logic, even dubious intelligence-gathering and correlation between elements was given substantial weight, because it was believed that the
next strike could be more lethal and perhaps even involve nuclear weapons.

   The declaration of emergency or derogation of the rule of law and exception by American, British, and Australian authorities is not the central element
of this call for immediate action. These declarations of emergency are not
changing the way we are governed, and they do not undermine the rule of law,
even if they seem to. In the United States these declarations were more of a
way to justify the militarizing of internal security, expanding the role of intelligence services, and downsizing the roles of the judiciary, the legislative body,
and international agreements. In the UK there were limited derogations in the
rule of law, which initiated a struggle between the executive and the judges. In
Australia, they generated more of a local agenda and a soul-searching among

Australians about who they really are or how they really related to the West. In the EU the unanimity of support for the United States after September 11 was shattered by the war in Afghanistan outside the purview of the UN. That war was nevertheless considered acceptable (even if not totally legally justified) by the majority of the member governments. However, the United States' refusal to wait for more information from UN weapons inspectors in Iraq severely fractured this unanimous support. After the UK and some other states decided to support the United States' invasion of Iraq, the strong refusal of the Germans, French, Belgians, and Russians to believe the dubious information provided by the United States and the UK had several effects. It stimulated a discussion about the role of politicians and their right to pass emergency legislation. It spurred debate about the capacity of security professionals, especially the intelligence services, to prevent any new attacks in a rational way. It generated a battle about the autonomy of the United States and the wisdom of solidarity with it.

The push for more coordination and collaboration between agencies at the national, transnational, and international levels and the pressure for them to provide information immediately has created considerable ambiguity in the decision-making process.[20] The respective responsibilities of political professionals and the network of agencies coordinated by intelligence services have become blurred. This is especially true in countries where political professionals at the head of government were accused of doctoring intelligence in order to justify a decision to go to war already taken for other reasons.[21] But it is not necessarily just cynicism that is at work here, even if that may be partly the case. What is central is the sense of being on the brink of disaster and the urgency of doing something to counter it. This frame of mind, which is directly rooted in the deeper belief of a rise in global insecurity, has been driving the decision-making process in both the United States and the UK.

This mindset has been augmented in both of these countries by a sense of crusade and a quasi-religious faith shrouded in the discourse of morality and freedom, which conceals a desire for revenge. There is the faith of the leaders in their own judgments and their refusal to admit they acted too quickly. Linked with the premise of this narrative of a rise in global insecurity there is the citizens' faith in their leaders, seen as the only ones who can act in time to protect them and safeguard their freedom. With both the leaders and those being led having this state of mind, the need for (global) security then prevails over (individual) freedom. To put it another way, security is the primary freedom; it is the right to live, the right to be "free from threat," to "survive."[22] This equation has been adopted by both political and security management professionals. It is the product of this "consensus" view of the world as a dangerous place oscillating between the tragic fate of Armageddon and the manifest destiny of the Anglo-American world.

Broadening the Enemy

The narrative of global terrorism extends beyond the Al Qaeda networks and the U.S. armed response. It pertains to all terrorists, all clandestine organizations using violent means against civilians as a way to attack or to retaliate against state oppression and the foreign policy of powerful nations. It requires all rational actors, regardless of their ideology, to collaborate in order to cope with the danger, but it produces a disturbing result. It makes the official lists of allegedly violent clandestine organizations so wide-ranging that they undermine the definition of terrorism as the work of primarily irrational or fanatical actors. Governments can anticipate doom and prevent it only by closer collaboration and better centralization of information within each country and, in the West, between liberal states. Governments can even go beyond this scope by collaborating with all state actors and groups who claim to have information about a clandestine organization. Thus constructed, global terrorism favors the idea of a virtually permanent state of revenge-minded fear engendered by a multiplicity of micro-actors involved in many different struggles. It creates a stock exchange of fears. The different transnational institutions (e.g., FBI, CIA, Homeland Security, Europol, Sitcen, Shangai Forum, G-8 Lyon group) dealing with counter-terrorism operate in an environment of mutually recognized fear, and that is why all these groups are creating long lists of groups and names. But of course the implication is that this cooperation is not just between liberal regimes but also with any state that has information on the groups suspected of terrorism, even if it means helping that state counter or repress its political opposition (whether violent or not).

Broadening the enemy is the best way to gain support. By doing so, one creates a shared interest in surveillance, as Russia immediately understood, thereby putting the Chechens on the list of terrorist groups. Yet broadening the enemy undermines the convenient notion of there being one central enemy coordinating all the other groups through personnel or ideology. It also undermines the legitimacy of democracies in battling terrorists as it enlists groups fighting against non-democratic states. Nevertheless, the decision was made to broaden the enemy, so every action in a remote part of the world led by an individual actor can then be seen as a new action of an Al Qaeda–related group. The Western governments involved in the Iraq war have been the first to insist that the number of actions attributed to Al Qaeda be as large as possible. This view conceals the reciprocity of violence and the rationality of targets by adding a plethora of data and giving the impression that bombings are global in scope and random in nature.

Having such a vast opposition in turn leads to the oft-repeated warning that there is a constant state of emergency, and in the name of efficiency one government must take charge of determining the actions of all other governments.[23] A more proactive stance against the different forms of violence used by small groups is therefore constantly required. This is the result of the view that September 11, 2001, definitively changed the world. Security, in the sense of survival, can no longer be provided by nuclear deterrence against other states as it could before. Nor is it any longer a question of calculating one's strength on the battlefield and whether the chances of winning are worth the cost of fighting. When fanaticism comes into play, rationality is "at risk." Erratic behavior combined with possession of weapons of mass destruction haunts the political imagination of the different agencies, and they can see no way to cope with such a threat. War has become a never-ending process. The only option that is presented, apart from waging a traditional war against rogue states, is to define the new security agenda as encompassing the surveillance and control of individuals on a global basis. Thus, patterns and profiles by which to differentiate the dangerous, the undesirable, and the normalized must be identified in order to prevent total destruction.

The meaning of freedom and the liberal state has been transformed. It incorporates wars and the war on terror. Policing at the global level is seen as the solution. A different form of governance is required—one which needs to be at the global level, with a coordinated center organizing the struggle against the enemy. The U.S. government naturally believes itself to be the best equipped to centralize the knowledge gathered by coordinated efforts. This knowledge must be used to prevent political violence rather than to react in its aftermath. This globally gathered information privileges the intelligence services over the police and the military. It privileges the more philosophical think-tanks over the scientists. It can even include some specialists in the art of prophecy, such as Alvin Toffler and Heidi Toffler, the futurologists.[24] It also bolsters the private industry of surveillance by insisting on the sharing of information through remote databases, the standardization of procedures, high-speed and reliable circuits of information, and better technology to determine the accuracy of information in the database. In brief, some actors profit more than others from the discourse of global insecurity and the war on terror. All the actors involved in transnational collaboration win more than those who remain involved at only the local level. The most powerful states feel justified in insisting that the other states obey them for their own safety.

The broadening of the image of the enemy has had another effect. Immigrants have become the unexpected victims of violent clandestine organizations as well as intelligence services in search of the suspicious activities of the greatly feared invisible enemy. They have paid a heavy price for a fight which was not theirs.[25] Of course, building a political spectacle around the idea that migrants are a source of danger has been one of the leitmotifs of contemporary governments for years. It has led to everyday racial profiling practices, to camps intended for deporting "illegal" foreigners, or to some sort of confinement in ghettos where the native-born children of foreigners live as second-class citizens. It is not a new phenomenon, but it has a new scale and a new appeal to political elites and security professionals, including the military. Yet, historically, strategic thinkers have always been uncomfortable with these internal political considerations. They preferred to associate "homeland" with the people to be defended, with those whom military professionals understand to be friends. The term "external" was defined as something dangerous, having to do with the enemy. The line between us and them, good and evil, citizens and foreigners, was then clear. On the other hand, the intelligence services have long had a feel for areas where the distinction is less clear—for infiltrated enemies, for "latent" agents, for the conquering power of hearts and minds. And after September 11 their influence over security issues has grown. Paradoxically, the end of a territorialized enemy has multiplied the anxieties of those security professionals. A new potential enemy lurks almost anywhere and everywhere.

In the absence of a well-defined enemy, intelligence services have regarded the risks and vulnerabilities brought to contemporary societies by the transnational flow of goods, people, and ideas as new "globalized" threats. Legal and illegal immigrants have come to be considered a risk to the welfare state and even to the national identity, at least since the mid-1980s and the end of the U.S.-USSR bipolarity. But generally the hostile foreigner was a rogue state, not individuals in a network within the homeland. All this has changed with the security and political scenario constructed following the terrorist attacks on September 11, 2001. The enemy was suddenly considered to be a small group of fanatics or religious extremists or an irrational, hostile individual inside the country, ready to commit suicide, and almost impossible to deal with using conventional methods. The fragmented nature of the threat at this "police" level, below the strategic level, has been answered with the use of surveillance. Any unusual behavior is considered suspect, especially after the transit bombings in London. Even well-known neighbors can be hostile foreigners, as can longtime residents who have acquired citizenship but refused to be integrated, insisting on speaking their own language at home and practicing their own religion. The term "Islamist" referring to Muslims or to aspects of Islamic religion, has been used as if the terms were homogenous, despite statements from university scholars that Islam, Islamic belief, and Islamists are not all the same. The term "immigrant" has taken on a pejorative meaning, one that connotes "suspect" and "potentially hostile foreigner." "Terrorist" and "immigrant" have been used in the same context of threat and extended to include any form of suspicion, changing the notion of migration itself into a sign of abnormality, more than of foreignness. It is then no longer the foreigner as such (the noncitizen) who is the one being targeted. It is instead all those, foreigners or not, who have an action profile judged to be a sign of potential danger. Such a profile could include buying an outbound airline ticket without purchasing a return ticket, buying that ticket with cash and not with a credit card, buying it from a third city and not from the point of departure, or having a record of having traveled to Islamic countries. All this information is being collected into databases for intelligence and profiling purposes. Cooperation between different intelligence agencies has been aided by this broadening of the image of the enemy, giving to the agencies the feeling they are protecting the homeland and that they are patriots in targeting migrants and even asylum seekers. Broadening the enemy has "embodied" the war on terror beyond symbolic politics by focusing on some migrants considered "abnormal" in the Foucauldian sense.[26]

The existence of technologies of mass surveillance using databases, profiling, body heat, and biometrics identifiers or face recognition software in some airports has pressured various ministries of interior and justice to justify the cost of this surveillance because the number of terrorism suspects proved so low. A new strategy of justification was needed. One such tactic was to convince the public that high-tech surveillance was also useful against any other form of illegality, such as organized crime, the trafficking of women and children, and illegal entries of migrants and asylum seekers. The rhetoric associating terrorism with migrants and asylum seekers by interior ministries has been a widespread phenomenon, but there have been some variations. In countries where the ministry of justice is more important than the ministry of interior, and in countries where the left was in power (with the partial exception of the UK), the stigmatization has been less significant. For example, Spain under Prime Minister Zapatero has not attempted to bridge terrorism and migration problems, even if they have been tough on both. In Australia, the United States, the UK, France, the Netherlands, and Austria, often because of the electoral importance of the far right and a climate of ultranationalism, all the political parties have played the game of merging the issues, as if they were all the same. The popular press has often jumped on the opportunity to launch campaigns against migrants and a generation of unemployed youth living in deprived areas, transforming them into the "public enemy" attacking the nation-state. These media campaigns and the inflammatory discourses of the political class have generated new tensions with minorities. The Muslim community in the UK experienced this tension after the London transit bombings and ensuing press coverage. It developed in the Netherlands after the murder of Theo van Gogh and the decision to send the army into the suburban neighborhoods that were home to many Moroccan immigrants. And it surged again when the youth (black, white, or Beur—that is, of Arabic origin) of the depressed suburbs in France erupted after the inflammatory speeches of Nicolas Sarkozy. The dialectic of mass surveillance, local and personalized controls in some specific areas, and strong resistance and even violence from the people targeted has had the effect of reinforcing feelings of insecurity, instead of reducing them. It had a negative effect on social cohesion by antagonizing community relations and freedom of movement, especially for third country nationals living in Europe or willing to enter, even legally, into it. Furthermore, when resistance from civil rights organizations, lawyers, and international organizations has been encountered, one common reply has been to claim that a global problem needed a global answer. But the need for global collaboration has actually generated the exchange of "worst" practices, reflected in the extraordinary renditions in Europe and the violations of the rules of data protection by the United States in an agreement concerning airlines' passenger name record (PNR) data, which was itself considered highly illegitimate by many lawyers.

Necessary but Unequal Collaboration at the International Level

As security is seen to be global, the leaders of small states have no option but to believe the information provided by bigger states. "Who decides" tends to become an oligopolistic or monopolistic matter, and thus small states cannot lead or participate on an equal footing in the coalition against global terror. The generalization of suspicion with respect to some groups as potential supporters of terrorism and the centralization of information entails abandoning the suspicion that the leaders of large states and their security experts might merely be promoting their own interests. In the fight against global terror, they cannot be wrong, and even if they really are wrong, they have acted for a just cause and therefore are absolved of blame. This narrative has been so overused that its credibility has been greatly diminished. Still, it continues to be at the heart of the idea of the "coalition of the willing" and drives a large part of U.S. foreign policy. This narrative is also a favorite of critics who label the United States a new "global empire" in the making. Unilateral American policy was developed by the neoconservative think-tanks largely before 2001, and not in connection with global terror, but it seems they were quick to jump on the opportunity to link the two.

The framing of the response to the attacks of September 11 as a "war on terror" has permitted the U.S. government to claim that it must assume the duty to lead and organize a coalition of the willing against terrorists all over the world. The United States was the first to take action, with the support of the UK and Australia, though Canada and New Zealand resisted.[27] But Germany, France, and Russia questioned the basis of this geopolitical vision, particularly its lack of substance concerning intelligence information and proposed alternative and more complex visions of the world concerning global and regional equilibrium. This alternate view was perceived as a challenge to the new cooperation between states. It was taken as evidence of "old" Europe's incomprehension of how the world had changed.[28] Any narrative framework other than the one given by American and British intelligence was dismissed as indirect support for the enemy camp or as a misunderstanding that needed to be corrected immediately. France launched a discussion about the independence and objectivity of the shared intelligence sources, and, even more importantly, it disagreed about fighting a war on terror in both Afghanistan and Iraq. These articulations by the French were perceived not as a fair discussion between allies but as acts of bad faith against the coordinators (Bush, Blair, Howard) in attempts to undermine their efforts.

In the UK, Tony Blair insisted on a centralized "pool" of "shared knowledge" between the Western leaders or the G-8 members. But when the Germans and the French wanted to employ their own sources to assess the objectivity of the intelligence, Blair found himself in a difficult position. That position was made worse by internal dissent in his own cabinet. And more importantly, Blair was seen as helping the United States build an "empire-like" challenge to the UN and the EU. The other European governments did not easily buy the "worst-case scenario" argument at the heart of the global terror thesis that the United States and the UK invoked to initiate the war in Iraq. They refused to accept, without clear evidence, the presence of weapons of mass destruction in Iraq and of the alleged links between Saddam Hussein and Osama bin Laden because they recognized the consequences for international leadership.

For all who believe that war is the answer to terror, the global security narrative leads to a state of mind that is highly pessimistic: the Apocalypse is coming tomorrow. The only way to delay it—at least for a while—is to unify and centralize all information about the enemy. As a result, the global security narrative leads inexorably to empire or at best to an unequal multilateralism with a strong leader or strong centralized institutions. The term "empire" is subject to discussion, but for those who doubt the now reigning paradigm of global security, only global and efficient governance can cope with the situation.[29] It is this stance of opposition that many states have chosen, which leads them to collaborate and exercise the free will to be outside of the imperial coalition. In the empire, if some states resist the assertions of others, if they dare to challenge the "evidence" of the foreseen future or the objectives of the "grand strategy" of the next century, they may not be traitors, but they are nevertheless under suspicion.[30]

For this reason, even when there is unanimity about the threats to security and survival, there are still quarrels about solutions. The narrative is never singular and straightforward. It frames a "discursive formation" that permits many discourses to exist.[31] Many governments want to maintain their own independent capacity to decide who is or is not a threat. The different security agencies do not want to give up their missions to others and are ready to compete to safeguard their budgets, their specific information, and their own bureaucratic power structures. The efforts at centralization and coordination falter at this point. Government leaders are not aware of or knowledgeable about the structure of the "field" of security professionals where the struggles are intense. It is important, however, to avoid a monolithic vision of the global security discourse leading to a kind of plot theory argument. On the contrary, the multiplicity of security discourses and the fierce oppositions gives rise to a wide debate masking the unanimous belief in the rise of global disorder and insecurity. The metanarrative of global security is then split by many lines of competition.

Professional Disputes about Borders and Migration or the "Classics" versus the "Moderns"

Arguments about the globalization of security have a considerable effect not only on international relations but also on the positioning of different institutions responsible for national (in)security. They destabilize the routines of different bureaucracies and create new competition and opportunities. They also help the agents and institutions that were on the margins of the police and military bodies to become central to the converging field of internal and external security. These debates reject the notion of the national border as a clear and legal way to delineate the missions of different agencies. The border is called into question as the jurisdictional limit for police, intelligence, and military activities and the protective barrier against enemies. New debates generate disputes about state boundaries as an organizing principle of life, favoring a more complex notion of boundaries linked to conceptions of freedom. They oblige some parties to carry out activities and missions with a different sense of duty and ethics. As power relations are transformed, the struggles over the correct response to global insecurity become even sharper. The main opposition to viewing borders in a conventional manner is found at a transnational level but exists in all states. Among security professionals, we may distinguish between at least two main kinds of security discourses, the Classics versus the Moderns.[32]

The present dispute about what constitutes security is partly ideological in character, but also reflective of the hierarchical position (and thus the bureaucratic power) of the agents, their habits, and their trajectories. It is a corporatist argument that simultaneously unites and divides all the professionals who want a role in assessing the threats and prioritizing the responses to them.

Using the metaphor of the Classics and the Moderns to describe the current debate is certainly an oversimplification, but it nevertheless has some advantages. It distinguishes but does not disconnect the academic discussions from the views expressed by security professionals. In addition, it allows for a better understanding of the convergence of discourses concerning internal security, law and order, and discourses of war. Finally, it allows us to understand who might have an interest in positing that defense and law and order must converge in a global security paradigm and who might benefit by defending that argument.

The quarrel is focused on the role of borders as barriers, as effective means of protection against a global threat. All the key debates since 2001, in Europe and the United States, whether about reorganizing and coordinating intelligence structures, about homeland security, or about immigration agents and border guards, as well as the priority given to military measures, follow the pathways inscribed by this discussion on borders and limits. One of the most powerful and consequential responses to recent acts of terror has been to try to seal the borders. The reasons given for this wide-ranging attempt are manifold. One goal is to create a U.S. and even a European homeland security zone (even as the leading motto of EU governance invokes the need to keep markets open and to facilitate freedom of movement). Another is to introduce new technologies for tracing individuals. Others are to toughen the requirements for people seeking to enter, to incarcerate potential suspects, to use the military and intelligence services to "police" inside a country, and to legitimate draconian measures to prevent a future cataclysm. The American development in 1999 of the policy concerning homeland defense was accelerated in 2001 and renamed "homeland security." A new cabinet-level secretary and department were created, followed by the implementation of the Computer Assisted Passenger Screening (CAPS) II system and the development of the Smart Borders program. In Europe, the European Council met in Thessalonica in June 2003 and instituted several new policies. The Hague Programme action plan reinforced the border control strategies of the Schengen information system, developed the Schengen visa policy, and proposed use of biometrics in visa and passport documents for better border controls. This specific focus on borders as a locus of control complements the definition of security as being related to foreigners with the idea of the individual living in the territory of a specific state.[33] It also defines the border as the place that militaries should occupy (even when not at war) when managing missions and operations, both externally and internally.

Two poles structure the political, media, and bureaucratic debates about security and terrorism. Classics stress national interests, sovereignty and borders, human knowledge, lessons from the past, and the importance of a balance between security and liberty. Moderns stress globalization, the need for maximum security regardless of territorial boundaries, for transborder collaboration and centralization of information, and new technologies of control and monitoring that, in order to be effective, must redraw the legal and ethical boundaries of liberal states.

These two standpoints are reflected in the media (television, radio, or newspaper) and in diverse political arenas (local, national, European, and international). They are truly transversal and oppose the institutions that traditionally had a monopoly on the "means for the use of force" (such as police, magistrates, and the military). Instead they speak to more specialized and transnationalized agencies of control and monitoring in which the important task is the detection of the enemy and the management of the flow of population (via intelligence services, the private security industry, risk management) more or less independently of the national culture of the country. Senior members of the institutions authorizing the sharing of knowledge on current or future threats legitimate the Classics by giving them more credibility. But the Moderns are in line with the politicians and some of the trends in public opinion.

The Internal/External Distinction Favored by the Classics

The Classics want to rely on the traditional solutions of the national state in case of emergency, stressing a reinforcement of controls at their national borders. They consider today's security the same as yesterday's, constituted by the nation-state's survival in the face of external armed aggression. Security is established between states (when the fundamental interests of the nation are concerned) and not inside the state, where security is simply a question of maintaining law and order. Security thus remains a "property" of the state. Only the threats regarding national security are worthy of interest. Matters of law and order and socioeconomic regulations that do not involve issues related to security are of secondary importance. The state is like the two-faced god, Janus: one face dispenses internal security within a precise territorial framework; the other face experiences insecurity and is under a permanent threat of aggression. The Classics share some of the postulates of the traditional realism of E. H. Carr and Hans Morgenthau, resurrected by Stephen Walt.[34]

For them, the world is still quite simple: the military forces take care of the outside, the police, the inside, and they collaborate from time to time for specific missions. In normal times, the police prevail. When they need quick and disciplined forces, public authorities may ask the military to intervene but only on special request and even then the military has little autonomy in such circumstances. The military forces are employed only where there is a real emergency, one that sometimes requires an inversion of the subordination to civil command. Such an inversion is limited to specific cases, such as invasion and revolution, which do not normally include terrorism.[35] Civil-military relations must be monitored by law and precise measures carefully drafted before any action is taken. Security is threatened in a military sense only when the nation's survival is at stake. Terrorism, even in the case of September 11, is a horrible event, but not a threat to the survival of the nation. To be secure was, for the Classics, to be protected from the external enemy, and the danger that enemy posed was "war," or at the very least the threat of military action at such a scale that collective survival is at risk. Individual survival was not "important" as long as the number of deaths remained acceptable. But now the main problem posed by September 11 is the possibility of infiltrated enemies with the capacity to seriously harm the country. This magnifies the importance of the border as the main locus of control. The idea of "homeland security" is plausible only if there are "secure borders," essentially a police matter, albeit with an important role for external intelligence services inside the national territory.

In spite of September 11, the Classics are not convinced of the globalization of threats and thus doubt the necessity of globalizing security. They prefer preserving the official national framework and subordinating the events to this reading, which has the advantage of classifying them and treating them on a familiar hierarchical basis. For them, the street corner criminal or the demonstrator, or even the terrorist, belongs to a different world than dissuasion directed toward the potential Russian or Chinese enemy. It seems incongruous to the Classics to view the functions of police officers as comparable to those of soldiers. There is hardly anything in common, except in terms of maintaining law and order where, sometimes, as in martial law, the extremes of a conflict oblige a resort to the army instead of the police. Terrorism is not global; it is a local event by definition, even if it has transnational implications. It is a crime and thus calls for the involvement of police, who then mix criminal detective work after the bombing with intelligence work both internally and externally to try to prevent other bombings.

Among the Classics are found many strategists coming from the armed services, politicians who have invested in nationalistic rhetoric, and pundits and think-tanks that are part of the institutional inheritance of the Cold War. These Classics still remain at the very top of the "establishment" in different Western countries, with the notable exception of the Bush administration in the United States. The Classics use their positions, the prevailing traditions, and the strength of law to limit changes in the conception of what constitutes security, as long as they consider change to have a potentially negative impact on their interests and ethics. Members of the military do not consider it their job to deal with matters other than deterrence and "real" wars—that is, war against other states. They refuse to deal with "subversive" agents and "dirty" wars. That is the task of the secret services, who deal with espionage, and the police, who fight terrorism and crime. From the military's perspective, combating organized political violence at the sub-state level or even at the transnational level is a matter for special squads, the intelligence services abroad, and counter-terrorism professionals and police at home. Meanwhile, the traditional police organizations have their own professional ethics and refuse to be involved in cases where there is no serious judicial evidence. They insist on strong links with magistrates in order to protect themselves from accusations of arbitrariness. They are suspicious about profiling and data-gathering and believe in their "people skills" and face-to-face relations, with a hint of technology for scientific policing but not policing by computer search or profiling.

Part of the U.S. response to September 11 was structured by initial choices based on these established patterns. Thus, the "solution" after September 11 was to defend the homeland. This meant striking the "bases," dismantling the "networks," and launching a territorial war against the Taliban with the unfounded hope that there would be no chain reaction and that such a war would prevent further attacks at home. The Classics are often strong proponents of sustained sovereignty and are highly suspicious of regional and international bodies that ask for more collaboration. In the European context, they do not consider efforts toward greater collaboration to be genuine and they believe that such requests mask the real interests of the new European institutions.

In the context of the present security debate, the advantage of the Classics is that they are the ones with the accumulated social prestige and institutional authority to lay claim to particular knowledge. Often less harmful in terms of civil liberties, their discourse is nevertheless considered by some politicians to be out of date. They only seek to intensify and enforce what already exists and ask for larger budgets and more human capital—exactly what politicians are reluctant to give. The politicians are thus inclined to prefer the Moderns and their call for emergency laws, more technology, and more control of the whole population because they think they can better demonstrate effective control. This preference of some political leaders for the Moderns partly explains the destabilization of the traditional hierarchy.

The Internal/External Fusion Favored by the Moderns

The Moderns believe that the national state is too weak to counter global danger. For them the only answer to global insecurity is to create global security through more surveillance of individuals, focusing on groups that are considered potentially dangerous because they are characterized as being the foundation for the proliferation of terrorism. To Moderns, borders are obsolete. Global networks are everything, especially when they are hidden.

These Moderns include an increasing number of "observers"—journalists or academics—who proclaim themselves to be "experts." They are often pretenders trying to challenge the Classic establishment. Others had previously been within, but consigned to the margins of, the security profession. In the military they often come from the ranks of those who were in colonial warfare, members of special forces units, or low-intensity warfare specialists—all marginalized during the Cold War and after the failure of Vietnam. In the police profession they are mainly in special squads dealing more with information than people; they put their faith in computerization and speed, as well as action at a distance via technological means. They are supported by the interests of a surveillance industry in full expansion, which includes, on one side, the ordinary civilian security companies, and on the other, private paramilitary companies. Both types of security companies now claim to have better knowledge than their public sector counterparts, especially with regard to high technologies ranging from satellite surveillance to management of databases, from profiling to correlation using biometric identifiers. Theirs is an industry that is recruiting at the crossroads of junior managers coming from the best universities and the retired professionals coming from the army, the intelligence agencies, or police forces. This trend explains the proliferation of risk analysis, performed by experts who are half private, half police, and often

transnational. Their aim is to anticipate the behaviors of individuals and targeted minorities using broad statistical series with multiple variables (data
mining) and the use of "expert" software that develops profiles. Many politicians—from the left or right, in the United States as well as in Europe—who
have built a part of their political career on law and order at the local level
have embraced the rhetoric of global terrorism. This rhetoric links the local
and the international levels. International and European institutions (e.g., the
G-8, OSCE, NATO, WEU, European Council, Europol, Interpol) have
strongly supported the Moderns, who insist on the role of coordination inside
and between states.

The Moderns all decry the secrecy preferred by the Classics and emphasize the importance of "open sources."[36] They come from very different institutional origins than the Classics. Intelligence or counter-espionage agencies,
anti-terrorist or narcotics task forces, the gendarmerie, and customs are common breeding grounds for Moderns. Other Moderns have served as administrative managers dealing with immigration and refugees, in expert groups
analyzing organized crime and its social impact, as military and civilian experts in low-intensity conflicts and terrorism, or as entrepreneurs selling surveillance or identification technology and secure databases. Despite the
variety of their origins, the Moderns all share the common view that, in spite
of increased controls, the border no longer protects the territory.

Moderns assert that the internal and external security concerns, which
have traditionally been distinct, are currently converging or even merging because the border is not functioning as a barrier. They also consider the notion
of keeping the population safe behind a wall or in a fortress (even an electronic one) to be outdated, a dream built on sand. So, according to these Moderns, one has to adapt to the "new distribution" of multiple lines of threats
and invisible enemies by changing the rules of the game between army and
police, and between sovereignty and collaboration. The new game is "glocal,"
both global and local. It is a game of networks that bypass the borders.[37]

In this view, the traditional missions of counter-espionage, of inside intelligence, of criminal investigations, of general information gathering for the
government, of data production concerning economic, sociological, and demographic trends are intertwined. External security agencies (the armies, secret services) have to look beyond the scope of spies and search inside the
borders for an enemy that comes from outside but has now infiltrated inside.
It is their job to analyze transnational threats. These external security agencies
use the term "transversal threat." It associates, in a supposed continuum, the
potential threat from migrants, second-generation citizens of foreign heritage,
or people from inner cities or disadvantaged suburbs, which are viewed as a

breeding ground for terrorism and organized crime. The idea of a fifth column or even of the enemy within is the assumption underlying the rhetoric, but it is not expressed officially. The Moderns want to "strategize" internal security and take over the control of information. Internal security agencies (national police, police with military status, border guards, customs) have to look beyond the borders to find criminals and to survey and infiltrate the networks of transnational organized crime (migrants, asylum seekers, displaced persons, Muslims who supposedly have links with crime, terrorism, drug trafficking). These internal agencies, however, must report to the foreign intelligence services and the army. Coordination structures like those that are standard in Western nations are needed, and it is an absolute necessity to have more and more agents abroad (in the form of liaison officers). So, for these Moderns, either European or American, it is unacceptable to watch the horizon, waiting gun in hand for the no-longer-coming enemy, while disorder insinuates itself at home. They criticize the Classics as out outdated, old-fashioned, and irresponsible on account of their blindness to the evidence of global insecurity. In fact, they say, the Classics are part of the problem because they take too long to understand and to act. They are attached to old-fashioned principles and ethics that have no place in the new world with all its dangers. Security institutions have to react to emergencies, whatever their level. If the enemy is now organized in transnational networks and has partly infiltrated into Western societies, coalitions ought to be organized. Friends and enemies ought to be identified in each country, in each locality, and no place should be left for the neutral, the unconcerned. The PATRIOT Act of the United States is the product of this philosophy. The Moderns' policy conclusions are therefore that institutions in charge of security should be restructured around intelligence departments, enabling them to coordinate armies, police, and customs according to their needs.

This second narrative concerning security beyond borders was created as a way to explain and combat the globalization of threats. It links diverse elements coming from social changes, the transformation of violence, the failure of public policies, and, last but not least, a fear of foreigners. The strength of these arguments lies in their ambiguity: they are not all pure lies or the product of overactive imaginations. They describe very real practices of making oneself invisible and of establishing networks of underground agents that institutional and diplomatic discourse seeks to conceal. They take into account the dark face of violent behavior that traditional diplomats prefer to gloss over. These arguments thus appear to undermine the legitimacy of a state that presents fact in contrast to state lies regarding the new international order. In doing so, their narratives appeal to the media and correspond easily with the views of journalists in search of provocative secrets that are easy to describe and to "investigate." Their capacity to be sustained by members of the news media looking for the exceptional and the sensational explains how they become matters of fact, a "consensus."

The news media succeed in giving a routine version of the exceptional by presenting their lack of knowledge as a way of describing events. The use of terms such as "gray area," "invisible threat," "mutant" and "metamorph guerrilla," or "underground fights" has a performative function of obscuring their ignorance and promoting it as a form of knowledge. With that they mobilize the disillusioned and the worried. They play with the idea that "the truth is out there." On the international level they fulfill a function more or less analogous to that of far right-wing parties on the national level.

And indeed, like the far right, they often make thoughtless amalgams that confuse victims and torturers. They create scapegoats and manufacture fictional causes, stimulated by the need to find an enemy behind each unpleasant social transformation (e.g., decrease in birth rate, unemployment, health care crisis, unstable urban areas, etc.). They often take one of the worst examples and extrapolate from it, as if it is routine, a general law. They then develop rhetoric based on a worst-case scenario about the future. Their demagogic stance and their dire view of the future seem to have been successful in making, at least on a rhetorical level, every element that involves a border crossing seem part of a virtually infinite criminal network. They have created a "continuum of insecurity," mixing demographic and social transformations, legitimate changes of values and behavior toward crime, and political violence and war. They have succeeded in creating in the public mind a "fear of having fears."

According to this logic, uncertainty and risks are not seen as an "exercise of freedom" or "opportunities" but as "dangers" and "threats." Migrants and refugees are "securitized" and become the object of police suspicion and intelligence service attention. Then they attract the attention of the strategic thinkers who characterize them as potential sleeper cells of terrorists or at least potential supporters linked by kinship or religious ties. In the aftermath of September 11, this so-called convergence of new threats and risks is the main justification for new structures and for closer cooperation among security agencies (internal as well as external). It also serves to rationalize large budgets in a period of financial crisis. The core of this new securitization is thus related to transnational flows and to the surveillance of boundaries that are not territorial, but societal and identity related. The whole project can be seen as an attempt to redraw a border between the inside and the outside. But this border is different from the frontier of the state. It is a border between the normalized and the "abnormal," a border between those who are banned, who are not part of humanity, and those who are good citizens, civilized, human.

A semantic study of the ever evasive and indefinable terms of this discourse shows to what extent their purpose is not to describe phenomena but to point fingers.[38] Very often the Moderns have chosen to create amalgams through the accumulation of diverse examples without any details providing depth to the analysis. The frequent use of metaphors is also very important to the Moderns, particularly when the facts are insufficient to support their position, and even when the metaphors are old and clichéd. Some of them come from the Cold War and others from a colonial mentality. Some were instrumental just after the end of the Cold War and were part of the roots of the interpretation of September 11. So, to understand the Moderns, we need to avoid focusing on post–September 11 and on the present as a new period. Their claim that "everything is different now" is a way to mask the fact that they are repeating old stories and proposing old solutions, which are often illiberal and destroy social solidarities. We have to refute the arbitrary construction of a "before" and an "after" as two different worlds. On the contrary, it is important to remember that the positions of both the Classics and the Moderns immediately after the fall of the Berlin Wall, after the end of the so-called bipolar world, consisted of discourses evoking global insecurity and the rise of transnational or nonterritorial threats. From the 1990s onward, journalists, "experts," and politicians have continuously developed a narrative concerning the emergence of new threats spreading "international disorder."

This chapter has developed four arguments. The first shows why the rhetoric of global security has become so credible that it is widely accepted as the truth about the modern world, a set of propositions that cannot be challenged, especially after the attacks of September 11, 2001, and the transit bombings that followed. This narrative has emerged as the new consensus and now has achieved a strength comparable to the one acquired by the term "Cold War" to specify the period of the 1950s, 1960s, and 1970s. Our political imagination is framed and limited by this narrative of global insecurity, which demands a global security response.

The second argument unpacks this "evidence," this "truth," and shows that it is a specific vision of how to understand political violence in modern society and how to cope with it. This specific vision is not as general as it claims to be and is, in fact, linked with a small but powerful group that advocates more collaboration between security professionals in the West. The intelligence services and the other national agencies already working in networks are favored over the local agencies in regard to missions and budgets.

The U.S. government and its closest allies see themselves as the center for this centralization of global information to fight global terrorism and believe that the age of equal sovereignty between states is definitively over. This centralization of information behind the rhetoric of shared information has been at the heart of the struggles at the UN between the United States and the UK on one side and France and Russia, supported by Germany, on the other. Clearly, that resistance signalled a refusal to "trust" the Anglo-American alliance and to weaken sovereignty by letting them decide who and what is good for all.

The third argument is that beyond the clash between countries, and sometimes ideologies, these conceptual struggles are internal to the world of security professionals. These professionals differ in the way they analyze the security situation depending on their positions within bureaucratic structures, their habits, and their ideology and political involvement. Based on their professional origins, they may have differing views of the relevance of national borders as forms of protection against enemies and as forms of delineation between an inside allocated to the police and justice professionals and an outside allocated to the military and diplomats. A dispute about the role of borders as an organizing principle has spread with the evident transnationalization of political violence, and it paves the way to see any global event as a threat to national identity.

The last argument shows that we have in fact a multiplicity of security discourses surrounding us and competing among themselves, supported by different agents and institutions. It is this proliferation of discourses, and the anxiety brought about by their lack of conclusive answers in the face of political violence, that leaves an overwhelming feeling of unease and the absence of any powerful counter-discourse on the side of civil liberties.

5

European Security and Counter-Terrorism

JOLYON HOWORTH

Since September 11, 2001, the EU and the United States have both been confronted—in very similar ways—by a new type of threat: Islamic terrorism organized on a global scale by a network of non-state actors structured in cells and located in approximately sixty countries. The transit attacks in Madrid (March 11, 2004) and London (July 7, 2005) as well as the failed plot to blow up civilian aircraft flying between Heathrow Airport and the United States (August 2006) furnish brutal proof of the vulnerability of Western societies in the teeth of this new scourge. The urgency of European coordination in the struggle against terrorism is difficult to overstate, as is the need to coordinate counter-terrorist activities between the EU and the United States. But the problems and the challenges are abundant. Interior ministries are not in the habit, to put it mildly, of cooperating across frontiers. Systems of criminal justice in different member states are not always compatible. Intelligence services jealously cling to the fruits of their own activities. The requirements of tracking Pakistan-based terrorism, which is the main concern of the British government, are very different from those appropriate for infiltrating North African jihadist networks, which preoccupy the French government. Between 2001 and 2004, the EU made genuine efforts to transcend these structural, institutional, and juridical constraints. But it was only after the Madrid transit bombings that these efforts began to come together. Despite the inherent difficulty in getting members of the EU Justice and Home Affairs Council (JHA) to cooperate on security matters, increasingly draconian measures were taken to demonstrate the member states' political commitment to challenging a form of terrorism that crossed borders more easily than did European public authorities themselves. In so doing, the EU provoked a backlash from human rights organizations. In its wake, the EU had to answer a number of questions. How could the correct balance be struck between repression and protection? What was the best method of coordinating policy areas as distinct and as different as immigration, refugee and asylum policy, international crime-fighting, border control, and counter-terrorism? Above all, how could the requirements of immediate responses to terrorist attacks and long-term solutions addressing the causes of terrorism best be articulated? This last question in particular gave rise to a difference in strategic approaches favored by the United States, which tended to prioritize the former objective, and the EU, which strove—at least rhetorically—to focus on the latter. I address the distinctiveness of the EU's approach to counter-terrorism by setting it in the framework of a transatlantic comparison.

Three basic differences between the EU and the United States can immediately be brought out:

• There is a tension between the two sides in terms of threat assessment, in particular the extent to which the new post-9/11 terror is or is not perceived as qualitatively different from previous types.
• The distinctiveness of EU counter-terrorism since 9/11, both in terms of what *has* been accomplished and in terms of the structural limitations to a specifically EU role in counter-terrorism, contrasts markedly with the centralizing capacity of the United States.
• Despite the administrative and juridical/legal cooperation that has been concluded between the EU and the United States since early 2004, there have been continuing differences in strategic approach. These differences are based on each side's overall understanding of the terrorism phenomenon. One of the key differences has been the EU's penchant for "soft" approaches and the United States' continuing reliance on military power.

"Old" Terrorism and "New" Terrorism

The first substantive point to make is that there is a major difference between the "old-style" terrorism, with which Europe has been familiar for more than

a century, and the new "superterrorism" epitomized by radical Islamic funda-
mentalists.[1] Two key differences stand out among many crucial distinctions.
With most old-style terrorism (anarchism being the exception that proves the
rule), there was a clear political demand, usually concerning a limited
geostrategic space, and the possibility of political negotiation. With superterrorism, none of that is true. The byword is "the jihad and rifle alone. No negotiations, no conferences, no dialogue." In addition, with old-style terrorism
the objective was, in the words of Brian Jenkins, "a lot of people watching,
not many people dead."[2] With superterrorism, the maximization of death is
a policy objective and the acquisition of weapons of mass destruction
(WMD) is perhaps only a matter of time. It is not surprising, therefore, that
counter-terrorism activities, as a consequence, have undergone fundamental
change in both methods and approaches. This has occurred on both sides of
the Atlantic.

The second substantive point is that Europe has refused to follow the
United States in declaring a "global war on terror" (GWOT).[3] In his address
to a joint session of Congress on September 20, 2001, President George W.
Bush not only declared "war" on "terrorism with a global reach" but also made
the remark that was to infuriate friends and allies around the world: "Every
nation, in every region, now has a decision to make. Either you are with us,
or you are with the terrorists."[4] This black-and-white approach to the world
was widely regarded in Europe not just as "simplistic" (according to French
foreign minister Hubert Védrine) but also, in the words of the eminently establishment British historian Sir Michael Howard, as a "terrible and irrevoca-
ble error." According to Howard, "to declare war on terror, or even more
illiterately, on terrorism, is at once to accord terrorists a status and dignity that
they seek and that is undeserving." Worse still, he argued, the "war" cannot
be "won" militarily, but the public will expect precisely such an outcome. And
that is to some extent what has happened. Despite official Bush administration disclaimers noting that this is not a war like any other, it has, in the words
of Gilles Andréani, now "acquire[d] a strategic reality."[5] The "war" has been
extended beyond terrorism to "rogue states" along the "axis of evil" (Bush) but
also, potentially, to a longer list of states now categorized as "outposts of
tyranny" (Condoleezza Rice).[6] Furthermore, that war—particularly the one
being fought in Iraq—has succeeded in *attracting* terrorists in numbers un-
seen in the past. It has in short *created* a "war" between terrorists and the United States that did not previously exist, a development that is now officially
recognized by U.S. intelligence sources.[7] All this has been widely perceived in
Europe not only as regrettable but also as highly counterproductive. It has, in
effect, according to many Europeans (and some Americans), amounted to a

massive distraction from the "real" fight against terrorism in general and against Al Qaeda in particular.[8]

The reports in July 2005 that the Bush administration had decided to re-brand its "war" under the new acronym SAVE (Struggle Against Violent Extremism) merely underlined the continuing gulf between the two sides.[9] The fact that it took the Bush administration more than four years to begin to emphasize that the "struggle" should be "more diplomatic, more economic, more political than it is military" (Gen. Richard Myers) cut little ice with most Europeans.[10] At a special operations seminar on June 8, 2005, in Tampa, Florida, UK officials attempted to demonstrate that the British experience of heavy-handedness in Northern Ireland had led to the conclusion "Kill five, recruit . . . how many?" But they suspected their U.S. audience of being deaf to such wisdom and doubted that U.S. officials genuinely believed that military instruments should take a backseat. They saw few signs of the United States accepting anything but a leading role in the ongoing struggle.[11] This U.S. acronymic shift (from GWOT to SAVE) was accompanied by the appointment of Karen Hughes as undersecretary of state for "public diplomacy." Hughes told senators during her confirmation hearings that she planned to turn around America's image in the Islamic world through astute deployment of the four Es (engagement, exchanges, education, and empowerment).[12] The challenge proved greater than she believed. A major challenge for the Europeans is to convince their U.S. allies that a holistic new approach to "new" terrorism is essential. Unfortunately, the Europeans, though convinced that a holistic approach is the right way to go, are still trying to figure out how the different parts of the whole fit together.

The Distinctiveness of EU Concepts of "Counter-Terrorism"

What is the distinctiveness of the European approach to contemporary counter-terrorism? In the immediate aftermath of 9/11, the EU held extraordinary meetings of both the Justice and Home Affairs Council (September 20, 2001) and the European Council (September 21, 2001). From these meetings were issued statements that the fight against terrorism had become a "priority objective" of the EU. The emphasis in these early days was clearly on intelligence sharing, judicial and police cooperation, and measures against terrorism financing. Yet it was already clear that the Union believed that a key dimension of the fight against terror must be a new approach to the EU's relations with third countries, particularly in the developing world. While supporting U.S. efforts to track down the perpetrators of 9/11 on the basis of UN Security Council Resolution 1368, the EU also stated its intention "systematically to evaluate [its] relations with third countries in the light of the support which those countries might give to terrorism," noting that "the integration of all countries into a fair world system of security, prosperity and improved development is the condition for a strong and sustainable community for combating terrorism."[13]

Thus a twin-track policy of immediate reaction/riposte and long-term international dialogue and negotiation was set in motion. This has been the main feature of the EU's approach ever since. A cardinal feature of this long-term approach has been its tight cooperation with the United Nations. As EU counter-terrorism coordinator Gijs de Vries told the UN Counter-Terrorism Committee in June 2005, "The EU regards the role of the UN in meeting and overcoming this challenge as vital. We are committed to supporting you in this, through unequivocal implementation of UN conventions and resolutions, through political and moral support in the world for the UN's role and, wherever possible, through practical co-operation on the ground."[14] In 2004–2005, EU and UN teams jointly visited Morocco, Kenya, Algeria, and Albania to identify counter-terrorism assistance programs, and EU member states pledged an additional 20 billion euros to help the UN meet its Millennium Goals by 2010. In addition, the EU strongly supported the rapid adoption of the UN's Comprehensive Convention against Terrorism and the universal ratification of the thirteen existing UN conventions in the field.[15] At least at the level of rhetoric, the EU appears to be prioritizing the structured attack against the root causes rather than a tactical onslaught against the symptoms. The United States, on the other hand, tends—at least overtly—to minimize this pathway.[16]

Although the U.S. *National Strategy for Combating Terrorism* document draws attention to what it calls "underlying conditions"—such as poverty, corruption, and religious and ethnic strife—that help foster terrorism, the emphasis is much less on these conditions per se than on the fact that terrorists can "exploit" them to attract recruits.[17] The EU *Declaration on Combating Terrorism* of March 2004 is much more explicit in stressing the need to adopt a long-term strategy to address root causes.[18] This difference can be detected also in the respective post-9/11 strategies of the two sides toward the tactical use of development aid in addressing terrorism. U.S. aid, in addition to enjoying a 38 percent increase, has been more tightly targeted at countries that are perceived foyers of terrorist recruitment. This tactic is employed with the hope that economic assistance will both reduce recruitment and help foster good governance, leading to better relations between the countries targeted and the United States. Afghanistan, Iraq, and Pakistan are prime examples. The EU, on the other hand, has not changed its basic aid philosophy, which is and always has been one of reducing poverty for its own sake. And it has not shifted focus to those countries that are believed to be hotbeds of terrorist recruitment. This amounts to a "long-term view that supporting institution-building and economic growth outside the current security hotspots will save new regions from becoming states that could breed terrorism five to ten years down the road."[19] However, this first long-term strategy of attacking the problem at the root exists mainly at the level of rhetoric.[20] No agencies or government departments have been established to deal with it; no armies of officials are toiling away in offices trying to come to grips with it. It remains a vital statement of principle. But acting on it is a challenge that remains in the hands of history rather than of human actors.

On the other hand, the second track of the EU's counter-terrorist strategy (immediate regulatory responses) has mobilized actors and officials by the thousands. A certain amount was accomplished between 2001 and 2004 in the EU's coordinated campaign against terrorism, and in the *European Security Strategy* document published in December 2003, terrorism was identified as the first of five key threats to European interests. Still, implementation (and especially coordination) of anti-terrorist measures was initially patchy and inadequate.[21] In a report issued in March 2004, Javier Solana noted that "the instruments are poorly used and/or poorly understood by law enforcement and judicial authorities in some member states."[22] It was not until the terrorist bombings in Madrid on March 11, 2004, that the Union ratcheted up its counter-terrorism activities considerably, notably with the appointment of an EU counter-terrorism coordinator, Gijs de Vries, whose main task was to ensure maximum coordination between the EU's Ministries of the Interior and Justice. On March 25, 2004, the EU published a *Declaration on Combating Terrorism,* which announced a revised plan of action involving seven strategic objectives and approximately 150 initiatives.[23] The Action Plan is audited and updated every six months.[24] A comprehensive Justice and Home Affairs Council package (The Hague Programme) was adopted in November 2004 at a special European Council meeting. Its objectives were summarized thus: "The European Council considers that the common project of strengthening the area of freedom, security and justice is vital to securing safe communities, mutual trust and the rule of law throughout the Union. Freedom, justice, control at the external borders, internal security and the prevention of terrorism should henceforth be considered indivisible within the Union as a whole."[25] (The highly problematic issue of indivisibility will be assessed below.) By the time of the European Council meeting in Brussels in December 2004, substantial progress was being reported in the following key areas:

the fight against financing of terrorism, law enforcement cooperation, border and transport security, external relations, intelligence cooperation, protection of critical infrastructure, and a long-term strategy to address issues of radicalization and recruitment of terrorists. On May 25, 2005, the long-awaited European Agency for the Management of Operational Cooperation at the External Borders of the Member States (aka "European Border Agency" or "Frontex") began work in Warsaw with a list of six very specific tasks.[26]

A superficial comparison of the EU's *Declaration on Combating Terrorism* (March 2004) and the U.S. *National Strategy for Combating Terrorism* (February 2003) suggests that the two blocs are very much on the same wavelength. Indeed, there is nothing in one side's approach that is not replicated in some form or another in that of the other side. Both recognize, for instance, that this is a long-term strategy, that it cannot lead to sudden "victory" or "defeat," and that military instruments constitute but a small part of the overall thrust. At a meeting in Dromoland Castle, Ireland, on June 26, 2004, EU and U.S. leaders issued the *EU-U.S. Declaration on Combating Terrorism*. It reads like a perfect synthesis of the two national documents, structured according to the seven strategic objectives of the EU text.[27] There is no doubt that the two sides' cooperation on counter-terrorism has been substantial and growing ever since 9/11. Intelligence sharing has been more intense and more effective than ever before—and this has included high-level Franco-U.S. flows, which President Bush acknowledged to have been crucial. Cooperation between law enforcement agencies and prosecutors has been massively stepped up. On June 25, 2003, the two sides concluded an Extradition and Mutual Legal Assistance Agreement facilitating extradition for many more offenses than previously.[28] Despite serious European misgivings, agreement was reached in May 2004 on communication of passenger name records (PNRs) in connection with international travel. In September 2004, wide-ranging agreements were reached on the safety of container transport (the Container Security Initiative), including extensive customs cooperation and the facilitating of inspection of container cargoes by U.S. officials in European ports. Joint investigative teams are being planned. A wide-reaching Policy Dialogue on Border and Transport Security is attempting to narrow the gap on issues such as sky marshals and biometric data. Substantial legal and banking cooperation has been agreed on to counter terrorist financing. New measures have been agreed upon for cooperation in response to the consequences of terrorist attack, including one with chemical, biological, radiological, and nuclear (CBRN) contaminants. This amounts to a substantial package of agreements, many of which would have been virtually unthinkable only five years ago.

However, the measure of agreement is essentially limited to the legal, administrative, and technical aspects of counter-terrorism—rather than harmonizing or reinforcing the strategy itself.

Moreover, recent events suggested that public authorities in Europe acted with undue haste in signing binding agreements with the United States. In the UK on November 9, 2005, the House of Commons threw out Tony Blair's proposal to extend the length of arrest without charges to ninety days, precisely on the grounds that this constituted an unnecessarily extended swing of the pendulum in the wrong direction.[29] On May 30, 2006, the European Court of Justice threw out the agreement between the Union and the United States on the transfer of passenger name records. This effectively nullified both the Commission's judgment that transferred data were adequately protected in the United States and the Council's decision to authorize the transfer of the data.[30] The year 2006 also witnessed a major row between the EU and the United States over CIA secret prisons and rendition flights, leading to the highly damaging Council of Europe report published in early June.[31] In other words, the transatlantic nexus, from one perspective, went from tense to worse.

Limitations to EU Anti-Terrorism Coordination

The agreements on counter-terrorism legislation outlined above look very impressive. However, it is important to understand the real limitations to coordination of EU activities on this front. A recent study argues that the EU is severely hampered in its collective campaign against terrorism by two major factors. First, the EU is not a state and thus can neither arrest nor prosecute terrorists, nor use spies and satellites to track them. The vast majority of counter-terrorism work is done at the nation-state level, and even cross-border cooperation is conducted overwhelmingly at a bilateral level rather than at the EU level. It is this situation that much of the flurry of legislation since 2004 aims to correct, but practice is running several steps behind theory. Secondly, and probably more importantly, "counter-terrorism" spans a vast number of policy areas involving most government departments. To quote Daniel Keohane, "National governments find it hard to coordinate their own ministries and agencies involved in counter-terrorism. Trying to coordinate the collective efforts of 25 governments at the EU level is exponentially more difficult."[32] Another major study concurs: "the EU's counter-terrorism effort has been more aspirational than substantive."[33]

Some of the challenges facing coordination may seem paradoxical. For instance, the EU's former "counter-terrorism coordinator," Gijs de Vries, has no effective power other than his own gifts of persuasion. He has no money, cannot propose legislation, and cannot chair meetings of EU justice or foreign ministers in an effort to set the counter-terrorism agenda. As with so many aspects of EU integration, the member states have understood the logical necessity of coordination, have established a position to facilitate it, but have then balked at giving the post-holder the political clout needed to carry out his or her mission effectively.[34] Not only did de Vries struggle to facilitate coordination between the Commission and the Council but he also had to navigate interagency rivalries. These conflicts were between such bodies as Europol, Eurojust, the EU's Terrorism Working Group (comprising national interior ministry officials), the Police Chiefs Task Force, the EU Counter-Terrorism Group (comprising national internal intelligence officials), the EU's Situation Centre, and many others. In spring 2007, de Vries announced that he was stepping down from his post at the end of his initial three-year mandate. He is unlikely to be replaced. The symbolism of creating a "counter-terrorism czar" in the wake of the Madrid bombings was high. The practical utility of this position, given all the competing agencies and powers involved in counter-terrorism, proved to be somewhat less evident. Several proposals have been formulated with a view to creating a transnational body with genuine authority for counter-terrorism. These proposals have come from bodies as diverse as the UK House of Lords and private think-tanks.[35] Yet these are unlikely to have the desired effect. Reluctance on the part of national authorities to share information too widely put an end to proposals, in the wake of the Madrid bombings, to establish a European-style CIA. All five major EU intelligence-gathering countries (UK, France, Germany, Italy, and Spain) refused to contemplate such a move. However, the fact that those same countries have, since May 2003, organized regular coordination meetings of their interior ministry officials (the G-5) demonstrates that they are not opposed to cooperation for its own sake. In March 2005, they took a step further and established a joint terrorist alert communications system, based in Granada. Such measures are highly contentious for civil and human rights organizations, despite the fact that to date (including with respect to the London bombings of July 2005) they have proved relatively ineffectual.[36]

The fundamental problem here is precisely the notion of "indivisibility" used in The Hague Programme, referred to earlier. The package of policy areas concerned covers a vast range of issues and actors and cannot so easily be rendered operationally "indivisible." Just to take two obvious categories of activities, terrorism and immigration, the problems of "indivisibility" are immediately obvious. Immigration policy has become indissociable from other—technically quite distinct—policy areas, including refugee policy, asylum policy, and policy on transnational crime, particularly human trafficking. As a result of various wars of destabilization around the EU's frontiers, "normal" pressures on migration have been joined since 1989 by massive pressures from refugees (the Balkan conflicts alone created approximately 3 million) and from asylum seekers. In addition, since the mid-1990s an increase in "people-trafficking" has added to these pressures.[37] The task of simultaneously attempting to both coordinate and disaggregate responses to these different migratory pressures is nigh on impossible. Elsewhere, Didier Bigo addresses the specifics of that problem.[38] If we take the other end of the spectrum—terrorism—we can see immediately that "indivisibility" poses as many problems as it solves. An article by Philippe Errera identified "three circles of threat" from Islamist terrorism that are being confused and conflated in operationally unhelpful ways. This is happening to some extent in response to George W. Bush's remark, in an interview with Bob Woodward, that, being a baseball fan, he needed a "scorecard."[39] The three circles identified by Errera are: (1) the Al Qaeda leadership; (2) locally based groups sharing some of Al Qaeda's ideology but that remain "territorialized" in important ways; and (3) jihadist individuals or groups of individuals who should be considered "home-grown bottom-up franchisees" of the greater Islamist cause. The London bombers of July 2005 and the airline plotters of August 2006 are classic examples of this last circle. They are arguably the biggest problem of all and yet probably have the least to do with immigration. These groups need to be understood—and tackled—in very different ways. Moreover, the relationship between policies appropriate to dealing with these different counter-terrorist challenges on one hand, and immigration policy on the other, is tenuous at best, nonexistent at worst. As one study suggests, the effective coordination of immigration policy is taking place in a rather ad hoc fashion. It is a mix of policy transfer modes characterized by unilateral emulation, adaptation by externality, and conditionality and not the result of "top-down" decision making emanating from the recent spate of legislation on counter-terrorism.[40]

Ongoing Differences between the EU and the U.S. Approaches to Counter-Terrorism

Philippe Errera, in his evaluation of the "three circles of threat," concludes by asking whether counter-terrorism efforts have the ability to bind together the approaches, methods, and fates of the United States and the EU in a way comparable to that of communism during the Cold War. He concludes—somewhat pessimistically—by suggesting that this might prove impossible, "but we cannot know until we have tried."[41]

There is no doubt that there continues to be a major difference of opinion between the two sides over the "newness" of the "new terrorism." U.S. officials tend to view the terrorism as exemplified by Al Qaeda or the jihadist phenomenon as "fundamentally different" from any prior threats faced by nations. The Europeans tend to see it as more of an "evolutionary phenomenon" than a dramatic shift in the nature of the threat.[42] Paradoxically, this argument can also be turned on its head in that Europeans, reacting to evolution, have themselves evolved very rapidly in their approaches to understanding and managing terrorism since 9/11. On the other hand, the United States, which sees things as fundamentally different, also tends to apprehend the threat in very traditional ways. The United States has tended, over the decades, to see threats as coming from a single identifiable source that has the country in its sights (e.g., the Soviet Union or China). Today, that "source"—the new *specific* enemy—is identified as a "*general* war on America" associated with particular regimes. Donald Rumsfeld has named it the "new fascism." Condoleezza Rice, in her testimony to the National Commission on Terrorist Attacks upon the United States, said,

> The U.S. and our allies are disrupting terrorist operations, cutting off their funding, and hunting down terrorists one by one. Their world is getting smaller. The terrorists have lost a home-base and training camps in Afghanistan. The governments of Pakistan and Saudi Arabia now pursue them with energy and force. . . . Because we acted in Iraq, Saddam Hussein will never again use weapons of mass destruction against his people or his neighbors. And we have convinced Libya to give up all its WMD-related programs and materials. And as we attack the threat at its sources, we are also addressing its roots.[43]

European countries in general, on the other hand, associate the recent upsurge with the consequences of long-term neglect of or failure in the Middle East. At the most general level, this helps account for the major difference in U.S. responses to terrorism. U.S. leaders believe it is appropriate to respond to the new terror with military instruments, whereas the EU tends to see terrorism as a phenomenon to be handled with almost any other instrument. After 9/11, this latter approach seemed for a brief moment to become the received wisdom: what was required above all else was intelligence sharing and law enforcement cooperation. Since Al Qaeda was internationally networked and decentralized, the response of the international community would have to be similar: multilateral, multilevel, cooperative, piecemeal, patient, and above all willing to share. However, the U.S. attack on Iraq, which grew directly from the Rice/Bush approach noted above (i.e., the belief that states are still primarily responsible for terrorist attacks) prevented such a consensus from setting in. The U.S. attack on Iraq was intended to put a stop to one major purveyor of terrorist activities (including the dangers of WMD). It would also suck into the Iraqi space large numbers of global jihadists so that they could be collectively killed by military means. That in its turn would make the world love the United States and would help Middle Eastern states to democratize. The result, as we now know, has been precisely the opposite. And yet the U.S. *Quadrennial Defense Review* for 2006 defines the key instrument in the global war on terror as being special operations forces engaged in kinetic and low-visibility military operations all around the world. This, to a large extent, explains (while it does not justify) the continuing reluctance of European countries to help out in Iraq—even though serious destabilization in the Middle East would have a more immediate and direct effect on European interests than on U.S. interests.

Beyond the differences over the global war on terror outlined above, there are many other European criticisms of the way the Bush administration has conducted this "war." One serious objection concerns the Bush administration's clear policy of forging "coalitions of the willing" instead of using the existing structures and resources of the Atlantic Alliance.[44] The slogan "the mission determines the coalition," with its unilateralist connotations, has been profoundly disruptive of NATO. Indeed, in its rush to prosecute the global war on terror, the United States is perceived by many Europeans (and by even more Americans) as having, in effect, abandoned multilateralism and sounded the death knell of NATO.

Another major objection formulated by Europeans concerns the Bush doctrine of "preemptive war" as outlined in the U.S. National Security Strategy document of September 2002. This is perceived as having abandoned the strategic approaches of deterrence and containment that characterized the post-1945 world. It is also viewed as having blurred the necessary distinctions between state and non-state actors and the most effective ways of dealing with them. This new strategy has, in effect, succeeded in undermining the solidarity of the West's traditional strategy against terrorism. Moreover, Europe, perceiving the Iraq war to have been a mistake, sees a number of major consequences. Those consequences include an increase rather than a decline in terrorist recruitment, the creation of a less stable rather than a more stable Middle East, and the exacerbation rather than the improvement of relations between the "West" and Islam.[45] As Chris Patten, EU external relations commissioner, put it in a speech to the European Parliament on September 15, 2004, "Is the world today safer than before the overthrow of the appalling

Saddam? Is global terrorism in retreat? Are we closer to building bridges between Islam and the West? Is the world's only super-power more widely respected? Have the citizens in our democracies been treated in a way that will encourage them to give governments the benefit of the doubt next time they are told that force needs to be used preemptively to deal with an imminent threat? I simply pose the questions. Honorable Members will have their own answers."[46] Indeed, the EU—a region in which Islam is a growing presence—is appalled at the extent to which the Bush "war" on terror has been perceived as a war against Islam, thus fueling jihadist tendencies among youth and other groups.[47]

Connected to this criticism has been widespread concern across Europe about U.S. approaches to "winning the peace" in Iraq. The United States has embarked on a crusade for democracy. The EU has sought—in areas outside its immediate purview (where it has in fact been the greatest force for the export of democracy that the world has ever seen)—to settle for greater stability. The United States has been perceived as having badly misjudged the challenge of democratization in Iraq and has been (perhaps unfairly) accused of wishing to move far too quickly toward an "exit strategy."[48] The EU stated from the outset that the instruments of its European Security and Defence Policy (ESDP) would play a part in the campaign against terrorism, and it has regularly insisted that a military component will be a necessary part of that campaign. However, it has never explained in any detail what specific role it foresees for military instruments.[49] This remains an unanswered question in the EU's approach to counter-terrorism. It is yet another—significant—contrast to the approach adopted by the United States.

A further area of European criticism has focused on U.S. disregard for the norms of international law, with respect to both the Geneva Convention and human rights.[50] There has been considerable disquiet about the PATRIOT Act and its restrictions on human rights and basic freedoms—all of which are explicitly protected in the EU Constitution's Charter of Fundamental Rights. This is a theme that is regularly—albeit diplomatically—brought up by EU counter-terrorism officials visiting the United States.[51] It has also constituted the main concern European analysts have about the impact of the GWOT on basic freedoms and human rights.[52] In part, this difference stems from yet another asymmetry. European countries have traditionally experienced terrorism as a domestic, national, or at most a continental phenomenon. The U.S. experience has been the opposite: the vast majority of attacks have come from global networks, attacking U.S. facilities almost anywhere in the world except within the continental United States (9/11 was the exception that proved the rule).

All EU officials expressed their desire to engage in a fresh start with the Bush administration after the November 2004 elections in the United States.[53] The "charm offensive" tour of Europe conducted by Condoleezza Rice in early 2005 set the scene for an even more constructive visit by George W. Bush in February. In his speech in Brussels, the U.S. president thanked his European allies for their "strong cooperation in the war on terror."[54] He was politely applauded. Two weeks later, Bush announced his support for the EU strategy of "constructive engagement" with Iran. Comment across Europe remained cautious. Editorialists welcomed the new tone of the second-term Bush administration and speculated that a new period of convergence was not impossible. Since then, however, analysts have awaited, with impatience, firm evidence of a breakthrough toward a new era of transatlantic harmony. There is still a very long way to go.

Signs of Hope for Cooperative Counter-Terrorism?

After the deadly transit bombings in London on July 7, 2005, and the failed bombings on July 21, both UK and European authorities introduced draconian measures to counter the new threat of what *Le Monde* called "Kamikazes Maison."[55] At an extraordinary meeting on July 13, the JHA Council outlined a twenty-five-point plan to strengthen the pursuit and investigation of terrorists across borders. Much of this plan involved speeding up implementation of existing plans.[56] France announced plans to reintroduce border checks on passports, with Spain rapidly following suit.[57] The UK government introduced new legislation. It included self-evident measures (such as preventing foreign supporters of terrorism from entering Britain) and more controversial proposals to criminalize not only direct incitement to terrorism but also anything that appeared to "condone," "glorify," or "justify" terrorism anywhere in the world. The deportation of "extremists"—apparently to be defined as individuals holding "what the government considers to be extreme views"—and the adoption of harsher measures against naturalized (as opposed to native-born) individuals was deplored not only by human rights organizations but also by the *New York Times*.[58] It seemed as though EU authorities, in their haste to be seen doing something robust to crack down on terrorism, were engaged in a headlong dash along the same lines as their strategies prior to July 7.

Many of these measures in fact enjoyed widespread public support in the UK. To a certain extent, the UK (one of the last bastions of liberal humanitarianism) had begun to align its counter-terrorism culture with that of a country like France. Under its then minister of the interior, Nicolas Sarkozy, and his "zero-tolerance" policy, France had for some time been uninhibitedly expelling (mainly to North Africa) Muslims found to be offering advice on how to beat one's wife in a "correct Islamic fashion," calling Jews "apes," or inciting jihad. However, cooler heads have wondered whether the remedy will not prove to be worse than the symptom. A UK government report in May 2004 suggested that there could be up to ten thousand active "Al Qaeda" supporters in the country. Similarly, a joint Home Office and Foreign Office report estimated that "only" 1 percent of UK Muslims were potential terrorists—a figure that translates to approximately sixteen thousand persons.[59] The danger was that the draconian legislation would produce precisely the result that UK specialists had witnessed in Ireland: terrorist recruitment would simply accelerate.[60] This was to some extent the reasoning behind the UK House of Commons rejection of Tony Blair's proposal to extend the length of arrest without charges to ninety days.[61] Any attempt to render "indivisible" the entire range of policies covered by The Hague Programme, in which terrorists, immigrants, asylum seekers, refugees, slave traffickers, and drug lords are covered by the same "freedom, justice, and security" program, is likely to prove operationally counter-productive.[62]

Given all this, one might have expected that the ongoing clashes I referred to earlier would simply exacerbate the difficulties in EU-U.S. cooperation. My final point (which introduces a glimmer of hope into the discussion) is that, paradoxically, the summer of 2006 may have witnessed the first signs of a return of the pendulum toward greater protection of human rights. It may also have seen the beginning of greater cooperation between the United States and the EU. The whole range of issues referred to above (Blair's defeat, the PNR debacle, the CIA renditions scandal, as well as the ongoing Iraq imbroglio) had two results. In Europe, some basic principles about the tipping point between human rights and homeland protection were restated. Gijs de Vries noted in a January 2006 speech otherwise devoted to outlining the many ways in which the EU collectively was coordinating its counter-terrorism activities, that core values are nevertheless a fundamental pillar in the overall campaign. "Qualified majority voting, stronger democratic and judicial control, and better protection under the ECHR [European Convention for Human Rights], " he stated, "are indispensable to fight terrorism effectively."[63] There were also signs of a similar reassessment in the United States. There was growing awareness in the U.S. intelligence community that the balance had swung too far in favor of military dominance of the intelligence world and that quality actionable intelligence had suffered greatly as a result. The first half of 2006 in fact saw an ever-greater monopoly of the Pentagon over U.S. intelligence activities, despite the creation of the national intelligence directorate. According to an International Institute for Strategic Studies (IISS) report published in June 2006, the Department of Defense succeeded in retaining control over some 80 percent of the federal intelligence budget. It also managed to cut the then national intelligence director, John Negroponte, out of the military chain of command. Yet CIA director Michael Hayden insisted that the agency should see it as a "top priority" to share information with foreign partners. While this was not (quite) a shift from a "need to know" approach to a "need to share" approach, it did betoken recognition that excess jealousy in guarding intelligence has proven counter-productive. Hayden also embarked on a campaign to claw his way back to greater control over the intelligence budget and activities for the civilian agencies. This meshes well with the statutory requirement under which Negroponte operated, which was to assert ever greater civilian control. As the IISS *Strategic Comment* put it, "Hayden's clear-eyed preoccupation with maintaining the high tempo of intelligence collection on emerging threats while simultaneously improving intelligence analysis, coupled with his premium on intelligence sharing, suggests tangible movement within the U.S. national security system in the direction of greater operational interdependence. . . . The U.S. and its partners may be settling into a new epoch of collegiality in the intelligence realm."[64] After a rather shaky start, there were some signs by the end of 2006 that both the EU and the United States were beginning to learn some of the basics of cooperation in counter-terrorism. But there is still a very long way to go.

6

Immigration Policy and Reactions to Terrorism after September 11

MARTIN SCHAIN

In reaction to security concerns following the events of September 11, 2001, new legislative initiatives to combat international terror are assumed to have had a deleterious effect on immigrants and immigration on both sides of the Atlantic. I address these assumptions by examining actual rules in place at the end of 2001 and subsequent changes to them in Britain, France, and the United States.

As in many countries in Europe, there were terrorist incidents and attacks in both France and Britain for decades before September 11, 2001. These attacks had begun to accelerate in the late 1960s as a radical response to domestic problems, often supported by international European networks. By the 1980s, terrorist incidents rooted in conflicts in other parts of the world began to increase in France as well as in other parts of Europe. It was not until a decade later, however, that incidents of jihadist terrorism linked new patterns of domestic conflict involving immigrant communities with conflicts and revolutionary challenges in other parts of the world.[1]

I have found that the reactions to patterns of terrorism since 2001 in the United States and Europe have generally been shaped by the ways that each country dealt with very different patterns of terrorism before 2001. After

1974, Britain wrote new laws to deal with the Irish Republican Army (IRA) and then refashioned that legislation to deal with broader terrorist threats even before 2001. The attack on the London transport system in July 2005 generated new legislation but did not alter the basic approach that had evolved until then.

In France, policy, and the organizational structure to pursue that policy, changed dramatically during the 1980s and has not been altered much since then. Although rooted in legislation, the French approach was quite different from that of the British. It was organized around a group of investigating judges granted broad discretionary powers of investigation, as well as power to impose penalties under law.

The reaction in the United States, constructed in the 1990s, was embedded in a long tradition of the way government has dealt with war powers. These powers do not derive from legislation but have been exercised directly by the president, with a claim that they are based on the president's constitutional prerogatives as commander-in-chief. Most such actions have been tested in the courts and have sometimes been reversed by court decisions after the fact. Compared with British and French laws, the American legislative initiatives to deal with terrorism have been relatively modest, with the strange exception of the passage of the Detainee Treatment Bill in September 2006. This legislation, which is generally portrayed as a Democratic victory that constrains presidential war powers, in fact affirmed prior presidential initiatives and placed them beyond the reach of court review.[2]

In general, the "war on terrorism" in Europe has been fought with draconian legislation that has legally compromised what Americans call civil liberties in ways that American legislation began to pursue only after the attacks of 2001. These compromises in civil liberties were made long before 2001, but the application of pre-2001 legislation has been reoriented and extended since then. In the United States, on the other hand, executive actions, only some of which have been successfully challenged in the courts, have had a similar effect. Unlike in the United States, in France and Britain 2001 does not constitute a sea change but rather the continuation of a process through which the balance between liberty and security has been changing in fits and starts for some time.

My focus is on the importance of these trends for immigration policy. On one hand, despite concerns about security, immigration policy has become more expansive throughout Europe and the United States since 2001. France, Britain, and other European countries have moved their focus away from the exclusionary "zero" immigration policies of the 1990s and have begun to devise ways of developing more normalized policies of immigration. On the other hand, the important anti-terrorism actions of governments on both sides of the Atlantic have increasingly focused on immigrant populations, particularly those originating from Muslim-dominated nations. This pattern has accelerated as attention has shifted from external threats of terrorism to internal threats based among immigrant populations—citizens, legal residents, and illegal aliens. Thus, increasingly, anti-terrorism actions are also actions that inevitably implicate immigrant populations.

Nevertheless, in general there has not been a public reaction against immigrants. Indeed, I present data from recent studies that indicate that immigrant populations have generally become more and not less accepted in Europe and the United States. There have certainly been political reactions to immigration in some European countries, including the Netherlands, Denmark, and Switzerland. However, among mass publics in most of Europe and the United States, the political priority of immigration is relatively low, although there has been a growing concern about illegal immigration on both sides of the Atlantic.

Britain

In many ways the British reaction is at once the most severe and the least changed from the pre-2001 pattern. The wave of sectarian violence that swept through Britain in 1974 provoked legislative initiatives that serve as a baseline for understanding the British reaction to terrorism.

The primary legacy of the "troubles" in Northern Ireland is an accumulation of broad powers of arrest and detention, powers that apply to all residents of the UK. In reaction to a wave of IRA violence throughout 1974, the Labour government rushed the Prevention of Terrorism Act through Parliament soon after the October elections.[3] The new act instituted several major changes. It gave the Home Secretary the power to issue a list of proscribed organizations and it applied penalties of imprisionment and fines to anyone belonging to these organizations or supporting them with financial and other means. It also outlawed the wearing of dress and symbols that could be linked to these organizations. In addition, it gave the police powers to detain people for up to seven days—if the police judged them to be a threat—without an arrest warrant and without any charge being brought against them. Finally, it allowed the authorities to "exclude" people from entering Britain, including citizens of the UK who ordinarily resided outside of the territory of the UK and its colonies and residents who had not ordinarily resided in the UK for the previous twenty years.

The legislation applied to citizens as well as residents but was far more constraining for noncitizens for purposes of exclusion and expulsion. Although the only proscribed organization initially named under the act was the IRA, the list was expanded to other militant organizations engaged in violent struggle, including those on the loyalist side.

Initially viewed as a temporary measure, the Prevention of Terrorism Act was renewed each year and modified in 1978, 1984, and 1989. Most of its major provisions were finally incorporated into the Terrorism Act of 2000 (although some of the exclusion and internment without trial provisions were dropped, at least until 2001). Critics of the legislation found that its provisions were used mainly as a means of monitoring the movements of Irish Catholics without having to go through the formalities of applying for warrants and bringing charges. Indeed, Home Office reports tell a story of several hundred people being stopped and examined each year; generally, never more than two were ultimately charged. Although the number of those actually detained each year fell during the decade of the 1990s, the number of those examined for suspected involvement with international terrorism grew each year, indicating a shift away from the Irish problem.[4]

The Terrorism Act of 2000 extended police stop-and-frisk powers, and it listed fourteen organizations involved in the struggle over Northern Ireland. However, at the end of February 2001, Home Secretary Jack Straw requested that twenty-one "international groups" be added to the list. By September, there were twenty-five groups on the proscribed organizations list, eighteen of which were Islamic.[5]

Therefore, a year before the attack on the World Trade Center, British policy—and the tools that had been developed during the long IRA emergency—had been reoriented toward transnational terrorism. This reorientation generalized extensive police powers that restricted several aspects of civil liberties, including freedom of movement and freedom of association. Perhaps more importantly, with the legislation in 2000 the temporary/emergency approach to terrorism was dropped entirely. The altered approach is evident from the report on the operation of the act in 2001, which indicated that only twelve of the thirty arrests under the act between January and the end of August 2001 were related to Irish terrorism.[6] Those more frequently targeted were immigrant residents and ethnic British citizens of immigrant families. The measures in place by 2000 were so extensive by European standards that in a variety of reports issued by European and international organizations Britain ranked as one of the most repressive countries in Europe.[7]

After the attacks in the United States on September 11, 2001, the focus was turned more fully on the question of transnational movements and more precisely on immigration and asylum. In fact the Anti-Terrorism, Crime, and Security Emergency Act (2001) was not a sharp break with the previous legislation. The changes, however, are important because of their impact on immigrants and immigration.

A key consequence of the legislation was to further separate citizens from foreign residents, with the focus being on foreign residents. As a continuation of the pattern begun in the 1974 legislation, foreign residents who were dubbed "suspected terrorists" could be detained without trial (or appeal), or—where the option existed—they could be deported. That option depended on whether the Home Office decided that they may be subject to actions by their "home" government that would be contrary to Article 3 of the European Convention on Human Rights (ECHR). If deportation was not possible, foreign residents could now be jailed indefinitely. This required that Britain opt out of Article 5 of the ECHR, which prohibits imprisonment without trial. This in turn required Britain to declare a "state of emergency," permitted by the treaty in case of public emergency or war. In fact, Britain was the only signatory of the treaty to opt out.

In the long run, opting out of Article 5 proved to be a crucial obstacle to the enforcement of the 2001 legislation. In December 2004, the British High Court—the Law Lords—found that the law was a breach of fundamental human rights, essentially rejecting the opt-out that had been written into the law.[8] This supported a previous decision that the treatment of foreign terror suspects was discriminatory because the law applied only to people who were not British citizens (i.e., subject to immigration control). At the time of the ruling, twelve terror suspects were being held in Britain without being charged (and had been held for three years).

To remedy the situation, the government proposed new legislation that finally replaced indefinite detention with limited (but renewable) judicially controlled detention—under "control orders," a form of house arrest—of citizens and foreigners alike. The Prevention of Terrorism Act 2005 was therefore meant to correct the act of 2001 by making what was unacceptable treatment for foreigners acceptable treatment for all suspects.[9]

The most recent legislation, the Prevention of Terrorism Act 2006, was passed in the aftermath of the July 2005 attacks in London. The act created a number of new offenses and increased police powers and the power of the Home Secretary to proscribe new groups. Once brought into force, it expanded the number of criminal offenses to include what are deemed acts preparatory to terrorism: incitement or encouragement of terrorism, the dissemination of terrorist publications, and being present where terrorist training is taking place. It also extended the powers of the police to search property and to detain suspects for up to twenty-eight days (though periods of more than two days must be approved by a judicial authority). Finally, the legislation extended the proscription regime to include the power to proscribe groups that glorify terrorism.

After more than thirty years of anti-terrorist legislation, the legal basis for arrest, detention, deportation, and proscription has been expanded cumulatively. To this, we must add the discretionary powers granted both to the Home Office and to the police themselves. All in all, one comparative study of anti-terror laws and civil liberties found that, on an eight-point scale, "Britain leads the 'scoreboard' with legislation introduced in seven out of the eight categories surveyed and a law that does not expire, followed by Germany with five out of eight categories affected and a law that expires very late and for the provisions introduced relating to the power of the secret services. Finally, there is France with a score of only three out of eight categories affected and a law that expires very late, two years after it has been invoked."[10] This evaluation is based on the assumption that the legislation passed since 2001 was a new departure. In fact, the judgment could be harsher if we consider the long accumulation of legislation since 1974.

France

France developed an approach to international terrorism far earlier than Britain, but it did so only after a series of attacks in the early 1980s indicated that the earlier policy—what has been called the "sanctuary doctrine"—was producing more violence than security. French authorities had concentrated their considerable efforts on combating home-grown terrorism of the anarchist left, Action Directe, as well as regional separatist groups in Brittany, the Basque area, and especially in Corsica. The French counter-espionage service (the SDECE) and the agency for internal surveillance (the DST) had long experience in dealing with internal terrorism, emanating from such sources as the Algerian war of independence, Action Directe, and Corsica. Still, it had no organizational means for dealing with international terrorism. Instead, "[the] sanctuary doctrine attempted to isolate the country from international terrorism by creating within France a sanctuary both for and from international terrorists. This policy required making French policy and soil as neutral as possible with respect to the issues that motivated international terrorism . . . [which] could operate with impunity, as long as they did not perpetrate acts of terrorism within France or against French interests."[11]

Jeremy Shapiro and Bénédicte Suzan argue that the policy was relatively successful, at least until the early 1980s, in part because it presumed that international terrorism was a foreign-policy problem, rather than a problem for law enforcement. The presumption was that the prevention of terrorism, at its core, depended on diplomacy. Increasingly, however, this approach seemed to convey a sense of weakness and invited conflicting countries and groups in the Middle East to play out their violent conflicts in the streets of Paris. Finally, fourteen attacks in 1986, twelve of them by one previously unknown group, provoked a change in policy and a major reorganization of the approach to terrorism.[12]

The Law Relative to the Struggle against Terrorism of 1986 refocused state efforts away from the Ministry of Foreign Affairs. It also increased the administrative capabilities of the Ministries of the Interior and Justice—the police and judicial authorities—that effectively coordinated the various intelligence and police agencies. The State Security Court, a secret military court that had been established during the Gaullist period to counteract the Secret Army Organization, had been abandoned after the left came to power in 1981 and never replaced. Under the new legislation in 1986, the fight against terrorism was centralized in Paris in a core group, the *juges d'instruction* (investigating magistrates), who then took both the judicial and investigative lead in the French struggle with terrorism for the next twenty years.

Under legislation that was passed in 1986, 1995, and 1996, the investigating magistrates gained tools that are similar to, if less draconian than, those developed at the same time in Britain. Thus, ordinary law permits stop and frisk, as well as detention without charge, for as long as four days in terror investigations. In addition, *juges d'instruction* can order preventive detention for long periods of time once suspects are under judicial investigation. In the 1994 roundup (see below), some defendants spent up to four years in prison before they went on trial in 1998.[13]

These police/judicial powers work in much the same way that they do in Britain, except that they are generally under the authority of a judge. During the worst of the Algerian civil war (1992–2000), played out once again in the streets of Paris, there were major roundups of Algerians in France in 1993, 1994, 1995, and 1998. In each case, the number of persons detained far exceeded the number finally held over for trial (with the exception of November 8, 1994, when seventy-eight of the ninety-three arrested were brought to trial, of which fifty-one were cleared).[14] The 1996 legislation created the crime of "conspiracy to commit terrorism," which gave the investigating magistrates considerable power to prevent acts from ever occurring.

The often cited virtues of this system are its specialization, centralization, flexibility, coordination, and political independence. Its virtues, however, are also its problems, since there is no political oversight and little oversight within the judicial system. Key magistrates, such as Jean-Louis Bruguière, make decisions on investigation and police action that are difficult to question.[15] On the other hand, after the attacks on the London transit system in 2005, British Home Secretary Charles Clarke stated a number of times that a French-style system in Britain could be more effective in detaining suspects while a case is being constructed against them.[16]

By 2001, the French system for dealing with terrorism was firmly set into place, and new legislation, the Law on Daily Security, which was passed in November 2001, changed relatively little. The ability of the police to stop and search was strengthened, at least in terms of the places where this could take place, and it allowed more types of police to carry out such security checks (private police, for example). September 11, however, did provide an opportunity—or an opening—to augment a campaign already under way against crime in France, and the police were given new powers to deal with petty crime. Police prerogatives were then reinforced with more specific legislation passed each year between 2001 and 2004.

While there have been few legislative changes since September 11, as in Britain, the focus of the system set in place after 1986 has shifted some focus toward internal aspects of terrorism. The dogged efforts of the Ministry of the Interior to develop relations with the Islamic community with the establishment of the Conseil Français du Culte Musulman (CFCM), and the sometimes contradictory efforts of then Interior Minister Nicolas Sarkozy (before he became president), are all indications of the importance of the European context of Islam. As Olivier Roy has stated, "So what is at stake is no longer immigrants, because there are no more immigrants. The guys we are speaking about are citizens."[17] But there are immigrant or ethnic communities.

Although the judicialization of the struggle against terrorism has no direct implications for immigration, the effectiveness of the system, combined with more generally enhanced policy powers, inevitably intrudes on immigrant communities and on the daily lives of immigrants who walk the streets and ride the metro. French police have poor training in "community relations," and little effort has been made to make this larger police presence more tolerable, as recent studies have pointed out.[18] In one reaction to the attacks in London, the French press pointed out that some fifteen groups under police surveillance "are somewhere between petty criminality and the radical Islamic movement."[19] Clearly all of these groups relate to French immigrant communities.

The United States

How, then, can we compare what has happened in Britain and France with what has happened in the United States? The U.S. case is at once the most radical in terms of the evolution of executive power, being relatively unchecked by either legislative or judicial constraint. It is less radical in terms of the evolution of legislated powers, with regard either to the struggle against terrorism or to immigration.

Prior to the passage of the PATRIOT Act in 2001, the U.S. approach to domestic terrorism was defined by the reaction to the bombing of the World Trade Center in New York in 1993, which in turn extended changes that had taken place a decade before. Both the FBI and CIA were reorganized, but domestic terrorism never became a priority. Although the counter-terrorism budget of the FBI tripled in the mid-1990s, spending remained constant between 1998 and 2001. According to the report from the commission assigned to investigate the terror attacks, "in 2000, there were still twice as many agents devoted to drug enforcement as to counter-terrorism." For the CIA, counter-terrorism appears to have become a priority by 1997, but its director testified that even by 2004 the agency was still five years away from being able to play a significant role in this effort.[20] Finally, the concern about terrorism had only minimal effect on immigrant entry into the United States. Legislation in 1996 authorized the use of classified information in removal hearings conducted by the Immigration and Naturalization Service (INS), which, however, had an impact on only a few cases.[21]

Before 2001, U.S. law did not permit the kind of preventive detention allowed under British and French law (if we do not consider the problem of bail) or most of the intrusive police powers permitted under French law. As we know from the 9/11 Commission report, terrorist activity within the United States was treated as criminal activity.[22] U.S. law did permit the effective outlawing of certain organizations (under the McCarran-Walter Act of 1952), and the FBI had a history of infiltrating domestic organizations that were labeled as being "subversive." Nevertheless, the 9/11 Commission report makes clear that, by the 1990s, these powers had been curtailed by legislation, as well as by court decisions.

The primary changes in the United States after the attacks of 9/11 have been legislative and organizational. However, the application of executive powers to the war on terrorism, to construct a system that is largely outside of the legislative purview, has been more far-reaching. One result has been the activation of judicial oversight in areas only rarely touched before (e.g., military tribunals at Guantanamo Bay) and judicial fine-tuning of the rights of U.S. citizens accused of terrorist activities.

Certainly the PATRIOT Act, first passed on October 26, 2001, and renewed in 2006, is the most visible change since 9/11.[23] Although the act enhances powers of the government and law enforcement authorities, it also constrains some of their worst impulses under law. For example, the law required that the hundreds of detainees (mostly immigrants), who were being held secretly without charges or hearings in October 2001, be released or charged. The act also granted special protection against deportation to noncitizen relatives of those killed or who had lost jobs in the attacks.

Nevertheless, the PATRIOT Act incorporates into American law many of the anti-civil-libertarian principles that have existed in European law for some time. The provisions granting enhanced surveillance powers to the FBI and other government agents are unchecked by either transparency or accountability. Wiretapping and searches, for example, can now be pursued without any requirement (previously imposed under Foreign Intelligence Surveillance Act [FISA] standards) that these actions be primarily for gathering intelligence against foreign conspiracies, rather than criminal investigatory purposes. In effect, this vastly broadens the basis for surveillance. In addition, the act either enhances or provides new tools for search warrants, the seizure of records, and the surveillance of bank, telephone, and Internet records (through so-called National Security Letters) in preliminary investigations.[24]

The act is not directed specifically against aliens or immigrants, but it specifically provides for noncitizens to be detained for up to seven days. If the government states its intention to deport, detention can be extended up to six months and be renewable. Indeed, most prominent in the claims made by Attorney General John Ashcroft in May 2003 was that 478 people had been deported and 211 criminal charges had been legally brought since October 2001.

On the other hand, a report by the NYU Center on Law and Security indicates that these claims may indicate less effective police work than they imply. Sweeping surveillance under the PATRIOT Act has produced very few arrests and fewer convictions. Thus, the report notes that "FISA warrants have mushroomed at an alarming rate; and the public sees only the tip of the iceberg, since FISA warrants and their fruits never see the light of day unless they are used in a criminal prosecution—which represents only an infinitesimal fraction of the total number of FISA wiretaps and searches."[25] Among the 211 criminal charges claimed by Ashcroft, the NYU Center on Law and Security documented 120 cases. Of the 84 people arrested on charges of terrorism between September 2001 and October 2004, 54 have been indicted for terrorism and/or support of terrorism, of which 27 have been convicted or accepted a plea (11 have been convicted). Only one person has been convicted of a direct act of terrorism (Richard Reid), and only 5 percent (18) of the charges brought before the courts have been for direct acts of terrorism.[26]

However, the alternative—perhaps the more serious—effort of the government to combat terrorism has been an extra-legal, ad hoc campaign, under cover of presidential war power, the results of which have been dubious. The PATRIOT Act specifically does not give the government the authority to incarcerate "enemy combatants" incommunicado, to detain illegal immigrants without filing charges, or to impose secrecy on the detention and hearings in immigration cases.[27] Although citizens, in principle, have greater claims on the legal system than noncitizens, there has been no consistency in the treatment of either. Thus, an American citizen, John Walker Lindh, who was captured in Afghanistan as an enemy combatant, was charged in federal court and given a plea bargain, while the government has simply detained two other citizens, Yasser Esam Hamdi and Jose Padilla, as enemy combatants without filing charges.[28] On the other hand, Richard Reid, a British citizen, was convicted, and Zacarias Moussaoui, a French citizen, was sentenced after pleading guilty in federal court on terrorism charges.

As for the impact on immigration and immigrant communities, it is clear from the arrest pattern detailed in the NYU CLS study that the focus of attention is on Muslim immigrant communities. The study also shows that, in general, increased detention and deportation have created hardships for undocumented aliens. Although the new legislation does not appear to be harsher than legislation already in place in France and Britain, it makes life more difficult for immigrants and aliens. This is not only because of new rules but also because of the new means of administering both the new rules and the old. Thus the follow-up Intelligence Reform Act of 2004 "is principally concerned with the reorganization of the intelligence community and the creation of a new 'czar,' the director of national intelligence, to oversee the intelligence operations of the Central Intelligence Agency, the Pentagon, and other agencies. In addition, however, it modifies many of the laws and regulations identified with the Patriot Act. It expands the scope of foreign intelligence surveillance, and strengthens the power to detain suspected terrorists prior to trial. It sets minimum federal standards for personal identity documents and attempts to bolster their security."[29]

The most high-profile detentions have included those of two sixteen-year-old girls, neither of whom was ever charged with a crime; one of them was released to her home, the other was deported to Bangladesh. From the perspective of new rules, however, all of these actions were undertaken on the basis of existing rules, enforced with greater vigor.[30] Thus, legal immigrants in the United States after September 11, from Arab and other Islamic countries, were required to register with the INS. Failure to register carried with it the danger of deportation.

As in Britain and France, all of these additional powers and administrative personnel create more hardships for immigrant communities. Although one target of legislation, reorganization, and ad hoc action has been undocumented aliens, the impact inevitably includes immigrants and even citizens, many of whom may be in the same family.

The American approach to combating terrorism in the post-9/11 period has therefore focused on means that have often been called extra-legal but that the government has viewed in the context of expanded executive powers. In effect, the executive has not only been using executive powers that have developed and been legally sanctioned over the years but also been testing new power, not yet sanctioned. As Valerie Caprioni, the general counsel of the FBI, noted at a seminar at New York University in November 2005,

> I think that anyone who reads the papers recognizes that this president in particular has a very broad view of executive power, and what is within his power as the executive, and has the authority to act unilaterally. And you may quarrel with that, there may be some people here who think that the federalist society view of the power of the executive is wrong and they are misreading the law, but there is nevertheless a legal structure for that, where there are lawyers at the Department of Justice and the Office of Legal Counsel whose job it is to opine whether particular things that the executive wishes to do are lawful or not, whether they are within his constitutional power as the commander-in-chief and as the executive.
>
> So we operate every bit as much within the parameters of the law when we are operating pursuant to an executive order that has been blessed by the Department of Justice's Office of Legal Counsel as when we are acting pursuant to a statute that has been passed by the United States Congress and signed by the President. So we stay within the legal parameters though those legal parameters can shift between being legal parameters that have been passed by Congress, and ones where we are operating pursuant to executive order. But it is no less legal from our perspective.[31]

In general, the anti-terrorism actions of the United States pursuant to law have touched relatively few people (as is indeed the case in Europe). However, the actions that have been undertaken under cover of executive power have touched many thousands of people, if we consider the scope of the warrantless phone taps first reported by the *New York Times* on December 16, 2005. Subsequent reports referred to thousands, "perhaps millions" of phone lines that were involved.[32]

President Bush's expansive use of executive power has been checked by two notable decisions by the U.S. Supreme Court, notably *Hamdi v. Rumsfeld* in July 2004 and *Hamdan v. Rumsfeld* in June 2006. Each of these decisions limited the prerogative of the president to authorize the unlimited detention of American citizens. The Guantanamo case (*Hamdi v. Rumsfeld*), decided together with the *Hamdan* case, also applied similar standards to noncitizens being held at Guantanamo Bay.[33] Nevertheless, although these court decisions were important landmarks, their impact has been to shape, rather than seriously constrain, presidential power in this area.

The president was forced to return to Congress and request authorization to do what he was already doing. The result was the Detainee Treatment Act in 2006, which gave congressional authorization for detention. Most newspaper reports in the United States focused on the challenge posed by a coalition of some Republicans and a majority of Democrats to the treatment of prisoners held at the American base in Guantanamo Bay. The Supreme Court, in *Hamdan v. Rumsfeld* in June 2006, had ruled that the military commissions organized under presidential authority to try these prisoners were invalid without congressional authorization. The European press, and a few American commentators, noted the affirmation of expanded presidential power.

The president could now authorize under law the identification of who is an enemy combatant (under a broadened definition) and their indefinite imprisonment outside the United States. The legislation does force the president to limit interrogation techniques but prevents Guantanamo prisoners from appealing to the courts. Of course the new law also reinstates the military tribunals.[34] The new legislation will be challenged in the courts. However, it appears that, at least for the moment, congressional action that was mandated by the Supreme Court has strengthened the ability of the president to act without being constrained by the courts in the future.

We find a similar pattern emerging in the case of the National Security Agency (NSA) warrantless searches that were authorized by the president in 2001. In August 2006, a federal district court declared that this surveillance, ordered by the president and undertaken by the NSA, was unconstitutional, but the case has been appealed and is now being considered by federal appeals courts.[35] A month later the House of Representatives passed the Electronic Surveillance Modernization Act, and that bill has been passed to the U.S. Senate, where three other competing, mutually exclusive bills are also being considered. For purposes of this analysis, what they all have in common is that in the name of constraining presidential prerogatives each would broaden the statutory authorization for electronic surveillance while still subjecting it to some restrictions.

Much of this debate was transformed, however, when then Attorney General Alberto Gonzales informed U.S. Senate leaders, by letter on January 17, 2007, that the program would not be reauthorized by the president. The letter further stated that "any electronic surveillance that was occurring as part of the Terrorist Surveillance Program will now be conducted subject to the approval of the Foreign Intelligence Surveillance Court."[36] The letter implied a compromise but one that conforms to the standards approved by the PATRIOT Act in 2006. Nevertheless, the president appeared to have emerged with reinforced prerogatives in the area of surveillance, powers that may yet be sanctioned by legislation.

New Immigration Departures

This is only part of the story of immigration since 9/11. In Britain, France, and the United States, the tendency since 2001 has been toward immigration expansion rather than exclusion.

In Britain, there have been new initiatives to increase at least some kinds of immigration. In 2002, the government launched a broader program to recruit skilled workers through the Highly Skilled Migrant Program based on a Canadian-style point system. Individuals who accumulate sufficient points, by scoring well on such criteria as educational qualifications, work experience, and professional accomplishment, are then free to look for a job and are thus free to enter the UK without a guarantee of employment.[37] This approach has quietly shifted the initiative for labor migration from the state to employers. The *Economist,* looking back on immigration policy after 2000, concluded that "over the past five years, the government has quietly liberalized the work-permit system: businesses, which used to have a tough time getting permits for foreigners, now find that applications go though pretty much on the nod. By and large, it is the employers who determine what kind of immigrants get jobs. They ask for permits, and the government responds, usually positively."[38]

In France, there was new cooperation among the G-5 interior ministers (France, Germany, Britain, Spain, and Italy) at the European level to transport undocumented aliens out of France and Europe on cooperatively sponsored charter planes.[39] At the same time, there are proposals emanating from France's Ministry of the Interior for developing a program "to determine the need for immigrant workers by profession categories, and a new organization of different services related to immigration."[40] These proposals resulted in the first wide-ranging debate on immigration policy in France since 1997.

Finally, in the United States, the Department of Homeland Security strengthened its control of the borders and has supported a national standard for drivers' licenses that would approximate an identity card for immigrants. On the other hand, there were contentious discussions within the Bush administration and Congress in the summer of 2007 about a program that would include both amnesty (that would benefit mostly undocumented Hispanic aliens) and an expanded guest-worker program.[41] Perhaps what is most notable about these proposals is that, like those in Britain and France, they imply increased, rather than reduced immigration.

Attitudes toward Immigrants

The other part of the story is that attitudes toward immigration have evolved in unexpected ways. Two patterns seem to have emerged since 2001. On one hand, attitudes toward *immigrants* seem to have either improved or not deteriorated in ways that might have been expected. In general, public opinion in many ways favorable to immigrants—and to legal immigration—has increased. For example, even as political concern about immigration has increased markedly in the United States in the second half of 2006 and first half of 2007, a series of surveys also indicate strong support (55–60 percent) for permitting illegal immigrants who are working in the United States to stay.[42] Furthermore, at least for the United States, public opinion has grown more, rather than less, favorable in some areas presumed to be affected by the current concern about illegal immigration (see tables 6.1 and 6.2).

On the other hand, attitudes toward the political importance of immigration, while somewhat more volatile, have not generally resulted in support for more restrictive policies. There has been some variation in the political importance of immigration among mass publics since 2001. For the EU 15, its importance has remained relatively low and relatively stable at about 14 percent, less than concern about unemployment (identified as the most important issue), the economy, crime, prices, terrorism, and health care.[43] In the Netherlands, for example, only 7 percent of those surveyed in 2004 ranked immigration among their most important political concerns.

The Eurobarometer surveys cited above are supported by country-based polls that generally show a decline in immigration as a political concern in France and low-level stability in the United States. In addition, immigration issues do not seem to be masked by attitudes toward law and order. Crime

Table 6.1
The perception of immigration from the third world
as "good" or "bad," 2002 versus 2005

	Good (%)		Bad (%)	
	2002	2005	2002	2005
United States	67.4	60	22.6	29
Britain	53	61	—	30
France	43	53	51.3	45

Source: Pew Research Center, Pew Global Attitudes Project, spring 2006 survey, question 4.
Note: Survey questions in the United States involved immigration from Mexico and Latin America; in Britain, from the Middle East and North Africa; and in France, from North Africa.

Table 6.2
Responses to the question of whether immigrants are having a
good or bad influence on the nation overall (%)

	United States	Britain	France
Very good	13	7	2
Somewhat good	39	36	43
Somewhat bad	29	26	40
Very bad	17	22	9

Source: Associated Press International Affairs Poll, IPOS Public Affairs, Washington, DC, May 2006.

does not register among the top political concerns for Americans; it has declined as a political concern for the French (see tables 6.3, 6.4, and 6.5).

Nevertheless, Britain stands out in this context. As the parliamentary elections of 2005 approached, both the concern about and the priority of immigration increased. In part, the issue was driven by the political campaigns in 2000 and 2005, when the Tories merged the issues of race and immigration, and in part by rising concerns about security and terror after 2001. However, neither the campaigns nor the public's increasing concern over immigration appeared to have any impact on British immigration policy.[44]

Where and How Policies Have Changed

Although there has been a certain amount of convergence of concerns between Europe and the United States with regard to international terrorism,

Table 6.3
Percentage of French voters motivated by particular issues,
by party affiliation, 1984–2004

Party affiliation	Law and Order						Immigration					
	1984	1988	1993	1997	2002	2004	1984	1988	1993	1997	2002	2004
Parti Communiste	9	19	29	28	29	23	2	12	16	15	7	6
Parti Socialiste	8	21	24	29	36	24	3	13	19	15	10	3
Droite	17	38	37	43	56	63	3	19	33	22	17	11
Front National	30	55	57	66	68	66	26	59	72	72	57	54
Total	15	31	34	35	48	43	6	22	31	22	21	15

Party affiliation	Unemployment						Social Inequality					
	1984	1988	1993	1997	2002	2004	1984	1988	1993	1997	2002	2004
Parti Communiste	37	59	77	85	41	66	33	50	52	46	56	43
Parti Socialiste	27	43	71	83	44	60	24	43	40	47	55	41
Droite	20	41	67	72	32	40	7	18	23	21	18	7
Front National	17	41	64	75	27	40	10	18	26	25	18	16
Total	24	45	68	75	36	52	16	31	32	35	33	25

Sources: SOFRES/TF1 exit poll, June 17, 1984; *Le Nouvel Observateur,* June 22, 1984; SOFRES, *État de l'opinion, Clés pour 1987* (Paris: Seuil, 1987), 111; Pascal Perrineau, "Les étapes d'une implantation électorale (1972–1988), in *Le Front National à découvert,* ed. Nonna Mayer and Pascal Perrineau (Paris: Presses de la FNSP, 1988), 62; Pascal Perrineau, "Le Front National la force solitaire," in *Le vote sanction,* ed. Philippe Habert, Pascal Perrineau, and Colette Ysmal (Paris: Presses de la FNSP/Dept. d'Etudes Politiques du Figaro, 1993), 155; CSA, "Les élections legislatives du 25 mai, 1997," Sondage Sortie des Urnes pour France 3, France Inter, France Info et Le Parisien, 5; CSA, "L'élection presidentielle: explication du vote et perspectives politiques" (April 2002); CSA, "Les élections régionales: explication du vote et perspectives politiques," March 22, 2004, 5–6.
Note: Since several responses were possible, the total across may be more than 100 percent. For 1988, the results are for supporters of presidential candidates nominated by the parties indicated.

Table 6.4
MORI Political Monitor: The three most important issues facing Britain (2001–2005) (%)

Date	Crime, law and order, violence	Economy	Education	Race relations, immigration, immigrants
October 2001	14	12	31	17
September 2002	28	10	31	21
September 2003	24	14	28	29
September 2004	27	10	29	26
June 2005	30	11	24	33

Source: The MORI Political Monitor, "Long-Term Trends: The Most Important Issues
Facing Britain Today, 1979–2005," http://mori.com/polls/trends/issues.shtml.

Table 6.5
**American responses to survey questions about the most important problem
currently facing the United States (%)**

	Iraq war	Terrorism	Economy	Unemploy- ment	Immigration/ illegal aliens
Oct. 2001	—	46	13	4	2
Jan. 2002	—	23	21	8	2
Nov. 2003	18	7	20	12	2
Oct. 2004	17	13	12	10	2
July 2005	25	17	10	8	4

Source: The Gallup Organization, Gallup Surveys, 2001–2005.

there has been less change in Europe than is generally thought. On the other hand, there has been considerable change in the United States, in part because there was little focus on terrorism before September 11. Nevertheless, the changes in American law have not gone as far as British and French laws had gone even before September 11, 2001. What is of more concern is not the number of changes in U.S. law but the use of the executive war power to deal with the struggle against terrorism. Moreover, as the episode of the Detainee Treatment Act of 2006 indicates, it is difficult for either the courts or Congress to seriously constrain the more creative aspects of executive power.

Convergence is most evident in the more widespread surveillance and other actions against immigrant populations. It is also evident in the awareness that, as terrorism emerges as a domestic problem, such an approach may be increasingly self-defeating, since the cooperation and trust of immigrant communities are essential tools in the fight against terrorist activities. However, the reactions in Britain, France, and the United States are complicated.

Britain and France have begun to move away from immigration policies that emphasized the goal of "zero" immigration. In the United States, more open immigration policies have been maintained since 1965. In addition, the conservative Republican president sought (unsuccessfully) to gain potential electoral points for his party by proposing policies that would regularize millions of illegal immigrants who reside in the country. Finally, in all three countries, mass publics are more accepting of immigrant populations than even a few years ago.

Of course, this apparent acceptance does not mean that the politics of immigration are necessarily fading. The French experience with the Front National indicates that, among those who deeply oppose immigration and immigrants, there may still be a durable subculture that can be mobilized for electoral purposes. Moreover, the effective opposition of conservative Republicans (and some Democrats) to the Bush proposals indicates the complexity of regularization.

However, the easy link that is often made between security policy and immigration policy needs to be reconsidered. The lives of immigrants in France, Britain, and the United States have certainly been changed in some ways by the denser security networks that have been put in place. Still, the general orientation of immigration policies has moved in a direction that could not have been anticipated if we presume that these policies are driven by security concerns. At a time when security administration on both sides of the Atlantic has been hardened, and even become more arbitrary, immigration policy, driven by other concerns, has become more expansive.

7

Migration and Security

Crime, Terror, and the Politics of Order

H. RICHARD FRIMAN

The intersection of migration and security ultimately entails questions of who is allowed access into the country and who can be removed. Migration scholars argue that the ability of policymakers in advanced industrial democracies to answer these questions—and ultimately deal with "unwanted" migration—has been constrained since the 1960s by the rise and institutionalization of rights-based protections for migrants.[1] In this context, the politics and the practice of immigration control since September 11, 2001, initially appear to have shifted dramatically. For the United States, the ramifications of who is trying to enter and who is already present clearly increased in importance. And in the aftermath of 9/11, rights protections for migrants seeking access to the United States, and especially for those already in the United States, appeared to be readily sacrificed in the name of security and order.

My argument is that the process of securitization of immigration control in the United States following 9/11 is better understood as an outgrowth of earlier politics, policy, and practice focused on criminal and terrorist aliens as existential threats to security and order. Immigration historians will correctly note that criminals and terrorists have long been the focus of state efforts to control the frontier. However, I am interested in the intersection of these efforts with the wave of rights protections that emerged for migrants in the 1960s. Exploring the politics of this intersection reveals a different watershed in the securitization of immigration control—the introduction in the late 1980s of aggravated felony offenses as excludable and deportable offenses under the Immigration and Nationality Act (INA) of 1952. The subsequent expansion of the categories of criminal and terrorist aliens and the erosion of rights protections for those so designated have had an impact on migration. However, the extent to which such steps have enhanced security remains unclear at best. This chapter briefly traces the origins of the securitization of criminal and terrorist aliens, explores the impact of 9/11 on this process, and addresses its continuation in legislation under consideration in Congress in 2006.

Securitization and Constraints

Securitization as explored in this chapter broadly refers to the presenting of an issue as "an existential threat requiring emergency measures and justifying actions outside the normal bounds of political procedure."[2] Securitization in practice often incorporates elements of "strategic social construction" of threats by governmental and nongovernmental actors for political or other gain and the creation of moral panics that exaggerate the extent of the threat to social order.[3] The securitization of migration is not a new phenomenon for the United States. Immigration policy from the individual states' measures of the late 1700s through the national-level policies of the mid-1900s linked restrictions to the need to combat threats to social order. These threats supposedly came from foreign prostitutes, convicts, anarchists, communists, and, more broadly, various ethnic groups equated with criminal activity and other sources of moral turpitude. Noncitizens deemed as falling into these categories often faced exclusion at the border or, for those noncitizens having attained entry to the United States, the prospect of arrest and imprisonment, detention on immigration charges, and/or deportation.[4] Elements of these earlier practices were incorporated into the Immigration and Nationality Act of 1952, and many continue to this day.

The securitization of migration in the United States tended to involve loose and inaccurate use of the term "immigration." U.S. immigration law includes distinctions between immigrants (legal permanent residents), nonimmigrants (a diverse category containing those temporarily and legally in the country), refugees and asylees, and illegal aliens (the illegality stemming from patterns of entry, stay, and/or activity). However, securitization arguments have blurred these distinctions between multiple paths and practices. In the

United States during the 1980s and 1990s, for example, calls for greater immigration control pointed to the threats posed by aggravated felons and alien terrorists, often making little distinction between the paths and processes of their migration. Securitization since September 11, 2001, similarly has focused on the linkages between immigration broadly (un)defined and the threats posed by criminal and terrorist aliens.

This chapter focuses on the intersection of securitization and the wave of rights-based protections seen by many scholars as inhibiting the ability of advanced industrial democracies to engage in immigration control. The growth of rights-based protections since the 1960s has stemmed from multiple sources. Wayne Cornelius, Philip Martin, and James Hollifield note the rise of a "liberal republicanism" in advanced industrial democracies, extending "rights to ethnic minorities and foreigners" through "legislative acts, partisan and interest group (especially ethnic) politics, and most important of all judicial rulings." The resulting liberal and democratic commitments became a primary source of what the authors posit as a gap between immigration policies and policy outcomes, especially policies seeking to control "unauthorized immigration and refugee flows from less developed countries."[5] Seeking to refine this "gap hypothesis," Gary Freeman reveals an interest group dynamic in which clientilist considerations of concentrated benefits from immigration mobilize employers and ethnic groups to work against state efforts designed to restrict immigration.[6] Christian Joppke stresses the importance of the judiciary and historically grounded "moral obligations" toward immigrants as providing a dominant counterweight against populist pressures for restriction. The impact of the judiciary lies in judges and courts "shielded" from populist pressures and "only obliged to the abstract commands of statutory and constitutional law." Historical patterns of immigration experiences also create moral obligations, with protections being more likely to accrue to immigrants where migration was solicited by the receiving country rather than tolerated for broader reasons of foreign policy.[7] James Hollifield links these arguments further by exploring historical patterns in immigration in advanced industrial democracies and their links to the development and institutionalization of "rights-based liberalism." The resulting legal and institutional frameworks that extend rights to foreigners make it difficult, although not impossible, to roll back protections in the face of economic and populist political pressures.[8]

Scholarship on the erosion of rights protections prior to the events of September 11, 2001, reveals rising anti-immigrant pressures during the 1990s. Yet Freeman, assessing the anti-immigrant backlash that spread from California to the national level during the 1990s, argues that the immigration act finally passed in 1996 was not only much less restrictionist than originally

envisioned by its supporters but that legislative and judicial challenges eroded these restrictions over time.[9] Virginie Guiraudon and Christian Joppke observe that policymakers in advanced industrial democracies have tended to
respond to domestic pressure for immigration restrictions with strategies of
"visibility" that create the "appearance of control" through high-profile actions at the border and with strategies of "remote control" through pressures
on source and transit countries and transportation carriers to prevent migrants from ever reaching the border.[10] In effect, though challenges to migrant
rights protections had taken place, by the turn of the millennium scholars
tended to characterize the protections as largely intact. However, this conclusion downplays the impact of securitization during the 1980s and early
1990s. As I argue in the following sections, this securitization eroded migrant
rights protections. It did so by expanding statutory conceptualizations of
criminal and terrorist aliens and related policies and practices of exclusion, detention, and deportation, and it provided the basis for subsequent expansion
after 2001.

Aggravated Felons and Terrorist Aliens

Securitization arguments during the 1980s reflected a combination of government officials who were exploring ties between immigration and the international drug trade and state and local government officials who were focused
on the impact of illegal migration on prison overcrowding and local crime. Interest groups, including the Federation for American Immigration Reform,
and the media fueled and echoed these concerns. Securitization arguments
initially converged in stressing the security threats posed by criminal aliens.
After the World Trade Center attack in 1993, securitization arguments began
to focus on threats posed by terrorists. By the mid-1990s, these arguments reflected increasing concerns over border security in the face of growing incidents of illegal immigration and state- and local-level anti-immigrant
initiatives such as California's Proposition 187 that stressed the criminal activities of illegal aliens. Another growing concern involved state efforts to obtain
federal compensation for incarceration and other costs for what officials saw
as the burden of a failed national immigration policy.[11]

The prominence of the drug trade in securitization arguments was not
new. Efforts to link migrants with drug trafficking and constructing drug
problems as primarily a foreign threat have had a long history in the United
States. Notable examples include linkages drawn between opium and Chinese
migrants in the mid-1800s and marijuana and Mexican migrants in the 1920s
and 1930s. As in most successful social constructions of threats to social order,

these arguments leveraged an element of truth—the involvement of *some* migrants in drug trafficking and consumption—into a broader moral panic. During the 1980s, securitization arguments pointed to both internecine violence between rival Colombian drug-trafficking organizations and fears of a crack epidemic fueled by migrant groups tied to urban street gangs. The result of these arguments was an image of America under siege. The Reagan administration's initial steps against drugs, including underfunded federal drug task forces and the rhetoric exhorting Americans to "just say no" to drugs and violence, did little to challenge this image.[12]

Members of Congress, Democrats and Republicans alike, responded to the limited policy steps by the Reagan administration and to the prospects for electoral gains in leveraging the drug issue by escalating their rhetoric and legislative initiatives. One result of the politics of the war on drugs was to turn to immigration law as a tool of drug control policy. In the deliberations leading up to the Anti-Drug Abuse Act (1988), Democratic members of the Senate and House introduced provisions for amending the INA (1952). The provisions called for designating aggravated felonies—narrowly defined as murder, drug-trafficking crimes, and firearms/explosive trafficking—as categories of offenses requiring the exclusion of migrants at the border. For those arrested within the United States, the provisions included mandatory detention after completion of sentence, expedited deportation, and criminal penalties for reentry. The proposals were introduced in April 1987 by Sen. Lawton Chiles (D-Florida) as Senate Bill 972. In October, Rep. Lawrence Smith (D-Florida) introduced the related bill, H.R. 3529, in the House. Florida had long been on the front lines of drug and illegal immigration issues, and Senator Chiles had been a vocal and leading advocate of restrictions on both.[13] The linkage between the issues resonated with members of Congress and the administration, resulting in the inclusion of the aggravated felony and immigration provisions under Title VII, Subtitle J, in the Anti-Drug Abuse Act (ADAA) of 1988.[14] Such steps helped to set in motion a tightening of immigration control.[15]

Aggravated felony provisions in the INA expanded during the 1990s, a pattern also explored by Jennifer Chacón in chapter 8 of this volume. More and more offenses were added to the list, ranging from drug abuse and money laundering to sexual abuse and theft. Sentencing thresholds qualifying for aggravated felony status were decreased from five years to one year, the definition of "conviction" was broadened, and changes were made retroactive. Moreover, protections against measures such as mandatory detention, expedited removal, and indefinite detention steadily eroded. In 1990, for example, Congress added language to the exclusion and deportation provisions of the

Immigration and Nationality Act. It also expanded the definition of aggravated felonies to include a broader array of drug offenses, including possession, as well as money-laundering offenses and "serious crimes" such as "crimes of violence for which the term of imprisonment imposed is at least five years."[16] In 1994, the Immigration and Nationality Technical Corrections Act added new offenses to the list of aggravated felonies, including offenses related to criminal enterprises and white-collar offenses such as fraud.[17]

In 1996, the Anti-Terrorism and Effective Death Penalty Act (AEDPA) expanded the INA list of aggravated felonies even further. The newly added offenses included "gambling, transportation for purposes of prostitution, alien smuggling, passport fraud, and other forms of documents fraud and expanded the definition to include new offenses involving obstruction of justice, perjury, or bribery offenses for which a sentence of at least five years or more may be imposed; commercial bribery, forgery, counterfeiting, and vehicle trafficking offenses for which a sentence of five years or more may be imposed; offenses committed by an alien previously deported; and offenses related to skipping bail for which a sentence of two or more years may be imposed."[18]

The Illegal Immigration Reform and Immigrant Responsibility Act (IIRIRA) of 1996, introduced a few months after the AEDPA, explicitly reconceptualized the linkage between immigration and crime as the threat posed by criminal aliens. The IIRIRA expanded the category of aggravated felonies under the INA still further, with new offenses including rape and sexual abuse. New provisions increased the reach of aggravated felony designations by lowering the qualifying sentencing threshold from five years to one year, essentially blurring the line with what had been treated as misdemeanor offenses—such as petty theft/shoplifting and drunk driving. New provisions also decreased the qualifying financial thresholds for money laundering, fraud, and tax evasion cases, from between $100,000 to $200,000 to only $10,000. The IIRIRA made all these changes to the INA retroactive—applying them "regardless of whether the conviction was entered before, on, or after the date of enactment of the 1996 Act." Furthermore, the IIRIRA redefined the concept of "conviction" to include adjudicated sentences, such as through delays and probation, as well as suspended sentences.[19]

During the 1990s, with growing concerns over terrorism, the United States followed a similar pattern of turning to immigration control as a tool of anti-terrorism policy. The Immigration Act of 1990, drawing in part on the 1988–89 Foreign Relations Authorization Act, added a definition of terrorism and a detailed list of "terrorist activities" to the INA as a subcategory for exclusion and deportation on security-related grounds. The list included activities ranging from hijacking, kidnapping, and use of a weapon of mass destruction to the provision of material support to individuals, organizations, or governments engaged in terrorist activities.[20] The AEDPA explicitly focused on the threat of "alien terrorists." New provisions also expanded the authority of the Department of State to designate groups as terrorist organizations and, in turn, to designate the grounds for exclusion and removal.[21] Noncitizens, for example, could be excluded if they were members of a terrorist organization or if they were "engaged in," "likely to engage in," or appeared to be "indicating an intention to" cause terrorist activity.[22]

The focus of securitization efforts on criminal and terrorist aliens, and the expansion of these categories under immigration law as a path to security and social order, converged in the 1996 IIRIRA and AEDPA. Leading Republicans of the House and Senate Judiciary committees successfully argued that flawed legal rights protections for criminal and terrorist aliens, including rights to judicial review and waivers from detention and deportation, were threatening the security and safety of the United States. In January 1995, Rep. William McCollum (R-Florida) introduced the Criminal Alien Deportation Improvements Bill (H.R. 668). The bill called for a wide-ranging expansion of aggravated felony offenses—from prostitution to document fraud and obstruction of justice—and the "strengthening" and "streamlining" of the deportation process. Such steps were necessary, Representative McCollum argued, to counter both the rise in organized alien smuggling and other serious crimes and to enhance a deportation system that was "allowing criminal aliens to escape" and undermining the safety of "citizens and noncitizens alike."[23] Speaking in support of H.R. 668, Rep. Lamar Smith (R-Texas), chair of the House Judiciary Subcommittee on Immigration, placed the bill in the broader context of promises made in the 1994 Republican Contract with America. Smith argued that the measures proposed were necessary to "counter the escalation of crime [*sic*] robbing Americans of the freedom to walk their streets, the right to feel secure in their homes, and the ability to feel confident that their children are safe in their schools."[24] The bill as passed by the House in February was referred to the Senate Judiciary Committee, and by 1996 its provisions had been incorporated into the AEDPA.[25]

In the Senate, Alan Simpson (R-Wyoming), chair of the Senate Judiciary Subcommittee on Immigration, pushed to curtail legal as well as illegal immigration. His proposals to amend the INA provisions on criminal aliens, introduced in 1994 (S. 2480) and reintroduced in early 1995 (as part of S. 269), called for expanding aggravated felony offenses and curtailing waivers and judicial review for aggravated felons.[26] By February 1996, as the Judiciary Committee turned to what would become the IIRIRA, Spencer Abraham

(R-Michigan), the influential junior member of the committee, emerged as the "principal architect of the 1996 aggravated felony provisions."[27] Senator Abraham derailed Simpson's efforts on legal immigration but supported measures for increasing the number of aggravated felony offenses and curtailing appeals and judicial review of deportation to redress the "problem we have with criminal aliens."[28] Abraham's testimony in support of such steps echoed a Senate Permanent Subcommittee on Investigations report from April 1995. He noted the roughly "half a million" convicted noncitizen felons that had been able to manipulate judicial review opportunities and waivers under the law to avoid deportation or had simply disappeared after being released from an overwhelmed detention system.[29]

As the categories of offenses for those designated as criminal and terrorist aliens widened, the rights accorded to those so designated narrowed. The IIRIRA reinstated mandatory detention provisions, which had been partially eased in early 1990s for legal aliens who were "not a threat to the community" and seen as "likely to appear for deportation hearings."[30] The AEDPA denied all aggravated felons, regardless of sentence, the right to appeal for waivers from deportation and removed court consideration of mitigating factors. The IIRIRA shortly thereafter shifted to the discretion of the attorney general all decisions concerning waivers from the courts to cancel deportations. It also prohibited the cancellation of deportation for aggravated felons.[31] The AEDPA and IIRIRA also added provisions to the INA for the expedited removal of noncitizens, including new courts and the use of classified information for terrorist aliens and accelerated proceedings to remove aggravated felons prior to completion of their prison terms.[32] Of even greater concern to immigration advocates, the IIRIRA's provisions on judicial review "removed all courts' jurisdiction to review final orders of removal against noncitizens ordered deported as aggravated felons."[33]

On the surface, the steps advocated by securitization arguments appeared to work. Noncitizens serving criminal sentences in U.S. correctional facilities increased from 25,250 in 1990 to 95,043 in 2000.[34] The average daily population of criminal aliens detained under INS jurisdiction increased from 3,300 persons in 1994 to 19,485 in 2000.[35] The numbers of criminal aliens deported or removed increased from 1,100 in 1988 to 72,297 in 2000.[36] However, looking below the surface, the effectiveness of such steps for securing the United States was less clear. As the categories of criminal and terrorist alien offenses increased, the absence of any mechanism to prioritize migrants within these categories by the severity of criminal offense or type of terrorist activity became problematic. The already overburdened immigration control system was quickly flooded. In addition, during the 1990s, those members of

Congress advocating greater security pointed to the greater number of incarcerations, detentions, and deportations of criminal aliens as metrics of success. Simultaneously, they pointed to the broader pool of aggravated felons who had avoided and evaded apprehension, detention, and deportation as confirmation of a growing security threat. Both observations were flawed, however, in that the numbers were in large part a reflection of the expanded definitions of aggravated felony offenses. Little attention was paid to this paradox.

Securitization and 9/11

In the aftermath of the terrorist attacks of September 2001, the United States again turned to immigration control as a path to security and social order. Members of the Bush administration and Congress posited the terrorist attacks as an existential threat requiring emergency measures. As is well known, the administration turned to targeted mass detentions, prioritized deportation, mandatory interviews and registration, and long visa waiting periods for those of Arab or Muslim background and origin.[37] However, broader efforts, such as those incorporated into the Uniting and Strengthening America by Providing Appropriate Tools Required to Intercept and Obstruct Terrorism (USA PATRIOT) Act, once again focused on criminal and terrorist aliens.

In deliberations over the PATRIOT Act, Bush administration and congressional officials emphasized that immigration threats to security necessitated expanding the definitions of terrorism and aggravated felonies. Bush administration proposals to Congress in mid-September 2001, for example, stressed how narrow definitions of terrorism, especially regarding the provision of material support "for a 'terrorist activity,'" had undermined the effectiveness of the Alien Terrorist Removal Court established in 1996. The desired and resulting broader language in section 411 of the PATRIOT Act included giving "material support" to a group that the "individual knows or reasonably should know" is a terrorist organization. It also added broad new definitions of a terrorist organization and expanded the authority of the secretary of state to designate groups as such.[38]

Administration proposals to Congress also turned to the issue of flawed legal rights for terrorist suspects and criminal aliens. The focus on the protection of rights called for steps to allow indefinite detention and limitations on judicial review. Congressional opposition in the House derailed administration efforts to obtain explicit authority for indefinite detention despite administration calls for the attorney general to be able to detain indefinitely individuals deemed threats to national security.[39] However, section 412 of the

PATRIOT Act did expand the attorney general's powers of detention under the INA. Section 236A greatly added to the INA, allowing for detention without arrest and the potential for indefinite re-detention.[40] Administration proposals also called for curtailing judicial review of detention and removal cases, noting the risks of the ability of terrorist aliens to exploit inconsistencies in habeas corpus proceedings. House opposition to administration calls for routing all such cases to the federal courts in the District of Columbia limited the PATRIOT Act to restricting appeals of habeas corpus decisions to the Appeals Court of the District of Columbia. The act did, however, preserve the right of detained terrorist aliens to file habeas corpus action in any district court that had jurisdiction.[41]

Securitization of immigration control policy and practice also blurred the line between terrorist and criminal aliens.[42] Although terrorist aliens were prioritized under the PATRIOT Act, the new Department of Homeland Security (DHS), which would play a central role in the act's implementation, prioritized the "apprehension and deportation" of criminal aliens as a central part of its mission in the war on terror.[43] The metrics of DHS success commonly include increases in the numbers of criminal aliens apprehended, detained, and removed. For example, according to the DHS primary investigative division, Immigration and Customs Enforcement (ICE) apprehensions of criminal aliens increased from 82,990 in fiscal year (FY) 2001 to 89,445 in FY 2004. Total apprehensions during the period from FY 2001 to FY 2004 reached 345,006 criminal aliens.[44] Daily average detention of criminal aliens increased from 20,429 in 2001 to 21,298 in 2004. Formal removals of criminal aliens increased from 72,679 in 2001 to 88,897 in 2004.[45]

Yet these figures say little about any success enjoyed by the government in fighting terrorism. For example, migrants from Central America, Latin America, and the Caribbean constitute the majority of criminal aliens apprehended from FY 2001 to FY 2004, with Mexico alone accounting for 257,718 or 75 percent. An ICE audit in 2006 notes that illegal aliens apprehended from countries "other than Mexico (OTM)" increased during the same period. It emphasizes OTM migrants that were from countries of "special interest" (SIC) or from "state sponsors of terrorism" (SST). The total number of SIC and SST aliens increased from 15,652 in FY 2001 to 15,795 in FY 2004; total apprehensions during the period from FY 2001 to FY 2004 reached 82,803 illegal aliens. Yet these apprehensions are not indicative of actual numbers of criminal or terrorist aliens. According to ICE, the apprehensions are intended "to determine whether they have a criminal record in the U.S. or are listed on various terrorist watch lists," and there can be difficulties with the "effectiveness of background checks." That said, more than 50 percent of those SIC and SST aliens apprehended from FY 2001 to FY 2004 were released.[46]

Expanding actionable criminal offenses offers the potential for a wider means to find terrorist suspects, but it is less clear that the blurring of the lines has led to success in this regard. Expanded enforcement measures at the border and within the United States intended to identify terrorist aliens more often have led to the exclusion, arrest, and detention of aggravated felons and other criminal aliens.[47] In Operation Tarmac, conducted in April 2002, enforcement agents raided "106 airports and identified 4,271 undocumented aliens," but no terrorists (those noncitizens with false documents) fell under the expanded aggravated felony definitions and were subject to deportation as criminal aliens.[48] Under Operation Predator, enforcement agents acting under the auspices of the Department of Homeland Security focused on "noncitizens with past sex offenses" as well as migrant traffickers and smugglers. This effort led to 1,300 arrests of noncitizens as aggravated felons between July and November 2003.[49] Immigration and Customs Enforcement's "Ten Most Wanted List of Fugitive Criminal Aliens" consists primarily of those wanted for violating deportation orders for past offenses ranging from assault to sex offenses rather than for crimes linked to terrorism. The "ICE Storm Most Wanted" list is focused on human smugglers.[50]

Administration statements on the effectiveness of enforcement efforts against terrorism have raised further questions about the blurring of crime and terror in the securitization of immigration control. President Bush, speaking in Ohio in July 2005, noted that since 2001 "federal terrorism investigations [had] resulted in charges against 400 suspects" and more than two hundred convictions. Subsequent investigations of these figures by reporters from the *Washington Post* revealed that only thirty-nine of the two hundred persons convicted were "convicted of crimes related to terrorism or national security" while the remaining had been convicted of immigration-related and other offenses.[51]

Securitization Redux

Securitization arguments have continued to play a prominent role in legislative steps intended to expand the number of criminal and terrorist alien offenses and challenge rights protections for suspected criminal and terrorist aliens in the name of security and social order. In 2005, citing the broad threat posed by illegal immigration to homeland security and the risks of terrorists exploiting asylum laws in particular, Rep. James Sensenbrenner (R-Wisconsin), chair of the House Judiciary Committee, played an influential role in introducing and facilitating the passage of the REAL ID Act.[52] In addition to a general tightening of asylum regulations and raising the burden of proof for asylum claims, the act expanded the INA's definitions of terrorist and terrorist-related activities as well as the definition of terrorist organizations. The act thus increased the ability of the U.S. government to deny asylum to those seeking entry or already in the United States.[53]

A broader wave of securitization arguments emerged later in the year as members of Congress turned to large-scale reform of U.S. immigration control. By mid-2006, the House and Senate were deadlocked in their advocacy of various approaches to reform: notably H.R. 4437, the Border Protection, Antiterrorism and Illegal Immigration Control Act, passed by the House on December 16, 2005, and the less restrictive S. 2611, the Comprehensive Immigration Reform Act, passed by the Senate on May 25, 2006. Although efforts to resolve the two positions prior to the 2006 mid-term elections stalled during the summer, several provisions in the bill are relevant to the arguments explored in this chapter.

Sections 201 and 203 of the House bill designated "unlawful presence" in the United States as a criminal rather than a civil offense, with the first offense subject to a year and day imprisonment. The length of sentence was not by accident. Such a sentence would automatically result in an estimated 12 million to 14 million migrants already illegally in the United States being designated as aggravated felons and faced with the erosion of rights protections such a designation entailed. Anything short of such a step was portrayed by House supporters of the bill as flawed amnesty for illegal aliens similar to that adopted in the Immigration and Refugee Control Act (IRCA) of 1986. With the parameters of the debate over immigration reform set by the House, Senate proposals initially took a compromise position. Under sections 203 and 206 of the proposed Securing America's Borders bill (S. 2454), introduced in mid-March 2006, the first offense of unlawful presence in the United States would be punishable by only six months imprisonment. It would thus fall short of an aggravated felony designation. However, subsequent legislation considered by the Judiciary Committee and eventually incorporated into S. 2611 made no changes to existing law and omitted measures designed to criminalize an illegal presence.[54]

Sections 201 and 202 of H.R. 4437 sought to expand the scope of aggravated felonies even further. They broadened the definition of facilitating migrant smuggling and designated as aggravated felons anyone who "assists, encourages, directs or induces a person to unlawfully reside or remain in the United States" or attempts to do so. Section 205 of S. 2454, as well as S. 2611, again took a different tack, focusing only on encouragement and inducement and excluding language regarding assistance and attempts at unlawful presence.[55] Other provisions in H.R. 4437, albeit attracting less attention in the public debate, included measures permitting indefinite detention for "dangerous aliens" (section 602), banned entry by aggravated felons and other criminal aliens, and precluded waivers and relief from such bans (section 604). Furthermore, it broadly interpreted "conviction" for aggravated felonies by giving no bearing to reversals or changes in sentences (section 613).[56]

The congressional hearings over the House and Senate bills highlighted familiar securitization arguments about the national security threats posed by terrorist and criminal aliens and the need for major new measures to address these threats. Republicans serving on the House Judiciary Committee and its Immigration Subcommittee played leading roles. For example, Rep. Lamar Smith (R-Texas), an active voice in earlier immigration control debates, argued in hearings leading up to the bill that determining who is in the country and why is "essential to our homeland security." As evidence of the purported threat to national safety, Smith pointed to "the fact that over 20 percent of all federal prisoners are illegal immigrants"; he did not offer insight into the nature of the crimes they had committed or the impact of expanded aggravated felony categories.[57] Rep. John N. Hostettler (R-Indiana), chair of the Immigration Subcommittee, pointed to the terrorist attacks of September 11 in arguing for measures against illegal aliens: "We should also not forget the national security danger to the country of having an estimated 10 million illegal aliens in the country, when no one knows who they are and what their intent is. Surely for most of them, they intend to work and perhaps settle here. But a small handful of undocumented illegal aliens may pose the danger of terrorists attacking our country once again. . . . Criminalization of illegal presence as an aggravated felony offense offered a dramatic step to address these problems."[58]

Observers of the immigration debate noted that the legal problems of Tom DeLay (R-Texas), leader of the House GOP Caucus, and the stalemate among Republicans in the Senate over immigration control provided an opportunity for Sensenbrenner to promote his interest in restricting immigration.[59] Sensenbrenner, who entered the House in 1979 and became chair of the Judiciary Committee in 2001, had long been at the forefront of efforts seeking to curtail legal as well as illegal immigration.[60] He was the author of H.R. 4437, and his stated intent for the bill was to "ensure the proper enforcement of immigration laws, create additional mechanisms to prevent illegal immigration, assist in the prohibition of hiring illegal immigrants and to enhance border security."[61] The report accompanying the bill, when introduced to the House, noted both the threats posed by illegal immigration, including "the drastic increase in crime committed by illegal aliens," especially among members of criminal gangs, and the growing numbers of illegal aliens in federal correctional facilities.[62]

The provisions for criminalization of illegal presence, however, caused an extensive backlash. Opposition to securitization efforts had taken place during the 1990s. In addition, court challenges to IIRIRA and the PATRIOT Act provisions focused on the denial of waivers from deportation, expedited deportation without judicial review, and indefinite detention, all with mixed results.[63] In June 2003, the Department of Justice inspector general released a "scathing" report on the administration's policies toward those detained in the immediate aftermath of 9/11, challenging practices of detention, access to legal counsel and evidence, and recommendations for policy changes.[64] Though an important step, the report fell far short of a broader indictment of the erosion of noncitizen protections that had taken place since 9/11. Within Congress prior to 2006, despite the arguments of immigrant advocacy groups, calls for protecting the rights of criminal and/or terrorist aliens had been the exception rather than the rule.

In the face of large-scale street protests across the country during the spring of 2006 and rising congressional opposition to the criminalization of unlawful presence, political maneuvering increased in the House. Sensenbrenner sought to amend the provisions, calling for continued criminalization but for reducing the offense from a felony to a misdemeanor imprisonment of six months. Democratic opposition to criminalization in the House helped lead to the defeat of the amendment. Charges and countercharges between Sensenbrenner and his critics over who was responsible for the aggravated felony provisions remaining in the House bill were played out in the media.[65] Despite the efforts of congressional Republicans to generate support for H.R. 4437 through a series of hearings held around the country, the combination of controversy over unlawful presence and other issues and the rapidly approaching mid-term elections temporarily derailed steps toward reform of immigration control.

The securitization of immigration control following September 11, 2001, has built extensively on steps that emerged in the 1980s and 1990s and positioned the threat of criminal and terrorist aliens. Securitization efforts by members of Congress and presidential administrations have successfully widened the statutory definitions of criminal and terrorism offenses for accused aliens. They also have successfully eroded rights protections that in the past have constrained efforts to exclude, detain, and remove migrants. Challenges to this securitization have emerged from advocacy groups, the courts,

Congress, and even some individuals within the executive branch. They have, however, had limited effect. That said, the proposals in 2006 to turn millions of migrants illegally in the United States, as well as those that assist them, into aggravated felons appeared to reveal the limits of securitization, at least in the context of an election year.

The extent to which such securitization has actually facilitated control over the frontier, and thus, the security of the United States, remains questionable at best. Broader categories of criminal and terrorist offenses and diminished rights protections for those so designated have increased the potential for greater exclusion at the border for those migrants seeking legal entry. These factors may well increase the numbers of migrants seeking to enter the United States illegally. Both trends will generate more pressure on the capacity of the U.S. immigration control system in at least three dimensions: (1) processing cases at the border, (2) engaging in background checks, and (3) meeting the needs of mandatory detention without the greater resources needed for more effective border control to prevent more illegal crossings. Within the borders of the United States, the expansion of criminal and terrorist alien offenses and the erosion of rights protections will allow for more initial apprehensions and detentions. However, by definition, such steps also will create larger pools of criminals and terrorists that, in the absence of prioritization by severity of offenses and a dramatic increase in resources, will overburden the immigration control system.[66] Finally, steps under consideration to expand cooperation of Immigration and Customs Enforcement officials with state and local law enforcement and to rely on state, local, and private detention facilities, raise still further security issues. Although intended to expand the numbers of de facto immigration enforcement agents within the United States, such steps have the potential to increase barriers between the police and migrant communities. In doing so, they will impede law enforcement and information sharing and overload the capacity of the broader criminal justice system—in effect, again undermining instead of enhancing security and social order.[67]

8

The Security Myth

Punishing Immigrants in the Name of National Security

JENNIFER M. CHACÓN

In times of national crisis, the U.S. government has a consistent history of responding by incarcerating, and in many cases removing, large numbers of foreign nationals or groups that are seen as "foreign" based on their national, racial, ethnic, or religious background.[1] The U.S. government's actions after the attacks on the Pentagon and World Trade Center on September 11, 2001, presented another example of the classic response to crisis in the United States. Many potential "suspects" were identified primarily on the basis of racial and ethnic profiling. As in the past, these suspects were detained on immigration-related charges on lower standards of proof than that which would have been required for criminal investigations. Their confinement was subject to far fewer procedural constraints than would have been required for criminal detention, and many were removed from the country without public hearings.[2]

While post–September 11 detentions and removals of noncitizens resembled many other historical moments of crisis in the United States, the "emergency" response to September 11 is not entirely of a piece with past responses. This is because the post–September 11 era of immigration enforcement has been not only a crisis response but also the continuation of an expansive trend in immigration enforcement that has been emerging for more than a decade. Prior to 2001, most lawmakers and their constituents viewed the expansion of immigration restrictions and immigration law enforcement primarily as a matter of crime control. While some U.S. lawmakers began to view immigration laws as an important vehicle for anti-terrorism efforts in the early 1990s, a national security rationale for immigration reform did not dominate legislative or national discussions in the pre–September 11 era.[3] Since September 11, however, the rationale of "national security" has provided the primary justification for more vigorous immigration law enforcement.

Al Qaeda's successful inflicting of massive damage on U.S. soil on September 11, 2001, revealed the shortcomings of the U.S. government's intelligence capabilities. Because the violent acts of September 11 were perpetrated by noncitizens, it is not surprising that immigration laws and the immigration enforcement bureaucracy came under scrutiny in the period that followed. At that point, an appropriate crisis response would have been to demand genuine changes in immigration enforcement, as well as other areas of law enforcement. Responsive reforms to the immigration bureaucracy could have included the implementation of uniform, comprehensive registration programs for noncitizens admitted or already present in the country. Another reform option would have been to ensure appropriate information sharing between immigration enforcement agencies and other law enforcement bodies.[4] Similarly, the government might have systematically increased the investigation of immigration crimes that provide the foundation for terrorist activity, such as alien smuggling and document fraud.[5]

Instead of rethinking immigration enforcement priorities, the U.S. government reorganized many of the immigration administrative institutions and consolidated them under the umbrella of the Department of Homeland Security.[6] The rhetoric of "national security" was then used to justify the ongoing expansion of the immigration enforcement apparatus and the implementation of harsh new immigration regulations that increasingly criminalized immigrants. Post–September 11 immigration "reform" has done little to enhance U.S. security, but national security rhetoric increasingly insulates the immigration enforcement apparatus from many of the constitutional constraints that apply to the criminal justice system.[7]

In this chapter, I discuss the origins and implications of the growing mismatch between the legal doctrines governing immigration enforcement and the realities of the post–September 11 immigration enforcement bureaucracy in the United States. I explain the historical evolution of the doctrinal link between national security and immigration enforcement in U.S. constitutional law. I also explore the legislative changes that have converted many aspects of immigration enforcement into an adjunct of domestic crime control—

changes that call into question the historical constitutional understanding of immigration enforcement. I then describe the post–September 11 security responses effectuated through immigration enforcement and explain how these responses illustrate the wide-ranging powers of the contemporary immigration enforcement bureaucracy. Finally, I discuss the threat to individual rights posed by the growth of a relatively unchecked immigration bureaucracy that conflates crime control with national security. In a "nation of immigrants," where 11.5 percent of the population is foreign born, the increasing reliance on the immigration bureaucracy to serve the ends of the criminal justice system has the potential to transform the general administration of criminal justice in the United States in fundamentally illiberal ways. These changes suggest increasing challenges to conventional civil liberties protections.[8]

Immigration and the Plenary Powers Doctrine

The link between security and immigration finds its roots in the earliest doctrines authorizing Congress to control immigration policy at the federal level. This is true even though the vast majority of the practices of immigration enforcement are not actually concerned with national security, at least as that notion has been traditionally conceived. According to Gerald L. Neuman, "the vast bulk of immigration enforcement involves such routine matters as poverty, crime, regulatory violations, and protection of the domestic labor market. These restrictions do not rely on sensitive foreign policy choices for their justification."[9]

Early in American history, the source and scope of federal congressional power over immigration law and policy were unimportant issues; Congress made no effort to regulate immigration through federal statute until 1875.[10] The only significant exceptions were the Alien Friends Act of 1798, which was never enforced and expired after two years, and the Enemy Alien Act of 1798, which has remained a part of the law through the present day.[11] The Enemy Alien Act authorizes the president to detain, expel, or otherwise restrict the freedom of any citizen of a country upon which the United States has declared war.[12] It was almost a century before this wartime provision was joined by other, more general federal immigration legislation.

The rise of federal immigration restrictions, and the legal challenges mounted against these restrictions, required the courts to answer the question of whether the U.S. Congress actually had the power to regulate immigration. The Constitution of the United States contains no express provision granting the federal legislature the power to regulate immigration. Courts variously have discussed the possibility of finding this power implicit in the Commerce Clause, the Migration or Importation Clause, the Naturalization Clause, and the War Clause.[13] But none of these sources is entirely satisfactory as a basis for congressional power over immigration. Thus, in granting the U.S. Congress tremendously broad authority to regulate immigration, the Supreme Court of the United States relied heavily upon the notion that immigration regulation was an inherent power of a sovereign nation. The Court rationalized that the power to regulate immigration was a necessary part of the power of a sovereign state to defend itself.

In 1882, Congress enacted the first general, federal immigration provision—the Immigration Act of 1882—which permitted the deportation of people who entered the United States without authorization and created the Office of Immigration within the Department of the Treasury.[14] The law imposed a head tax of fifty cents per immigrant and excluded "idiots, lunatics, convicts, and persons likely to become a public charge."[15] The Congress also enacted the Chinese Exclusion Act of 1882, suspending all future immigration of Chinese laborers.[16] In the so-called Chinese Exclusion Case of 1889, the Supreme Court first upheld Congress's authority to pass laws excluding "foreigners" as "an incident of sovereignty belonging to the government of the United States."[17]

Cases decided shortly after the Chinese Exclusion Case made clear that this "sovereign" power was not only the broad power to exclude noncitizens from entering the United States but also the power to deport noncitizens from within the United States. In 1893, in *Fong Yue Ting v. United States,* the Court extended the holding of the Chinese Exclusion Case, taking a deferential stance toward congressional decisions to deport noncitizens residing in the United States without authorization.[18] In *Fong Yue Ting v. United States,* the Court upheld a law that required a noncitizen seeking to avoid deportation to produce a "credible white witness" to vouch for their physical presence in the United States prior to a certain time.[19] "The right of a nation to expel or deport foreigners who have not been naturalized, or taken any steps towards becoming citizens of the country, rests upon the same grounds, and is as absolute and unqualified, as the right to prohibit and prevent their entrance into the country."[20]

The Court continued to justify the political branch's plenary power over immigration. This plenary power included the authority to deport noncitizens physically present in the United States, by characterizing such power as "an inherent and inalienable right of every sovereign and independent nation, essential to its safety, its independence, and its welfare."[21] The rationale is that immigration is inextricably tied up with foreign policy. The protection of the national interest in such areas is "so exclusively entrusted to the political branches of government as to be largely immune from judicial inquiry or interference."[22] The view of immigration administration as a function of sovereignty, and as inextricably tied to the nation-state's foreign powers and right of self-defense, has immunized immigration law from a great deal of the judicial scrutiny that usually applies when state actions affect individual rights. This is true despite almost universal scholarly condemnation of the plenary powers doctrine.[23]

The vision of immigration control articulated in these early rulings also resulted in the legal treatment of deportation as distinct from—and requiring fewer procedural protections than—criminal punishment. The legal distinction between removal and "punishment" has its roots in very early immigration cases. For example, in the *Fong Yue Ting* case, even as the Court recognized Congress's seemingly unlimited authority to deport noncitizens in the name of sovereignty and security, the dicta of the 1893 *Fong Yue Ting* decision also distinguished the deportation of noncitizens from "transportation."[24] In contrast to transportation or banishment, the Court found that "[t]he order of deportation is not a punishment for crime." Instead, deportation was "a method of enforcing the return to his own country of an alien who has not complied with . . . conditions" for residence in the United States.[25] In this circumscribed context, the Court recognized Congress's broad power to deport noncitizens and constructed deportation not as punishment but as an administration of the sovereign immigration function.[26]

The deliberate distinction between deportation and criminal punishment was again a theme in the 1896 case of *Wong Wing v. United States*. In that case the Court upheld the deportation of a noncitizen and also held that his detention pursuant to his deportation was constitutional and did not constitute punishment. But the Court struck down the portion of the law that authorized that a deportable noncitizen could be subject to up to a year of hard labor, which could be imposed as a part of the order of deportation. The Court considered imprisonment at hard labor to be the imposition of punishment, requiring a jury trial. The Court held that "[i]t is not consistent with the theory of our government that the legislature should, after having defined an offense as an infamous crime, find the fact of guilt and adjudge the punishment by one of its own agents."[27]

At the time the Court decided *Wong Wing*, deportation by and large looked to be a measure meant to cure inadvertent failures in admission and exclusion policies. It was not linked to offenses committed after entry. It was a backward-looking remedy. In this context, the distinction between deportation and punishment had some basis in reality. Over time, the distinction between deportation when used to expel those who never should have entered and deportation when used as punishment for post-entry conduct has faded.[28]

Immigration Control Measures Become a Means of Crime Control

The line between administrative policy and criminal punishment has blurred since the deportation of Wong Wing. Over the course of the past one hundred years, immigration detention and removal increasingly have become tools for achieving domestic crime control ends. However, the Court has continued to maintain that immigration control is a security function and that deportation is not criminal punishment but an administrative means to achieve national security through border control. A look at the evolution of immigration law in the United States over the past century reveals that these legal doctrines are increasingly out of step with the realities of immigration enforcement. Even though certain immigration enforcement measures legitimately and necessarily serve the ends of security, the security rationale has come to justify a host of immigration laws and enforcement measures that are properly characterized as criminal law enforcement and that are, as such, clearly distinct from security concerns.

The shift in immigration enforcement began as long ago as 1903. The immigration law of 1903 barred entry to "anarchists, or persons who believe in or advocate the overthrow of the Government of the United States or of all government or of all forms of law."[29] The consequence of this provision was that foreign nationals could be excluded from entry on the basis of speech or actions that were protected by the First Amendment when undertaken by a citizen in the United States.[30] More significant shifts followed. In 1917, Congress extended the exclusion provisions to those who advocated the unlawful destruction of property, disbelieved or were opposed to organized government, or were members of organizations espousing such ideas.[31] A year later, Congress added a new category of immigrant subject to exclusion: subversives. The Anarchist Act of 1918 provided for the exclusion of "subversive" aliens and also authorized their expulsion without time limits.[32] At this point, deportation began its shift from a purely corrective administrative tool to one sometimes used to complement the criminal law in sanctioning certain post-entry conduct. The shift to the use of immigration law as a means of punishing the deviant noncitizen was doubly masked—it was constructed as a security issue and its remedy was constructed as an issue of immigration control. Since deportation of the "subversive" was not legally understood as criminal punishment, the deportation provisions had an advantage over criminal law: Congress could subject noncitizens engaged in certain conduct to deportation even when that conduct was constitutionally protected from criminal punishment. And by that time, it was already becoming apparent that the flexible notions of due process that governed deportation proceedings did not

carry the same degree of procedural protections guaranteed in criminal proceedings.[33] Thus, the Immigration Act of 1917 and the Anarchist Act provided a quick and effective means of detaining thousands of noncitizens and
deporting hundreds of them in a series of raids—the Palmer Raids—carried
out in 1919 and 1920 in response to a series of violent domestic attacks, even
when no evidence existed to link most of these people to the crimes.[34]

A few short years after the raids, the Immigration Act of May 26, 1924,
changed the face of U.S. immigration forever. Before 1920, very few people
had been deported from the United States.[35] This changed with the enactment of strict racial quotas that were included in the 1924 law. The 1924 immigration law eliminated the statute of limitations on deportation for nearly
all forms of unlawful entry and entry without a valid visa. It also created a
land Border Patrol, the principal function of which was to police the southern border. In 1929, the act of illegal entry itself was criminalized for the first
time.[36] Congress enacted a law making entry at a point not designated by the
U.S. government, or by means of fraud or misrepresentation, a misdemeanor.[37] A previously deported "alien" who reentered the country could be
convicted of a felony.[38] In other words, the act of immigration itself, when
performed outside of legal channels, became a violation of criminal law.

The change in law was followed by a change in the discourse around irregular migrants.[39] Until the 1930s, immigrants were categorized descriptive-
ly as either "legitimate" immigrants on the one hand or "illegitimate" or
"ineligible" immigrants on the other.[40] But the changes in the immigration
laws that Congress enacted in the 1920s created the "illegal alien." Over time,
would-be Mexican immigrants greatly outnumbered lawfully available immigrant visas.[41] Those who entered without visas violated the new immigration
laws. According to Mae Ngai, "[p]ositive law thus constituted undocumented immigrants as criminals, both fulfilling and fueling nativist discourse."[42]
By the 1950s, the phrases "illegal immigrant" and "illegal alien" had become
a staple of the popular lexicon.[43] Today, the phrases illegal alien and illegal immigrant are still commonly used in the press and by politicians when describing unauthorized migrants in the United States.[44] One result is that the
linkage between alien status and illegal status is cemented in the public
mind.[45] With their entry and eventually their labor criminalized, certain
groups of people—most commonly Mexicans—have increasingly been constructed as illegal aliens, whether or not that label applies to them.[46]

The labeling of certain groups of immigrants so as to convey their "illegality" has left these groups particularly vulnerable to deportation, which can be
seen as a natural and appropriate means of dealing with the transgressions of
perceived outsiders. Thus, it is perhaps unsurprising that as the illegality of

certain immigrants was constructed by legal definition and cemented by popular discourse, Congress expanded deportation grounds based on post-entry
conduct. The list of deportable offenses came to include a laundry list of
mundane post-entry criminal or quasi-criminal actions. Immigration law became an effective tool not only for barring the admission of undesired "aliens"
but also for punishing through deportation many noncitizens (either lawfully admitted or illegally present). The law was simple to use because there was
no need to adhere to the due process norms of criminal procedure institutionalized in a series of Supreme Court rulings during the civil rights revolution
of the 1960s.[47]

Two 1996 laws—the Anti-Terrorism and Effective Death Penalty Act
(AEDPA) and the Illegal Immigration Reform and Immigrant Responsibility
Act (IIRIRA)—resulted in a significant expansion of grounds for removal
under criminal law.[48] These laws altered prior national policies by increasing
penalties for violations of immigration laws, expanding the class of noncitizens subject to removal for the commission of crimes, and imposing a system
of tough penalties that favor removal even in cases involving relatively minor
infractions or very old crimes.[49] The changes applied retroactively, so even if
an offense would not have rendered a noncitizen removable at the time of its
commission, the noncitizen was subject to removal if the offense was a removable offense under the new law.[50]

Following the enactment of these laws, noncitizens can be removed and
permanently barred from reentry for the commission of an "aggravated
felony." This category, as Nancy Morawetz has explained, has an "Alice in
Wonderland"–like quality in that such offenses need be neither aggravated
nor a felony.[51] These include not only things like "murder, rape, or sexual
abuse of a minor" but also a crime of violence or a theft offense "for which
the term of imprisonment is at least a year."[52] The limits of the law are still
being tested. For example, hundreds of noncitizens—many legal residents,
many long-term residents—were deported for driving under the influence before the Supreme Court found that such an act did not qualify as an "aggravated felony."[53] Aggravated felons are statutorily barred from seeking virtually
any form of relief from removal.[54] There is no statute of limitations on these
provisions, so noncitizens can be removed for "aggravated felonies" committed years ago. The more than 156,000 "aggravated felons" who have been removed from the United States since 1997 had been in the country an average
of fifteen years prior to being put into removal proceedings; 25 percent had
been in the United States more than twenty years.[55]

Nor do the penalties stop with noncitizens convicted of "aggravated
felonies." The 1996 laws, operating in conjunction with a host of immigra-

tion restrictions that have evolved over the past century, create harsh immigration consequences for committing many other crimes as well. The commission of two or more "crimes involving moral turpitude" at any time after entry subjects a noncitizen to deportation, no matter how long that person has been present in the United States.[56] After 1996, relief from removal is not available for anyone falling into this category who has not been a lawful permanent resident for at least five years.[57] Before 1996, a single crime involving moral turpitude within five years of entry was not a ground of deportability for lawful permanent residents unless the individual was actually sentenced to at least one year of incarceration. However, after 1996 removal turned not on whether the sentence was for one year but on whether a sentence of a year or more was possible. In New York, for example, a person could receive mandatory deportation for such offenses as jumping a turnstile or the unauthorized use of cable television service.[58]

Status offenses such as drug addiction are the basis for removal even though the U.S. Constitution prohibits the criminalization of status.[59] Certain forms of constitutionally protected associational conduct are also removable offenses, as are failures to comply with technical special registration provisions.[60] Immigration violations involving document fraud and false claims of citizenship are also removable offenses, and relatively minor drug convictions under state law also render noncitizens removable.[61]

At the same time that the 1996 laws massively expanded the number of removable offenses, they also greatly decreased the power of judges to exercise discretion in cases involving the deportation of noncitizens who had committed certain crimes.[62] For example, during the period between 1989 and 1995, immigration judges and the Board of Immigration Appeals had collectively waived deportation in about 51 percent of the cases in which a noncitizen had committed a deportable offense. To do so, they relied on the discretionary waiver of deportation permitted by section 212(c) of the Immigration and Nationality Act.[63] But the 1996 law eliminated relief under the former section 212(c).[64] In its place, the 1996 law provided for much more limited "cancellation of removal" under section 240A of the Immigration and Nationality Act.[65] Explicit in the *Congressional Record* is the fact that section 240A(a) relief is intended only for "highly unusual cases involving outstanding aliens."[66] Among its many limitations, cancellation of removal is not available to anyone who commits any offense that falls under the expansive "aggravated felony" umbrella.[67] Finally, in a twist that rendered the immigration law quite detrimental to the liberty interests of noncitizens, the law vastly expanded the number of instances in which a noncitizen would be subject to mandatory detention during the course of removal proceedings.[68]

As a practical matter, these changes in law and policy mean that tens of thousands of noncitizens in the United States are now vulnerable to removal based on post-entry criminal conduct. They are also vulnerable to lengthy detention, pending the outcome of their immigration proceedings. In enacting these provisions, members of Congress clearly viewed the measures as a means of punishing the criminal conduct of noncitizens. Nevertheless, the Supreme Court has not revisited its generic nineteenth-century pronouncement that deportation is not punishment.[69] Consequently, widespread detention and removal for post-entry criminal conduct is carried out through administrative bodies of the executive branch and is subject to relatively few procedural constraints and limited judicial review. The government's response to the attacks of September 11, 2001, illustrates the absence of procedural protections available to noncitizens subject to punitive immigration detentions and removals in times of national crisis.

In light of the legal and political developments of the 1990s, September 11, 2001, cannot accurately be labeled a watershed for U.S. immigration policy. Most of the expansive removal provisions had already been enacted into law prior to that time. The spike in American immigration enforcement began in the 1990s, not after 2001. But the response to September 11 that was carried out through immigration policy is still worth examining. It demonstrates the degree to which the criminalization of immigration, which reached its legal zenith with the 1996 laws, blurred easily into the "securitization" of immigration policy that took place after September 11. The post–September 11 response illustrates the degree to which the long-standing rhetoric of security in the area of immigration law enforcement has created a startling degree of insularity for the immigration bureaucracy. This insularity is not limited to "national security" issues but comfortably extends just as readily to basic crime control functions carried out by the immigration enforcement bureaucracy.

Post-9/11 Changes to the Substantive Law

In response to the September 11 attacks, the U.S. Congress enacted a wide range of legislation, including the USA PATRIOT Act in 2001, the Homeland Security Act (HSA) and the Enhanced Border Security and Visa Entry Reform Act (EBSVERA) in 2002, the Intelligence Reform and Terrorism Prevention Act in 2004, and the REAL ID Act of 2005.[70]

Many of the post–September 11 laws are aimed primarily at increasing the ease with which the government can monitor noncitizens. EBSVERA mandated the creation of an integrated entry and exit data system and specified the technological standards for such a system, including the use of biometric indentifiers.[71] It also mandated the creation of a detailed database for monitoring noncitizens who entered the country on student visas.[72] Both of these programs are being integrated into a single comprehensive database called the U.S. Visitor and Immigration Status Indication Technology System (US VISIT).

The HSA rolled all of the functions of the Immigration and Naturalization Service (INS) into a newly created Department of Homeland Security. The DHS is responsible not only for immigration enforcement and oversight but also for the oversight of such agencies as the Federal Emergency Management Agency (FEMA), which is charged with responding to disasters, including hurricanes, floods, and tornadoes. As with most of the other post–September 11 legislation, the Homeland Security Act focused on consolidating governmental immigration functions with other security-related functions.

Congress also enacted several notable changes to the law of removal. First, both the PATRIOT Act and later the REAL ID Act expanded the definition of "terrorist aliens" who would be subject to removal as security threats. The PATRIOT Act retroactively amended the INA, expanding the reach of the terrorism definition to subject to removal aliens who provided "material support" to terrorism. This includes support to organizations that are not designated as terrorist organizations in the INA or through publication in the Federal Register but were deemed to have engaged in "terrorist activity." That category includes actions involving the use of any "dangerous device" (not just explosives and firearms) for anything other than "mere personal monetary gain."[73] The REAL ID Act greatly expanded the definition of "terrorist organization" to include "a group of two or more people, whether organized or not, which engages in or has a subgroup which engages in any form of terrorist activity." It thus further expanded the grounds for inadmissibility based on support of terrorism as well as being a member of a terrorist organization.[74] Although these provisions are purportedly security related, their impact on security is dubious. The definitions sweep so broadly that they can clearly encompass not just "terrorism" but general criminal acts as well. The expanded provisions thus imbue immigration enforcement agencies with tremendous discretion but do not provide a more effective tool for identifying and removing people who engage in acts of terrorism. Indeed, the expansive provisions have had a demonstrably negative effect on U.S. asylum policy. The United States is excluding thousands of refugees who are victims of terrorism because many refugees flee after being forced to give food, shelter, or other support to armed or terrorist groups or authoritarian regimes that qualify as "terrorist organizations" under the law. Ironically, the law bars them from admission for precisely the same reason that they are seeking refugee status.[75]

One additional post-9/11 legal provision was aimed directly at facilitating the arrest and removal of noncitizens who purportedly posed security risks. Section 412 of the PATRIOT Act added a section to the Immigration and Nationality Act that would allow the attorney general to "certify" noncitizens when there are "reasonable grounds to believe" that the person is inadmissible or deportable on certain national security grounds.[76] The provision mandates detention for anyone so certified, and the government has up to seven days to initiate removal proceedings against any individual detained under this provision.[77] These detentions may be indefinite, so long as the case is reviewed every six months.[78] In contrast to the procedures permitted under section 412, standard immigration and criminal procedures generally limit detention to two days prior to the commencement of proceedings.[79] This legal change sounds significant, if not drastic. In reality, however, section 412 has never been invoked. Immigration enforcement officials do not need section 412 because the vast power of the executive branch in the area of immigration law enforcement has allowed the federal government to arrest and detain noncitizens for lengthy periods even without invoking section 412. Indeed, by the time the provision was enacted, the Immigration and Naturalization Service had already amended its own regulations to allow for the possibility of extended detention of noncitizens beyond the standard two-day period for a "reasonable period of time" in the event of an "emergency or other extraordinary circumstances."[80]

The post-9/11 legislative changes with the most practical significance have taken place not in substantive immigration law but in appropriations bills, in which Congress has steadily increased the budget of Immigration and Customs Enforcement (ICE) to an all-time high. Large increases in the immigration enforcement budget began before September 11 but accelerated in the wake of the events of that day. From fiscal year (FY) 1993 to FY 2005, the Border Patrol budget quadrupled from $362 million to $1.4 billion, with the largest annual increase taking place after the events of September 11, 2001.[81] Since the creation of ICE in 2003, the budget for that agency has grown each year. In FY 2006, that budget totaled $3.9 billion in direct appropriations and fees for ICE—an increase of more than $216 million or 6.3 percent above FY 2005.[82] The resulting enforcement bureaucracy touches millions of lives, including the lives of thousands of noncitizens who pose no security threat of any kind.

Changes in Immigration Enforcement

After 9/11, Attorney General John Ashcroft made this pronouncement: "Let the terrorists among us be warned: If you overstay your visa by even one day we will arrest you. If you violate local law, you will be put in jail and kept in custody as long as possible."[83] The surveillance of certain noncitizens and the enforcement of immigration laws continue to expand. The entire immigration bureaucracy has been reorganized through the prism of security concerns. Despite these changes, neither legislation nor executive enforcement efforts have been efficiently tailored toward the elimination of security threats. Furthermore, changes in immigration enforcement have increased racial and ethnic profiling in newly expanded immigration enforcement efforts and flooded an overburdened administrative and judicial system with detainees and cases that are unrelated to security concerns. The most troubling aspects of the U.S. government's response to September 11 in the area of immigration were not the result of new legislation. Instead they were the result of changes in administrative rules governing immigration enforcement and of exercises of prosecutorial power that sometimes seemed contrary to existing law.

"Security" and Prosecutorial Discretion

Ashcroft's warning to the "terrorists among us" summarizes the Justice Department's clear policy of using the immigration enforcement bureaucracy as a means of preventively detaining any perceived terrorists. Immigration law already provided an effective tool for widespread detention and removal of noncitizens. Therefore, simple changes in immigration enforcement practices, rather than changes to law or regulation, truly account for the bulk of the most troubling post–September 11 changes to the immigration landscape.

For example, on November 9, 2001, Attorney General Ashcroft called on thousands of resident noncitizens from countries suspected of harboring terrorists to participate in "voluntary" interviews. Those in violation of the immigration laws could be subjected to jail without bond. A second wave of such interviews was carried out in March 2002.[84] No change in law was needed to allow this discriminatory application of immigration laws. Nor were changes in the law needed to enact the so-called "Operation TIPS" (Terrorism Information and Prevention System), which encouraged U.S. citizens to report "suspicious" activity.

Young male Arabs and Muslims were prioritized in immigration investigations on the basis of their race, ethnicity, and national origin. On October

31, 2001, Ashcroft announced the creation of a Foreign Terrorist Tracking Task Force (FTTTF) aimed at detaining potential terrorists on the grounds of alleged immigration violations. The task force targeted Arab and Muslim immigrant communities.[85] One important tool for accomplishing the stated goal was the initiation of the National Security Entry-Exit Registration System (NSEERS) programs. The Department of Justice initiated the NSEERS program in September 2002. The program required noncitizen men from certain—predominantly Arab and Muslim—countries to register with the INS.[86] Many who registered were detained on the basis of immigration violations. Those who failed to register could also be detained for that failure. It is difficult to estimate how many noncitizens were detained under these programs aimed at alleged immigration violators meeting certain profiles. David Cole writes,

> [T]he government admits that there were 1,182 detentions in the first seven weeks of the campaign. As of May 2003, it had also detained some 1,100 more foreign nationals under the Absconder Apprehension Initiative, which expressly targets for prioritized deportation the 6,000 Arabs and Muslims among the more than 300,000 foreign nationals living [in the United States] with outstanding deportation orders. As of May 2003, another 2,747 noncitizens had been detained in connection with a Special Registration program [NSEERS] also directed at Arab and Muslim noncitizens. A conservative estimate would therefore place the number of domestic detentions in the war on terrorism as of May 2003 at over 5,000.
>
> Sadly, this program has been a colossal failure at finding terrorists.[87]

U.S. law enforcement agencies thus arrested and interviewed thousands of noncitizens in the wake of September 11. Immigration detention became the central tool of this enforcement effort. When the FBI suspected that their detainees had violated immigration law, those individuals were transferred into INS custody. In the eleven months following September 11, 2001, the INS detained 738 such individuals.[88] To justify their detention on immigration charges, the FBI sent routine, boilerplate memoranda to the Executive Office of Immigration Review stating that "the FBI has been unable to rule out the possibility that the respondent is somehow linked to, or possesses knowledge of, the terrorist attacks."[89] Detention in many cases continued while the investigation of the person in detention proceeded under a controversial "hold until cleared by the FBI" policy.[90] When the Office of the Inspector General later conducted an investigation of post–September 11 detention policy, it found problems with the length of detention and the INS's automatic opposition to bond. It also found significant problems in the treatment of the detainees. These problems included physical and verbal abuse by some correctional officers, twenty-four-hour lighting in certain cells, and the imposition of a "communications blackout" that deprived detainees of the opportunity to make their confinement known to family members or counsel.[91]

The obvious problem with the strategy of pursuing national security through expansive immigration enforcement techniques is that it ensures that many innocent people will be detained, mistreated, and pressed into removing themselves from the country. The federal government is currently in the process of trying to address some of the wrongs committed in the frenzy of post–September 11 activity. In February 2006, the federal government reached its first settlement in a lawsuit arising out of its treatment of noncitizens in the days following September 11. The government agreed to pay $300,000 to settle a lawsuit brought by an Egyptian citizen, Ehab Elmaghraby, who was among dozens of Muslim men swept up and detained in the New York City area.[92] Elmaghraby and a co-plaintiff, Javaid Iqbal of Pakistan, faced tremendous barriers to filing their lawsuits since they had already been sent back to their home countries.[93] Unfortunately, for this and other reasons, many noncitizens will never receive compensation for their unjust detentions and coerced "voluntary" departures from the United States.

Another significant policy shift occurred in March 2003. At that time, Tom Ridge, head of the Department of Homeland Security, announced the beginning of an operation that mandated detention for asylum applicants from more than thirty countries designated as harboring terrorists—countries the government declined to identify. The controversial policy was terminated after only a month.[94] Unilateral executive branch action had resulted in a policy that expressly discriminated against certain asylum seekers in a manner clearly at odds with U.S. law and international treaty obligations. This fact illustrates the degree to which the administrative bodies charged with immigration enforcement have been able to shape the practice of immigration policy without changes in the immigration laws.

Administrative Rulemaking

In addition to changes in practice, the government also changed some of the implementing regulations that governed the enforcement of immigration laws. Sometimes these changes were of questionable legality.

One example can be found in ICE's detention policies. Prior to 2001, if an immigration judge found that a noncitizen was entitled to release on bond pending immigration proceedings, that person was generally freed unless the INS made a strong case to the contrary. After September 11, Attorney General Ashcroft oversaw a change in administrative regulations requiring that the individual be detained through the appeal of the decision to the Board of Immigration Appeals, even after an immigration judge ordered a noncitizen's release from detention.[95] Additionally, as previously noted, the regulations were amended to allow for protracted pre-hearing detention in cases of emergency.

A second example of an expansive administrative rule change is the alteration of the Department of Justice's regulation on racial profiling. Attorney General Ashcroft strengthened the power of the administrative bodies responsible for immigration enforcement. He did so through the issuance of regulations expressly authorizing executive officials to engage in certain forms of racial profiling in immigration enforcement, even though such profiling was formally prohibited in other federal law enforcement endeavors.[96] Even before those regulatory changes, racial profiling had become an important component of the law enforcement response to September 11. However, in June 2003, with the passage of new guidelines on racial profiling, the Justice Department formally sanctioned the use of race in the context of "national security" investigations. It simultaneously continued an earlier ban on racial profiling in traditional domestic criminal investigations.[97]

Unfortunately, this rule provides few real limitations on the use of profiling. The problem extends well beyond the selective (and overly aggressive) enforcement of immigration laws against Arabs and Muslims. As domestic crimes and national security concerns are conflated, other ethnic groups are becoming targets for aggressive crime control measures undertaken through immigration laws.[98]

Generally, the legislative and administrative changes enacted after September 11, 2001, reflect the sort of crisis response that has been deployed against noncitizens in the United States at various points in history. As such, although these examples are deeply troubling, they are not surprising. More surprising is the degree to which this security response subsequently has become blurred and been altered into a more general mechanism for effectuating domestic crime control.

The Rhetoric and Reality of Immigration Policy and National Security

The perceived link between immigration and security is driving a massive effort to deport noncitizens, but there does not appear to be any systematic effort to apply these enforcement procedures to the most serious offenders or the most dangerous security threats. As "national security" is defined with increasing breadth, virtually all noncitizens can be targeted based on national, ethnic, and racial profiling. Such profiling generally tends to affect the rights of citizens as well.[99] The resulting frenzy of activity to deport or prosecute immigration violators usurps resources—prosecutorial, bureaucratic, and judicial—which might be better spent on identifying and incarcerating those who pose genuine threats to security. Rather than increasing security, the current approach seems more likely to undermine due process protections and individual rights.

As previously noted, the security and terrorism grounds for removal were expanded with the passage of the 1996 laws and further expanded after September 11. The breadth of the resulting provisions raises serious questions as to whether the law is tailored to address an appropriately narrow class of security threats.[100] Paradoxically, despite the significant expansion of these categories, the number of immigrants removed on security and terrorism grounds has contracted, not expanded, over the course of the past decade. In the early 1990s, removals on security and terrorism grounds numbered approximately fifty each year. After the 1996 enactment of AEDPA and IIRIRA, these numbers dropped drastically; by 1999, there were only ten.[101] Given the rhetorical linkage of immigration enforcement and national security in the wake of September 11, 2001, one would anticipate a spike in security-related removals after that date. Yet there is no such spike.[102]

At the same time, however, the number of people processed through the immigration enforcement bureaucracy is large and growing. On any given day in the United States, there are more than four million foreign nationals authorized to be present in the country for a temporary period of time, usually on "nonimmigrant visas."[103] Additionally, in 2005 alone, more than four million people became legal permanent residents of the United States.[104] The average number of lawful permanent residents admitted each year for the past ten years is approximately eight hundred thousand.[105] Given that the average time between obtaining legal permanent residency and citizenship is about eight years, this means that there are more than ten million noncitizens lawfully present at any given time in the United States, in addition to an estimated twelve million people who are in the country without legal authorization.[106] The administrative bodies charged with immigration enforcement have potential jurisdiction over all of these noncitizens.

Large numbers of people are processed through administrative immigration enforcement mechanisms in the United States. In 2004, Immigration and Customs Enforcement completed 202,842 removals of noncitizens from the United States. Of those removed, 88,897 were classified as "criminal aliens."[107] The Department of Homeland Security detained a total of 1,241,089 foreign nationals during 2004, although many of them "voluntarily departed" without further proceedings.[108] That year is not anomalous; it simply continues a significant upward trend that began in 1997 and accelerated after 2001.[109]

Furthermore, the detention of noncitizens is the most rapidly expanding segment of the prison system in the United States. As of March 2004, on an average day, 22,812 individuals were in the custody of the Department of Homeland Security.[110] That number fell slightly to 21,919 in 2004. These averages—although significant in and of themselves—mask the scope of immigration detentions in the United States. The Department of Homeland Security estimates that it detained 235,247 noncitizens in 2004.[111] The boom in immigration detention has spurred an accompanying boom in the private industries responsible for building and managing immigration detention facilities in the United States.[112]

In addition to the removals and detentions effectuated through administrative channels, there has also been a significant increase in the criminal prosecution of immigration violations. In 2004, federal prosecutors filed charges in 37,854 cases on the basis of criminal immigration law violations. This is a 300 percent increase since 2000; immigration violations now surpass even drug prosecutions, constituting the single largest category of federal crimes.[113] Although noncitizens in criminal proceedings are entitled to many of the same procedural rights as citizens in criminal proceedings, their conviction exposes them to removal under the less protective administrative system, since many of those convicted of crimes become eligible for removal as "criminal aliens."

If security removals are on the decline and represent a small portion of ever-expanding immigration enforcement efforts, why does the rhetoric of security dominate the U.S. justifications for its immigration policy? The simple answer seems to be that general crime control measures achieved through immigration enforcement are now depicted and understood as national security matters. As previously noted, in the wake of the September 11 attacks, the U.S. government detained and removed large numbers of people on immigration violations under the pretext of national security concerns. This was done even where a national security threat had not been, and perhaps could not be, substantiated. Moreover, as the events of September 11 recede, the government has been able to continue to use the language of security to justify immigration detentions and removals on security grounds. This was possible not only because of the apparently endless character of the "war on terror" but also because, in the context of immigration enforcement, the boundaries between national and personal security have become blurred.

After September 11, 2001, crime control efforts through immigration have increasingly been discussed as "security measures"—suggesting that national security is at stake—when in fact the policies are aimed at basic crime control. ICE's strategic plans reflect the complete conflation of its security and crime control agenda.[114] This conflation is echoed in the halls of Congress. For example, the immigration bills debated in Congress during the 2006 session were almost universally referred to as "security" measures, even though they contain numerous anti-crime measures, including further proposed expansions to the definition of the "aggravated felony" category.[115] The media has accepted these characterizations of expanded alien removal provisions and proposals to militarize the border region and reported them as efforts to "protect the border."[116] The consequence is that immigration enforcement has become a powerful adjunct to the criminal justice system, but one that lacks comparable judicial oversight and operates to facilitate arbitrary and excessive forms of punishment.

In the post–September 11 era, the powerful rhetoric of security masks the degree to which contemporary immigration enforcement improperly blurs the boundaries between external security measures and internal crime control in the United States. Historically contingent notions of who is really a "citizen" and who is an "alien" ensure that many Latinos, Asian Americans, Arabs, and Muslims—citizens, legal permanent residents, authorized noncitizens, and the undocumented—have been and will continue to be subjected to crime control measures achieved through the highly punitive and insufficiently protective immigration enforcement bureaucracy. Although the result is a developing two-tier system of criminal justice administration, U.S. courts have generally ignored the problem by relying on age-old notions that immigration policy and security policy are one and the same. The changing nature of crime and security demands a new approach.

9

National Security and Political Asylum

ELENA A. BAYLIS

Since September 11, 2001, the United States has made significant changes in its political asylum policy, restricting access to asylum for many applicants in the name of the war on terror. The debate over these reforms draws from two competing visions of national security. The first views national security as essentially aligned with international human security and emphasizes the need to ensure protection for asylum applicants by approving legitimate claims. The second views national security as dependent primarily on defending a domestic safe zone against threats that are primarily foreign, identifiable, and excludable, so long as sufficiently stringent measures are adopted. The current predominance of the second view puts U.S. policy at odds with its international legal obligations, with some EU practices, and with the internal structure and realities of the U.S. asylum system itself.

Links between Asylum and Security

International Links

The international asylum and refugee systems were founded in the recognition of a link between international and human security and were initiated to address the humanitarian crisis of displaced peoples following World War II.[1] The 1951 UN Refugee Convention, the fundamental legal document establishing the rights of refugees, recognized the cyclical pattern of refugee movements as both a response to and a catalyst of conflict. It accordingly urged states "recognizing the social and humanitarian nature of the problem of refugees, to do everything within their power to prevent this problem from becoming a cause of tension between states."[2] The very definition of a refugee—one who "owing to well-founded fear of persecution on account of race, religion, nationality, membership in a particular social group, or political opinion, is outside the country of his nationality and is unwilling or, owing to such fear, unable to avail himself of its protection"—points to situations of dire human insecurity as the source of asylum-seeking populations.[3]

Today, the connection between international and human security manifests itself in the correspondence between flows of refugees and asylum seekers, and the failed states, political oppression, and conflict areas that pose threats to international security. According to the UN High Commissioner for Refugees (UNHCR), in the first half of 2006 the most significant sources of asylum seekers (those who have "left their country of origin . . . [and] applied for recognition as a refugee in another country") were China, Iraq, Serbia and Montenegro, Russia, Turkey, Haiti, and Iran.[4] In 2004, the primary source countries for refugees (those whose applications to be recognized as such have been granted and who are therefore entitled to all the rights corresponding to refugee status under national and international law) were Afghanistan, Sudan, Burundi, Democratic Republic of Congo, Somalia, Palestinian populations, Vietnam, Liberia, Iraq, and Azerbaijan.[5] Just as when the Refugee Convention was drafted, the relationship between national and international security, human security, and refugee movements continues to be cyclical and dynamic. A UNHCR report issued in 2006 describes spikes in refugee and asylum seeker numbers in regions that are hotspots for the war on terror. It also specifically identifies new refugee populations created by counterterrorist military offensives in regions such as Chechnya and Pakistan.[6]

National Links

On a national level, while September 11 is often identified as a watershed moment refocusing America's attention on security issues, national security and foreign policy have long been defining concerns in U.S. asylum and refugee law. Throughout the Cold War, the United States used political asylum as a tool of foreign policy, granting asylum primarily to refugees from communist states as part of a deliberate national security strategy. In this strategy "U.S. intelligence services engaged in a campaign to encourage defections from behind the Iron Curtain as a means of destabilizing communist regimes."[7] Similarly, national security and foreign policy concerns were at work in the changing treatment of Cuban refugees as U.S.-Cuban relations shifted. They were also apparent in the contrast between the warm welcome of asylum seekers from Cuba and the cooler reception of those from Haiti, given the lack of a perceived U.S. national security interest in Haiti.[8]

The need to address influxes of asylum seekers has often been in the first instance an unintended consequence, rather than a deliberate strategy, of U.S. foreign policy. An example of such was when U.S. policy in Central America in the 1980s contributed to sharply increased refugee flows to the United States from that region.[9] However, just as refugee movements operate cyclically, both in response to and in catalyzing conflict, so have foreign policy concerns historically affected both the initial development of refugee movements and also the eventual granting or denial of refugee status. In the 1980s, "the rate of acceptance of asylum claims from Nicaragua, El Salvador and Guatemala continued to reflect foreign policy considerations." In that decade, 26 percent of Nicaraguan claims were being granted in contrast to 2.6 percent of Salvadoran and 1.8 percent of Guatemalan claims.[10]

However, attempting to secure U.S. foreign policy goals through strategic admission of asylum seekers has proved to be a double-edged sword. It inevitably entails favoring applicants from what are often, by virtue of the purpose and definition of asylum itself, hostile or even enemy states.[11] These conflicting interests can play out in ironic and counterproductive ways. One obvious example is the Iraqi opposition. They were brought to the United States by the U.S. government to seek asylum after their CIA-encouraged plot to overthrow Saddam Hussein failed. Rather than gaining asylum, they found themselves detained and initially ordered deported based on secret, classified evidence that they were threats to national security.[12] As the latest development in this convoluted relationship between political asylum and foreign policy interests, the emphasis on security since September 11, 2001, has further exposed and legitimized the expression of security concerns in the rhetoric about asylum policy.

Convergences in U.S. Asylum Policy before and after September 11

Pre–September 11 Security Measures in Asylum Policy

The post–September 11 reforms in U.S. asylum law do not represent a sea change in asylum policy. Instead they follow upon earlier measures directed at limiting access to political asylum and incorporate the long-standing though fluctuating linkages between asylum and security. Concerns that fraudulent claims were overwhelming a too permissive asylum system instigated a round of regulatory reforms that began in 1993 and were finalized and implemented in 1995.[13] This was followed in 1996 by another round of changes. This round was catalyzed by the bombing of the World Trade Center, the murders of several CIA agents by asylum seekers, and the unrelated but nonetheless galvanizing Oklahoma City bombing, which was carried out by an American citizen.[14] The role of the Oklahoma City bombing in spurring immigration reform in the mid-1990s reveals the complexity of the relationship between security fears and immigration reform. It is particularly revealing of the tendency to conflate even domestic attacks with foreign threats. The Anti-Terrorism and Effective Death Penalty Act, which Congress hastily passed on the one-year anniversary of the bombing, contained numerous measures restricting the rights of immigrants, although the Oklahoma City bombing had no foreign connection.

The effectiveness of these prior measures and the security concerns that fueled them have become a focal point for renewed debate. The overall effect of these changes was to make the asylum process a considerably more lengthy and difficult mechanism for entering the United States than it had been in the previous decade. The government complicated the process by detaining arriving asylum seekers, imposing new limits on eligibility for asylum, requiring waiting periods for employment authorization, and excluding those associated with designated foreign terrorist organizations.[15] Supporters of further restrictions argue that terrorists nonetheless continue to enter the United States through the asylum system. Opponents contend that the security hole was plugged by the earlier round of reforms and that further restrictions will come at the cost of legitimate asylum seekers, not would-be terrorists.[16] Here, each side has anecdotes to offer, either of terrorists who slipped through the asylum system or of persecuted refugees whose claims were denied.[17] Notably, while several of the prominent terrorist attacks that took place before the reforms of the mid-1990s were carried out by asylum seekers or refugees, not one of the September 11 attackers had entered the United States through the asylum system.

Post–September 11 Changes in U.S. Asylum Policy

The post–September 11 changes to asylum law have taken several forms.[18] Perhaps the most sweeping and telling change was the transfer of immigration authority, including the asylum processing system, from the former Immigration and Naturalization Service to the Department of Homeland Security. Asylum adjudication was thus integrated into the heart of the federal government's security apparatus.[19] Critics have decried this move. They argue that it put asylum adjudication into the hands of an agency with a mission unrelated to the purposes of political asylum and that it divided asylum processing into three different bureaus, making effective coordination and application of uniform legal standards difficult.[20]

Some measures have been targeted directly at the issue of identifying and excluding terrorists, building on the laws of the mid-1990s. In 2001, the USA PATRIOT Act expanded the existing definitions of terrorist organizations and of associations with them that would derail applications for asylum. Under the USA PATRIOT Act definitions, an asylum seeker could be found to have provided material support to a terrorist organization even if that organization had never been officially designated as such. So long as an organization had ever used, threatened, attempted, or conspired to use a weapon or "dangerous device" for any reason other than "mere personal monetary gain," with the intent to endanger personal safety or cause substantial property damage, it could be deemed a terrorist organization. An asylum seeker could then be barred from gaining asylum for having provided it with support.[21]

In 2005, the REAL ID Act extended these definitions even further, so that a "terrorist organization" no longer has to be "organized" at all. It can be any "group of two or more individuals, whether organized or not," that engages in the broad definition of terrorist activity described above. It also expands the kind of relationship that renders an asylum applicant inadmissible. This wider definition includes not only members of terrorist organizations and those who have supported such but also those who have provided support even to members of terrorist organizations. The only exception is if the asylum seeker has clear and convincing evidence that he or she "did not know and should not reasonably have known" of the person's association with the organization in question.[22]

Numerous critics have objected to the sweeping breadth of these provisions. Perhaps the most adverse and counterproductive aspect of these standards is that they encompass not only willing but also unwilling supporters of terrorist organizations in their home countries. These unwilling supporters are forced, in fear of their lives, to aid such groups and are thus themselves victims of terrorism. While it sounds fantastical, commentators cite instances of applicants statutorily barred from asylum for providing money, food, shelter, or housework to terrorist groups who had either violently attacked them and their families, abducted them, or extorted this aid under threat of their lives.[23] In an article on the subject in 2006, Jennie Pasquarella pointed to 512 asylum cases "on indefinite hold at the Asylum Office because of material support concerns."[24]

Other measures are not specifically security oriented but alter the basic standards under which asylum will be granted.[25] These changes build on pre–September 11 asylum policy in a very direct way: several of the specific provisions adopted represent previously contested standards that gained new currency under the pressure of the terrorist threat. For example, a central question presented by the asylum standard, and one of the elements addressed by the 2005 REAL ID Act, is the notoriously difficult issue of motive. The adjudicator must assess not merely the facts establishing whether the applicant was persecuted or has a fear of future persecution but also the reason for that persecution.[26] Before the REAL ID Act, the case law had coalesced around a standard that required claimants to offer some proof of the reason for their persecution. Still, it recognized and tolerated the potential for persecutors to have multiple motives; applicants need not prove that a prohibited category was the sole motive for their persecution but only that this was one of the motives for it.[27] The REAL ID Act, in contrast, requires that asylum applicants prove that race, religion, national origin, political opinion, or membership in a social group was not just a reason but a "central" reason for their persecution. This requirement stems from regulations that were proposed but never adopted in December 2000 and which the Department of Homeland Security itself subsequently failed to support.[28] Similarly, before 2005, U.S. courts were divided on the questions of when corroborating evidence should be required and on the extent of the fact-finder's discretion in assessing credibility.[29] In both instances, the REAL ID Act adopted the most demanding of the standards presented in the case law.

Supporters of these and other reforms argue that they represent "narrow" changes intended to "ensure that all courts better scrutinize asylum claims so that legitimate claims survive and fraudulent claims get thrown out." Opponents argue that the law is "potentially detrimental to legitimate asylum seekers."[30] The rhetoric of both camps has converged upon this question of "legitimacy" and upon a basic, unanswered question of fact: do U.S. asylum procedures effectively distinguish genuine from fraudulent asylum seekers? From the terms of the debate, one would think that everyone agrees on the line that should be drawn by the asylum system between authentic and inauthentic asylum seekers. One might also think that the disagreement concerns only the question of whether that line is in fact properly drawn now.

But while both sides in the debate deploy the concept of legitimacy to promote their policy goals, in the past other critics have problematized the very concepts of legitimacy and genuineness. They have argued that the motive aspect of the asylum test is at odds with the nature of much political violence and therefore fails to legitimize claims and applicants who need protection. Considering the case studies of asylum seekers fleeing the Salvadoran and Guatemalan civil wars, Susan Bibler Coutin concluded that "continual violence, surveillance[,] and interrogation made the causes of persecution unclear and defined average people as potentially subversive." These conditions created a "gap between legal definitions of persecution and the repressive tactics that are directed at suspect populations."[31] Similarly, the new standards imposed by the REAL ID Act "allow adjudicators to base an adverse credibility determination on inconsistencies, inaccuracies or falsehoods . . . that are not material," that is, not related to the legitimacy of the plaintiff's claim for asylum at all.[32]

The current discussion props up the illusion that asylum seekers have a fixed identity as genuine or fraudulent, terrorist or nonterrorist. It suggests, basically, that all would agree on which claimants were eligible for asylum if only the proper procedures were followed and the correct standards applied. But there is little reason to think that this is so. The motives of applicants for asylum may or may not map onto the relative strength of their legal claim. Applicants with terrorist intentions may in fact have been persecuted in their home countries, whereas innocuous and genuinely fearful applicants may have been persecuted on a basis not recognized by the law or may lack essential evidence for their claims. Applicants with mixed motives for their migration may have some aspect of their personal history that strongly grounds an asylum claim. Furthermore, the motives of an applicant may change over time. Applicants who applied in good faith, for example, may later develop hostile intentions, or vice versa. The question of legitimacy thus obscures more than it reveals. It operates as a stratagem for claiming the high ground in the debate rather than as an actual point of debate in itself. The question also obscures the fundamental philosophical differences dividing those who focus on the harm done by "illegitimate" claimants who are granted asylum and those who focus on the harm done to "legitimate" claimants who are denied.

Finally, pro-asylum advocates have long contended that economic and social concerns are at work under asylum policy discussions that ostensibly concern security, fraud, and other issues.[33] On the national level, Eleanor Acer contends that security fears have provided "a new vocabulary" for immigration opponents to use "to advance long desired objectives." She points to policies disfavoring Haitian asylum applicants as an example of anti-immigration measures with no clear security objective but nonetheless put forward under a national security guise.[34] The UNHCR observes that the currently heightened security rhetoric has converged with public fears of "pressure on scarce resources such as jobs, housing, education, and healthcare," on government funds, illegal entries, and overstays, and "'bogus' claims." Together they constitute a worldwide trend toward "a growing degree of public suspicion and . . . increasingly rigorous state controls" on asylum seekers.[35]

Divergences of U.S. Policy from International and National Norms and Practices

It is of course too early to do more than speculate about the long-term effects of these security-related restrictions on asylum. However, they do diverge considerably from other policies and principles, raising red flags about their likely ineffectiveness in promoting national security and their possible detrimental effect on the asylum system itself. The primary issues are divergences from the United States' international obligations, from the direction of EU reform, and from the observed limits that legal processes face in assessing asylum claims in practice.

International Legal Obligations

As a party to the 1967 Protocol, the United States has international legal obligations to refugees and asylum seekers, in addition to its domestic legal responsibilities. States that were parties to the 1951 Convention and the 1967 Protocol that incorporates it promise a range of rights to refugees within their borders. These rights include, most importantly, the prohibition on *refoulement,* that is, returning refugees to a state where they would face persecution on one of the prohibited grounds.[36] These responsibilities are, of course, in addition to the obligations the United States bears under other international human rights treaties, such as the Convention against Torture. It specifically forbids returning an individual to a state where "there are substantial grounds for believing he would be subjected to torture"; there are also obligations under domestic law.[37]

It is a foregone conclusion under international law that asylum applicants who pose a threat to national security have no right to refugee status. Since the very foundation of the international refugee system in 1951, even the core right of non-refoulement can be denied to "a refugee whom there are reasonable grounds for regarding as a danger to the security of the country in which he is."[38] A crucial question, of course, is whether the legal standards established in post–September 11 legislation constitute such "reasonable grounds."

On that question asylum advocates contend that the recent changes in U.S. asylum law may put it in contravention of its Convention against Torture duties. Anwen Hughes has suggested that the REAL ID Act's expansion of the "grounds of deportability related to terrorism [to be] coextensive with the grounds of admissibility" may "conflict with U.S. obligations under the Refugee Convention."[39] Likewise, Eleanor Acer has argued that the Department of Homeland Security is shirking its obligations to the asylum principle. She cites its "sweeping approach" to barring asylum applicants on the basis of such remote associations with terrorist organizations as making payments garnered only by extortion. Such an action is "not consistent with the Refugee Convention's precise approach in assessing whether an individual refugee should be excluded from its protection."[40]

The lack of a duress exception to U.S. provisions making asylum applicants ineligible because of associations with terrorist organizations is particularly problematic. As discussed above, under new, broader definitions, people may be deemed ineligible for asylum due to their unwilling associations with terrorist organizations. Gregory Laufer has argued that "the lack of a duress exception violates the Convention Relating to the Status of Refugees . . . and its successor, the Protocol Relating to the Status of Refugees."[41] This failing is certainly at odds with the UNHCR's own interpretation of the grounds of inadmissibility under the Refugee Convention. The Refugee Convention provides that "serious non-political crimes" such as support for terrorism are grounds for excluding an otherwise eligible refugee from the Convention's protections. However, "the Article 1(F) exclusion does not apply 'where the act in question results from the person concerned necessarily and reasonably avoiding a threat of imminent death, or of continuing or imminent serious bodily harm to him or herself or another person.'"[42]

Similarly, under the broader definitions of terrorism, those persecuted by their governments may find themselves excluded from seeking asylum in the United States. Such restrictions could be based not on association with terrorist organizations having ill will toward the United States, or even on association with designated terrorist organizations. They could be based instead on involvement with predominantly peaceful organizations that have at any time used any violent means against oppressive regimes.[43] In the same vein, the UNHCR has noted that, ironically, refugees who have been displaced by military offensives in the name of the war on terror also find it more difficult to seek asylum. Their way is barred by new anti-terrorism efforts, and many have faced "accelerated and/or involuntary returns due to 'anti-terror' measures in asylum states."[44] Any or all of these measures may put those who, under international law, ought to be designated as refugees at risk of being returned by the United States to countries where they have a genuine fear of persecution. Thus, these policies put the United States in contravention of its international legal obligation to harbor refugees within its borders.

European Union Practice and Rhetoric

At the EU level, the role of security in influencing asylum law and policy diverges considerably from that in the United States. In the United States, the security threat posed by asylum seekers is conceptualized in the context of terrorism as the risk of individual terrorists penetrating the country through the asylum system and perpetrating violent attacks. In Europe, in contrast, discussions of security and asylum take place primarily in the context of migration, rather than terrorism, and with a broader understanding of security.

Specifically, European discussions seem to focus on the threat to European social, cultural, and economic security and on security from crime and criminal networks generated by large-scale patterns of migration across European borders, of which asylum seekers are a part. It is striking, for example, that EU asylum policy documents refer all in one breath to "the ongoing development of European asylum and migration policy" and "development of a common policy in the field of asylum, migration and borders." The EU thus conceptualizes asylum as an aspect of migration policy, rather than as an aspect of the war on terror.[45] Accordingly, much of the asylum-related legislation in the EU has focused on questions of coordination, harmonization, and burden sharing. Since 2001, European Council directives and regulations have, for example, established minimum standards for receiving asylum seekers and criteria for determining which member state has responsibility for adjudicating an asylum seeker's claim.[46] Most recently, the European Commission Communication on Strengthened Practical Cooperation, issued in February 2006, promotes increased harmonization and interaction among member states.[47]

In the same vein, terrorism, while a serious concern in its own right, is not one that crops up nearly so frequently in European discussions of asylum as in the American context. In Europe, terrorism concerns seem to be addressed primarily through a set of measures directed specifically at interdicting that phenomenon, rather than operating indirectly through the asylum system.[48] Of course, in the European context, as in the American, neither terrorism nor counter-terrorist measures are new developments. The continuity between pre– and post–September 11 policies is, however, perhaps better recognized in Europe. In Europe, terrorism was far more prominent in the public eye before September 11, and post–September 11 events such as the Madrid and London transit attacks in 2004 and 2005 both extend the impact and blunt the singularity of the September 11 attacks.[49]

This is not to say, of course, that national and regional security and terrorism are of no concern whatsoever in European immigration policy—both are, for example, mentioned in the introduction to The Hague Programme (2005).[50] The point is that the emphasis of the security debate is different. For example, the EURODAC database of asylum applicant fingerprints is intended to promote European security. This security is seen as a protection against the overall effect of asylum seekers moving across and within European borders to evade adverse decisions or go "asylum shopping," not security from terrorist attack.[51] Use of the database is limited to its designated purpose of "comparison of fingerprints of asylum applicants" to "identify third country nationals who have already lodged an asylum application in another Member State." It is not available for counter-terrorist activities.[52]

In another sense, however, the concepts of security in the EU and U.S. debates converge in the tension between the two competing visions of national security outlined at the outset of this chapter. Undoubtedly, evidence of the first vision, which emphasizes human security as necessary to national security, is far more prominent in European rhetoric and policy than in that of the United States. The Hague Programme of 2005, which, among other things, established a plan for developing and implementing the European Common Asylum System, offers a focal point for illumination and critique of the perceived links between immigration and security in Europe. In its introduction, The Hague Programme sets forth a list of goals. In them, security-oriented aims—"to control the external borders of the Union, to fight organized cross-border crime and repress the threat of terrorism"—stand side by side with other concerns—"to guarantee fundamental rights, minimum procedural safeguards and access to justice," for instance.[53] Here, the tension between the two visions of national security in the asylum context is evident in the juxtaposition of two contrasting goals: the intention "to provide protection in accordance with the Geneva Convention on Refugees and other international treaties to persons in need" is followed immediately by the aim "to regulate migration flows and to control the external borders of the Union."[54] Thus, as Didier Bigo has noted, the "European agenda is a lighter-handed version of the U.S. homeland security strategy, with more considerations concerning the dignity of the 'others,' their humane conditions, and with less antagonism."[55]

This divergence on the level of theory also finds its way into practice. Some of the counter-terrorist measures the United States has deployed within its asylum system are at odds with both EU and European national practices. Specifically, in contrast to the U.S. practice of disregarding evidence of duress when assessing an individual's connections to terrorist organizations, Gregory Laufer notes that "while vigorously combating terrorism, the Commission of the European Union has promoted considerations of duress in assessing an asylum applicant's case." He adds that "Belgium, Denmark, the

Netherlands, Switzerland, and the United Kingdom all focus on the individual's intent and actual role in light of a terrorist organization's activities."[56]

Although there seems to be more of an interplay between the two visions in Europe than in the United States, on both the theoretical and pragmatic levels, the role of the defensive, dichotomized vision of national security is not insignificant in Europe. In his critique of The Hague Programme, Didier Bigo identifies the image of "an 'essentialized' us under threat by unknown others." They must be defended through "the creation of a 'safe area without intruders'" that emerges not only in the context of asylum but also throughout the discussion of migration and border policy.[57] In the asylum context, two developments in particular highlight the contrast between the European security concern with large-scale migration and the American fear of individual terrorists. Those developments are the EU's new minimum standards for asylum procedures and its efforts to externalize asylum restrictions to third countries.

On December 1, 2005, the European Council adopted a long-debated Asylum Procedures Directive, setting minimum standards for member states' asylum-processing procedures.[58] Observers within and outside the EU have critiqued the directive, in draft and in final form, for its lowest common denominator approach. UNHCR has expressed concerns that the directive does not offer adequate protections for asylum seekers, raising the risk of refoulement of refugees and thus violation of their fundamental rights under the 1951 UN Refugee Convention.[59] Critiquing the draft proposed by The Hague Programme, the Immigration Law Practitioners Association pointed to the "safe countries of origin" list as creating particular risks where there are in fact "serious human rights concerns in the countries concerned." It also posited that mandating universal use of such a list represents an illegal dilution of standards in member states that did not currently use such lists.[60]

In this context, observers contend that efforts at creating common procedures have catalyzed already intense national debates over asylum. In addition, they argue, these moves have legitimized and reinforced a defensive, border-focused view of European social, economic, and cultural security that emerged much earlier.[61] Ariel Meyerstein describes a growth in asylum rates in the 1980s and 1990s that catalyzed more restrictive national-level policies on asylum, particularly in those states that received a disproportionate share of asylum seekers.[62] These legal shifts were followed by a sharp drop in the number of asylum applications, "from a high of nearly 700,000 in 1992 to 288,000 in 2004," which she attributes to "restrictive measures" at the national and EU level.[63] Without the political will among member states to accept more asylum applications, the "lowest common denominator" approach observed in The Hague Programme and the Asylum Procedures Directive is the only way to accommodate the pre-existing restrictive national policies on asylum in some member states. These are policies that seem to stem from these ongoing economic and social concerns.

The European goal of externalizing asylum policy illustrates both the severity of the external-internal approach to security that it shares with the United States and the emphasis on mass rather than individualized deterrence of migration, in which it diverges from U.S. security concerns. This externalization takes several forms. The one most directly focused on asylum is the externalization of asylum determinations to third countries. The Hague Programme calls for a study to "look into the merits, appropriateness, and feasibility of joint processing of asylum applications outside EU territory, in complementarity with the Common European Asylum System."[64] Other forms include partnerships with "countries and regions of origin" and "countries and regions of transit" to provide funding and support to source and transit countries for better migration management.[65]

The Hague Programme asserts that such measures should be carried out "in compliance with the relevant international standards" and that partnerships with third countries should include "[s]upport for capacity-building in national asylum systems" as well as in "border control and wider cooperation on migration issues." But advocacy groups object that these measures will outsource asylum processing to states known to have inadequate opportunities for seeking asylum and will, in effect, deny many refugees the right to seek asylum.[66] The Immigration Law Practitioners Association has raised concerns that "[c]alling upon non-EU States to ratify and adhere to the Geneva Conventions" may serve as "a justification for making expulsions to these countries easier." Such a move would thus not ensure protection for asylum seekers in those states.[67] Whatever the risks for asylum applicants, the contrast in strategy between the externalized European approach and the policy in the United States, where asylum determinations have been internalized deep in the federal government's Homeland Security apparatus, could not be starker.

Most recently, the designation of funding for Libya to manage migration across its borders illustrates the contrasting dynamic of security and asylum concerns in the EU versus the United States. In late 2005, the European Commission announced a "joint EU-Libya action plan" to address, not the risk of terrorist entry, but "migration pressure on the EU."[68] This pressure was illustrated, not by terrorist activity or threats, but by the deaths of migrants at Ceuba and Melilla, Spanish enclaves that provide prominent entry points for "Africans who pour into Morocco from all over the continent in an effort to enter the European Union." These enclaves are also where, in 2005, a number of migrants were crushed and others were shot in mass efforts to push through border fences.[69] Human Rights Watch has long protested that "Italy, the country most affected by migration from Libya . . . egregiously flouted international laws intended to protect migrants, asylum seekers, and refugees." It was accused of doing so by "collectively expel[ling] groups of people back to Libya, . . . conduct[ing] thousands of expulsions since 2004 in a hasty and indiscriminate manner" without "provid[ing] all individuals with an opportunity to present an asylum claim," and permitting its navy to force migrant ships out of its territorial waters with "no consideration for identifying asylum seekers."[70] Amnesty International has raised new concerns about the EU's decision to provide funding to Libya "without seeking any guarantees that the rights of asylum seekers and migrants will be upheld in the process."[71]

What is striking about these measures is not a contrast to actions taken under U.S. policy, for certainly the United States has been similarly criticized for turning back potential asylum seekers en masse. Rather, it is the divergence in the justifications offered for these choices that is remarkable. Contrast the "migration pressure" rationale deployed by the European Union with the rhetoric used by Attorney General John Ashcroft when faced with an influx of Haitian refugees in 2003: national security. Attorney General Ashcroft justified deterring potential asylum seekers from departing Haiti on the grounds that intercepting migrant boats would "divert valuable Coast Guard and [Department of Defense] resources from counterterrorism and homeland security responsibilities." Another reason given was the "national security interest in curbing use of this migration route" by "third country nations (Pakistanis, Palestinians, etc.)."[72] While there is some overlap between security concerns in the United States and the EU, the emphasis is entirely reversed, with national security playing the role of a trump card in U.S. but not EU asylum policy and rhetoric.

U.S. Legal Structure and Processes

Asylum applications are particularly challenging cases for legal adjudication, even apart from the problem of deterring terrorism. To some extent, this is inherent in the legal questions at the heart of the refugee definition and in the acute circumstances in which asylum cases arise. Returning to the example discussed above, about the REAL ID Act's change in the motive requirement, the effect of this change depends on the strength of the evidence that can be offered to meet it. As Anwen Hughes has noted, "[p]ersecutors often fail to make their motivations clear, creating evidentiary obstacles for their victims as they seek protection in this country."[73] Similarly, David Martin contends that "the unique elusiveness of the facts" in asylum cases complicates the adjudicator's evaluation of evidence, as genuine as well as nongenuine claims are likely to lack extensive evidentiary support.[74] Because the key events took place in other countries and often in situations of great turmoil, and because the applicant is likely to have left his or her home country in something less than a deliberate and measured fashion, corroborating evidence tends to be in short supply in legitimate as well as illegitimate claims. Efforts to assess credibility are made more difficult by the often horrific nature of the experienced atrocities, which may affect the applicant's perception and memory of the events in question. Credibility judgments are also complicated by the cultural and language differences dividing the adjudicator from the applicant. These differences create uncertainty concerning the internal consistency or inconsistency of an applicant's testimony as well as other, less tangible characteristics, such as the meaning of the applicant's demeanor.[75]

Arguably, this degree of factual "elusiveness" constrains the fact-finding processes to such a degree that any adjudicative process, however designed, can assess such claims only with some margin of error. If so, within this margin of error the choice of legal test and evidentiary standard will serve primarily to determine where the cost of error will fall. In the asylum context, some critics have identified lax evidentiary standards as presenting an avenue for fraudulent claims and abuse of the process by would-be terrorists, among others.[76] Counterbalanced against the risks posed by granting asylum based on fraudulent claims (particularly those made by potential terrorists) is the grave risk that applicants whose genuine claims are denied will face deportation and then further persecution in their home countries.[77]

Accordingly, these questions of where to draw the line between caution and compassion return us to the fundamental question of the relationship between national security and human security. The heightened refugee definition and evidentiary standards promulgated since September 11 will almost certainly result in diminished numbers of successful asylum claims in the aggregate. If the only goal of these reforms is to increase the raw numbers of denied terrorist claims, these changes seem likely to produce at least some improvement. This might be expected so long as there are any terrorists among those applicants who could have met the previous standards but cannot meet the newer ones. But if we take into account other concerns, such as the effect of these changes on genuine claimants or on the integrity of the adjudication system, it is far less clear whether the new standards will produce any marginal improvement in the system's ability to identify fraudulent or dangerous applicants.[78]

UNHCR has argued vigorously for the "need to safeguard the principle of asylum" in this "context where governments and electorates are unable to draw a clear distinction between the victims of persecution and the perpetrators of terrorist violence."[79] The most optimistic assessment by asylum advocates has been that, if interpreted in the light most favorable to asylum applicants, many of these standards could represent only minor changes in the law and will not affect most claims.[80] However, even under this view of the matter, at least some of the changes seem likely to "provide statutory cover for shoddy decision-making."[81]

Finally, as David Zaring and I have argued elsewhere, the post–September 11 legislation diverges sharply from basic principles of administrative law and from the underlying structure of the asylum system. This trajectory leads in ways that are likely to undermine the effectiveness of these structures, whether for improving national security or the functioning of the asylum system.[82] A cardinal error in these changes in asylum standards was to expand dramatically the discretion of the weakest link in the asylum processing chain: immigration judges. Compounding the effects of this shift, the Board of Immigration Appeals has substantially reduced its review of decisions by immigration judges, moving from review by three-judge panels to review by individual judges who issue one-sentence decisions affirming or denying the opinion. The result has been a dramatic drop in the effectiveness of the review of immigration judges' decisions provided by the Board of Immigration Appeals.[83]

The results can be measured according to several criteria, but by any standard they are dire. The range of grant and denial rates among immigration judges is so broad as to create the appearance of arbitrariness in the system. A study based on data from the Executive Office of Immigration Review found that the denial rates for 208 immigration judges hearing asylum claims between 2000 and 2005 ranged from 10 to 98 percent. Even when attempting to account for potential regional differences in the sources and strengths of asylum claims by narrowing the data to focus solely on claims from Chinese applicants, the study still found a range of 6.9 percent of claims denied by one judge to 94.5 percent denied by another.[84]

The reactions of those who have been in a position to observe this trend have included considerable criticism. Federal judges have deplored the repeated incompetence displayed by immigration judges in the asylum cases they have reviewed. The Seventh Circuit's Judge Posner found in 2005 that "the adjudication of these cases at the administrative level has fallen below the minimum standards of legal justice."[85] The U.S. government itself has been forced to confront and admit these lapses in the performance of immigration judges. Following the outcry from the federal judiciary, Attorney General Alberto Gonzales called for reforms, "voicing concern about 'intemperate or even abusive' conduct" by immigration judges.[86] In this context, vesting greater discretion in immigration judges to promote delicate matters of national security seems less than prudent.

Another glaring problem with these reforms is that raising standards within the asylum process is a highly inefficient way to find terrorists. On average, more than sixty-four thousand people apply for asylum every year, and few, if any, of those who apply each year are terrorists.[87] While it certainly makes sense to subject asylum applicants to standard security screenings, scrutinizing each claim according to heightened standards in hopes of catching a marginally greater number of terrorists is the quintessential search for a needle in a haystack. Here, it is worth noting that a 2005 report identified only sixteen people with purported terrorist associations among the more than one million people who have applied for asylum in the United States between 1980 and 2005. This number included several "friends" of accused terrorists who were themselves never accused of any terrorist involvement. It also included several others who entered the United States through other means and filed asylum claims only as defensive measures after they were already in deportation proceedings.[88] All in all, by focusing on the asylum process as a point for interdicting terrorists, the U.S. government is operating against the observed limits of the asylum process in adjudicating individual claims, against basic principles of administrative laws, and against the known weaknesses in the structure of its asylum system.

Within and outside the United States, two visions of national security compete in forming asylum policy: one that links national security to broader human security, and another conceptualizing internal security as being at odds with distinct external threats. While September 11 is often treated as a turning point between the two perspectives, in fact the second view has distinct roots in pre–September 11 policies, and the first view continues to carry some weight, although more so in Europe than in the United States. A comparison of U.S. and European policies reveals a second dichotomy in conceptualizations of security threats, between the narrow American focus on terrorism and the broader European fear of the disruption of social, economic, and cultural norms. Whether by comparison with international norms, European practices, or practical experience within the U.S. asylum system, the security strategy implemented in U.S. asylum policy since September 11 appears at best to fail to promote and at worst to risk undermining the human security goals for which the international political asylum system was founded.

10

Immigration Enforcement and Federalism after September 11, 2001

ANIL KALHAN

Since 2001, the U.S. federal government and Congress have proposed and, in some cases, adopted policy initiatives that aggressively seek to involve state and local government institutions more extensively and directly in the day-to-day regulation of immigration status and the so-called "interior enforcement" of federal immigration laws. Traditionally, federal immigration enforcement efforts in the United States have tended to prioritize enforcement activities at the border itself, rather than focus on interior enforcement. Interior enforcement has increased since enactment of the Immigration Reform and Control Act of 1986 (IRCA), which instituted civil and criminal sanctions against employers who hire non-U.S. citizens without authorization to work in the United States. These enforcement efforts have remained relatively limited, however, when compared with the vast resources devoted to border enforcement.[1]

Interior enforcement efforts also have been implemented almost exclusively by federal immigration agents. The role of state and local governments, by contrast, has been highly constrained. The states played an active role in the regulation of immigration to the United States prior to the enactment of the first federal immigration statutes in the late nineteenth century. Until recently, scholars, advocates, and government officials have largely agreed that under the legal regime in place since then, state and local governments lack any general legal authority to engage in activities to enforce federal immigration statutes.

However, since the mid-1990s, and to an even greater extent since 2001, the federal government and members of Congress have increasingly sought to involve state and local governments in federal immigration enforcement initiatives. Some of these initiatives have attempted to facilitate direct enforcement of immigration laws by state and local law enforcement officials, such as police, highway patrol, or corrections officials, in cooperation with federal immigration agents. Other initiatives have sought to operate less directly. These have been designed to employ a range of means to induce officials from welfare agencies, educational institutions, public hospitals and health agencies, motor vehicle licensing agencies, and others to restrict noncitizens' access to various benefits and public services. These initiatives have also sought state and local involvement in collecting immigration status information and reporting suspected civil immigration violators to federal officials. Still other initiatives impose federal standards, in circumstances where state and local institutions might otherwise apply their own, in order to advance federal immigration policy objectives. The strategies relied upon to induce states and municipalities to participate in these efforts have varied. Examples include simple attempts to persuade state and local officials to act voluntarily, devolution of discretionary authority to states and localities, imposition of conditions on federal funding, promulgation of federal standards that states and localities may avoid only with great difficulty, and even, in some proposals, direct imposition of federal mandates upon state and local governments.

Two sets of recent federal initiatives challenge conventional assumptions about the relationships between state and local governments and their noncitizen residents. These initiatives include efforts to involve state and local law enforcement officials in routine, civil immigration enforcement and the development of mandatory federal issuance and eligibility standards for state driver's licenses. The level of resistance to those initiatives by some states and localities also challenges conventional assumptions. Some states and localities have welcomed these federal initiatives. In some instances they have even gone further by attempting to regulate and enforce federal immigration statutes entirely on their own. Others have actively resisted these federal efforts to enlist their involvement in immigration-related matters.[2] The extent and potential implications of these more protective impulses by states and localities remain underexplored.

U.S. immigration law has traditionally been interpreted as an attempt to constrain state and local involvement in the regulation of immigration status.

One way it has done so is through laws involving "immigration" policy; these laws purport to regulate and enforce immigration status and the right to entry and presence itself. Another way is through laws involving "alienage" or "immigrant" policy; these laws regulate the day-to-day rights and obligations of noncitizens who are already present in the United States. In many cases such laws have been enacted as an indirect form of immigration regulation.[3] These limitations on state and local authority have been explained as resting, at least in part, on the premise that noncitizens are more likely to face hostility, discrimination, or disadvantage at the hands of state or local institutions than at the hands of the federal government. This premise is consistent with conventional understandings about federalism and the role of state and local governments in the United States more generally.

Recent federal initiatives intended to involve states and localities in immigration enforcement matters have engendered debate over the legality and wisdom of such initiatives as a matter of policy. Supporters have argued that security imperatives demand greater involvement of state and local officials in the regulation of immigration status. Critics have raised concerns that such initiatives will increase the likelihood of racial profiling and other civil rights violations, and they have questioned the extent to which these initiatives meaningfully improve security. Notably, among these critics are many state and local officials themselves. They have emphasized that such aggressive efforts to enlist state and local government agencies in routine federal immigration enforcement activities threaten to distort those institutions' priorities and undermine their autonomy. To the extent that the federal government can impose immigration enforcement responsibilities upon them, these critics have warned, state and local institutions may become increasingly obliged to shift their priorities. They may be forced to devote scarce resources to pursue federal policy objectives that have little to do with their own central purposes under state and local law.

The broader implications of these post-2001 developments include conventional assumptions concerning immigration and federalism. Certainly, as a number of recent examples make clear, it remains the case that noncitizens may often be vulnerable to hostility or discrimination by state and local government actors. As the federal government more aggressively regulates immigration and emphasizes security rather than traditional aspects of immigration policy, non-U.S. citizens are seeking protection in state capitals and city halls. In some instances they are finding greater concern for rights and liberties in those locales than they have in Washington. In this context, the traditional assumptions concerning immigration, citizenship, and federalism may be incomplete.

Background

Traditional doctrinal assumptions about immigration law place significant limits on the authority of states and localities to regulate immigration and federal citizenship status. Immigration was regulated almost exclusively by the states during the nation's first century. At the end of the nineteenth century, the first major federal immigration statutes were enacted and the Supreme Court handed down its first immigration-related decisions. Since then it has been presumed that authority to regulate immigration in the United States is exclusively the province of the federal government.[4] According to this paradigm, Congress has been recognized by the courts as having the "plenary power" to enact laws governing the admission and removal of non-U.S. citizens and the conditions under which they may remain in the United States. The specific source of this authority is not altogether clear. However, the Supreme Court has recognized this power over immigration as arising from the inherent sovereignty of the national government. It has also pointed to several specific textual sources within the Constitution that confer to the federal government power over foreign commerce, foreign affairs, and naturalization. Under the plenary power doctrine, the power of Congress over immigration has been subject to relatively few constitutional limits and only limited judicial scrutiny.[5] The breadth of this power has been widely recognized when Congress has directly regulated immigration—at its core, the "determination of who should or should not be admitted into the country, and the conditions under which a legal entrant may remain." This breadth has also been apparent when Congress enacted alienage-based laws governing the day-to-day rights and obligations of non-U.S. citizens.[6]

By contrast, direct state and local efforts to regulate immigration or to formulate other policies on the basis of alienage-based classifications have been found unlawful (or at a minimum, have been scrutinized closely). Although the extent to which the Constitution limits the authority of the states to directly regulate matters involving immigration is not entirely clear, some cases have invalidated state and local laws on the basis of structural, federalism-based principles. In the nineteenth century, before Congress had enacted its first major immigration laws, the Supreme Court invalidated several immigration-related state laws as unconstitutional. In doing so it suggested that those laws infringed upon the federal government's power to regulate foreign commerce or to conduct foreign relations.[7] Since the enactment of comprehensive federal immigration legislation at the end of the nineteenth century, courts have been able to avoid developing these constitutional principles further by invalidating state laws, which broad federal statutes preempted.[8]

With respect to alienage-based classifications, while states and localities have been permitted to formulate and implement policies that discriminate against non-U.S. citizens when the discrimination excludes non-U.S. citizens from involvement in the state's "political functions," courts have otherwise exercised heightened scrutiny over such classifications. They invalidated on equal protection grounds laws that discriminate on the basis of alienage unless they have been sufficiently tailored to advance a legitimate and compelling state interest.[9] On this basis, for example, the Supreme Court has applied strict scrutiny to invalidate state laws denying legal immigrants eligibility for state welfare programs and commercial fishing licenses.[10] Undocumented immigrants have not been extended the same degree of equal protection. Nevertheless, the Supreme Court did apply an intermediate standard of heightened scrutiny to invalidate a state law authorizing local school districts to deny educational access to children who were not lawfully admitted to the United States.[11] Moreover, like U.S. citizens, non-U.S. citizens, whether lawfully present or not, are protected in their day-to-day lives by other provisions of the U.S. Constitution. Those provisions guarantee the fundamental rights of all "persons," such as the Due Process Clause and the prohibition against cruel and unusual punishment.[12]

The principles underlying these decisions to some extent presume that non-U.S. citizens are more likely to face hostility, discrimination, or disadvantage at the hands of state or local institutions than at the hands of the federal government. Premises of this sort are by no means limited to the area of immigration. Indeed, the dominant, modern view of American federalism has conceived of the national government as a "bulwark" against violations of individual rights by the states. According to this view, states are regarded as probable "constitutional wrongdoers" in a broad range of contexts.[13] There is certainly much historical support for this interpretation with respect to non-U.S. citizens. As Gerald Neuman has noted, the Supreme Court "began denying powers of immigration regulation to the states" during the late nineteenth century "in part because they were visibly abusing those powers."[14] Since then, non-U.S. citizens have periodically experienced a variety of similar abuses at the hands of state and local governments.[15]

Doctrinally, this notion is reflected most clearly in the context of equal protection where the Supreme Court has self-consciously justified strict scrutiny of alienage-based classifications. It has done so on the ground that non-U.S. citizens "as a class are a prime example of a 'discrete and insular' minority" vulnerable to invidious discrimination, and for whom "heightened judicial solicitude" under the federal constitution is appropriate.[16] However, echoes of this rationale also may be found in cases invalidating state laws because they are inconsistent with the federal powers over foreign commerce and foreign relations. For example, in *Chy Lung v. Freeman*, the Supreme Court expressed concern that mistreatment of non-U.S. citizens by state officials might antagonize foreign governments. The concern was that this might render the federal government liable for claims arising from such mistreatment.[17]

As observers have noted, the equal protection and structural limits on state and local authority sit together somewhat uneasily.[18] The equal protection cases place limits on the ability of states and localities to discriminate on the basis of alienage. But the Supreme Court has left open the possibility of sustaining state and local involvement in the direct regulation of immigration status to the extent harmonious with federal law.[19] More complicated questions may arise, therefore, from situations in which the federal government exercises its broad plenary power over immigration in a way that might invite state and local involvement. Depending upon the nature of those federal initiatives, the assumption that non-U.S. citizens will be more vulnerable to mistreatment by states and localities may or may not be true.

Recent Efforts to Induce State and Local Immigration Enforcement

Like other immigration-related initiatives introduced after 2001, recent efforts by the federal government to involve states and localities in federal immigration enforcement have not been entirely a product of the aftermath of the terrorist attacks of September 11, 2001. Instead, they have roots in the immigration policy debates of the 1980s and 1990s.[20] During the 1980s, amid intense public debate over illegal immigration, at least twenty-four local governments and one state adopted policies prohibiting their officials from reporting immigration status information to or cooperating with federal immigration authorities.[21] Other political forces—first in the states, and then eventually in Washington—soon pushed in the opposite direction, seeking to involve state and local officials more directly in federal immigration enforcement activities.[22] Most prominently, in 1994, California voters approved Proposition 187. This ballot initiative attempted to create a comprehensive, state-level immigration enforcement system. It was intended to restrict the access of undocumented non-U.S. citizens to a variety of public services, including education and nonemergency health care. It would also require state and local officials to collect immigration status information from members of the public and to inform federal immigration officials about anyone they suspected of being in the country unlawfully.[23]

In 1996, Congress itself acted to encourage or mandate various forms of state and local involvement in immigration enforcement activities. Provisions in the immigration legislation enacted that year banned states and localities from adopting policies restricting the disclosure of immigration status information to federal immigration officials. The legislation thereby purported to preempt the policies adopted by states and localities during the 1980s.[24] Other legislative provisions authorized (but did not require) states to deny social service benefits to non-U.S. citizens, restrict driver's license eligibility for non-U.S. citizens, and involve their law enforcement officials on a structured and limited basis in federal immigration enforcement activities.[25]

These efforts by Congress and the federal government have gained momentum since 2001. National security has explicitly served as the principal justification for many of the post-2001 incarnations of these initiatives, part of the broader trend in which security considerations have come to dominate the formulation of policies concerning immigration and alienage.[26] Two examples illustrate the post-2001 trend of seeking to enlist states and localities more aggressively in immigration enforcement efforts, at least in part in the name of national security.[27] The first involves the efforts to induce state and local law enforcement officials to enforce civil violations of the federal immigration laws. The second involves the promulgation of mandatory federal issuance and eligibility standards for state driver's licenses.

State and Local Law Enforcement

Prior to 2001, the extent to which state and local law enforcement officials were involved in day-to-day enforcement of the civil provisions of federal immigration laws (as opposed to their criminal provisions) was highly limited.[28] While individual police departments had occasionally engaged in some immigration-related enforcement activities, these activities were relatively isolated. To the extent that Congress explicitly authorized some state and local participation in civil immigration enforcement activities, these programs were carefully structured and relatively constrained. For example, Congress authorized emergency deputization of state and local police officials as federal immigration enforcement officers in the event of a "mass influx" of non-U.S. citizens at the border.[29] Congress expanded these provisions to apply in nonemergency situations. In doing so, it set forth a structured set of conditions under which state and local jurisdictions may voluntarily enter written, cooperative agreements with the federal government to permit their officers to participate in certain designated immigration enforcement activities under federal supervision.[30] As the 1980s and 1990s proceeded, the federal government also sought greater cooperation from state and local officials in identifying potentially deportable non-U.S. citizens in state or local criminal custody.[31] The number of immigrants detained increased rapidly in the mid-1990s. Faced with tremendous constraints on their own available detention space, federal immigration officials increasingly entered into voluntary agreements with state and local governments to house federal immigration detainees in their jails.[32]

Beyond these limited, highly structured modes of state and local participation in immigration enforcement activities, state and local law enforcement officials have played a limited sustained role in civil immigration enforcement matters. In fact, whether states and localities have any broader, general legal authority to enforce federal immigration laws remains a matter of considerable doubt. The long-standing view of the U.S. Department of Justice was that state and local police lacked any general "recognized legal authority to arrest or detain aliens solely for purposes of civil immigration proceedings as opposed to criminal prosecution." Commentators reached similar conclusions.[33] Some state and local officials themselves concluded that their law enforcement officials lacked authority under state law to enforce the civil provisions of the federal immigration laws.[34]

Courts still have not resolved the question definitively. One court suggested early on, in the nonbinding, explanatory portion of the decision, that state and local police may indeed have the authority to enforce civil immigration laws. But at least one other court assumed that any state or local authority was preempted by the comprehensive federal immigration enforcement scheme enacted by Congress.[35] In the years since the 1996 immigration legislation, some courts have continued to characterize the existence of any broader, more general state and local immigration arrest authority as "doubtful," "questionable," and "uncertain." These characterizations are based in part on the likely preemption of such authority by Congress's comprehensive approach to immigration enforcement.[36]

Since the terrorist attacks of September 11, 2001, however, the federal government has taken a series of steps aimed at reshaping the role of state and local law enforcement officials in ordinary federal immigration enforcement matters. The federal government has effectively recast these day-to-day, *civil* immigration enforcement efforts as security-related, *criminal* enforcement priorities. In doing so, it has, in effect, sought to reposition its civil immigration enforcement activities within the long-standing, extensive set of federal-state-local partnerships designed to combat violent crime, organized crime, drugs, and terrorism.[37]

First, the executive branch, on its own initiative, has sought to encourage the voluntary cooperation of state and local police in federal immigration enforcement efforts. In 2002, the Department of Justice (DOJ) withdrew the portions of the 1996 legal opinion stating its long-standing position on state and local immigration arrest authority. Instead, the DOJ announced that it had reached the opposite conclusion. Its new conclusion was that state and local police have "inherent authority" to enforce and make arrests for civil violations of the immigration laws. The DOJ proceeded to encourage subfederal jurisdictions to accept such enforcement responsibilities.[38] The government also issued regulations implementing the 1996 statutory provision authorizing cooperative deputization agreements, which had not yet been implemented. Since then the DOJ has entered into several agreements with particular jurisdictions to authorize some of their law enforcement officers to perform certain specified federal immigration enforcement functions.[39]

Second, the Department of Justice has attempted to induce state and local police officers to engage in de facto immigration enforcement activities in an indirect fashion. The DOJ has done so by entering hundreds of thousands of civil immigration records into the FBI's main criminal database, the National Crime Information Center (NCIC). The NCIC database is a nationwide clearinghouse of largely crime-related records that is maintained by the FBI but accessed for the most part by state and local officials. The purpose behind the creation of this clearinghouse, which Congress originally authorized in 1930, was twofold. It would facilitate an efficient means for police in one jurisdiction to learn about a person's criminal history in another jurisdiction. It would also enable law enforcement agencies to respond to similar inquiries from police in other countries. The clearinghouse has existed in the form of a computerized database since 1967. It currently offers approximately ninety-four thousand law enforcement agencies in the United States and Canada the ability to access records on approximately fifty-two million individuals. State and local police query the NCIC database millions of time each day as they conduct their normal policing duties.[40] Congress has, on occasion, authorized specific categories of noncriminal information to be included in the database, such as specific categories of immigration-related information. Nonetheless, the database continues to consist primarily of crime-related records, in accordance with Congress's statutory mandate.[41]

Since 2001, however, the Justice Department has dramatically expanded the categories of individuals whose records are being entered into the NCIC. In particular, the government has begun to enter and disseminate to local police nationwide information concerning so-called absconders. These are individuals with outstanding orders of deportation, exclusion, or removal whom the government believes have remained in the United States (a category that totals approximately four hundred thousand individuals). The category also includes individuals whom the government believes have failed to register with the government under the National Security Entry-Exit Registration System (NSEERS). This is the "special registration" program announced in June 2002 by Attorney General John Ashcroft for certain nationals of a few dozen predominantly Muslim countries as well as North Korea.[42] The federal government also announced its intention to enter information on suspected foreign student visa violators and individuals previously deported for misdemeanor convictions. It has, however, deferred the final decision on those categories for the time being. Proposals in Congress would go much further by specifically requiring the entry and dissemination (through the NCIC) of these and several other categories of immigration records.[43]

The government's apparent purpose in using the NCIC in this manner seems to be to induce individual police officers to arrest and detain suspected civil immigration violators whose names appear when officers make routine queries in that database. This inducement appears to be without regard to the scope of the police officers' immigration arrest authority as a matter of federal, state, or local law. The initiative to employ the NCIC is currently the subject of litigation challenging the government's authority to use the database for civil immigration enforcement purposes not authorized by Congress.[44] In the interim, however, the government has apparently continued to enter these immigration records into the NCIC. Since it commenced doing so, thousands of non-U.S. citizens have been arrested by state and local police for suspected civil violations of immigration laws.[45]

As a result of these initiatives, state and local police have increasingly found themselves enmeshed in civil immigration enforcement activities under circumstances in which they previously would not have been.[46] Even more aggressive proposals to involve state and local police enforcement have come from members of Congress. Over one hundred of them cosponsored legislation in 2003 that purported to provide timely authorization for state and local participation in immigration enforcement and the inclusion of immigration records in the NCIC. Proposed initiatives would also have cut off certain federal funding streams from states that failed to enact legislation of their own specifically intended to authorize their police to enforce federal immigration laws. Other proposals would criminalize a number of immigration law violations that are currently only subject to deportation and civil penalties. Still others required states and localities to develop and implement policies to provide federal authorities with identifying information about non-U.S. citizens who are suspected of violating immigration laws. The proposed legislation would also have conferred immunity upon state and local agencies in the case of any suit for any noncriminal wrongdoing that allegedly arose from federal immigration enforcement activities.[47]

Variants of these proposals have periodically been reintroduced and incorporated into other proposed immigration legislation in the course of the debates over comprehensive immigration reform in 2005 and 2006. The most extreme of these proposals would have criminalized unlawful presence in the United States altogether, largely eliminating the traditional distinction between civil and criminal violations of immigration laws.[48] Such proposals would facilitate the implementation of immigration provisions by state and local law enforcement, since state and local police do have recognized authority in many jurisdictions to make arrests for criminal violations of immigration laws.[49] To date, none of these proposals has been enacted into law.

Driver's License Issuance and Eligibility Standards

The United States has no uniform national identification document. Filling this vacuum, state driver's licenses and, to a lesser extent, other state identification documents have become the default means of establishing one's identity in a broad range of contexts. Without a state-issued identification document, one is effectively excluded from banking, check cashing, boarding airplanes, establishing eligibility for employment, and many other common activities. Traditionally, states have set their own requirements and eligibility criteria for their residents to obtain a driver's license and identification card. In many cases, states have not explicitly restricted eligibility on the basis of immigration status. State governments typically recognize valid driver's licenses issued by other states or, indeed, other countries. They do, however, typically require individuals to obtain state licenses within a certain period after becoming a state resident if they wish to remain eligible to drive within the state. For example, in New York, an individual must obtain a New York driver's license within thirty days of becoming a New York resident in order to be authorized to operate a motor vehicle within the state.[50]

In 1996, as part of a comprehensive package of changes to the immigration laws, Congress authorized the states to conduct pilot programs for a period of three years. The intention was to deny driver's licenses to non-U.S. citizens who are unlawfully present in the United States. While the attorney general was required to submit a report on those pilot programs within three years, no report was submitted, and it is not clear that any pilot programs were in fact conducted under these provisions.[51] As part of the same legislation, Congress also attempted to set forth substantive minimal standards for state driver's licenses as prerequisites for their use for federal purposes. The legislation proposed required states either to include the licensee's Social Security number on the document itself or to verify each license applicant's Social Security number with the federal government. This second provision proved unpopular, however, and as a result Congress blocked funding to implement these provisions and ultimately repealed the provision itself.[52]

In addition, prior to 2001 active movements sought to expand noncitizen access to driver's licenses in at least fifteen states. Advocates variously sought to modify requirements that served as barriers to access for non-U.S. citizens. These barriers included evidence of lawful presence, a Social Security number, and other documentation requirements. Advocates also sought to expand two categories: non-U.S. citizens eligible for driver's licenses and documents that could be used to obtain driver's licenses.[53] These efforts stalled somewhat after the terrorist attacks of September 11, 2001, as state legislators and administrators introduced new proposals to limit eligibility for non-U.S. citizens. However, only a few of these proposals succeeded and became law, and a number of states even sought to expand eligibility to undocumented non-U.S. citizens. As of May 2002, one leading immigrants' rights organization could claim that the pre-2001 campaigns to expand eligibility for driver's licenses had made "surprising progress" even after the terrorist attacks.[54]

The legislative catalyst for action by Congress was the final report of the September 11 Commission. It recommended that the federal government "set standards for the issuance of birth certificates, and sources of identification, such as driver's licenses."[55] Accordingly, the intelligence reform bill that Congress enacted in December 2004 to implement the commission's recommendations did precisely that. It provided that in order for a driver's license or state identification card to be accepted for any official purpose by a federal agency, the state had to satisfy certain minimum standards for application procedures. Among these criteria were documentation of an applicant's identity and verification of that documentation. The September 11 Commission did not recommend any restrictions on a noncitizen's eligibility for driver's licenses. The Intelligence Reform Act of 2004, accordingly, did not include any. On the contrary, the relevant statute explicitly provided that the implementing regulations, to be established through a negotiated rulemaking process, could not infringe upon any state's authority to set and enforce its own criteria for the categories of individuals eligible for driver's licenses or identification cards.[56]

However, only six months later, Congress repealed these provisions and enacted the REAL ID Act.[57] The REAL ID Act terminated the Intelligence Reform Act's negotiated rulemaking process midstream. It also banned the use of negotiated rulemaking to develop implementing regulations for the

REAL ID Act. In addition to the kinds of criteria required under the Intelligence Reform Act—with which states now must comply within three years, at tremendous expense to their treasuries—the REAL ID Act also set forth certain alienage-based eligibility requirements. Under the REAL ID Act, within three years driver's licenses may be issued only to U.S. citizens and non-U.S. citizens with certain categories of immigrant visas.[58] Lawfully present non-U.S. citizens with nonimmigrant visas or certain pending or approved applications may obtain only "temporary" licenses or identification cards. Those cards must expire on the same date as the individual's visa (or, for visas of indefinite length, must expire one year from the date of issue). Temporary licenses and identification documents must visibly indicate that they are temporary. They must also clearly display the expiration date, in order to facilitate the ability of law enforcement personnel to inspect and verify the document.[59] States may issue "driver's certificates" to undocumented non-U.S. citizens, but these documents must indicate clearly that they may not be accepted for federal purposes.[60] The REAL ID Act requires state motor vehicle department officials to adhere to minimum federal standards regarding issuance and identity verification for driver's license and identification card applicants. This requirement includes the eventual use of a federal immigration database to determine whether applicants are lawfully present in the United States.[61]

The enactment of REAL ID by Congress has led to a flurry of legislative activity in the states on the subject of driver's licenses. Many states must enact new legislation and appropriate significant amounts of money to comply with the REAL ID Act's stringent issuance and verification standards. It has been estimated that implementation of the act will cost the states as much as $11 billion.[62] As of March 2006, at least sixty-six bills were pending in twenty-four different states that would have some effect on the ability of non-U.S. citizens to obtain driver's licenses.[63]

Policy Considerations

The debates over the federal government's efforts to enlist the help of state and local law enforcement in enforcing immigration law and in applying federal eligibility and issuance standards for state-issued driver's licenses have involved related, if not identical issues. In both instances, the purpose and effect of these initiatives—like their precursors in the early 1990s—would be to make immigration status more salient on a day-to-day basis. The initiatives thus increase the likelihood that individuals other than federal immigration enforcement agents will directly engage in, or at minimum cooperate with, federal enforcement activities. In both instances, an unusual constellation of voices—including conservatives, libertarians, immigrant community and civil rights advocates, law enforcement organizations, and some state and local government officials themselves—has coalesced to criticize these initiatives. Their argument is that these initiatives distort and potentially undermine important state and local policy priorities, with little, if any, corresponding gain in national security.

Proponents of these initiatives have emphasized the importance of supplementing the federal government's limited immigration enforcement resources with the considerably more extensive resources of state and local governments. For example, while there are only a few thousand federal immigration enforcement agents, there are well over seven hundred thousand state and local police officers nationwide. Proponents characterize this much larger pool of enforcement officials as a potential "force multiplier" whose use would result in more effective immigration enforcement and, they argue, greater security. They also contend that state and local police are in a better position to enforce the immigration laws, given their knowledge of local communities.[64] Similarly, with respect to driver's licenses, proponents of restricting eligibility for non-U.S. citizens go well beyond the concerns expressed by the September 11 Commission. It emphasized the need to standardize and safeguard the integrity of state driver's license and identification cards, given their tremendous importance as the default means of establishing identity across a broad range of social contexts. REAL ID Act supporters argue instead that non-U.S. citizens who are unlawfully present should legitimately be hindered in their ability to engage in the full range of day-to-day activities that driver's licenses facilitate—including, for that matter, driving.[65] As with the use of state and local police, the implicit goal and apparent result would be to make immigration status—and unlawful presence—more salient on a day-to-day basis in situations in which it currently is not. Through the use of such policies, proponents hope not only to increase the number of undocumented immigrants who may be detected and deported but also to induce others to depart the country on their own. This is what immigration restrictionists refer to as "self-deportation." Proponents also hope that more restrictive policies will deter prospective migrants from entering or remaining in the United States illegally.[66]

Opponents have criticized these initiatives from a variety of perspectives.[67] In the spring of 2006, hundreds of thousands of people—including U.S. citizens and both documented and undocumented non-U.S. citizens, from many different racial and ethnic backgrounds—took to the streets en masse. They demonstrated in favor of legalization and against the enforcement-driven approaches to immigration reform advocated by many in Congress.[68]

With respect to the use of state and local police in particular, immigrant community advocates and community leaders have raised rights-based concerns about the potential for racial profiling and violations of due process. Given how complicated immigration law can be, these advocates argue, state and local police whose primary responsibilities involve completely different objectives will likely find it difficult to properly ascertain the immigration status of individuals whom they encounter. For example, as Gerald Neuman has noted, "'[i]llegal alien' gestures toward a concept of noncompliance with law, but [immigration] law is more complex than most politicians and voters realize. There are different manners in which an alien's presence could be said to violate the law, and there are different forms of curative government action that may impart degrees of legality to the alien's presence."[69] Some states and localities that have implemented immigration-related laws on their own are already wrestling with these sorts of complexities.[70] Unschooled in these intricacies, state and local law officials may resort all too quickly in some cases, whether consciously or unconsciously, to racial and national origin profiling rooted in stereotypes, in direct violation of state law.[71] Indeed, evidence suggests that even federal immigration officials themselves—who are trained to understand the immigration laws and whose sole responsibility is immigration enforcement—have engaged in racial profiling of this sort.[72]

Even if the conduct of state and local officials were no worse than that of their federal counterparts, the negative consequences could be more significant, given the broader set of responsibilities of state and local governments within immigrant communities. Advocates and community leaders have noted with concern that members of immigrant communities may be discouraged from cooperating with police (for example, if they are crime victims or witnesses) and other local institutions if they perceive those institutions to be in the business of federal immigration enforcement. Preliminary research suggests that this concern may be well founded.[73] In other instances, it has been reported that individual officers have used the threat of deportation as a means of intimidating non-U.S. citizens.[74]

State and local government officials have themselves echoed these same concerns. Police have emphasized in recent years the importance, when seeking to protect public safety, of building and maintaining trust and cooperation with immigrant communities. They face a number of barriers in creating that sense of trust—not least of which is the fear within immigrant communities that cooperating with the police might lead to deportation.[75] The baseline level of trust of the police in some immigrant communities is frequently quite low to begin with. Those individuals may have had negative experiences with the police in their home countries. There may be language and cultural barriers. Some evidence suggests that in jurisdictions where local police have become involved in immigration enforcement, police-community relationships have suffered even further as a result.[76] The recent federal initiatives to enlist state and local law enforcement in immigration enforcement matters also have come at a time when local and state governments have been forced to bear significant costs associated with other federal homeland security initiatives. At the same time, federal funding that previously had been granted to localities to fund the hiring of new police officers and fight violent crime has been shrinking dramatically.[77] In this context, some state and local officials have acutely sensed that the imposition of federal immigration enforcement responsibilities upon them would constitute an unfunded mandate. It would have the potential to improperly "commandeer" state and local institutions for federal policy purposes that are unrelated to—and indeed, may undermine—the core criminal justice and public safety objectives that state and local law enforcement agencies are charged to advance.[78]

Critics have also questioned the extent to which involving state and local police in routine immigration enforcement represents an effective means of protecting national security at all. They note that beyond the potential distortion of state and local law enforcement priorities, devoting scarce law enforcement resources to large-scale immigration enforcement efforts simply multiplies the "haystacks" in which police must search for those "needles" who pose the most serious national security threats. Instead, these critics argue, state and local police cooperation should be tailored to focus more narrowly on those particular individuals and groups who pose the greatest threats to public safety. They argue that immigration status alone is neither a necessary nor a sufficient proxy for that purpose.[79] Moreover, Dan Richman and others have noted that transforming local police into "a potential source of personal ruin" in the eyes of many within immigrant communities would be counterproductive. The federal government's efforts to delegate ordinary immigration enforcement responsibilities would "in all likelihood result in a net intelligence loss" of information relevant to potential terrorism and other serious crimes.[80]

With respect to the limitation of eligibility for driver's licenses, critics have sounded similar notes of concern. Critics have emphasized that the principal purpose for states in issuing driver's licenses is not to create a document to be used as a form of federal identification. It is rather to ensure that state residents are qualified to drive and possess automobile insurance. By rendering millions of non-U.S. citizens ineligible for driver's licenses, critics argue, the REAL ID Act may make roads less safe and increase insurance rates. Many non-U.S. citizens would likely drive even without a valid license because they need to do so in order to work. At the same time, individuals in immigrant communities who are legitimately eligible for driver's licenses may be discouraged from applying for them.[81] Moreover, like state and local police, state motor vehicle department officials have no particular immigration expertise and will thus find it difficult to make proper eligibility determinations. And as discussed earlier, the implementation of the REAL ID Act will require state governments to expend tremendous sums of money to fulfill federal immigration policy objectives that have nothing to do with their own policy purposes.[82]

Critics have also questioned whether denying non-U.S. citizens driver's licenses represents sound security policy. Taking millions of undocumented non-U.S. citizens out of state motor vehicle databases dramatically increases the numbers of people living "in the shadows," without any government agencies having information about their presence. This may make the tasks of law enforcement and identification of individuals who may be security threats more difficult, not easier.[83] Critics point out that it is not necessary to restrict noncitizen eligibility to ensure the integrity and reliability of the identification documents that states issue. At the same time, committed terrorists scarcely need driver's licenses to board aircraft, since any number of other identification documents can suffice, including U.S. or foreign passports.[84]

Immigration and the Liberty-Enhancing Potential of Federalism

The post–September 11 efforts to involve state and local officials in federal immigration enforcement activities—and the responses to these initiatives—raise questions about the appropriate model of federalism upon which U.S. immigration law should rest. These efforts also raise questions about the continued strength of traditional doctrinal assumptions concerning the appropriate role for state and local governments in the regulation of immigration. Given the persistence of non-U.S. citizens' vulnerability to hostility and abuse at the hands of state and local governments, the traditional presumption in favor of exclusive federal regulation and enforcement of immigration status retains tremendous force.[85]

Still, this perspective may be incomplete. As scholars of U.S. federalism have discussed, the importance of federalism is not simply its role in advancing and facilitating values associated with any decentralized system of administration—such as the promotion of public participation, citizen choice, efficiency, and experimentation. Its importance instead lies in the establishment of multiple centers of power with the capacity to exert independent checks upon the power of the national government.[86] Subfederal institutions accordingly can play significant roles in the protection of liberty. They can do

so as focal points for the expression of political opposition to national policies, as "seedbeds for political change" at the national level, as sources of alternative and potentially broader conceptions of federal rights, and as potentially
moderating influences on the federal actors who seek their cooperation.[87]

This liberty-enhancing potential may be particularly important when a
strong national government itself needs to be checked or fails to protect liberties sufficiently.[88] Legislative and judicial developments during the past fifteen years have enhanced the power of state governments. This has occurred
through the imposition of substantive and procedural limits on Congress's
legislative authority, limits on the ability to subject state governments to suit
in federal court, restrictions on the ability of the federal government to
"commandeer" state government institutions for federal policy objectives,
and the shift of decision making to the states in certain policy areas. As a result, the capacity of state and local governments to play this counterbalancing role may be greater than it previously had been, at least with respect to
some policy areas.[89]

Discussions of immigration and federalism have inadequately accounted
for these potentially liberty-enhancing dimensions of federalism and (to a
somewhat lesser extent) localism.[90] A number of scholars in recent years have
explored the potential roles that state and local governments might play in
immigration regulation and enforcement, either on their own or pursuant to
delegations of power by the federal government.[91] Others have discussed the
ways in which federalism can facilitate the recognition of multiple identities
and affiliations through overlapping conceptions of citizenship in both federal and subfederal political communities.[92] By contrast, comparatively little
emphasis has been placed on the myriad ways in which state and local governments might actively play a role in protecting the rights and liberties of
non-U.S. citizens. More specifically, this active role would be *resisting* potential abuse of non-U.S. citizen residents by the federal government.[93]

And yet, the increasing aggressiveness of the federal government in its
regulation and enforcement of immigration and citizenship status makes the
liberty-enhancing role of state and local governments potentially more
salient.[94] The status of non-U.S. citizens as "citizens" of those state and local
communities is relevant here. Though often discussed as if it were a unitary
concept, citizenship encompasses a range of discrete institutions and practices, both formal and informal.[95] As Linda Bosniak has noted, non-U.S. citizens are not "entirely outside the scope of those institutions and practices and
experience we call citizenship."[96] On the contrary, non-U.S. citizens can and
often do engage in a broad range of citizenship-like practices at the state and
local levels. Non-U.S. citizens bear the same rights, exercise the same respon-

sibilities, and engage in the same participatory practices within state and local communities as any other state or local residents. They do so without regard to their formal immigration or citizenship status under federal law. This is true to varying extents within many state and local communities—and at least to some minimal extent within *all* state and local communities.

In some instances, this citizenship-like status at the state or local level may even be *formally* recognized as a matter of state or local law. Some recent discussions of subfederal citizenship have emphasized dimensions of citizenship other than its formal legal status. However, the divided nature of sovereignty in the United States means that the formal, legal dimension of state citizenship—formal membership in the political community of a particular state—remains a potentially significant category within which to understand the rights and privileges available to non-U.S. citizens.[97] State citizenship for non-U.S. citizens could not lawfully justify state efforts to block or interfere directly with the enforcement of federal immigration law; this is due to the supremacy of federal law under the U.S. Constitution. And under the Citizenship Clause of the Fourteenth Amendment, state governments are not constitutionally permitted to *deny* state citizenship to individuals who are U.S. citizens.[98] However, in particular policy areas, states may retain some ability to affirmatively *grant* state citizenship to non-U.S. citizen residents. Less formally, they may retain some ability to define affirmatively the nature of their relationships with all state residents without regard to U.S. citizenship or immigration status. This would occur, for example, when states implement laws of general applicability that have been adopted in the exercise of their traditional police powers to protect the health and safety of their communities.[99]

The extent to which states and localities might be able or willing to incorporate non-U.S. citizens into their political communities in any meaningful way as "citizens," or to play the role of resisting potential abuses by the federal government, at this point remains difficult to assess. This ability or willingness may depend upon the context: in some states and localities non-U.S. citizens may fare better, while in others they may fare worse. However, some states and localities manifestly are doing so already. In some cases this is taking place through policies of general applicability, while in others, through policies designed specifically to incorporate non-U.S. citizens as members of state and local communities. As Peter Schuck has observed, it already is the case that some states and localities "embrace legal aliens at least as warmly as the federal government does."[100] Even immigration restrictionists at times have complained that "it is the states and local governments that are rolling out the welcome mat for illegal aliens once they are here."[101]

For example, as Rebecca Smith, Amy Sugimori, and Luna Yasui have observed, states often have "latitude to act in areas that are as yet subject only to state regulation, and to offer benefits and protections beyond what the federal government has made available."[102] Accordingly, some states and localities have acted to protect the rights of their non-U.S. citizen residents to an extent greater than the federal government in a number of policy areas. These areas include equal employment and labor rights, language access and confidentiality protections for non-U.S. citizens seeking government benefits and services, and eligibility for workers' compensation benefits.[103] Similarly, in the aftermath of Congress's devolution to the states of authority to determine non-U.S. citizen eligibility for certain categories of welfare benefits, some states have continued to provide immigrants with these benefits to a considerable extent. This has occurred particularly (though not exclusively) in states with large non-U.S. citizen populations.[104] At least ten states have extended eligibility for in-state college and university tuition rates to undocumented, non-U.S. citizens.[105] In December 2006, Illinois announced plans to implement a comprehensive set of initiatives spanning a range of different policy areas. These initiatives were designed to improve integration of immigrants within the state by improving language access to state agencies, increasing resources for English education programs, providing job training, and ensuring access to health care, education, and other state services without regard to immigration status.[106] Some states and localities have even extended political rights to non-U.S. citizens.[107]

These political and legal skirmishes over the federal government's burgeoning efforts to involve state and local governments in federal immigration enforcement activities provide a vivid illustration of these dynamics. On the one hand, as discussed above, non-U.S. citizens who have opposed these initiatives, in partnership with U.S. citizens and community organizations, have engaged in citizen-like political action. In some contexts they have been recognized as legitimate, citizen-like political actors.[108] In turn, states and localities that have opposed these initiatives have in effect asserted the right to implement their traditional police powers to protect the health and safety of their communities through laws of general applicability. They have done so without regard to the U.S. citizenship or immigration status of the residents within their communities. Notably, such opposition by states and localities has not always or necessarily been driven by an explicit goal of protecting the rights of non-U.S. citizens as such. Rather, their efforts have been animated in many cases by concern that the incorporation of federal immigration policy objectives would grossly interfere with their ability to advance the welfare of their citizenries as a whole.[109]

On the other hand, by aggressively pushing state and local governments to incorporate federal immigration enforcement activities into their day-to-day work, the federal initiatives discussed here challenge the potential salience of state citizenship altogether. This is true insofar as they seek to extend and impose the institutions and standards for federal citizenship upon state and local communities seeking to protect and advance the welfare of their own citizenries. By asserting the predominance of federal over state and local policy objectives, these enforcement initiatives in effect seek to diminish any independent significance that state and local citizenship-like institutions might have.

"Denationalized" Citizenship and the Changing State-Federal Equilibrium

The debates over the role of state and local governments in the regulation and enforcement of federal immigration status illustrate what Saskia Sassen has termed the partial "denationalization" of formal national citizenship in the wake of globalization. By "denationalization," Sassen is not referring to the supplanting of national citizenship altogether by new forms of "postnational" citizenship existing "outside the confines of the national." Denationalization refers instead to a transformation of national citizenship itself, in a manner that "remains deeply connected to the national, as constructed historically, and is indeed profoundly imbricated with it but is so on historically new terms of engagement."[110] As the role of the national state changes, notes Sassen, the possibility has emerged for "new forms of power [to be exercised] at the subnational level."[111] In resisting federal efforts to enlist subfederal institutions in immigration enforcement activities, non-U.S. citizens and state and local governments are seeking to exercise the "new forms of power" that Sassen identifies.

As Sassen recognizes, however, national citizenship itself remains important, and the extent to which these processes will in fact result in greater subnational power over immigration and citizenship remains highly uncertain.[112] Denationalization may indeed make state and local citizenship more salient, as some scholars have tentatively suggested. It may create spaces for state and local governments to exercise power on behalf of their non-U.S. citizen residents against potential encroachments by federal authorities. However, the U.S. experience in any number of policy areas since the New Deal makes clear that Washington, relying upon various degrees of coercion and cooperation, has often been successful in its efforts to enlist state and local institutions in implementing federal policy objectives. It has done so when political will and leverage at the federal level has been sufficiently strong.[113]

It is too early to tell whether the federal government will prevail in its ef-

forts to incorporate state and local institutions in its immigration enforcement efforts. However, even if the assertion of federal predominance over
state and local prerogatives ultimately succeeds, these incipient processes of
denationalization may yet play a role in shaping the form that those federal
enforcement initiatives ultimately take. Even if successfully induced to cooperate in federal immigration enforcement activities, many states and localities
will continue to recognize the critical importance of fully integrating and
maintaining strong relationships with their non-U.S. citizen residents. They
may need to do so in order to implement fundamentally important policies
designed to protect and promote the health and safety of *all* of their residents—whether U.S. citizens or non-U.S. citizens, documented or undocumented. In an era in which the power of the federal government may be
diminishing, and the power of subfederal institutions correspondingly increasing, states and localities may retain sufficient influence to ensure that
federal authorities are attentive to these imperatives. Over time, therefore, any
cooperative equilibrium that ultimately emerges between federal and subfederal authorities with respect to immigration enforcement may yet incorporate
these state and local concerns in some manner and to a significant extent.[114]

11

Immigration, Security, and Integration in the European Union

ARIANE CHEBEL D'APPOLLONIA

A series of paradoxes illustrates the evolution of immigration policy in Europe. First, European governments and, to a larger extent, public opinion support policies designed to lower overall immigration levels. But immigration is crucial to Europe for demographic and economic reasons. According to the UN's Population Division, the population of the EU is projected to decline by forty-one million between 2005 and 2050.[1] The contribution of immigrants to sustaining the size of the labor force and the solvency of European welfare systems is therefore crucial.

The second paradox is related to the ambivalent immigration policies implemented for the last twenty years at the national level and, since the mid-1990s, at the EU level. While focusing on lowering overall immigration levels in order to stabilize resident foreign populations, European governments allowed family reunification, which encouraged immigrants to adapt to their new host society. Yet national governments largely neglected to improve the "social engineering" of integration. The main results were restrictive immigration policies unable to curb legal immigration and unanticipated flows of asylum seekers and refugees, inefficient (if not ineffective) integration policies for existing minority groups, and the politicization of "immigration issues" fueled by anti-migrant groups.

The third paradox, which today raises the most urgent concerns, is the result of the prior incoherence that has characterized national and European immigration policies. EU member states were so obsessed by the regulation of immigration flows that they neglected to consider what needs to happen after immigration: the management of migrant stocks in order to enhance their integration. The issue of integration goes far beyond the regulation of immigration and asylum policy, as illustrated by the London bombings of 2005. These terrorist attacks have generated a new catchphrase for frequent use in the media and a new priority for national policy agendas: the "enemy inside." This "enemy" not only lives in Europe but is itself European. The "others" are apparently among "us." Tony Blair's reaction to the bombings was symptomatic of the inadequacy that today characterizes the post-immigration process. Blair condemned immigrants who refuse to "share and support the values that sustain the British way of life" and who do not "have a rudimentary grasp of the English language." The broad Yorkshire accent heard in the suicide video of one of the terrorists who carried out the London bombing sounded like an ironic illustration of the presumed success of the "British multicultural model." Similarly, during the urban riots that took place in France in November 2005, Nicolas Sarkozy suggested new limitations on immigration, with no reference to the spatial segregation and poor housing conditions that ethnic groups in France endure.

Two maxims could summarize the combined effects of these three paradoxes: "more security creates more insecurity" and "more security leads to fewer civil liberties." As I argue in this chapter, there is strong evidence that European governments have become singularly obsessed with the task of controlling their external borders. As a result they have been distracted from addressing a deep-rooted origin of insecurity: the failure to effectively integrate immigrants and nationals of foreign origin into their national societies. Current national and EU policies are dysfunctional; they do not actually strengthen either internal or external security. Furthermore, in implementing these policies, governmental authorities have unintentionally encouraged discriminatory attitudes and introduced measures that have eroded the civil and human rights of asylum seekers, immigrants, and their descendants. This trend, in turn, undermines integration and fuels terrorist recruitment.

Facing new terrorist threats, European governments are still more inclined to strengthen security measures than to admit that they are unable to address the dilemmas posed by the so-called second and third generation of immigrants. These are the immigrant descendants who are predominantly nationals—by birth or by acquisition—in many EU countries. Yet the issue of integration encompasses not only the "immigration problem" but also issues that are at the very heart of European societies. Integration does concern immigrants, especially the "newcomers," but it also affects nationals. What happens today is obviously the result of prior immigration policies, but responses to the current problems should not be limited to adjustments of immigration policy. Integration focuses on what happens after immigration and must be distinguished from immigration policy per se. As Gilles Kepel, the French academic, wrote, "neither the blood spilled by Muslims from North Africa fighting in French uniforms during both world wars nor the sweat of migrant laborers, living under deplorable living conditions, who re-built France (and Europe) for a pittance after 1945, has made their children full fellow citizens."[2] In response to Blair's plan, Trevor Phillips (chair of the Commission for Racial Equality) argued that integration "will prove to be our best defense against the extremists' assaults." He further noted that "it is a disgrace that in 2003 there were fewer ethnic minority people on public bodies than previously, and that in 2004 there were fewer local councilors than in 2001."[3]

In this chapter I provide a critical analysis of the "communautarization" of immigration policies in Europe and examine the mix of both its inclusive and exclusive components. Inclusion refers to all measures guaranteeing the fundamental rights of Europe's citizens (country nationals and broader EU nationals), which are designed to ensure fair treatment for non-EU citizens legally resident in Europe. By contrast, exclusive measures are intended to ensure that distinctions remain between nationals and "foreigners." This categorization varies from one country to another and is based on objective or legal factors and the subjective perception of foreigners (ranging from a view of their "otherness" to a view of foreigners as "scapegoats" for the ills of society). From a theoretical perspective, my approach in this chapter combines elements from the two dominant schools of thought. One is globalist or postnational theory, and the other is state-centered theory. Synthesizing them in this way allows an evaluation of EU immigration policy along a continuum ranging from intergovernmentalism to supranationalism. While these theories mainly focus on the nation-states, using this tool allows me to answer the main question addressed in this study: "What are the main consequences of the recent constitution of an immigration and anti-discrimination 'policy domain' at the EU level, not only for member states but also for immigrants, in terms of status and perceptions?"

I also analyze the EU's contribution to the emergence of a new anti-discrimination framework, arguing that EU immigration policy in itself does not encourage discrimination. It has, however, institutionalized the exclusive trends imposed by member states. In addition, the anti-discrimination framework has been too limited to balance the prejudices embedded in the "securitization" of immigration and asylum issues.

This chapter also addresses the integration debate revived by recent terrorist threats. So far, the EU is far from having articulated a coherent and comprehensive policy in this field. At the national level, governments have envisaged and applied only anti-terrorist measures. In practice, they risk applying policies that are detrimental to the integration of ethnic minorities but are unrelated to terrorism. On the basis of the recent challenges posed by the expanded notions of "internal security," we are developing a clear idea of how immigration policies have been affected by national security interests. We are also learning how immigration has affected national security concerns. What we urgently need, however, is to study how the issue of "internal security" is going to affect the definition and implementation of integration policy in the near future.

The Social Construction of Immigration as a Security Issue

The perception of immigration in the EU is usually based on opposing stereotypical assumptions. On one side, European immigration and asylum policy is perceived as being too restrictive and that the building of a "Fortress Europe" has been detrimental to immigrants. On the other, European immigration and asylum policy is depicted as being too liberal, if not lax. In this view, EU policy has led to growth in the number of legal or illegal immigrants and "bogus" asylum seekers, all of whom threaten internal security, national identities, and social cohesion. The truth is that these contradictory assumptions are both simplistic and yet relevant. A more sophisticated understanding of the current situation suggests that all the major components of the "area of freedom, security, and justice" (AFSJ) must be studied. This study must be at the empirical level—examining the dynamics of inclusion and exclusion that have supported the gradual emergence of this new framework. The evaluation of both of these aspects of the AFSJ needs to pay attention to the ways, and to the timing by which, European integration has accommodated national and EU interests.

The shift from national policies to intergovernmental cooperation, and from intergovernmental cooperation to supranationalism, took place in three stages. In the first, from the mid-1970s to the mid-1980s, immigration policies were designed and implemented exclusively by the member states. Then, from the mid-1980s to the mid-1990s, national governments began to coordinate their policies with the intergovernmental Schengen Agreement. The third stage was initiated by the Maastricht Treaty and the Treaty of Amsterdam. These treaties gave the EU competence over immigration, visa, and asylum policy. The changes initiated during each stage were motivated by differing but interrelated goals: to achieve "zero immigration," to implement the single market, and to strengthen external border controls. The rationale behind each goal contributed to the securitization of immigration as an issue. Immigrants were first perceived to be threatening, to be competitors for jobs and the likely recipients of social benefits. They were subsequently accused of perverting national identity and mounting a challenge to social cohesion. With the subsequent blurring of the distinction between immigrants and terrorists, the third stage then further aggravated the exclusionary dimension of the AFSJ. More detailed descriptions of these three historic phases follow.

Phase 1 (from the mid-1970s to the mid-1980s)

From the late 1970s onward, the goals of both curbing illegal immigration and asylum applications and stopping the recruitment of migrant workers were shared by countries with historically different immigration policies and with contrasting conceptions of migrants and minority groups.[4] Similar restrictive measures were implemented in various countries to limit immigration flows and encourage repatriation. These measures affected the arrival, admission, and entitlements of immigrants and asylum seekers. They also included new visa requirements, sanctions on companies responsible for the arrival of "undocumented aliens," new measures to reject "economic migrants" and "bogus" asylum seekers, broader powers of detention, and new provisions for expulsion.

The main argument used to justify these new restrictive measures was a recent spike in unemployment. But there were clear signs that concerns over the social and political costs associated with immigration had been growing for several years. Indeed, most restrictions on immigration were passed during periods of relatively low unemployment, as illustrated by the British and Dutch cases. Political concerns had actually played a more important role. For example, the British Nationality Act of 1981 was largely motivated by the evolution of Britain's relationship with the New Commonwealth and by the increasing number of Hong Kong Chinese who demanded the right of residency in the UK prior to the colony's transfer to China. The debate over British national identity also influenced immigration controls, notably after the urban riots of 1980–1981, which involved many immigrants. In France, the Netherlands, Austria, and Germany, the politicization of immigration issues was mainly the result of the emergence of anti-immigrant parties. These included the Nederlandse Volks Unie or Dutch People's Union (NVU) and the Centrumpartij or Center Party (CP) in the Netherlands, the Front National (FN) in France, and the Republikaners in Germany.

If the common objectives were to restrict migration, the means adopted were both exclusionary and inclusive. In the UK, the exclusionary effects of the Immigration Act of 1971 and the British Nationality Act of 1981 were balanced by new inclusive measures in the field of anti-discrimination. An example would be the Race Relations Act of 1976. It prohibited discrimination on "racial grounds" (race, color, nationality, ethnic, or national origins) and established the Commission for Racial Equality (CRE) to promote and enforce the legislation.[5] In 1984, this commission introduced the Code of Practice for Eliminating Racial Discrimination. In the Netherlands, the Law on Foreign Workers (1976) and the Act on the Employment of Foreign Workers (1978) were complemented by new legislation primarily oriented toward equal treatment. In 1985 the Independent National Bureau against Racist Discrimination was created. In France, new restrictive measures designed to limit access to citizenship were counterbalanced by the creation of the Social Action Fund (FAS) for immigrants and their families.

The coexistence of exclusionary and inclusive measures produced ambivalent results for migrants and minority groups. In Germany, for example, the government gave preference to the social integration of the second- and third-generation immigrants in the early 1980s. At the same time, it stated the need for immigrants to maintain strong ties with their countries of origins in order to facilitate repatriation and maintained a very restrictive citizenship policy. German policy was also ambiguous with regard to the issues of family reunification and to the right of family members to find employment. Policy alternated between restrictive (1974–1979, 1982) and liberal (1979–1981) modes. In Italy, Spain, and Portugal, restrictive measures alternated with regularization programs.[6]

There were two main results of these "stop-and-go" policies at the European level. First, they were unable to curb either legal or illegal immigration or to regulate the flow of asylum seekers. In Europe, the aggregate number of immigrants rose by 4.1 million in the 1980s, reaching 26.3 million in 1990. Some countries were more affected than others. In Italy, for example, the number of foreigners increased from 183,000 in 1980 to 781,000 in 1990. The objective of achieving "zero immigration" was not feasible, having been undermined by contradictory trends. European states had to cope with unpredictable migrant flows after the end of the Cold War as Western Europe received a growing number of applications for asylum from citizens of Eastern and Central European countries. Furthermore, European states faced the issue of family reunification. Denmark, France, and Sweden, for example, admitted between 50 and 70 percent of their long-term immigrants on that basis. However, the combination of the immigration of non–EU nationals, family reunification, and their natural increase raised the number of ethnic minorities everywhere. With the sources of immigrants growing ever more diverse, European societies became increasingly multiethnic. In France, for example, the number of North Africans tripled between 1982 and 1990. The gross figures illustrating these trends are listed in table 11.1.

The second result was the mounting sense of an "immigration problem," which fueled the politicization of immigration issues in a context characterized by growing debates over national identity. An upsurge in racism and xenophobia followed. This trend was first noted by the Evrigenis Report of 1985 and confirmed by the Ford Report of 1990. Resentment among natives to old and new immigrant communities alike increased during the 1980s despite all the restrictive immigration measures. The transformation of immigration into a security issue was fueled by the idea that immigrants posed a threat to social cohesion. Urban problems, such as violence, segregation, and "ghettoization," were subsequently connected to "immigration issues," with reference to the most visible signs of social and spatial dysfunctions ("inner-city riots" in the UK, the "*crise des banlieues*" or crisis of the suburbs in France). Despite the fact that immigration was mainly an urban phenomenon, neither the EU nor its member states addressed these twin issues in a coherent or concerted way for many years. While the linkages among immigration, discrimination, and urbanization were partially acknowledged, the specific needs and problems of immigrants were often ignored. Only five of the fifteen member states (Denmark, France, Ireland, the Netherlands, and the UK) had a national area–based urban policy when the URBAN program was introduced by the EU in 1994.

Phase 2 (from the mid-1980s to the mid-1990s)

Increasingly aware of their inability to regulate immigration, European states agreed to coordinate their actions through the initiatives introduced in

Table 11.1
Population by citizenship groups in the EU 15 (by million)

	Nationals	EU nationals	Non–EU nationals
1985	344.9	5.2	8.4
1990	348.9	5.5	9.4
1995	353.5	5.8	12.3

Source: EU Commission, European Social Statistics, Migration, 2002, 25.

the Schengen Agreements and the Dublin Convention.[7] In anticipation of the Single European Act, the first agreement between the five original members (the Benelux countries, France, and Germany) was signed in June 1985 and was subsequently extended to include every member state.[8]

Two major trends characterized this period. First, prior restrictive national policies were reinforced by the new provisions introduced by the Schengen Agreements. The need to ensure the free movement of workers within the Single Market generated a debate about the meaning of the concept of "free movement of persons." The introduction of new external border checks therefore compensated for the suppression of internal border checks. As a result, during this decade, EU policy reflected and refracted some of the most pressing immigration-related political issues and transferred to the European level the exclusionary aspects of the national policies of belonging.

The second major trend of this period—long before September 11, 2001—was the "securitization" of immigration issues. In order to reconcile freedom and security, the freedom of movement was accompanied by compensatory measures designed to improve cooperation between the police, customs, and the judiciary. These measures included activities intended to combat terrorism and organized crime. Cooperation in the field of Justice and Home Affairs (JHA) led to the creation of Europol, which became operational in 1999, and the implementation of the Grotius Program. This increasing amalgamation of immigration and security issues (such as drug smuggling, organized crime, and terrorism) fueled discrimination and encouraged extreme right-wing propaganda activities. To a great extent, this period constituted the dark ages of integration and anti-discrimination.

National governments introduced new provisions regarding both immigration and access to citizenship. In Italy, for example, legislation was amended after the admission to "Schengenland." During this period, the average Italian's attitude toward non-EU immigrants was characterized by the absence of a sense of social obligation and a claim for differential treatment. Immigrants were needed but not welcome and were still perceived as "foreigners." The imposition of income requirements as a prerequisite for resident status (which could be revoked) contributed to the uncertain status of legal immigrants. In the UK, the government imposed new visa requirements, introduced limitations to both family reunification and the right of appeal against deportation, and created restrictions on welfare benefits and public housing. Other restrictive measures converted asylum seekers into irregular migrants. In addition, the British Nationality Act (1981) introduced three types of citizenship in order to limit non-white immigration: British citizens, individuals with citizenship in the "British Dependent Territories," and people of

British descent. When Labour came back into power in 1997, it abolished several restrictive policies enacted by the Conservatives. However, the Immigration and Asylum Act (1999) limited asylum applicants to one appeal after rejection, extended carrier liability to truck drivers, and sought to disperse asylum seekers around the country while their claims were being considered. In France and the Netherlands, the restrictive regulations on immigration were accompanied by a reform of the conditions governing access to citizenship. The liberalization of naturalization policy, introduced by the Dutch government in 1984, was limited by a new law on family reunification in 1993. Further measures followed in 1994 and 1996. The French government reformed its nationality code in 1993, and the Pasqua laws and the Chevène-ment law followed. Germany also amended its constitution and revised its asylum policy, preserving a constitutional right to asylum but instituting new regulations that severely restricted its application. In 1994, stricter border controls were applied and Kurds were deported from Germany with the approval of the Supreme Court.

Despite the introduction of new restrictive intergovernmental measures, the number of asylum applicants in Europe continued to grow. The number of applications peaked in 1992, and after a period of decline it increased again between 1997 and 1999 (see table 11.2).

Legal experts expressed three concerns about asylum policy. The new arrangements restricted asylum seekers' access to a fair hearing of their case (in violation of the Geneva Refugee Convention [1951]). Also, the concept of "safe country" (designed to permit states to return asylum seekers without strictly violating the non-refoulement provision in international refugee law) remained contested. This dispute occurred because the criteria by which they defined a "safe country" were controversial. The British government, for example, put Sri Lanka and Nigeria—with their record of human rights abuses—on the list of "safe countries." The notion of "safe *third* country" (the last through which asylum seekers had transited and to which they could be returned for processing) was also unclear. This concept created the potential for a growing number of "chain deportations" or "refugees in orbit," to use Gil

Table 11.2
Asylum applicants in the EU 15 (per 1,000 population)

	1985–89	1990–94	1995–99	1996	1997	1998	1999	2000
EU 15	211.7	491.4	275.9	227.8	242.8	295.5	352.2	363.1

Source: EU Commission, European Social Statistics, Migration, 2002, 24.

Loescher's terminology. Furthermore, many asylum seekers traveling from states sharing borders with the EU faced a *cordon sanitaire* or buffer zone. The EU had asked the Visegrad Group to establish this zone in order to protect Western European nations against a flood of refugees from Eastern Europe.

Net migration slightly decreased after 1992. Yet the number of EU nationals and non-EU nationals in all EU member states steadily increased between 1985 and 1995 (see table 11.3).

Meanwhile, the total number of people acquiring citizenship in the EU member states more than doubled during the 1990s, from almost 200,000 in 1990 to about 475,000 in 1999. During that decade, more than 3 million people acquired citizenship in an EU member state. In some countries, a large majority of them were non-EU nationals. Largely ignoring statistics, the media and some political parties increased the public's confusion about the difference between immigrants (illegal and legal) and asylum seekers. They also blurred the public's view of the actual composition of minority groups legally resident in the EU territory (third country nationals [TCNs] or "foreigners" naturalized by birth or by acquisition). Attitudes toward immigrants and refugees remained hostile. Many were viewed as "bogus," that is, economic migrants trying to circumvent controls on labor migration, or were depicted as illegal immigrants. An EU survey conducted in 1997 showed a worrying level of racism and xenophobia in member states, with nearly 33 percent of those interviewed openly describing themselves as "quite racist" or "very racist." Forty-five percent considered that there were "too many people from minority groups living in their country"; 53 percent said that "in schools where there are too many children from these minority groups, the quality of education suffers." In addition, 59 percent believed that "minorities abuse the system of social benefits," and 63 percent said that "the presence of people from these minority groups increases unemployment."[9]

Efforts at intergovernmental cooperation proved unable to resolve the so-

Table 11.3
Net migration in the EU 15 (per 1,000 population)

1992	3.6
1993	2.8
1994	2.0
1995	2.0
1996	1.9
1997	1.3

Source: EU Commission, European Social Statistics, Migration, 2002, 19.

called immigration problem. Moreover, the "securitization" of immigration and asylum policies aggravated the negative effects of the politicization of the debate over the "threats" to national identity posed by migrant communities in member states. As Jef Huysmans explains, "in speaking of the migrant as a security problem, he/she becomes an actor in a security drama. . . . In this drama, there is always a risk that the interaction between the natives and the migrants turns to violence."[10]

Phase 3 (since the mid-1990s)

Under the terms of the new framework provided by the Maastricht Treaty, subsequently modified by the Treaty of Amsterdam, immigration has become an issue of common interest for the EU. This common interest in immigration can be seen in the creation of the new Area of Freedom, Security, and Justice (AFSJ). The Maastricht Treaty pronounced asylum policy to be among the matters of common interest to member states defined in Title VI (the "third pillar"). Then, the Treaty of Amsterdam included these issues in the EC Treaty (articles 61 to 69), intended to establish a common set of standards to be implemented. These standards include such things as controls at the Union's external borders, visa regulation, asylum policy, and immigration flows.[11] A protocol attached to the Treaty of Amsterdam incorporated the Schengen Acquis into the EU framework. Under the Treaty of Nice, visa, asylum, and immigration policy were to be decided mainly by the codecision procedure.[12]

The inclusive and exclusive aspects of the new EU framework entailed a comprehensive integration of the three main components of the AFSJ.[13] It combined the former immigration and asylum policies with both the old "security issues" and new "humanitarian" measures that were intended to balance the exclusionary effects of the "security issues." As a result, the AFSJ now has three distinctive features that explain the current perception of immigrants as a security threat.

First, the AFSJ reaffirms at the EU level the most restrictive controls on immigration and asylum policy previously imposed by the member states, notably in terms of protecting external borders and in addressing the threat of terrorism. This development is illustrated by a series of new institutional and policy initiatives. The first is the development of the Schengen Acquis with the second-generation Schengen Information System (SIS II). It operates in thirteen member states and two non-member states (Norway and Iceland). There are also new functions for the Schengen system in the fight against terrorism, based on a Spanish initiative in 2002.[14] A second initiative was the creation of the European Agency for the Management of External Borders.[15] Third were new visa requirements for TCNs and the establishment of a list of countries whose nationals must be in possession of a visa when crossing the external borders of the EU territory.[16] Fourth were the integration of biometric features in passports and travel documents and new airport transit arrangements.[17] The final initiative was the establishment of minimum standards for the conditions governing eligibility for refugee status or international protection.[18]

The securitization of immigration issues was subsequently strengthened by a series of measures adopted in the field of Justice and Home Affairs. The Council adopted a Joint Action in 1996 intended to create a directory of specialized counter-terrorism skills. The Action Plan of 1997, designed to combat organized crime, led to the creation of the European Judicial Network.

As Didier Bigo and Elspeth Guild suggest, these components of the AFSJ have collectively created a "new form of policing: policing at a distance. This policing in the name of freedom moves the locus of the controls and delocalizes them from the borders of the states to create new social borders both inside and outside of the territory, which is envisioned as a European territory."[19] Furthermore, the blurring of the distinction between "terrorist," asylum seeker, and immigrant raises fears that national security procedures now serve to regulate the flow of asylum applications—to the detriment of the fundamental rights of the applicants. Several cases before the Court of Justice have recently confirmed these fears. The case of *Segi and others v. The Council of the European Union,* for example, highlighted procedural abuses related to the registration of persons on the EU's 2004 anti-terrorism list. Another case, *Xhavara and others v. Albania and Italy,* concerned the deaths of a number of Albanians seeking to enter Italy by boat, one of which was intercepted and sunk. The EU Network on Independent Experts on Fundamental Rights analyzed the recent evolution of those rights in relation to the implementation of the internal market and the AFSJ. It then underscored the fact that "initiatives adopted in this area must be carefully monitored, especially insofar as they should not lead to deprive potential asylum seekers from having access to the procedure for the determination of their status as refugees."[20] Other concerns have been expressed about the scope and the implementation of the directive on the status of "refugees." Because of its new provisions on the revocation of refugee status, this directive increased both the risk of expulsion and the possibility of refoulement.[21]

Another feature of the AFSJ is the way in which it combines inclusive and exclusive measures in adjudicating and regulating the treatment of TCNs, asylum seekers, and refugees. The relevant exclusive measures include all the limitations imposed on non-EU nationals relating to freedom of movement for workers, resident permits, and family reunification. In 1994, for example, the member states agreed on a resolution concerning employment limitations affecting the admission of TCNs. Two years later, in 1996, they agreed on further limitations for the admission of self-employed persons. In other words, paradoxically, there would be no free movement for legal TCNs who had been given the right of admission and residence on the basis of their employment. That same year, the EU adopted a resolution on the status of TCNs residing on a long-term basis in the territory of the member states. TCNs had to prove that "they have been resided legally and without interruption in the territory of the Member State concerned for a period specified in the legislation of that Member State and, in any event, after 10 years."[22] In addition to the lengthier new residency requirement, this legislation did not include social assistance benefits. Restrictions on TCNs' admission, their skills, their movement, and their access to welfare provisions had begun piling up.

Among the most recent inclusive measures, a distinction must be made between asylum seekers and long-term legal residents (especially TCNs). The provisions of the process for granting asylum attempt to balance the restrictive effects of harmonization with a guarantee of fundamental rights.[23] So far, only a few measures specifically addressing such rights have been adopted, for example, common minimum standards on the reception of applicants for asylum in member states and the creation of the European Refugee Fund in 2000.[24] The situation of TCNs differs. While still being denied equal access to all rights, they tend to enjoy the same rights as EU nationals in some areas. In 2001, the EU Commission suggested that the conditions for entry and residence of TCNs should be liberalized.[25] A directive adopted in April 2004 granted residency permits to TCNs who are determined to be victims of human trafficking or who immigrated illegally but cooperate with the relevant authorities. Another example of an inclusive initiative was Directive 2004/83/EC of April 2004 (on minimum standards for the status of TCNs or stateless persons and refugees in need of international protection). The convergence in the treatment of EU nationals and TCNs was completed by a directive adopted in September 2003 on the right to family reunification. Once this directive was introduced into national legislation (with a deadline of October 2005), TCNs residing lawfully in the territory of member states were able to exercise the right to family reunification. Another directive, adopted in November 2003 and implemented by January 2006, modified the status of TCNs who had been long-term residents.[26] TCNs now benefit from having long-term resident status after five years of continuous legal residence but still have to prove that they have sufficient economic resources and medical insurance. Finally, access to social security benefits has been liberalized. New regulations on the application of social security schemes to employed persons and their families moving within the EU has been extended to include TCNs legally resident in a member state. This regulation ensures that all legal TCNs have the right to normal health care when they move to another member state.

An additional feature of the AFSJ is the varied status afforded to nationals, EU nationals, and TCNs in several areas. Under the terms of the Maastricht Treaty and successive regulations, nationals and EU nationals are EU citizens. As EU citizens, they enjoy comparable rights, such as the right to vote and to stand as a candidate in European elections, the freedom of movement, and equality before the law. The equal treatment of EU nationals has been enhanced as a result of a directive on the rights of citizens of the Union and their family members to move and reside freely within the territory of member states. The European Parliament and the Council adopted this directive in April 2004.[27] This directive also included the right to family reunification. In other fields, notably those of civic and political integration, however, the results were less widespread. EU citizenship was characterized by scholars such as Yasemin Nuhoğlu Soysal and Jürgen Habermas as the first step toward the emergence of a "postnational citizenship," a measure designed to facilitate the integration of certain "foreigners." This measure, however, affected only a tiny minority (4.5 million EU citizens, or 2 percent of the total voters in the EU 15) and excluded the vast majority of TCNs (8 million to 10 million) by creating a new ethnic barrier.

To date, the purported emergence of postnational citizenship has not served as a realistic avenue to integration. From the immigrant's perspective, access to citizenship has not guaranteed functional integration. Nationals of foreign origin are not protected against discrimination because they possess an identity card. Young members of ethnic groups, especially young Muslims, consequently feel that they are being treated as second-class citizens. Meanwhile, TCNs continue to be denied EU citizenship and their access to specific social and economic rights remains limited as a result of national legislation. Despite the liberalization of the status of TCNs who are long-term legal residents, member states are allowed to set ceilings restricting the number of permits issued. They also reserve the right to make special rules on employment access in the public sector or other activities connected with the exercise of official authority. Some categories of individuals are excluded from the scope of the 2003 directive for economic reasons. As a result, notes Elspeth Guild, "the poor who are most in need of security and support are those most likely to be excluded from the benefits" of the new legislation.[28]

The EU's Responses to "Immigration Issues" and Discrimination

What many studies have ignored is the relationship between the consolidation of the AFSJ and the most recent initiatives related to the integration of immigrants. As a result of the new provisions in the Amsterdam Treaty (articles 12 and 13), the Commission suggested new legislative proposals. These proposals included the Racial Equality Directive of June 2000 and the Employment Equality Directive of November 2000.[29] The former prohibited discrimination based on racial or ethnic origin. It would "apply to all persons, as regards both the public and private sectors, including public bodies" in broad areas (such as employment, education, access to goods and services, social protection, and social security).[30] The latter directive established a general framework for equal treatment in employment and occupation. Both directives draw a distinction between direct and indirect discrimination. Both also underscore the binding obligations of the member states to ensure that judicial and/or administrative procedures are available everywhere to all persons who consider themselves denied the principle of equal treatment. In addition to an expressed concern about effective enforcement, the second directive promoted both dialogue with nongovernmental organizations (NGOs) and the dissemination of information to the general public. It addressed the sensitive issue of the burden of proof because the defendant is responsible for proving that the principle of equal treatment has not been infringed. Each member state must also adopt measures to protect the plaintiff against retaliation. The Commission also suggested a third new element, the Community Action Program (2001–2006), adopted by the Council in November 2001 and intended to support and supplement the member states' efforts in combating discrimination.

Some countries went beyond the minimum standards set by the two directives and by article 13. Furthermore, in some member states there is a legal basis for other anti-discrimination initiatives, such as constitutional provisions dealing with equality and racial discrimination. In many member states, the fight against discrimination has been reinforced by new criminal laws and penal provisions combating racism. In some countries, such as France and the UK, racially motivated offenses are now regarded as being aggravated in nature, and the concept of "hate crimes" has been adopted. Additionally, the level of government consultation with representatives of social groups and NGOs was extended in countries such as Belgium, Denmark, the Netherlands, and the United Kingdom.

The adoption of new EU measures to fight discrimination might be regarded as a major improvement. According to Andrew Geddes, this initiative has opened a door for supranational legislation and created the opportunity for groups representing immigrant populations to gain access to the material and symbolic resources of the EU and to press for representation at the national level.[31] The Commission can also use its right of initiative with respect to new measures in the fight against discrimination. Such measures include those that are part of Title VI of TUE (article 29 refers to the prevention of racism and xenophobia) and Title IV of TCE (notably in the fields of asylum and immigration). Certainly, in advocating common solutions to common problems, this shift to action at the EU level is promising.

Europe's long-standing commitment to equal treatment is unquestionable. Unfortunately, the EU framework suffers from severe limitations at both the continental and national levels. The first limitation deals with the scope of the two directives passed in 2000, whose provisions do not address differences in treatment based on nationality. As a result, anti-discrimination legislation has become part of the EU's legal framework while rights for legally resident TCNs remain partially outside its scope. While not reluctant to extend rights to TCNs, unlike some member states, the EU is precluded from involvement in drafting the nationality laws of member states because of declarations attached to the Treaty of Amsterdam and the Maastricht Treaty. The two directives are consequently "without prejudice to provisions and conditions relating to the entry into and residence of TCNs and stateless persons on the territory of member states." This exclusion seems more anomalous when recalling that a key component of the EU's legal system is the right to "equal treatment." But, in this case, exercising the rights of EU citizenship is contingent on national citizenship in a member state.

The second limitation of the EU legal framework for equal treatment involves the stance of national governments. The directives of 2000 clearly emphasized that all the provisions on legal action and enforcement are "without prejudice to national rules of procedure concerning representation and defense before the courts." They are also "without prejudice to national rules relating to time limits for bringing actions as regards the principle of equality of treatment." Member states adopted different means by which to implement the two directives, with the result being very different legal provisions. Furthermore, a comprehensive and effective implementation of the two directives in all member states has proven more difficult than expected.[32] As the European Commission noted in September 2005, "a challenge identified in many member states is the application of anti-discrimination laws in practice." Exceptions to the principle of equal treatment permitted under the two directives were generally integrated into national laws.[33]

This implementation problem led to a third limitation of the equal treatment policies. It is clear that, in reality, only a fraction of the numerous victims of discrimination actually lodge a complaint. As noted by the European Union Monitoring Centre on Racism and Xenophobia (EUMC), "as for court cases, victims of discrimination may be skeptical as to the efficiency of lodging a complaint, may fear dismissal, or may simply not be aware of existing complaint mechanisms."[34] Several member states have failed to adopt a burden of proof provision consistent with the intent of the two directives. Even in countries where a complaint mechanism does exist, only a fraction of victims lodge complaints, with only a small portion of those eventually leading to formal court cases.

A 2005 EUMC report identified a fourth limitation to the new anti-discrimination framework, pointing out that "at present, the integration of fundamental rights in the law and policy-making of the Union remains inadequate. Of course, the acts of the institutions of the Union, in most cases, may be subject [to] judicial review before the Court of First Instance or the European Court of Justice. However, this remains an exclusively *post hoc* form of control. It is reactive and remedial in nature rather than proactive and preventive."[35]

In addition to the new legal provisions' limitations in scope and enforceability, the question of integration remains unresolved. As Anna Triandafyllidou notes, "the European dimension may open identity and institutional space for minorities and provide alternative dimensions for inclusion."[36] But ethnicity is even more salient as a political and social cleavage in Europe because of conflict between majority and minority populations and between the new ethnic minorities and the state. Despite the EU's improved legislation in the field of anti-discrimination, these efforts have failed to integrate all ethnic minorities. The two directives address the most visible and concrete aspects of unequal treatment, such as unequal access to employment, housing, and public goods and services. These moves toward an effective anti-discrimination policy should not be underestimated. Nonetheless, they are insufficient to remedy the problem because discrimination is based on prejudices that often have more to do with the characteristics of host societies than those of migrants. These prejudices fuel a new "xenophobic culture," to use Gilles Ivaldi and Pierre Brechon's term. This culture is rooted in a series of factors: dissatisfaction with life circumstances, fear of unemployment, insecurity about the future, and a low confidence in public authorities. The Eurobarometer (EB) surveys and the European Social Surveys (ESS) collectively provide useful insights that promote a better understanding of the current European "ethnic exclusivism." These surveys, conducted in 2003, offered insight into some of the important characteristics that are associated with negative attitudes toward immigrants and ethnic minorities (see tables 11.4 and 11.5).

The first important conclusion that we can draw from the data is that European public opinion has continued to express strong anti-immigrant feelings despite the measures European states have taken to restrict immigration. In 2003, 50 percent of survey respondents expressed opposition to immigrants.[37] The results also showed a desire to limit the number of "newcomers" (legal or illegal immigrants, asylum seekers, and refugees). This desire was illustrated by the fact that an increasing minority of respondents favor new repatriation policies for legal immigrants (22 percent in 2003 compared to 18 percent in 1997 and 20 percent in 2000).[38] Another observation is that resistance to a new influx of immigrants is linked to a growing intolerance of asylum seekers. The latter are still more tolerated than immigrants (legal and, of course, illegal): "only" 29 percent of those interviewed in 2003 expressed resistance to asylum seekers compared to the 50 percent who oppose immigrants. But the "right of asylum" is increasingly questioned by the general public in many Western European countries and perhaps, more surprisingly, in some Eastern European countries as well.[39]

The second important conclusion to be drawn from the data is that the scope of xenophobia is now both much wider (in terms of targeted populations) and broader (in relation to the other dimensions of "ethnic exclusivism") than it was in years past. Notably, anti-immigrant feelings are increasing but are now coupled with strong xenophobic attitudes. Several pieces of evidence support this assertion. First, legal immigrants (EU nation-

Table 11.4
Attitudes toward minorities in Western and Eastern European societies

Attitudes	Percent affirming
Resistance to immigrants	50
Resistance to asylum seekers	29
Resistance to diversity	48
Favor ethnic distance	21
Favor repatriation for criminal migrants	70
Perceived collective ethnic threat	58

Source: European Social Survey, 2003. See also European Union Monitoring Centre on Racism and Xenophobia (EUMC), *Majorities' Attitudes towards Minorities: Key Findings from the Eurobarometer and the European Social Survey,* Report 4, 2005.

als or TCNs) were relatively well tolerated in 1997. Today, the distinction between legal and illegal migrant populations has become blurred in the minds of the public. Xenophobic feelings now target all categories of "foreigners" without distinction. Second, 60 percent of the respondents disagreed in 1997 that members of minority groups "are so different" that they could never be fully integrated, and only 14 percent said there were "too many" people from minority groups living in their countries. By 2003, 39 percent opposed the idea that "legal TCNs should have the same rights as the national citizens," which suggests that the notion of "civic integration" supporting a successful socioeconomic integration is losing ground. "Opposition to civil rights for legal immigrants" has significantly increased in Finland, Spain, and Greece. Third, resistance to diversity appears linked to the widening influence of xenophobic feelings and attitudes, with a growing preference for a homogeneous society.[40] In 2003, 48 percent of European respondents expressed resistance to diversity, registering a strong preference for a monocultural society in which the majority of people share the same values and traditions. Furthermore, 21 percent suggested they wished to avoid social interaction with members of minority groups. Resistance to multicultural society implies that people oppose the idea that cultural, ethnic, and religious diversity enriches society as a whole.[41] In 2003, the rejection of multiculturalism reached 25 percent in the EU 15 and 28 percent in the EU 10. Finally, this resistance to multiculturalism is complemented by the increasing feeling, shared by a large majority of Europeans, that their country has reached the limits of cultural or ethnic diversity, a number that significantly increased between 1997 and 2003. By 2003, 60 percent of respondents (from the EU 15) believed that

Table 11. 5
Attitudes of majorities versus minorities regarding immigrants and the law

Attitudes surveyed	Percentage affirming
Resistance to multicultural society	25 (EU 10: 28)
Limits to multicultural society	60 (EU 10: 42)
Opposition to civil rights for legal migrants	39 (EU 10: 38)
Repatriation policies for legal migrants	22 (EU 10: 19)
Insistence on conformity to law	67 (EU 10: 45)

Source: Standard Eurobarometer 59.2, 2003. See also European Union Monitoring Centre on Racism and Xenophobia (EUMC), *Attitudes towards Minority Groups in the European Union* (Vienna, 2003), Report 2.

"there is a limit to how many people of other races, religions, or cultures a society can accept" and "if there were to be more people belonging to these minority groups, we would have problems." This result is consistent with the
ESS findings in which 58 percent of respondents expressed the belief that immigrants constitute a "collective ethnic threat."

Integration Policy and the Impact of Terrorism

The new EU immigration and asylum policy raises two concerns. The first
one is related to limited implementation of the most urgent provisions concerning equal treatment and effective social inclusion. As the prior discussion
suggests, member states are more inclined to standardize their restrictive asylum laws and visa rules than their labor policies or social welfare systems.
States readily institute restrictive immigration policies. They show greater reluctance when provisions are related to the rights and economic integration
of TCNs. The second concern is related to the lack of coherence that characterizes national policies when dealing with the notion of "internal security."
Even if it is clear that failed integration policies facilitate extremism and
violence, European governments have decided to use their "security toolbox"
in the aftermath of terrorist attacks rather than their integration toolbox. The
preferred new security measures are ineffectual and counterproductive; they
fail to address the issue of internal security while undermining the integration
of some targeted minority groups.

Integration involves not only access to some formal rights but also effective economic and social integration. It therefore raises the issues of poverty,
social and urban exclusion, unemployment, civic participation, education,
and religion. The issue of the integration of immigrants and their descendants
remains sensitive because it questions the ability of national governments to
address problems at the very heart of their sovereignty. National governments
have preserved their competence in many fields related to integration, such as
social policy, citizenship requirements, housing policy, and education. The
failure of integration thus reflects the failure of these governments to maintain national cohesion, social equity, economic equity, and respect for fundamental rights—aspects of core competency.

For many years, European governments have justified restrictive immigration measures as a way to better integrate existing ethnic communities. In the
case of young Muslims recruited by jihadist networks, this approach has
proved to be a complete failure. However, focusing on Islamic militants, a tiny
minority among the estimated 15 million to 20 million Muslims living in Europe, should not disguise the fact that integration is a complex matter that af-

fects all categories of ethnic minorities. It concerns individuals who are often citizens in name but do not exercise social citizenship and who, sometimes, are not culturally integrated. It deals with the descendants of guest workers, who are born and raised in Europe, who are socially and spatially excluded, and who suffer from discrimination and racism. Among them, only a tiny minority constitutes a reservoir of militant Islamic resentment toward "Western dominance."

The London bombings of July 2005 did not illustrate just the inability of the British government to deal with terrorist threats. The incident also put an end to the celebration of the continued success of the British multicultural model. While the overall unemployment rate in Britain stood at 6.2 percent in 2000 (5.8 percent for whites and 13 percent for ethnic minorities), it was 23 percent for Bangladeshi and 20 percent for Pakistani ethnic groups. The Bangladeshi ethnic minority today has a labor force participation (LFP) rate of only 45 percent compared to 79.8 percent for the white majority population. The situation in other European countries is quite similar. Grandiose declarations about the excellence of the French republican model of integration conflict with strong evidence of social deprivation, economic inequality, and urban segregation. The narrow definition of immigrants as "resident non-nationals" adopted by the French government has the virtue of entirely obfuscating the integration issue. Naturalized second- and third-generation immigrants are lost to statistical studies once they leave the immigrant household. But, even if they disappear from official statistics, the sons and daughters of ethnic immigrants are many times more likely to be unemployed than natives (*Français de souche*). They also underperform at school and are overrepresented in the prison system. The employment situation is best characterized by high structural unemployment, which particularly affects young people, especially young immigrants. According to the EUMC, "Youth of North African origin (mostly born in France) are twice as often unemployed as their peers."[42] In the locations where the riots of 2005 took place, the unemployment rate stood at 40 percent for people under the age of twenty-five.

Copycat riots took place in Germany and Belgium. Romano Prodi, former president of the European Commission, stated that deprived suburbs in Italy constituted a similarly fertile ground for the cultivation of urban violence. The Dutch minister Sybilla Dekker, in charge of national development and housing policy, said it was not a peculiarly French issue and called for new measures designed to promote the social and spatial integration of immigrants in the Netherlands. The European Commission head, José Barrosso, indicated that youth employment was a key challenge, saying that having 60 percent of youths in suburbs unemployed was a serious problem. He added that other big cities had similar problems and that European governments must figure out how to address them. In Germany, for example, the LFP rate of foreigners has decreased by 10 percent since the mid-1980s and is now significantly below that of native Germans. In Denmark, the LFP rate for immigrants and their descendants from third countries is 34 percent below that of the ethnic Danes. The LFP rate of all foreigners in Austria is 12 percent lower than that of nationals.

In the aftermath of the terrorist attacks, European governments adopted new security packages. At the EU level, post-9/11 counter-terrorism work included broadening the definition of terrorism and making it very flexible, introducing a European arrest warrant, and setting up an EU-wide database containing the fingerprints of asylum seekers.[43] FRONTEX was the agency created in 2004 to integrate national border security systems against "all kinds of threats that could happen at or through the external border of the member states of the EU."[44] National governments developed parallel measures, such as those included in the Anti-Terrorism Crime and Security Emergency Bill adopted in Great Britain in December 2001. The Second Security Package of laws (Sicherheitspaket II) was adopted in Germany in December 2001. France's parliament approved a series of exceptional amendments in October 2001, after only two weeks of deliberation, as part of the Day-to-Day Security Law (Loi de la Sécurité Quotidienne).

These new security measures do not address the issue of integration, and they also raise additional concerns. First, many experts express doubts about the efficiency of the security measures adopted, both at the EU and the national level.[45] Secondly, restrictions on the freedom of assembly, religion, speech, and the right to privacy generate claims by critics that the new measures undermine civil liberties. The EU office of Amnesty International, for example, claims that "miscarriages of justice arising from violations of human rights in terrorism cases not only create the potential that the real perpetrators of terrorist acts remain at liberty, but also have a significant impact on public confidence in the rule of law. This can in turn lead to a sense of alienation within certain sectors of society that feel as though they are being unfairly targeted in the fight against terrorism."[46]

So far, a common justifiable criticism is that little attention is being paid to the socioeconomic roots of support for terrorism while the "criminalization" of immigrants is making integration increasingly difficult. The EU's recent initiatives regarding integration have been notable for a lack of coordination with the efforts of national governments. This is not to suggest that policymakers have not tried. In March 2000, the European Council of Lisbon launched the EU strategy against poverty and social exclusion. The EU Commission focused on the Action Program (2002–2006), which is today the main financial instrument of the EU strategy against poverty and social exclusion. Other instruments include the EES (European Employment Strategy), the NAPs/incl (national action plans to fight poverty and promote social inclusion), and several programs managed by the Commission (such as URBAN II, EQUAL, and CULTURE). In 2003, the Commission published a communication on "Immigration, Integration, and Employment," which defined the EU conception of integration and specified policy orientations and priorities.[47] Finally, the Commission presented a green paper on an EU approach to managing the economic migration of TCNs.[48] The strategy of putting integration at the top of the EU agenda has been reflected in the activities of the Commission, the Economic and Social Committee, and other agencies. There have been other structural initiatives as well, such as the Athens Migration Policy Initiative and the European Social Forum (ESF).[49]

A question nonetheless remains: has the "comprehensive approach" adopted by the EU over the last several years contributed to greater integration? Its innovative and relevant dimensions are certainly worth noting. The first advantage of the EU's approach is that it takes into account not only the economic and social aspects of integration but also issues related to cultural and religious diversity, citizenship, participation, and political rights. Its scope has consequently been enlarged. A second advantage is that it offers a systematic and comprehensive categorization of immigrants: labor migrants, family members admitted under family arrangements, asylum seekers, refugees, and persons enjoying international protection. The third advantage is that this new approach underscores the fact that integration is a two-way process. This process involves not only the characteristics, attitudes, and behaviors of immigrants but also those of the members of the receiving society (i.e., its characteristics and reactions to newcomers). It raises questions regarding the context in which immigrants are supposed to integrate. It also urges national authorities to recognize that it is the interaction between the minority and majority groups that determines the final outcome of the integration process. The EU's "comprehensive approach" recognizes that institutional structures, the perception of immigrants, and patterns of socialization all matter.

Furthermore, in contrast to the attitudes of the majority of European national governments, the EU directly addresses the problems of the second- and third-generation descendants of migrants. The Commission pointed out that "while many immigrants in the EU are well integrated, there are nevertheless growing concerns in a number of countries about the situation of the second and third generation." The diagnosis offered by the Commission is harsh: "social and racial discrimination prevent 2nd and 3rd generation immigrant youth from acceding on an equal footing with nationals to the jobs and places in society for which they are qualified. The failure of integration policies plays a part in enabling these phenomena to develop."[50]

Nonetheless, the concept of integration as developed by the EU has several limitations. There is no agreement about the criteria for evaluating sociological or functional integration/segregation among the member states. Is integration to be measured in economic or noneconomic terms? Is cultural diversity the best way to promote integration, or is integration better achieved by means of "assimilation," defined as cultural and religious homogeneity? Furthermore, should policymakers aim for national integration? These are widely debated questions with no consensus in sight even among proponents of integration, as illustrated by the plethora of national policies. Progress has been made in evaluating segregation and, conversely, integration.[51] There remains, however, an urgent need for a clarification agreement about the meaning of integration.

More importantly, while immigration and asylum policies are now part of the EU framework, a large number of integration policies (addressing such areas as education, access to citizenship, and access to social rights and the welfare state) still remain outside of the EU's sphere of competence. The Commission is not allowed and is thus unable to act in many fields included in its new comprehensive strategy. The EU intends to overcome these "competency" limits, at least in principle, by promoting three projects on the political agenda: cultural diversity, civic citizenship, and labor integration. They are, however, sensitive issues, and the Commission's progress has been incremental and diplomatic. In a recent communication, the Commission advocated a "gradual and smooth move from national to Community rules." It emphasized that "EU legislation on the admission (and integration) of economic migrants should therefore be conceived as a 'first step legislation' while leaving the Member States to respond to the specific needs of their labor markets."[52]

Increasingly aware of the need to address the roots of terrorism, in November 2004 the EU adopted The Hague Programme, which includes a list of ten priorities.[53] Only two of them, however, refer directly to the protection of human rights and civil liberties and to the positive impact of immigration. Among the measures designed to achieve the "strengthening of fundamental rights and citizenship," the only concrete measure in the program entails the conversion of the EUMC into a Fundamental Rights Agency. With regard to immigrant integration, the Commission can only "encourage member states to push ahead with their integration policies in order to help improve mutual understanding and dialogue between religions and cultures." In 2005, the Commission adopted a communication on the "factors contributing to violent radicalization," which clearly recognized the significance of the relationship between failed integration and terrorist recruitment in Europe.[54] However, its scope is limited to "soft measures," such as intercultural exchanges among young people, rather than tackling the harder tasks of cultural regulation, political representation, and social acceptance.

The Failure of Integration Becomes a New Security Issue

The movement toward the securitization of immigration in Europe began before September 11, but it has accelerated since 2001 with the introduction of a wave of new measures after the Madrid and London transit bombings in 2004 and 2005. The redefinition of immigration as a security question is embedded in a wider political process in which immigrants and asylum seekers are portrayed as people who generate a challenge to national identity, the provision of welfare benefits, and internal security. Since the mid-1980s, the use of immigration policy to counter terrorism has proven to be ineffective. Furthermore, the recent use of anti-terrorism measures to curb immigration has proven to be not only ineffective but also detrimental to the fundamental rights of immigrants, particularly to asylum seekers and TCNs.

Furthermore, anti-immigrant propaganda, which conflates "terrorists" with "foreigners" (including those who are actually native born) has been fueled by all the consequences of failed integration. These consequences include unemployment and "*insécurité*" (a French word signifying the combination of vandalism, delinquency, and hate crimes arising from immigrant enclaves). These phenomena are also exploited by anti-immigrant groups, with reference to a "clash of cultures," to prove that ethnic minorities are unable to integrate, not qualified to be integrated, and even reluctant to do so. The vicious circle is therefore complete.

Recent surveys and reports confirm the growth in xenophobic attitudes—and incidents. Included among these is the EUMC report on Islamophobia in the EU after September 11, 2001. It reported that Islamic communities have become the target of growing hostility: "a greater sense of fear among the general population has exacerbated already existing prejudices and fueled acts of aggression and harassment in many European member states."[55] Relatively low levels of physical violence were identified in most countries, with the exception of Denmark and Great Britain, where the EUMC noted a dramatic and prolonged upsurge in physical attacks on Muslims. According to the report, "visual identifiers" of Islam (such as the hijab, chador, or turban) appeared to explain why certain groups (not only Muslims but also those who "look Arab," such as Sikhs) were targeted for aggression.[56] Mosques and Islamic cultural centers were also targeted for damage and retaliatory acts. Verbal abuse, harassment, and aggression were even more widespread. In most EU countries, negative feelings against Muslims (and others visually identified as "Arab") were reinforced by the disproportionately large amount of publicity the media generated by focusing on some of the extremist fringes of the Muslim community. The EUMC noted "instances of sensationalism and stereotypical representations of Muslims."[57]

Concerns about asylum seekers have also increasingly overlapped with issues related to September 11. Asylum seekers have constituted the second most prevalent group of discrimination victims because of the perceived threat that they are potential "internal terrorists." In France and the UK, for example, asylum seekers and refugees have been largely characterized by the media as a threat and described as the "enemy within." Of course, their vulnerability to xenophobia is not solely due to the events of September 11, but that particularly dramatic day of terrorism gave new force to the hostilities directed toward them. Subsequent events have raised concerns about the balance between the exigencies of security and the minimal requisites of civil liberties, reflected in the development of a new rhetoric of exclusion and in public debates on security/identity challenges. The new linkage between those who "are foreign" and those "who threaten" has changed the nature of identity politics in both old and new countries of immigration. This change has become evident to new immigrants themselves and poses a dilemma for each country as it attempts to redefine its own formal rules for citizenship and, perhaps more importantly, its concept of nationality.

There is strong evidence that terrorist threats are not only external but also deeply rooted in domestic issues. European governments, nonetheless, still emphasize the external dimension of terrorism by using border controls and restrictive asylum policies as a way to improve their internal security. Using some aspects of urban policy (in the guise of integration policy), the problem has remained outside the scope of their strategy. Meanwhile, most of the measures adopted to improve internal security have proved detrimental to immigrants and their descendants because they limit opportunities to integrate successfully. Recent EU initiatives represent a shift toward greater awareness of the problem. However, there is a gap between rhetoric and action in EU and national policies in this area. This gap is expected to last as long as European governments refuse to acknowledge historic policy failures and remain reluctant to address the deep-seated social malaise from which they suffer.

12

Muslims and the State in Western Europe

JONATHAN LAURENCE

The state has been an ascendant and indispensable actor in Muslim integration in contemporary Europe, in particular through successive governments' development of representative councils for the Muslim religion. I argue against the current tide of postnationalism, in which migrants are said to appeal to powers higher than the national state for access to cultural and legal rights. I find that even in an age of globalization and transnational movements, the state is alive and well. This view militates an increasing political consensus that this relatively new Islamic presence challenges not only the integrative capacity of democratic institutions but also Enlightenment values *and* Europe's Christian heritage (ignoring, for the moment, any tensions between those legacies).

Contemporary scholarly accounts of Islam in Europe have tended to portray one of two extreme visions. In the pessimistic view, foreign policy analyses and the scholarly literature are in rare concurrence about the meager chances for either interreligious dialogue or Muslim integration. These accounts bear witness to a showdown between intransigently secular states and an ambitious, fundamentalist religion whose followers aim to transform the continent into "Eurabia."[1] To justify their gloom, these authors cite Islam's unhierarchical nature and the impossibility of establishing legitimate representatives—or "one phone number"—for Muslim communities in Europe.[2] Compounding this difficulty, these scholars emphasize, is the inadequacy of Europe's nineteenth-century state-church institutions, which stumble from crisis to crisis with this new and agile religious challenger.[3] The optimistic voices, on the other hand, come from the camps of postnationalist theorists and from proponents of a reformed "Euro-Islam" that is divorced from overseers and financiers in the Muslim world.[4] But those authors' cheerfulness is founded, respectively, on two formidable hypotheses: the diminishing importance of "host" state institutions for immigrant integration and the "sending" states' renunciation of religious influence over the Muslim diaspora.[5] More than a decade after they were first expounded, neither of these scenarios has been played out.

Surprisingly few studies (and virtually none in English) systematically compare how different national interior ministries have used political and institutional processes to organize Islam for state-religion relations.[6] This chapter sidesteps the warring bands of pessimists and optimists and instead sketches the character of state-Islam interaction in the first thirty years (1974–2004) of government consultations with foreign and native-born Muslim representatives in Europe. Based on thirty months of fieldwork and more than 150 interviews with religious leaders and policymakers in France, Germany, Italy, Belgium, and the UK, I argue that European nation-states have reasserted their sovereign prerogative. They have done so to manage the transnational threats associated with their citizens' religious membership.[7] My research examines the theoretical and practical significance of contemporary efforts to nationalize Muslim religious communities. These are political and institutional processes intended to provide a more amenable context for the sociopolitical integration of all Muslims, religious or not. Three decades of increasingly assertive policies toward organized Islam in Europe militate against the image of states being overrun by the unplanned or undesired mass settlement of Muslims. This finding is in line with Steven Krasner's contrarian view that "globalization and state activity have moved in tandem" and that this occurs across institutional models that might be expected to have dramatically distinct policy outcomes.[8] A portrait emerges of the contemporary European nation-state not as a "weathervane" or a neutral broker among competing interests but rather as an actor in its own right that structures the nature of group-state relations in crucial ways.[9]

The Challenge of Integration

There is no shortage of bad news to comfort the pessimists. A sense of foreboding and an atmosphere of failed integration and social conflict hang like a cloud over the 15 million or so Muslims living in Western Europe. Second- and third-generation immigrants suffer disproportionately high unemployment, widespread social discrimination, and feeble political representation in local and national institutions. This is coupled with the impression of imported threats from abroad, taking the form of cultural clashes over head scarves worn by schoolgirls or civil servants, or imams preaching hatred or violence, or violence and vandalism targeting the Jewish community.

There have been hair-raising incidents of assassination and exile (e.g., Theo Van Gogh and Ayaan Hirsi Ali in the Netherlands). There has been attempted censorship—from lawsuits against the works of Oriana Fallaci and Michel Houellebecq in France, to the caricatures of the prophet Mohammed published in Denmark in 2005. And there have been threats of violence (against a production of Mozart's *Idomeneo* at the Deutsche Oper in Berlin, in response to Pope Benedict's Regensburg address, and after Toulouse high school teacher Robert Redeker's opinion piece in *Le Figaro* in September 2006).

At best, this pattern of crisis suggests systemic bad communication between host societies and their Muslim minorities. At worst, it seems like the political and social integration of Muslims in Europe has failed spectacularly. Indeed, many observers see a grave crisis of previous models of immigrant integration.[10] At worst, they see evidence of a "reverse colonization" that will lead to the "Islamization" of Europe.[11] Gilles Kepel, an authority on the Muslim world, has commented that Europe now faces a grave choice: "either we train our Muslims to become global citizens, who live in a democratic, pluralist society, or on the contrary, the Islamists win, and take over those Muslim European constituencies. Then we're in serious trouble."[12]

To use an analogy from the first era of modern state building, how do today's governments attempt to make Muslims French, or German, or Italian? This was basically how authors have described the state-building process—turning "peasants into Frenchmen," "*juifs*" into "*Israélites*," or Christians into "good citizens."[13] There are different kinds of integration—socioeconomic indicators tell one story, for example—but political integration is the underlying impulse of this historical process. To discover the true nature of European governments' strategies toward organized Islam begs a look beyond the repressive measures that states can (and do) take. These measures might include deporting extremist prayer leaders or arresting individuals who threaten public order. Instead, what are the constructive steps that make up the path to citizenship and a measure of integration for this new minority? In twentieth-century Western Europe, three arenas ensured the gradual political integration of immigrants and new citizens from Southern and Eastern Europe. Traditional participation through elections and civil society associations is one, civic inculcation through the national education system is the second, and identification with the nation-state through service in the armed forces is the third.[14] But today, party systems have largely failed to transmit social diversity into parliaments, public schools are in financial crisis, and mandatory conscription is a thing of the recent past. How have national governments granted some degree of representation to these sizeable minority populations when traditional civic institutions have failed to do so? The answer lies in the unexpected revival of a fourth arena: religious community. In an era of advanced secularization in Western Europe, ironically, governments there have fallen back on religion policy—via national state-church institutions—as a central tool of immigrant integration.

The Attempts to Nationalize Muslim Organizations

The most striking evidence of this development is a Europe-wide move toward "nationalization" of Islam through the development of national consultations with Muslim civil society. The thousands of mosques, prayer rooms, and religious associations that have popped up in the last several decades are nearly all under de jure or de facto foreign influence—as is characteristic of major world religions. The local and national Islam Councils that have emerged to manage these prayer rooms, from the Conseil Français du Culte Musulman, the Comisión Islámica de España, the Exécutif des Musulmans de Belgique, the Consulta Islamica or Consultative Council in Italy, to the Deutsche Islam Konferenz, and so on, are the culmination of a fifteen-year push. Muslims and public authorities alike pushed for the legal recognition of Islam and the protection of freedom of worship that other major religions enjoy.

The interior ministries do not presume the existence of some essential "Muslim" to be trained and formed into a mythical "citizen." But regardless of Muslims' diversity of national origin, piety, and religious affiliation, policymakers have nonetheless come to see "their" Muslims as a community, a collectivity, and the object of public policymaking. These administrations are not engaged in the special accommodation of *Muslims;* they are incorporating *Islam* into pre-existing institutional state-church relations. It is in this domain that European governments are trying to create the institutional conditions for the emergence of an Italian Islam or a German Islam rather than just tolerating Islam within Italy or Germany. The religion bureaus of European interior ministries structure and mediate the activities of religious organizations. As Don Baker writes in reference to another part of the world, such efforts aim to "ensure that the centrifugal push of religious loyalties that transnational religious regimes foster . . . does not overcome the centripetal pull toward national unity that the state must nurture."[15] The institutionalized relations between state and religion are predicated on the assumption that national laws take priority over religious texts. They are intended to steep religious leaders in the secular precepts of a society in which church and state are separate. In practical terms, national interior ministries accomplish these lofty goals by overseeing and helping coordinate various activities. These include the financing and construction of mosques, the training of imams, the appointment of Muslim chaplains in prisons and hospitals, the setting of religious curriculum in publicly funded schools, and the celebration of major holidays and religious events—from the orderly slaughter of lambs for Eid al-Adha to the orderly departure of pilgrims traveling to Mecca. This guarantees equal access to religious exercise at the same time that it favors the transparency of community ties with foreign governments and international NGOs.

The state's challenge has been to establish these nascent councils as legitimate interlocutors for public authorities. It is important to note that these are not "Muslim" councils, any more than the conference of French bishops can claim to represent Catholics on nonreligious matters or the Jewish central councils or grand rabbis can speak for all Jews. Nor does this stem from a desire to impose a Catholic-style hierarchy on Islam. After all, Protestants and Jews do not naturally gravitate toward centralized representation either, but they were required to reorganize to obtain full legal recognition. The creation of Islamic Councils reflects governments' desire to mold Islam into an organizationally homologous shape, as the modern secular state has asked all major religions and cults to do. Governments behave toward Islam as they have toward previous transnational religious challenges: they seek to weaken ties abroad and strengthen institutional connections at home in the hope of enhancing the authority of the nation-state over competing demands on citizens' sociopolitical loyalties. Religious belonging has persistently posed challenges to the meaning of territory and citizenship by setting constitutions in competition with a higher law. Nancy Rosenblum calls this the "tensions between the obligations of citizenship and the demands of faith." This is remarkably similar to Locke's concerns over the suitability of Christians as republican citizens, as well as the Enlightenment-era logic of Mirabeau or

Von Dohm, who argued that emancipated and domestically oriented Jews would be more useful members of society as full citizens.[16] In Michael Mc-Connell's apt paraphrasing of Rousseau, "your citizenship can be in Heaven or in France, but not in both."[17] Faced with a dual system, priest and prince, Rousseau doubted that believers could be trusted which to choose: "The sacred cult of Christianity aimed to become independent of the sovereign, and had no natural or necessary bond with the body of the state. . . . Far from attaching citizens' hearts to the State, it detaches them from it as from all worldly things."[18] Following the liberal democratic revolutions of eighteenth- and nineteenth-century Europe, the consolidating nation-states often tried to weaken—and domesticate—the powerful transnational Catholic network. Their new state-church frameworks eliminated the Church's monopolistic or dominant position, the clergy was subjected to a civil code, and church property and wealth was taxed or seized. The development of national institutions to regulate religious life sought to reduce the risks of radical anti-state influences and, indirectly, to make better citizens of church faithful.

The results of my empirical research suggest that the same kind of effort is the major background to Muslim integration in Europe today. Rather than reflecting the postnational dynamics that some scholars claim to observe, the most significant measures of Muslim accommodation have occurred in reaction to organized Islam's challenge to the authority of modern, secular states. What emerges as the major through-line of this story are European states' parallel efforts to confront the transnational nature of Muslim organizations operating under their national public law. These efforts to assert authority over transnational Islam look very similar to earlier moves to create centralized interlocutors for religious affairs. Public recognition has provided a tool kit to modify or sever transnational ties; as Patchen Markell writes about the Prussian emancipation legislation of 1812, the recognition of difference can be seen as "an instrument of, rather than a threat to, [state] sovereignty."[19] Markell views institutionalization as a "double bind," a trade-off at the highest theoretical level of state building: "[Emancipation] was not conceived merely as the fulfillment of liberal principles of fairness or equality, nor was it simply the gift of an indifferent king who expected nothing in return. It secured recognition for the Jews, yet it also secured recognition for Prussia by placing Jews into a new relationship with the state."[20]

Charting Attempts at Nationalization

Scholarly attempts to explain and typologize new policies toward organized Islam have not closely examined the links between national state-church regimes, on the one hand, and the Muslim world's state-led and civil society networks that make up global Islam, on the other. Instead, they have focused on points of conflict and coercion. The existing literature offers little guidance for understanding these governments' efforts to grapple with the new social and political reality. Given my emphasis on the nation-state's enduring importance to the integration of Islam in Europe, surprisingly little of my account flows from the particular national arrangements for the organization of religion. Instead, we are witnessing a broad, uncoordinated effort of institution building. I argue against three prevailing (and competing) misconceptions in the literature on the state accommodation of Islam in the West: the determinism of political opportunity structures, the impossibility of reconciling Islam and democracy, and the relevance of postnational dynamics.

One tendency has been to characterize the policy responses of European nation-states as falling into national models in an entirely predictable fashion. This school of thought holds that the best predictor of Islam's integration is national, institutional, or ideational trajectories.[21] Authors of this school argue that policies can be explained according to resource mobilization and opportunity structures. Jocelyne Cesari, for example, writes that "different institutional arrangements tend to shape the agendas of Islamic mobilization and claims in different countries."[22] Using a similar logic, Long Litt Woon and Aristide Zolberg predicted that any improvements in the official status of Islam in Europe would follow a routine trajectory of pluralist minority incorporation in its respective national settings.[23] And Joel Fetzer and Christopher Soper suggest that conflict over the head scarf and school curriculum in France is merely the product of that country's "long and contentious state-church history." Similarly, they find that "inherited state-church institutions best explain how" Germany has accommodated Muslims.[24] This makes little sense given the spread of "head scarf affairs" and related controversies to the UK, Germany, Italy, and elsewhere since the French ban on religious symbols in public schools began in 2004. The avowal of discomfort with various types of veils and head coverings expressed by officials in each of these countries— and their stated intention to adopt restrictive administrative practices— underscores their similar concerns. Notwithstanding the different historical backgrounds and distinct institutional legacies with regard to religion in the public sphere, government officials across Europe face common challenges regarding the integration of Muslims in politics and society.

Another misconception authors have advanced is the notion that Islam is doctrinally unsuited for state-church separation in contemporary Western democracies. They have also taken the pessimistic view that Islam may simply be incompatible.[25] They argue that it is impossible to politically integrate

Islam within secular Western nation-states and point to the novelty of the challenges posed by Islamic doctrine. A notable example is the reluctance to accept basic liberal precepts that distinguish spiritual rule from temporal authority.[26] In this view, Muslim leaders' refusal to allow Islam to be relegated to the private sphere is compounded by their systemic incapacity to produce centralized representatives for the government to address—that is, a single organization that can "communicate and negotiate" on behalf of Muslims.[27] "In contrast to Catholicism," write Carolyn Warner and Manfred Wenner, "the Islamic religion is not conducive to large-scale collective action. . . . [Islam is among] decentralized, non-hierarchical religions with multiple, competing schools . . . [and has] no central authority to enforce cooperation or structure activity."[28] Thus, any state concessions to recognize Islam or to create "multicultural" policies benefiting Muslims' religious identity are seen to weaken the foundations of liberal democracy because of Islam's tendency to fuse religion and politics.[29] This perspective predicts that governments will be hostile to demands made by Muslim communities and will avoid integrating Islam. Muslims, in turn, will be unable to take advantage of opportunities presented to them because of internal disunity. These authors predict continuous conflict between Islam and the state and a reluctance to make religious accommodations.

The other misconception is an argument that transnational forces are overcoming old national institutions and that accommodation of Islam would occur only over the dead body of the nation-state. Yasemin Nuhoğlu Soysal's study of the incorporation of guest workers into Western European social systems in the late 1980s and early 1990s—why states "extended rights and privileges of their citizens to migrant workers"—led to her theory of "postnational" rights acquisition. She opposed this development to Tomas Hammar's concept of "denizenship," which focuses on the changes in citizenship on a territorial, nation-state basis—which Soysal called the "mere expansion of the scope of national citizenship." Instead, she claimed, the state is "no longer an autonomous and independent organization closed over a nationally defined population."[30] Thus immigrants turn to international actors and acquire rights only thanks to the increasing irrelevance of national citizenship regimes. The erosion of national institutions' pertinence occurs by way of "constitutionally interconnected states with a multiplicity of memberships." Examples include state membership in supranational organizations like the EU and European Court of Justice (ECJ), or by way of international human rights norms established via the Universal Declaration and European Convention on human rights. According to this view, the integration of Islam takes place when national governments lose power and institutions associated with postnational processes gain authority.

But Soysal's framework ignores the cultural conflict and demands for religious accommodation that cause controversy at local and national levels. Her theory does not adequately address how states manage the mundane details of family law and state-church laws in religiously plural societies, domains that are still solidly under the competence of national governments. Her evocation of new postnational rights "to express and develop their cultural heritage" avoids sticky areas. These include the applicability of *fatwa*s across borders, the propriety of wearing a head scarf in public institutions, the civil recognition of religious marriage and divorce, the obligation to wage holy war, the source of financing for prayer space and the training of imams, and so forth. These are all challenges of a distinctly transnational nature, but the basis for policy responses to them cannot be found in international institutions or human rights norms. After all, the European Convention for Human Rights (ECHR) respects national states' rights to legislate the details of religious expression if public order is deemed to be threatened. The court upheld head scarf bans in Turkish public universities, and that precedent was cited by French officials who drafted a law on religious symbols in public schools. Similarly, the French government felt secure enough to promote the 2005 treaty for a European constitution, even though the document included a clause on freedom of religious expression "in private and in public."

My view is that governments have not treated Islam as doctrinally impossible to integrate and that states across Europe, in fact, "jump" outside the purported categories of inherited institutional patterns. This goes against Soysal's prediction for French state–Islam relations, for example, when she argues that the "unit of incorporation" is the individual citizen and that "statist" strictures prevent "systematic representation or consultation with immigrant groups that would promote a unified structure."[31] Indeed, I find that the question is not how Muslim groups adapt to the state's institutions. She claims they "adopt predominant national organizational models" and that a more centrally organized Islam will emerge in countries where the state actively incorporates or defines Islam as a functional group. The question is, rather, how does the state actively *encourage* such centralized structures to emerge as a reaction to the challenge of transnational religion?

My argument also contradicts Fetzer and Soper's perspective, in which the institutional opportunity structure alone determines the shape of Muslim accommodation. Governments have recognized that many of their integration challenges with regard to populations of Muslim origin require reining in certain transnational characteristics of religious communities. It is precisely in reaction to transnational forces that state action is framed. Where regime types matter is in the institutional opportunity structure: for example, whether public recognition entails the creation of a council, a corporation of public law, or a treaty between religious community and state. The importance of national structures and historical state-church settlements does determine which institutional actors will lead the process of nationalization—for example, the national interior ministry in France or courts of law in Germany. And the specific narrative of national accommodation of Islam is of course particular to the historical circumstances of the given country's interaction with the main Muslim "sending states." French colonialism left a different legacy than did Germany's *Gastarbeiter* program. But I find the *similarity* in the patterns of institutional outcomes to be surprising, given distinctive national approaches to citizenship, divergent state-religion regimes, and the political traditions of state-society relations. The outcomes are far from identical, but governments whose doctrines would normally steer them away from religious affairs have all recognized the need to confront the transnational nature of this neglected religious community. By resorting to corporatist-style mechanisms of political integration, governments have shown that the state is alive and well. This chapter must forgo the rich detail of the options for public legal status that influence the precise path of Islam's national institutionalization. Instead it identifies the commonalities and draws attention to the broader themes at play and the mechanisms at work in state-Islam relations.

Charting Transnational Muslim Organization

These governments' pursuit of state-centric agendas has required managing the competing interests and formal demands of Muslim organizations both at home and abroad. It is helpful to view this story in terms of an evolving supply of and demand for religious leadership for the activity of state-church relations. For reasons related to the nature of civil society in the Arab-Muslim world, Olivier Roy argues, European states naturally looked to mosques and prayer rooms—not trade unions or political parties—as the "spontaneous form of organization" of Muslims in the West.[32] The mirror image of European governments' strategy with regard to Islam is the organized Muslim world's pursuit of its own interests. Since the early 1970s, governments have been faced with a shifting supply of foreign and native-born Muslim religious representatives who operate through embassies or local organizational nodes of transnational movements. The first category of Muslim organizations, broadly speaking, represents the "official Islam" of sending states in the Muslim world. These organizations are concerned with protecting spheres of influence among émigré populations and neutralizing threats to their own sovereignty from the growing Muslim diaspora. The second category of organizations can be classified as "political Islam": the dissident movements that sought refuge from repressive regimes and that have staked out an operational base in Western Europe.

Official Islam—also known as the "Islam of the Embassies"—is characterized by a sending state's foreign policy of ensuring "a cleric in every consulate catchment." The enduring examples of such organizations are the Muslim World League (MWL), the Algerian and Moroccan consular services, and the Turkish Directorate for Religious Affairs. Although Saudi Arabia did not send labor migrants to Europe, its government has sought to expand the kingdom's religious influence outside the Arab world in part through the MWL, a Mecca-based NGO founded in 1962. King Faisal bin Abdul Aziz (who reigned from 1964 to 1975) sought to enable independent Islamic diplomacy through commissioners in Saudi embassies who would serve as MWL representatives. The MWL Paris bureau chief, for example, simultaneously served as an ambassador to UNESCO. Its charter called for making "direct contact with Muslim minorities and communities wherever they are . . . to close ranks and encourage them to speak with a single voice in defense of Muslims and Islam." The MWL receives dozens of annual funding requests across Europe and has provided major financing for mosques across the continent, from Mantes-la-Jolie, Evry, and Lyon to Madrid, Rome, Copenhagen, and Kensington. The boom in Saudi proselytizing around the world— through the construction of grand mosques, the circulation of free Wahhabi prayer books, and the dispatching of missionaries and imams—was funded by petrodollars. It is estimated that more than $85 *billion* was spent between 1975 and 2005, reflecting a determined effort to establish spiritual and political hegemony over Muslim practice.[33]

In addition to this kind of grand strategy, there is also the everyday engagement of embassies and consulates that try to maintain control over émigré populations abroad. Algerian, Moroccan, and Turkish consulates, for example, keep tabs on associations founded by their nationals abroad. They compile lists of friendly and unfriendly prayer associations and either offer their support or report potential troublemakers to authorities of the home country or the host government. This "Islam of the Embassies" seeks to retain a guardian status over religious practice in the diaspora. The emergence of Turkish, Algerian, and Moroccan federations in Europe that remain loyal to the official Islam of the homeland was no spontaneous event. Rather, consulates and embassies have encouraged—and even helped to administer—organizational structures that bring together the existing prayer associations founded in different European countries under a homeland banner. Examples may be found in Algerian Islam in France and Turkish Islam in Germany.

The French president inaugurated the Grande Mosquée de Paris (GMP) and an association in charge of holy sites in French Algeria shortly after World War I. Though its first board of directors included Algerians, Moroccans, Tunisians, and Senegalese, the GMP gradually came under Algerian domination in the two decades that followed that country's independence in 1962. The Algerian government took over responsibility for the GMP's finances in 1982 and began using the mosque as a conduit for spreading its official state version of Islam. It did so by creating prayer spaces and attempting to co-opt existing ones following the post-1981 boom in prayer associations. The GMP is organized as a federation with five regional muftis, and it currently controls 250 prayer spaces and associations around France. The GMP's rector has authority over 150 imams (just over 10 percent of all imams in France), most of whom are from Algeria.

Alongside the GMP, one can look to the Turkish directorate for religious affairs (the DIB) for a quintessential model of exported "official" Islam. Founded in 1950, this special administration in the prime minister's office is responsible for the construction, administration, and staffing of mosques. Its 70,000 clerics/civil servants help organize *Qur'an* courses and the publication and censorship of liturgical prayers. The DIB's mission statement indicates that the directorate's purpose is to "instill love of fatherland, flag, and religion"; portraits of Atat–rk hang in the front offices and foyers of DIB prayer spaces. Like Algerian state Islam, the DIB lays claim on all Turkish citizens living abroad. It underwrites prayer space and religious education for Turks living abroad through local offices (DITIB), staffing them with diplomats from Turkish consulates. The president of DIB in Turkey is the honorary chairman of every DITIB, and he may participate in DITIB membership and executive meetings.[34] Its prayer spaces in Europe are considered sovereign Turkish territory; when they join the national DITIB umbrella organization, the property is transferred to DIB and comes under the control of the Turkish interior ministry. The organization's first German office was founded in 1982 in West Berlin, home to a large Turkish guest worker population. Within two years, the federation had assembled 250 associations under its umbrella. In 1995 the DITIB in Germany employed 760 imams, each of whom is hired as a public servant with a salary from the Turkish state for six-year terms. The DIB indirectly controls half of all Turkish mosques in Europe (it is known as the CCMTF in France).

Europe's two most influential international networks of "political" Islam—also known as "dissident" Islam—are the Muslim Brotherhood (Ikhwan al-Muslimin or MB), of Egyptian origin, and the Germany-based Islamische Gemeinschaft Milli Görüs (IGMG), of Turkish background. The commonality among these political Islam organizations is their broad ideological outlook regarding the ultimate "inseparability of religion and politics" and their recruitment patterns. They attract individuals "far removed from traditional ulemas," or religious authorities.[35] The MB consists of a loose ideological network of like-minded leadership figures, whereas the IGMG provides formal organizational and financial support to Muslim associations across Europe. The MB was founded in 1928 by Hassan al-Banna (1906–1949) in Egypt, the intellectual and political center of Islamism. The movement aimed to Islamize society from below by taking control of religious, academic, cultural, and social institutions. In the words of al-Banna, "Islam is faith and religion, country and nationality, religion and state, spirituality and action, book and spade."[36] The MB, in turn, is influential over Moroccan organizations in France (such as the Union des Organisations Islamiques de France or UOIF). The NGOs based in the Arab-Muslim world—the MB (Egypt and Syria), the Refa party (Turkey), the Jam'at-I Islami party (Pakistan)—maintain the "international nodes" of transnational forms of Islam.[37] These are not simply political movements, Roy writes, but also a sort of religious brotherhood. These movements were able to spread in Western countries through the 1970s and 1980s, Roy argues, thanks to globalized migration and communication technologies.[38]

The IGMG was originally linked to the Refa party through the son of party founder Necmettin Erbakan. Established in Cologne since 1976 as the Islamic Union of Europe (Islamische Union Europa), IGMG currently has fourteen branches in Europe, including one in Brussels. The Cologne office is responsible for finances, while the Bonn office oversees religious issues and mosque construction. Local Milli Görüs branches (called Islamic Federations in Germany) have emerged as a major organizational force among Turks in Europe, principally as the arch-rival of the Turkish state's directorate for religious affairs (DITIB). The IGMG defines itself in contrast to the DITIBs, which consider themselves to be foreign organizations operating under diplomatic cover and which the IGMG views as an obstacle to integration.

The Union des Organisations Islamiques de France (UOIF) is the French branch of the Federation of Islamic Organisations in Europe (FIOE). Headquartered in a defunct factory in the Paris suburbs, the federation was founded in 1983 as a rejection of the Grand Mosque of Paris's monopoly on representation and as a result of other schisms among dissidents of "official" Franco-Algerian Islam. It federates approximately 250 of the many cultural, religious, and professional associations that have appeared since the 1981 reform that allowed foreigners to found associations. It claims control over 150 prayer spaces but directly owns less than a third of these. The UOIF also runs a small theological seminary. Its current president and general secretary are both from Morocco, and both came to France to pursue advanced degrees in Bordeaux. Though the organization has no formal links to the Muslim Brotherhood, its president has used an MB slogan in interviews ("The Qur'an is our constitution") and its general secretary meets regularly with a roving MB ambassador in Europe. UOIF representatives go on regular fundraising trips to the Persian Gulf states and Saudi Arabia, partly with the help of the French offices of the Muslim World League and private donors. There are conflicting accounts as to whether it is one-third or two-thirds foreign financed, but the organization's directors speak openly of their wish to decrease their dependence on foreign aid. The federation maintains a "policy of non-intervention" with regard to its donors: the UOIF independently owns and administers the prayer spaces paid for with Saudi or Gulf-state money. The UOIF has sought to dispel any ambiguity that its sympathies lie with its adopted country, however, and in 1990 changed its name to the Union of Islamic Organizations of France (rather than "in" France).

Two Phases of Strategies in Europe

European governments have evolved from a laissez-faire policy of "outsourcing" state-Islam relations to Muslim diplomats (1974–1989) toward a proactive policy of "incorporation" (1989–2004). The goal of incorporation is to co-opt the competing representatives of *both* "official" and "political" Islam. There were at first geopolitical and domestically rooted disincentives to engage Muslim minorities as if they were a permanent segment of national society. But this period was followed by major incentives to end the laissez-faire policy. Just as the German government came to view the Turkish population in Germany as worthy of *Einbürgerung* (naturalization) by the late 1990s, Muslim religious representatives went from being treated as exogenous actors to serving as local government interlocutors. This shift from outsourcing to incorporation led to a change in the demand for representative organizations in the practical and politically symbolic realm of state-church relations. State-Islam relations emerged as the primary category of integration policy, replacing the emphasis on nationality or citizenship.[39] This has led to sustained efforts to institutionalize relations between religion offices and Muslim organizations along the lines of existing arrangements for other religions.

It was not long after the end of mass migration (1973–1974) that national and local governments in Europe realized they would require an interlocutor in order to attend to the basic religious needs of their newly settled foreign populations. These needs included prayer spaces, imams, facilities for ritual lamb slaughter, and travel visas for pilgrimage to Mecca. But host societies' ambivalent attitudes toward the permanence of these new populations manifested themselves in the type of interlocutor that governments sought out—official "return migration" incentives were in place into the early 1980s.[40] A template of temporary migration defined the governments' demand during the first phase. Guest workers and their offspring were not destined for citizenship, and Islam, as the religion of foreigners, was "an exogenous reality," as Claire de Galembert writes.[41] Governments thus largely entrusted embassies and representatives of the "official Islams" of the Muslim world, whether sending states (e.g., Algeria, Morocco, Turkey) or centers of religious authority (e.g., Egypt, Saudi Arabia), to cater to religious needs. Faced with a community of modest means, and given the legal and political difficulties of providing public funding, European governments encouraged the use of foreign funds for religious practice. From an electoral perspective, local officials undoubtedly viewed this as a safer route in the short term, at a time when extreme right-wing parties were finding their bearings in response to the increasingly visible presence of immigrants in big cities by the late 1970s and early 1980s. This encouragement of a "home country" identity in the domain of religion dovetailed with a mutual fiction of an eventual "return home" for migrants and even their locally born children.

European governments tolerated the Islamic proselytism of foreign envoys from the DITIB, MWL, and GMP, for example, for a clear set of pragmatic reasons. The large, classical mosques that were planned and built across Europe during this period were justified as a fix for the practical needs of local Muslims. It made sense to rely on homeland governments for the material requirements of religious observance since those states had experience in its practical administration. Additionally, those homeland governments attended to the matter of combating extremism in their own national interest. The implantation of official Islam into European national landscapes thus offered a security guarantee. As one French interior ministry official recalled, "Algeria, Morocco, Turkey, and Senegal were able to offer France a common front that was perhaps not pro-Western but at least anti-terrorist."[42]

The minimal accommodation of Islam that took place in the first phase (1974–1989) should be seen in this context. With the minor exception of prayer spaces created in some workplaces and public housing units, governments outsourced relations to Muslim representatives to the embassies and consulates of sending states and the regional religious powerhouse, Saudi Arabia. When the local government in Bavaria created Turkish-language religious instruction in public schools in the early 1980s, for example, Turkish consular officials from DITIB were responsible for curriculum and instruction. In the absence of religious education for Muslims in public schools in North Rhine–Westphalia, the Saudis created the King Fahd Akademie. French authorities allotted funds for Arabic-language radio programs through the Fonds d'Action Sociale, and the foreign ministry created theological scholarships for foreign imams through a program known as Enseignement des Langues et Cultures d'Origine (ELCO). A rare European Community (EC) directive concerning migrant populations in 1976 allowed for language classes to be sponsored by sending countries and taught by foreigners for third country nationals in the EC. What might ostensibly look like multicultural programs, however, were in fact the opposite: the relation with state Islam and homeland culture was intended to facilitate eventual repatriation of migrants and their locally born children.

This laissez-faire policy also served as a diplomatic nod to regional powers in the Muslim world. A reshuffling of the power balance had taken place in the aftermath of Egypt's 1973 defeat in its war against Israel and, in 1979, the Iranian revolution and the religiously inspired coup attempt in Saudi Arabia.[43] European countries sought to contain the regional aspirations of newly theocratic and Shi'ite Iran by supporting its Arab Sunni rivals in Saudi Arabia and in the Maghreb area of North Africa. Tokens of good faith were offered by European governments eager to be on good terms with regional powers in the Arab world, who were the source not only of immigration but also of oil. In the aftermath of OPEC's oil embargo of the United States and the Netherlands in 1973–1974, the Euro-Arab Dialogue (EAD) was institutionalized between twenty-one Arab states and the ten countries of the European Community. The EAD met several times a year to discuss trade issues alongside the theme of "cultural cooperation."[44] Grandiose diplomatic gestures and monuments to the Islamic presence in Europe soon followed. Rome got an enormous mosque at Monte Antenne, authorized by the local city council in 1974 in cooperation with Prime Minister Giulio Andreotti, who had personally asked for the pope's blessing of a minaret in the heart of western Christendom. Belgium recognized Islam as a national religion in 1974. The MWL created major Islamic centers in Brussels and Vienna in 1975. The funds for mosque construction, decorations, and personnel salaries were provided either by Saudi, Moroccan, Algerian, and Turkish embassies and donors from the Gulf states—who were solicited by the non-state Islam groups—or through the collaboration of state Islam with wealthy backers.

The year 1989 was a watershed that initiated the second phase of state-Islam relations, in which governments sought to reassert state sovereignty over transnational Muslim networks. There were several confrontational events involving Islam in the international arena that year. First, the Ayatollah Ruhollah Khomeini pronounced an unfavorable fatwa against Salman Rushdie for his allegedly blasphemous novel *The Satanic Verses*. Then, three head scarf–wearing girls were expelled from a junior high school outside Paris. Finally, that same year, Soviet troops withdrew from Afghanistan.[45] The postcommunist void in central Asia would soon reveal to Europe the extent of Saudi (and later, Turkish) institutional and financial deployment and proselytizing outside the Arab world. These events turned all eyes toward the European territory itself and reverberated within Muslim communities across the continent. They also opened local governments' eyes to the reality of transnational memberships among minority populations. Soon thereafter, the war to drive Iraq out of Kuwait sent further ripples across Muslim populations—where there were a few expressions of sympathy for Saddam Hussein and a lack of understanding about the Saudi alliance with the U.S.-led coalition. Several incidents of Algerian jihadist terrorism occurred in France in the mid-1990s and culminated in a deadly shootout between French special forces and a young Frenchman of Algerian origin.

Cumulative integration failures among young Muslim Europeans contributed to the crystallizing sentiment that, as Hugh Heclo describes the moment preceding policy shifts, "spread a general conviction that something must be done."[46] By the mid- to late 1980s, the children and grandchildren of labor migrants had grown up, and the largely civic-based integration strategy had failed to achieve results in the second and third generations. The half-hearted strategies of inclusion that had stressed anti-racism or citizenship and electoral participation had, to a large extent, fallen flat. Schools in the large urban centers that are home to populations of immigrant origin suffered from budgetary crises, military service was no longer obligatory, and voting rights had not led to much parliamentary representation. The shortcomings of the promise of integration and socioeconomic mobility were clear for all to see. Most significantly for the purposes of this chapter, however, by the late 1980s the convenient bargain of outsourcing was ultimately judged to be counterproductive in terms of the integration of Muslims. NGOs associated with the political Islam movements of transnational Muslim civil society in the diaspora—such as the UOIF and IGMG discussed above—were increasingly assertive and behaved in the manner of the most prominent associations of official Islam. They conglomerated sympathetic prayer rooms and cultural associations under common-law umbrella organizations that were ineligible for the status of state-church associations and were therefore beyond the oversight and control of the government.

In this same period, the second and third generations who had been expected to assimilate (or to "return home") instead discovered religious identity in their new societies. Surveys have shown that many of these young people identified more with their inherited religion than with their nationality, place of residence, or even gender. This might be called re-Islamization or the "Ummah phenomenon" (Ummah refers to the larger Muslim community).[47] Jean-Pierre Chevènement, who as interior minister initiated the final round of consultations leading to the Conseil Français du Culte Musulman, pointed to this development in an interview: "It was only upon discovering that Islam was a form of identity affirmation for people who do not have much else that I [realized] it was important to engage in dialogue with these young people, who are having an identity crisis—we must not leave Islam outside."[48] This observation is emblematic of a broader change among public authorities, who adjusted their view of second and third generations from "youth of immigrant origin" and came to see them, for limited public policy purposes, as "Muslims."

Authorities' attitudes toward "official" Islam changed significantly during this period. It is not that European governments suddenly discovered the Islam of sending states to be anti-democratic or even fundamentalist. Indeed, as "official" Islams they aim by definition for a peaceful relationship between religion and state. But their religious emissaries perpetuated a competing foreign tie among populations of immigrant origin—an Islam "in" rather than "of," in politicians' shorthand. The maturation of migrant Muslim communities that retained strong organizational ties to homeland governments and nurtured connections with almost entirely unregulated dissident organizations of "political" Islam combined with a growing perception of transnational threats linked to global Islam.[49]

In this second phase of state-Islam relations, interior ministries initiated consultations with a broader swath of Muslim representatives, expanding their contacts with Muslims well beyond the "official" Islams of the homeland. This required delicate negotiations in which officials felt a need to tread lightly. These negotiations involved not just diplomatic representatives (though they remained crucial) but also civil society organizations—including international NGOs affiliated with political or dissident Islam. This period has seen the reassertion of nation-state sovereignty over the informal influence of international religious NGOs and foreign embassies. This phase of Muslim incorporation has been about "de-transnationalization," or undoing the power arrangement of the 1970s and 1980s that had privileged Saudi Arabia and other Muslim sending states in the practice of Islam in Europe. This phase has also involved reining in the unregulated associations of transnational "political" Islam active on national territory. Interior ministries provided the first impetus to organize Islam as a "national" religion, and the government-led consultations established a variety of national councils. In 1989, France began its fifteen-year journey to the Conseil Français du Culte Musulman (CFCM). By 1992, Spain had a Comisión Islamica. By 1998, Belgium had an Exécutif Musulman. By 2000, there were special councils to guide state-Islam relations in seven German *Länder,* and the Deutsche Islam Konferenz was launched in 2006. By 2002, official encouragement led to a newly consolidated Muslim Council of Britain, and by 2003, the Consulta Islamica was initiated to assign an interlocutor among the newly arrived Muslim communities In Italy.

These national processes are not identical. Some place more weight on the role of "official" Islam and foreign government representatives (Belgium is seen as one case of this), while others rely more heavily on hand-picked local civil society organizations (Italy is a good example). There are some striking differences. For example, the French administration has been content to concentrate solely on *religious* representation: the CFCM is designed to represent only the 6 to 8 percent of observant Muslims who regularly attend prayer services.[50]

Italy has proposed something less official than a council: an informal consultation, or *consulta,* which has the goal of not only religious representation but also social and political representation of the Muslim minority. Italian officials are focusing their consulta on what Giuseppe Pisanu, Italy's former interior minister, called the "95% of moderate Muslims," whether observant or not. They include civil society representatives, secular Muslims, women's groups, and so forth. Previous sluggishness in granting recognition to Muslim communities was intended to avoid the unknown consequences of ending the representative monopoly of the Saudi- and Moroccan-dominated Centro Culturale Islamico d'Italia (CCII) in Rome, which had served as a de facto representative for organized Islam since 1974. Chartered well before the settlement of any significant number of labor migrants, the CCII's administrative council is made up mostly of ambassadors from most Muslim countries accredited with the Italian state and Vatican City. CCII boasts the largest mosque in Europe (5,000-person capacity, including outdoor spaces) but counts only 25 other prayer spaces under its organizational umbrella. The government has been loath to jeopardize diplomatic relations with these international guardians of Islam, who oversaw the creation of prayer spaces for labor migrants in the 1970s and 1980s. Italian administrators shared the same anxieties as their counterparts in other European countries regarding the integration of a new religious community that outgrew the "Embassy Islam" that emanates from the guardian states. Several other umbrella organizations claiming to represent Islam in Italy have competed for government recognition since the 1990s. The largest is the Ancona-based Unione delle Comunità ed Organizzazioni Islamiche in Italia (UCOII, founded in 1990), which is associated with the political Islam of the Muslim Brotherhood. The UCOII claims to represent 200 to 300 Muslim associations and approximately 70 to 120 prayer spaces.

In a crucial change from previous models of consultation in Italy that relied almost exclusively on representatives of "Embassy Islam," the new Consultative Council includes a representative of the UCOII. It also includes "lay" civil society leaders and non-prayer associations in Italy. The UCOII secretary general, Mohamed Nour Dachan, had previously been snubbed in official meetings. But he increasingly tried to burnish the UCOII's image as a moderate organization, including organizing nationwide demonstrations on September 11, 2004, "against war and terrorism." Dachan also volunteered his aid in negotiations to free Italian hostages in Iraq and, more recently, Yemen. Pisanu said of his decision to include Dachan, "I took into account what the UCOII is today—not its past—and the efforts it has made for a positive evolution of the Muslim Brotherhood in the whole world."[51]

The interior ministry eliminated the earlier embargo on Dachan's political Islam federation participating in the Consultative Council. But the Italian government has proceeded slowly, crafting its response without rushing headlong into a final institutional arrangement. The Consultative Council does not, for now, benefit from the status of a recognized community body as outlined in the Italian constitution. The interior ministry argued that the Muslim population is not ripe for formal representation via the existing state-church mechanism, called an *Intesa*. It is used with assorted Christian and Jewish communities and can be formalized only with Italian citizens. Instead, the interior minister used a nontraditional formula to make individual appointments to the Consultative Council. The chosen participants are thus not restricted to religious leadership. The Consultative Council reflects the range of Muslim civil society in Italy without any pretense of "representing" Muslims in Italy. Sixteen members were named in November 2005 and approved by the government in February 2006. They include a UCOII representative, a CCII/Muslim World League representative, and a representative of the Comunità Religiosa Islamica d'Italia (COREIS) alongside three association leaders, three journalists, two health-care workers, an imam, a literature professor, a student leader, an author, and a charity worker. There are four women; one member is a twenty-two-year-old student; twelve national origins are represented (only nine of the sixteen members are of Arab origin); and eight of the sixteen are Italian citizens (several have been naturalized). This is a sharp departure from the short-lived Consiglio Islamico d'Italia (Islamic Council of Italy, 1998–2001). It included just five leaders from religious federations and fell apart because of differences between representatives of the Muslim World League and the UCOII before it could present a common request for an *Intesa*.

In their first meeting, the Consultative Council members condemned violent protests against caricatures of the prophet Mohammed, as well as the caricatures themselves. Like their French counterparts, the UCOII has requested that laws against inciting racial hatred (Legge Mancini) be enforced against newspapers that reprinted the cartoons. The Danish embassy released a common declaration with UCOII. Pisanu commented, "[A]nyone participating in this meeting would have understood that there is a moderate Islam in Italy."[52] In their second meeting, one month later, leaders asked the government to develop an optional Muslim religious hour in public schools (seen by many as an alternative to Qur'an schools).

In Germany, by contrast, the councils in various *Länder* (since religion is a local competence) have resembled single-issue coalitions uniting to accomplish specific tasks, such as organizing religious education in public schools. German accommodation of Islam has also heavily relied on court cases. In addition, the office entrusted with upholding the constitution has played a special role, in effect excluding "political" Islam participants from consultations. The two-year German Islam Conference (Deutsche Islam Konferenz or DIK) was launched in September 2006. It is the first national effort to gather representatives of national and local governments together with the leaders of major Muslim federations as well as hand-picked individuals who embody a "modern, secular Islam," in the words of the interior minister, Wolfgang Schäuble. With the government's Deutsche Islam Konferenz, which got under way in Berlin's Charlottenburg Castle, there is at long last a national initiative to formally recognize interlocutors for Islam. The makeup of the DIK belies the German Interior Ministry's dual agenda of recognition *and* religious reform. The membership of the conference consists of fifteen state representatives (from the federal, *Länder,* and municipal levels) and fifteen representatives of Islam in Germany.[53] On the Muslim side, the five main federations invited to the consultation (Islamrat, ZMD, DITIB, VIKZ, and the Alevis) together are estimated to represent from 15 to 20 percent of the general Muslim population. Alongside these membership organizations are ten ministerial appointees, including, in Schäuble's words, "representatives of a modern secular Islam" from business, society, science, and culture. Schäuble explained the consultation's guiding principles in a 2006 interview: "Our state order is not unfamiliar with religion [but] we have the separation of state and religion. We will make constitutional standards clear in the DIK."[54] Whether or not the DIK is in fact inspired by grand designs of religious reform, the everyday agenda of the consultation will be practically oriented. The DIK has much to recommend it as a representative body that will allow for regular discussions. These discussions, between Muslims and the highest administrative levels, will be about the practical policy issues relating to religious observance, from mosque construction and religious education to *halal* slaughter and chaplains in public institutions. By agreeing to meet with these federations to discuss practical matters of Islamic observance, the Angela Merkel government expects these organizations to produce a more or less united front on behalf of prayer spaces and observant Muslims in Germany. The government's decision to introduce a standard for Islamic religious education, in particular, has been welcomed across the board, from the chair of the Central Council of Jews in Germany to Schäuble's CDU and CSU colleagues (although some contend it is properly the jurisdiction of the *Länder*).

The government has given the DIK an initial time frame of two to three years, after which Muslim leaders may agree to "make a kind of round table, elect a leader and rotate, along the model of the charity organizations that have several umbrella organizations."[55] The conference will be divided into four thirty-person working groups, which will issue reports twice annually (the first met in November 2006).[56] The IGMG has even been invited to participate in a DIK working group, though not as an official participant in the conference. Nonetheless, the DIK represents a radical departure for a CDU minister. Schäuble opened his summary to the Bundestag the day after the DIK by citing the Turkish-German film director Fatih Akin: many of Germany's Muslims "have forgotten about going back home." They are "no longer a foreign population group," Schäuble said, but rather "have become a component of our society . . . their children and grandchildren have long felt themselves to be Germans of Turkish or Arab origin." However, he also expressed his agenda for transformation by quoting the French-Lebanese author Amin Maalouf, saying that if a country grants recognition and acceptance then it "also has the right to ask [Muslims] to renounce certain aspects of [their] culture."[57]

A good first opportunity to illustrate Schäuble's point came with the uproar over the cancellation of Mozart's *Idomeneo* at the Deutsche Oper, which is within walking distance of the Charlottenburg Castle, where the DIK held its first meeting. A proposal was made that all thirty DIK members go to see the opera together. The Islamrat representative demurred, saying that "even though it would have pleased the Minister, artistic freedom doesn't mean you have to go see everything."[58] The government has been lauded for its effort to elicit a single body representing Muslims for religious purposes; there is gen-

eral agreement with Schäuble's assertion, "better now than later or not at all."
It is an open question whether the DIK will be the forum for an "emancipa-
tory march through institutions" earlier envisioned by the German-Turkish
author Zafer Senoçak. To say this is not to downplay the practical advantages
of the DIK. As the Green party politician Omid Nouripour, one of the interior ministry appointees, remarked, "[I]f inner-Muslim controversies come to
further light in the public sphere, then Muslims and Germans will become
more aware that there is not one Islam—that is as valuable as a contract with
the state."[59]

The commonalities of these national consultations with Islam in the second phase are striking. European nation-states have undertaken a gradual institutional process of "de-transnationalizing" the practice of Islam. These
governments have gone about integrating Islam into state-church relations by
negotiating a delicate settlement between "official" and "political" Islam. They
have also used several specific instruments of nationalization familiar from
previous instances of institutional incorporation. Space constraints prevent a
full discussion of these instruments, but they include three crucial steps. The
first is a charter or founding document in which participating Muslim organizations confirm their respect for the rule of law. The second is the establishment of technical working groups that include representatives of the two
competing Islams alongside state representatives. The third is, crucially, the
nomination or election of a representative council that can serve as an interlocutor for state-church affairs.

The emergence of organized Islam as a permanent fixture in the European religious landscape was under way long before September 11, before a surge in
anti-Semitic acts or the departure of young British and French Muslims on
suicide missions in Israel and Iraq. Contrary to the announcement of the
state's imminent death in the face of globalization and transnationalism, we
can see that government activity has not diminished but increased. European
nation-states have established routine contacts with Muslim leaders, leading
to a new level of mutual acquaintance and a slow but steady process of nationalization of religious authority.

Muslims in Europe today are still far from experiencing full political integration, but increasing numbers of leaders are being received in the halls of
power. The predominant scene of state-Islam interactions is not just one of
unabated conflict but of government officials sitting down with Muslims—
the pope at Castelgandolfo, the French interior minister at Château Nainville-
les-Roches in 2003, the German interior minister at Charlottenburg Castle in
2006, and the Italian president at the Quirinale Palace in 2004. As a result of

meticulous institution building by interior ministries across the continent, these post-crisis sit-downs are no longer the random, ad hoc gatherings of foreign dignitaries they once were. In practice, authorities have effectively opened up communication channels. These channels serve both as a first response of the putative Muslim community and as a temporary substitute for the millions of citizens and residents of Muslim origin who are, for the time being, without significant electoral representation.

The brief history of confrontations between the sensibilities of some Muslim leaders and majority societies in the last several years alone has afforded observers several chances to test the thesis of a "clash of civilizations." It has also offered a chance to test the institutions that were born of the shift from "outsourcing" to state-led strategies of incorporation. The controversies over the Danish caricatures and the pope's remarks have been universally acknowledged as "proof" of a clash. On the one hand, these instances were indeed a sign of "failure" in Europe. The failure of local dialogue in Denmark led Muslim leaders to appeal for support abroad, with consequences clear to all. But these have also been accompanied by a measure of success. During the caricatures controversy, Europe's Muslim populations engaged in nothing like what took place in cities across the Arab-Muslim world, from Lebanon to Libya, Nigeria to Pakistan. Instead, Muslims in Europe expressed their outrage and offense lawfully, through the new and old institutions created to govern state-Islam relations. Members of the CFCM in France, the Consulta in Italy, and the future German DIK, for example, all condemned the cartoons *and* the violence, and several pursued lawsuits against newspapers and magazines that reprinted the cartoons. In other words, they behaved like any other aggrieved minority group in those countries.

Church-state relations are of vital importance because these institutional links with religious communities provide key elements of political integration. If not attended to, as in the first period of "outsourcing," transnational religious networks have the potential to threaten the state and its maintenance of social order. By taking the initiative to incorporate and nationalize Islam in their respective institutional orders, European states have attempted to influence what kind of Islam young people discover—whether they search out religion as a reaction against European societies or whether they are just satisfying curiosity about their heritage or carrying on family traditions. Church-state relations are instrumental in achieving the state's core duties of stability and security. Governments took into consideration the unintended consequences of their previous laissez-faire strategies in state-Islam relations and took stock of unanticipated developments among the immigrant populations. Of course, these populations did not "go home," and the networks of embassies and NGOs whose religious activities and proselytism European governments had uncritically tolerated for fifteen years turned out to be more tenacious than expected. But the strategy in the first period of keeping religion private, of keeping Islam out of the public sphere, and of using international diplomacy to manage the religion of immigrants was judged to be a failure. The national governments have assumed an active posture in state-religion affairs because Islam has emerged as a major factor of individual and group identity among the descendants of labor migrants.

13

Dissonance between Discourse and Practice in EU Border Control Enforcement

The Spanish Case

FRANCISCO JAVIER MORENO FUENTES

In October 2005, the images of hundreds of potential migrants from sub-Saharan Africa trying to jump over the fences that separate the Spanish North African enclaves of Ceuta and Melilla from Moroccan territory made headlines around the world. Officials strengthened border controls in these two cities, but those trying to reach Spain turned toward the coasts of the Western Sahara, Mauritania, Senegal, and Gambia. They hoped to board rafts that would take them to the Canary Islands, creating a new humanitarian crisis over the summer of 2006. Beyond the temporary media attention granted to those seeking new lives in Western Europe, those dramatic images drew attention to the strong migratory pressures felt by the European Union in general and, more specifically, by Spain.

Like the other southern member states of the EU, Spain has shifted in status from a traditional "sending" country to net receiver of migratory flows over the last two decades. This change in position in the international migration system was determined by three interconnected processes. The first was an important transformation of Spain's economic structure. The second was a relatively smooth political transition from a right-wing dictatorship to a liberal parliamentary democracy. The third process was the country's entry into the European Economic Community (EEC) in 1986. In this context of large economic and political changes, the direction of migratory flows reversed and, together with considerable numbers of returned migrants, an initially small but increasingly growing number of foreign nationals settled in Spain.

The response of Spanish authorities to this phenomenon was initially determined by goals and objectives defined at the European level. During the 1980s, European objectives of tightening external border controls were readily accepted by Spanish administrations. In an example of "Europeanization," domestic policies were adapted to meet explicit European requirements. The result was a very restrictive immigration policy that did not correspond to the migratory processes that were affecting Spain. Over time, tension developed between the externally induced restrictive policy and the immigration situation at the national level. Spain was seeing large numbers of undocumented immigrants, high demand for unskilled labor, changes to foreign policy and economic interests in sending regions, and so forth. The growing tension led to the increasing importance of immigration on Spain's political agenda and the gradual development of a more comprehensive set of policies. While complying with EU requirements for strict border policing, these policies increased the degree of Spanish authorities' intervention in this area.

In this chapter I contextualize the position of Spain within the world migration system. I also frame the analysis of Spanish immigration policies within the European context. Finally, I analyze the evolution of Spanish policies toward migration that are caught between the need to comply with the EU's tough discourses on migration and the confluence of supply and demand that made Spain among the largest receivers of migrants during recent years. By reviewing the combination of border control discourses and policy measures together with the policies intended to integrate populations of immigrant origin, I reveal the complex picture of migration policies in Spain over the last two decades. I also address the challenges Spanish authorities face, paying particular attention to the implications that Spain's changing position in the world migration system will have for Spanish society in the future.

The Changing Position of Spain in the World Migration System

In the last quarter of the twentieth century, the countries of Southern Europe, until then net exporters of labor, progressively became countries of immigration. This was due to the end of outgoing migration and the arrival of growing numbers of migrants from less developed countries. In the Spanish case, the closure of Western European economies to further labor migration after the 1973 oil crisis marked the end of the cycle of mass emigration. Taking advantage of the schemes set up by some European countries, more than 300,000 Spanish nationals returned to Spain between 1974 and 1977.[1] After that inflection point, Spain started to receive migration flows that have considerably accelerated during recent years. The total figures of foreign residents in Spain remained relatively modest during the 1980s and 1990s (especially when compared to other European countries). Those numbers began growing very fast in the early 2000s (foreign-born individuals represented 1.8 percent of the Spanish population in 1978; in 2006 they constituted more than 9 percent).[2] Coming from all continents, these groups settled in the two largest cities (Madrid and Barcelona) as well as in the most economically dynamic areas along the Mediterranean coast (Valencia, Murcia, and Andalucía).

A series of interrelated factors account for the migratory pressures experienced by Spain. During the 1980s the Spanish economy faced a series of important reforms (tertiarization, a crisis in labor-intensive activities, deregulation) linked to Spain's entry into the EEC in 1986 and subsequent opening of its economy to international markets. Despite the high unemployment rates resulting from those transformations, the Spanish economy gradually generated jobs both at the top and at the very bottom of the occupational scale, positions that were partly occupied by foreigners. At the upper end of the social and occupational scale, the removal of barriers to foreign capital implied the arrival of highly qualified professionals to occupy managerial positions. In addition, Northern European pensioners in search of milder winters at an affordable price contributed to the increasing number of foreigners living in Spain. The size of these privileged groups increased eightfold between 1975 and 2005. In general terms, foreigners from developed countries (most of them nationals of other EU member states) did not represent an issue for Spanish public opinion.

At the other end, a series of labor market niches, composed of low-skilled, poorly paid jobs not readily accepted by Spanish nationals, were occupied by immigrants from developing countries. Table 13.1 lists immigrants living in Spain according to their region of origin based on data drawn from official figures regarding legal residents rather than on census data. In addition to the rapid increase in the number of foreign residents, two aspects deserve particular attention. One is the differential growth rates in the number of Latin American and Eastern European residents with relation to those coming from Africa. The other is the considerable discrepancies between the data on legal residents (provided by the Ministry of Interior), and that on residency (generated by the census and gathered without regard to individuals' administrative or legal status), particularly for the 2002–2003 period.

The number of Latin American migrants living in Spain increased nearly

Table 13.1
Foreigners living in Spain by region of origin

Year	Total	EU[1]	Rest of Europe	North America	Latin America	Africa	Asia
	Foreign legal residents (data from the Ministry of Interior)						
1975	165,289	92,917	9,785	12,361	35,781	3,232	9,393
1980	182,045	106,738	11,634	12,363	34,338	4,067	11,419
1985	241,971	142,346	15,780	15,406	38,671	8,529	19,451
1990	407,647	—	—	21,186	59,372	25,854	29,116
1995	499,773	235,858	19,844	19,992	88,940	95,718	38,352
1997	609,800	260,600	28,500	21,000	106,000	142,800	49,100
1999	801,339	312,203	41,353	17,138	149,571	213,012	66,340
2001	1,109,060	331,352	81,170	15,020	282,778	304,109	91,552
2002	1,324,001	362,858	107,574	15,774	364,569	366,518	104,665
2003	1,647,011	406,199	154,001	16,163	514,484	432,662	121,455
2004	1,977,291	498,875	168,900	16,964	649,122	498,507	142,762
2005	2,738,932	569,284	337,177	17,052	986,178	649,251	177,423
2006[2]	2,873,250	598,832	359,840	17,446	1,037,110	671,931	185,355
	Data from the census[3]						
2002	1,977,944	489,813	212,132	22,103	730,459	423,045	98,942
2003	2,664,168	587,949	348,585	25,963	1,047,564	522,682	128,952
2004	3,034,326	636,037	404,643	24,613	1,237,806	579,372	142,828
2005	3,691,547	766,678	561,475	28,404	1,431,770	705,944	186,227
2006[4]	3,884,600	916,100	645,600	30,000	1,350,000	741,600	202,100

Source: Ministerio del Interior, "Anuario de Extranjería," 2002; Instituto Nacional de Estadística, "Boletín informativo del INE," no. 3, 2006; and Ministerio de Trabajo y Asuntos Sociales (MTAS), "Anuario de Migraciones 2005," Dirección General de Migraciones, Madrid, 2005.
Notes: [1] EU data includes nationals of the new member states after the enlargement processes of 2001 (EU 15) and 2004 (EU 25).
[2] Data for March 31.
[3] Includes all those registered in the census, regardless of their legal status.
[4] Temporary data for January 1, 2006.

fifteenfold between 1997 and 2005, and that of Eastern Europeans by a factor of almost twenty. The number of immigrants coming from the African continent over the same period increased fivefold. Following this shift, Moroccans, traditionally the most numerous foreign community from a developing country living in Spain, fell to second in the ranking of immigrant communities after the year 2000 (with some 14.2 percent of the total foreign population). This change in the relative position of North Africans was fundamentally the consequence of a massive arrival of immigrants from Latin America. Those from Ecuador became the largest migrant community, representing 14.6 percent of the foreign population. Large numbers also came from Colombia, Bolivia, and Argentina and from Eastern Europe (e.g., Rumania, Bulgaria). These differences in the growth rates of different immigrant communities were to a large extent the result of the border control policies implemented by Spanish authorities.

In September 2005, the number of foreigners administratively included in the Spanish social security system was 1.7 million (about 9.4 percent of the total social security working force). This figure does not take into consideration the important role of foreigners in the informal economy. A more precise depiction of the labor market situation is provided by the census. It shows that in 2001, foreigners represented more than 8.4 percent of the work force in the agricultural sector, nearly 7 percent of the construction labor force, and more than 3 percent of industrial workers. In specific sectors (domestic service, with more than 26 percent, and catering, more than 10 percent), foreigners constitute a significant share of the work force.

As we can see in table 13.2, the segmentation of labor markets by origin of the migrants is quite strong. Latin American migrants are overrepresented in the service sector (where Africans have a much lower presence), and Africans are particularly present in the agriculture and construction sectors. This segmentation is the consequence of a very complex combination of factors. These factors include the different skills and qualifications (academic and linguistic) of the migrants and the prejudices, stereotypes, and expectations of the receiving society in relation to each group. Another factor is the availability to take those jobs by being physically present in Spanish territory (even if, or actually preferably, as undocumented migrants).

The gradual development of a common European market, with the weak-

Table 13.2
Participation in different economic sectors by origin (%)

	Agriculture	Industry	Construction	Services
All foreigners	11.4	12.1	17.2	59.2
Non-EU Europeans	14.1	13.3	23.1	49.4
Africans	23.8	15.0	24.0	37.1
Latin Americans	8.6	10.0	16.0	65.4
Asians	5.5	11.5	12.0	71.0

Source: Instituto Nacional de Estadística, "Boletín informativo del INE," no. 3, 2006.

ening of internal boundaries and the creation of a common external border, forced national policymakers to take steps to try to coordinate their immigration policies. In the Spanish case, this European debate has had an extremely important role, since Spain did not have a specific way of handling migration prior to its incorporation into the European supranational integration process.

EU Immigration Policies and the Concept of "Fortress Europe"

The common market clearly placed strong pressures on national policymakers to coordinate their immigrant integration policies with those of other EU countries.[3] The development of a common European immigration policy has been the result of an incremental process. It began with the granting of free movement for workers within the EEC and led to the definition of common procedures in asylum, border control, or family reunification. The nature of this increasingly communitarized area of policy could be defined as an uneasy equilibrium. It must balance between a restrictive trend, revolving around the strict control of the EU external borders, and more inclusive tendencies, which promote policies such as giving third country nationals the same rights as European citizens or integrating foreign populations into European societies.

With the implementation of the Schengen Agreement by a group of European countries, the restrictive tendencies took the shape of a strong emphasis on border control issues. Such issues include common visa policies, coordination of police forces, and exchange of computerized personal data. Another restrictive outcome was the conceptualization of illegal immigration and international crime as illicit activities to be prevented through the intervention of police forces. The implementation of the Dublin Convention also resulted in a restrictive shift in asylum policies in most EU member countries.

The Maastricht Treaty of 1991 (the Treaty of the European Union or TEU) represented a significant step toward creating "Fortress Europe" within the new institutional framework of the so-called "third pillar." Moreover, the introduction of the concept of European citizenship for nationals of member states fueled fears that the process of European integration would exclude third country nationals living within the Union.

The entry into force of the Amsterdam Treaty, in May 1999, represented an additional step forward in the process of coordinating immigration policy within the EU. The creation of an Area of Freedom, Security, and Justice shifted issues of asylum, admission, and residence of third country nationals and of immigration from the third (intergovernmental) pillar, to the first. The whole Schengen scheme (up to then an intergovernmental agreement outside of the EU structure) was then incorporated into the EU framework. In addition, the Amsterdam Treaty attributed competences to European institutions to combat discrimination based on sex, racial or ethnic origin, religion or belief, disability, age, or sexual orientation. The EU Commission elevated a series of reports and communications to the Council and to the European Parliament on the social integration of immigrants in the member states.[4] It did so with the objective of counterbalancing the emphasis on border control measures and coordinating immigration and asylum policies across the Union. The Commission under the TEU had relatively little power to set an agenda. The result was poor implementation of these proposals. The governments of member states strongly resisted increasing the competences of the Commission and the European Parliament in issues related to the integration of immigrant populations. That resistance resulted in little development of more inclusive policies at the EU level and, therefore, more policies aimed at regulating and controlling migratory flows to the Union.

The Plan of Action of the Council and the Commission on the implementation of the Amsterdam Treaty made a distinction between measures to be taken within two years and those to be taken within five years of the treaty's entry into force. In the first group were issues of readmission and return, combating illegal immigration, procedures and conditions for issuing visas and the list of countries whose nationals are subject to visa requirements, and carriers' liability. Among those policies to be developed within five years were long-term residence permits, family reunification, conditions of entry and residence, and movement of third country nationals across the EU. Between these two groups of policy objectives the division introduced between control and integration was quite explicit, as was the priority granted to the first over the second in terms of timing. For the first time, however, integration issues were at least recognized as an area of policy that should be addressed at the European level.

Despite the explicit recognition of the need to move toward standardizing integration policies in the EU, as specified by the conclusions of the Tampere Summit, the specific mechanisms through which those objectives should be achieved remained uncertain. Even agreeing that there should be a common policy to control the EU's external borders proved to be a difficult task. The development of a common set of policies to promote the integration of immigrants in the EU provoked even stronger resistance from member states. The reluctance on the part of state authorities to further EU intervention in this policy area can be traced to two sources. One is the existence of nationally specific philosophies of integration. The other is the perception that integration policies are intimately connected to the notion of state sovereignty (these policies define the *demos,* that is to say, those who belong to the polity and are entitled to participate).[5]

The tensions between policies of restriction versus integration have been reproduced in a very country-specific manner in all member states. It is thus extremely difficult to characterize immigration policies in the EU under a single label. Similarly, some might consider the impact of the EU in policymaking procedures at the national level only as the result of the implementation of EU directives or regulations. Doing so, however, would underestimate the impact of the complex and subtle processes of policy learning and emulation that take place in a political entity such as the EU.[6] As Patrick Weil points out, the convergence of national immigration policies in Western Europe occurred because of international constraints and similar conditions during the policymaking process. He notes, however, that there have in fact been very different policy outcomes in each country.[7] Several factors in the immigration policy sphere could explain those different outcomes. Another reason for the diverging outcomes could include the different policy tools chosen by each state for the implementation of those policies.[8]

Evolution of Spanish Migration Policies

During the 1980s, EU objectives in border control policies were implemented in a relatively straightforward manner in Spain. This was possible because they did not challenge previously existing policies, seriously damage articulated interests, or openly question other areas of policies applied by the Spanish state. It was a clear example of "direct Europeanization," that is, domestic policy changes in response to a series of explicit requirements defined at the EU level.[9]

With regard to integration policies, the lack of a well-defined guideline emanating from the supranational level, and/or of any external pressure to implement policies in a specific direction, implied that Spanish authorities had more room for maneuver while designing those policies. Although domestic considerations determined when those types of policies could be implemented, Spanish authorities used the European Commission's proposals for coordinating integration policies as a basic frame of reference. This is an example of "indirect Europeanization," because national policymakers conceived a domestic issue within a European frame of reference and adapted their policies to fit that framework, even though no specific reason to do so existed.

Spain as Guardian of the EU's Southern Border

Up to 1985, Spanish legislation on immigration was characterized by two main features. First, issues related to immigration were defined as matters of "public order" (and therefore were the exclusive responsibility of the Ministry of Interior). The other feature was that all other issues related to the settlement of foreign nationals in Spain had been subject to extremely weak regulations. (These related issues included the defining of rights and duties, regulation of their incorporation into the labor market, access to social services, and so forth.) This situation determined, to some extent, the context in which the first legislation on immigration was to be defined and implemented.

In July 1985, the government passed the first law aimed at regulating immigration to Spain. The legislation was presented as an urgent bill, and the proceedings were considerably shortened, thus facilitating its passage before the formal incorporation of Spain into the EEC in January 1986. The urgency, together with the extremely low profile of this policy area in the political agenda, made for a very poor debate in Parliament, with virtually no amendments to the bill being presented. The Ley Orgánica 7/1985 sobre derechos y libertades de los extranjeros en España (commonly known as Ley de Extranjería, Alien Act) was passed in Parliament almost unanimously (only five members voted against it).

The new legislation had a very restrictive character, with a strong emphasis on issues of border control. Despite its title, evocative of the rights and freedoms that were to be enjoyed by foreigners in Spain, the policing aspects of the legislation, and its inability to deal with issues arising from the daily presence of immigrant populations, were soon quite apparent. During the debate on the 1985 law, MPs had made many references to the importance of preventing the activities of international criminal organizations, terrorist groups, and drug smugglers. There was hardly any mention of the need to integrate the newly arrived immigrants into Spanish society. In line with that emphasis on control, several articles of the law explicitly limited the rights of foreigners living in Spain to associate and to hold meetings. The new law also defined presence on Spanish soil without authorization as an offense punishable by expulsion from the territory.

In many other respects, the law fell short of what a comprehensive immigration law should have been. One of its main limitations was the extremely restrictive character of the system of work and residence permits that it established. While it did not recognize the existence of permanent permits, the law introduced a highly demanding set of requirements for the renewal of the temporary permits already granted. Paying little attention to the need to integrate immigrant populations, the 1985 law did not recognize immigrants' right to family reunification. Similarly, it did not address the issue of immigrants' rights to access social security services (health care, education, personal services, housing), leaving this issue unregulated and in the hands of regional governments. As a result of the conditions under which the 1985 law was passed, the Ley de Extranjería clearly placed Spain in the role of gatekeeper at the EEC's southern border. The strong emphasis on border control issues responded explicitly to that responsibility, while it left unresolved the real needs arising from the presence of a still small but growing number of immigrants from less developed countries living and working in Spain.

The strict rules that began regulating labor migration to Spain in 1985 resulted in a significant rise in demand for asylum because many immigrants tried to legalize their status by applying for asylum. This situation, which reached a peak in 1993, was answered with a tightening of the requirements for gaining asylum. The result was a drastic decline in the rate of acceptance for asylum status. In 1994, the government introduced significant changes in ten-year-old legislation that was considered to be too generous to asylum seekers. The main argument used to justify the restrictive shift in the legislation was the need to comply with compromises signed at the EU level. With the objective of adapting Spanish legislation to the requirements of the Schengen Agreement and the Dublin Convention, the government introduced an abbreviated process of admission. This admission would be allowed prior to formal acceptance of application for asylum and was designed to act as a filter and to eliminate those demands considered "clearly abusive." This system of "pre-filtering" was implemented in accordance with the resolutions adopted in December 1992 at the London meeting of EU ministers in charge of immigration issues.

As we can see in table 13.3, those changes in the legislation resulted in a very sharp decline in the number of applications for asylum. Despite that decrease in the number of applications, and the existence of the filtering mechanism that considerably reduced the number of demands ultimately considered, the acceptance rate remained at the very low levels established in the mid-1980s.

The extremely restrictive impact of the legislation on political asylum can be perceived in table 13.4. The data show that Spain was one of the European countries that received the smallest number of applications for political asylum during the 1990s while also having one of the lowest acceptance rates.

The development of restrictive legislation with a strong emphasis on issues of border control was supposed to be matched with an increase in resources allocated to police the borders. The evidence for this arrangement is slightly

Table 13.3
Evolution of political asylum in Spain, 1986–2006

Years	Requests submitted	Requests considered	Requests accepted	Acceptance rate	Number of people
1986	—	709	401	56.6	850
1987	2,500	843	262	31.1	513
1988	4,516	1,379	303	22.0	555
1989	4,077	1,515	134	8.8	264
1990	8,647	2,236	246	11.0	490
1991	8,138	3,808	156	4.1	313
1992	11,708	7,357	296	4.0	543
1993	12,615	14,954	592	4.0	1,287
1994	11,192	11,045	345	3.1	627
1995	5,678	4,941	276	5.6	464
1996	4,730	3,521	143	4.7	243
1997	4,975	3,822	105	2.7	156
1998	6,764	4,475	123	2.7	238
1999	8,405	2,661	172	2.04	294
2000	7,926	1,688	218	2.75	370
2001	9,074	2,539	167	3.28	298
2002	6,309	1,729	—	2.80	175
2003	5,248	4,598	153	2.91	227
2004	4,929	1,977	111	2.25	161
2005	5,254	—	—	3.05	202

Source: Compiled by the author with data from Ministerio de Trabajo y Asuntos Sociales, "Informe sobre la inmigración y el asilo en España," Foro para la Integración Social de los Inmigrantes, 1998; Ministerio del Interior, "Anuario Estadístico de Extranjería," Comisión Interministerial de Extranjería (Madrid, 1998); and CIDOB Fundación,"Anuario internacional CIDOB 2005" (Barcelona, 2006).

less than conclusive. Up to the late 1980s, Spanish authorities maintained a relatively flexible stand on the implementation of effective policies of border closure.[10] The complex nature of relations with Morocco and the close historical connections with Latin America made Spanish authorities adopt a more relaxed attitude toward the flows of migrants coming from those areas. The government thus facilitated the development of significant communities of Moroccan and Latin American immigrants working and living in Spain.

The attitude of the Spanish authorities with respect to policing the borders changed gradually in the early 1990s. In May 1991, coinciding with the expiration of agreements with Morocco and Tunisia for mutual limits on visas, the Spanish government reintroduced the requirement of visas for nationals of countries from the Maghreb region. This change was again related

Table 13.4
Political asylum cumulative statistics, 1989–1998

Country	Applications for asylum	Requests accepted	Acceptance Rate (%)
Germany	2,024,960	163,178	8.0
France	324,150	82,180	25.3
Belgium	153,060	11,386	7.4
Spain	77,620	4,371	5.6
Italy	44,460	4,610	10.3

Source: United Nations High Commissioner for Refugees (UNHCR), "Asylum Levels and Trends in Industrialized Countries: First Quarter 2006," July 2006, 6, www.unhcr.org/statistics/STATISTICS/ 44d74d9c2.pdf.

to immigration policies designed at the European level because the closure of external borders appeared to be a precondition for the incorporation of Spain into the Schengen Agreement, formalized a few weeks later. That change in visa policy resulted in the tightening of external border controls, especially in Ceuta and Melilla (the only land borders between the EU and Morocco). In the years that followed, Spanish authorities invested considerable resources in trying to build an effective system of border control around those two enclaves, as well as along the hundreds of kilometers of the Iberian Peninsula coast.[11]

In more recent years, Spanish authorities have also introduced visa requirements for citizens from a series of Latin American countries. Here again Spanish EU membership was crucial. It was a factor compelling the introduction of that measure (aimed at limiting the growing number of economic migrants who had entered the country ostensibly as tourists but stayed on, joining the ranks of undocumented migrants). It was also a way of attributing problems to rules emanating from EU headquarters in Brussels. Spanish authorities needed a scapegoat for a measure that was strongly criticized both in Spain and in Latin American countries (particularly Colombia in 2001 and Ecuador in 2003).[12]

After the introduction of visa requirements for North Africans and Latin Americans and the strengthening of the external borders, the number of people rejected at the borders or sent back to their country of origin significantly increased. For Spanish authorities the responsibility of exercising strict border control was the direct result of a compromise Spain made with its European partners. This was clearly reflected in their numerous requests for the

EU to co-finance the border policing efforts. These demands were answered positively with the allocation of EU funds to strengthen the borders of Ceuta and Melilla and through the development of several initiatives for cooperative patrolling of the Estrecho (Strait of Gibraltar).[13]

Since 1991, Spanish authorities have invested considerable material and human resources in trying to build an effective system of border control. The SIVE system (an integrated system of radars, infrared cameras, planes, helicopters, and boats) was gradually deployed to prevent the influx of *pateras* and *cayucos* (different types of rafts) loaded with undocumented migrants on the Andalucian and Canary Islands shores. The control of access to the cities of Ceuta and Melilla was also strengthened. The army was also deployed along the border at times of particular pressure. The idea of fulfilling a European mission was clearly reflected in the allocation of EU funds for the deployment of those complex and expensive schemes of border control.

A curious segmentation of potential illegal migrants has also taken place. One distinction is based on nationality. If caught, Moroccans are returned to their country of origin, but that is not often the case with other nationalities. Minors are not returned because of Spanish child protection regulations, while pregnant women and mothers of very young children are also allowed to stay in Spain for humanitarian reasons. Inevitably, those with more money have a greater chance of entering Spain. They might use falsified papers or pay to board a raft departing from the West African coast and heading for the Canary Islands—where the SIVE system has not been fully deployed. In contrast, those with less money pay to try to reach the Andalucian coasts, and finally, those without much in the way of monetary resources try to jump the fences of Ceuta or Melilla.

Contrary to the images of mayhem at Ceuta, Melilla, and the Canary Islands, table 13.1 shows that the policies implemented on the southern EU border have been relatively effective in controlling unwanted migration from the African continent. This can be seen in the differential growth of the stocks of undocumented migrants coming from Latin America and Eastern Europe (arriving legally and overstaying their permits) versus those from Africa.[14]

Toward a More Comprehensive Migration Policy

As the 1990s progressed, it became increasingly clear that immigrants were not only using Spain as a transit platform to move toward other European countries. Migration was clearly not a temporary phenomenon, and the demand for unskilled labor that had strongly contributed to bringing those immigrants to Spain in the first place was not disappearing. Despite the restrictive family reunification policy applied, primary migrants had managed to bring their relatives to Spain, and their children represented a growing proportion of the pupils in certain schools. The development of increasingly diverse immigrant communities within Spain implied an altogether different image of immigration and a series of brand new challenges to public services.

The tensions between the border control philosophy embedded in the 1985 law and respect for the basic rights of the individual was in fact addressed by the Spanish judiciary on several occasions. It intervened in several ways. Different courts issued rulings criticizing specific aspects of the legislation as well as their application by public administrations. These rulings addressed in particular issues related to expulsions, denial of the rule of habeas corpus, and detention of undocumented immigrants beyond the time limits established by the law. A Constitutional Court ruling declared unconstitutional several articles of the 1985 law that limited the rights of foreigners to hold meetings and form associations. In several of his annual reports, the ombudsman had expressed his concern over marginalization suffered by immigrants from less developed countries, in particular those without permits.

In absolute terms, immigrants from developing countries still represented a relatively small portion of the total Spanish population. However, the novelty of their presence, their high concentration in certain regions, media attention, and the activities of some uncoordinated but locally powerful xenophobic entrepreneurs contributed to the salience of immigration in Spanish public opinion polls in the early 2000s. Several racist incidents had taken place in different Spanish towns since the late 1990s (notably in El Ejido, Terrassa, and Figueres). Those cases highlighted the need for public authorities to help integrate immigrant populations into Spanish society and to retard xenophobic and racist sentiment within the Spanish population. Spanish authorities developed three basic strategies in order to reconcile a strict policy of border control with satisfying some of the demands that Spanish society had expressed in relation to migration.

Regularization Processes

The most ambitious measure taken by Spanish authorities to facilitate the integration of immigrants into Spanish society has traditionally been the development of initiatives to bring undocumented migration to the surface. Regularizing the legal and administrative situation of undocumented migrants gives them access to basic rights deriving from residency. Having those rights facilitates their access to markets (labor, housing, banking, etc.) and public services (social security, education, health care, personal social services, etc.).

Since the first law regulating immigration issues in 1985, several regularization processes have been developed with the explicit objective of legalizing all immigrants living in Spain without legal residency status or a work permit (see table 13.5).

These processes, common in many other European countries (notably in Italy, France, and Belgium), have been strongly criticized by the EU Council because they supposedly provide incentives for further illegal immigration.[15] Despite those critiques, Spanish authorities have used these procedures to bring to the surface the undocumented foreigners who, due to their lack of a recognized legal status, were pushed toward the underground economy and did not enjoy the most basic rights.

The first of those procedures was conducted in 1986 (right after the first immigration law was passed) with the objective of legalizing the undocumented foreigners generated by the previous legislative vacuum. This process was implemented in a very uncoordinated manner, and its effects did not last very long; many of those who obtained a permit had it revoked shortly thereafter due to the strict rules regulating the renewal of those permits. Of the nearly 44,000 applications for a work or residence permit that had been presented by March 1986, only 23,000 were granted (the others were not even answered).[16]

Between 1986 and 1991, when the second regularization process took place, the number of undocumented immigrants grew considerably. Trade unions periodically denounced the exploitation and marginalization suffered by those undocumented immigrants. Community organizations tried to provide relief for some of those immigrants' more elementary needs while advocating for a change in the legislation that condemned them to social exclusion.

Table 13.5
Regularization processes implemented in Spain, 1986–2006

Year	Applications	Work permits granted
1986	44,000	23,000
1991	133,000	116,000
1996	25,000	22,000
2000–2001	250,000	220,000
2002 ("*arraigo*")	350,000	240,000
2005	690,000	580,000

Source: Ministerio de Trabajo y Asuntos Sociales (MTAS), "Anuario de Migraciones 2004," Dirección General de Migraciones, Madrid, 2004; MTAS, "Borrador del Plan Estratégico de Ciudadanía e Integración," Madrid, 2006.

Despite those domestic pressures, the main rationale for the implementation of the second regularization process came from the domain of foreign policy. It came in the form of an agreement with Morocco in which Spanish authorities agreed to develop a process to legalize the status of undocumented migrants (many of them Moroccans). Spain would, in return, benefit from the introduction of visa requirement for nationals of that country.[17] More than 133,000 applications were made during this process, and some 116,000 new work permits were granted (nearly 50,000 of them to Moroccans).[18] Apart from the much larger scale of this regularization effort, other changes resulted in a more effective execution of this process (closer cooperation with community organizations and associations of immigrants for distributing information, better coordination of the process, etc.). It also had a more lasting effect because officials used a more flexible approach to renewing permits that had been issued during the process.

In 1996, in conjunction with a new regulation introduced under the original 1985 law, a new regularization process was developed with the objective of granting permits to those who had previously held permits and then had them revoked because of the restrictive character of the regulation. It granted more than 14,000 work permits in response to nearly 25,000 applications.

Beginning in March 1998, and for nearly two years, a parliamentary commission debated a new immigration bill aimed at replacing the 1985 law with more comprehensive legislation. The new legislation would take into account the complexity and structural character of immigration in contemporary Spain. That bill was negotiated in a consensual manner by all parties up to its very last stages. At that point certain factions of the conservative Partido Popular (PP) in the government started to oppose some aspects of the bill drafted with the participation of their own MPs. After voting against it in the first instance, the PP tried to introduce a series of changes in the bill during its discussion in the Senate (112 amendments were presented for a bill of 77 articles). However, its relatively weak situation in Parliament (without an absolute majority and depending on the support of the Catalan and Basque nationalist parties) resulted in a defeat of its proposals. The bill was accepted as it had been initially drafted by the parliamentary commission. Part of the PP's opposition to the new law was in fact related to the mechanisms for regularization recognized in that text, which were considered too generous.

The 4/2000 Law established a new regularization process to bring forward those undocumented migrants who could show proof of residency in Spain before June 1, 1999. This fourth regularization process started in March 2000, and by October 2001 it had legalized some 164,000 out of a total of nearly 250,000 applications. Some 60,000 rejected applications were reevaluated a few months later, and 36,000 of them were finally accepted. A special procedure was also initiated for Ecuadorian undocumented migrants, and of the nearly 25,000 files analyzed some 20,000 received a positive reply. Finally, the 4/2000 Law also established a mechanism of regularization based on the concept of *arraigo* (literally, "rooting"). This mechanism was aimed at legalizing those migrants who could prove they were integrated into Spanish society (by having family in the country or producing a job offer) and who had arrived in Spain before January 23, 2001. By late 2002, some 240,000 out of a total of more than 350,000 applications had been approved based on this clause. Altogether, some 460,000 undocumented migrants were regularized directly following the implementation of the 4/2000 Law. The PP argued that some aspects of the 4/2000 Law were openly contrary to the spirit of the Tampere Summit (particularly the conditions for *arraigo*). During the buildup to the March 2000 general elections, the PP campaigned for the introduction of restrictive clauses to the new immigration law. After winning those elections, the new conservative government toughened conditions for regularization in the so-called 8/2000 Law.

More than a million undocumented migrants were estimated to be living in Spain at the beginning of 2004. After its victory in the general elections of March 2004, the Socialist Party government designed a new regularization process. Between February and May 2005, those undocumented migrants who could produce a work contract and proof of residency in Spain for the previous six months could apply to have their legal status regularized. More than 800,000 applications were processed and some 650,000 work permits were granted. The novelty of this process lay in the fact that potential employers were responsible for actually initiating the procedure for regularizing the migrants. Thus the link between the work permit and the labor market was reinforced and that portion of the underground economy based on undocumented labor was legitimized.

In addition to the "exceptional" regularization process described, Spanish authorities established a quota system to issue a certain number of work permits every year to fill those jobs not taken by nationals. Those permits were supposed to be distributed through Spanish consulates and embassies, but in practice they ended up functioning as mechanisms for the regularization of undocumented immigrants already present in Spain. Since 1993, and virtually every year thereafter, between 20,000 and 40,000 work permits were issued to undocumented immigrants already present in Spanish territory. This system did not accomplish its original objective of regulating and controlling the inflows of immigrants. It did, however, help to provide the unskilled labor demanded by certain sectors of the Spanish economy while simultaneously bringing to the surface the undocumented immigrants working in the informal sector.

Immigration issues continued to be increasingly politicized in the Spanish political arena. The EU remained reticent toward legalization programs as a way of handling the issue of illegal immigration. Still, Spanish policymakers implemented mechanisms for the regularization of undocumented immigrants (exceptional regularization processes, yearly quotas, automatic regularization by residence) as a way of answering some of the demands being made by Spanish society.

The Expansion of Rights

The limitations of the 1985 law forced Spanish policymakers to consider developing policies to facilitate the integration of migrants. To respond to the growing political mobilization of the left wing and to the demands of community organizations working with immigrants, in December 1994 the Socialist Party government approved a plan for the social integration of immigrant populations.

This plan defined three main strategies relative to immigration issues: (1) preventing migratory flows by cooperating to promote the social and economic development of the countries where those flows originate; (2) increasing knowledge of those flows and of the demand for unskilled labor in the Spanish economy, with the objective of regulating immigration effectively; and (3) facilitating the integration of immigrant populations into Spanish society.

The structure and content of this plan replicated the goals defined by the European Commission in its failed attempt to coordinate integration policies within the EU.[19] Despite this declaration of good intentions, the multidimensional nature of the issues at stake and the decentralized nature of the semifederal Spanish state resulted in inconsistent coverage of the basic needs of immigrant groups, especially those with a more precarious administrative status.

The area where those failures were most evident was in social rights (access to health care, education, etc.), and the 4/2000 Law had been intended to introduce significant changes in the area of rights for immigrants living in Spain. That law gave the same civil and social rights to legal foreign residents that Spanish nationals enjoyed. It also established the possibility of voting rights at the local level based on the existence of reciprocity agreements with sending countries. The 4/2000 Law also extended rights to public health care, education, and public housing schemes based on the criterion of residence (inscription of the census), moving somehow in the direction of decoupling nationality and citizenship rights.

During the parliamentary debate over the new immigration law, tensions over the two approaches to immigration issues (closure versus integration) appeared. These conflicts developed not only between the different political parties but also within the parliamentary group of the party leading the government and among the different ministers of the Cabinet. On the one hand, the MPs of the PP that participated in the drafting of the bill, together with the minister for Labor and Social Affairs, praised the atmosphere of consensus in which the bill had been drafted. They also praised the positive steps toward integrating immigrant populations within Spanish society that the new law represented. On the other hand, a series of ministers (of Economy and Finance, Interior, and Foreign Affairs), backed by the president of the government, showed their concern for the unexpected consequences that might occur as a result of the new immigration bill. For the minister of Economy and Finance, the cost of extending social benefits to undocumented immigrants would be an extremely heavy burden on the Spanish welfare state. For the ministers of Interior and Foreign Affairs, the new law would be by far the most progressive in the EU. In their view it would pose a considerable challenge to the country, which was already attracting major inflows of illegal immigrants and having to guard the EU's southern border. In that context, the argument of the immigration policies being promoted by the EU played an important role in the debates, although every party played up whichever aspect of the issue better suited their interests. For those defending the need to expand immigrants' rights, EU documents and drafts for common policies emphasized the need to integrate immigrant populations. In this argument, those defending more restrictive positions argued that all measures promoted by the EU to integrate immigrants referred only to legal residents and explicitly excluded undocumented immigrants.[20]

Although the PP promised to change the law to comply with the agreements made at the Tampere Summit, that is, to exclude undocumented immigrants from all social services programs, the 8/2000 Law did not represent a significant change in the conditions for accessing social rights.

Bilateral Agreements for the Import of Labor

The signing of bilateral agreements with sending countries channeling migratory flows toward Spain in recent years was in response to a combination of demographic, economic, and political conditions. It also reflected Spanish authorities' interest in increasing control over the influx of migrants into their territory.

A report by the population division of the UN pointing out the aging and declining population of Spain (and Europe as a whole) was the starting point for a debate about the consequences of having one of the lowest fertility rates on the planet for more than a decade.[21] According to UN projections, in the year 2050 Spain would have the oldest population in the world, and it would need some 12 million immigrants to keep a ratio of four workers for every retired person.[22] Although UN experts recognized that the levels of migration predicted by that report would be socially and politically unthinkable in Europe, they stressed the importance of those demographic trends and pointed out that substitution migration will be a reality in Western Europe in the near future.

The highly segmented demand for labor, quite strong in sectors such as domestic service, construction, and labor-intensive agriculture, has been one of the most powerful factors in creating migratory flows (very often illegal) toward Spain in the recent past. For many years, employers in those sectors found in the undocumented immigrants a cheap and flexible supply of labor with no additional costs (e.g., social security contributions, severance or unemployment insurance payments, or paid holidays). They took advantage of this situation and hired large numbers of undocumented immigrants who were often exploited at work and socially marginalized in the cities and villages where they lived. Spanish authorities did not show much interest in controlling and imposing sanctions on employers who hired undocumented immigrants. The argument was that there were not enough resources at the Ministry of Labor to control those areas of activity in which the hiring of irregular immigrants was more common. The lack of political will to pursue a more strict policy of labor market control may be related to the will to show a lax attitude toward the black-market economy (extremely important in certain regions and in specific areas of activity). It was very often made up of businesses struggling to survive in an increasingly internationally competitive environment (e.g., textiles, shoe manufacturing, etc.).[23] Families, which could not afford to buy services in the regular labor markets (cleaning, caring for dependent relatives) and did not receive much support from the underdeveloped welfare system, also benefited from the tolerant stance of Spanish authorities when hiring undocumented immigrant women for those activities.

But that model, based on the exploitation and marginalization of the undocumented immigrants, is not sustainable. Social groups expressed their concern for the negative consequences deriving from such a system, such as shanty towns, increasing marginalization, and crime, together with xenophobic feelings and racism directed at the immigrant population.[24] Even employers who greatly benefited from the unlimited supply of undocumented workers have expressed their preference for stronger regulation of migratory inflows. They have also called for the establishment of mechanisms to improve the extremely precarious conditions in which undocumented immigrants live.[25] In that context, the Spanish government announced in October 1999 the signing of an agreement with Morocco for the development of a strategy to regulate temporary migration to Spain. According to that agreement (broadly defined, although initially intended for the agriculture sector), those jobs not covered by Spanish, Communitarian, or legal foreign workers already present in Spain would be offered to potential immigrants from Morocco. Spanish authorities would grant a temporary work permit (for a maximum of nine months a year), would offer health care insurance, and would subsidize transportation costs and decent housing (which would be the responsibility of the employers).

Although similar agreements were signed with other countries such as Ecuador, Colombia, Romania, the Dominican Republic, and Poland, the bilateral agreement with Morocco was by far the most important. Among the reasons for that importance were the country's geographical proximity, its large flows of illegal immigration, and its being the source of the largest immigrant community in Spain. Foremost among the reasons, though, were foreign policy concerns.

The Challenge Ahead for Spanish Society

The most important factor generating the migratory flows into contemporary Spain is the extreme development differential between it and its former colonies. According to the UN Human Development Report (2005), the border between Spain and Morocco constitutes the largest development gap in the world (Spain occupies the number 21 spot on that index, Morocco, number 124). In terms of strict economic differential (measured in gross domestic product [GDP] per capita, purchasing power parity with U.S. dollars [PPP US$]), the wealth gap between Spain ($22,391) and Morocco ($4,004) is 25 percent larger than the one between the United States ($37,562) and Mexico ($9,168). If we conceptualize the border between Spain and Morocco as the cleavage, not only between both shores of the Mediterranean but also between the wealthy metropolises of Europe and its former African colonies, the wealth gap becomes much larger. For example, GDP per capita in Mali is $994, in Ivory Coast, $1,492, in Gambia, $1,859, and in Ghana, $2,238.

Many things help to explain the growing migratory pressures that Spain and the EU suffer. One is the existence of settled African communities in many Western European countries (which provide the information, financing, support, and solidarity networks that encourage migration). Another is the stagnant (and often receding) economies of the countries of origin of those migration flows. Political instability is widespread in many African countries as are environmental adversities (droughts, plagues, desertification). Demographic factors (extreme differentials in age structures, fertility rates, etc.) are also causal factors for this migration dynamic. To the complex of incentives that lead many Africans to make the arduous journey north and face the associated risks of life as a new immigrant, we should add the strong demand for unskilled workers in the Spanish and European labor market (mainly for the underground economy). Certainly Spain's geographical proximity to Morocco (separated by only nine miles at one point) makes it the natural entrance to the EU's southwestern flank.

In recent years, migration has gained considerable salience within the already charged bilateral political agenda between Spain and Morocco. Relations between these two neighboring countries had traditionally been very complex. Protracted issues include the future of the Western Sahara, the sovereignty of Spanish possessions on the North African coast, the smuggling of illicit drugs (particularly hashish) from Morocco to Spain and of consumption goods from Ceuta and Melilla to Morocco, and Spanish access to Moroccan fisheries.[26] The incorporation of Spain into the EEC in 1986 was also perceived with suspicion by Moroccan authorities. That event added new issues to the political agenda, such as competition for European markets in agricultural products, the growing political leverage of the Spanish government in the EU, and the transit through Spain of Moroccan immigrants settled in other European countries. The gradual development of a Moroccan migrant community in Spain introduced some additional dimensions to that already very long agenda. Those dimensions include visas, control of unwanted migratory flows, living conditions of Moroccans in Spain, undocumented migrants, remittances, and social security transfers.

In this context of complex bilateral relations, Spanish authorities tried to involve Moroccan authorities in the control of migratory flows not only of Moroccan nationals but also of other Africans trying to enter Europe. With that objective, the authorities of both countries signed an agreement in 1992 for the readmission of illegal immigrants who crossed to Spain from Morocco. The implementation of that agreement, though, has depended on the mood of the Moroccan authorities, who used this issue as leverage when negotiating other issues on the bilateral agenda. Within that broad process of negotiation, the bilateral agreement for the importation of temporary workers to Spain could be understood as a way of regulating the inflows of migrants (an objective for Spanish authorities), while improving the working and living conditions of Moroccan immigrants in Spain (in the interest of Morocco).

For Spanish authorities, the main objective was getting Moroccan authorities to enforce border control measures to prevent the arrival of unwanted migratory flows. Bilateral cooperation in this matter was marked by the signing of agreements to regulate the introduction of visas for Moroccan nationals in 1991 and by the agreement in 1992 for the readmission of migrants illegally arriving in Spain from Moroccan territory. The agreement in 1999 for the importation of Moroccan temporary workers constituted another step toward managing the inflows of migrants and improving the living conditions of Moroccan immigrants in Spain. Initiatives such as the deployment of joint sea patrols or the agreement in 2002 for the repatriation of unaccompanied Moroccan minors strengthened bilateral cooperation in this policy area.[27]

As border control policies were tightened, the smuggling of undocumented migrants developed, increasing the price and the risks of the migratory enterprise.[28] In addition to using rafts to cross the Strait, undocumented migrants tried to enter Spain by jumping the fences or swimming to the beaches of Ceuta or Melilla. Some tried clinging to the undercarriage of trucks or hiding in their cargoes or stowing away in the trunks of cars or the holds of fishing boats.

The actual implementation of those agreements was determined by the status of bilateral relations, with migration-related issues becoming a bargaining element in the negotiation process. Moroccan authorities adjusted their level of cooperation in the readmission of undocumented migrants depending on the status of relations between the two states.[29] In fact, they systematically refused to accept the repatriation of sub-Saharan undocumented immigrants even though it was part of the 1992 agreement. The bilateral agreement for the importation of temporary Moroccan migrants also languished due to the Spanish authorities' lack of a clear political will to make it work.[30]

At the Tampere Summit, the High Level Group on Asylum and Migration, set up by the European Council in January 1999, presented its progress report as well as drafts of different action plans for a series of countries considered to be of special interest. The report on the action plan for Morocco, coordinated by Spain, emphasized the idea of the latter country being a buffer zone that could reduce migratory pressures on the southern external border of the EU. To accomplish that objective, several proposals were made that included the primary elements of Spanish policy toward Morocco. These were cooperative measures to facilitate the socioeconomic development of the country, the signing of agreements to implement mechanisms for readmission of illegal immigrants trying to get into the EU through Moroccan territory, and the development of temporary migration strategies. EU officials initiated negotiations with Moroccan authorities to link the control of migration flows to issues of financial aid and the export of Moroccan products to European markets. The idea of establishing European-financed and supervised reception areas for potential migrants in transition countries (including Morocco) has also been openly discussed in EU institutions as a way of diminishing migratory pressures on Europe.

In addition to the challenges related to border control, Spanish authorities and society have to address a series of issues arising from the presence of immigrant communities settled in Spanish territory. In recent times the definition of the migratory situation as a mass "invasion" of the poor from the south has generated anxieties within the Spanish population and reinforced negative prejudices, particularly against North Africans. Playing to popular fears, some politicians of the conservative party in government between 1996 and 2004 pointed to a "causal" link between the increase in crime and the growing presence of immigrants. Their doing so suggested an attempt to siphon off some of the xenophobic vote and thus prevent the appearance of an extreme-right party. The idea that the disenfranchised character of those migrants would push them to do "anything" in order to get what they sought favors the development of a discourse centered around the issue of "security." The same phenomenon has been observed in many Western societies in recent years.[31]

The terrorist attacks in Madrid on March 11, 2004, conducted by radical Islamists of Moroccan nationality, resulted in 192 deaths and thousands wounded. Up to now no survey has been published on Spanish society's evolving perceptions of North African migrants, so we cannot estimate the impact of those attacks on the already relatively negative image of this group.[32] In the aftermath of those attacks, Spanish public opinion appeared quite able to dissociate the actions of a minority group of fanatical Islamist militants from those of the North African community of law-abiding immigrant workers. Nevertheless, that event may have contributed to reinforcing feelings of mistrust toward migrants from that region. When asked to rank their sympathies for groups from different world regions on a scale of 0 to 10, Spaniards have consistently chosen North Africans as the least liked group, ranking them at around number 6 during the second half of the 1990s and down to around 5 in 2002 and 2003.[33] A similarly suspicious attitude toward North Africans is expressed by Spaniards when asked if they would mind having them as neighbors, colleagues, or relatives. Qualitative research based on focus groups of individuals living in neighborhoods with a marked presence of North African migrants shows a clear concern among Spanish nationals about the cultural differences of this migrant community. The focus groups also had concerns about North Africans' perceived hostility toward Spaniards and expressed a moral judgment about the way Muslim men treat women, all within a general perception of losing control of the public space in their neighborhoods.[34]

As table 13.6 shows, the general attitude toward the presence of migrant communities during a recent four-year period has evolved toward a growing reluctance and a smaller degree of indifference. It remains impossible to untangle the reasons for that evolution (factors like the growth of the immigrant community may be playing a major role). However, the savage attack against civilian commuter trains may have contributed to the "activation" of xenophobic feelings toward migrant communities in general and toward North Africans in particular.[35]

There is also evidence that points to the existence of discriminatory practices in relation to the working conditions (e.g., promotions, salary, etc.) of Muslim migrants.[36] Those practices have been studied in detail in relation to the incorporation of Moroccan workers into the construction sector. That employment sector, according to a study by Lorenzo Cachón Rodríguez, is one of the least prone to discriminate against Moroccan workers in its hiring practices. This research also showed the buffer function of this migrant group in relation to the evolutions of the economic cycle (Moroccan workers are more likely to be fired during the periods of lower activity). It further pointed to the importance of the employers' prejudices and stereotypes in assigning tasks, responsibilities, and promotions. Moroccan workers were consistently overlooked, while Polish workers—considered to be more reliable, hard working, and skilled—were more likely to be pushed up the professional ladder.[37]

The negative attitudes toward migrants materialized in several racist incidents in different Spanish towns and neighborhoods (notably in El Ejido, An-

Table 13.6
Evolution of attitudes toward migrants in Spain, 2000–2004

	Feb. 2000	Feb. 2001	June 2002	May 2003	May 2004
Reluctant	10	19	20	30	32
Ambivalent	49	36	28	32	29
Tolerant	41	45	44	38	39

Source: M. A. Cea D'Ancona, *La activación de la xenofobia en España: ¿qué miden las encuestas?* (Madrid: Centro de Investigaciones Sociológicas, 2004).

dalucía, in 2002, and Terrassa, Catalonia, in 2003) during recent years. Though different in nature and evolution, they were based on a common rejection of the presence of North African communities. The Terrassa incidents developed in a peripheral urban working-class neighborhood where growing numbers of Moroccans had settled since the early 1990s. The process of competition for scarce resources (public services, use of the public space, etc.) previously described ended with the rejection of the presence of the North Africans by a traditionally communist constituency that had turned xenophobic. Only the intervention of public authorities promising to invest in public services in that underprivileged area calmed the rioting against North Africans.

Despite the eruptions of racism previously mentioned, Spanish authorities do not seem particularly concerned about this phenomenon. They are reassured by the lack of electoral support for extreme-right parties in Spain (a positive fact considering the menacing shadow of those parties in European countries such as France, Belgium, the Netherlands, and Denmark). They also find reassurance in the relatively benevolent image that surveys give of Spaniards when compared with other Europeans (according to Eurobarometer, Spain appears as one of the countries less prone to racist and discriminatory attitudes). Amnesty International, SOS Racismo, and the European Network against Racism (ENAR) periodically report that the relatively widespread negative attitudes toward some migrant groups in Spain, particularly North Africans, are also reflected in the behaviors of public officials, notably the security forces. Despite this, the issue of the existence of institutional racism has not yet appeared on the Spanish political agenda, and therefore no systematic study of the magnitude of the phenomenon has been undertaken. In fact, Spanish authorities are rather delayed in their required compliance with EU regulations relative to the establishment of mechanisms to monitor and fight discrimination.[38]

The "Europeanization" of immigration policy appears to be one of the key elements for understanding immigration policies in Spain in the last two decades. Either through direct pressure (e.g., requirements to join the Schengen Agreement) or indirect influences (e.g., emulating the policies of other institutions), the participation of Spain in the process of building a common market without internal borders has strongly conditioned the shape of its policies with regard to immigration issues. The convergence of national immigration policies in Western Europe resulted in very different policy outcomes in each country. The position of Spain at the southern border of the EU emphasized the need to control the borders. However, historical interaction with North Africa and Latin America and the economic and diplomatic interest in both areas contributed to relaxing the implementation of border control policies.

Spanish authorities have been particularly sensitive to the opinion of other European governments in issues related to border control policies, for that area of policy is strongly based on reciprocal trust among EU member states. This resulted in restrictive border control legislation aimed at counterbalancing the geographical position of Spain at the edge of one of the sources of the highest migratory pressures on the Union. Nevertheless, its historical, diplomatic, and economic links to and interests in Latin America and North Africa, as well as the need for unskilled labor, selectively relaxed the implementation of the strict border control regulation adopted. Thus, the policies applied in recent years seem to point to the existence of a preference for some migratory flows. Such policies might include the delay in the introduction of visa requirements for certain Latin American nationalities known to be migrating to Spain in large numbers. Another might be the relatively blind eye turned toward Eastern Europeans. Those policies indicate a preference for those migrants at the expense of flows from the African continent, which face much more strict border controls.

Other policies not explicitly related to border control but directly linked to the conditions that determine the right to live in the territory of the country, notably the rules on naturalization, show differential treatment between nationalities. Latin American nationals need two years of legal residency before being able to apply for Spanish nationality while North African and other national groups have to wait for ten years.[39]

Spain has not yet developed its own philosophy of integration, and the creation of such a model may in fact be impossible due to the strongly decentralized character of the Spanish state. In those autonomous communities with their own language and cultural traits, migration may pose a very specific set of challenges. They risk dilution of their specificities (language, culture, etc.) when culturally and ethnically different migrants embrace a general Spanish (Castilian-speaking) umbrella identity instead of a combination of regional (Catalan, Basque, Galician) and Spanish identities. The attitude of minority nationalist forces in relation to migration will be extremely important in the resolution of those challenges.

Among the new policies implemented in recent years, the development of temporary migration programs to fill the need for unskilled labor is perceived to be of critical importance in certain sectors of the Spanish economy. Some authors have suggested that the Spanish state was turning a blind eye toward the issue of undocumented workers. However, a recent consensus among employers, trade unions, and the state subordinated the legality of migratory flows to the perceived needs of the Spanish economy. In this respect, the negative experiences with guest worker schemes in other European countries did not seem to act as a discouraging factor for the design of the bilateral agreement with Morocco.

Although the administrative skills of the Spanish state in relation to immigration issues did not exist fifteen years ago, the handling of programs such as regularization and the yearly quotas have considerably increased its capacities. Integration policies have remained only on paper to a large extent. Still, a network of agencies, research bodies, and forums have started to develop the capabilities to implement a more sophisticated set of policies to facilitate the incorporation of immigrant populations into Spanish society. "Third sector" organizations played a significant role in that effort by fulfilling the tasks that the state was not willing or prepared to accomplish while still retaining their role as advocacy groups in the interest of immigrant populations.

Immigration policies and the extension of civil and social rights to populations of immigrant origin generally have a low profile in the Spanish public and political agenda. Some have explained that low profile by pointing to the liberal-democratic character of other Western societies and the universal idiom of liberalism.[40] In their argument, the relatively weak nature of liberalism in a young democracy like Spain would account for the lack of mobilization to fight explicit violations of immigrants' rights or the different forms (both implicit and explicit) of discrimination against these groups.[41] The fight against discriminatory treatment constitutes a very important dimension for the present in terms of justice. It is also a key aspect for the future if the second generation of North Africans, born and reared in Spain, are to be fully incorporated into Spanish society.

The level of politicization of immigration issues in Spain has remained relatively low, with no extreme-right party capitalizing on the issue. But the appearance of some local xenophobic entrepreneurs in areas with a higher concentration of immigrants (e.g., Ceuta and Melilla, El Ejido, Vic) and the eruption of racist incidents have helped to gradually raise the profile of this area of policy. Since the general elections of March 2000, all political parties have been forced to express their opinion on immigration issues, and this area of policy is quite likely to occupy a growing role within the Spanish political scene, just as it has in the rest of Europe.

The situation at the border in Ceuta and Melilla must be understood as more than simply poor people from the Global South storming the barricades. It is part of a complex system of migration. While the flow of migrants may have temporarily slowed at this one locus of entry, the broader context is one that has stimulated illicit activity. The flow of migrants has often simply been diverted to other locations. The fundamental, underlying problems that stimulate the northward flow, however, have not been addressed. The global dimension of the issue has thus remained unresolved. Realistically, migratory pressures at the southern EU border are unlikely to decrease in the foreseeable future. Long-term measures that go beyond transforming migration transition countries like Morocco into buffer areas to prevent migratory flows from reaching Europe will have to be implemented. Current EU policies fail to link immigration, integration, and development policies in an adequate manner. They focus largely on staffing geographic barriers rather than providing a long-term solution. It may be time to rethink the fundamentals of this approach.

The challenges for Spanish authorities and society in relation to the incorporation of immigrant communities are quite complex. The general climate of public opinion is generated by the (to a certain extent) self-fulfilling prophecy of the "clash of civilizations." That climate is combined with the troubled situation in the Middle East–North Africa (MENA) region. Additionally, the traditionally complex relations between Spain and its North African neighbors and the feeling of being forced to guard the EU's southern border present a rather difficult situation. In this turbulent situation, a peaceful and mutually beneficial process must be found to integrate North African migrant communities into Spanish society. Reaching this objective will require more proactive policies aimed at counterbalancing the negative vestiges of long-lasting prejudices and misinformation.

14

The Challenge to Integration in France

SYLVAIN BROUARD AND VINCENT TIBERJ

September 11, 2001, shed new light on multiculturalism in France and in Europe. Before these tragic events, immigration and cultural and ethnic diversity were issues raised only by the extreme-right parties, the best known being the Front National, and only a small part of the French electorate considered terrorism to be the nation's most important political issue.[1] After the reelection of Jacques Chirac in 2002, the situation changed dramatically. France has since engaged in serious debate on the relationships between Islam and the Republic (the Islamic scarf, the Mohammed cartoons and freedom of speech, the creation of the Conseil Français du Culte Musulman, etc.). Recently a new theme has emerged: the question of the Islamization of French society, popularized by Philippe de Villiers, leader of Mouvement pour la France (MPF), a right-wing, anti-European political party. The MPF propagates the fear that Islamist organizations would take advantage of the increasing number of Muslims to legitimize and impose their values and way of life on the rest of the national community.[2]

Simultaneously, doubts have been cast on the desire of the latest immigrant waves—mostly from the Maghreb as well as other parts of Africa—to join the French mainstream. Traditional critics of immigration state that im-

migrants try to take advantage of the French welfare system and steal jobs
from French-born citizens. Current criticism of immigration focuses on the
belief that immigrants refuse to enter into mainstream French society. The
public perception is that France would become a "communautarist" society,
like the Anglo-Saxon nations (following the characterization of these polities
offered by many French academics and politicians). In such a society, specific groups would demand and obtain special treatment, thus ignoring the Republican ideal of equality among citizens. French essayist Alain Finkielkraut
interpreted the riots of November 2005 as an ethnic and religious uprising
against the rest of society.

Preoccupation with the French immigration question is not limited to the
elite. In two opinion surveys conducted at the beginning and end of a six-
month period (April 2005 to December 2005) the percentage of respondents
who answered that the number of immigrants was too high in France rose
from 49 to 64 percent. When asked whether they thought that "France has a
debt toward those who come from its former colonies," the percentage of
those who disagreed rose from 36 to 48 in December. Such dramatic changes
in opinion polls can best be explained by the rioting in the suburbs. In fact,
after running a hierarchical classification using several values questions (both
socioeconomic and cultural), we identified a particular class of voters that
constitutes two-thirds of the rightist electorate, which we named the "closed
right." These voters are characterized by a very specific interpretation of the
November 2005 riots. The remainder of the electorate stressed the socioeconomic reasons behind the riots and blamed French society's discrimination
against the youth in the suburbs. The closed right, on the other hand, blamed
the riots on problems resulting from immigration and integration. They believe that those living in the suburbs rather than French society at large are
mainly responsible for the crisis. For them, the primary reason for the riots is
anti-French racism (41 percent of responses), beating out the effects of television news (38 percent), Islamic organizations and gangs (35 percent each,
multiple answers allowed). The closed right explained the crisis by a lack of
parental control (47 percent), unemployment (29 percent), immigration (26
percent), and an insufficient number of police officers in the suburbs (24 percent). For the rest of the sample, unemployment and discrimination were the
primary reasons. The closed right favors conservative or repressive policies to
solve the problems in the suburbs. Such policies include more restrictive laws
against illegal immigration (96 percent), requiring parents to enter contracts
of responsibility for their children (88 percent), increasing the number of police officers (87 percent), automatic expulsion of foreign rioters (84 percent),

and more restrictions on bringing immigrants' family members to France (76 percent). The rest of the electorate focused on social responses such as increased funding for public schools, better public housing, and education to fight discrimination.

The context surrounding immigration and multiculturalism leads scholars to wonder if the French are suffering an identity crisis, if they question their capacity to integrate the "new" waves of immigration (which in some cases go back three generations), and if French public opinion reflects the debate over Huntington's "clash of civilizations" theory. We address these questions by examining the opinions of the French electorate regarding the integration of immigrants. Several points of tension between the French electorate and those of immigrant origin are apparent, including Islamophobia. We compare the attitudes and behaviors of the "new French" (i.e., those of immigrant origin) to determine whether the integration process in France has failed.

Data

Our data come from the CEVIPOF survey, "Rapport au politique des Français issus de l'immigration" (Political Implications of the French of Immigrant Origin) or RAPFI.[3] The field institute TNS-SOFRES conducted the poll, using the questionnaire drawn up by the CEVIPOF research team, between April 8 and May 7, 2005, with a representative sample of 1,003 French citizens who emigrated from Africa and Turkey and were at least eighteen years of age. A "mirror" survey was also conducted, between April 13 and April 21, 2005, with a representative sample of the French electorate—the control sample—of 1,006 individuals at least eighteen years old. Both surveys consisted of a telephone interview that lasted thirty-five minutes on average. In both cases, a base of surveys representative of the two types of households was set up using the quota method (INSEE EHF survey and INSEE Employment survey, respectively).[4] From this base, telephone numbers were randomly selected. With the exception of a few necessary adaptations, the questionnaires used in both surveys were identical, in wording as well as in the order of the questions. The methodology used ensures a reliable and systematic comparison of the two samples.

The RAPFI survey is unique in the field of minority studies in France. First, the population of interest was defined to avoid bias. Previous surveys defined the population by selecting only individuals of the Islamic faith or only by birthplace. Both these criteria are biased. They preclude individuals such as the French of immigrant origin who are atheist or practice another religion and the *pieds-noirs* of Algeria (Algerians of European descent), who do not consider themselves immigrants. Our study includes individuals of French citizenship having at least one parent or grandparent who held or still holds the nationality of one of the following countries: Turkey, Tunisia, Algeria, Morocco, or any other African nation. We therefore include in our sample naturalized immigrants, the first and second generation born in France, whether of mixed heritage or not. Second, by using the INSEE EHF survey and the computer assisted telephone interviewing (CATI) procedure, we have made this survey the first to be controlled by quotas, thus correcting the methodological errors of previous polls.[5] Most previous polls were based on face-to-face interviews and are biased since densely populated urban areas were chosen to minimize the cost of the polls. These areas have disproportionately high numbers of foreigners. Our method, though more labor intensive, remedies this bias: 28,000 individuals were interviewed to make up a representative sample of 1,003 respondents. Lastly, the RAPFI survey is the first to explore not only specific dimensions such as integration, perceptions of racism, and attitudes toward Islam but also general dimensions such as politics, value systems, and policy preferences, whereas the French of immigrant origin were surveyed only on matters such as Islam or secularization.

The French and Their Models of Integration

A Preliminary Assessment of Integration

Several differences between the French of immigrant origin and the rest of the electorate are noteworthy (see table 14.1). First, the French of African, Maghrebian, or Turkish origin responded more often than the mirror respondents that French society is color-blind and that immigrants can be easily assimilated. They also said less often that they were prejudiced against immigrants (not because they are of a particular ethnic origin but because they are younger and therefore better educated). They believed that integration difficulties are due to societal attitudes rather than immigrants' behavior.

Second, respondents in the mirror sample focused more on the question of religion. Their perception of whether the number of immigrants is excessive does not change their position on the difficulty of immigrants' integration (roughly a third of the respondents think that immigrants can easily integrate into the French mainstream). This is not the case when Islam is considered. Among the mirror respondents, 43 percent felt slightly or very negative toward Islam (compared with 17 percent in the RAPFI survey), and negativity toward this particular religion colors their attitude about immi-

Table 14.1
Opinions about integration

	RAPFI survey (immigrant-origin French) (% agreeing)	Mirror sample (French electorate) (% agreeing)
The immigrants' situation will worsen in the future.	27	26
There are too many immigrants in France.	37	47
In France, everybody can succeed regardless of skin color.	49	43
Immigrants can easily integrate into French society.	41	33
Concerning the problem of integration, the responsibility lies mostly with the immigrants who do not try hard enough.	26	48
Concerning the problem of integration, the responsibility belongs mostly to French society.	59	39

grants' capacity to join the French mainstream. When respondents in the mirror population judged the Muslim religion positively, 48 percent of them said that integration of immigrants would be easy, whereas among those who viewed Islam most negatively, this proportion drops to 28 percent.

Furthermore, on the issue of responsibility for integration problems in France, the differences between the "new French" and the rest of the electorate are even greater. French of immigrant origin, whatever their ideological leaning or level of ethnocentrism, blamed society more often than they did immigrants. Among the electorate as a whole, the variations are even more dramatic. If French society is considered color-blind by respondents, immigrants are held responsible for immigration problems and not society. On the other hand, when respondents recognize racial discrimination in France, the society as a whole, rather than immigrants in particular, is blamed for the problems   of integration. In addition, when the mirror respondents answer questions on the integration process, they simultaneously answer questions on the compatibility of Islam with French society. When respondents view this religion positively, society is blamed, and when they view Islam negatively, immigrants are blamed. In the current climate, the integration issue encompasses not only the traditional debate over politics and the economy but also religion in the secular state. The fundamental question is whether Islam, the French identity, and the French mainstream can cohabit in the same national space.

The French Models of Integration

The French are clearly divided over the issue of the integration process in France and the capacity of immigrants to join the mainstream because the general public holds several different views of integration (see table 14.2).

In both samples, the responses of the majorities are the same for two of three questions. The sample groups' answers differ sharply, though, on the choice between equal treatment for every French person or the struggle against discrimination, the general public being focused on the first issue and the RAPFI respondents on the second. This could be the consequence of demands for special treatment or evidence of immigrants' resistance to assimilation. This divergence of opinion is not as simple as it appears, as we will demonstrate.

Using a hierarchical classification based on these three issues and the item concerning responsibility for the integration problem, we have identified three specific groups of French voters, each of them with different models of integration. The first group, the assimilationists, make up 46 percent of the

Table 14.2
Issues selected as being of primary importance by survey respondents (%)

	That immigrants join the rest of society without conflict	Or that they petition for special rights even if it creates tensions	Don't know	Total
RAPFI survey	54	43	3	100
Mirror survey	65	32	3	100

	Treating every French person equally	Or struggling against discrimination	Don't know	Total
RAPFI survey	41	59	0	100
Mirror survey	58	41	1	100

	Valuing the cultural differences among the French	Or highlighting what the French have in common	Don't know	Total
RAPFI survey	43	55	2	100
Mirror survey	31	67	2	100

Note: Survey respondents were asked, "For you today, which of these issues is the most important?"

mirror sample; the second group, the republicans, count for 36 percent of the sample; and the third, the multiculturalists, constitute 8 percent. Each group helps to shed light on the question of integration.

The assimilationists believe the following: immigrants, not society, are responsible for the integration problem (100 percent of their responses), immigrants should not receive special treatment to assist in their assimilation (78 percent), they should be treated no differently than others (70 percent), and they should participate in the common culture of the country (72 percent). Ethnocentrism is highest among this group (67 percent think there are too many immigrants in France, in comparison with 49 percent at the sample level). Assimilationists also score high on two traditional questions measuring authoritarianism in the sociological field: 66 percent of them value discipline over the development of critical thinking at school, and 41 percent of them believe in the reestablishment of capital punishment, versus 50 and 32 percent of the overall sample, respectively. They most often belong to the Catholic Church (76 percent) and are the most critical toward Islam: 55 percent of them feel negatively toward this religion, in comparison with less than 40 percent of negative feelings among the two others groups. Clearly, they are the least open to a society made up of many cultures and religions. For them, immigrants must be assimilated and thus abandon that which makes them different from the rest of French society. Integration means accepting the French way of life.

Assimilationists and republicans share some common beliefs. They particularly share a preference for equal treatment (75 percent of their responses), a preference for what the French have in common rather than their cultural diversity (77 percent of responses), and a wish for integration to be achieved without immigrants' demanding special rights. The major difference with the first group is their opinion that society is responsible when integration is problematic (78 percent of republicans blame society, the remaining 22 percent think that responsibility for problems is shared by immigrants and society). The republicans clearly voice their commitment to the traditional model of the French Republic, or at least the one to which political elites refer when talking about the Republic, and cannot be portrayed as anti-immigrant. In contrast to the assimilationists, only 29 percent of them consider the number of immigrants in France too high and only 37 percent feel negatively toward the Muslim religion. These respondents are mostly left wing (48 percent in comparison with 27 percent of the first group) and are opposed to the death penalty (80 percent). The republicans also rated the development of critical thinking (61 percent) as more important than discipline in the schools. They share with the assimilationists the wish that migrants join the French mainstream, but their definitions of this mainstream differ greatly from those of the first group.

The gap between republicans and assimilationists is wide on several topics (e.g., tolerance toward Islam, the death penalty, and responsibility for problems with integration). The republicans value a society based on tolerance toward ethnic diversity at the private level and on republican neutrality at the public level. Assimilationists are more intolerant in matters of ethnic and religious diversity (even in the realm of private practice) and favor a more traditional vision of French society, where authority is strong. Furthermore, republicans are much more in favor of public policies to promote integration, which demonstrates their judgment that society is responsible for difficulties in the integration process. Assimilationists disagree on that point. Among republicans, 30 percent support public funding for building mosques in France, 70 percent favor budgetary increases for schools with a high proportion of immigrants, and 51 percent agree with quotas for social housing dedicated to immigrant families. Among assimilationists, only 16, 48, and 36 percent gave the same answers to questions on those issues. Republicans are in favor of state intervention for helping immigrants join the French mainstream, whereas assimilationists consider migrants to be solely responsible for their destiny.

The multiculturalists share certain beliefs with the republicans. They both have positive attitudes toward Islam (62 percent) and think that society is responsible for failures in the integration process (86 percent). They also reject the reestablishment of the death penalty (75 percent), the focus on discipline rather than the development of critical thinking at school (62 percent), and ethnocentric prejudice (only 25 percent think immigrants are too numerous in France). As for the republicans, they are left wing in their politics (53 percent) and are highly educated (63 percent of them earned the *baccalauréat* or college degree).[6] They favor a particular model of integration, though. The multiculturalists are equally divided between acceptance and rejection of immigrants' demands for special rights. They unanimously believe in the fight to end discrimination and promote cultural diversity rather than commonality. Not surprisingly, the multiculturalists are in favor of public and state intervention to promote both cultural diversity and the integration of immigrants. Among multiculturalists, 81 percent support increased public spending on schools with high immigrant populations and quotas for public housing for immigrant families. Fifty-eight percent promote affirmative action for immigrants in the private and public sectors, and 55 percent favor public funding for mosques in France. Their model of integration is clearly grounded in a society that recognizes and even promotes ethnic, religious, and cultural diversity, in contrast to the public neutrality favored by the republicans.

The various groups of French that we polled view integration differently. The multiculturalists readily accept immigrants and even view their cultural differences as a benefit to the nation. Assimilationists believe that immigrants must merge into the French mainstream and that they are solely responsible for that process. The particular hallmarks of assimilationists are their ethnocentricity and their religious prejudice. Rejection of Islam is not new, but this survey demonstrates its connection with this particular model of integration. Among the republicans, the religious factor could also preclude a positive evaluation of the immigrants' integration. As previously shown, republicans are less accepting of religious differences when those differences become public. The numerous public stances voiced by Islamic organizations such as the Union des Organisations Islamiques de France (UOIF) could, in the long run, polarize republicans. Furthermore, among both assimilationists and republicans, integration has a shared common goal: immigrants must become "French citizens just like the others." This means no preferential treatment or rights for them. In both groups, integration would be considered unsuccessful if immigrants do not try to join the mainstream and instead remain apart from the rest of society. But is that true? Those views about what constitutes a failure to integrate raise several questions: Do people of the Islamic faith demand special treatment? Can Islam and French secularization coexist? How realistic is the threat of ethnic separation?

The Representation versus the Reality of Islam

Diversity among Muslims

Several scholarly studies have addressed the question of Islam in French society, usually by relying on in-depth interviews of French and non-French Muslims.[7] One problem with this method is that it exaggerates the weight of religious identity in individual value systems. It is also noteworthy that in dealing with a marginal part of the French population (4 percent), quantitative analysis is often complex. The RAPFI survey is therefore a very useful tool for examining the conclusions of these scholars. Among them, Jocelyne Cesari hypothesizes that the new French and their children do not abandon Islamic culture.[8] Our findings contradict this assumption. First, there are strong differences in terms of modal denomination (Catholics stand out in the electorate as a whole and Muslims among the RAPFI respondents). It is false, however, to categorize French people as Catholics or to categorize Maghrebian-, African-, and Turkish-French individuals only as Muslims. Second, though less numerous in proportion than the electorate as a whole, atheists account for 20 percent of the new French (see table 14.3).

Furthermore, the social logic that follows from Islamic religious practice must be examined. Three phenomena found among religious Muslims are opposed to the traditional findings of the sociology of religion, particularly in the study of Catholics.[9] First-generation renewal does not attenuate the religious affiliation of this population. Among the mirror respondents, atheists account for 45 percent of the eighteen- to twenty-five-year-old individuals and 19 percent of those fifty and older, whereas among the new French the proportion of atheists remains more or less the same for all ages. Second, education level is positively correlated to atheism. This is true for both populations, but the relationship is weaker among the new French. Among the RAPFI respondents, 17 percent of the less educated and 25 percent of the college educated practice no religion. Among the mirror respondents, 17 percent of the less educated and 33 percent of the college educated are atheist. The practice of religion in general, and Islam in particular, is therefore more widespread among the immigrant French and their children than in the overall electorate.

Finally, religiosity in Islam does not follow the same trend that it does among Catholics. To analyze the strength of religious belief among the

Table 14.3
Religious affiliations of survey respondents (%)

	Catholic	Muslim	Other religions	Atheist
RAPFI survey	13	60	7	20
Mirror survey	66	2	4	28

Table 14.4
A comparison of the importance of religion among Catholics and Muslims

Religion is very or extremely important (% agree)	Regular attendees	Irregular attendees	No attendance
Mirror survey Catholics	61	19	—
RAPFI survey Muslims	95	75	55

Catholic French, scholars usually study mass attendance because devout Catholics believe they have an obligation to go to church regularly. Using only this indicator, French Catholics and French Muslims would have similar levels of regular attendees: nearly 20 percent of them go to church or the mosque at least once a month. But the percentages among all those who are irregular attendees differ markedly between Catholics and Muslims. Among French Catholics surveyed, 87 percent attend only for marriage, funeral services, or religious holidays and 3 percent never go to church. Among Muslims, the respective proportions are 45 and 35 percent. Following the traditional analysis of religiosity, these secularized Muslims would be seen as being in conflict with their religious beliefs, but this is not the case. As shown in table 14.4, when asked whether religion is important in their everyday lives, Catholics were deeply divided between those who attend mass regularly and those who do not. This clearly demonstrates that among the "unchurched" group, religious denomination should not be taken as an indicator of religiosity. It is more of a cultural distinction than a sign of religious faith.[10] But Muslims are different: religion plays a bigger role in their everyday lives regardless of whether they attend mosque services. There are therefore various ways of being a Muslim in France, and the indicators used to assess Catholic religiosity are not applicable to Muslim religiosity. So, considering all the different indicators, we set up a hierarchical clustering analysis comprising four groups of Muslims. The different dimensions of involvement in Islam can be summed up by three criteria: the importance of religion, the level of compliance with some religious norms in private, and the level of mosque attendance. The four groups—nominal Muslims, customary believers, private followers, and the orthodox (i.e., those who regularly attend mosque services)—present some different and systematic features related to these three dimensions (see table 14.5). The four features are as follows: (1) the lowest level of involvement in every indicator characterizes the nominal Muslims; (2) regular mosque attendance distinguishes orthodox worshipers from other types of Muslims; (3) systematic individual compliance with religious rules in private distinguishes the private followers from the customary believers; and (4) the customary believers limit their religious involvement to cultural tradition.

These results shed new light on the public policies designed by the French state. Former Interior Minister and current French president Nicolas Sarkozy created the Conseil Français du Culte Musulman (CFCM) based on the election of representatives of the mosques, not of the entire Muslim community. These representatives are not even elected by all regular mosque attendees but by a minority of electors designated by the local imams. This

Table 14.5
Typology of French Muslims' involvement in Islam (%)

	Nominal Muslims	Customary believers	Private followers	Orthodox attendees
Religion extremely important	0	31	28	52
Religion very important	12	56	53	46
Religion more important than before	16	40	50	62
Religion less important than before	39	12	9	11
Better worshiper than their parents	1	6	26	30
Worse worshiper than their parents	82	82	50	40
Never drink alcohol	49	73	94	95
Pray every day	0	0	92	84
Never pray	76	39	0	1
Fast throughout Ramadan	66	87	86	96
Do not want to go on pilgrimage	42	8	9	1
Want to go on pilgrimage	58	92	90	88
Have already gone on pilgrimage	0	0	2	10
Attendance at least once a week	0	0	0	93
From time to time	2	39	45	0
Only for religious ceremonies	22	28	18	0
Never	76	31	33	0
Number surveyed	101	179	164	112
Percentage in the sample of Muslims	18	32	30	20

institutional framework is not by itself troublesome, since one of the CFCM's missions is to organize the conditions of the Muslim faith. But the CFCM is also used by political, social, and media actors to represent the whole Muslim community. Islamic groups, including the UOIF, exploit the legitimacy created through this institution to impose their views regarding various issues such as wearing the Islamic veil in school. And clearly they draw their legitimacy on a very unrepresentative sample of Muslims, as the analysis of values and attitude systems will demonstrate.

The Relationship between Islam and Attitudes toward Secularization and Cultural Issues

The relationship between Islam and French culture has raised many questions. Some question whether the Islamic faith is incompatible with French Republican values, as most French citizens think. Some wonder whether French Muslims consider French secularization to be an obstacle or if Islam is systematically associated with conservative beliefs that create tensions with the rest of the polity. Some ask if assimilationists are correct in their view that Islam is not part of the French way of life and if republicans are correct in thinking that religion should not be a public matter. To address these questions, we have analyzed the attitudes of the different groups of French Muslims and other French of immigrant origin on what are often referred to as the cultural issues.

The results concerning secularization are not as straightforward as some may think. The general attitude of French Muslims toward secularization is as positive as that of the rest of the society. This is also the case when the role of secularization is seen as a means of bringing together people with different beliefs and religions. Differences appear when secularization and religious freedom are linked. First of all, Muslims view secularization as an obstacle twice as often as the electorate as a whole. This could be interpreted as tension between the French way of life and that of Muslims, but Muslims themselves respond differently to this question (49 percent of the orthodox versus 22 percent of the nominal Muslims). Second, some Muslims support adapting certain secular practices rather than rejecting them outright, as shown by the strong support for enrolling their children in the current French public school system. Expressing the wish to adapt cafeteria menus to the religion of the pupils is not as opposed to secularism (*laïcité*) as it may seem. Third, a strong gap exists between the orthodox and the rest of the Islamic community. Regular mosque attendees are the only group containing a majority who support wearing the Islamic scarf in school, and they are the strongest supporters of "religion-friendly" public schools. In conclusion, Islam, as a whole, and secularism are not considered antagonistic by a significant majority of Muslims, but a small minority is requesting major changes in the way immigrants are treated by French society.

It is therefore not surprising to find that the orthodox are more conservative in terms of sexual tolerance (both for women and gays) and are also more anti-Semitic.[11] This is not to say that regular attendance at a mosque is systematically associated with conservatism, as shown by the questions on the death penalty or ethnocentrism. But clearly on several points the orthodox

Table 14.6
Religious issues and religious affiliation

	Muslims				Other religions	Atheists	Mirror survey
	Nominal Muslims	Customary believers	Private followers	Orthodox attendees			
Secularization (% positive view)	88	83	79	77	83	81	80
Christian religion (% positive view)	84	91	87	94	86	69	72
Secularization is an obstacle for religious freedom (% agree)	22	42	42	49	27	25	20
Muslims do not have problems practicing their faith in France (% agree)	51	56	56	62	57	54	54
Secularization is the only way for people with different beliefs to live harmoniously (% agree)	94	84	79	77	78	85	81
Specific religious menus in public school cafeterias (% agree)	56	81	80	89	58	59	41
Wearing the Islamic scarf in class (% agree)	33	52	52	76	22	22	17
Wish to enroll children in public secular school (%)	84	72	63	45	63	87	66
Wish to enroll children in public school where religious education is allowed (%)	6	14	21	38	11	4	14
No sexual relations for women before marriage (% agree)	20	51	59	67	14	7	8
Homosexuality is an acceptable way to express one's sexuality (% agree)	65	53	45	35	72	83	81
Jews have too much power in France (% agree)	41	51	46	55	38	26	21
There are too many immigrants in France (% agree)	32	37	44	44	38	24	47
Death penalty should be reestablished (% agree)	17	23	25	15	33	17	32

differ strongly from the rest of Muslims and the rest of society (among the orthodox, 65 percent have homophobic attitudes versus 35 percent among nominal Muslims and 19 percent among the electorate as a whole). It also shows that simply being Muslim cannot be equated with being conservative and that the CFCM should not be viewed as representative of the entire Muslim community.

In summary, tensions between Islam and the French way of life are too often exaggerated. A majority of Muslims express no particular resentment toward the French way of life, some ask for small but not radical changes. Only a minority of them, mostly regular mosque attendees, place the French model in question. When the religious factor is considered, the results are positive in terms of integration.

The Concept of a Clash of Identities

While the religious identity of immigrants may not be as threatening as politicians and a significant part of the electorate claim, other questions about the integration process remain. Is the French polity significantly pressured by an increase in minority-specific demands? Does the communautarist threat correspond to a real claim voiced by the French of immigrant origin, particularly by the Muslim French? As shown before, the electorate as a whole strongly opposes demands for special treatment and recognition of cultural diversity. Behind these attitudes, the survey respondents express their opposition to what they perceive to be a growing movement of ethnic and religious pressure against Republican neutrality. They view special treatment as separation from the rest of society, that is, that some members of the Republic would live by specific rules and not by general laws. For them, cultural diversity would mean being of a particular origin or religion rather than being French and a member of the national community. One must ask if that would necessarily be the case. Are the French of immigrant origin less "French" than the rest of society? Can an individual have distinct political, national, religious, and social identities and still be identified as French, or are those identities mutually exclusive?

These are complex questions for both theoretical and empirical reasons. The wording and ordering of the questions in the survey could influence the level of "communautarism" by either overestimating or underestimating the phenomenon.[12] We therefore chose not to mention the population targeted by the survey. We also asked the identity questions at the beginning of the interview, before questions concerning affirmative action, discrimination, religious beliefs, and attitudes could influence their thinking and exaggerate a feeling of belonging to a specific group. Finally, the identity questions take the form of a battery of queries regarding their proximity to different groups (their generation, social milieu, ethnic and religious groups, nationalities).[13] If the Turkish-, African-, and Maghrebian-French differ from the rest of the electorate in terms of identity, the inter-sample comparison will reveal that.

Once again, the perception developed by a significant portion of French society does not fit with reality. The differences between the two samples on these indicators are often marginal. The impression of being close to the French is even more widespread among the French of immigrant origin than in the electorate as a whole, though the difference is statistically insignificant. The most widespread feeling of closeness is toward members of the same social background and generation. Religion or ethnic origin lag far behind these two groups. The samples differ for only two groups: feelings of closeness toward one's religious group and toward immigrants (a 12 and 22 percent difference, respectively). The religious closeness can be easily explained by the more intense religiosity among the RAPFI respondents in contrast to the rest of the electorate and particularly the movement of secularization among Catholics. Country of origin also matters greatly for the RAPFI respondents. Nevertheless, the intensity of these feelings of belonging should not be overstated. Most of them merely feel close rather than very close to these two groups. There is therefore still some distance between the respondents and these groups. The feeling of closeness toward the country of origin is also widespread, even more so than to the religious group.

But closeness to these particular things or persons (coreligionists, country of origin, immigrants in general) does not conflict with feelings of closeness

Table 14.7
Inter-sample comparison of reported feelings of closeness to several groups

Survey question: Do you feel close or very close to . . .	RAPFI survey (% positive responses)	Mirror survey (% positive responses)
Residents of your neighborhood	69	73
The French	85	84
Citizens of other European countries	56	59
Citizens of the country from which your family emigrated	77	—
People of your age	89	87
People of your social background	87	88
People who share your religion	71	59
Immigrants in France	76	64

to the national community. Fewer than 30 percent of the RAPFI respondents state more intense feelings of closeness toward their country of origin than toward their country of citizenship. As far as religion and immigrants are concerned, this schema holds for, respectively, fewer than 25 and 20 percent of the RAPFI respondents. Consequently, closeness toward the French community prevails among a large majority of the French of immigrant origin. Finally, feelings of closeness based on religion and nationality are not mutually exclusive; on the contrary, the two variables are not correlated, demonstrating that religious and national dimensions are evaluated independently by respondents.

To summarize, transnational, religious, or ethnic identities are not in conflict with the national feeling of belonging. Once again, regarding the question of Islam in France, the representation and the reality differ greatly. Furthermore, communitarianism includes a strong sense of belonging to a minority (which is stronger than the sense of being close to the French) and demands for special treatment. Only 4 percent of the RAPFI respondents fit this definition.

To conclude, France is facing an integration crisis, as shown by the division of the electorate between assimilationists, republicans, and multiculturalists. This crisis focuses mainly on two points: the religious factor and the rise of communautarism. But as demonstrated in these pages, it is unclear whether the crisis is real or perceived. France is caught in a real paradox. On the one hand, politicians, intellectuals, and a major part of the electorate believe that the integration process has failed and hope for greater assimilation and fewer multicultural demands from the French of immigrant origin. On the other hand, the new French demonstrate a high level of religious accommodation when they belong to one denomination yet perceive themselves as being part of the French community. This discrepancy is troublesome, since it could threaten the French Republic with communautarism and ethnic separation.

15

"Weak Immigrants" in Britain and Italy

Balancing Demands for Better Support
versus Tougher Constraints

MANLIO CINALLI

The presence of political refugees and undocumented immigrants is a contentious issue in many contemporary democracies. These immigrants are also at the core of the ongoing construction of a common policy framework across Europe. They are also intertwined with other contentious issues on which contributors to this volume have shed some valuable light. These issues include the enforcement of border controls, threats to national security, the radicalization of Islam, and the position of Muslims in democracies. Despite their decreasing numbers, asylum seekers and undocumented immigrants have gained salience in recent years. Their presence has brought about similar political developments across different states, such as increasingly restrictive measures, growing resentment, and a stimulus to the growth of the far right.[1] As targets of restrictive policies, stigmatizing discourses in the public sphere, and abusive attacks by the far right, asylum seekers and undocumented immigrants can thus be considered among the constituency of "weak immigrants." Both groups are equally passive protagonists since their situation renders them incapable of speaking on their own behalf. Facing social and economic exclusion, psychological distress, and a series of limitations to their most basic rights, asylum seekers and undocumented immigrants have no means by which to oppose the hostile initiatives of a wide range of anti-immigrant protagonists (including state actors).

This chapter focuses on the role of the main pro-immigrant activists, including nongovernmental organizations (NGOs), independent organizations, charities, and movements within the host society that mobilize altruistically on behalf of asylum seekers and undocumented immigrants.[2] It aims to evaluate whether the support offered by these advocacy groups plays an important role in explaining varying responses to the demand that tougher constraints be imposed on "weak immigrants." My argument draws on an analysis of interorganizational dynamics in two national contexts, Britain and Italy. I thus offer a different perspective from other approaches that have instead focused on the supranational political context to explain the treatment of migrants.[3] Do these relational patterns reveal specific dynamics that account for cross-national variations in terms of answers and solutions to the paradox of growing grievances and tougher constraints for weak immigrants? The main answer I suggest is that specific relational dynamics within different countries may well account for different degrees and forms of contention over weak immigrants. I also suggest that politicized issues such as asylum and undocumented immigration do not imply a necessary confrontation between political elites and their most concerned opponents. Rather, these multi-organizational fields may be crucial locations for the engagement of a broader civil society in a bottom-up process of policy formation.

The selection of Britain and Italy as cases allows for meaningful comparison. Multicultural Britain stands out for its relatively inclusive stance toward legal migrants and their descendants. Civic criteria for individual access to citizenship and the acknowledgment of cultural differences and group rights are indeed at the core of its political and institutional arrangements in the field of immigration and ethnic relations.[4] In Italy, numerous actors at the national and local level have accepted the "integration challenge" by engaging in a search for effective provisions, arrangements, and ideas to address the recent transformation of Italy into a country of immigration.[5] Both countries, however, have stood out in Europe for their hard stance against asylum seekers and undocumented immigrants, blurring any significant distinction between these two different groups. The British debate revolves around the contentious issue of "bogus asylum." This is a rhetoric that bridges the gap existing between the (lawful) application for refugee status and the (unlawful) sneaking of economic immigrants into the country. In Italy, the discussion has focused on "clandestine immigration," even when referring to the rescuing of castaways fleeing civil war and starvation. Furthermore, the variety of obstacles asylum seekers face in trying to claim refugee status means that they soon

become undocumented immigrants by failing even the most trivial procedure.

Initially I map out the exchanges between advocacy groups mobilizing on
behalf of "weak" immigrants (henceforth, pro-immigrant groups) and the immigrants themselves, as well as their exchanges with other organizations from
civil society. These networks can be regarded as "endogenous resources."
These are sources that serve as channels for the optimal sharing of assets
among pro-immigrant activists and for support from broader civil society in
defense of weak immigrants. In the next part of the investigation, however,
the analysis focuses on the patterns of exchanges among pro-immigrant organizations and policy elites in the institutional domain. The utility of this
analysis lies in comparing the different combinations of "exogenous opportunities" that pro-immigrant groups have for bringing weak immigrants' interests to the core of policy processes. Subsets of research questions can thus be
formulated along two main dimensions of investigation. The first dimension
consists of "networks of resources." Questions from the first dimension in-
quire as to the pattern of mutual exchanges among pro-immigrant activists in
Britain and Italy, respectively, and their exchanges with other organizations
from civil society. The second dimension consists of "networks of opportunities." In this dimension we are inquiring about the patterns of these exchanges
in each country and how they are sustained. There are other lines of questioning as well. One asks about the roles that specific pro-immigrant protagonists
play in each network. Another concerns whether contention over weak immigrants divides certain types of activists in the same fashion, say, policymakers
from pro-immigrant organizations, or, alternatively, if activists of different
types build crucial relationships that reduce the traditional pattern of disagreement between them.

The first two sections of this chapter establish the basis for national comparison, by presenting legal frameworks, relevant numbers, and public discussions. I also focus attention at the supranational level, since in recent years the
European Union has successfully reinforced its impact upon member states
on the specific issues of asylum and illegal immigration. The third section
deals with the theoretical foundations of the comparison. Using concepts
drawn from resource mobilization theory and political opportunity structure,
this section emphasizes the distinct roles of networks of resources and networks of opportunities. The next two sections compare the main empirical
findings, focusing on networks of resources and networks of opportunities.
These two types of networks are at the core of my research. They reveal
whether different network patterns, as they are developed among similar sets
of activists in different national contexts, are significant factors in explaining

the differences in the empowerment of weak immigrants and in the inclusion of their demands. While advocating further research to study the crucial role of networks, the final section contains a policy-oriented conclusion. In particular, it proposes that the EU adopt a more prominent role, emphasizing both the EU's limits and potential.

Comparing Weak Immigrants in Britain and Italy

There are a number of potential justifications for comparing the contentious politics of asylum and undocumented immigration in Britain and Italy. In the last decade, weak immigrants have been at the core of many legislative reforms and political discussions in both countries. In particular, they have been the object of a series of restrictive measures, underscoring the British and Italian governments' agendas of deterring more arrivals in both countries. In Britain, three main pieces of legislation have come into force with New Labour in power: the Immigration and Asylum Act (1999), the Nationality, Immigration, and Asylum Act (2002), and the Asylum and Immigration Act (2004). These laws have extended penalties on carriers, introduced (and then changed) the voucher scheme as the main instrument of welfare support, extended policies to prevent the arrival of weak immigrants at British ports, and made provisions for a new system of compulsory dispersal to reduce asylum seekers' presence in London and the southeastern part of England. In particular, the 2002 and 2004 laws have followed in the footsteps of the 1999 act in extending the application of non-suspensive appeals and withdrawing welfare support for in-country applicants.

The introduction of restrictive measures has been matched by an increasing politicization of the issue, with New Labour and Conservative party politicians regularly throwing facts, figures, and mutual accusations at each other about entries, deportations, and overstayers. The heightened rhetoric has focused on asylum due to the growing number of applicants for refugee status. From the mid-1990s until 2002, applications rose sharply, reaching a peak of 103,000 in 2002. Since then, however, the government has used new, tighter rules to curb entries, reject more applications, and compel the expulsion of failed asylum seekers. In a time span of only two years, total numbers have decreased by more than half, to approximately 40,000 applications in 2004, decreasing further in the following two years.[6] Undocumented immigration has been intertwined with, and mostly undistinguishable from asylum seeking, thus blurring any major distinction between them.[7] The British Home Office, for example, provided an official estimate of 430,000 undocumented immigrants, but this figure has been publicly contested because it included failed and amnestied asylum seekers.[8] In the lead-up to the 2005 general elections, the New Labour and the Conservative parties debated extensively about "asylum shoppers." This debate prompted a general warning from the Commission for Racial Equality regarding their decision to campaign on such a sensitive issue. The Conservative party has even proposed to impose an annual limit on the number of asylum seekers, beyond which all applicants for refugee status would be illegal immigrants by default. Proposals have gone as far as to contemplate British withdrawal from the 1951 UN Convention on Refugees, which, it is maintained, unjustly constrains the UK's freedom to expel unlawful intruders.[9]

Unlike Britain, Italy has no comprehensive legislation on asylum but only a limited series of specific clauses within its immigration laws. While provisions on asylum were included in the "Martelli law" (1990) it is only over the past ten years that immigration laws have paid more attention to asylum seekers, first, with the "Turco-Napolitano law" (1998) and then, with the "Bossi-Fini law"(2002).[10] As in Britain, however, the stance against asylum seekers has become stricter over time, especially during Prime Minister Silvio Berlusconi's center-right government between 2001 and 2006. Restrictive measures on asylum, with draconian provisions on illegal entry, residence, and working permits, have brought about an increasing number of deportations, long detentions, and coercive policing interventions. Indeed, as in Britain, confusion reigns over the distinction between asylum seekers and undocumented immigrants. Specific claims for asylum are much less numerous in Italy than in Britain, but overall numbers of weak immigrants are similar due to higher estimates of undocumented immigrants.[11] Indeed, it is argued that many potential refugees have been forced to become undocumented immigrants because of deficient legislation on asylum, ever-changing restrictions, scarce information, and a broad range of administrative impediments to their applications.[12] It is noteworthy that there were only 13,460 applications for asylum submitted in Italy in 2003, and yet 20,000 arrivals in the same year were registered in Sicily alone. The Italian authorities can detain weak immigrants for up to sixty days to distinguish between those who are economic illegal immigrants and those who have a genuine asylum case under the 1951 Convention. Perhaps in a gesture intended to placate the northern EU member states, Italy has done the most to deter new arrivals, deporting several tens of thousands of weak immigrants in the last few years alone.[13] Following a controversial agreement between Berlusconi and Libya's Colonel Gheddafi, the Italian government has sent thousands of weak immigrants to detention camps in Libya, where their most basic human rights have been abrogated.[14] Allegedly, Italy has also resorted to regular mass expulsions in breach of its international obligations. This behavior has raised growing concerns among several intergovernmental and interparliamentary bodies. These include the UN Special Rapporteur for the Human Rights of Migrants, the UN High Commissioner for Refugees (UNHCR), the Council of Europe's Committee for the Prevention of Torture and Other Cruel, Inhuman or Degrading Treatment or Punishment, the European Parliament, and the European Court of Human Rights.

At the same time, weak immigrants in Britain and Italy have faced intense resentment, open racism, and threatening labels, including "bogus asylum seekers," "welfare scroungers," "job thieves," "bingo-bongo," and even "terrorist bombers."[15] In Italy, some leaders of the Lega Nord (Northern League) political party have tried to use the media to poison the public debate. In their own words, detention centers are five-star hotels and the navy should fire on boats carrying immigrants as they approach Italian shores. In Britain, popular tabloids have conducted a hate campaign against asylum seekers, describing them as foreign killers, rapists, pedophiles, terrorists, or, at best, as gangs jumping the queue for homes and welfare.[16] Several opinion surveys and studies on prejudice have documented the spread of xenophobic sentiments among British and Italian citizens. Terrible racial attacks have marred the reputation of some cities in both countries with images of the hunting and deliberate killings of innocent immigrants.[17] Not surprisingly, anti-immigrant movements and far-right parties have gained operational capacities and increasing political leverage. The 2006 local elections in Britain marked a political triumph for the British National party (BNP) in terms of votes and seats gained throughout constituencies of traditional New Labour influence. Crucially, the BNP has long been campaigning against asylum seekers and undocumented immigrants, building on its own success in widespread anti-immigrant public discourse. In Italy, the very endorsement of the Bossi-Fini law in 2002 was considered to be an attempt by Prime Minister Berlusconi to placate his coalition partners, namely, the Lega Nord and Alleanza Nazionale, and their broader anti-immigration electorates.

In addition, the two countries have met extensive criticism from international institutions and independent organizations for the conditions in their detention camps. Amnesty International (AI) has highlighted that detention policy in Britain permits the imprisonment of any asylum seeker. British detention, it is argued, is often unlawful as it is applied indiscriminately to those who are patently fleeing persecution, to families with young children, and to people with severe mental illness. These circumstances are exacerbated by several factors. These include the lack of legal representation, by the remoteness of the detention centers, which prevents contact between detainees and their families and legal representatives, and above all by the fact that there is no limit on the length of possible detention and that no judicial authorization is required.[18] The Italian detention centers have also come under attack for their appalling conditions. Medici Senza Frontiere (MSF) conducted an extensive review of the centers in 2003 and discovered vandalism, self-mutilations, and excessive use of sedatives on the detainees by center personnel.[19] Amnesty International's 2005 reports also condemned physical assault by law enforcement officers, unhygienic living conditions, deficient medical care, and great difficulties in gaining access to the asylum determination process. Not surprisingly, Italian center-right officials have been extremely reluctant to allow inspections of detention centers. They have delayed or denied access to UNHCR representatives, members of the Italian Parliament, lawyers, pastoral workers, journalists, and the majority of the key NGOs in the field.

Lastly, it should be noted that both Britain and Italy are EU members. Political developments on asylum and undocumented immigration, including increasingly restrictive measures, overall confusion between asylum and undocumented immigration, widespread resentment in the public sphere, and growing popular support for the far right are common throughout Europe. An analysis of entries, asylum rejections, and deportations in Britain and Italy reveals similarities with the rest of Europe. One example is the number of asylum applications, which has risen sharply, reaching a peak of nearly 400,000 in both 2001 and 2002 in the fifteen countries that were part of the EU at the time. Since then, however, applications have been halved in a time span of only a few years.[20] These common developments parallel the increasing Europeanization of asylum and (illegal) immigration. The Treaty of Amsterdam has reinforced the main supranational institutions in the third pillar (Justice and Home Affairs), increasing important access points for the European Commission, Parliament, and Court of Justice. The Schengen Agreement has been included in the EU treaty framework, transferring immigration and asylum policy from the third to the first pillar of the Union. This process has thus strengthened exchanges and cooperation between EU member states, bringing about the approval of the first multi-annual program to build a "Union of Freedom, Security, and Justice" on the occasion of the European Council of Tampere in 1999.

Following the Tampere Summit, the first of a two-stage process for developing a common asylum policy was completed between 2004 and 2005. This first stage focused on EU-wide minimum standards on asylum through the elaboration of a comprehensive package of four directives and two regulations. More precisely, in 2001, the Temporary Protection Directive addressed crises that forced people to leave their homes temporarily. It was followed by the Eurodac Regulation in 2002, which introduced systematic fingerprinting of asylum seekers across EU member states. A substantial step toward policy harmonization was made in 2003, when specific criteria to determine responsible countries for processing asylum applications were formalized under the Dublin Convention. In the same year, the EU 15 also agreed to minimal reception rights for asylum seekers with the Reception Conditions Directive. The 2004 Qualification Directive provided a common EU interpretation of the Geneva Convention definition of a refugee.[21] Lastly, the Asylum Procedures Directive was adopted in 2005, establishing minimum standards on procedures for granting or withdrawing refugee status. While both the UNHCR and the European Parliament have expressed their serious concerns in terms of full respect for the Geneva Convention, this directive represented the conclusion to the first stage of developing a common asylum policy.[22] Indeed, the European Council of The Hague in 2004 officially began another multi-annual program for the second stage of the process, that is, the setting up of a single asylum system for the whole of the EU, including a unified status for all refugees. This second stage saw the twenty-five EU member states abandon the unanimity rule in the Council of Ministers and grant "co-decisionmaking" to the European Parliament.

Conceptual Foundations and Operational Framework

The previous section argued that asylum seekers and undocumented immigrants face difficult constraints for autonomous mobilization both in Britain and Italy. Not surprisingly, weak immigrants have refrained from mobilizing in the public domain, with the exception of a few symbolic individual protests. In fact, most choose not to vocalize their grievances because of seclusion and fear. Some, however, have expressed their despair by self-mutilation or even suicide.[23] This highlights the critical need for independent organizations, charities, NGOs, and other advocacy groups to mobilize on behalf of weak immigrants. This pro-immigrant focus is here combined with study of the conceptual and methodological tools that are increasingly applied in the scientific literature. Some European scholars are in fact pursuing a research agenda that focuses on ethnic communities in order to assess the extent to which political participation of immigrants can be explained with ethnic capital as it is reflected in the social networks of immigrants' organizations.[24] These scholars also focus on the connections between different ethnic communities and, more specifically, on the concept of cross-cultural social capital.[25] At the same time, research has been focused on how institutions may

channel and influence generalized trust and, in particular, on channels between the macro-level of the political and the discursive context and the
micro-level of individual immigrants themselves.[26]

Building on this research, it is possible to provide key insights on relational dynamics impacting empowerment and inclusion of weak immigrants' demands across different national contexts. Political contention over weak
immigrants is thus considered to be dependent upon network patterns, which
are built differently by activists in each national context. Since all these activists are not distinct and isolated units but mutually connected via an extensive set of interactions, networks can be considered to be crucial along two
main dimensions. First, a wide range of embedded resources can be accessed
through "networks of resources." These are exchanges that facilitate the flow
of information among pro-immigrant movements and organizations, reinforce their mutual recognition, and allow for their public acknowledgment
across civil society. From this perspective, the analysis of networks fits into "resource mobilization theory" since ties provide a valuable "resource" that rational activists can use to balance their scarce control of other resources,
having evaluated the costs and benefits of different strategies.[27] Second, the
analysis of exchanges can be used to assess the extent to which actors "from
below" seize key opportunities to engage in processes of decision making
alongside policy elites and institutions. These "networks of opportunities"
may also lead to a dynamic renegotiation of boundaries between movements,
civil society, and the state. Put simply, "networks of opportunities" refer to
channels between pro-immigrant activists and the political context within
which they operate. They thus offer a different perspective from the analysis
of "networks of resources" (in which exchanges are an internal resource to mobilize for sustaining pro-immigrant action). From this perspective, the investigation of networks fits the "political opportunity structure" approach since
ties provide opportunities (and constraints) for pro-immigrant activists, impacting their mobilization.[28]

In particular, many types of exchanges among activists can be simplified
into two main relationships at the core of classic studies of network analysis,
that is, ties of cooperation and ties of disagreement.[29] It follows that the relational dynamics (both cooperation and disagreement) beyond the contentious
politics of weak immigrants can be analyzed in terms of "networks of resources." This can be both inwardly, among pro-immigrant organizations,
and outwardly, between these organizations and other activists from civil society. Having compared British and Italian pro-immigrant activists in terms
of their networks of resources, the analysis can then turn to "networks of opportunities." They can be analyzed by focusing on cooperation and disagree-

ment between advocacy organizations and elites in the policy domain. Put simply, each pro-immigrant organization is taken as a focus from which lines radiate to other nodes in the multi-organizational field. This latter node may represent another advocacy group, a civil society organization, or policy activists. In particular, these lines are sets of cooperative and disagreement ties connecting a set of activists, that is, they depict activists connected by relations of close cooperation and close disagreement.

Network analysis can be extremely valuable for focusing on the entire field, main subgroups, and the specific situation of pro-immigrant organizations.[30] Starting with the last, I refer to a relation between any two actors as an "edge." If there is an edge joining two actors, these actors are adjacent. A "path" is a chain of edges that connect two actors. The number of actors adjacent to an actor expresses its "degree," that is, the measure of an actor's centrality within the network. Regarding the analysis of entire multi-organizational fields, the most important structural characteristic of a network is "density."[31] The use of density, however, can be problematic when comparing different networks due to the sensitivity of this measure to network size.[32] I thus decided to rely on measures of "average degree" of all actors in order to make systematic comparisons between different networks. The average degree is the number of exchanges that each actor on average shares within a network, to be computed by dividing the total number of ties by the total number of actors. Combinations of measures of average degree are extremely useful in appraising the extent to which cooperation prevails over disagreement, along the dimensions of both resources and opportunities.

Empirical Findings on Networks of Resources in Britain and Italy

Having divided the two national fields into relevant network portions, I focus first on an analysis of the interorganizational ties that pro-immigrant activists have built among themselves on the issues of asylum and undocumented immigration. Figure 15.1 shows the map of edges between sixteen pro-immigrant organizations that have mobilized on behalf of weak immigrants in Britain; each edge indicates the existence of a close cooperative relationship between a pair of these actors.

The most evident characteristic of this group of networks among British pro-immigrant organizations is its high density, demonstrating that many activists interact with each other. The majority of these organizations have forged ties of cooperation with more than half of the activists in the network. Some of them (namely, the Joint Committee for the Welfare of Immigrants, Refugee Council, Amnesty International, and Oxfam) stand out for their high degree of cooperation. At the same time, all the organizations with the lowest degree of cooperation (namely, the Children's Society, the Jesuit Refugee Centre, and the Commission for Racial Equality) interact directly with two or more organizations with the highest degree. Hence, they are no more than one edge away from any other organization within the network. In addition, extensive ties of cooperation are in no way counterbalanced by ties of disagreement among the same organizations. Figure 15.2 shows in fact that there is hardly any disagreement among British advocacy groups. This prevalence of mutual ties of cooperation and absence of disagreement thus promotes not only a fast and efficient flow of information among the different nodes but also the reinforcement of solidarity and a stronger sense of unity in the overall network. British advocacy groups can access, exchange, and rely on crucial resources through their extensive web of mutual interorganizational exchanges of cooperation. These networks of resources are particularly useful not only for increasing the flow of information across the nodes and for facilitating allocation of responsibilities and flexibility of action but also for elaborating mutual understanding and common goals.

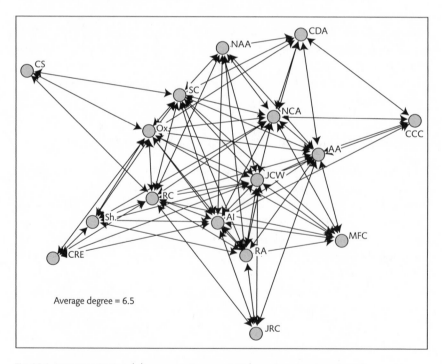

Fig. 15.1. Interorganizational disagreement among British pro-immigrant groups.
See chapter appendix on page 320 for a list of defined acronyms for interviewed actors for figures 15.1–15.8.

Hence, many organizations together decided to establish a coordinating umbrella, namely, the Asylum Rights Campaign, which keeps members informed about the campaigning work of each group. The importance of mutual networks is particularly evident when considering solidarities and the sense of unity that have been mobilized at crucial times. For example, a large number of pro-immigrant organizations have stood together to boycott the implementation of the government's food voucher scheme.[33] This campaign has proved that advocacy groups can successfully unite in their efforts for political change. It has demonstrated in particular that the instrumental function of networks of resources is only a part of the resources themselves, since overwhelming feelings and common identities can at times be mobilized through these same networks. The resolute participation of the Refugee Council in the campaign of protest—notwithstanding its role as an assistance agency under the same act that had introduced the vouchers—provides key evidence of this direction.

Turning to the analysis of ties among advocacy groups mobilizing on behalf of weak immigrants in Italy, it is noteworthy that they have decided to shape their reciprocal exchanges in a different pattern. Figure 15.3 shows the map of edges between advocacy groups, where each edge represents a close cooperative relationship between a pair of them. The lower density of the Italian pro-immigrant network compared to the same network for Britain is clearly visible; interactions among pro-immigrant organizations in Italy are considerably less extensive than in Britain.

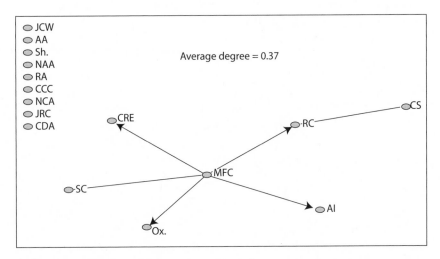

Fig. 15.2. Interorganizational disagreement among British pro-immigrant groups.

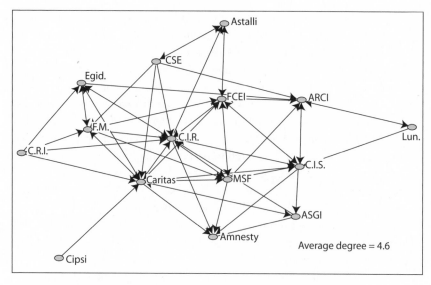

Fig. 15.3. Interorganizational cooperation among Italian pro-immigrant groups.

For example, it is evident that many activists have forged only few ex-changes and hence, they are connected with other activists only through long paths. Of course, some organizations are clearly distinguished to a significant degree, namely, Caritas, the Consiglio Italiano Rifugiati or Italian Council for Refugees (CIR), and the Federation of Evangelic Churches in Italy (FCEI). By interacting with one of these few organizations, many activists can still communicate with each other. Nevertheless, the British network of pro-immigrant organizations stands out for its larger volume of nodes of a high degree and for its shorter paths of communication among different activists.

Regarding disagreement, figure 15.4 shows that there is no significant dif-ference between the British and the Italian fields. While Italian activists are somewhat more argumentative than their British counterparts, pro-immigrant organizations in both countries rarely engage in disputes.

However, the most revealing figures are obtained by weighting coopera-tion on disagreement in order to precisely measure their prevalence in each national field. That is, the prevalence of cooperation expresses the ratio of the average degree of cooperation in the network to the average degree of dis-agreement. This measure is 17.57 for the British issue-field of asylum (i.e., 6.5/0.37) and 8.68 for the Italian issue-field of undocumented immigration (i.e., 4.6/0.53). The prevalence of cooperation among British pro-immigrant activists is thus double the rate of that in Italy. Networks of resources are less

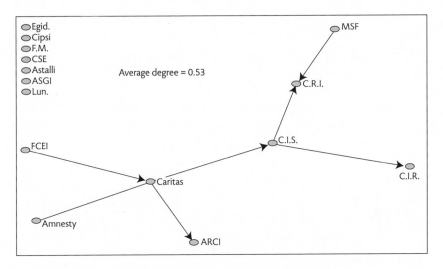

Fig. 15.4. Interorganizational disagreement among Italian pro-immigrant groups.

extensive in Italy when they are assessed by focusing inwardly on mutual exchanges between advocacy groups. Of course, these activists are still aware of the importance of mutual connections in promoting the flow of information among themselves. These connections are useful in reaching mutual agreement on different roles and duties but are ineffective in mobilizing shared feelings and common identities.

Turning our attention to networks of resources that on the surface bridge the gap between pro-immigrant activists and their potential allies from broader civil society, it is crucial to assess the extent to which they complement the network patterns examined above. In this case, the analysis focuses on relationships of cooperation and disagreement between pro-immigrant activists and trade unions, political parties, churches, and professional and other independent organizations from civil society. Figures 15.5 and 15.6 compare network patterns between advocates and civil society allies across the two national fields. The focus is exclusively on networks of resources that bridge these two different sets of activists, rather than on reciprocal ties forged among activists within the same set.

The data confirm that British and Italian pro-immigrant organizations differ in terms of their networks of resources. In particular, Italian pro-immigrant organizations have built fewer outward connections with broader civil society than have their British counterparts. Nearly all Italian advocates have built at

least one tie of cooperation with trade unions, churches, and/or political parties. Yet no node is characterized by high point-centrality, with the exceptions
of Caritas and CIR. Pro-immigrant organizations in Britain have developed a
denser network structure, characterized by extensive networks of resources
with civil society allies.

In particular, it is noteworthy that the high degree of the Joint Council for
the Welfare of Immigrants (JCWI) and the Refugee Council (RC) within the

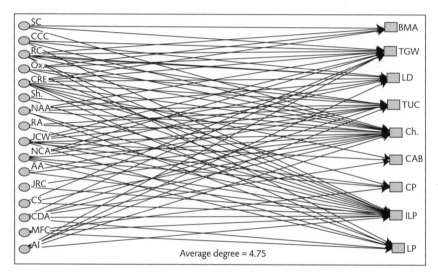

Fig. 15.5. Interorganizational cooperation between British pro-immigrant groups and civil society.

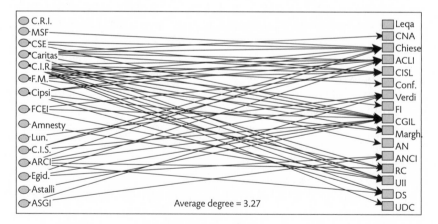

Fig. 15.6. Interorganizational cooperation between Italian pro-immigrant groups and civil society.

advocacy network is matched by similar high values when considering this larger portion of network. JCWI and RC emerge as the main organizations that have pulled resources outwardly across advocacy groups and civil society. At the same time, the Council for Racial Equality (CRE) occupies a strategic position of exchange with civil society allies and should therefore be considered a central organization within the overall network in spite of its more limited internal ties with other advocacy groups. It is clear that British pro-immigrant activists can rely on more extensive networks of resources, both inwardly and outwardly, thus standing out as a unified advocacy sector which is at the same time well integrated within the broader civil society.

Empirical Findings on Networks of Opportunities in Britain and Italy

My analysis has so far demonstrated that pro-immigrant activists can make different decisions when shaping their interorganizational networks among themselves and with other organizations from civil society. In particular, I have found some interesting variations in terms of networks of resources, both inwardly and outwardly, between the British and the Italian models. Indeed, one could expect even more significant variations if we extend this kind of investigation to other national case studies. The main argument, up to this point, has been that extensive networks of resources provide a distinct advantage not only in terms of material exchanges and efficient use of assets but also in the development of solidarities and the strengthening of common identities. In particular, the data have shown that in the British issue-field of asylum, the extensive number of ties among advocacy groups, as well as with civil society allies, has been matched by the substantial flow of information and other material resources. The data also show the gradual development of a cohesive sense of unity within the network. In the case of Britain's voucher campaign, this pursuit of a common goal prevailed over the interests of separate groups of pro-immigrant activists. By contrast, pro-immigrant organizations in Italy seem to be less unified by common solidarities. Although they have at times organized national day parades to make immigrants' claims more visible in the public sphere, Italian pro-immigrant organizations have not yet united in widespread and cohesive mobilizations.

However, networks of resources represent only one dimension of pro-immigrant groups' actions for the empowerment and inclusion of weak immigrants' claims in their host societies. This first dimension needs to be integrated with the analysis of networks of opportunities, which are indeed crucial for putting advocacy groups in communication with their institutionalized political environment. Networks of opportunities may be useful for explaining, for example, how some institutional provisions (rather than others) can favor (or not favor) pro-immigrant activists in their effort to include weak immigrants' demands both in the public debate and in the policy domain. Networks of opportunities could be essential in transmitting public discourse on the renegotiation of interpretations among pro-immigrant organizations. They could also be useful in evaluating how pro-immigrant activists come to absorb new ideas or to be challenged to reevaluate their own practices. An indirect impact may also concern the weak immigrants themselves, since they still face rules, policies, and discourses that have grown out of continuous interaction between pro-immigrant organizations and their political environment. Ultimately, a detailed study of exchanges between pro-immigrant groups and policy activists would be useful for systematically assessing what remains to be accomplished before including weak immigrants' demands within contemporary societies.

Figures 15.7 and 15.8 compare ties of cooperation between advocacy groups and core influential policy actors in each national field. The main finding is that pro-immigrant organizations in Britain have developed more extensive links to the policy domain than have their Italian counterparts, which is consistent with previous findings about networks of resources. In opposition to many government policies, British organizations mobilizing on behalf of weak immigrants have forged direct links with policy elites and institutions so as to play some crucial role in the decisionmaking process. One example is the CRE's work, in which it coordinated efforts with public bodies to promote laws, policies, and practices to prevent discrimination. Another example is the RC, which was established as a result of the Immigration and Asylum Act (1999). In fact, the RC is part of a multi-agency partnership that, with other advocacy groups, aims to plug weak immigrants into the national institutions of welfare support and provide them with independent advice on a wide range of questions. Networks of opportunities in Britain are crucial for enabling advocates to enter processes of governance through direct contact with institutions, thus strengthening their intervention on behalf of asylum seekers. Taken together with extensive networks of resources, these networks of opportunities allow pro-immigrant organizations to mobilize on behalf of weak immigrants in order to affect policy change to improve their situation.

In Italy, advocacy groups must rely on less extensive, less structured networks of opportunities. That is, Italian pro-immigrant activists are not only less well connected among themselves and across civil society than their British counterparts but also further removed from policymaking because they are only loosely connected to political elites and institutions in the policy domain. Of course, a few specific organizations can rely much more than

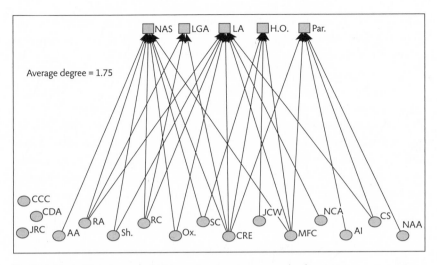

Fig. 15.7. Vertical links between British pro-immigrant groups and policy actors.

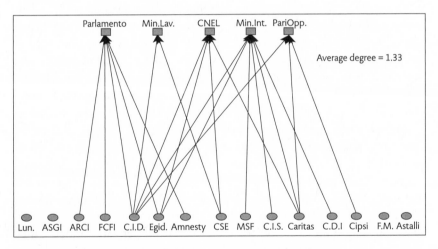

Fig. 15.8. Vertical links between Italian pro-immigrant groups and policy actors.

others on crucial networks of opportunities. The CIR and Caritas, for example, play a crucial role in the processes of governance. Policymakers are obviously interested in the support that these central organizations provide in terms of welfare services, knowledge, expertise, and public legitimization. In turn, CIR and Caritas themselves can obtain privileged access to political opportunities so as to reinforce their organizational strength and public profile.

Nevertheless, most Italian advocacy groups acting in the name of weak immigrants either share few links with policy actors or are disconnected from the policy domain altogether.

Policy disputes and public contention over asylum seekers and undocumented immigrants are at the core of most recent political developments in both Britain and Italy. In the campaign for the 2005 general election, the UK's former prime minister, Tony Blair, debated fiercely with members of the Conservative opposition on the issues of border controls, asylum quotas, and even withdrawal from the Geneva Convention. Italian debate has focused at length on these issues, and they continue to dominate the political agenda. At the time of this writing, heated debates in the Italian Parliament surround the formulation of a new Italian asylum law, which the newly elected center-left government considers to be part of a wider and necessary reform of the restrictive measures implemented by the previous center-right government. This chapter has demonstrated that asylum seekers and undocumented immigrants can be taken as representatives of the same constituency of "weak immigrants." Both groups are excluded from social, political, and legal entitlements and are thus incapable of autonomous interventions in the public sphere. The role played by pro-immigrant activists, and particularly the networks of resources and networks of opportunities that these activists have forged in each national context, form patterns. The patterns of these networks are thought to be the main reasons for the differences in mobilization on behalf of weak immigrants and possible inclusion of their interests and demands in policymaking.

In fact, a main goal of this chapter is to encourage further research on the relational dynamics behind mobilization and contention over politicized issues. The analysis of networks of resources indicated that they are important in terms of not only the instrumental advantages of single organizations but also in the diffusion and sharing of feelings of solidarity and unity. In particular, mutual exchanges among pro-immigrant organizations may enable them to develop and unite in collective movements, while networks bridging their distance from potential allies in civil society may enhance their scope of action and lead to wider acknowledgment of their objectives. Regarding networks of opportunities, analytical inquiry can offer a new and effective representation of the dynamics of formulation and integration of weak immigrants' demands in their host societies. Indeed, the development of exchanges across different levels of political power may facilitate flows of information about policy preferences otherwise not available, allow agents who play a critical role in the policy domain to capitalize on opportunities, and reinforce the internalization of public discourse and political legitimization. Networks of opportunities may enable pro-immigrant activists to influence decisionmaking, thus shaping de facto new patterns of governance for the bottom-up inclusion of weak immigrants' needs and demands.

Regarding policy challenges, it is clear that the politics of weak immigrants are not marginal but indeed central in the broader field of immigration and ethnic relations. At the core of broader political (and economic) processes, issues such as asylum and undocumented immigration hardly represent a restricted space for the intervention of few specific institutions and ad hoc organizations. The analysis of networks has indeed emphasized the relevance of a broader multi-organizational field. This is a field whose relational dynamics play a key role in finding different solutions to the paradox of growing grievances versus stricter constraints for weak immigrants. Major policy efforts should be directed to foster these networks. Contention over weak immigrants is a complex dynamic that is not simply played across a definite dividing line between friends and enemies.

On the one hand, pro-immigrant organizations need to be fully aware of their vital altruistic function of empowering weak immigrants and including their demands in the formation of public policy. These activist groups need to carefully consider the effective resources that they can mobilize through their exchanges among themselves and with other organizations from broader civil society. These networks are an important signal of their genuine advocacy as well as a defense against frequent criticism of their work. This criticism includes charges of victimization, paternalism, creating new forms of dependence, and increasing weak immigrants' vulnerability through altruistic aid, all of which are serious risks that need to be considered. On the other hand, policymakers must be aware that their exchanges with pro-immigrant organizations need to be safeguarded and nurtured not only in an opportunistic fashion. Pro-immigrant activists can provide them with vital channels toward more fully understanding the main issues at the core of our modern democracies. This would enable them to offer solutions that strike a virtuous balance between respect for weak immigrants' rights and preferences and the costs and commitments for individual governments.

This leads to a final point: the role of the EU. The establishment of a single asylum system for the whole of the EU, including a unified status for all refugees, is currently at the top of the EU agenda. The single system would hold a much greater role for supranational institutions such as the European Parliament. Yet these important political advancements at the European level seem to contradict notions such as "safe country" or "manifestly unfounded" claims, which in fact do little to meet the needs of weak immigrants. It is sufficient to emphasize widespread concern for issues affecting weak immigrants. These include the lack of respect for the "non-refoulement" principle, for the different types of legal detentions that have been sanctioned, for the growing allocation of EU funds to border management and control, and for the externalization of procedures to keep asylum seeking and undocumented immigration from the public view. The EU needs to state more clearly its support for a fair policy for all parties involved, considering the burdens, responsibilities, and legitimate concerns of member states while effectively addressing the need for consideration of weak immigrants' demands. The main implication of this chapter is that pro-immigrant organizations and their allies from civil society should always be key protagonists within this broader European design.

Nation-states need to come to a similar shared understanding of issues and solutions since they are still the primary voices of Europe and are well able to resist, if they choose, the most compelling European developments in the field. Indeed, in response to the two most recent pieces of EU anti-discrimination legislation, the Racial Equality Directive (2000) and the Employment Equality Directive (2000), the specific aspects concerning social and civil dialogue have proved to be particularly difficult to implement. Member states have easy recourse to flexible measures and exceptions to suit their own particular desires. Pro-immigrant organizations have an important role to play where the paths of weak immigrants, civil society, and policymakers cross at both the national and the European level. Contemporary democracies need to acknowledge and reinforce specific aspects of this role if they want to overcome the rhetoric of "emergence" and "illegality." They must do so to find long-lasting solutions, which may involve listening to the voices of weak immigrants in our polities, finally resolving their unsustainable position between growing grievances and stricter constraints.

Appendix

List of Interviewed Actors with Abbreviations (UK)

AA=Asylum Aid; **AI**=Amnesty International; **BMA**=British Medical Association; **CAB**=National Association of Citizens Advice Bureaux; **Ch.**=Churches' Commission for Racial Justice; **CCC**=Campaign to Close Campsfield; **CDA**=Committee to Defend Asylum Seekers; **CP**=Conservative Party; **CRE**=Commission for Racial Equality; **CS**=Children's Society; **H.O.**=Home Office; **ILP**=Immigration Law Practitioners' Association; **JCW**=Joint Council for the Welfare of Immigrants; **JRC**=Jesuit Refugee Service; **LD**=Liberal Democrats; **LA**=Local Authority; **LGA**=Local Government Association; **LP**=Labour Party; **MFC**=Medical Foundation for the Care of Victims of Torture; **NAA**=National Assembly Against Racism; **NAS**=National Asylum Support Service; **NCA**=National Coalition of Anti-Deportation Campaigns; **Ox.**=Oxfam; **Par.**=Parliament; **RA**=Refugee Action; **RC**=Refugee Council; **SC**=Save the Children; **Sh.**=Shelter; **TGW**=Transport and General Workers Union

16

Immigration

Tensions, Dilemmas, and Unresolved Questions

ARIANE CHEBEL D'APPOLLONIA AND SIMON REICH

Much has been made on both sides of the Atlantic about the current debates over immigration. These debates focus mainly on the economic and social impact of immigration as well as on the relationship between border controls and state sovereignty. Each debate replays controversies that have been going on for decades in Europe and the United States. The perception of immigrants as a threat is therefore unoriginal. The securitization of immigration issues began before 9/11, but the terrorist attacks of that day reinforced the linkage to border control and national security. The linkage between immigrants and security is perhaps more emphasized in public rhetoric in the United States and more emphasized in identity and civil violence in Europe. Yet in neither place is there a comprehensive linkage made between immigration, national security, and integration. The contributors to this book suggest that this is an important oversight in at least three ways.

First, a failure to comprehend that there is an important holistic linkage between the three elements detracts from our understanding of how they influence each other. Examining the individual components of this relationship may be understandable from a theoretical perspective, however, because it may make any analysis more manageable. If domestic behavior regarding social programs actually has a significant influence on national security, then studying border controls or internal surveillance alone risks missing a key component of the equation. The London and Madrid transit bombings suggest that marginalized domestic actors play into the relationship in an important way. The conventional view is that security challenges often begin externally, or that the primary way in which terrorists recruit domestic support is by infiltrating from abroad. Bluntly stated, that conventional way may incorrectly specify the problem. The problem may begin with insufficient integration of minority groups who feel excluded and whose resentment provides fertile ground for terrorist recruitment. Although the work in this volume provides no definitive answers, it does suggest that we need to explore and analyze the claim further.

Second, and of course, relatedly, the implications of this lack of a linkage between the three components of immigration, integration, and security are problematic in terms of public policy. As chapter 11, by Ariane Chebel d'Appollonia, illustrates, immigration debates in Europe have been largely disconnected from—and often in conflict with—attempts to integrate first-, second-, and even third-generation immigrants. Security policy is certainly attenuated from debates about integration. The effects of this decoupling are often cross-cutting, dysfunctional, counterproductive, and generally unintended. Security policies encourage xenophobic tendencies, the rhetoric of policymakers focuses on the need for assimilation and acceptance, and social policies do not address the particular needs of migrants and their descendants. These countervailing tendencies often lead to alienation and, not too subtly, establish the foundations for the legitimization of widespread xenophobia on one side and violent radicalism on the other. In the United States, the assumption is made that national security is more about border control than cultural, social, and economic integration. Many Americans believe that once legal migrants have been granted domicile, the power of the U.S. melting pot can be relied upon to ensure that they do not respond to the lure of radical (read jihadist) ideas and engage in terrorist acts. This complacency may come at a heavy cost if Americans are mistaken and experience the same form of "terrorism from within" that their European counterparts have.

Finally, public debate in the United States has focused on the civil liberties and political rights of terrorist suspects and insurgent combatants held as prisoners. To a lesser (if growing) extent, opponents have voiced concern about the growth of intrusive state powers under the PATRIOT Act. Relatively little attention has been paid, however, to the consequences of new security measures for legitimate immigrants and for asylum seekers. As the chapters by Baylis, Kalhan, and Chacón all illustrate, this burden has been a significant one—in terms of both the changes in due process and the redefinition of the boundaries of criminality. New instruments of state power have not been off-set by new measures designed to ensure against their abuse. The Bush administration's oft-articulated claim that new security measures offer a guarantee against the diminution of freedom appears unpersuasive when it comes to applicants for immigration, domiciled immigrants, and asylum seekers.

In Europe, the debate on the adoption of minimum standards for "the qualification, status, and reception conditions of asylum seekers" began in September 2001. It is noteworthy that the EU Commission's proposal was adopted on September 12, 2001, and was therefore negotiated in the political climate of the attacks in the United States the previous day. The agreed provisions reflect an emphasis on the exigencies of security to the detriment of human rights obligations.[1] Security concerns thus create limits on the right to asylum. EU Council Directive 2004/83/EC, for example, contains provisions on exclusion, revocation, and non-refoulement that arguably fall short of existing and evolving international law and standards. Article 14, paragraphs 4 and 5, includes what constitutes de facto provisions on exclusion, going beyond what is permissible according to the Geneva Convention.[2] Similar human rights concerns are raised by new regulations adopted by EU member states. German laws, for example, allow for the rejection of individuals requesting entry into the country (through visa or asylum application) if the applicant is suspected of supporting a terrorist group or if the applicant is suspected of being violent. Suspicion is therefore a sufficient ground to deny the right to asylum. Several countries have enacted new limits on entry and residence and have developed new powers of expulsion. In Austria, an amendment to the Asylum Act (1997) adopted in 2003 restricts the period during which a preliminary assessment of the refugee's case is made. In the Czech Republic, the Law on Employment (435/2004) requires the payment of a fee from those seeking work permits—a measure intended to restrict entry. In Luxembourg, an asylum law adopted in 2004 accelerates the procedure for "unfounded claims" and places limits on the right to appeal.[3] The British Asylum and Immigration Act of 2004 reinforced the government's ability to detain and expel asylum seekers.

Furthermore, calls for greater assimilation by domiciled immigrants, coupled with fears of the dilution of Europe's identity, have often translated into more stringent formal requisites for immigrants and asylum seekers. Language training and citizenship tests are conditions for the acquisition of nationality in many countries. But other requisites still further limit third country nationals' (TCNs) access to citizenship. These include various requirements related to their income level, the stability of their employment, and a broader, vaguer notion of being a threat to national security. Several states impose fees and other restrictions for the application and the renewal of permits regarding residency status, reducing its accessibility. Furthermore, tests on integration are now intended to allow national authorities to revoke a previously granted residency status. The Dutch government, for example, declared in December 2004 that recent immigrants would have to pass an "integration test" within three-and-a-half years; failure to successfully complete the test would affect their residency status. The Netherlands also introduced a pre-entry language test in February 2006 for both non-European immigrants and asylum seekers. Thus, as Europeans discuss the prospects for residency (rather than citizenship) being the basis for electoral enfranchisement, in the same breath they voice support for the denial of basic rights to—and even the repatriation of—legal migrants.

Just as in the United States, restrictive measures enforced against immigrants and asylum seekers tend to affect the life of domestic populations in Europe. Internal surveillance has a long and complicated history, as reflected in the chapter by Martin Schain. The expanded use of closed-circuit television in Britain is only one example of the expansion of public and private monitoring into the broader public sphere. Indeed, arguably, many European domestic populations have become familiar with (and accepting of) the idea that state intrusion is inevitable if justified by the exigencies of public security. Nonetheless, the new security measures raise concerns about the balance between the exigencies of security and the respect for civil liberties. Great Britain, France, and Germany are the three European countries most frequently listed among the top five on the "shame list" compiled by several NGOs concerned with the protection of human rights. The "security packages" adopted by these three countries affect various categories of civil liberties, such as the civil right to privacy.[4] Authorities can access bank accounts, airline data, and postal data. Internet providers and telephone companies are required to keep records for six to twelve months. In Germany, the IMSI catcher has been legalized.[5] The introduction of biometric technologies (through digitized fingerprints, facial recognition, and retinal scans) is now part of the wider post-9/11 "securitization of the inside," facilitating the emergence of "surveillance societies."[6] The securitization of immigration has encouraged a broader process of criminalization. Yet there is no evidence that the "securitization of the inside" will prevent the threat of the "enemy within."

So where does the linkage between immigration, integration, and security emphasized in this volume leave Europe and the United States? We suggest that it highlights two major conundrums. The first is the economic need for tax-paying immigrants to support an aging population on both continents. The second is the cultural and legal need to recognize that not all migrants are alike and that migrants only constitute a terrorist, criminal, or economic threat to the extent that public policy fails to adequately address questions about their integration. To that extent, urban policies and national security policies may be directly related. An examination of these issues follows.

The Importance of Immigrants in America and Europe

Europe's "demographic gap" highlights many of these key tensions between external and internal security, civil liberties, and economic necessity. A recent report published by the Council of Europe anticipates that the population will decline from 808 million in 2005 to 763 million in 2050 (i.e., by a total of 6 percent) in the forty-two European countries studied.[7] While there will be national variations in the rate and extent of decline, many countries have to deal with long-term declines of birth rates, to the point where populations are not replacing themselves.

Correspondingly, the average age of the same European population will increase significantly. The old-age dependency ratio, for example, is expected to double by 2050.[8] The proportion of the population over the age of eighty years is projected to increase from 5 percent in 2005 to 15 percent in 2050. The most notable age-cohort decline (27 percent) will take place among those between twelve and forty-four years of age. The population of older age groups is going to increase (by 41 percent for the population between sixty-five and seventy-nine years of age, and by 155 percent for the oldest cohort).

The impact of immigration on sustaining Europe's population is therefore quite stark. Within the EU, net migration accounted for 65 percent of all population growth in 2000. In the EU, the annual average population increase of 1.8 million between 2000 and 2004 was due mainly to higher net migration. In the future, immigration will have a dramatic impact on the capacity of governments to support an aging population in the context of a diminishing labor force. Studies suggest that "replacement migration" will prove insufficient to redress the effects of low European fertility rates.[9] In its green paper, "An EU Approach to Managing Economic Migration," the EU Commission emphasized that "while immigration in itself is not a solution to demographic aging, more sustained immigration flows could increasingly be required to meet the needs of the EU labor market and ensure Europe's prosperity."[10]

The European Union and the United States are, however, projected to follow starkly contrasting demographic paths in forthcoming decades. According to the UN Population Division, while the population of the United States would increase by 82 million between 1995 and 2050, that of the European Union would decline by 41 million. As a result, the population of the United States, which in 1995 was 105 million smaller than that of [the] European Union, will become larger by 18 million in 2050. The same trends will characterize their working-age population: While the number of people aged 15–65 years will decline by 61 million in the European Union, in the United States it will increase by 39 million. By 2050, the working-age population in the United States will outnumber that of the European Union by 26 million, while in 1995 it was outnumbered by 75 million.[11]

Yet despite these differing population projections, the debate on the demographic impact of immigration raised similar issues on both sides of the Atlantic.[12] Immigration is less critical to sustaining population growth in the United States than it is in Europe. While the fertility rate in the United States has declined (dropping from 3.45 births per woman in 1950–1955 to 2.02 in 1970–1975), it still remains higher than in Europe. In the last three decades (apart from a temporary period when it decreased to 1.8 during the late 1970s and early 1980s), the United States has sustained a fertility rate of around 2, slightly below "replacement level."[13] Evidence suggests that the United States will not experience a dramatic population decline in forthcoming years. If historic inflows of immigrants are also sustained, the fertility rate will remain above the number needed to prevent a decline. The UN Population Division, using a "zero migration" scenario, has projected that the U.S. population will stand at 290 million in 2050, slightly below current levels. The same analysis, however, suggests that maintaining the average historic intake of 760,000 migrants per year between 1995 and 2050 will result in a population increase of 50 million.[14] Net migration is therefore less vital in preventing a slowdown in population growth in the United States than it is in Europe.

As in Europe, the U.S. population will age, though not as rapidly. By the middle of the twenty-first century, the median age is likely to be as high as 52.7 years in Europe, while it will be around 40 in the United States.[15] Despite this significant difference, the terms of the debate are quite similar with regard to the "old-age" dependency ratio and the future of the working-age population.[16]

Americans may be less cognizant of their demographic gap and its financial implications. But Ben Bernanke, chairman of the Federal Reserve, is one who recognizes that it has growing implications for the United States. In a statement before a congressional budget committee in January 2007, he suggested that the United States faces an unsustainable fiscal crisis. Reliance on

growth, he suggested, was not the solution. While not offering recommendations, and thus not focusing on the importance of immigration as a solution,
implicit in Bernanke's statement is a recognition of the reality of drastic problems if the age distribution of the American population is left unaddressed.[17]

The contribution of immigrants to sustaining the size of the labor force,
and thus the solvency of U.S. and European welfare systems, is therefore vital.
Despite the potential positive effect of immigration, however, a growing number of Europeans express xenophobic feelings toward minority groups already
domiciled in Europe. These sentiments particularly target the members of the
so-called second generation of immigrants who were born in their respective
European countries. Furthermore, restrictive measures designed to limit the
number of "newcomers" are gaining ground. The European Social Survey of
2003 revealed that 50 percent of the respondents expressed "resistance to the
influx and admittance of immigrants belonging to a different race or ethnic
group than the majority population." About 60 percent of the respondents in
the EU 15 believed that "there is a limit to how many people of other races,
religions, or cultures a society can accept." The same share believed that "if
there were to be more people belonging to these minority groups, we would
have problems."[18]

Domestic concerns about their societies' inability to integrate relatively
poor and uneducated migrants have engendered xenophobic or anti-Muslim
views about immigration policies, even in the most historically tolerant of EU
member states. Fifty-nine percent of Germans oppose more immigration
from the Middle East and North Africa; more than 40 percent of the French
feel the same, as do about a third of those polled in Spain and the UK.[19] The
primary electoral beneficiaries of this growing intolerance (and often outright
hostility) have often been extremist right-wing parties. However, discussion
about the foundational principles of integration (multiculturalism and assimilation) has moved to the center of the political debate among both mainstream politicians and scholars. The bevy of claims are familiar. Some argue
that first-generation migrants—and even their second- and third-generation
native-born children—are alleged to be the undeserving beneficiaries of state
welfare. These migrants are accused of stealing jobs from domestic workers,
characterized as refusing to integrate into the dominant national cultures, and
suspected of supporting the goals and methods of jihadists. Poor educational
programs and (informal) discrimination often create a vicious circle. In it,
migrants often suffer from higher unemployment rates, accept jobs in the informal sector, and do retain strong community links as a way of coping with
their poverty and alienation.[20] These responses reinforce the stereotypical view

that immigrants are disloyal, fringe members of society with separatist tendencies; the circle is therefore complete.

The alleged correlation between immigration and higher unemployment
rates among domestic populations is gaining popularity in Europe. Despite a
slight decrease in unemployment levels in some countries in the first half of
2006, a Eurobarometer survey taken at that time showed that 49 percent of
the respondents saw unemployment as one of the two most important issues
facing their country. In contrast, only 14 percent of the respondents thought
that immigration was the most important issue.[21] Yet negative perceptions of
the economic impact of immigration were nevertheless increasing. Approximately 50 percent of Europeans expressed resistance to immigrants, and 58
percent thought immigrants posed a collective threat to the socioeconomic
situation in their country.[22]

Yet those same European countries where anti-immigrant sentiment is
often the strongest are the ones who need their migrants the most because of
aging populations. They generally prefer to reject the Victorian values of marriage and parenthood in favor of the postmodern values of consumption (albeit a "green-conscious" variant) and leisure. Germany epitomizes this tension:
its population is among Europe's oldest and yet is the most hostile to immigration.[23] In the absence of immigration, Germany, Greece, Italy, Sweden, the
Czech Republic, and Slovenia would have experienced a population loss over
the last fifteen years. While the required replacement fertility rate is 2.1, the
total fertility rate for the EU was 1.53 in 2000 and around 1.7 in 2005. Fertility rates do of course differ among European countries. In the Mediterranean
countries (Spain, Italy, Portugal, and Greece), fertility dropped relatively late
but has done so to very low levels. Spain (1.19) and Italy (1.23) now have the
lowest fertility rates in the EU. Ireland (1.89) and France (1.89) have relatively high fertility rates. All, however, are still below the replacement level.[24]

Similar polls among Americans present a decidedly mixed picture. In contrast to European polling conducted at about the same time, only 14 percent
of all Americans pointed to unemployment as the biggest problem facing the
country. Furthermore, just 4 percent mentioned immigration as their biggest
concern.[25] Fifty-two percent, however (up from 38 percent in 2000), believe
that immigrants are a burden, taking jobs and housing and creating strains on
the health care system. Sixty-five percent believe that immigrants take jobs
that Americans do not want, while only 24 percent are convinced that the
newcomers compete with natives for jobs. Concerns about wages and taxes,
however, are increasing. A majority (56 percent) expressed the view that most
recent immigrants do not pay their fair share of taxes, and 52 percent believe

that immigrants hurt the economy more than they help it, by driving down wages for native workers.

As in Europe, the debate in the United States focuses on the issue of job security. The claim that migrants displace domestic workers often looks like a populist, disingenuous political ploy in the context of the relatively regulated markets of the European Union. The well-publicized case of French fears that Polish plumbers would invade France in the aftermath of Polish accession did not materialize. Indeed, the Polish tourist board developed a humorous riposte by distributing posters of a handsome, virile Polish man, semi-clothed in plumbers' garb, inviting Europeans to come visit *him* in Poland. From the agricultural sector to the industrial, from education to health care, employment in many European markets is so regulated by EU and national government procedures and requirements that labor mobility is much less flexible than the fears of a migrant invasion would suggest. True, immigrants are disproportionately represented in the service sector and the "gray" economy. Most people cannot remember the last time they were served by a native in a London coffee bar or restaurant. But, like the Californian who complains about migrant Mexicans working in the agricultural sector, there are relatively few Germans who would accept the menial jobs held by Eastern Europeans and Turks.

Nonetheless, many Americans look at the reported figures of between 9 million and 12 million illegal immigrants in the United States and feel pessimistic about immigration. They conclude that the "race to the bottom" initiated by NAFTA through outsourcing will be accelerated by uninterrupted illegal migration and a lack of new measures to repatriate those already illegally present.[26] This fear is particularly acute, although not exclusively so, in southern American states bordering Mexico and among the relatively uneducated proportion of the native population who potentially compete for the same jobs.

The evidence to substantiate such fears, however, is not compelling since there is no obvious correlation between immigration and the level of unemployment in a host country. In the United States, for example, the unemployment rate stood at 4.6 percent in September 2006 despite increasing numbers of immigrants. In the EU 25, it stood at 8 percent. The lowest unemployment rates were in Denmark (3.5 percent), the Netherlands (4 percent), Ireland (4.2 percent), Estonia (4.4 percent), and Austria (4.7 percent). Unemployment rates were highest in Poland (14.1 percent), Slovakia (12.8 percent), Greece (9 percent), France (8.9 percent), and Germany (8.7 percent).[27] High unemployment rates were not correlated with high numbers of immigrants in many countries. Non-nationals represented only 1.8 percent of the total population in Poland and 0.6 percent in Slovakia, where unemployment was high (14 percent and 13 percent, respectively). By contrast, in Estonia and Luxembourg, low unemployment rates (4.4 percent and 4.9 percent, respectively) coincided with the presence of large numbers of immigrants: non-nationals represented 20 percent and 38.6 percent of the total population, respectively. Indeed, the authors of the EU's 2002 report on aging concluded that at the EU level, "immigration can contribute to filling certain specific gaps [in] the European labor market."[28]

In the United States, a growing labor market belies the belief that immigrants and native workers compete for a stable number of jobs. More than 15 million new jobs were created between 1999 and 2003. According to a Bureau of Labor Statistics report in 2001, about 33 million jobs will be created in the decade preceding 2010, mainly in sectors that employ large numbers of low-skilled workers. Furthermore, native workers tend to migrate out of local areas into which immigrants move. Geographical mobility thus attenuates the pressures on the local labor market. Finally, in specific sectors of the economy, there is no convincing evidence that immigrants significantly displace natives: either immigrants and native workers do not compete for the same jobs (high-skilled versus low-skilled jobs) or they compete in growth sectors where there are expanding job opportunities. Jeffrey Passel's review of studies on the subject found that "the majority find no more evidence of displacement than is revealed by the aggregate data. Even studies of more high-skilled occupations find no strong evidence of displacement."[29] Immigrants often complement native workers, even in sectors that employ large numbers of workers with lower levels of formal education. Estimates of low-skilled jobs for the coming years reveal that immigrants will be the only labor source able to address shortages in many sectors. According to the National Academy of Sciences, "the most plausible magnitudes of the impacts of immigration on the economy are modest for those who benefit from immigration, for those who lose from immigration, and for total gross domestic product. The domestic gain may run on the order of $1 billion to $10 billion a year. Although this gain may be modest relative to the size of the U.S. economy, it remains a significant positive gain in absolute terms."[30]

A large number of studies have concluded that migrants play an increasingly important role in generating the tax base upon which the provision of future social welfare benefits will rest. However, solutions designed to address the tension between the popular impulse to stem the large-scale influx of migrants and the need to sustain a demographic balance for economic reasons remain problematic—and elusive. Furthermore, those same immigrants also form an increasingly significant political constituency. Their views regarding Middle Eastern politics are often hard to ignore because of both their potential electoral influence and possible propensity toward terrorist recruitment if they are ignored.

Leaving these immigrants' economic and political concerns unaddressed therefore creates one set of risks: that of a Europe unable to support itself economically or guarantee its population's security. Excluding them by a process of repatriation, however, creates another set of risks. It would reinforce the gap between European countries and those of the Middle East on which Europe relies for most of its natural resources and security intelligence (which could thwart terrorist activity aimed at European targets). Many European countries therefore need hard-working, tax-paying, politically loyal, and socially integrated immigrant populations in the long term. Those immigrants are vital, even as large segments of domestic populations, and many politicians, currently balk at their presence.

Despite the fact that immigrants are playing an increasing role in the growth of the labor force, opponents of mass immigration reject the idea that it addresses essential labor-market needs in the United States and Europe. Supporters of restrictive immigration measures argue that tougher border controls would protect native workers, consolidate the national identity, and strengthen internal security. This restrictive approach is gaining ground on both sides of the Atlantic, as discussed by many authors in this volume. The debate between pro- and anti-migrant groups about the impact of new migration concerns its demographic, economic, and ethno-cultural aspects—and is likely to continue as a critical open-ended controversy.

The purpose of this book is to provide balance to this often polemical debate. Clearly, immigration has direct and indirect socioeconomic costs and benefits. Immigrants are both competitors in, *and* a needed supplement to, the native work force. They also avail themselves of social benefits *and* contribute to the tax foundation of the welfare system. Immigration is neither the sole cause nor the unique solution to current demographic imbalances and socioeconomic problems. Immigration will not solve, for example, the aging population problem in Western societies. Without immigration, however, this problem will get worse and other policy tools commonly used to sustain the overall labor force will become less efficient.

Those who emphasize the costs of immigration need to recognize comparable costs associated with the implementation of other policy options. Among them, one can list the increasing percentage of both women and older people (men and women) in the work force and a drastic reform of the health care and pension systems that will inevitably ensue as fewer workers support an aging population. By contrast, those who claim that immigration is bene-ficial to host countries are obliged to recognize the societal issues raised by im-migrant integration, both from society's viewpoint and from the immigrant's perspective.

Not All Migrants Are Created Alike

Although politicians often cite economic issues in defense of their position on immigration, neither the actual number of immigrants nor a variety of eco-nomic indicators can fully explain the immigration agenda in Europe or the United States. A third influential factor in the debate is the ethnic character of arriving immigrants. As the prior discussion suggested, demographic con-siderations often clash with social and political concerns when the challenge is incorporating nonwhite, non-Western, and often non-Christian immi-grants into predominantly white and Christian Western societies. A sense of "invasion" is palpable among a segment of Europe's and America's domestic populations in which immigrants constitute "others." Critics of the process fear that immigrants form the vanguard of a population shift likely to chal-lenge their cultural and national identities.

Those who fear that their country is already "swamped" by immigrants are even more upset when they extrapolate from current trends into the future. Pat Buchanan has recently claimed, for example, that America was becoming "Mexamerica" and that an "immigration tsunami will make whites a minori-ty in the U.S."[31] David Coleman has provided scenarios of changing ethnic and racial composition for seven European countries (covering half of the population of Western Europe) and the United States. Assuming that immi-gration flows remain stable and that the children of migrant populations will be fully assimilated, Coleman's findings envisage widespread ethnic shifts that he regards as a "third demographic transition." If the composition of the pop-ulations of Europe and the United States continues to change as he projects, the foreign-origin proportions of these populations would rise to between 15 percent and 30 percent or more by mid-century.[32]

Many of these migrants originate from the Arab and Muslim populations of Asia, Africa, and the Middle East, deepening the division between natives and those arriving at Europe's shores along racial, ethnic, and religious lines. Superimposed on the economic and cultural conundrum is therefore an in-creasing concern about the "security threat" presented by the influx. New mi-grant settlement has often historically been associated with greater crime rates (regardless of the accuracy of the claim). In the current context, it is associated with support for both the methods and objectives of Al Qaeda (and other terrorist groups in the case of Arab and Muslim populations) in Europe and the United States.[33] The tone and tenor of this last claim is reflected in comments by Robert Leiken, in which he says that from Amsterdam to Brussels, London, Paris, Madrid, and Milan,

> [a]s a consequence of demography, history, ideology, and policy, Western Europe now plays host to often disconsolate Muslim offspring, who are its citizens in name but not culturally or socially. In a fit of absentmindedness, during which its academics discoursed on the obsolescence of the nation-state, Western Europe acquired not a colonial empire but something of an internal colony, whose numbers are roughly equivalent to the population of Syria. Many of its members are willing to integrate and try to climb Europe's steep social ladder. But many younger Muslims reject the minority status to which their parents acquiesced. . . . The very isolation of these diaspora communities obscures their inner workings, allowing mujahideen to fundraise, prepare, and recruit for jihad with a freedom available in few Muslim countries.[34]

Evidence, albeit anecdotal—generated by the operation of criminal syndicates, the violent street protests by marginalized and unemployed youths, and, most markedly, the suicide bombers in Europe—gives apparent credence to the notion reflected in Leiken's view. This is the idea that migrant populations (or rather, a segment of them) form the basis for what is collectively characterized as the "enemy within." They are often associated with what the British used to call a "fifth column"—saboteurs mingling with the domestic population and comprising:

> a group of alienated citizens, second- or third-generation children of immigrants, . . . who were born and bred under European liberalism. Some are unemployed youth from hardscrabble suburbs of Marseilles, Lyon, and Paris or former mill towns such as Bradford and Leicester. They are the latest, most dangerous incarnation of that staple of immigration literature, the revolt of the second generation. They are also dramatic instances of what could be called adversarial assimilation—integration into the host country's adversarial culture. But this sort of anti-West westernization is illustrated more typically by another paradigmatic second-generation recruit: the upwardly mobile young adult, such as the university-educated Zacarias Moussaoui, the

so-called 20th hijacker, or Omar Khyam, the computer student and soccer captain from Sussex, England, who dreamed of playing for his country but was detained in April 2004 for holding, with eight accomplices, half a ton of explosives aimed at London.[35]

More systematic substantiation of the accuracy of any claims about the widespread nature of such support is closely guarded by security and intelligence forces—and therefore beyond the bounds of public discourse. General support for such extremism can only be inferred. Indeed, one major survey of Muslims across Europe found the opposite, that Muslims were primarily concerned with unemployment and favored religious and political moderation rather than extremism. Nonetheless, findings of the same poll among Europeans suggest that a majority worry about Islamic identity and extremism. Indeed, "substantial majorities in Germany (76%), Great Britain (64%), Spain (67%), and Russia (69%) say that Muslims in their country want to remain distinct from the larger society."[36] Presumably, it is from among the ranks of the disaffected minority of Muslims that terrorists are likely to be recruited, and it is they who are the focus of Leiken's comments. This situation produces an apparent paradox. Despite the fact that a majority of Europeans in most countries polled think that immigration from the Middle East and North Africa is a net positive, the securitization of immigration seems to progress unabated in Europe. It proceeds through a combination of internal surveillance, policing, (ineffectual) border controls, and limited attempts at socioeconomic integration.

Europeans have implicitly learned to accept that there is a trade-off in the eastward expansion of the EU. On the one hand, enlargement enhances the likelihood of peripheral regional stability and offers the opportunity for greater regulation of domestic markets (and with that, domestic labor). It also increases the prospects for greater cohesion and autonomy, at least in the long term, as a global actor, and serves as a mechanism for the consolidation of democracy among new members. It is generally recognized, however, that the shift from the EU 15 to the EU 25 also brought with it new problems, principal among them a reduced capacity to regulate the borders of the EU. Stated bluntly, the border between Germany's Federal Republic and the GDR prior to 1985 was far less porous than Poland's borders are with Ukraine or Belarus, or Estonia's borders are with Russia today. Indeed, the problem is not simply confined to Eastern European states with limited resources and neighbors in the throes of crises. As Francisco Javier Moreno Fuentes's contribution to this volume vividly demonstrates, the problem is just as grave along the southern contours of the EU, as refugees risk their lives for the promise of greater economic and political security.

The securitization of immigration often takes on differing characteristics in the United States, at least according to the rhetoric of policymakers and commentators. But the problem it poses is considered just as acute. As in Europe, the politicization of border controls and the securitization of immigration issues have induced increasing resistance to foreigners (both legal and illegal immigrants but also nationals of foreign origin). There is also increasing hostility to multiculturalism, and there is the growing feeling that immigrants constitute a threat to national identity.[37] Americans deny the existence of any comparable trade-off between more human and economic flows and less control of their borders. They (often implicitly) see their membership in NAFTA as complementary with the effective operation of border security—whether the barrier is a physical fence or, as is increasingly likely, a virtual one—along thousands of miles of (primarily) the southern but also the northern border. The rhetoric of American politicians is reminiscent of King Canute attempting to turn back the tide. That rhetoric often suggests that while they recognize that current border security is a problem, they believe that they can geographically isolate themselves effectively against both Middle Eastern terrorists and impoverished Mexican and Central American workers. Even British policymakers, geographically isolated from the rest of Europe on an island with a relatively diminutive shoreline, do not delude themselves with the belief that this forms an effective deterrent to determined migrants. Evidence from Europe's experience, however, does little to daunt American advocates of the utility and efficacy of border security. Facing the challenge of the "construction of both a borderless economy and a barricaded border," both the United States and the EU must reconcile two antagonistic goals.[38] The first goal is the relaxation of state controls for the purpose of developing legal economic flows (through NAFTA and the Single Market). The second is strengthening border controls for the purpose of fighting illegal flows—whether of humans, drugs, or weapons.

Americans couple their faith in the power of new technologies and sufficient man power to secure their borders with an unquestioning belief in the capacity of their national "melting pot" culture to assuage subversive tendencies. While Europeans worry about the power of Islamic identity to draw their Muslim minorities toward radicalism, relatively few Americans express concerns that legal foreign inhabitants will become alienated and responsive to fractional, violent ideologies in the United States. American public discourse is heavily imbued with the fears of Islamic radicals infiltrating the United

States and carrying out large-scale acts of terrorism. That same rhetoric, however, largely ignores or rejects the idea that disaffected legal migrants will riot in the streets or are susceptible to recruitment as suicide bombers by fringe domestic groups tenuously linked to global jihadists or other forms of radicalism. The foiled plot of June 2007 to attack facilities at New York's John F. Kennedy Airport may be a forerunner of this potential pattern.

Yet, the immigration debate is as vibrant today in the United States as it is in Europe, dividing both political parties and the general population along nontraditional lines. Allied with the first debate about border security is a second debate about internal security. In this common characterization, illegal terrorists, posing as tourists or migrants, are generally profiled as the most likely source of a threat. There are a number of preferred tools of choice in dealing with the threat. One tool is a stricter set of migration rules and regulations for screening migrants and asylum seekers. Another is an aggressive foreign policy designed to locate and destroy terrorist enclaves. A technological tool would be an enhanced surveillance system that focuses on links between internal cells and their foreign sponsors. The last tool in this kit might be the effective denial of civil liberties and human rights in the process of administering the regulation of migrants and asylum seekers. All these procedures have been described as "draconian" in style and effect by both H. Richard Friman and Jennifer Chacón in their contributions to this volume. Furthermore, as both authors conclude, the administrative demarcation lines distinguishing legal from illegal migrants in the application of these instruments have become blurred. The securitization of immigration in the United States has therefore had far-reaching consequences. It has affected those seeking entry to the United States, those legally domiciled who have not transgressed the law, those legally domiciled who have done so, and illegal migrants—whether their primary goals are simply employment or are criminal or terroristic in nature.

The Issue of Integration

It is unlikely that Western countries will be able to dramatically curb immigration. They can do little to influence the push factors that drive immigration: poverty, war, persecution, and the desire for family reunification. Despite the enforcement of restrictive new measures, Western nations still face a "global crisis of immigration controls." The more that states and international or supranational bodies do to manage immigration, the less successful they seem to be.[39] Restrictive policies designed to curb the number—and to control the "quality"—of immigrants paradoxically seem to result in increasing flows of "newcomers" allegedly unable to integrate. This is often due to increased illicit flows of migrants.

Furthermore, Western countries need immigrants to support their aging populations and to address labor shortages in various sectors. These countries therefore face the prospect of an increasing ethno-racial diversity among their populations. The recurring cycle of conflicting expectations (such as "more workers but fewer immigrants" or "more immigrants but less ethnic and religious diversity") partially explains the various apparent reversals in policies implemented by the United States and European countries over the last thirty years. The emphasis on limiting the "diversity" of newcomers remains in place because of new eligibility regulations, new requirements related to language proficiency, and an insistence that the newcomers adopt the cultural values of the host country. The efforts to screen newcomers are insufficient, however, because the core issue is in fact the integration of settled immigrants, particularly their children. Historically, cultural assimilation was made possible through socioeconomic integration. Today, the explicit goal of cultural assimilation has proved elusive as a result of the failure to integrate immigrants socially, politically, and economically.

The diverse chapters of this volume examine the two dimensions that currently link immigration and security policies: the use of restrictive immigration measures to combat or prevent terrorism and the use of counter-terrorism policy to control immigration. While the contributors develop different approaches in addressing this linkage and tend to focus on various specific aspects of this securitization of immigration issue, they all agree that efforts to do so have proven a failure. Indeed, these efforts may have generated or exacerbated the problems associated with greater immigration flows and enhanced insecurity for at least three reasons.

One reason is that the strengthening of border controls has paradoxically tended to increase rather than reduce the number of illegal immigrants and humans being trafficked. Neither desperation nor the search for profit are motives easily deterred by border surveillance. Tighter controls have produced more demand for the services of smugglers. More illicit activity has therefore produced more unregulated traffic and thus more of a pervasive sense of insecurity that, in turn, fuels anxieties about immigration and concerns about the ability of the state to control the borders.

A second reason is that the securitization of immigration may support the radicalization of minority groups who feel alienated and are actually suffering from discrimination. The roots of insecurity are not only abroad but also in our backyard. Internal security is therefore more closely linked with the inability to provide equal opportunities for all than is currently recognized.

Finally, the securitization of immigration issues may result in the crisis of legitimacy. As Jef Huysmans argues, "evoking emergencies and dangers may generate a need to control the fears by reassuring the members of the political community that one has the capacity to control the emergency. The latter can undermine governmental legitimacy because a continuation of insecurity may be interpreted as a sign of the incapacity of the government to manage the security problem."[40] To borrow an example from another context, many Americans have cynically suggested that there is a correlation between the Bush administration's propensity for raising the terror alert level around the same time that it encounters dips in its popularity in opinion polls.

More generally, the securitization of immigration issues has produced the same critical results on either side of the Atlantic: discrimination against "foreigners" (nationals of foreign origin included) and an increasing level of political distrust. A recent poll conducted by the Pew Research Institute showed that the American public lacked confidence in its political leadership's capacity to deal with the immigration issue. Only 42 percent have a lot or some confidence in President Bush to act effectively with regard to this issue, and 62 percent fully disapproved of the way President Bush is handling the nation's immigration policy.[41]

A similar distrust is noticeable in Europe, where the low efficacy of border controls has fueled suspicion about the possibility of any effective immigration policy at the national level. According to the MORI Social Research Institute, 44 percent of the British public and 42 percent of the Spanish public expressed concern about the lack of efficiency in immigration controls. Only 25 percent of the respondents in the UK—and 32 percent in Italy—expressed confidence in the government when it came to the issue of promoting the integration of foreign populations.[42] Indeed, a large majority of the EU 25's population want more active EU policy designed to control external borders (72 percent) as well as tighter asylum and migration policy (65 percent).[43]

In essence, a vicious cycle ensues. Concerns about government incapacity are likely to feed anti-migrant alarmism; perceptions of government weakness make host societies more vulnerable to fears about the "intrusion" of outsiders and subsequently raise concerns about ethnic balance. Migration phobia, in turn, fuels discrimination and makes integration more difficult to achieve, thus feeding a sense of governmental inefficacy.

It is now widely accepted that there must be reform in order to achieve a better management of immigration and to contain terrorism more effectively. Different options are currently debated. One claim is that integration issues will be solved by better management of immigration flows. Yet there is strong evidence that neither border controls nor restricted access to public services have deterred legal and illegal immigration. Moreover, the absence or failure of integration policies have created major social problems that Western democracies must address. Finally, the declared objectives of receiving states are often misleading because of their unwillingness to acknowledge past policy failures. This is why, as Wayne Cornelius suggests, it is essential to ask why a failed policy persists.[44]

Another suggestion is that countries revert to a "guest worker" policy. Both the United States and European countries have attempted to reform their immigration legislation in that direction. There are controversies about defining the criteria for "wanted" immigrants, but supporters of temporary immigration strongly believe that this option will solve the issue of integration. Paradoxically, however, if immigrants are guest workers, they are presumably not supposed to integrate. They are supposed to go home.

Leaving aside the issue of whether governments can enforce this option, it constitutes a major component of President Bush's immigration reform (as well as a source of contention in Congress) and inspires European countries such as France and Germany. The EU Commission has recently promoted the idea of "circular migration," without any right for immigrants to bring their families or to claim welfare benefits.[45] Even if this policy is successful (although previous failures raised suspicion about its efficacy), it will leave unaddressed the problems faced by existing minority groups. Furthermore, European countries are still dealing with the unintended consequences of similar measures, such as Germany and the Netherlands, where the *Gastarbeiter* programs created major obstacles to the integration of guest workers who, in fact, never left.

The contributors to this volume express varied degrees of optimism about the opportunities afforded to immigrants seeking to integrate. They have raised a series of questions related to this multifaceted concept that need to be addressed. How can we revise or generate theories that account for the new exigencies of security and enhanced cross-cultural cleavages in the context of large immigrant populations whose historic origins lie outside the foundations of Western society? Why has integration alternatively failed or been ignored as a security issue in Europe and the United States? Why is it that the "securitization of immigration" has become such a potent political force in debates on both continents? Correspondingly, why have the vast bulk of domestic measures focused on internal surveillance rather than on providing the socioeconomic platform that might integrate new immigrants and both isolate and identify any radical fringe? Can the exigencies of security and the aspirations for integration be reconciled and, if so, how?

We believe that the urgent need to address these questions stems from the fact that the failure of integration has become a major source of insecurity. If our assessment is correct, national governments will have to adopt a more comprehensive approach that includes social, educational, and urban policies. Moreover, effective integration is not the sole responsibility of states but one shared with social actors. It is therefore crucial that alternative means for managing the immigrant-host society interaction be negotiated and elaborated in broader forums. The current climate of enmity will not secure societal security nor prevent external threats in the long run. That, however, is the subject of further analysis and debate.

Notes

Chapter 1: The Securitization of Immigration

1. An immigrant can be defined as a foreigner who moves from his or her country of origin to another country for the purpose of settlement. This basic definition has been adopted—and promoted—by international organizations such as the United Nations and the Organization for Economic Cooperation and Development (OECD). See UN Recommendations on Statistics of International Migration, ST/ESA/STAT/SER.M/58/Rev.1, 1998; and Michel Poulain and Nicolas Perrin, "Can UN Migration Recommendations Be Met in Europe?" *Migration Information Source,* Migration Policy Institute (MPI), July 2003. However, international comparisons remain difficult because migration flows and stocks pose particular challenges to the production of reliable and widely comparable statistics. Technical reasons for statistical uncertainty include the use of inappropriate sources of data, the inability of administrative systems to collect information, or the lack of comparability due to different national views concerning who is an "immigrant."

2. The first major counter-terrorism measures were adopted in the United States in the 1980s (such as the *Act to Combat International Terrorism Law* in 1984 and the *Antiterrorism Act of 1986*) and strengthened during the 1990s (with, for example, Presidential Decision Directive [PDD] 39 on "U.S. Policy on Counterterrorism," Executive Order [EO 1015], the *Anti-Terrorism Act of 1996,* the *Defense against Weapons of Mass Destruction Act of 1996,* and the Nunn-Lugar-Domenici amendment to the National Defense Authorization for 1997). In Europe, countries facing domestic and/or international terrorist threats (such as France, Germany, Italy, and Spain) have enacted counter-terrorism measures since the 1970s. At the EU level, the main initiatives included the Europol Convention supplemented by the Council decision (1998), the Joint Action 96/610/JHA on the creation of a Directory of Specialized Counter-Terrorist Skills, the Joint Action 98/428/JHA on the creation of a European Judicial Network, the Joint Action 98/733/JHA on making it a criminal offense to participate in a criminal organization, the Council Recommendation of December 1999 on Cooperation in Combating the Financing of Terrorist Groups, and the Council Directive (June 2001) supplementing the provisions of article 26 of the Convention implementing the Schengen Agreement of June 1985.

3. See BBC News, "MI5 Chief Reveals Terror Threat," Oct. 17, 2003, http://news.bbc.co.uk/2/hi/uk_news/3198828.stm; and "MI5 Tracking 30 UK Terror Plots," Nov. 10, 2006, http://news.bbc.co.uk/2/hi/uk_news/6134516.stm.

4. On this alleged "transatlantic divide," see for instance Timothy Garton Ash, "Anti-Europeanism in America," *New York Review of Books* 50, no. 2 (Feb. 13, 2003), www.nybooks.com/articles/16059; Francis Fukuyama, "The West May Come Apart," *Straits Times,* Aug. 10, 2002; Michael Cox, "Beyond the West: Terrors in Transatlantia," *European Journal of International Relations* 11, no. 2 (2005): 203–33; Robert Kagan, *Of Paradise and Power: America and Europe in the New World Order* (New York: Knopf,

2003); T. R. Reid, *The United States of Europe: The New Superpower and the End of American Supremacy* (New York: Penguin Press, 2005).

5. Kagan, *Of Paradise and Power.*

6. Rumsfeld quoted in ibid., 4.

7. Kagan, *Of Paradise and Power,* 5.

8. Ash, "Anti-Europeanism in America."

9. Tony Judt, "Europe v. America," *New York Review Books* 52, no. 2 (Feb. 10, 2005), www.nybooks.com/articles/17726.

10. See Jeremy Rifkin, *The European Dream: How Europe's Vision of the Future Is Quietly Eclipsing the American Dream* (New York: Tarcher Penguin, 2004); Reid, *The United States of Europe.*

11. See European Union Monitoring Centre on Racism and Xenophobia (EUMC), *Majorities' Attitudes Towards Minorities: Key Findings from the Eurobarometer and the European Social Survey,* Mar. 2005; EUMC, *Report on Racism and Xenophobia in the EU,* Vienna, 2005; Pew Hispanic Center, *America's Immigration Quandary,* Mar. 2006.

12. See David Goodhart, "Too Diverse?" *Prospect* 95 (Feb. 2004): 30–37.

13. Madeleine Bunting, "Jack Straw Has Unleashed a Storm of Prejudice and Intensified Division," *Guardian Unlimited,* Oct. 9, 2006, www.guardian.co.uk/commentis free/story/0,,1890821,00.html.

14. Barry Buzan, Ole Wæver, and Jaap de Wilde, *Security: A New Framework for Analysis* (Boulder, CO, and London: Lynne Rienner, 1998), 32–33.

Chapter 2: Identity Discourse in Western Europe and the United States in the Aftermath of 9/11

The epigraph is a quotation that appears in an article by Steve Sailer, "Fragmented Future," *American Conservative,* Jan. 15, 2007.

1. See Richard Wolin, "September 11 and the Self-Castigating Left," *South Central Review* 19, no. 2/3 (summer–autumn 2002): 39–49.

2. Lutz Niethammer, *PostHistoire: Has History Come to an End?* (New York and London: Verso Press, 1992), 8.

3. For the prevailing counter-argument, in which humanity's cultural makeup is of no consequence in modern capitalist society, see Herbert Marcuse, *The One-Dimensional Man: Studies in the Ideology of Advanced Industrial Society* (Boston: Beacon Press, 1964). See also Dankwart Rustow, "Transitions to Democracy: Toward a Dynamic Model," *Comparative Politics* 2 (Apr. 1970): 337–63.

4. Francis Fukuyama, *The End of History and the Last Man* (New York: Avon Press, 1992); Samuel P. Huntington, *The Clash of Civilizations and the Remaking of World Order* (New York: Touchstone Press, 1996).

5. Amartya Sen, *Identity and Violence* (New York: Norton, 2006).

6. Kwame Anthony Appiah, *Cosmopolitanism: Ethics in a World of Strangers* (New York: Norton, 2006).

7. See Yitzhak Nakash, *Reaching for Power: The Shi'a in the Modern Arab World* (Princeton, NJ, and London: Princeton University Press, 2006).

8. See Perez Zagorin, *How the Idea of Religious Toleration Came to the West* (Princeton, NJ, and London: Princeton University Press, 2003).

9. "Living Together Apart: British Muslims and the Paradox of Multiculturalism," *Daily Telegraph,* Jan. 29, 2007 (47 percent of Muslims, sixteen to twenty-four, want

Shaaria as the law of the land compared to 17 percent among those more than fifty-five years of age; 36 percent of the young group supported capital punishment to apostate Muslims, and 74 percent endorsed the wearing of the veil).

10. Virtually every major city in the industrial world has "no-go" areas dominated by immigrant gangs, and as many as 200 million immigrants are under the sway of criminal gangs. See Barbara Crossette, "U.N. Warns That Trafficking in Human Beings Is Growing," *New York Times,* June 25, 2000.

11. Jan-Werner Müller, *Memory and Power in Post-War Europe: Studies in the Presence of the Past* (Cambridge: Cambridge University Press, 2002).

12. See Jean François Lyotard, *The Postmodern Condition: A Report on Knowledge* (Manchester, England: University of Manchester Press, 1984); Richard Wolin, *The Frankfurt School Revisited* (New York and London: Routledge, 2006); and Pierre Nora, "The Tidal Wave of Memory," *Project Syndicate,* June 2001, www.project-syndicate.org/commentary/nora1.

13. Nicolas Tenzer, "Is Freedom Enough?" *Project Syndicate,* Sept. 2004, www.project-syndicate.org/commentary/tenzer2.

14. See Tony Judt, *The Burden of Responsibility: Blum, Camus, Aron, and the French Intellectual Century* (Chicago and London: University of Chicago Press, 1993); Franz Fanon, *The Wretched of the Earth* (New York: Grove Press, 1963), esp. the preface by Sartre and chap. 1; and Edward W. Said, *Orientalism* (New York: Vintage Books, 1978).

15. Whereas the icons of the generation of Sartre and Picasso were Lenin and Stalin, by the late 1960s the icons of the European left were Che Guevara, Ho Chi Minh, Mao Tse-tung, and later Khomeini and Yasser Arafat.

16. Shalom Lappin, "How Class Disappeared from Western Politics," *Dissent* (winter 2006), www.dissentmagazine.org/menutest/articles/wi06/lappin.htm.

17. See Andrei Markovits, *Uncouth Nation: Why Europe Dislikes America* (Princeton, NJ: Princeton University Press, 2007).

18. See Jefferson Chase, "Europa, Europa . . . ," *Boston Globe,* July 20, 2003; Pascal Bruckner, "Europe: Remorse and Exhaustion," *Dissent* (spring 2003), www.dissentmagazine.org/article/?article=499; and Philippe Roger, *The American Enemy: History of French Anti-Americanism* (Chicago and London: University of Chicago Press, 2005).

19. Pascal Bruckner, "The Paradoxes of Anti-Americanism," *Dissent* 53, no. 3 (summer 2006): 10.

20. John Fonte, "Fracturing of the West?" *Policy* 18, no. 3 (spring 2002): 16–20.

21. Exact figures are hard to get due to the refusal of some governments to collect information based on religious affiliation (France), while others (Spain, Italy, and Greece) have poor mechanisms to account for informal immigration. But estimates indicate that the Muslim population rose from 300,000 in 1960 to more than 20 million in 2005 and is currently increasing at the rate of 1 million per year.

22. Byatt quoted in Max Hastings, "Who Do We Think We Are?" *Times* (London), Dec. 17, 2006; Greer quoted in BBC News, "MPs Attack Greer on Circumcision," Nov. 25, 1995; Janet Afary and Kevin Anderson, *Foucault and the Iranian Revolution: Gender and the Seduction of Islamism* (Chicago: University of Chicago Press, 2005).

23. Ali quoted in Pascal Bruckner, "Enlightenment, Fundamentalism or Racism of Anti Racists," *Sign and Sight,* Jan. 24, 2007, www.signandsight.com/features/1146.html.

24. Mirza quoted in Graeme Wilson, "Young, British Muslims 'Getting More Radical,'" *Daily Telegraph,* Jan. 30, 2007.

25. Michael Collins, *The Likes of Us: A Biography of the White Working Class* (London: Granta, 2005); Oriana Fallaci, "Rage and Pride," *Il Corrierre della Sera,* Sept. 29, 2001.

26. Hans Kundnani, "Goodbye to the 68rs," *Prospect,* no. 113 (Aug. 2005), www.prospect-magazine.co.uk/article_detailsuphp?id=6969.

27. See Andrei Markovits, "The European and American Left since 1945," *Dissent* (winter 2005).

28. Michel Houellebecq, *Elementary Particles* (New York: Vintage International Editions, 2000); Martin Amis, "The Age of Horrorism," *Observer,* Sept. 10, 2006; Henryk M. Broder, *Hurra, Wir Kapitulieren* (Berlin: Wolf Jobst Siedler Verlag, 2006).

29. Anthony Shadid, "Remarks by the Pope Prompt Muslim Outrage," *Washington Post,* Sept. 16, 2006. Benedict quoted the emperor as saying, "Show me just what Muhammad brought that was new, and there you will find things only evil and inhuman, such as his command to spread by the sword the faith he preached."

30. All Lafontaine quotes are from Henryk Broder, "The West and Islam: Hurray! We're Capitulating," *Spiegel Online,* Jan. 25, 2007, www.spiegel.de/international/spiegel/0,1518,462149,00.html.

31. Livingston quoted in Amis, "The Age of Horrorism."

32. Paul Berman, *Terror and Liberalism* (New York: Norton, 2004); see also Berman, *Power and the Idealists: The Passion of Joschka Fischer and Its Aftermath* (New York: Norton, 2003); Berman, *A Tale of Two Utopias: The Political Journey of the Generation of 1968* (New York: Norton, 1996); and Joschka Fischer, *Die Ruckkehr der Geschichte* (The Return of History) (Cologne, Germany: Kiepenheuer & Witsch, 2005).

33. On Dewinter see Adi Schwartz, "Between Haidar and a Hard Place," *Haaretz,* Aug. 28, 2005; Helmut Schmidt, "Europe and the Clash of Civilizations" *Globalist,* Mar. 15, 2004; Sonia Mikich, "What Next, Bearded One?" *Tageszeitung,* Feb. 6, 2006.

34. Yael Tamir, *Liberal Nationalism* (Princeton, NJ: Princeton University Press, 1993).

35. I owe the term "fantasies of salvation" to Vladimir Tismaneanu, *Fantasies of Salvation: Democracy, Nationalism, and Myth in Post-Communist Europe* (Princeton, NJ: Princeton University Press, 1998).

36. Stephen Castle, "Nationalists in the European Parliament: Growing in Strength and Numbers," *Independent,* Jan. 17, 2007.

37. Roger Griffin, "Interregnum or Endgame? The Radical Right in the 'Post-fascist' Era," *Journal of Political Ideologies* 5, no. 2 (2000): 163–78.

38. Benedict XVI, "Europe and Its Discontents," *First Things,* Jan. 2006.

39. Hélène Mulholland, "Muslim Extremists Are a Mirror Image of the BNP, Cameron says," *Guardian,* Jan. 29, 2007.

40. G. M. Tamas, "On Post-Fascism: How Citizenship Is Becoming an Exclusive Privilege," *Boston Review,* summer 2000, 42–46.

41. Israel Zangwill, *The Melting Pot: A Drama in Four Acts* (New York: Macmillan, 1909), act I, 33, 34; Aristide R. Zolberg, *A Nation by Design: Immigration Policy in the Fashioning of America* (New York: Sage, and Cambridge, MA: Harvard University Press, 2006).

42. Samuel P. Huntington, *Who Are We? The Challenges to America's National Identity* (New York: Simon & Schuster, 2004).

43. The Irish were the first immigrant group to resist "melting"; the St. Patrick's Day parade became the first minority ethnic celebration.

44. Nathan Glazer and Daniel Patrick Moynihan, *Beyond the Melting Pot: The Negroes, Puerto Ricans, Jews, Italians, and Irish of New York City* (Cambridge, MA: Harvard University Press, 1963).

45. See Arthur Schlesinger Jr., *The Disuniting of America: Reflections on a Multicultural Society,* rev. ed. (New York: Norton, 1998); Nathan Glazer, *We Are All Multiculturalists Now* (Cambridge, MA: Harvard University Press, 1997); Huntington, *Who Are We?* See also Francis Fukuyama, "Identity and Migration," *Prospect* 131 (Feb. 2007).

46. Mark Noll, "The American Revolution and Protestant Evangelism," *Journal of Interdisciplinary History* 23, no. 3 (winter 1993): 615.

47. Isaiah Berlin in his book *Two Concepts of Liberty* (Oxford: Clarendon Press, 1958) argued that while European polities are based on "freedom to," which demands consensus, the Anglo-Saxon notion of freedom is a far more individualistic "freedom from."

48. Harold Bloom, *The American Religion: The Emergence of the Post-Christian Nation* (New York: Simon & Schuster, 1992), 28.

49. Laurence Moore, *Selling God: American Religion in the Marketplace of Culture* (New York: Oxford University Press, 1994); Eldon J. Eisenach, *The Next Religious Establishment: National Identity and Political Theology in Post-Protestant America* (Lanham, MD: Rowman and Littlefield, 2000).

50. Allan Bloom, *The Closing of the American Mind* (New York: Simon & Schuster, 1987).

51. Thus, whereas the UK and Italy were by the far largest source of immigrants between 1950 and 1970 (Germany, accounting for nearly half of all immigrants historically), by 1996, both Mexico and Vietnam each sent more immigrants to the United States than did all of Europe combined. Of the 605,793 legal immigrants to the United States in 1996, only 147,581 were from Europe (U.S. almanac at www.infoplease.com).

52. Michael J. Thompson, "Beyond the Vote: The Crisis of American Liberalism," *Logos* 3/4 (fall 2004); Robert Putnam, "Who Killed Civic America?" *Prospect,* Mar. 1996.

53. John Kekes, *Against Liberalism* (Ithaca, NY: Cornell University Press, 1997). See also John Kekes, *A Case for Conservatism* (Ithaca, NY: Cornell University Press, 1998).

54. "The Kindness of Strangers," *Economist,* Feb. 26, 2004.

55. Gregory Melleuish, "Globalised Religions for a Globalised World," *Policy* (Australia), winter 2005.

56. Garry Wills, "Fringe Government," *New York Review of Books,* Oct. 6, 2005.

57. It is noteworthy that in the last decade more than a million Mexicans joined the Mormon Church.

58. Paul Johnson, "America's New Empire of Liberty," *Hoover Digest,* July 16, 2003.

59. Beecher quoted in John Micklethwait and Adrian Woolridge, *The Right Nation: Conservative Power in America* (New York: Penguin, 2004).

60. Micklethwait and Woolridge, *The Right Nation.*

61. Ralf Dahrendorf, "After Assimilation," *Project Syndicate,* Sept. 2004, www.project-syndicate.org/commentary/dahrendorf30/English.

62. Russell Kirk, *America's British Culture* (New Brunswick, NJ, and London: Transaction Books, 1994).

Chapter 3: Religious Legacies and the Politics of Multiculturalism

1. Samuel P. Huntington, *The Clash of Civilizations and the Remaking of World Order* (New York: Touchstone, 1996).

2. Ulrich Willems and Michael Minkenberg, "Politik und Religion im Übergang—Tendenzen und Forschungsfragen am Beginn des 21. Jahrhunderts," in *Politik und Religion,* special issue 33/2002 of *Politische Vierteljahresschrift,* ed. Michael Minkenberg and Ulrich Willems (Wiesbaden, Germany: Westdeutscher Verlag, 2003), 13–41; Pippa Norris and Ronald Inglehart, *Sacred and Secular: Religion and Politics Worldwide* (Cambridge: Cambridge University Press, 2004).

3. Tomas Hammar, *Democracy and the Nation State: Aliens, Denizens, and Citizens in a World of International Migration* (Aldershot, England: Avebury 1990), 49–51.

4. Rogers Brubaker, *Citizenship and Nationhood in France and Germany* (Cambridge: Cambridge University Press, 1992).

5. Joel Fetzer and J. Christopher Soper, *Muslims and the State in Britain, France, and Germany* (Cambridge: Cambridge University Press, 2005); Riva Kastoryano, *Negotiating Identities* (Princeton, NJ: Princeton University Press, 2002).

6. Francis Castles, *Comparative Public Policy: Patterns of Post-War Transformation* (Cheltenham, England: Edward Elgar, 1998).

7. Fetzer and Soper, *Muslims and the State in Britain, France, and Germany.*

8. One such study on the Christian Democratic model is Kees van Kersbergen, *Social Capitalism: A Study of Christian Democracy and the Welfare State* (London and New York: Routledge, 1995).

9. Michael Minkenberg, "Religion and Public Policy: Institutional, Cultural, and Political Impact on the Shaping of Abortion Policies in Western Democracies," *Comparative Political Studies* 35 (Mar. 2002): 221–47; Michael Minkenberg, "Religious Effects on the Shaping of Immigration Policies in Western Democracies," paper presented at the ECPR joint sessions workshops, Uppsala, Sweden, Apr. 2004.

10. Willems and Minkenberg, "Politik und Religion im Übergang"; see also Willems and Minkenberg, *Politik und Religion,* special issue 33/2002 of *Politische Vierteljahresschrift.*

11. Steve Bruce, *Fundamentalism* (Oxford: Polity Press, 2000); Gilles Kepel, *Allah in the West: Islamic Movements in America and Europe* (Stanford, CA: Stanford University Press, 1997); Martin E. Marty and R. Scott Appleby, eds., *Fundamentalisms Observed* (Chicago and London: University of Chicago Press, 1991); Michael Minkenberg, *Neokonservatismus und Neue Rechte in den USA* (Baden-Baden, Germany: Nomos, 1990).

12. José Casanova, *Public Religions in the Modern World* (Chicago and London: University of Chicago Press, 1994).

13. Steve Bruce, *God Is Dead: Secularization in the West* (Oxford: Blackwell, 2002).

14. Huntington, *The Clash of Civilizations and the Remaking of World Order.*

15. Bruce, *God Is Dead;* Grace Davie, *Religion in Modern Europe: A Memory Mutates* (Oxford: Oxford University Press, 2000).

16. Lahouari Addi et al., *Islam et démocratie,* special issue 104 of *Pouvoirs* (Paris: Seuil, 2003); Alexandre Escudier, ed., *Der Islam in Europa: der Umgang mit dem Islam in Frankreich und Deutschland* (Göttingen, Germany: Wallstein Verlag, 2003); Wilhelm Heitmeyer and Rainer Dollase, eds., *Die bedrängte Toleranz: Ethnisch-kulturelle Konflikte,*

religiöse Differenzen, und die Gefahren politisierter Gewalt (Frankfurt: Suhrkamp, 1996); Kastoryano, *Negotiating Identities;* Jørgen S. Nielsen, *Muslims in Western Europe,* 2nd ed. (Edinburgh: Edinburgh University Press, 1995); Jørgen S. Nielsen, "Muslims, the State, and the Public Domain in Britain," in *Religion und Politik in Deutschland und Großbritannien,* ed. Richard Bonney et al. (Munich: K. G. Saur, 2001), 145–54; Steven Vertovec and Ceri Peach, eds., *Islam in Europe: The Politics of Religions and Community in the United States,* 2nd ed. (Washington, DC: CQ Press, 1997).

17. Fischer Weltalmanach, *Der Fischer Weltalmanach 2000* (Frankfurt: Fischer Verlag, 1999), 163.

18. Gerhard Robbers, "Status und Stellung von Religionsgemeinschaften in der Europäischen Union," in *Politik und Religion,* special issue 33/2002 of *Politische Vierteljahresschrift,* ed. Michael Minkenberg and Ulrich Willems (Wiesbaden, Germany: Westdeutscher Verlag, 2003), 88–112; José Casanova, "Religion, European Secular Identities, and European Integration," in *Religion in an Expanding Europe,* ed. Timothy A. Byrnes and Peter J. Katzenstein (Cambridge: Cambridge University Press, 2006), 65–92.

19. Francis Castles, ed., *Families of Nations: Patterns of Public Policy in Western Democracies* (Aldershot, England: Dartmouth, 1993); Castles, *Comparative Public Policy;* Kersbergen, *Social Capitalism.*

20. Michael Minkenberg, "Staat und Kirche in westlichen Demokratien," in *Politik und Religion,* special issue 33/2002 of *Politische Vierteljahresschrift,* ed. Michael Minkenberg and Ulrich Willems (Wiesbaden, Germany: Westdeutscher Verlag, 2003), 115–38; Michael Minkenberg, "The Policy Impact of Church-State Relations: Family Policy and Abortion in Britain, France, and Germany," in *Church and State in Contemporary Europe: The Chimera of Neutrality,* special issue of *West European Politics,* ed. John Madeley and Zsolt Enyedi, (London: Frank Cass, 2003), 195–217.

21. Göran Gustafsson, "Church-State Separation—Swedish Style," in *Church and State in Contemporary Europe: The Chimera of Neutrality,* special issue of *West European Politics,* ed. John Madeley and Zsolt Enyedi (London: Frank Cass, 2003), 51–72; Tariq Modood, ed., *Church, State, and Religious Minorities* (London: Policy Studies Institute, 1997).

22. Will Kymlicka and Wayne Norman, eds., *Citizenship in Diverse Societies* (Oxford: Oxford University Press, 2000); Kenneth Wald, *Religion and Politics in the United States* (Lanham, MD: Rowman and Littlefield, 2003); Justin Watson, *The Christian Coalition: Dreams of Restoration, Demands for Recognition* (Basingstoke, England: Macmillan, 1997).

23. Jeff Haynes, *Religion in Global Politics* (London and New York: Longman, 1998); Roland Robertson and William R. Garrett, eds., *Religion and Global Order* (New York: Paragon House, 1991); Roland Robertson, "Religion und Politik im globalen Kontext der Gegenwart," in *Politik und Religion,* special issue 33/2002 of *Politische Vierteljahresschrift,* ed. Michael Minkenberg and Ulrich Willems (Wiesbaden, Germany: Westdeutscher Verlag, 2003), 581–94.

24. Huntington, *The Clash of Civilizations and the Remaking of World Order;* Benjamin Barber, *Jihad vs. McWorld* (New York: Ballantine, 1996).

25. Gabriel A. Almond and G. Bingham Powell Jr., eds., *Comparative Politics: System, Process, and Policy,* 2nd ed. (Boston and Toronto: Little, Brown, 1978), 283–314; Gabriel A. Almond and G. Bingham Powell Jr., eds., *Comparative Politics Today: A Worldview* (New York: HarperCollins, 1992), 107–15.

26. Almond and Powell, *Comparative Politics Today*, 113.

27. Almond and Powell, *Comparative Politics,* 309.

28. Hammar, *Democracy and the Nation State.*

29. Yasemin N. Soysal, *Limits of Citizenship: Migrants and Postnational Membership in Europe* (Chicago and London: University of Chicago Press, 1994); Andrew Geddes, "The Development of EU Immigration Policy: Supranationalisation and the Politics of Belonging," in *The Politics of Belonging: Migrants and Minorities in Contemporary Europe,* ed. Andrew Geddes and Adrian Favell (Aldershot, England: Ashgate, 1999), 176–91.

30. James F. Hollifield, *L'immigration et l'état nation à la recherche d'un modèle national* (Paris: L'Harmattan, 1997); James F Hollifield, "Migration, Trade, and the Nation-State: The Myth of Globalization," *UCLA Journal of International Law and Foreign Affairs* 3 (1998): 595–636; Dietrich Thränhardt, "Der Nationalstaat als migrationspolitischer Akteur," in *Migration im Spannungsfeld von Globalisierung und Nationalstaat,* ed. Dietrich Thränhardt and Uwe Hunger (Wiesbaden, Germany: Westdeutscher Verlag, 2003), 8–31.

31. Ruud Koopmans et al., *Contested Citizenship: Immigration and Cultural Diversity in Europe* (Minneapolis: University of Minnesota Press, 2005); Ruud Koopmans and Paul Statham, eds., *Challenging Immigration and Ethnic Relations Politics: Comparative European Perspectives* (Oxford: Oxford University Press, 2000).

32. Tomas Hammar, ed., *European Immigration Policy: A Comparative Study* (Cambridge: Cambridge University Press, 1985), 7 (first quote), 9 (second quote). The earlier study is Minkenberg, "Religious Effects on the Shaping of Immigration Policies in Western Democracies."

33. Almond and Powell, *Comparative Politics.*

34. Kastoryano, *Negotiating Identities;* Koopmans and Statham, *Challenging Immigration and Ethnic Relations Politics.*

35. Ruud Koopmans and Paul Statham, "Migration and Ethnic Relations as a Field of Political Contention: An Opportunity Structure Approach," in *Challenging Immigration and Ethnic Relations Politics,* ed. Koopmans and Statham (Oxford: Oxford University Press, 2000), 13–56; Koopmans et al., *Contested Citizenship.*

36. Han Entzinger, "The Dynamics of Integration Policies: A Multidimensional Model," in *Challenging Immigration and Ethnic Relations Politics,* ed. Ruud Koopmans and Paul Statham (Oxford: Oxford University Press, 2000), 97–118.

37. Stephen Castles and Mark Miller, *The Age of Migration*, 3rd ed. (New York: Palgrave, 2003), 80–81.

38. Koopmans et al., *Contested Citizenship,* 55–64.

39. Entzinger, "The Dynamics of Integration Policies," 97–118.

40. Michael Minkenberg, "Religion, Immigration, and the Politics of Multiculturalism: A Comparative Analysis of Western Democracies," paper presented at the Immigration Policy Post-9/11 workshop at the University of Pittsburgh, Sept. 9–10, 2005; T. Alexander Aleinikoff and Douglas Klusmeyer, eds., *Citizenship Policies for an Age of Migration* (Washington, DC: Carnegie Endowment for International Peace, 2002); Koopmans et al., *Contested Citizenship.*

41. Koopmans et al., *Contested Citizenship,* 71–73.

42. See the chapter appendix; also Koopmans et al., *Contested Citizenship,* 73.

43. See contributions to Thränhardt and Hunger, *Migration im Spannungsfeld von Globalisierung und Nationalstaat.*

44. Michael Minkenberg, "The Politics of Citizenship in the New Republic," *West European Politics* 26 (Oct. 2003): 219–40.

45. Ibid.; Minkenberg, "Religion, Immigration and the Politics of Multicultural-ism."

46. See chap. 11, by Ariane Chebel d'Appollonia, in this volume.

47. Minkenberg, "Religious Effects on the Shaping of Immigration Policies in West-ern Democracies."

48. Castles, *Families of Nations;* Castles; *Comparative Public Policy.*

49. Michael Minkenberg, "Religion and Public Policy: Institutional, Cultural, and Political Impact on the Shaping of Abortion Policies in Western Democracies," *Comparative Political Studies* 35 (Mar. 2002): 221–47; Minkenberg, "Staat und Kirche in west-lichen Demokratien"; Minkenberg, "The Policy Impact of Church-State Relations."

50. Bruce, *Fundamentalism,* 3.

51. David Martin, *A General Theory of Secularisation* (London: Blackwell, 1978); Steve Bruce, *Religion in the Modern World: From Cathedrals to Cults* (Oxford and New York: Oxford University Press, 1996); Ronald Inglehart, *Modernization and Postmodernization* (Princeton, NJ: Princeton University Press, 1997); Ronald Inglehart and Wayne E. Baker, "Modernization, Cultural Change, and the Persistence of Traditional Values," *American Sociological Review* 65 (2000): 19–51.

52. David Martin, *A General Theory of Secularisation,* 119.

53. Inglehart and Baker, "Modernization, Cultural Change, and the Persistence of Traditional Values"; Ronald Inglehart and Michael Minkenberg, "Die Transformation re-ligiöser Werte in entwickelten Industriegesellschaften," in *Religion und Politik-zwischen Universalismus und Partikularismus,* vol. 2 of *the Jahrbuch für Europa- und Nordamerika-Studien,* ed. Heinz-Dieter Meyer and Michael Minkenberg (Opladen, Germany: Leske+Budrich, 2000), 115–30; Norris and Inglehart, *Sacred and Secular.*

54. Minkenberg, "Religion and Public Policy," 238.

55. Francis Castles, *Comparative Public Policy,* 8f.; Martin Baldwin-Edwards, "Immi-gration after 1992," *Policy and Politics* 19 (1992): 199–211.

56. Thomas Faist, "Immigration, Integration und Wohlfahrtsstaaten: die Bundesre-publik Deutschlnad in vergleichender Perspektive," in *Migration in nationalen Wohlfahrtsstaaten: theoretische und vergleichende Untersuchungen,* ed. Michael Bommes and Jost Halfmann (Osnabrück, Germany: Universitätsverlag Rasch, 1998), 152.

57. Minkenberg, "Religion and Public Policy," 221–47; Minkenberg, "The Policy Impact of Church-State Relations," 195–217; Fetzer and Soper, *Muslims and the State in Britain, France, and Germany.*

58. Mark Chaves and David E. Cann, "Regulation, Pluralism, and Religious Market Structure," *Rationality and Society* 4 (1992): 272–90; Minkenberg, "Staat und Kirche in westlichen Demokratien."

59. For details, see Minkenberg, "Religion and Public Policy"; Minkenberg, "The Policy Impact of Church-State Relations"; Fetzer and Soper, *Muslims and the State in Britain, France, and Germany.*

60. On the relevance of church-state relations for immigration policies, see Minken-berg, "Religious Effects on the Shaping of Immigration Policies in Western Democra-cies."

61. For the evidence presented elsewhere, see Kastoryano, *Negotiating Identities;* and chap. 12, by Jonathan Laurence, in this volume.

62. Russell J. Dalton, *Citizen Politics: Public Opinion and Political Parties in Advanced Industrial Democracies,* 2nd ed. (Chatham, NJ: Chatham House, 1996), 176–85; Minkenberg, *Neokonservatismus und Neue Rechte in den USA;* Inglehart, *Modernization and Postmodernization.*

63. For details, see Minkenberg, "Religion and Public Policy."

64. See Minkenberg, "The Policy Impact of Church-State Relations."

65. See Kersbergen, *Social Capitalism.*

66. See Minkenberg, "Religious Effects on the Shaping of Immigration Policies in Western Democracies."

67. Arend Lijphart, *Patterns of Democracy: Government Forms and Performance in Thirty-six Countries* (New Haven, CT, and London: Yale University Press, 1999); Manfred G. Schmidt, *Demokratietheorien,* 3rd ed. (Opladen, Germany: Leske+Budrich, 2000), chap. 3.3.

68. Hammar, *European Immigration Policy,* 294.

69. Grete Brochmann and Tomas Hammar, eds., *Mechanisms of Immigration Control: A Comparative Analysis of European Regulation Policies* (Oxford and New York: Berg, 1999); Kees Groenendijk and Elspeth Guild, "Converging Criteria: Creating an Area of Security of Residence for Europe's Third Country Nationals," *European Journal of Migration and Law* 3 (2001): 37–59; Rey Koslowski, *Migrants and Citizens: Demographic Change in the European State System* (Ithaca, NY, and London: Cornell University Press, 2000).

70. Koopmans et al., *Contested Citizenship,* 72.

71. See the chapter appendix; see also Robert Manne, *The Howard Years* (Melbourne: BlackInc. Agenda, 2004).

72. Fernando Soares Loja, "Islam in Portugal," in *Islam, Europe's Second Religion: The New Social, Cultural, and Political Landscape,* ed. Shireen T. Hunter (Westport, CT : Praeger, 2002), 191–203.

73. Koopmans et al., *Contested Citizenship.* See also the appendix to this chapter; Kevin Boyle and Juliet Sheen, eds., *Freedom of Religion and Belief: A World Report* (London and New York: Routledge, 1997); Alexandre Escudier, ed., *Der Islam in Europa: der Umgang mit dem Islam in Frankreich und Deutschland* (Göttingen, Germany: Wallstein Verlag, 2003); Steven J. Monsma and J. Christopher Soper, *The Challenge of Pluralism: Church and State in Five Democracies* (Lanham, MD: Rowman & Littlefield, 1997).

74. Koopmans et al., *Contested Citizenship,* 73.

75. Marion Maddox, *God under Howard: The Rise of the Religious Right in Australian Politics* (Crows Nest, NSW, Australia: Allen & Unwin, 2005); Manne, *The Howard Years,* appendix.

76. Michael Minkenberg, "Mobiliser contre l'Autre: la nouvelle droite radicale et son rôle dans le processus politique," in *Les codes de la différence,* ed. Riva Kastoryano (Paris: Presses de la FNSP, 2005), 263–96.

77. Fetzer and Soper, *Muslims and the State in Britain, France, and Germany,* 143f.

78. Ibid., 145.

79. EUMC, *Majorities' Attitudes towards Minorities in European Union Member States* (Vienna: EUMC 2003), 42f; see figure 3.1.

80. EUMC, *The Impact of 7 July 2005 London Bomb Attacks on Muslim Communities in the EU* (Vienna, 2005).

81. Francis Castles, *Comparative Public Policy;* Kersbergen, *Social Capitalism.*

82. Kastoryano, *Negotiating Identities.*

83. Hunter, *Islam, Europe's Second Religion.*

Chapter 4: The Emergence of a Consensus

1. There is a long list of authors who share this view. Among those who directly address the question of global threats and who profess a belief in growing global terrorism are Louis Rene Beres, *Terrorism and Global Security: The Nuclear Threat* (Boulder, CO: Westview Press, 1979); Steve Kovsky, "Corporate Terrorism: A New Global Threat," *Management Review* 79 (1990): 4ff.; Paul Wilkinson, "The Lessons of Lockerbie," *Conflict Studies* 226 (1990): 1–30; Frank Barnaby, "Weapons of Mass Destruction: A Growing Threat in the 1990s?" *Conflict Studies* 235 (Oct.–Nov. 1990): 1–26; Arnaud de Borchgrave, "Transnational Crime: The New Empire of Evil," *Strategy & Leadership* 24 (1996): 6; Linnea P. Raine, Frank J. Cillufo, and Center for Strategic and International Studies, *Global Organized Crime: The New Empire of Evil* (Washington, DC: Center for Strategic and International Studies, 1994); Amy Borrus and Dean Foust, "In a World of Trouble, Can He Cope?" *Business Week* 3594 (Sept. 7, 1998): 32–33; Phil Cerny, "The New Security Dilemma: Divisibility, Defection, and Disorder in the Global Era," *Review of International Studies* 26 (2000): 623–46; Ronald D. Crelinsten, "Terrorism and Counter-Terrorism in a Multi-Centric World: Challenges and Opportunities," *Terrorism and Political Violence* 11 (2000): 170–96; Laurent Goetschel, "Globalisation and Security: The Challenge of Collective Action in a Politically Fragmented World," *Global Society* 14 (Apr. 2000): 259–77; Joseph A. Camilleri, "Terrorism, Anti-Terrorism, and the Globalization of Insecurity," *Arena Journal* 19 (2002): 7–19; Xavier Raufer, "New World Disorder, New Terrorisms: New Threats for Europe and the Western World," *Terrorism and Political Violence* 11 (2000): 30–51; Majid Tehranian, "Global Terrorism: Searching for Appropriate Responses," *Pacifica Review* 14 (2003): 57–65; Rohan Gunaratna, *Inside Al Qaeda* (New York: Columbia University Press, 2002).

2. Paul Wolfowitz, "The Gathering Storm: The Threat of Global Terror and Asia/Pacific Security," *Vital Speeches of the Day* 68 (2002): 674–79; Lisa Hoffman, "U.S. Targets Global Terror Hot Spots," *Washington Times,* Dec. 24, 2001; United States, Office of the White House Press Secretary, "Address to a Joint Session of Congress and the American People by George Bush" (press release), Sept. 20, 2001.

3. The beliefs, policies, and actions of George Bush, Tony Blair, and John Howard regarding the buildup to the Iraq war have been the object of many books, perhaps too many. Critical discussion of the role of intelligence and the conceptualization of the war on terror as they relate to the Iraq war is less common but nevertheless well documented. See Lawrence Freedman, "War in Iraq: Selling the Threat," *Survival* 46 (summer 2004): 7–49; Simon Chesterman, *Just War or Just Peace? Humanitarian Intervention and International Law* (Oxford and New York: Oxford University Press, 2001); Roger Burbach and Jim Tarbell, *Imperial Overstretch: George W. Bush and the Hubris of Empire* (New York: Zed Books, 2004); Robert C. Byrd, *Losing America: Confronting a Reckless and Arrogant Presidency* (New York: Norton, 2004); Jeff Danziger, "Safeguarding Our Freedoms" (drawing), Tribune Media Services, June 24, 2002; Ivo H. Daalder and James M. Lindsay, *America Unbound: The Bush Revolution in Foreign Policy* (Washington, DC: Brookings Institution, 2003); Craig R. Eisendrath and Melvin A. Goodman, *Bush League Diplomacy: How the Neoconservatives Are Putting the World at Risk* (Amherst, NY: Prometheus Books, 2004); Gary C. Jacobson and Samuel Kernell, *The Logic of American*

Politics in Wartime: Lessons from the Bush Administration (Washington, DC: CQ Press, 2004); Douglas Kellner, *From 9/11 to Terror War: The Dangers of the Bush Legacy* (Lanham, MD: Rowman and Littlefield, 2003); Saul Landau, *The Pre-Emptive Empire: A Guide to Bush's Kingdom* (London and Sterling, VA: Pluto Press, 2003); Frances Fox Piven, *The War at Home: The Domestic Causes and Consequences of Bush's Militarism* (New York: New Press, 2004); John Newhouse, *Imperial America: The Bush Assault on the World Order* (New York: Knopf, 2003); Wayne Wilson and Jim Whiting, *Tony Blair: A Real Life Reader Biography* (Bear, DE: Mitchell Lane Publishers, 2003); Bob Woodward, *Bush at War* (New York: Simon & Schuster, 2002); Bob Woodward, *Plan of Attack* (New York: Simon & Schuster, 2004). I wish to address a concept that goes beyond the impact of September 11 and counter-terrorism policy. That is, I address the use of the label "terrorism" and the common belief among security experts that there is a growing list of reasons to fear the future. On that list are terrorist networks, failed states and rogue governments, dissemination of weapons of mass destruction, hatred of U.S. foreign policy, the so-called clash of Western and Islamic civilizations, and the conflict over political and democratic values on one side and Islamo-fascism on the other.

Among many works, valuable insights can be found in Ken Booth and Tim Dunne, eds., *Worlds in Collision: Terror and the Future of Global Order* (New York: Palgrave Macmillan, 2002); Craig J. Calhoun, Paul Price, and Ashley S. Timmer, *Understanding September 11* (New York: New Press, 2002); Eric Hershberg and Kevin W. Moore, *Critical Views of September 11: Analyses from around the World* (New York: Norton, 2002); Richard Johnson, "Defending Ways of Life: The (Anti-) Terrorist Rhetorics of Bush and Blair." *Theory, Culture, and Society* 19 (2003): 211–32; William Rosenau, Kemper Gay, and David Mussington, "Transnational Threats and US National Security," *Low Intensity Conflict and Law Enforcement* 6 (1999): 144–61; Nancy Chang, Center for Constitutional Rights, *Silencing Political Dissent* (New York: Seven Stories Press, 2002); David Cole, *Enemy Aliens: Double Standards and Constitutional Freedoms in the War on Terrorism* (New York and London: Free Press, 2003); Ronald J. Daniels, Patrick Macklem, and Kent Roach, eds. *The Security of Freedom: Essays on Canada's Anti-Terrorism Bill.* Toronto: University of Toronto Press, 2001; Monica Den Boer and Jorg Monar, "Keynote Article: 11 September and the Challenge of Global Terrorism to the EU as a Security Actor," *Journal of Common Market Studies,* annual review issue, (2002): 11–28; Takis Fotopoulos, "The Global 'War' of the Transnational Elite," *Democracy and Nature* 8 (2003): 201–40; Jürgen Habermas, Jacques Derrida, and Giovanna Borradori, *Philosophy in a Time of Terror: Dialogues with Jürgen Habermas and Jacques Derrida* (Chicago: University of Chicago Press, 2003); Murray Hiebert, "The Cost of Security," *Far Eastern Economic Review* 165 (2002): 18–19; Michael Dillon, *Politics of Security: Towards a Political Philosophy of Continental Thought* (London and New York: Routledge, 1996).

4. The Latin roots for the word "terrorism" mean to frighten, terrify, run away (while frightening); to be driven out by fear, to be prevented from acting because of fear; to strike, to intimidate.

5. This focus on the ordinary nature of the victims seems rather likely to be the reason why the World Trade Center rather than the Pentagon became the symbol of September 11.

6. See François Heisbourg, "De l'après-guerre froide à l'hyperterrorisme," *Le Monde,* Sept. 12, 2001; François Heisbourg, *L'Hyperterrorisme* (Paris: Odile Jacob, 2002); Frederic Megret, "Justice in Times of Violence," *European Journal of International Law* 14

(2003): 327–45; Thérèse Delpech, "One Year After: Four Reactions Regarding September 11," *Internationale Politik* 57 (2002): 39–46; Alexandre Adler, *J'ai vu finir le monde ancien* (Paris: Grasset, 2002); Richard L. Garwin, "The Technology of Megaterror," *MIT Technology Review,* Sept. 2002; Andre Glucksmann, "The World of Megaterrorism: Mad Is the European Who Thinks Himself Immune to Terror for Having Opposed Saddam's Overthrow," *Wall Street Journal,* Mar. 21, 2004. For a more serious account see Graham Allison, *Nuclear Terrorism: The Ultimate Preventable Catastrophe* (New York: Times Books, 2004).

7. The perception of novelty in the 9/11 attacks and the resulting narrative of hyper-terrorism are perhaps why it was so important, after the failure to find a link between 9/11 and the anthrax attacks, to find a new link. We have seen weak assertions of Al Qaeda working on atomic bombs and chemical weapons from the caves of Afghanistan and plans inside computers hawked at the Peshawar market, but no one seriously believed in such a "discovery." The narrative of hyperterrorism is why the supposed 9/11 connection to Iraq was such a crucial argument, not only as a basis for the decision to go to war in Iraq but also for the discourse about the "global war on terrorism." The dossier prepared to convince the British parliament that Saddam Hussein's palace was the location of chemical plants insisted on the link. We still don't know if it was a deliberate lie (and if so, why) or a "no-risk policy in case of doubt," a "shoot-to-kill policy" at the international level in the name of preventing catastrophe. We must wait for evidence about Iraqi weapons of mass destruction, but at least we can understand why the original argument for war was not regime change but to find these weapons.

8. I am not arguing that this narrative was instrumental. It really appeared for many people in shock that a global war had been launched, and as soon as some experts gave evidence that it was effectively the case, they were believed to be true. Thousands of victims in one day in a country which has no modern record of war casualties at home, thousands of victims televised and shown again and again in the world media gave a strong image of war and especially of global war. And security experts have been convinced that they were correct, that their ominous forebodings before September 11 were revealed to have been perfectly justified when the airplanes struck their targets. The need for an immediate response to the attacks has condensed and framed the meaning of the attacks themselves. As the attacks were not followed by the attackers' open claims of specific objectives, such as the withdrawing of U.S. troops from Saudi Arabia, the September 11 violence was full of "silence." The meanings were totally open-ended, so the United States' emphasis went from point A (an attack on the Pentagon or the World Trade Center), to point B (blaming Saudi Arabia), to point C (blaming Afghanistan). In other words, the shift in emphasis meant a shift in options, away from the option of referring to the attacks as odious criminal acts to speaking of them as acts of undeclared war.

9. Interviews during 2003 and 2004 with U.S. officials in the White House, Defense Department, and Department of Homeland Security.

10. The decision to make the reprisal attack against Afghanistan rather than Saudi Arabia explains why the nationality of the suicide bombers was kept secret as a matter of national security and not released until later on.

12. Stella Remington, *Open Secret: The Autobiography of the Former Director-General of MI5* (London: Arrow, 2002), xi.; Didier Bigo et al., *Illiberal Practices of Liberal Regimes: The (In)security Games* (Paris: L'Harmattan, 2006).

13. See several works by René Girard: *The Scapegoat* (Baltimore, MD: Johns Hopkins University Press, 1986); *Violence and the Sacred* (Baltimore, MD: Johns Hopkins University Press, 1977), originally published as *La violence et le sacré* (Paris: Grasset, 1972); and *Violences d'aujourd'hui, violences de toujours: textes des conférences et des débats* (Lausanne, Switzerland: L'Age d'Homme, 2000).

14. This perspective is actually shared by many European scholars and think-tanks, such as Louis Rene Beres, Arnaud de Borchgrave, Linnea P. Raine, Frank J. Cillufo, and the Center for Strategic and International Studies.

15. Habermas, Derrida, and Borradori, *Philosophy in a Time of Terror,* 137.

16. The relationship between the anthrax scare and Al Qaeda is not obvious. After four years of intensive research by the FBI, it is still highly problematic to correlate anthrax and Al Qaeda. It seems more plausible that the anthrax came from someone within the U.S. military establishment attempting to generate bigger research budgets rather than from Al Qaeda. A suspect was arrested, but FBI agents complained about outside pressure on the case. The possible trial entered a juridical limbo, and no one seemed willing to accelerate the investigations (interviews with FBI, 2004).

17. U.S., Office of the President, "President Bush Outlines Iraqi Threat: Remarks by the President on Iraq," Cincinnati Museum Center, Cincinnati, OH, Oct. 7, 2002, www.whitehouse.gov/news/releases/2002/10/20021007-8.html, accessed Aug. 27, 2007; Secretary of Defense Donald Rumsfeld, speech, Nov. 21, 2003, www.defenselink.mil/transcripts/transcript.aspx?transcriptid=2981.

18. References to Armageddon are common: Martin Schram and Ted Turner Documentaries, *Avoiding Armageddon: Our Future, Our Choice,* companion to the PBS series from Ted Turner Documentaries (New York: Basic Books, 2003); D. W. Brackett, *Holy Terror: Armageddon in Tokyo* (New York: Weatherhill, 1996); Rensselaer W. Lee, *Smuggling Armageddon: The Nuclear Black Market in the Former Soviet Union and Europe* (New York: St. Martin's Press, 1998); *Through Our Enemies' Eyes: Osama Bin Laden, Radical Islam, and the Future of America* [by Anonymous] (Washington, DC: Brassey's, 2002). Some authors have made money with handbooks describing how to survive terror on a massive scale or have ridden the wave of fear with a sense of humor: Sam Scheinberg, *Survive Bio-Terrorism: A Basic Handbook* (Newport, OR: CYA Publications, 2001); Elizabeth Terry and J. Paul Oxer, *Survival Handbook for Chemical, Biological, and Radiological Terrorism* (Philadelphia: Xlibris, 2003); Joshua Piven and David Borgenicht, *The Worst-Case Scenario Survival Handbook: Travel* (San Francisco: Chronicle Books, 2001).

19. United Kingdom, Parliament, House of Commons, Foreign Affairs Committee, *The Decision to Go to War in Iraq: Ninth Report of Session 2002–03.* H.M.S.O. 2003, http://image.guardian.co.uk/sys-files/Politics/documents/2003/07/07/WMD%5Freport.pdf. See the Butler report, "Review of Intelligence on Weapons of Mass Destruction: Report of Privy Counsellors," July 14, 2004, House of Commons, London, 198, www.butlerreview.org.uk/report/report.pdf. See United States, Congress, Senate, Select Committee on Intelligence, *Report of the Select Committee on Intelligence on the U.S. Intelligence Community's Prewar Intelligence Assessments on Iraq Together with Additional Views* (Washington, DC: GPO, 2004); Geoffrey Barker, *Sexing It Up: Iraq, Intelligence and Australia, Briefings* (Sydney: University of New South Wales, 2003).

20. Concerning the merging, or the concentration and centralization of the development of homeland security in the United States, the centralization of information and

reform of the intelligence service in the UK and Australia, the coordination of police and gendarmerie in France, and the project of coordination and centralization of intelligence at the European level, see Laurie Mylroie, *Bush v. the Beltway: How the CIA and the State Department Tried to Stop the War on Terror* (New York: Regan Books, 2003); Douglas Kellner, *From 9/11 to Terror War: The Dangers of the Bush Legacy* (Lanham, MD: Rowman and Littlefield, 2003).

21. See the discussion in the *New York Review of Books* (Mark Danner, "The Secret Way to War," *NYRB*, June 9, 2005) about the Downing Street memo of July 23, 2002. Also relevant of course is the "Kelly affair" (in which weapons expert David Kelly was found dead after he was revealed as the source of a BBC story that the British government had a "fixed-up" dossier on WMD in Iraq). It was followed by the "Hutton inquiry" (which concluded he had taken his own life) and the reaction of the judges against the Hutton "result." See http://news.bbc.co.uk/2/hi/uk_news/3472361.stm

22. See Barry Buzan, *People, States, and Fear: The National Security Problem in International Relations* (Chapel Hill: University of North Carolina Press, 1983).

23. Ulrich Beck, "The Terrorist Threat: World Risk Society Revisited," *Theory, Culture, and Society* 19 (2003): 39–56; Jean-Claude Monod, "Destins du paulinisme politique: K. Barth, C. Schmitt, J. Taubes" (Pauline Political Thought and Its Destiny: K. Barth, C. Schmitt, J. Taubes), *Esprit* 292 (Feb. 2003): 113–24; James Der Derian, "Global Events, National Security and Virtual Theory," *Millennium* 30 (2002): 669–90; David P. Forsythe, "The United States and International Criminal Justice," *Human Rights Quarterly* 24 (2003): 974–91; Stanley Hoffmann, "American Exceptionalism: The New Vision," in *American Exceptionalism and Human Rights,* ed. Michael Ignatieff (Princeton, NJ: Princeton University Press, 2005), 225–40; "War on Terrorism: America Takes Action in a Changed World—Pro & Con: Should the Congress Approve Emergency Funding and Military Force in Response to Terrorist Attacks?" *Congressional Digest* 80 (Nov. 11, 2001): 257–88.

24. Alvin Toffler and his wife and coauthor Heidi Toffler were invited to be keynote speakers at a meeting on September 11, 2002, which was designed to address new threats (interview with CIA officer, Oct. 2002). In the final statement about the Madrid transit bombing, issued on Mar. 10, 2004, Alvin Toffler was quoted heavily as the first to have predicted that terrorism would be the next global enemy. The 9/11 anniversary meeting gathered about two dozen presidents, prime ministers, or monarchs, with two hundred experts from fifty countries presenting research on extremism and sectarian violence. Interestingly enough, this statement about terrorism being the next enemy is not present in the Tofflers' books *The Third Wave* or *Future Shock.* Toffler was speaking of computer attacks as the new form of terrorism, and he completely dismissed physical violence, considering an attack inside the United States to be impossible. Physical violence from terrorism uses Toffler's "second wave" technology, whereas information attacks would fall within the "third wave" paradigm. The Tofflers have set up a private company, Toffler Associates, with the promise "we help you create your future." See also National Intelligence Council, *Mapping the Global Future: Report of the National Intelligence Council's 2020 Project* (Washington, DC, 2005).

25. Elspeth Guild, "International Terrorism and EU Immigration, Asylum and Borders Policy: The Unexpected Victims of 11 September 2001," *European Foreign Affairs Review* 8 (2003): 331–46; L. Wacquant, "Des 'ennemis commodes,'" *Actes de la recherche en sciences sociales* 129 (1999): 63–67; Didier Bigo, *Les nouveaux enjeux de l'(in)sécurité*

en Europe: terrorisme, guerre, sécurité intérieure, sécurité extérieure (Paris: L'Harmattan, 2005).

26. M. Foucault, *Abnormal: Lectures at the College de France, 1974–1975* (New York: Picador USA, 2003); Jasbir K. Puar and Amit S. Rai, "Monster, Terrorist, Fag: The War on Terrorism and the Production of Docile Patriots," *Social Text* 20, no. 3(72) (2002): 117–48.

27. Concerning Australia's stance on this relationship, see the statement given by Mr. Howard to justify the position taken before the commission investigating 9/11 (Philip Flood, *Report to the Inquiry into the Australian Intelligence Agencies* [Australian government, July 2004; www.globalsecurity.org/intell/library/reports/2004/australia_intell-inquiry_intro.htm]). See also the Canadian position, which maintained a more neutral tone but was consistent with that nation's refusal to accept the "evidence" given by the United States, and the French position, which also indicated its skepticism of American and British intelligence concerning Iraq and its decision to rely instead on their technologies. The French stance on the Iraq intelligence solidified its decision to employ satellite surveillance totally independent of U.S. involvement.

28. The framing of "old" and "new" Europe is more than a tactical move against the resistance of Germany and France. It is a culturalist vision linked with the vision that the leaders of these countries are "Classics" (see note 32 below) out of touch with the "new" reality of the post-9/11 world. In addition, "old Europe" is in some corners synonymous with welfare states, pensions, and bureaucracy.

29. Concerning the debate over a U.S. "empire" after 9/11 see Michel Drancourt, "Anti-Americanism French Style: But What Have the Americans Done to the French?" *Futuribles* 280 (Nov. 2002): 51–59; Danny Goldberg, Victor Goldberg, and Robert Greenwald, *It's a Free Country: Personal Freedom in America after September 11* (New York: RDV Books, 2002); Walter LaFeber, "The Post September 11 Debate over Empire, Globalization, and Fragmentation," *Political Science Quarterly* 117 (2002): 1–17; Ronnie D. Lipschutz, "The Clash of Governmentalities: The Fall of the UN Republic and America's Reach for Empire," *Contemporary Security Policy* 23 (2002): 214–31; Cesare Merlini, "U.S. Hegemony and the Roman Analogy: A European View," *International Spectator* 37 (2002): 19–30; Toni Negri, "Ruptures within Empire, the Power of Exodus: Interview with Toni Negri," *Theory* 19 (Aug. 2002): 187–94; John O'Neill, "Empire versus Empire: A Post-Communist Manifesto," *Theory* 19 (Aug. 2002): 195–210; Martin Walker, "America's Virtual Empire." *World Policy Journal* 19 (2002): 13–20; Mariano Aguirre, "Defense Strategy in the New Bush Epoch: Preventive War and the Empire Ideology," *Revista Internacional de Filosofía Política* 21 (July 2003): 236–42; Peter Bender, "America: The New Roman Empire?" *Orbis: A Journal of World Affairs* 47 (2003): 145–59; Bruce Cumings, "Is America an Imperial Power?" *Current History* 102 (2003): 355–60; Richard Falk, "Will the Empire Be Fascist?" *Global Dialogue* 5 (2003): 22–31; John Foran, "Confronting an Empire: Sociology and the U.S.-Made World Crisis." *Political Power and Social Theory* 16 (2003): 213–33; John D. Kelly, "U.S. Power, after 9/11 and before It: If Not an Empire, Then What?" *Public Culture* 15 (2003): 347–69; Saul Landau, *The Preemptive Empire: A Guide to Bush's Kingdom* (London and Sterling, VA: Pluto Press, 2003); Ann Larabee, "Empire of Fear: Imagined Community and the September 11 Attacks," *Research in Social Problems and Public Policy* 11 (2003): 19–31; Ravi Arvind Palat and Mark Selden, "Introduction: 9/11, War without Respite, and the New Face of Empire," *Critical Asian Studies* 35 (2003): 163–74; Leo Panitch, "September 11 and the American

Empire," *Interventions* 5 (2003): 233–40; Dimitri K. Simes, "America's Imperial Dilemma," *Foreign Affairs* 82 (2003): 91–102; Robert Hunter Wade, "The Invisible Hand of the American Empire," *Ethics & International Affairs* 17 (2003): 77–88; Michael Walzer, "Is There an American Empire?" *Dissent* 50 (2003): 27–31; Ernst R. Zivier, "Pax Americana—Bellum Americanum: On the Way to a New International Law or to a New International Injustice?" *Recht und Politik* 39 (2003): 194–201; Julian Reid, "War, Liberalism, and Modernity: The Biopolitical Provocations of 'Empire,'" *Cambridge Review of International Affairs* 17 (2004): 63–79; Ronnie D. Lipschutz, "Imitations of Empire," *Global Environmental Politics* 4 (2004): 20–23.

30. See Frederic Ramel and Charles-Philippe David, "'Yes But'—The Image of Europe according to the Bush Administration: From Ambivalence to Rigidity," *Etudes Internationales* 33 (2002): 31–55; Dany Deschenes, "French Security Experts and 11 September 2001," *Etudes Internationales* 33 (2002): 763–74; Thérèse Delpech, "One Year After: Four Reactions Regarding September 11," *Internationale Politik* 57 (2002): 39–46; Shaun Gregory, "France and the War on Terrorism," *Terrorism and Political Violence* 15 (2003): 124–47; Anatol Lieven, "In the Mirror of Europe: The Perils of American Nationalism," *Current History* 103 (2004): 99–106.

31. On "discursive formation" see Michel Foucauld, *The Order of Things: An Archaeology of the Human Sciences* (New York: Pantheon Books, 1971), originally published as *Les mots et les choses: une archéologie des sciences humaines* (Paris: Gallimard, 1966); and Gilles Deleuze, *Foucault: un nouvel archiviste* (Montpellier, France: Fata Morgana, 1972).

32. The "Classics" versus "Moderns" debate refers to a very famous academic dispute about the use of the French language in the seventeenth century. As analyzed by Marc Fumaroli, the dispute initiated by Perrault on his poem "Le grand siècle de Louis XIV" opposed the Classics, seen as the Bees, and the Moderns, seen as the Spiders. The former, represented by Boileau, Racine, and Molière, insisted that Louis XIV was great because of his classicism. The latter group, represented by Perrault and his friends, insisted on the contrary that modernity was the mark of Louis XIV's greatness, and they made their argument a discourse praising the enthroned power who was helping industry and technology. In the Moderns' narrative, current affairs triumph—the latest news commands the present and the future; technical innovation is linked with moral innovations and the adaptation of customs and laws. In the Classics' narrative, however, the events of the present must be read through the memory of the past. They are reluctant about the imperative of the present and the conformity of the mind after a specific event and consider that length of time, rather than speed, is the best friend of reflection. Jonathan Swift describes the Classics as bees because Plato identifies them as symbols of memory and because they use nature (flowers) for their product (honey). The Moderns are spiders because they use their own excrement to produce their thread, and this geometric and technological knowledge is also a trap. They seem to trap the others and therefore be winners, but they are trapped in the lifestyle they have set up. The academic dispute is not only about the use of French instead of Latin in literary works or about the fame of Louis XIV; it also has to do with trying to cope with the future and to analyze exceptional events as well as their consequences, which explains why it pertains to the present situation. Do we need to analyze the present by considering what may happen in the future or do we study events of the past to give meaning to the present? Do we have to believe that technology will answer our questions? Do we have to believe that moments of unanimity are moments of truth?

33. Mark B. Salter, "Passports, Mobility, and Security: How Smart Can the Border Be?" *International Studies Perspectives* 5 (2004): 71–91.

34. The Classics are often but not always "realist" in the sense of international relations theory. They may be "liberal" and even "idealist." But they believe in the divide between the interior and exterior of the state as the summa divisio of the world. They often make the distinction between security as defense and security as law and order and consider that the two do not overlap. At the theoretical level Stephen Walt provides good examples of what they think. See Stephen M. Walt, "The Renaissance of Security Studies," *International Studies Quarterly* 35 (1991): 211–39; "Hegel on War: Another Look," *History of Political Thought* 10 (1990): 113–24; "Beyond bin Laden: Reshaping U.S. Foreign Policy," *International Security* 26 (2002): 56–78; and John J. Mearsheimer and Stephen M. Walt, "An Unnecessary War," *Foreign Policy* 134 (Jan.–Feb. 2003): 50–59.

35. For a detailed account of the differences in the role of armies in internal security, see Didier Bigo, Jean Paul Hanon, and Anastasia Tsoukala, *La participation des militaires à la sécurité intérieure: France, Italie, Allemagne, Etats-Unis* (Paris: Rapport du Centre d'Études sur les Conflits pour la DAS, 1999).

36. This is the case even if the Moderns reintroduce secrecy into the core of their argument when they encounter an opposing view.

37. At the theoretical level the Moderns are inspired by transnationalist international relations theory, but often they are also culturalists and neo-realists who changed their views after the end of bipolarity. See James N. Rosenau, *Turbulence in World Politics: A Theory of Change and Continuity* (Princeton, NJ: Princeton University Press, 1990); Bertrand Badie, *La fin des territoires: essai sur le désordre international et l'utilité sociale du respect* (Paris: Fayard, 1995). Other works are Jurgen Turek, "The Global Threat: New Dangers of Terrorism," *Internationale Politik* 56 (2001): 81–82; Quintan Wiktorowicz, "The New Global Threat: Transnational Salafis and Jihad," *Middle East Policy* 8 (2001): 18–38; Robert Bussiere, "After 11 September: America, Europe, and Global Antiterrorism Strategy," *Commentaire* 25 (2002): 301–309; Christopher Coker, "Globalisation and Insecurity in the Twenty-First Century: NATO and the Management of Risk," *Adelphi Papers* 345 (June 2002): 7–103; Der Derian, "Global Events, National Security and Virtual Theory"; Stanley Hoffmann, "Clash of Globalizations," *Foreign Affairs* 81 (2002): 104–15; Douglas Kellner, "Theorizing September 11: Social Theory, History, and Globalization," *Social Thought & Research* 25 (2002): 1–50; Audrey Kurth Cronin, "Transnational Terrorism and Security," in *Grave New World: Security Challenges in the 21st Century,* ed. Michael E. Brown (Washington, DC: Georgetown University Press, 2003); Dario Kuntic, "Terrorism in a Changing World," *Croatian International Relations Review* 9 (2003): 199–204; Samuel M. Makinda, "Global Governance and Terrorism," *Global Change* 15 (Feb. 2003): 43–58; Thomas M. Sanderson, "Transnational Terror and Organized Crime: Blurring the Lines," *SAIS Review* 24 (2004): 49–61.

38. See Didier Bigo, *Sécurité intérieure, implications pour la défense* (Paris: Rapport établi pour la DAS, French Ministry of Defense, 1998).

Chapter 5: European Security and Counter-Terrorism

1. Ken Booth and Tim Dunne, eds., *Worlds in Collision: Terror and the Future of Global Order* (New York: Palgrave Macmillan, 2002); Jan Oskar Engene, *Terrorism in Western Europe: Explaining the Trends since 1950* (London: Edward Elgar, 2003);

Lawrence Freedman, ed., *Superterrorism: Policy Responses* (Oxford: Blackwell, 2002); Brian Jenkins, *Terrorism: Current and Long-Term Threats* (Santa Monica, CA: Rand, 2001).

2. Andrew McGregor, "Jihad and the Rifle Alone: 'Abdullah' Azzam and the Islamist Revolution," *Journal of Conflict Studies* 23, no. 2 (fall 2003): 92; Brian Jenkins, Quest for Peace Interview, University of California Irvine, 1988, www.lib.uci.edu/quest/index.php?page=jenkins.

3. For a comprehensive European critique of this quintessentially American notion, see Gilles Andréani, "The 'War on Terror': Good Cause; Wrong Concept," *Survival* 46, no. 4 (winter 2004–2005): 31–50.

4. Bush's speech was accessed at www.whitehouse.gov/news/releases/2001/09/2001 0920–8.html.

5. Michael Howard, "What's in a Name? How to Fight Terrorism," *Foreign Affairs* 81, no. 1 (Jan.–Feb. 2002): 8; Andréani, "The 'War on Terror,'" 31.

6. This war psychosis is aptly epitomized by the remark attributed to Radek Sikorski of the American Enterprise Institute: "Baghdad is for wimps. Real men go to Tehran" (quoted in Steven Everts, "Engaging Iran: A Text Case for EU Foreign Policy," CER working paper, Mar. 2004).

7. National Intelligence Council, *Mapping the Global Future: Report of the National Intelligence Council's 2020 Project* (Washington, DC: CIA, 2005), 93–95, www.foia.cia.gov/2020/2020.pdf. For a European view of this report, see Philip Stephens, "An American Map of the Future Bush Cannot Ignore," *Financial Times,* Jan. 21, 2005. See also Anthony H. Cordesman, *Iraq's Evolving Insurgency and the Risk of Civil War* (Washington, DC: CSIS, 2006) (327 pages), accessed at www.csis.org/index.php?option=com_csis_pubs&task=view&id=3304.

8. Toward the end of his presidential election campaign John Kerry repeatedly made the point about some Americans agreeing with the European view. On the distraction from the "real" fight, see Harald Muller, *Terrorism, Proliferation: A European Threat Assessment*, Chaillot Paper 58 (Paris: EU-ISS, 2003); Philip H. Gordon and Jeremy Shapiro, *Allies at War: America, Europe, and the Crisis over Iraq* (Washington, DC: Brookings, 2004).

9. In some versions, the new "brand" name was G-SAVE (G being for Global, rather than for God). See Eric Schmitt and Thom Shanker, "New Name for 'War on Terror' Reflects Wider U.S. Campaign," *New York Times,* July 26, 2005; Fred Kaplan, "Say G-WOT?" *Slate,* July 26, 2005.

10. In fact, this message was made clear in United States, Office of the President, *National Strategy for Combating Terrorism,* issued in February 2003, as early as page 1: "The struggle against international terrorism is different from any other war in our history. We will not triumph solely or even primarily through military might" (accessed at www.whitehouse.gov/news/releases/2003/02/20030214–7.html).

11. Robert Fox, "GWOT Is History: Now for SAVE," *New Statesman,* Aug. 8, 2005.

12. Anne Applebaum, "Think Again, Karen Hughes," *Washington Post,* July 27, 2005.

13. Council of the European Union, "Conclusions and Plan of Action of the Extraordinary European Council Meeting on 21 September 2001," www.consilium.europa.eu/ueDocs/cms_Data/docs/pressdata/en/ec/140.en.pdf.

14. Gijs de Vries, address to the Counter-Terrorism Committee, New York, June 23, 2005, http://ue.eu.int/uedocs/cmsUpload/06_23_final_1373.pdf.

15. Ibid. It is noteworthy that the very first item on the EU's 150-point Action Plan involves "support for the key role of the UN" in counter-terrorism.

16. There is only one explicit mention of the UN in the U.S. *National Strategy* document (p. 11), although there is frequent reference to UNSC 1373 (Sept. 28, 2001) on international cooperation against terrorism.

17. U.S., Office of the President, *National Strategy for Combating Terrorism*, 6, 22.

18. EU, *Declaration on Combating Terrorism*, Mar. 2004, accessed at http://ue.eu.int/uedocs/cmsUpload/79635.pdf. Objective 6: "to address the factors which contribute to support for, and recruitment into terrorism." It is noteworthy that, in the combined U.S.-EU *Declaration* of June 2004, key issues mentioned in the EU document ("the links between extreme religious or political beliefs, as well as socio-economic and other factors, and support for terrorism") were dropped, to be replaced by objectives such as the promotion of "democracy, increased trade and freedom" (www.consilium.europa.eu/uedocs/cmsUpload/10760EU_US26.06.04.pdf).

19. Center for Strategic and International Studies, *The Transatlantic Dialogue on Terrorism: Initial Findings* (Washington, DC, Aug. 2004), 10. This report highlights the points of agreement and disagreement between the United States and the EU over the struggle against terrorism.

20. Moreover, it should be noted that in most lists of issues to be addressed, it usually figures close to the bottom (sixth out of the EU's seven objectives).

21. See "European Union Factsheet: The EU and the Fight against Terrorism" (update Feb. 2005), http://ue.eu.int/uedocs/cmsUpload/europa.pdf; European Council, *A Secure Europe in a Better World: European Security Strategy*, http://ue.eu.int/uedocs/cmsUpload/78367.pdf.

22. Solana report accessed via www.statewatch.org/news/2004/mar/10eu-intel-centre.htm. As late as March 2004, five EU countries had failed to adopt the EU-wide arrest warrant, three countries had failed to approve the common definition of terrorism, and only nine countries had adopted the framework decision on joint investigation teams.

23. The seven strategic objectives are (1) to deepen the international consensus and enhance international efforts to combat terrorism; (2) to reduce the access of terrorists to financial and other economic resources; (3) to maximize capacity within the EU bodies and member states to detect, investigate, and prosecute terrorists and prevent terrorist attacks; (4) to protect the security of international transport and ensure effective systems of border control; (5) to enhance the capability of the EU and of member states to deal with the consequences of a terrorist attack; (6) to address the factors that contribute to support for, and recruitment into, terrorism; and (7) to target actions under EU external relations toward priority third countries where counter-terrorist capacity or commitment to combating terrorism needs to be enhanced (accessed at http://ue.eu.int/uedocs/cmsUpload/79635.pdf).

24. Action Plan: http://ue.eu.int/uedocs/cmsUpload/web097781.en.pdf.

25. www.consilium.europa.eu/uedocs/cmsUpload/EU_4.5_11.pdf.

26. The six tasks were to: coordinate operational cooperation; train national border guards; do risk analyses; develop research; assist member states with technical and operational facilities; and organize joint return operations (http://europa.eu.int/scadplus/leg/en/lvb/l33216.htm).

27. *EU-U.S. Declaration on Combating Terrorism,* http://ue.eu.int/uedocs/cmsU
pload/10760EU_US26.06.04.pdf.

28. There is a special clause (article 13) on capital punishment, making it clear that
the EU will not extradite an offender if he or she would be subjected to the death penalty.

29. "Blair Bashing," *Economist,* Nov. 12, 2005, 13; "After the Defeat," *Economist,*
Nov. 12, 2005, 59–60.

30. "Growing European Rejection of Bush's Phony 'Terrorist' Rules: EU Court
Scraps Passenger Data Transfers to US," TBR News, May 30, 2006, www.tbrnews.org/
Archives/a2368.htm.

31. Council of Europe, Parliamentary Assembly, *Alleged Secret Detentions and Unlawful Inter-State Transfers Involving Council of Europe Member States,* June 7, 2006, accessed at www.washingtonpost.com/wp-srv/world/specials/coerenditionreport.pdf.

32. Daniel Keohane, *The EU and Counter-Terrorism* (London: Centre for European
Reform, 2005), 3. For a shorter version of these same arguments, see International Institute for Strategic Studies, "The EU's Role in Counter-Terrorism: Coordination and Action," *Strategic Comments* 11, no. 2 (Mar. 2005).

33. Jonathan Stevenson, *Counter-Terrorism: Containment and Beyond,* Adelphi Paper
367 (Oxford: Oxford University Press, 2004), 53.

34. The limits to the real powers of the High Representative for the Common Foreign and Security Policy (HR-CFSP), Javier Solana, constitute another interesting case.

35. House of Lords (UK), European Union Committee, "After Madrid: the EU's
Response to Terrorism," Mar. 2005, www.publications.parliament.uk/pa/ld200405/ldse
lect/ldeucom/53/53.pdf; Daniel Keohane and Adam Townsend, "A Joined-Up EU Security Policy," *CER Bulletin* (Dec. 2003–Jan. 2004).

36. For civil and human rights organizations, see, e.g., www.cybertime.net/~ajgood/
places.html.

37. Valsamis Mitsilegas, Jorg Monar, and Wyn Rees, *The EU and Internal Security*
(New York: Palgrave Macmillan, 2003); see also Wyn Rees, "The External Face of Inter-
nal Security," in *International Relations of the European Union,* ed. Christopher Hill and
Michael Smith, 4th ed. (Oxford: Oxford University Press, 2005).

38. Didier Bigo and Elspeth Guild, eds., *Controlling Frontiers: Free Movement into
and within Europe* (Burlington, VT: Ashgate, 2005); Didier Bigo, *Les nouveaux enjeux de
l'(in)sécurité en Europe: terrorisme, guerre, sécurité intérieure, sécurité extérieure* (Paris:
L'Harmattan, 2005).

39. Philippe Errera, "Three Circles of Threat," *Survival* 47, no. 1 (spring 2005);
Bob Woodward, *State of Denial* (New York: Simon & Schuster, 2006).

40. Sandra Lavenex and Emek M. Uçarer, "The External Dimension of Europeanization: The Case of Immigration Policies," *Cooperation and Conflict* 39, no. 4
(2004).

41. Errera, "Three Circles of Threat," 85.

42. Martha Crenshaw, "The Transatlantic Campaign against Terrorism," speech
delivered to NATO Conference, "New Tasks and Responsibilities," July 11, 2005,
www.nato.int/docu/speech/2005/s050711h.htm.

43. Condoleezza Rice, Opening remarks to the National Commission on Terrorist
Attacks upon the United States, Apr. 8, 2004, http://whitehouse.gov/news/releases/
2004/04/20040408.html.

44. See Jolyon Howorth et al., "L'impact sur les organisations de défense du concept de 'Coalition de Circonstance'" (Paris: IFRI/DAS, 2004).

45. François Heisbourg, "A Work in Progress: The Bush Doctrine and Its Consequences," *Washington Quarterly* 26, no. 2 (spring 2003): 75–88; Lawrence Freedman, "Prevention, not Preemption," *Washington Quarterly* 26, no. 2 (spring 2003): 105–14; Jolyon Howorth, "The U.S. National Security Strategy: European Reactions," in *Security Strategy and the Transatlantic Alliance,* ed. Roland Dannreuther and John Peterson (London: Routledge, 2006), 30–44. A BBC poll conducted in January 2005 showed that as many as 80 to 90 percent of respondents in many European countries believed the Iraq war to have been a mistake.

46. Chris Patten, speech to the European Parliament, Sept. 15, 2004, accessed Aug. 23, 2007, http://europa.eu/rapid/pressReleasesAction.do?reference=SPEECH/04/399&format=HTML&aged=1&language=EN&guiLanguage=en. See also Chatham House Middle East Programme Report, *Iraq in Transition: Vortex or Catalyst?* (London: Royal Institute of International Affairs, 2004).

47. According to one source, "bin Laden . . . has been able to capitalize on the growing resentment of the Muslim diaspora, especially in Europe" (Center for Strategic and International Studies, *The Transatlantic Dialogue on Terrorism,* 6).

48. Simon Chesterman, "Bush, the United Nations, and Nation-Building," *Survival* 46, no. 1 (spring 2004): 101–16; Toby Dodge, "A Sovereign Iraq?" *Survival* 46, no. 3 (autumn 2004): 39–58.

49. At the Extraordinary Council Meeting of September 21, 2001, the EU stated that the effectiveness of the fight against terrorism would require "making the ESDP operational at the earliest opportunity." That a military component would be a necessary part of that campaign against terrorism was first made explicit in the Declaration on the Contribution of the CFSP, including the ESDP, to the Fight Against Terrorism, issued as Annex V to the Presidency Conclusions of the June 22, 2002, Seville European Council.

50. Adam Roberts, "Law and the Use of Force after Iraq," *Survival* 45, no. 2 (summer 2003): 31–56; Christopher Greenwood, "International Law and the 'War against Terrorism,'" *International Affairs* 78, no. 2 (Apr. 2002): 301–18.

51. Hence the statement by Gijs de Vries on his first visit to Washington in May 2004: "We must be careful to preserve and protect the rights and liberties, the principles and values terrorists are seeking to destroy" (CSIS speech, May 13, 2004, 2–3, www .consilium.europa.eu/uedocs/cms/Upload/CSIS_Washington.13_May_2004.pdf).

52. Monica Den Boer, *9/11 and the Europeanisation of Anti-Terrorism Policy: A Critical Assessment,* Notre Europe Policy Paper 6 (Paris: Notre Europe, 2003).

53. See, for example, "A Letter to America" written by French foreign minister Michel Barnier, *Wall Street Journal,* Nov. 8, 2004, and Thomas Ferenczi, "L'Union Européenne veut adresser un message positif," *Le Monde,* Jan. 21, 2005.

54. Bush speech at the Concert Noble, Brussels, Feb. 21, 2005, www .whitehouse.gov/news/releases/2005/02/20050221.html.

55. "Home-Grown Kamikazes" (editorial), *Le Monde,* July 15, 2005.

56. http://ue.eu.int/ueDocs/cms_Data/docs/pressData/en/jha/85703.pdf.

57. Michel Radu, "London 7/7 and Its Impact," *Watch on the West* (Philadelphia, Foreign Policy Research Institute), 6, no. 5 (July 26, 2005).

58. Consultation Paper on Exclusion or Deportation from the UK on Non-Conducive Grounds: Response from the Muslim Council of Britain, www.mcb.org.uk/

uploads/Response_2nddraft.pdf, accessed Aug. 23, 2007; "Tony Blair's Antiterrorism Package" (editorial), *New York Times,* Aug. 19, 2005.

59. Figure cited by David Leppard and Nick Fielding, "The Hate," *Sunday Times* (London), July 11, 2001.

60. "Intercommunal tension fuelled by tough intelligence and law enforcement efforts, and the implementation of more intrusive counter-terrorist legislation, could make radicals all the more inclined towards violence in the medium term" (International Institute for Strategic Studies, "Islamist Terrorism in London: Unsettling Implications," *Strategic Comments* 11, no. 5 [July 2005]).

61. "Blair Bashing," *Economist,* Nov. 12, 2005, 13; "After the Defeat," *Economist,* Nov. 12, 2005, 59–60.

62. In a major editorial in *Le Monde,* Jean-Marie Colombani offered ten fundamental lessons that he hoped would help Europeans learn to "live with terrorism" ("Vivre avec le Terrorisme," *Le Monde,* July 27, 2005).

63. Gijs de Vries, "The European Union and the Fight against Terrorism," Seminar of the CER, Brussels, Jan. 19, 2006.

64. International Institute for Strategic Studies (IISS), "Cooperative Intelligence: Renewed Momentum?" *Strategic Comments* 12, no. 4 (May 2006).

Chapter 6: Immigration Policy and Reactions to Terrorism after September 11

1. See Olivier Roy, *Globalized Islam: The Search for a New* Ummah (New York: Columbia University Press, 2006).

2. See Scott Shane and Adam Liptak, "Shifting Power to a President," *New York Times,* Sept. 30, 2006, and "Le Congrès 'légalise' le programme secret de la CIA," *Le Figaro,* Sept. 23–34, 2006.

3. Prior to 1974, states of emergency, in which the cabinet had power to issues orders, were declared under the Defense of the Realm Act of 1914 and its successor, the Emergency Powers Act, which was passed after the war. See Tony Bunyan, *The Political Police in Britain* (London: Quartet, 1977), 51–56.

4. United Kingdom, Home Office Report, review of the *Operation of the Prevention of Terrorism Acts,* chap. 12, Mar. 7, 2000, http://security.homeoffice.gov.uk/news_publi cations/publication_search/terrorism_act_2000..

5. United Kingdom, Home Office, *Report on the Operation in 2001 of the Terrorism Act 2000,* by Lord Carlile of Berriew QC (2002), annex I. This report is available for each year since 2002.

6. Ibid., annex F.

7. See United Kingdom, House of Lords, Joint Committee on Human Rights, "Anti-terrorism, Crime and Security Bill: Further Report" (2002), 37. For a summary of some of these criticisms, see Ronald Dworkin, "Political Freedom in Britain," Democratic Findings No. 1, Democratic Audit of the United Kingdom, Human Rights Centre, University of Essex, 1996.

8. Of course, this was only possible because of the legislation in 1998 that integrated the ECHR into British law.

9. The fix was tentative, since a backbench revolt and resistance by the House of Lords forced the government to accept a sunset clause by which the law could have expired within a few months. However, according to the Home Office, "to date the Government has not sought to make a control order requiring derogation from Article 5 of

the European Convention on Human Rights" ("The Facts about Control Orders," United Kingdom Home Office, www.homeoffice.gov.uk/security/terrorism-and-the-law/prevention-of-terrorism/).

10. Dirk Haubrich, "September 11, Anti-Terror Laws, and Civil Liberties: Britain, France and Germany Compared," *Government and Opposition* 38, no. 1 (Jan. 2003): 19. Other comparisons (cited in *Le Nouvel Observateur,* Jan. 21, 2002) yield roughly the same result, while placing the United States first on the list. It should be noted that these comparisons are based on new legislation after September 11 and therefore do not seriously consider the question of change.

11. Jeremy Shapiro and Bénédicte Suzan, "The French Experience of Counter-Terrorism," *Survival* 45, no. 1 (spring 2003): 69.

12. The attacks in 1986 were organized by groups close to Iran, probably on the instigation of the Iranian government, which was demanding that France fulfill its commitment (made to the deposed shah) to provide it with technology for the development of atomic energy. At the same time, France was also giving material support to Iraq. See the article by Laurent Greilsamer, "La logique de l'improvisation du Hezbollah," *Le Monde,* Jan. 30, 1990.

13. Henri Astier, "Profile: France's Top Anti-terror Judge," BBC News on Line, Jan. 7, 2003, http://news.bbc.co.uk.

14. Shapiro and Suzan, "The French Experience of Counter-Terrorism," 80–82.

15. Bruguière, around whom the press has constructed a considerable legend, indicated that he was considering resigning to run for the National Assembly in the 2007 elections. See *Le Monde,* Dec. 6, 2006.

16. *Sunday Express* (London), July 17, 2005.

17. Olivier Roy, "Euro-Muslims in Context," *NYU Review of Law and Security,* summer 2005, 20.

18. See Sophie Body-Gendrot and Catherine Wenden, *Police et discriminations raciales: le tabou français* (Paris: Éditions de l'atelier, 2003); Didier Bigo, "Reassuring and Protecting: Internal Security Implications of French Participation in the Coalition against Terrorism," in *Critical Views of September 11,* ed. Eric Hershberg and Kevin Moore (New York: New Press, 2002).

19. *Le Monde,* July 9, 2005, 6.

20. *Final Report of the National Commission on Terrorist Attacks upon the United States* (New York: Norton, 2004), 77, 81.

21. Ibid., 80.

22. See ibid., chap. 3.

23. The best critical account of the PATRIOT Act is Stephen J. Schulhofer, *Rethinking the Patriot Act: Keeping America Safe and Free* (New York: Century Foundation Press, 2005).

24. See presentation by Sophie Body-Gendrot, "The USA Patriot Act and the Threat to Civil Liberties," Center for European Studies, New York University, Apr. 12, 2004.

25. Karen Greenberg, "The Courts and the War on Terror," NYU Center on Law and Security, Apr. 2005.

26. NYU Center on Law and Security, "Terrorist Trials: A Report Card," Feb. 2005.

27. Schulhofer, *Rethinking the Patriot Act,* 3.

28. Hamdi gave up his American citizenship and was deported to Saudi Arabia in

September 2004, after the U.S. Supreme Court remanded his case in June (124 S Ct. 2633 2004). The Padilla case is more complicated. In November 2005, the U.S. attorney general decided to charge him, apparently to avoid another reversal by the Supreme Court. The indictment, that he "conspired to murder, kidnap and maim people overseas," had little to do with the original charges made by the administration—an alleged plot to use a dirty bomb in the United States and that he engaged in terrorist activity. Padilla's lawyers resisted his transfer to civilian prison, as well as the new charges and instead pursued a case before the Supreme Court that questioned his initial and continuing imprisonment in a military brig without being charged. In April 2006, a divided Supreme Court refused to hear the case. Padilla is now in civilian prison awaiting trial on the new charges.

29. Schulhofer, *Rethinking the Patriot Act,* 5.

30. *New York Times,* June 17, 2005.

31. This statement was in answer to a question that I posed in a public discussion about the legal bases of American actions during the post-9/11 period.

32. See *USA Today,* May 1, May 10, 2006.

33. *Washington Post,* June 30, 2006.

34. See *New York Times,* Sept. 30, Oct. 18, 2006.

35. *ACLU vs. NSA* (06 CV 10204).

36. Quoted in *New York Times,* Jan. 18, 2007.

37. See Andrew Geddes, *The Politics of Migration and Immigration in Europe* (London: Sage, 2002), 43.

38. "Why the British Government's Plan for Controlling Immigration Is a Bad Idea," *Economist,* Feb. 10, 2005.

39. *Le Monde,* July 7, July 27, 2005.

40. *Le Monde,* Jan. 14, Jan. 20, Feb. 24, 2005.

41. The most comprehensive proposal has been made in the Senate by Senators John McCain and Edward Kennedy: *The Secure America and Orderly Immigration Act of 2005.* See *New York Times,* Feb. 11, 2005.

42. See *USA Today,* Apr. 3, 2006; *Washington Post,* May 15, 2006.

43. Eurobarometer 62 (2004): 6 and Q33 in annex.

44. "A New, Improved Race Card," *Economist,* Apr. 7, 2005.

Chapter 7: Migration and Security

1. For example, see Wayne Cornelius, Philip Martin, and James Hollifield, eds., *Controlling Immigration: A Global Perspective* (Stanford, CA: Stanford University Press, 1994); Christian Joppke, "Why Liberal States Accept Unwanted Immigration," *World Politics* 50 (1998): 266–93; and Gary Freeman, "Client Politics or Populism? Immigration Reform in the United States," in *Controlling a New Migration World,* ed. Virginie Guiraudon and Christian Joppke (London and New York: Routledge, 2001), 65–95.

2. Barry Buzan, Ole Wæver, and Jaap de Wilde, *Security: A New Framework for Analysis* (Boulder, CO, and London: Lynne Rienner, 1998), 32–33.

3. For example, see Erich Goode and Nachman Ben-Yehuda, "Moral Panics: Culture, Politics, and Social Construction," *Annual Review of Sociology* 20 (1994): 149–71; and Gary W. Potter and Victor E. Kappeler, *Constructing Crime: Perspectives on Making News and Social Problems* (Prospect Heights, IL: Waveland Press, 1998). For a discussion of "strategic social construction," see Margaret Finnemore and Kathryn Sikkink, "Inter-

national Norm Dynamics and Political Change," *International Organization* 52 (1998): 887–917.

4. The literature here is extensive and includes Keith Fitzgerald, *The Face of the Nation: Immigration, the State, and National Identity* (Stanford, CA: Stanford University Press, 1996); Michael Welch, *Detained: Immigration Laws and the Expanding I.N.S. Jail Complex* (Philadelphia: Temple University Press, 2002); and Kevin R. Johnson, *The "Huddled Masses" Myth: Immigration and Civil Rights* (Philadelphia: Temple University Press, 2004).

5. Wayne Cornelius, Philip Martin, and James Hollifield, "Introduction: The Ambivalent Quest for Immigration Control," in *Controlling Immigration: A Global Perspective,* ed. Wayne Cornelius, Philip Martin, and James Hollifield (Stanford, CA: Stanford University Press, 1994), 8–10. See also James Hollifield, "The Politics of International Migration: How Can We 'Bring the State Back In'?" in *Migration Theory: Talking Across the Disciplines,* ed. Caroline Brettel and James Hollifield (London: Routledge, 2000), 148–49.

6. Gary P. Freeman, "The Decline of Sovereignty? Politics and Immigration Restriction in Liberal States," in *Challenge to the Nation-State: Immigration in Western Europe and the United States,* ed. Christian Joppke (Oxford: Oxford University Press, 1998), 86–108.

7. Christian Joppke, "Asylum and State Sovereignty: A Comparison of the United States, Germany, and Britain," *Comparative Political Studies* 30, no. 3 (June 1997): 261–62; Joppke, "Why Liberal States Accept Unwanted Immigration," 268–71.

8. Hollifield, "The Politics of International Migration," 150–51.

9. Freeman, "Client Politics or Populism?" 65–95.

10. Virginie Guiraudon and Christian Joppke, "Controlling a New Migration World," in *Controlling a New Migration World,* ed. Virginie Guiraudon and Christian Joppke (London and New York: Routledge, 2001), 12–13. See also Peter Andreas, *Policing the U.S.-Mexico Divide* (Ithaca, NY, and London: Cornell University Press, 2000).

11. For example, see James G. Gimpel and James R. Edwards Jr., *The Congressional Politics of Immigration Reform* (Boston and London: Allyn Bacon, 1999); Freeman, "Client Politics or Populism?" 69; Welch, *Detained;* Nora V. Demleitner, "A Vicious Cycle: Resanctioning Offenders," in *Civil Penalties, Social Consequences,* ed. Christopher Mele and Teresa A. Miller (New York and London: Routledge, 2005), 185–201; and Teresa A. Miller, "By Any Means Necessary: Collateral Civil Penalties of Non-U.S. Citizens and the War on Terror," in *Civil Penalties, Social Consequences,* ed. Christopher Mele and Teresa A. Miller (New York and London: Routledge, 2005), 52–53.

12. For example, see Elaine Shannon, *Desperados* (New York: Signet, 1991), 420–29; and Diana R. Gordon, *The Return of the Dangerous Classes: Drug Prohibition and Policy Politics* (New York: Norton, 1994).

13. See *Anti-Drug Abuse Act of 1988,* Pub. L. 100-690; and information regarding House Resolution 3529 and Senate Resolution 972, http://thomas.loc.gov/cgi-bin/bdquery/z?d100:HR03529:l/bss/100search.html/, accessed Aug. 24, 2007, and http://thomas.loc.gov/cgi-bin/bdquery/z?d100:SN00972:l/bss/100search.html/, accessed Aug. 24, 2007.

14. *Anti-Drug Abuse Act of 1988,* Pub. L. 100-690. The ADAA further required the Immigration and Naturalization Service "to begin and, to the extent possible, complete deportation proceedings for aggravated felons before their release from prison." See Nor-

man Rabkin, "Criminal Aliens: INS Efforts to Identify and Remove Imprisoned Aliens Need to Be Improved," testimony before the Immigration and Claims Subcommittee, Committee on the Judiciary, House of Representatives, July 15, 1997, 4.

15. For example, see Susan Martin, "The Politics of U.S. Immigration Reform," *Political Quarterly* 74 (Aug. 2003): 132–49; Michael John Garcia and Larry M. Eig, *Immigration Consequences of Criminal Activity,* CRS Report for Congress (Washington, DC: Congressional Research Service, July 6, 2005); Miller, "By Any Means Necessary," 53.

16. Juan P. Osuna, "The 1996 Immigration Act: Criminal Aliens and Terrorists," *Interpreter Releases: Report and Analysis of Immigration and Nationality Law* 73, no. 47 (Dec. 16, 1996): 1714; Miller, "By Any Means Necessary," 54.

17. Miller, "By Any Means Necessary," 54.

18. Ibid.

19. Osuna, "The 1996 Immigration Act," 1714–15 (quote); Welch, *Detained,* 3; Melissa Cook, "Banished for Minor Crimes: The Aggravated Felony Provision of the Immigration and Nationality Acts as a Human Rights Violation," *Boston College Third World Law Journal* 23, no. 2 (2003): 307–309; Miller, "By Any Means Necessary," 54–55.

20. See *Immigration Act of 1990,* Pub. L. 101-649, Title VI (Exclusion and Deportation). Proposals influencing these shifts include the *Terrorist Alien Removal Act of 1989* (H.R. 1451H) and comparable language found in S. 953 (A Bill to amend the Immigration and Nationality Act to revise the grounds for exclusion from admission into the United States, 1989).

21. See Title IV, section 401 (Terrorist and Criminal Alien Exclusion and Removal: Alien Terrorist Removal), Pub. L. 104-132. The criteria for designation are a "foreign organization" that "engages in terrorist activity" (as defined in the INA) and "threatens the security of U.S. nationals or the national security of the United States" (Osuna, "The 1996 Immigration Act," 1720).

22. Osuna, "The 1996 Immigration Act," 1721.

23. William McCollum, statements on the "Criminal Alien Deportation Improvements Act of 1995," *Congressional Record,* House, Friday, Feb. 10, 1995, 104th Cong., 1st sess., 141 *Cong Rec* H 1586, vol. 141, no. 27.

24. Lamar Smith, statements on the "Criminal Alien Deportation Improvements Act of 1995," *Congressional Record–Extension of Remarks,* Monday, Feb. 13, 1995, 104th Cong., 1st sess., 141 *Cong Rec* E 330, vol. 141, no. 28.

25. H.R. 668, *Criminal Alien Deportation Improvements Act,* Bill and Summary Status for the 104th Congress.

26. Gimpel and Edwards, *The Congressional Politics of Immigration Reform,* 238. For example, see S. 2480, 103rd Cong., 2nd sess., 1994, "To amend the Immigration and Nationality Act to add provisions relating to the treatment of criminal aliens under the immigration laws of the United States, and for other purposes."

27. Gimpel and Edwards, *The Congressional Politics of Immigration Reform,* 245–47; Martin, "The Politics of U.S. Immigration Reform," 143 (quote).

28. Spencer Abraham, statements on the "Immigration Control and Financial Responsibility Act of 1996," *Congressional Record–Senate,* Thursday, May 2, 1996, 104th Cong., 2nd sess., 142 *Cong Rec* S 4592, vol. 142, no. 59.

29. Ibid.; William Roth, statements on the "Immigration Control and Financial Responsibility Act of 1996," *Congressional Record–Senate,* Thursday, May 2, 1996, 104th

Cong., 2nd sess., 142 *Cong Rec* S 4592, vol. 142, no. 59.

30. Rabkin, "Criminal Aliens," 4 (quotes); Miller, "By Any Means Necessary," 54.

31. Cook, "Banished for Minor Crimes," 301–302, 312.

32. Osuna, "The 1996 Immigration Act," 1721–22; Cook, "Banished for Minor Crimes," 310n.163.

33. Cook, "Banished for Minor Crimes," 312n.186.

34. Drug offenders comprised the primary group in federal prisons. More than two-thirds of noncitizens under incarceration were in state and private facilities (U.S. Department of Justice, Bureau of Justice Statistics, *Census of State and Federal Correctional Facilities, 1995*, Aug. 1997, v; and U.S. Department of Justice, Bureau of Justice Statistics, *Census of State and Federal Correctional Facilities, 2000*, revised Oct. 15, 2003, 8.

35. Alison Siskin, *Immigration-Related Detention: Current Legislative Issues*, CRS Report for Congress (Washington, DC: Congressional Research Service, Apr. 28, 2004), 12; Alison Siskin et al., *Immigration Enforcement within the United States*, CRS Report for Congress (Washington, DC: Congressional Research Service, Apr. 6, 2006), 23.

36. Miller, "By Any Means Necessary," 55–56; U.S. Department of Homeland Security, *Yearbook of Immigration Statistics 2004* (Washington, DC: U.S. Department of Homeland Security, Office of Immigration Statistics, 2006), table 43 (Aliens Removed by Criminal Status and Region and Country of Nationality, 1998–2004); Siskin et al., "Immigration Enforcement within the United States," 16. These figures do not include voluntary departures.

37. David Firestone and Christopher Drew, "Al Qada Link Seen in Only a Handful of 1,200 Detainees," *New York Times*, Nov. 29, 2001; David Cole, *Enemy Aliens: Double Standards and Constitutional Freedoms in the War on Terrorism* (New York and London: Free Press, 2003), 22–50; "DHS-ICE Sanctions, Registration," *Migration News*11, no. 1 (Jan. 2004), http://migration.ucdavis.edu/mn/more.php?id=2968_0_2_0_c/, accessed Aug. 24, 2007; and Miller, "By Any Means Necessary," 59–60.

38. U.S. Department of Justice, "Anti-Terrorism Act of 2001: Section by Section Analysis," Sept. 19, 2001; Cole, *Enemy Aliens*, 61–76; and *USA PATRIOT Act*, Title IV (B) (411), Pub. L. 10756, 115 *Stat.* 272, codified at *INA* § 212(a)(3)B).

39. U.S. Department of Justice, "Anti-Terrorism Act of 2001," 8; United States, Congress, House Judiciary Committee, "Majority Staff Description of the Latest Version of the Patriot Act," Oct. 12, 2001, 4, www.cdt.org/security/011012patriot info.pdf.

40. The attorney general was empowered to detain without arrest for up to seven days, after which the attorney general must release the alien or certify, by "demonstrating reasonable ground to believe," that the alien meets the definition of terrorist activity or is engaged in "any other activity that endangers the national security of the United States." If the alien is so certified, he or she must be charged with a criminal offense or placed in removal proceedings. However, if "removal is unlikely in the foreseeable future" and the alien's release is deemed a threat to the "national security of the United States or the safety of the community or any person," the alien can be detained for a period of up to six months and, following review of the certification, re-detained (U.S. Department of Justice, "Anti-Terrorism Act of 2001," 9; U.S. Congress, House Judiciary Committee, "Majority Staff Description," 4; *USA PATRIOT Act*, Title IV [B] [412]).

41. U.S. Department of Justice, "Anti-Terrorism Act of 2001," 9; U.S. Congress, House Judiciary Committee, "Majority Staff Description," 4; *USA PATRIOT Act*, Title IV (B) (412).

42. For example see Mary Beth Sheridan, "Immigration Law as Anti-Terrorism Tool," *Washington Post,* June 13, 2005.

43. Miller, "By Any Means Necessary," 47; Siskin et al., *Immigration Enforcement within the United States.*

44. Of those apprehended, 27,497 were released "due to lack of detention bed space or for some other reason" (U.S. Department of Homeland Security, Office of Inspector General, *Detention and Removal of Illegal Aliens: U.S. Immigration and Customs Enforcement* [Washington, DC: DHS Office of Audits, Apr. 2006], 7).

45. U.S. Department of Homeland Security, *Yearbook of Immigration Statistics 2004,* table 43; Siskin et al., *Immigration Enforcement within the United States,* 15–16, 23.

46. U.S. Department of Homeland Security, Office of Inspector General, *Detention and Removal of Illegal Aliens,* 9–10.

47. Rosemary Jenks, "The USA Patriot Act of 2001," Center for Immigration Studies, Dec. 2001, www.cis.org/articles/2001/back1501.html; Miller, "By Any Means Necessary," 47.

48. Miller, "By Any Means Necessary," 59.

49. Christopher Mele and Teresa A. Miller, "Collateral Civil Penalties as Techniques of Social Policy," in *Civil Penalties, Social Consequences,* ed. Christopher Mele and Teresa A. Miller (New York and London: Routledge, 2005), 20.

50. Miller, "By Any Means Necessary," 48–49; U.S. Department of Homeland Security, "Department of Homeland Security Launches Operation 'Ice Storm'" (DHS press release), Nov. 10, 2003, www.dhs.gov/dhspublic/display?content=3008.

51. Dan Eggan and Julie Tate, "U.S. Campaign Produces few Convictions on Terrorism Charges," *Washington Post,* June 12, 2005.

52. James Sensenbrenner, "Real ID Legislation Introduced in the House" (press release), Jan. 2005, www.house.gov/sensenbrenner/wc20050127.html.

53. Michael John Garcia, Margaret Mikyung Lee, and Todd Tatelman, *Immigration: Analysis of the Major Provisions of H.R. 418, the REAL ID Act of 2005,* CRS Report for Congress (Washington, DC: Congressional Research Service, Feb. 2, 2005).

54. Michael John Garcia, *Criminalizing Unlawful Presence: Selected Issues,* CRS Report for Congress (Washington, DC: Congressional Research Service, May 3, 2006), 1–3; Federation for American Immigration Reform, "Comparison of H.R. 4437 and S. 2611," July 3, 2006, 4, www.fairus.org/site/DocServer/amnesty_bill_condensed.pdf?docID=1061.

55. See H.R. 4437, *Border Protection, Antiterrorism and Illegal Immigration Control Act,* http://frwebgate.access.gpo.gov/cgi-bin/getdoc.cgi?dbname=109_cong_bills&docid=f:h4437eh.txt.pdf; S. 2454, *Securing America's Borders Act,* www.nilc.org/immlawpolicy/CIR/saba_frist_2006-3-16.pdf; and S. 2611, *Comprehensive Immigration Reform Act,* http://frwebgate.access.gpo.gov/cgi-bin/getdoc.cgi?dbname=109_cong_bills&docid=f:s2611es.txt.pdf.

56. H.R. 4437, *Border Protection, Antiterrorism and Illegal Immigration Control Act;* American Immigration Lawyers Association, "The Border Protection, Antiterrorism and Illegal Immigration Control Act of 2005 (H.R. 4437), as Amended and Passed by the House on 12/16/05: Section-by-Section Analysis," http://policycouncil.nationaljournal.com/NR/rdonlyres/8B648050-C027–4E13-BB8D-9C9498F8CBF1/35796/The borderprotection.pdf.

57. Lamar Smith, statements on "How Illegal Immigration Impacts Constituencies: Perspectives from Members of Congress (Part I)," Hearing before the Subcommittee on

Immigration, Border Security, and Claims of the Committee on the Judiciary, House of Representatives, 109th Cong., 1st sess., Nov. 10, 2005 (Washington, DC; GPO, 2006), 30, http://judiciary.house.gov/media/pdfs/printers/109th/24507.pdf.

58. John N. Hostettler, statements on "How Illegal Immigration Impacts Constituencies: Perspectives from Members of Congress (Part I)," Hearing before the Subcommittee on Immigration, Border Security, and Claims of the Committee on the Judiciary, House of Representatives, 109th Cong., 1st sess., Nov. 10, 2005 (Washington, DC; GPO, 2006), 1, http://judiciary.house.gov/media/pdfs/printers/109th/24507.pdf.

59. For example, see Gary Endelman, "After the Fall: Making Sense Out of Sensenbrenner," *Immigration Daily,* Jan. 4, 2006, www.ilw.com/articles/2006,0104-endelman.shtm.

60. For example see Numbers USA, "Immigration Profile of Rep. James Sensenbrenner," http://profiles.numbersusa.com/improfile.php3?DistSend=WI&VIPID=880. In contrast to the migration patterns facing Florida representatives in the 1980s, Wisconsin's migrant population was relatively low. Even in 2003 estimates of illegal migrants in the state were 64,000 compared to the estimated national total of 11 million. See Federation for American Immigration Reform, "Distribution of the Illegal Alien Population," June 2003, www.fairus.org.

61. U.S. Congress, House of Representatives, "Border Protection, Antiterrorism and Illegal Immigration Control Act of 2005, Report of the Committee on the Judiciary House of Representatives, to Accompany H.R. 4437, together with Additional and Dissenting Views," Dec. 13, 2005, 44, http://frwebgate.access.gpo.gov/cgibin/getdoc.cgi?dbname=109_cong_reports&docid=f:hr345p1.109.pdf.

62. Ibid., 45. These arguments had been raised in earlier hearings over illegal immigration; no hearings were held on the bill itself.

63. For example, see Freeman, "Client Politics or Populism?" 95; Welch, *Detained,* 177; Cook, "Banished for Minor Crimes," 310–11.

64. For example, see Cole, *Enemy Aliens,* 30–31; U.S. Department of Justice, Office of Inspector General, *The September 11 Detainees: A Review of the Treatment of Aliens Held on Immigration Charges in Connection with the Investigation of the September 11 Attacks,* June 2003, www.usdoj.gov/oig/special/0306/index.htm.

65. For example, see "Sensenbrenner Statement on Border Security and Immigration Reform" (news advisory), Mar. 27, 2006, http://judiciary.house.gov/media/pdfs/immcorrectingrecord32706.pdf.; and "Media Repeated GOP's False Claim That Democrats Are to Blame for Plan to Make Illegal Immigrants Felons," Media Matters for America, Apr. 17, 2006, http://mediamatters.org/items/200604170005.

66. Prioritization as an essential component of immigration control reform had long been recommended by critics of the Immigration and Naturalization Service. For example, see U.S. Commission on Immigration Reform, "U.S. Immigration Policy: Restoring Credibility: Executive Summary," 1994, www.utexas.edu/lbj/uscir/exesum94.html; and Susan Martin, "Politics and Policy Responses to Illegal Migration in the U.S.," Institute for the Study of International Migration, Georgetown University, Washington, DC, 1998.

67. For example, see National Immigration Forum, "Legislation: State and Local Police Enforcement of Immigration Laws," www.immigrationforum.org/DesktopDefault.aspx?tabid=737.

Chapter 8: The Security Myth

1. See, e.g., Kevin R. Johnson, *The "Huddled Masses" Myth: Immigration and Civil Rights* (Philadelphia: Temple University Press, 2004), 20–22, 62–69 (discussing the internment of Japanese and Japanese-Americans as a wrongheaded response to the Japanese attack on Pearl Harbor; the deportation of Eastern and Southern European immigrants in the wake of the Palmer Raids of 1919–1920; the exclusion and deportation of politically undesirable foreigners during the "Red Scare" of the 1950s); David Cole, *Enemy Aliens: Double Standards and Constitutional Freedoms in the War on Terrorism* (New York and London: Free Press, 2003), 85–179 (discussing the use of the Sedition Act to punish perceived "enemy aliens" in the United States during World War I and the deportations and internments in response to the Palmer Raids and Pearl Harbor).

2. See Cole, *Enemy Aliens,* 17–82; Johnson, *The "Huddled Masses" Myth,* 78–85; see also Victor C. Romero, *Alienated: Immigrant Rights, the Constitution, and Equality in America* (New York: New York University Press, 2005), 26–47.

3. See Jennifer M. Chacón, "Unsecured Borders: Immigration Restrictions, Crime Control and National Security," *Connecticut Law Review* 39 (July 2007): 1830–31, 1850–56.

4. For these and other recommendations, see Muzaffar A. Chishti et al., *America's Challenge: Domestic Security, Civil Liberties, and National Unity after September 11* (Washington, DC: Migration Policy Institute, 2003), 153–60.

5. Ibid., 147–50.

6. Bill Ong Hing, "Misusing Immigration Policies in the Name of Homeland Security," *New Centennial Review* 6, no. 1 (spring 2006): 195–224.

7. On security enhancement, see generally Hing, "Misusing Immigration Policies in the Name of Homeland Security"; see also Cole, *Enemy Aliens,* 184–97.

8. On the percentage of foreign-born citizens, see Thomas Alexander Aleinikoff, David A. Martin, and Hiroshi Motomura, *Immigration and Citizenship: Process and Policy,* 5th ed. (St. Paul, MN: Thomson/West, 2003), 266.

9. Gerald L. Neuman, *Strangers to the Constitution: Immigrants, Borders, and Fundamental Law* (Princeton, NJ: Princeton University Press, 1996), 137 (quote).

10. Stephen H. Legomsky, *Immigration and Refugee Law and Policy,* 4th ed. (New York: Foundation Press; St. Paul, MN: Thomson/West, 2005), 105 and n.3; compare Aristide Zolberg, *A Nation by Design: Immigration Policy in the Fashioning of America* (New York: Sage; Cambridge, MA: Harvard University Press, 2006), contending that throughout American history, immigration policy was a major instrument of American nation building; and Gerald L. Neuman, "The Lost Century of American Immigration Law (1776–1875)," *Columbia Law Review* 93, no. 8 (Dec. 1993): 1833–1901, discussing immigration restrictions imposed by state governments during this period.

11. An Act Concerning Aliens (*Alien Friends Act of 1798*), June 25, 1798, ch. 58, 1 Stat. 570; Charles Gordon, Stanley Mailman, and Stephen Yale-Loehr, *Immigration Law and Procedure* § 2.02[1] (Newark, NJ: Matthew Bender, 2004); 50 U.S.C.A. §§ 21–24 (2006); see Gregory Sidak, "War, Liberty, and Enemy Aliens," *NYU Law Review* 67, no. 6 (Dec. 1992): 1402.

12. Sidak, "War, Liberty, and Enemy Aliens," 1402.

13. For the Commerce Clause, U.S. Const., art. I, § 8, cl. 3 (granting Congress the power to "regulate commerce with foreign nations"); see, e.g., *Henderson v. Mayor of*

New York, 92 U.S. (2 Otto) 259 (1875), striking down, on Commerce Clause grounds, a state statute imposing a tax on arriving noncitizen passengers; the *Head Money Cases,* 112 U.S. 580 (1884), upholding the constitutionality of a federal statute regulating immigration. For the Migration or Importation Clause, U.S. Const., art. I, § 9, cl. 1 ("The Migration or Importation of such Persons as any of the States now existing shall think it proper to permit, shall not be prohibited by the Congress prior to the year one thousand eight hundred and eight"). In spite of early disagreement on the scope of the clause, see the *Passenger Cases,* 48 U.S. (7 How.) 283, 452–54, 474–78, 511, 540–41 (1849); the clause is now largely assumed to pertain only to the regulation of the slave trade (Legomsky, *Immigration and Refugee Law and Policy,* 106). For the Naturalization Clause, U.S. Const., art. I, § 8, cl. 4 (authorizing Congress "to establish an uniform Rule of Naturalization"). The provision does not expressly grant the power to regulate admission, but read in conjunction with the "necessary and proper" clause, U.S. Const., art. I, § 8, cl. 18, it might reasonably be read to afford the federal legislature such power. For the War Clause, U.S. Const., art. I, § 8, cl. 11 (granting Congress the power "[t]o declare War"). This provision has been interpreted to authorize Congress to regulate "alien enemies"—the nationals of countries with which the United States is at war—but not to extend further. See the *Passenger Cases,* 48 U.S. (7 How.) at 509–10 (Daniels dissenting).

14. "An Act to Regulation Immigration" (*Immigration Act of 1882*), Aug. 3, 1882, 22 Stat. ch. 376.

15. Ibid.; see also Gordon et al., *Immigration Law and Procedure* § 2.02[2].

16. See *Chae Chan Ping v. United States* (Chinese Exclusion Case), 130 U.S. 581, 589 (1889). The act was not repealed until 1943 (Gordon et al., *Immigration Law and Procedure,* § 2.02[2]).

17. *Chae Chan Ping v. United States* (Chinese Exclusion Case), 130 U.S. 609.

18. *Fong Yue Ting v. United States,* 149 U.S. 698 (1893).

19. Ibid., 732.

20. Ibid., 707.

21. Ibid., 711.

22. *Harisiades v. Shaughnessy,* 342 U.S. 580, 589 (1952).

23. See, e.g., Neuman, *Strangers to the Constitution;* Sarah H. Cleveland, "Powers Inherent in Sovereignty: Indians, Aliens, Territories, and the Nineteenth Century Origins of Plenary Power over Foreign Affairs," *Texas Law Review* 81, no. 1 (2002); Robert Pauw, "Plenary Power: An Outmoded Doctrine that Should Not Limit IIRIRA Reform," *Emory Law Journal* 51 (2002): 1095; Gabriel J. Chin, "Segregation's Last Stronghold: Race Discrimination and the Constitutional Law of Immigration," *UCLA Law Review* 46, no. 1 (1998): 12–16; Stephen H. Legomsky, "Immigration Law and the Principle of Plenary Congressional Power," *Supreme Court Review* (1984): 255, 258; Hiroshi Motomura, "Immigration Law After a Century of Plenary Power: Phantom Constitutional Norms and Statutory Interpretation," *Yale Law Journal* 100 (1990): 545; Louis Henkin, "The Constitution and United States Sovereignty: A Century of Chinese Exclusion and Its Progeny," *Harvard Law Review* 100 (1987): 853.

24. Daniel Kanstroom, "Deportation, Social Control, and Punishment: Some Thoughts about Why Hard Laws Make Bad Cases," *Harvard Law Review* 113 (2002): 1889, 1901–1902.

25. 149 U.S. 730 (1893).

26. Kanstroom, "Deportation, Social Control, and Punishment," 1901–1902.

27. *Wong Wing v. United States,* 163 U.S. 228 (1896).

28. Kanstroom, "Deportation, Social Control, and Punishment," 1901–1902; see also Robert Pauw, "A New Look at Deportation as Punishment: Why at Least Some of the Constitution's Criminal Procedure Protections Must Apply," *Administrative Law Review* 52 (2000): 305.

29. *Immigration Act of 1903,* ch. 1012, § 2, 32 Stat. 1213, 1214 (1903) (repealed by *Immigration Act of Feb. 5, 1917,* ch. 29, § 38, 39 Stat. 874, 897 [1917]).

30. Cole, *Enemy Aliens,* 107–109.

31. *Immigration Act of Feb. 5, 1917,* ch. 29, § 19, 39 Stat. 874 (1917). Illustrating the racist sentiments that fueled these laws was the literacy requirement designed to bar non-English-speaking immigrants and the creation of the "Asiatic Barred Zone," excluding all Asian immigrants aside from the Japanese, who were already barred by the so-called "gentlemen's agreement" between the Japanese and U.S. governments (*Immigration Act of Feb. 5, 1917,* ch. 29, § 38, 39 Stat. 874, 897 [1917]); see also Gordon et al., *Immigration Law and Procedure,* § 2.02[3].

32. *Anarchist Act of 1918* (*Immigration Act of Feb. 5, 1917*), ch. 29, § 19, 39 Stat. 874 (1917); see also Gordon et al., *Immigration Law and Procedure,* § 2.02[3].

33. See *Yamataya v. Fisher,* 189 U.S. 86 (1903), on requiring procedural due process in removal proceedings but finding that a proceeding conducted without a translator and in the absence of sufficient notice met the flexible standards of procedural due process required in removal proceedings; see also Kanstroom, "Deportation, Social Control, and Punishment," 780, explaining how the flexible procedural due process notion outlined in the *Yamataya* case provided a basis for later legislative evisceration of procedural protections in removal proceedings.

34. Following a rash of mail bombs aimed at prominent government officials and May Day riots and bomb explosions in several major cities in the spring of 1919, the Department of Justice, at the direction of J. Edgar Hoover, launched a series of raids aimed at deporting foreign nationals. Between 4,000 and 10,000 foreign nationals were arrested, mainly without warrants in a series of dragnet raids, even though there was no evidence as to who had perpetrated the criminal acts that prompted the raids. A total of 556 people were ultimately deported, again without evidence linking any of the deportees to the violent crimes that prompted the round-ups. See Cole, *Enemy Aliens,* 117–23; see also Kevin R. Johnson, "The Antiterrorism Act, the Immigration Reform Act, and Ideological Regulation in the Immigration Laws: Important Lessons for Citizens and Noncitizens," *St. Mary's Law Journal* 28 (1997): 833.

35. "Between 1892 and 1907 the Immigration Service deported only a few hundred aliens a year and between 1908 and 1920 an average of two or three thousand a year—mostly aliens removed from asylums, hospitals or jails" (Mae M. Ngai, *Impossible Subjects: Illegal Aliens and the Making of Modern America* [Princeton, NJ: Princeton University Press, 2004], 59–60).

36. Ibid., 59–60.

37. Act of Mar. 4, 1929, 45 Stat. 1551 (1929).

38. The term "alien" has been an entrenched feature of immigration law throughout its history in the United States. According to U.S. immigration law, "any person not a citizen or national of the United States" is an "alien" (8 U.S.C.A. § 1101[a][3] [2000]). The concept of the "alien" is thus "the nucleus around which the comprehensive immi-

gration law, the Immigration and Nationality Act, is built" (Kevin R. Johnson, "'Aliens' and the U.S. Immigration Laws: The Social and Legal Construction of the Nonperson," *University of Miami Inter-American Law Review* 28 [1997]: 263). In addition to the myriad legal consequences of being an "alien," in the United States the use of the term "alien" has come to be used in ways that reinforce and strengthen nativist sentiment toward members of new immigrant groups, which in turn influences U.S. responses to immigration and human rights issues. Gerald Neuman has observed that "[i]t is no coincidence that we still refer to noncitizens as 'aliens,' a term that calls attention to their 'otherness,' and even associates them with nonhuman invaders from outer space" (Gerald L. Neuman, "Aliens as Outlaws: Government Services, Proposition 187, and the Structure of Equal Protection," *UCLA Law Review* 42 [1995]: 1425, 1428 [footnote omitted]). Gerald Rosberg acknowledged that "[t]he very word, 'alien,' calls to mind someone strange and out of place, and it has often been used in a distinctly pejorative way" (Gerald M. Rosberg, "The Protection of Aliens from Discriminatory Treatment by the National Government," *Supreme Court Review* [1977]: 275, 303).

39. The International Organization for Migration (IOM) defines an irregular migrant as "someone who, owing to illegal entry or the expiry of his or her visa, lacks legal status in a transit or host country. The term refers to migrants who infringe a country's admission rules and any other person not authorized to remain in the host country" (International Organization for Migration, *International Glossary on Migration,* vol. 1 [Geneva: IOM, 2004], 34).

40. Joseph Nevins, *Operation Gatekeeper: The Rise of the "Illegal Alien" and the Making of the U.S.-Mexico Boundary* (New York: Routledge, 2002), 95; see also Anna Marie Gallagher, "The Situation of Undocumented Migrants in the United States," *Immigration Briefings* no. 5–6, (2005): 1. The Great Depression greatly slowed the rate of immigration into the United States, initially slowing the nation's preoccupation with irregular migration (Gallagher, "The Situation of Undocumented Migrants in the United States," 5). However, with the rise of anti-communist sentiments in the late 1930s came another wave of anti-immigrant measures. "By the middle of 1939, Congress had over 100 anti-immigration proposals under consideration" (Cole, *Enemy Aliens,* 130).

41. In the 1940s, labor shortages resulted in the creation of the *bracero* program, a labor contract system that brought more than 200,000 Mexican workers into the country in the 1940s. That program was extended in various forms until 1964, and more than 5 million Mexican workers entered the country during the twenty-two-year span of the program (Cole, *Enemy Aliens,* 130). This program helped to entrench the labor market mechanisms still in place today that draw Mexican workers north to the United States to perform agricultural labor.

42. Ngai, *Impossible Subjects,* 61.

43. Gallagher, "The Situation of Undocumented Migrants in the United States," 1.

44. See, e.g., Nina Bernstein, "Invisible to Most, Women Line Up for Day Labor," *New York Times,* Aug. 15, 2005, A1 ("nationally men account for about two-thirds of labor migration among illegal immigrants"); David Brooks, "Two Steps Toward a Sensible Immigration Policy," *New York Times,* Aug. 14, 2005 ("What do you say to the working-class guy from the south side of San Antonio? He feels his wages are stagnating because he has to compete against illegal immigrants").

45. See, e.g., Johnson, *The "Huddled Masses" Myth,* 43 (discussing the phenomenon in the context of California's debate over Proposition 187).

46. Ngai, *Impossible Subjects,* 59 ("Mexicans emerged as the iconic illegal aliens").

47. See chap. 7, by H. Richard Friman, in this volume.

48. *Antiterrorism and Effective Death Penalty Act of 1996* (AEDPA), Pub. L. No. 104-132, 110 Stat. 1214 (1996); *Illegal Immigration Reform and Immigrant Responsibility Act of 1996* (IIRIRA), Pub. L. No. 104-208, Div. C, 110 Stat. 3009–546 (codified as amended in scattered sections of 8 U.S.C. and 18 U.S.C.).

49. See generally Margaret H. Taylor, "The 1996 Immigration Act: Detention and Related Issues," *Interpreter Releases* 74, no. 5 (1997): 209. IIRIRA also stripped the term "deportation" of much of its legal significance. Prior to IIRIRA, those who had previously entered the United States were subject to deportation and were placed in deportation proceedings. Those who were seeking to enter the United States were subject to exclusion and placed in exclusion proceedings. After IIRIRA, both categories of individuals are subject to "removal" and are placed in "removal proceedings." Regarding the commission of crimes see, e.g., AEDPA § 441(e), 8 U.S.C. § 1101(a) (2000) (expanding the "aggravated felony" definition to include gambling, alien smuggling, and passport fraud); IIRIRA § 321, 8 U.S.C. § 1101(a)(43) (2000) (adding crimes and lowering the sentence requirement of removable violent crimes to one year). There are no statutes of limitations for many criminal offenses. See generally Dawn Marie Johnson, "The AEDPA and IIRIRA: Treating Misdemeanors as Felonies for Immigration Purposes," *Journal of Legislation* 27 (2001): 477.

50. See AEDPA § 441(e), 8 U.S.C. 1101(a) (2000); IIRIRA § 321(b), 8 U.S.C. § 1101(a) (2000); but compare *INS v. St. Cyr,* 533 U.S. 289 (2001) (limiting retroactivity to guilty verdicts and barring retroactive application of the removal provisions for convictions based on plea agreements).

51. Nancy Morawetz, "Understanding the Impact of the 1996 Deportation Laws and the Limited Scope of Proposed Reforms," *Harvard Law Review* 113 (2000): 1936, 1951; see also *United States v. Pacheco,* 225 F.3d 148 (2d Cir. 2000) (J. Straub dissenting).

52. 8 U.S.C.A. § 1101(a)(43)(A) (2000); 8 U.S.C.A. § 1101(a)(43)(F)&(G) (2000).

53. *Leocal v. Ashcroft,* 543 U.S. 1 (2004).

54. See, e.g., 8 U.S.C.A. § 1229b(a)(3) (2000) (barring cancellation of removal for aggravated felons).

55. TRAC Immigration, "How Often Is the Aggravated Felony Statute Used?" http://trac.syr.edu/immigration/reports/158/ (accessed July 22, 2006).

56. 8 U.S.C.A. § 1227(a)(2)(A)(ii) (2000). Historically, removal on the basis of a crime involving moral turpitude was subject to a five-year statute of limitations. See *Immigration Act of Feb. 5, 1917,* Pub. L. No. 64-301, ch. 29, § 19, 39 Stat. 874, 889–90 (repealed 1952).

57. 8 U.S.C.A. § 1229b(b)(1)(C) (2000).

58. See Kati L. Griffith, "Perfecting Public Immigration Legislation: Private Immigration Bills and Deportable Lawful Permanent Residents," *Georgetown Immigration Law Journal* 18 (2004): 273, 291.

59. 8 U.S.C.A. § 1227(a)(2)(B)(ii) (2000) ("Any alien who is, or at any time after admission has been, a drug abuser or addict is deportable").

60. 8 U.S.C.A. § 1227(a)(4)(B) (2000) (relating to the removal of aliens for terrorist activities); 8 U.S.C.A. § 1227(a)(3) (2000). By and large, these laws were ignored before September 11, 2001. However, on June 5, 2002, Attorney General John Ashcroft an-

nounced the National Security Entry-Exit Registration System (NSEERS), which required nearly all male nonimmigrants who were at least sixteen years of age and the nationals of certain designated countries to be fingerprinted and photographed upon entry; to report periodically to DHS for stays longer than thirty days; and to appear at one of several specified ports upon departure, so the departure could be recorded (8 C.R.R. § 264 [2006]).

61. 8 U.S.C.A. § 1227(a)(3)(C)&(D) (2000); 8 U.S.C.A. § 1227(a)(2)(B)(i) (2000). Furthermore, drug trafficking convictions constitute "aggravated felonies," with all the harsh consequences that the designation entails (8 U.S.C.A. § 1101 [a][43][B] [2000]).

62. See, e.g., 8 U.S.C. § 1252(a)(2)(C) (2005) (barring judicial review of any "removal order" if a noncitizen is removable on virtually any crime-related ground); 8 U.S.C. § 1252(a)(2)(B) (2005) (barring judicial review of discretionary decisions to grant certain relief from removal and other discretionary decisions of the attorney general); see also Stephen H. Legomsky, "Deportation and the War on Independence," *Cornell Law Review* 91 (2006): 369, 380–84 (discussing the significance of these jurisdiction-stripping provisions).

63. Julie K. Rannik, "Comment, 'The Anti-Terrorism and Effective Death Penalty Act of 1996': A Death Sentence for the 212(c) Waiver," *University of Miami Inter-American Law Review* 28 (1996): 123, 132n.52 (citing 142 *Cong. Rec.* S12,294–01, S12,295 [daily ed. Oct. 3, 1996] [statement of Senator Abraham]).

64. *Immigration and Nationality Act (INA) of 1952,* Pub. L. No. 82-414, § 212(c), 66 Stat. 181, 187 (codified at 8 U.S.C. § 1182(c) [repealed 1996]).

65. INA § 240A, 8 U.S.C. § 1229b (2000).

66. Rannik, "Comment, 'The Anti-Terrorism and Effective Death Penalty Act of 1996,'" 139 (quoting 142 *Cong. Rec.* H10,841- 02, H10,896 [daily ed. Sept. 24, 1996] [Joint Explanatory Statement of the Committee of Conference]).

67. INA § 240A, 8 U.S.C. §§ 1229a(a)(3); 1229a(b)(1)(C) (2000). There are also limitations on the availability of the waiver for noncitizens committing other crimes, such as crimes of moral turpitude. See note 56 above and accompanying text.

68. See Taylor, "The 1996 Immigration Act," 209; see also Margaret H. Taylor, "Dangerous by Decree: Detention without Bond in Immigration Proceedings," *Loyola Law Review* 50 (2004): 149 (discussing problematic post-9/11 reliance on mandatory detention provisions).

69. See generally Pauw, "A New Look at Deportation as Punishment."

70. *Uniting and Strengthening America by Providing Appropriate Tools Required to Intercept and Obstruct Terrorism Act of 2001* (USA PATRIOT Act), Pub. L. No. 107-56, 115 Stat. 272 (2001); *Homeland Security Act* (HSA), Pub. L. No. 107-296 §§ 442, 451; 6 U.S.C.A. §§ 252, 271 (2002); *Enhanced Border Security and Visa Entry Reform Act of 2002* (EBSVERA), Pub. L. No. 107-173, 116 Stat. 552, §§ 201–203, 8 U.S.C. §§ 1721-23 (2002); *Intelligence Reform and Terrorism Prevention Act of 2004,* 108 Pub. L. No. 458, 118 Stat. 3638 (2004); *REAL ID Act,* Division B of *Emergency Supplemental Appropriations Act for Defense, the Global War on Terror, and Tsunami Relief,* Pub. L. No. 109-13, 119 Stat. 231 (2005).

71. *EBSVERA,* §§ 302, 303.

72. This is known as the Student Visitor Information System, or SEVIS (Ibid., § 501). The *USA PATRIOT Act of 2001* allowed schools to disclose individual student

records to government officials pursuant to *ex parte* court orders on suspicion of terrorism, even when such information would not have been obtainable absent student consent under prior law (*USA PATRIOT Act* § 507).

73. *USA PATRIOT Act* § 411 (codified as amended at 8 U.S.C.A. § 1226a(a)(3) (2001)).

74. *REAL ID Act,* § 103.

75. Susan Benesch and Devon Chaffee, "The Ever-Expanding Material Support Bar: An Unjust Obstacle for Refugees and Asylum Seekers," *Interpreter Releases* 83, no. 11 (Mar. 13, 2006): 465; "Terrorist Support Exception Made for Karen Refugees," *Interpreter Releases* 83, no. 20 (May 15, 2006): 930–31; see also the Immigration and Refugee Clinic and International Human Rights Clinic, Harvard Law School, "Preliminary Findings and Conclusions on the Material Support for Terrorism Bar as Applied to the Oversees Resettlement of Refugees from Burma" (Feb. 2006), www.humanrights first.org/pdf/06619-asy-mat-sup-terr-bar-study.pdf; www.humanrights first.info/pdf/06619-asy-mat-sup-terr-bar-study.pdf (accessed July 22, 2006).

76. 8 U.S.C.A. §1226a.

77. 8 U.S.C.A. § 1226a(a)(5).

78. 8 U.S.C.A. § 1226a(a)(6).

79. See David Cole, "In Aid of Removal: Due Process Limits on Immigration Detention," *Emory Law Journal* 51 (2002): 1003, 1026–28.

80. See Chishti et al., *America's Challenge,* 52–53.

81. Walter Ewing, *Border Insecurity: U.S. Border-Enforcement Policies and National Security,* Immigration Policy Center Report, Washington, DC, spring 2006.

82. U.S. Immigration and Customs Enforcement, Public Information, "ICE Budget Gains 6.3 Percent in FY 06 DHS Spending Bill," *Inside ICE* 2, no. 23 (2006), www.ice.gov/pi/news/insideice/articles/insideice_111405_Web3.htm.

83. Attorney General John Ashcroft, quoted in U.S. Department of Justice, Office of Inspector General, *The September 11 Detainees,* 12.

84. Hing, "Misusing Immigration Policies in the Name of Homeland Security," 199.

85. Cole, *Enemy Aliens,* 25.

86. Designated countries included Afghanistan, Algeria, Bahrain, Eritrea, Iran, Iraq, Lebanon, Morocco, North Korea, Oman, Pakistan, Qatar, Saudi Arabia, Somalia, Syria, Tunisia, United Arab Emirates, and Yemen. See Registration of Certain Nonimmigrant Aliens from Designated Countries, 67 *Fed. Reg.* 67,766 (Nov. 6, 2002); 67 *Fed. Reg.* 70,526 (Nov. 22, 2002); and 67 *Fed. Reg.* 77,642 (Dec. 18, 2002) (modifying registration requirements).

87. Cole, *Enemy Aliens,* 25n.1; see also Hing, "Misusing Immigration Policies in the Name of Homeland Security," 202–207.

88. U.S. Department of Justice, Office of the Inspector General, *The September 11 Detainees* (June 2003), www.usdoj.gov/oig/special/0306/index.htm. Other noncitizens were held as material witnesses or on terrorism-related charges.

89. American Immigration Lawyers Association (AILA), "Boiling the Frog Slowly: Executive Branch Actions since September 11, 2001," *Bender's Immigration Bulletin* 7 (Oct. 15, 2002): 1236.

90. U.S. Department of Justice, *The September 11 Detainees,* 46.

91. Ibid., chap. 7.

92. Nina Bernstein, "U.S. Is Settling Detainee's Suit in 9/11 Sweep," *New York Times,* Feb. 28, 2006, A1.

93. Ibid. Some of the former detainees were allowed to return to the United States to give depositions in their lawsuits, but they were subject to extraordinary security measures, such as remaining in the constant custody of federal marshals and calling no one. The lawsuit has not been settled with regard to many of the plaintiffs in the suit.

94. Cole, *Enemy Aliens,* 51n.1.

95. 8 C.F.R. § 1003.19(i)(2). Attorney General Ashcroft also announced a rule overriding state court decisions that would have precluded certain detentions of noncitizens in state and local detention facilities on state constitutional grounds. See chap. 10, by Anil Kalhan, in this volume.

96. See Susan M. Akram and Kevin R. Johnson, "Race, Civil Rights, and Immigration Law after September 11, 2001: The Targeting of Arabs and Muslims," *NYU Annual Survey of American Law* 58 (2002): 295, 351–55 (describing the use of racial profiling as basis for adoption of enforcement measures after September 11).

97. U.S. Department of Justice, Civil Rights Division, "Guidance Regarding the Use of Race by Federal Law Enforcement Agencies" (June 2003), 1–2 (hereinafter DOJ, "Guidance Regarding the Use of Race"), www.usdoj.gov/crt/split/documents/guidance_on_race.htm; see also Kevin R. Johnson, "Racial Profiling after September 11: The Department of Justice's 2003 Guidelines," *Loyola Law Review* 50 (2004): 67. Under the guidelines, "traditional law enforcement activities" cannot involve reliance on race unless the reliance on race is a response to actual reports that the perpetrator is of a particular race. By contrast, for "national security and border integrity" activities, race can be considered to the full extent permitted by the U.S. Constitution and other federal laws (Johnson, "Racial Profiling after September 11," 82).

98. See Chacón, "Unsecured Borders."

99. See Johnson, *The "Huddled Masses" Myth,* 32–39.

100. See, e.g., "Terrorists or Victims?" (editorial), *New York Times,* Apr. 3, 2006, A16 (noting that the absence of a statutory exception in the law's bar on those who have provided material support for terrorism contains no exceptions for those acting under duress or providing *de minimus* support).

101. U.S. Department of Homeland Security, Office of Immigration Statistics, *2003 Yearbook of Immigration Statistics* (Sept. 2004).

102. U.S. Department of Homeland Security, Office of Immigration Statistics, *2004 Yearbook of Immigration Statistics* (2005), table 42 (recording the number of security removals as thirteen in 2000, twelve in 2001, eleven in 2002, fourteen in 2003, and eleven in 2004).

103. Elizabeth M. Greico, Report of the Department of Homeland Security Office of Immigration Statistics, *Estimates of the Nonimmigrant Population in the United States: 2004* (June 2006), 1, www.uscis.gov/graphics/shared/statistics/publications/NIM_2004.pdf; www.uscis.gov/graphics/shared/statistics/index.htm.

104. Kelly Jeffreys and Nancy Rytina, Report of the Department of Homeland Security Office of Immigration Statistics, *U.S. Legal Permanent Residents: 2005* (June 2006), www.uscis.gov/graphics/shared/statistics/publications/USLegalPermEst_5.pdf.

105. See U.S. Department of Homeland Security, Office of Immigration Statistics, *Yearbook of Immigration Statistics: 2005* (2006), table 3, Legal Permanent Resident Flow

by Region and Country of Birth, Fiscal Year 2003, www.uscis.gov/graphics/shared/
statistics/yearbook/LPR05.htm.

106. John Symanska and Nancy Rytina, Report of the Department of Homeland
Security Office of Immigration Statistics, *Naturalizations in the United States: 2005* (June
2006), 3, www.uscis.gov/graphics/shared/statistics/publications/2005NatzFlowRpt.pdf;
Jeffrey S. Passel, "Size and Characteristics of the Unauthorized Migrant Population in
the U.S.," Pew Hispanic Center Report, Mar. 7, 2006, http://pewhispanic.org/
reports/report.php?ReportID=61.

107. Mary Dougherty, Denise Wilson, and Amy Wu, U.S. DHS Management Directorate, Office of Immigration Statistics, *Immigration Enforcement Actions: 2004* (Nov.
2005), 1, www.uscis.gov/graphics/shared/statistics/publications/
AnnualReportEnforcement2004.pdf. The streamlined "expedited removal" process accounted for 41,752, or 21 percent, of these removals. It is important to note that these
statistics measure "events," not "individuals." It is possible that some individuals are subject to removal proceedings or voluntary departure more than once in a given year
(Dougherty, Wilson, and Wu, *Immigration Enforcement Actions,* 1).

108. Dougherty, Wilson, and Wu, *Immigration Enforcement Actions,* 1. In the
process of "voluntary departure," a noncitizen agrees that his or her entry was illegal,
waives his or her right to a hearing, and remains in custody until he or she is removed
under supervision. Many, but not all, of these voluntary departures occur shortly after
entry.

109. By way of contrast, in 1993 only 42,452 noncitizens were removed. In 1996,
this number was 69,317, after a series of relatively gradual increases. In 1997, the number ballooned to 114,060 removals, and that number has generally expanded since that
time. See U.S. Department of Justice, Immigration and Naturalization Service, *1997
Statistical Yearbook of the Immigration and Naturalization Service* (Oct. 1999), 166.

110. Allison Siskin, *Immigration Related Detention: Current Legislative Issues,* CRS
Report for Congress (Apr. 28, 2004), ii, www.fas.org/irp/crs/RL32369.pdf.

111. Dougherty, Wilson and Wu, *Immigration Enforcement Actions,* 5.

112. See, e.g., Rachel L. Swarns, "Halliburton Subsidiary Gets Contract to Add
Temporary Immigration Detention Centers," *New York Times,* Feb. 4, 2006, A7 (reporting on Kellogg Brown & Root contract worth up to $385 million for the building of
immigration detention centers).

113. Transactional Records Access Clearinghouse, Syracuse University, TRAC Re-
port, "Timely New Justice Department Data Show Prosecutions Climb during Bush
Years: Immigration and Weapons Enforcement Up, White Collar and Drug Prosecutions
Slide" (2005), http://trac.syr.edu/tracreports/crim/136 (accessed July 22, 2006).

114. In 2006 ICE released a report unveiling a "comprehensive immigration enforcement strategy for the nation's interior." The report states that one goal is to "[t]arget
and remove aliens that pose criminal/national security threats." The report elaborates:

There are numerous illegal aliens at large in this country that pose criminal
and/or national security threats. ICE has created several programs to combat this
problem. ICE's Operation Community Shield targets foreign-born gang members and has resulted in the arrest of 2,400 gang members since its inception in
2005. ICE has requested 322 position enhancements for Operation Community
Shield in Fiscal Year 2007. ICE also launched Operation Predator in 2003 to target, among others, illegal alien child sex offenders. This effort has resulted in

more than 7,500 arrests, most of whom were alien child sex offenders. ICE also has more than 200 agents assigned to the nation's Joint Terrorism Task Forces. Last year, these agents made roughly 270 arrests for criminal or administrative immigration charges.

None of the arrests or detentions listed actually involve "security" threats. All involve crime (like street gang activity or sex offenses) or administrative immigration violations (U.S. Department of Homeland Security, "Department of Homeland Security Unveils Comprehensive Immigration Enforcement Strategy for the Nation's Interior" [press release], Apr. 20, 2006, www.dhs.gov/dhspublic/display?content=5546).

115. See, e.g., John Holusha, "In Mexico, Bush Presses Congress on Immigration," *New York Times,* Mar. 31, 2006, www.nytimes.com/2006/03/31/washington/31cndimmig.html (referring to the "border security" bill of Sen. Bill Frist).

116. See Rachel L. Swarns, "Hastert Hints at Compromise," *New York Times,* Mar. 30, 2006, A22, www.nytimes.com/2006/03/30/politics/30immig.html; see also "It Isn't Amnesty," *New York Times,* Mar. 29, 2006, A22 ("The bill does not ignore security and border enforcement. It would nearly double the number of Border Patrol agents, add resources for detaining illegal immigrants and deporting them more quickly, and expand state and local enforcement of immigration laws").

Chapter 9: National Security and Political Asylum

1. The United States is a party to the 1967 United Nations Protocol Relating to the Status of Refugees, which incorporates the 1951 United Nations Convention relating to the Status of Refugees (United Nations, Treaty Series, United Nations Protocol Relating to the Status of Refugees, 267, no. 8791, vol. 606).

2. UN Convention Relating to the Status of Refugees, adopted July 28, 1951, entered into force Apr. 22, 1954, Preamble.

3. 1951 UN Refugee Convention, art. 1(A)(2); 1967 Protocol, art. 1(2).

4. UN High Commissioner for Refugees (UNHCR), "Definitions and Obligations: Basic Definitions," www.unhcr.org.au/basicdef.shtml; UNHCR, "Asylum Levels and Trends in Industrialized Countries: First Quarter 2006" (July 2006), 6; UNHCR, "Asylum Levels and Trends in Industrialized Countries: Second Quarter 2006" (Sept. 2006), 5.

5. UNHCR, "Definitions and Obligations: Basic Definitions." The 2004 data is the latest provided (UNHCR, *The State of the World's Refugees 2006* [Oxford: Oxford University Press, 2006], 16, www.unhcr.org/cgibin/texis/vtx/template?page=publ&src=static/sowr2006/toceng.htm).

6. UNHCR, *State of the World's Refugees 2006,* 10.

7. Kenneth J. Franzblau, "Immigration's Impact on U.S. National Security and Foreign Policy" (Research Paper, U.S. Commission on Immigration Reform, Oct. 1997), 12 (quotation). See also Michael J. McBride, "Migrants and Asylum Seekers: Policy Responses in the United States to Immigrants and Refugees from Central America and the Caribbean," *International Migration* 37 (1999): 289; Mark Krikorian, "Who Deserves Asylum?" *Commentary* 52 (June 1996): 101.

8. Franzblau, "Immigration's Impact," 12–13; McBride, "Migrants and Asylum Seekers," 293–95.

9. Franzblau, "Immigration's Impact," 13–14; McBride, "Migrants and Asylum Seekers," 295–96.

10. McBride, "Migrants and Asylum Seekers," 296.

11. Bill Ong Hing, *Defining America through Immigration Policy* (Philadelphia: Temple University Press, 2004), 233–35; Franzblau, "Immigration's Impact," 3–6.

12. Federation for American Immigration Reform, "National Security Considerations in Asylum Applications: A Case Study of 6 Iraqis," Oct. 8, 1998, www.fairus.org/site/PageServer?pagename=leg_.

13. "Asylum and Withholding of Removal," 8 Code of Federal Regulations (hereafter CFR) §208.

14. *Illegal Immigration Reform and Immigrant Responsibility Act of 1996,* Pub. L. 104-208, Div. C. (1996) (IIRIRA); *Anti-Terrorism and Effective Death Penalty Act of 1996,* Pub. L. 104-132, 110 Stat. 121 (1996) (AEDPA).

15. IIRIRA; 8 CFR §208.

16. Janice L. Kephart, "Immigration and Terrorism: Beyond the 9/11 Report on Terrorist Travel," Center for Immigration Studies Paper 24 (Sept. 2005); Marisa Silenzi Cianciarulo, "Terrorism and Asylum Seekers: Why the REAL ID Act Is a False Promise," *Harvard Journal on Legislation* 43 (winter 2006): 101–38.

17. See Kephart, "Immigration and Terrorism"; Cianciarulo, "Terrorism and Asylum Seekers."

18. A comprehensive review of the anti-terrorism measures since September 11, 2001, is well beyond the scope of this chapter. Dinah Shelton has provided an excellent analysis of a broader range of these measures in light of international human rights standards in "Shifting the Focus of U.S. Law from Liberty to Security," in *September 11th, 2001: A Turning Point in International and Domestic Law?* ed. Paul Eden and Thérèse O'Donnell (Ardsley, NY: Transnational Publishers, 2005), 497–532.

19. Eleanor Acer, "Refuge in an Insecure Time: Seeking Asylum in the post-9/11 United States," *Fordham International Law Journal* 28 (May 2005): 1362; U.S. Department of Homeland Security Web site, "Immigration and Borders," www.dhs.gov/dhspublic/theme_home4.jsp.

20. Acer, "Refuge in an Insecure Time," 1373–74.

21. *Uniting and Strengthening America by Providing Appropriate Tools Required to Intercept and Obstruct Terrorism Act (USA PATRIOT Act) of 2001,* Pub. L. 10756, 115 Stat. 272, codified at INA §212(a)(3)B); Anwen Hughes, "Asylum and Withholding of Removal—A Brief Overview of the Substantive Law," 158 PLI/NY 289 (Practising Law Institute, Mar. 2006): 318.

22. Hughes, "Asylum and Withholding of Removal," 319; *REAL ID Act of 2005,* 119 Stat. 231, PL 109–13 (HR 1268), Div. B, Title I, §§103, 105 (May 11, 2005).

23. Gregory F. Laufer, "Admission Denied: In Support of a Duress Exception to the Immigration and Nationality Act's 'Material Support for Terrorism' Provision," *Georgetown Immigration Law Journal* 20 (2006): 437; Jennie Pasquarella, "Victims of Terror Stopped at the Gate to Safety: The Impact of the 'Material Support to Terrorism' Bar on Refugees," *Human Rights Brief* 13, no. 3 (2006): 28.

24. Pasquarella, "Victims of Terror Stopped at the Gate to Safety," 32.

25. *REAL ID Act,* §§101(a)(3) and (e). The act also vests discretion over asylum decisions in the director of Homeland Security in addition to the attorney general; eliminates a planned study on vulnerabilities in the asylum system; and, in a pair of changes

benefiting asylum applicants, lifts the caps on applicants whose claims are based on coercive population controls and on the number of asylees permitted to change their status to permanent residents each year (*REAL ID Act*, §§101[b]–[d] and [f]–[h]).

26. "Aliens and Nationality: Immigration and Nationality: General Provisions: Definitions," 8 United States Code Annotated §1101(a)(42)(A).

27. E.g., *Osorio v. INS*, 18 F.3d 1017 (2nd Cir. 1994); *Singh v. Ilchert*, 63 F.3d 1501 (9th Cir. 1995); *Yazitchian v. INS*, 207 F.3d 1164 (9th Cir. 2000); *Eduard v. Ashcroft*, 379 F.3d 182 (5th Cir. 2004); *Matter of Fuentes*, 19 I&N Dec. 58 (BIA 1988).

28. *REAL ID Act; Immigration and Nationality Act*, §208; 65 Federal Register 76,588, 76,598 (proposed Dec. 7, 2000); Hughes, "Asylum and Withholding of Removal," 317.

29. On corroborating evidence, compare *Ladha v. INS*, 215 F.3d 889 (9th Cir. 2000), and *Sidhu v. INS*, 220 F.3d 1085 (9th Cir. 2000) with *Alvarado-Carrillo v. INS*, 251 F.3d 44 (2d Cir. 2001), *Abdulai v. Ashcroft*, 239 F.3d 542 (3rd Cir. 2001), and *Mukanusoni v. Ashcroft*, 390 F.3d 110 (1st Cir. 2004). On credibility, see *Damaize-Job v. INS*, 787 F.2d 1332 (9th Cir. 1986); *Dia v. Ashcroft*, 353 F.3d 228 (3rd Cir. 2003); *In re S-S-*, 21 I. and N. Dec. 121 (BIA 1995); *Balasubramanrim v. INS*, 143 F.3d 157 (3rd. Cir. 1998); *Singh-Kaur v. INS*, 183 F.3d 1147 (9th Cir. 1999); *Matter of A-S-*, 21 I. and N. Dec. 1106 (BIA 1998).

30. Kephart, "Immigration and Terrorism," 26; Cianciarulo, "Terrorism and Asylum Seekers," 115.

31. Susan Bibler Coutin, "The Oppressed, the Suspect and the Citizen: Subjectivity in Competing Accounts of Political Violence," *Law and Social Inquiry* 26 (2001): 65 (second quote), 75 (first quote).

32. Hughes, "Asylum and Withholding of Removal," 318.

33. McBride, "Migrants and Asylum Seekers," 289.

34. Acer, "Refuge in an Insecure Time," 1362–63.

35. UNHCR, *State of the World's Refugees 2006*, 33.

36. 1951 UN Refugee Convention, art. 33(1); 1967 Protocol, art. 1(1).

37. Convention against Torture and Other Cruel, Inhuman or Degrading Treatment or Punishment, Adopted and opened for signature, ratification and accession by General Assembly resolution 39/46 of Dec. 10, 1984, entry into force June 26, 1987, in accordance with art. 27(1), art. 3(1), www.unhchr.ch/html/menu3/b/h_cat39.htm.

38. 1951 UN Refugee Convention, art. 33(2).

39. Hughes, "Asylum and Withholding of Removal," 319.

40. Acer, "Refuge in an Insecure Time," 1365.

41. Laufer, "Admission Denied," 437n.12.

42. Pasquarella, "Victims of Terror Stopped at the Gate to Safety," 31n.56, quoting UNHCR, Guidelines on International Protection: Application of the Exclusion Clause: Article 1F of the 1951 Convention Relating to the Status of Refugees, HCR/GIP/03/05 (September 4, 2003) at para. 12; Refugee Convention, art. 1(F)(b); UNHCR Handbook on Procedures and Criteria for Determining Refugee Status under the 1951 Convention and the 1967 Protocol Relating to the Status of Refugees, HCR/IP/4/Eng/REV1, Reedited, Geneva, Jan. 1992, UNHCR 1979, www.unhcr.org/cgi-bin/texis/vtx/home/open doc.pdf?tbl=PUBL&id=3d58e13b4.

43. Acer, "Refuge in an Insecure Time," 1365.

44. UNHCR, *State of the World's Refugees 2006,* 10.

45. "The Hague Programme: Strengthening Freedom, Security and Justice in the European Union," *Official Journal C 053, 03/03/2005 P. 0001 – 0014,* 52005XG0303(01), (2005/C 53/01); "1.2 Asylum, Migration and Border Policy," 4, http://europa.eu.int/eur-lex/lex/LexUriServ/LexUriServ.do?uri=CELEX: 52005XG03 03(01):EN:HTML.

46. Council Directive 2003/9/EC of Jan. 27, 2003, laying down minimum standards for the reception of asylum seekers (Official Journal L 31 of 06.02.03); Council Regulation (EC) No. 343/2003 of Feb. 18, 2003, establishing the criteria and mechanisms for determining the member state responsible for examining an asylum application lodged in one of the member states by a third country national (Official Journal L 50 of Feb. 25, 2003).

47. Commission of the European Communities, Communication from the Commission to the Council and the Parliament on Strengthened Practical Cooperation, SEC(2006) 189, Brussels 17.2.2006, COM(2006) 67 Final, http://eur-lex.europa.eu/ LexUriServ/site/en/com/2006/com2006_0067en01.pdf#search=%22communication% 20on%20strengthened%20practical%20cooperation%22.

48. European Union, Justice and Home Affairs, "EU Fights against the Scourge of Terrorism," http://ec.europa.eu/justice_home/fsj/terrorism/fsj_terrorism_intro_en.htm.

49. "The Hague Programme, I. Introduction," 2.

50. Ibid.

51. Commission of the European Communities, Commission Staff Working Paper, Second Annual Report to the Commission and the European Parliament on the Activities of the EURODAC Central Unit, Brussels 20.6.2005, SEC(2005) 839: 5–7.

52. Commission of the European Communities, Commission Staff Working Paper, First Annual Report to the Commission and the European Parliament on the Activities of the EURODAC Central Unit, Brussels 5.5.2004, SEC(2004) 557: 4; Europa, "Eurodac: A European Union-wide Electronic System for the Identification of Asylum-Seekers" (press release), MEMO/06/334, Brussels, Sept. 19, 2006, http://europa.eu/ rapid/pressReleasesAction.do?reference=MEMO/06/334&format=HTML&aged= 0&language=EN&guiLanguage=en.

53. "The Hague Programme," I. Introduction, 2.

54. Ibid.

55. Didier Bigo, "Liberty? Whose Liberty? The Hague Programme and the Conception of Freedom," www.libertysecurity.org/article339.html#nb2, posted July 20, 2005.

56. Laufer, "Admission Denied," 475–76.

57. Bigo, "Liberty? Whose Liberty?"

58. Asylum Procedures Directive, Council Directive 2005/85/EC of Dec. 1, 2005, on minimum standards in procedures in member states for granting and withdrawing refugee status, *Official Journal of the European Union* L326/13, 13.12.2005.

59. UNHCR, *State of the World's Refugees 2006.*

60. Immigration Law Practitioners Association (ILPA), "ILPA Response to the Hague Programme: EU Immigration and Asylum Law and Policy," www.libertysecurity .org/article72.html, posted Dec. 20, 2004.

61. "02092005—Commission proposes new rules on asylum and immigration," Europa Web site, http://europa.eu.int/comm/justice_home/news/intro/news_intro_

ent.htm; Ariel Meyerstein, "Retuning the Harmonization of EU Asylum Law: Exploring the Need for an EU Asylum Appellate Court," *California Law Review* 93 (Oct. 2005): 1509; Bigo, "Liberty? Whose Liberty?"

62. Meyerstein, "Retuning the Harmonization of EU Asylum Law," 1512.

63. Ibid., 1516–17.

64. "The Hague Programme, 1.3 A Common European Asylum System," 4.

65. Ibid., "1.6 The External Dimension of Asylum and Migration," 5–7.

66. Ibid., "1.3 A Common European Asylum System," 4; and "1.6.3 Partnerships with Countries and Regions of Transit," 7.

67. ILPA, "ILPA Response to the Hague Programme," sec. 3.

68. Franco Frattini, vice president of the European Commission Responsible for Justice, Freedom and Security, "Recent Developments of Immigration and Integration in the EU and on Recent Events in the Spanish Enclave in Morocco," SPEECH/05/667, Konrad Adenauer Foundation, Brussels, Nov. 3, 2005, http://europa.eu/rapid/pressReleasesAction.do?reference=SPEECH/05/667&format=HTML&aged=1&language=EN&guiLanguage=en.

69. BBC News, "Africans Die in Spanish Enclaves," Sept. 29, 2005, http://news.bbc.co.uk/2/hi/africa/4292490.stm.

70. Human Rights Watch, "Stemming the Flow: Abuses against Migrants, Asylum-seekers and Refugees," 18, no. 5(E) (September 2006): 5, www.libertysecurity.org/IMG/pdf/libya0906web.pdf.

71. Amnesty International, "JHA: Closing Eyes to Human Rights Leaves Asylum Seekers and Migrants at Risk" (press release), Oct. 4, 2006, www.amnesty-eu.org/.

72. *In re D-J,* Respondent, decided Apr. 17, 2003, U.S. Department of Justice, Office of the Attorney General, Interim Decision #3488, 23 L&N Dec. 572 (A.G. 2003): 579.

73. Hughes, "Asylum and Withholding of Removal," 300.

74. David Martin, "The 1995 Asylum Reforms: A Historic and Global Perspective," *Backgrounder* (Center for Immigration Studies) (May 2000): 3; Cianciarulo, "Terrorism and Asylum Seekers."

75. Dr. Gregor Noll, "Proof and Credibility," Danish Institute for Human Rights, www.humanrights.dk/departments/research/rrp/repr.doc/proofandcred.doc.

76. Krikorian, "Who Deserves Asylum?" 52.

77. Martin, "The 1995 Asylum Reforms," 3.

78. In assessing incentives and effectiveness, other considerations are of course also at play, including, for example, incentives for forum-shopping, the risks and effects of backlogs, and costs of adjudication in comparison to costs of other interventions. See, e.g., Charles K. Keely and Sharon Stanton Russell, "Response of Industrial Countries to Asylum-Seekers," *Journal of International Affairs* 47 (1994); Jonas Widgren and Philip Martin, "Managing Migration: The Role of Economic Instruments," *International Migration* 40, no. 5 (2002): 213; Matthew J. Gibney and Randall Hansen, "Asylum Policy in the West," Discussion Paper No. 2003/68, World Institute for Development Economics Research (Sept. 2003).

79. UNHCR, *State of the World's Refugees 2006,* 33.

80. Hughes, "Asylum and Withholding of Removal," 315–22; Cianciarulo, "Terrorism and Asylum Seekers."

81. Hughes, "Asylum and Withholding of Removal," 318.

82. David Zaring and Elena Baylis, "Sending the Bureaucrats to War," *Iowa Law Review* 92, no. 4 (2007).

83. Acer, "Refuge in an Insecure Time," 1384–86.

84. Transactional Records Access Clearinghouse, Syracuse University, TRAC Immigration Report, "Immigration Judges," http://trac.syr.edu/immigration/reports/160/.

85. Adam Liptak, "Federal Courts Criticize Judges' Handling of Asylum Cases," *New York Times,* Dec. 26, 2005. Other sharp critiques are found in *Pasha v. Gonzales,* No. 044166 (7th Cir. 2005); *Sukwanputra v. Gonzales* (3d Cir. 2006), 17.

86. Jason Ryan, "Attorney General Chastises Immigration Judges," ABC News, Jan. 11, 2006, http://abcnews.go.com/US/LegalCenter/story?id=1492671.

87. United States Citizenship and Immigration Service, *2003 Yearbook of Immigration Statistics,* 45–46, 56, http://uscis.gov/graphics/shared/aboutus/statistics/Asylees.htm. The 9/11 Commission itself noted that "very few people" among all the immigrants to the United States pose a threat to national security (National Commission on Terrorist Attacks against the United States, *The 9/11 Commission Report* [Washington, DC: Government Printing Office, 2004], 383).

88. Kephart, "Immigration and Terrorism," 27.

Chapter 10: Immigration, Enforcement and Federalism after September 11, 2001

1. *Immigration Reform and Control Act* (IRCA), Pub. L. No. 99-603, 100 Stat. 3359 (1986) (codified in scattered sections of 8 U.S.C.); see David Dixon and Julia Gelatt, Migration Policy Institute, "Immigration Facts: Immigration Enforcement Spending since IRCA," Task Force Fact Sheet No. 10 (Nov. 2005), 1 (analyzing dramatic increases between 1985 and 1992 in appropriations and staffing for federal immigration enforcement activities and noting that these resources "have been concentrated heavily on border enforcement"), www.migrationpolicy.org/ITFIAF/FactSheet_Spending.pdf. Border enforcement accounted for approximately 58 percent of all spending in 2002, compared to 9 percent for interior investigations and 33 percent for detention and removal operations.

2. See, e.g., Peter Whoriskey, "States, Counties Begin to Enforce Immigration Law," *Washington Post,* Sept. 27, 2006, A1, www.washingtonpost.com/wp-dyn/content/article/2006/09/26/AR2006092601319_pf.html. Several states and localities have enacted laws and ordinances prohibiting, among other things, hiring or renting property to undocumented immigrants and denying business permits, contracts, and grants to those who assist undocumented immigrants. See, e.g., Daniel Gonzalez, "States Fight Illegal Migration," *Arizona Republic,* Aug. 2, 2006, www.azcentral.com/arizonarepublic/news/articles/0802statelaws.html (noting that over half of all states had passed immigration-related measures in 2006 "aimed at denying undocumented immigrants access to jobs and benefits"); see also David Migoya, "New Era on Immigration," *Denver Post,* Aug. 1, 2006, www.denverpost.com/search/ci_4813481 (discussing new Colorado laws requiring proof of legal residence in the United States to be eligible for public benefits and professional licenses); "Perdue Signs Georgia Security and Immigration Compliance Act," *Chattanoogan,* Apr. 17, 2006, www.chattanoogan.com/articles/article_83961.asp (discussing comprehensive new Georgia law requiring proof of lawful residence to be eligible for public services, requiring state contractors to verify lawful residence of new employees, and authorizing state law enforcement to enforce federal immigration laws).

These laws and ordinances are currently the subject of litigation. See, e.g., Michael Rubinkam, "Federal Judge Blocks Town's Crackdown on Illegal Immigrants," Associated Press, Nov. 1, 2006, at http://news.findlaw.com/ap/o/51/11–01–2006/ 2b42000fb270c1a6.html; Laura Parker, "Court Tests Await Cities' Laws on Immigrants," *USA Today*, Oct. 9, 2006, www.usatoday.com/news/nation/2006–10–08-immi gration_x.htm (discussing ordinances in Hazleton, Pennsylvania, and other localities).

3. On the distinction between "immigration" law and policy and "alienage" or "immigrant" law and policy, see Linda Bosniak, *The Citizen and the Alien: Dilemmas of Contemporary Membership* (Princeton, NJ: Princeton University Press, 2006), 37–76; Hiroshi Motomura, *Americans in Waiting: The Lost Story of Immigration and Citizenship in the United States* (Oxford: Oxford University Press, 2006), 46–47, 113–14.

4. See, e.g., Gerald Neuman, "The Lost Century of American Immigration Law (1776–1875)," *Columbia Law Review* 93 (1993): 1833 (discussing regulation of immigration by states before 1875); *De Canas v. Bica*, 424 U.S. 351 (1976) ("power to regulate immigration is unquestionably exclusively a federal power"); Gerald L. Neuman, "Aliens as Outlaws: Government Services, Proposition 187, and the Structure of Equal Protection Doctrine," *UCLA Law Review* 42 (1995): 1425, 1436; Michael J. Wishnie, "State and Local Police Enforcement of Immigration Laws," *University of Pennsylvania Journal of Constitutional Law* 6 (2004): 1084, 1088–90 (discussing the "widely understood and accepted" conclusion that state and local governments lack power to enforce provisions of federal immigration laws); Peter J. Spiro, "The States and Immigration in an Era of Demi-Sovereignties," *Virginia Journal of International Law* 35 (1994): 121, 134 ("it has long been assumed that control of immigration and the treatment of aliens within the United States are exclusive federal responsibilities").

5. On the plenary power doctrine, see, e.g., Michael J. Wishnie, "Laboratories of Bigotry? Devolution of the Immigration Power, Equal Protection, and Federalism," *NYU Law Review* 76 (2001): 493, 502–504, 532–33.

6. *De Canas v. Bica*, 424 U.S. at 355 (quote); see, e.g., *Mathews v. Diaz*, 426 U.S. 67 (1976).

7. See, e.g., *Chy Lung v. Freeman*, 92 U.S. 275 (1875); the *Passenger Cases*, 48 U.S. 283 (1849); Spiro, "The States and Immigration in an Era of Demi-Sovereignties," 134–45; Gerald L. Neuman, *Strangers to the Constitution: Immigrants, Borders, and Fundamental Law* (Princeton, NJ: Princeton University Press, 1996), 44–51.

8. See, e.g., *Hines v. Davidowitz*, 312 U.S. 52, 66–67 (1941) (invalidating Pennsylvania alien registration law on the basis of federal preemption); Wishnie, "Laboratories of Bigotry?" 510; Peter H. Schuck, "The Message of Proposition 187," *Pacific Law Journal* 26 (1995): 989, 990 (discussing invalidation of main provisions of California's Proposition 187 in part on the ground of preemption).

9. See Harold Hongju Koh, "Equality with a Human Face: Justice Blackmun and the Equal Protection of Aliens," *Hamline Law Review* 8 (1985): 51.

10. *Graham v. Richardson*, 403 U.S. 365 (1971); *Takahashi v. Fish & Game Commission*, 334 U.S. 410 (1948).

11. *Plyler v. Doe*, 457 U.S. 202 (1982).

12. E.g., *Wong Wing v. United States*, 163 U.S. 228, 237–38 (1896) (non–U.S. citizens may not be subjected to criminal punishment without being afforded due process of law and other constitutional protections); see Neuman, "Aliens as Outlaws," 1441–42, 1445–46.

13. Akhil Reed Amar, "Five Views of Federalism: 'Converse-1983' in Context," *Vanderbilt Law Review* 47 (1994): 1229, 1230–31; see also Daniel Richman, "The Past, Present, and Future of Violent Crime Federalism," *Crime & Justice* 34 (2006): 421 ("We are accustomed to the idea that the federal government is responsible for monitoring local abuses—stepping in with civil suits or civil rights prosecutions whenever the local are derelict in their attention to such matters—not local monitoring of the feds"); Michael W. McConnell, "Evaluating the Founders' Design," *University of Chicago Law Review* 54 (1987): 1484, 1501 (under modern assumptions underlying the Fourteenth Amendment and New Deal legislation, "it is the federal government, not the states, that appears to be our system's primary protector of individual liberties").

14. Neuman, "Aliens as Outlaws," 1436.

15. See, e.g., Mae M. Ngai, *Impossible Subjects: Illegal Aliens and the Making of Modern America* (Princeton, NJ: Princeton University Press, 2004), 71–75 (discussing state and local government initiatives during the 1930s to exclude Mexicans and Mexican Americans from state and local government services and to expel them from the United States); Joan M. Jensen, *Passage from India: Asian Indian Immigrants in North America* (New Haven, CT: Yale University Press, 1988), 42–47 (discussing inaction of local police in response to violent expulsions of South Asians and other Asian immigrants from Pacific Coast communities during late nineteenth and early twentieth centuries); Wishnie, "Laboratories of Bigotry?" 555 and nn.318–19 (discussing anti-immigrant movements at state and local levels).

16. *Graham v. Richardson,* 403 U.S. at 372; see also Neuman, "Aliens as Outlaws," 1435 (arguing that "dynamics of the political process" render non-U.S. citizens "more vulnerable at the state level than the federal level").

17. *Chy Lung v. Freeman,* 92 U.S. at 279 (1875) (noting that mistreatment of non-U.S. citizens by state officials "may bring disgrace upon the whole country, the enmity of a powerful nation, or the loss of an equally powerful friend"). Similar principles underlie the availability of federal court jurisdiction for cases involving non-U.S. citizens. As Kevin Johnson has explained, the nation's founders provided for alienage jurisdiction in the federal courts "to avoid the potentially adverse foreign relations consequences caused by allowing state courts, fueled by a mixture of anti-British and anticreditor sentiment, to resolve disputes involving noncitizens" (Kevin Johnson, "Why Alienage Jurisdiction? Historical Foundations and Modern Justifications for Federal Jurisdiction Over Disputes Involving Noncitizens," *Yale Journal of International Law* 21 [1996]: 1, 6).

18. See, e.g., Wishnie, "Laboratories of Bigotry?"

19. For example, in *De Canas v. Bica,* the Supreme Court concluded that Congress did not intend to preclude states from restricting the employment of unauthorized migrants, and on that basis it left open the possibility that a California statute making it illegal to "knowingly employ" undocumented immigrants if it would have "an adverse effect on lawful resident workers" might be sustained (*De Canas v. Bica,* 424 U.S. at 351). See also Bill Ong Hing, *Defining America through Immigration Policy* (Philadelphia: Temple University Press, 2004), 156–57 (discussing *De Canas*).

20. See, e.g., Jennifer M. Chacón, "The Security Myth: Punishing Immigrants in the Name of National Security" (chap. 8 in this volume, where she argues that in light of legal developments during 1990s, "September 11, 2001, cannot accurately be labeled a watershed for U.S. immigration policy"); H. Richard Friman, "Migration and Security: Crime, Terror, and the Politics of Order" (chap. 7 in this volume, discussing the pre-2001 trend toward "securitization" of immigration law).

21. Some of these policies were adopted in direct response to the federal government's failure to grant asylum to thousands of individuals fleeing civil wars in Guatemala and El Salvador, the overwhelming majority of whose claims were denied apparently on account of the federal government's support of the political regimes from which they had fled. Following the lead of religious congregations that had pledged "sanctuary" to these refugees, these cities explicitly stated their opposition to the deportation of these Guatemalan and Salvadoran refugees and prohibited city officials from cooperating in their arrest or deportation. In other instances, localities acted in response to concerns within their immigrant communities about the barriers to fair and equal access to government services that might be put in place if local officials cooperated with federal immigration enforcement activities, which many individuals perceived to involve racial discrimination and other abuses. See Ignatius Bau, "Cities of Refuge: No Federal Preemption of Ordinances Restricting Local Government Cooperation with the INS," *La Raza Law Journal* 7 (2004): 50, 50–53 and nn.4, 10–11; Craig B. Mousin, "A Clear View from the Prairie: Harold Washington and the People of Illinois Respond to Federal Encroachment of Human Rights," *Southern Illinois University Law Journal* 29 (2005): 285, 293–96; Linda Reyna Yañez and Alfonso Soto, "Local Police Involvement in the Enforcement of Immigration Law," *Hispanic Law Journal* 1 (1994): 9, 33–34.

22. See, e.g., Spiro, "The States and Immigration in an Era of Demi-Sovereignties," 130–32 (noting state laws criminalizing employment of undocumented immigrants, requiring prison and mental health authorities to share immigration status information with federal officials, preempting local "sanctuary" ordinances, and discussing state legislative proposals in the early 1990s to regulate immigration status more aggressively). In the states, some of these political efforts were driven by concern that illegal immigration was imposing significant fiscal burdens upon state and local governments. While accounts differ concerning the extent of the costs and benefits to states and localities associated with illegal immigration, a number of states filed lawsuits during the early 1990s seeking compensation from the federal government for the costs they claimed to have incurred (Spiro, "The States and Immigration in an Era of Demi-Sovereignties," 126–29).

23. See Schuck, "The Message of Proposition 187," 989, 990. Federal court litigation over Proposition 187 initially led to the invalidation of most of its main provisions, on the grounds that they either were preempted by the federal immigration laws or constituted an impermissible regulation of federal immigration status by the state of California. Litigation ended with a settlement agreement. See *League of United Latin American Citizens v. Wilson,* 997 F. Supp. 1244 (C.D. Cal. 1997); *League of United Latin American Citizens v. Wilson,* 908 F. Supp. 755 (C.D. Cal. 1995).

24. *Illegal Immigration Reform and Immigrant Responsibility Act of 1996* (IIRIRA), § 642(b)(2), Pub. L. No. 104-208, Division C, 110 Stat. 3009–546, 8 U.S.C. § 1373; see *City of New York v. United States,* 179 F.3d 29, 37 (sustaining provision against constitutional challenge, but reserving decision as to whether a broader confidentiality policy "more integral to the operation of City government" might be constitutionally protected under the Tenth Amendment).

25. *Personal Responsibility and Work Opportunity Reconciliation Act of 1996* (PRWORA), Pub. L. No. 104-193, 110 Stat. 2105 (codified in scattered sections of 8 U.S.C. and 42 U.S.C.); see Wishnie, "Laboratories of Bigotry?" 513–16; IIRIRA § 502, 8 U.S.C. § 1621 note (authorizing pilot programs to limit issuance of driver's licenses to undocumented non-U.S. citizens); IIRIRA § 133 (codified at 8 U.S.C. § 1357[g]).

26. See Muzaffar Chishti et al., *America's Challenge: Domestic Security, Civil Liberties, and National Unity after September 11* (Washington, DC: Migration Policy Institute, 2003); see also Chacón, "The Security Myth" (chap. 8, this volume).

27. See generally Wishnie, "State and Local Police Enforcement of Immigration Laws"; Michael J. Wishnie and Doris Meissner, "Policing Immigrants Post-September 11" (unpublished manuscript, 2005); *Forcing Our Blues into Gray Areas: Local Police and Federal Immigration Enforcement, A Legal Guide for Advocates* (Washington, DC: Appleseed, 2006); Kevin R. Johnson, "Driver's Licenses and Undocumented Immigrants: The Future of Civil Rights Law?" *Nevada Law Journal* 5 (2004): 213; Maria Pabon Lopez, "More Than a License to Drive: State Restrictions on the Use of Driver's Licenses by Noncitizens," *Southern Illinois University Law Journal* 29 (2004): 91, 95, and n.11.

28. Federal immigration law consists of both *civil* provisions, which authorize deportation, fines, and other civil penalties for violations, and *criminal* provisions, which authorize criminal punishment for a subset of immigration violations deemed to be more serious. See Wishnie, "State and Local Police Enforcement of Immigration Laws," 1089–90. Congress has authorized state and local law enforcement officials to make arrests for violations of the *criminal* provisions of the immigration laws. See 8 U.S.C. § 1324(c) (authorizing criminal arrests for harboring, smuggling, or transporting unauthorized immigrants); 8 U.S.C. § 1252c(a) (authorizing criminal arrests for illegal reentry by previously deported felon).

29. See 8 U.S.C. § 1103(a)(8) (conferring on the attorney general emergency powers to certify the existence of "an actual or imminent mass influx of aliens arriving off the coast of the United States, or near a land border," and on that basis to authorize state and local law enforcement officials to enforce federal immigration laws).

30. IIRIRA §§ 133 (codified at 8 U.S.C. § 1357[g]); IIRIRA § 373 (codified at 8 U.S.C. § 1103); see also 8 U.S.C. § 1103(a)(8) (authorizing the attorney general, in event of a "mass influx of aliens" into the United States, "to authorize any State or local law enforcement officer," with the consent of the head of the state or local agency, "to perform or exercise any of the powers, privileges or duties conferred or imposed [upon]" federal immigration officers).

31. See Peter H. Schuck and John Williams, "Removing Criminal Aliens: The Pitfalls and Promises of Federalism," *Harvard Journal of Law and Public Policy* 22 (1999): 367, 427–31, 434, 448–49.

32. See Mark Dow, *American Gulag: Inside U.S. Immigration Prisons* (Berkeley: University of California Press, 2004), 9–10, 207–11 (discussing use of state and local jails for federal immigration detention); Human Rights Watch, "Locked Away: Immigration Detainees in Jails in the United States," report issued Sept. 1998, 16–17, www.hrw.org/reports98/us-immig/. As of August 2006, 57 percent of all federal immigration detainees, or approximately 130,000 individuals per year, were housed in county jails, which received between fifty and ninety dollars per day for each detainee (Meredith Kolodner, "County Jails Boost Their Income," *News 21,* Aug. 30, 2006, http://news.yahoo.com/s/news21/20060831/ts_news21/county_jails_boost_their_in come).

33. Theresa Wynn Roseborough, Deputy Assistant Attorney General, Office of Legal Counsel, "Assistance by State and Local Police in Apprehending Illegal Aliens," Memorandum Opinion for the U.S. Attorney, Southern District of California, Feb. 5, 1996; Douglas W. Kmiec, Assistant Attorney General, Office of Legal Counsel, "Han-

dling of INS Warrants of Deportation in Relation to NCIC Wanted Person File," 4 and n.11 (Apr. 11, 1989); see generally *Bronx Defenders v. U.S. Dep't of Homeland Sec.*, No. 04 Civ. 8576(HB), 2005 WL 3462725, *2-*3 (Dec. 19, 2005) (discussing series of legal opinions by federal government officials between 1974 and 1996 concluding that "state and local officers could not 'arrest' a person against whom an administrative [civil] warrant of deportation had been issued" by federal immigration authorities). See, e.g., Wishnie, "State and Local Police Enforcement of Immigration Laws," 1090; Jeff Lewis et al., Migration Policy Institute, "Authority of State and Local Officers to Arrest Aliens Suspected of Civil Infractions of Federal Immigration Law," *Bender's Immigration Bulletin* 7 (2003): 944.

34. See, e.g., Office of the Attorney General, State of New York, Informal Op. No. 2000–1, 2000 N.Y. Op. Atty. Gen. (Inf.) 1001, 2000 WL 420372 (N.Y.A.G. Mar. 21, 2000) (concluding that state and local law enforcement officers in New York lack authority to make arrests for civil violations of federal immigration laws, but do have authority to make arrests for criminal violations); Chishti et al., *America's Challenge*, 85 (discussing legal conclusions by officials in other states, including California, Texas, and Oklahoma).

35. Compare *United States v. Vasquez-Alvarez*, 176 F.3d 1294, 1296 (10th Cir. 1999) (state and local police have authority to enforce civil violations of federal immigration laws), with *Gonzales v. City of Peoria*, 722 F.2d 468, 475 (9th Cir. 1983) (states and localities do not have such authority).

36. E.g., *Mena v. City of Simi Valley*, 332 F.3d 1255, 1265 n.15 (9th Cir. 2003), vacated on other grounds, 544 U.S. 93 (2005); *Carrasca v. Pomeroy*, 313 F.3d 828, 836–37 (3d Cir. 2002).

37. See Richman, "The Past, Present, and Future of Violent Crime Federalism," 377; see also William A. Geller and Norval Morris, "Relations Between Federal and Local Police," *Crime & Justice* 15 (1992): 231; Malcolm L. Russell-Einhorn, U.S. Dept. of Justice, National Inst. of Justice, "Fighting Urban Crime: The Evolution of Federal-Local Collaboration" (Dec. 2003), www.ncjrs.gov/pdffiles1/nij/197040.pdf.

38. See Jay S. Bybee, Assistant Attorney General, Office of Legal Counsel, "Non-Preemption of the Authority of State and Local Law Enforcement Officials to Arrest Aliens for Immigration Violations" (Apr. 3, 2002); see *Bronx Defenders v. U.S. Dept. of Homeland Sec.*, 2005 WL 3462725, *3 (stating that the DOJ "flip-flopped" by opining in 2002 that "state and local law enforcement could, in fact, lawfully enforce the civil provisions of the immigration law"). While the government initially attempted to withhold the 2002 DOJ legal opinion from the public, it was ordered to release the document in the course of litigation under the Freedom of Information Act. See *National Council of La Raza v. Department of Justice*, 411 F.3d 350 (2d Cir. 2005).

39. Agreements with the federal government were initially concluded by Florida and Alabama, each of which has designated a small number of state troopers to participate in certain immigration enforcement activities (Wishnie and Meissner, "Policing Immigrants Post-September 11," 18–19, 23–24). Since then, several other jurisdictions have entered or considered entering into similar agreements involving specific categories of state officials (see, e.g., Peggy Lowe, "Deal Guts O.C. Sheriff's Immigration Enforcement Plan," *Orange County Register*, Oct. 6, 2006 [regarding officials in Orange County jails], www.ocregister.com/ocregister/homepage/abox/article_1299610.php; Heather MacDonald, "ICE, ICE, Baby," *National Review Online*, Aug. 7, 2006, http://article.nationalre

view.com/?q=YjRiYzRlYTM4ZjlhOThjYmRlNDUzNjQ3NjRmY2RlZGY= [on jail officials in Arizona and Los Angeles, San Bernardino, and Riverside Counties in California];
see also Bill Turque, "Herndon Police May Join Immigration Enforcement," *Washington
Post,* Sept. 22, 2006, B1, www.washingtonpost.com/wp-dyn/content/article/2006/09/
21/AR2006092101562_pf.html [noting consideration of deputization agreement by
town of Herndon, Virginia]). As of September 2007, at least twenty-eight state and local
jurisdictions had entered into these agreements with the Justice Department. See U.S.
Immigration and Customs Enforcement, Fact Sheet, Delegation of Immigration Authority, section 287(g), Immigration and Nationality Act (Sept. 24, 2007), at www.ice.gov/
pi/news/factsheets/factsheet287gprogover.htm. At least one jurisdiction, however, has already reversed course. Recently, upon election of Deval Patrick as its new governor,
Massachusetts rescinded the decision of its previous governor, Mitt Romney, to assign
thirty state police troopers to participate. See Jonathan Saltzman, "Governor Rescinds
Immigration Order," *Boston Globe,* Jan. 12, 2007, www.boston.com/news/local/massa
chusetts/articles/2007/01/12/governor_rescinds_immigration_order.

40. In recent years, the NCIC has processed more than 4 million queries per day—
most from state and local police—with an average response time of approximately 0.06
seconds. See Federal Bureau of Investigation, "An NCIC Milestone" (press release), Aug.
9, 2006, www.fbi.gov/pressrel/pressrel06/ncic080906.htm.

41. See Wishnie and Meissner, "Policing Immigrants Post-September 11," 19–20;
Wishnie, "State and Local Police Enforcement of Immigration Laws," 1095–1101.

42. On the Absconder Apprehension Initiative and NSEERS, see Chishti et al.,
America's Challenge, 40–45.

43. See Lisa M. Seghetti et al., Congressional Research Service, "Enforcing Immigration Law: The Role of State and Local Law Enforcement" (Jan. 27, 2006), 23.

44. *National Council of La Raza v. Ashcroft,* 468 F. Supp. 2d 429 (E.D.N.Y. 2007),
appeal pending, No. 07-0816 (2d Cir.). I serve as co-counsel for the plaintiffs in that
lawsuit.

45. Wishnie and Meissner, "Policing Immigrants Post-September 11," 19.

46. See, e.g., ibid.; Whoriskey, "States, Counties Begin to Enforce Immigration
Law," *Washington Post,* Sept. 27, 2006. Other initiatives implemented after the 2001 terrorist attacks have induced state and local officials to enforce federal immigration policy
objectives at the expense of state laws of general applicability that have been enacted in
the exercise of state police powers. For example, an emergency administrative order by
the INS—which was hastily issued without an opportunity for notice and comment
under the Administrative Procedures Act, 5 U.S.C. § 553, in the midst of litigation in
New Jersey state courts seeking to learn the identities of non-U.S. citizens detained after
September 11, 2001, in New Jersey county jails—prohibited all nonfederal facilities
housing federal immigration detainees, including state and local jails, from disclosing the
identities of any detainees in their custody (Interim Rule, Release of Information Regarding Immigration and Naturalization Service Detainees in Non-Federal Facilities, 67
Fed. Reg. 19, 508 [Apr. 22, 2002], as confirmed at 68 Fed. Reg. 4365 [Jan. 29, 2003]
[codified at 8 C.F.R. § 236.6]). The regulation thereby purported to preempt a set of
state laws in New Jersey requiring county jails to record and publicly disclose the identities of all individuals committed to their care—thereby displacing state policies concerning county jail operations and open government in the name of federal immigration

policy objectives. See Ronald K. Chen, "State Incarceration of Federal Prisoners after September 11: Whose Jail Is It Anyway?" *Brooklyn Law Review* 69 (summer 2004): 1335.

47. *Clear Law Enforcement for Criminal Alien Removal Act of 2003,* H.R. 2671; *Homeland Security Enhancement Act of 2003,* S. 1906.

48. *Border Protection, Antiterrorism, and Illegal Immigration Control Act of 2005,* H.R. 4437; see Seghetti et al., Congressional Research Service, "Enforcing Immigration Law," 20–24.

49. See notes 28 and 34 above.

50. See, e.g., New York Vehicle and Traffic Law § 250(2).

51. IIRIRA § 502; see Pabon Lopez, "More Than a License to Drive," 95n.11.

52. IIRIRA § 656; Michael John Garcia et al., Congressional Research Service, "Immigration: Analysis of the Major Provisions of H.R. 418, the REAL ID Act of 2005" (Feb. 2, 2005), 29n.89.

53. See National Immigration Law Center, "Immigrant Driver's License Proposals and Campaigns: Surprising Progress since 9/11," *Immigration Rights Update* (May 14, 2002), www.nilc.org/immspbs/DLs/DL002.htm.

54. See ibid.; National Immigration Law Center, "Most State Proposals to Restrict Drivers' Licenses for Immigrants Have Been Unsuccessful," *Immigration Rights Update* (July 15, 2002), www.nilc.org/immspbs/DLs/DL003.htm.

55. National Commission on Terrorist Attacks upon the United States, Final Report 390 (2004), www.9-11commission.gov/report/911Report.pdf.

56. Negotiated rulemaking brings administrative agency representatives together with concerned interest groups to negotiate the contents of proposed regulations. See *Negotiated Rulemaking Act of 1990,* Pub. L. 101-648, 104 Stat. 4970 (1990). In this case, the negotiated rulemaking process included state officials, law enforcement, and other experts, including privacy and immigrant community advocates. See also *Intelligence Reform and Terrorism Prevention Act of 2004,* Pub. L. 108-408, § 7212(b), 118 Stat. 3638 (2004); Todd B. Tatelman, Congressional Research Service, "Intelligence Reform and Terrorism Prevention Act of 2004: National Standards for Drivers' Licenses, Social Security Cards, and Birth Certificates" (Jan. 6, 2005).

57. The statute was enacted as part of an emergency supplemental appropriations bill to provide aid for victims of the December 26, 2004, tsunami in the Indian Ocean and to fund military operations in Iraq and Afghanistan (*REAL ID Act,* Pub. L. 109-13, Div. B., 119 Stat. 303–23 [May 15, 2005]).

58. *REAL ID Act,* § 202(a)(1), (c)(2)(B).

59. *REAL ID Act,* § 202(c)(2)(C). As a practical matter, these requirements also may induce state and local officials such as the police—and for that matter, private actors who may have occasion to review a driver's license for identification purposes—to enforce federal immigration laws in much the same way as the government's use of the NCIC database, since they make immigration status a salient and apparent fact in the eyes of those officials in the course of their day-to-day, non-immigration–related duties.

60. *REAL ID Act,* § 202(d)(11).

61. *REAL ID Act,* § 202(c)(1) (setting forth minimum issuance standards), (c)(3) (setting forth minimum requirements for verification of documents).

62. See National Governors Association, National Conference of State Legislatures, and American Association of Motor Vehicle Administrators, "The Real ID Act: National

Impact Analysis" (Sept. 2006), 3, www.ncsl.org/print/statefed/Real_ID_Impact_Report_
FINAL_Sept19.pdf.

63. National Immigration Law Center, "Twenty-four States Introduce Driver's License Bills," *Immigration Rights Update* (Mar. 23, 2006), www.nilc.org/immspbs/DLs/DL031.htm.

64. See, e.g., Kris W. Kobach, "The Quintessential Force Multiplier: The Inherent Authority of Local Police to Make Immigration Arrests," *Albany Law Review* 69 (2005): 179; Jeff Sessions and Cynthia Hayden, "The Growing Role for State & Local Law Enforcement in the Realm of Immigration Law," *Stanford Law and Policy Review* 16 (2005): 323; Kris W. Kobach, Center for Immigration Studies, "State and Local Authority to Enforce Immigration Law: A Unified Approach for Stopping Terrorists" (2004); Federation for American Immigration Reform, "State of Insecurity: How State and Local Immigration Policies Are Undermining Homeland Security" (Sept. 2003) (cited hereafter as FAIR Report 2003), 3; Seghetti et al., Congressional Research Service, "Enforcing Immigration Law," 28–30; Richman, "The Past, Present, and Future of Violent Crime Federalism," 409.

65. See FAIR Report 2003, 4.

66. As Gerald Neuman has noted, an approach taken to an extreme such would justify the treatment of undocumented immigrants as de facto outlaws, individuals who are disentitled from a whole range of basic legal protections altogether, in a manner analogous to the treatment of individuals declared "outlaws" under old English law. See Neuman, "Aliens as Outlaws," 1440–52.

67. See generally Michele Waslin, National Council of La Raza, "Immigration Enforcement by Local Police: The Impact on the Civil Rights of Latinos," Issue Brief, Feb. 2003; Craig E. Ferrell Jr., "Immigration Enforcement: Is It a Local Issue?" *Police Chief* (Feb. 2005); Craig E. Ferrell Jr., "The War on Terror's 'Absconder Initiative,'" *Police Chief* (Oct. 2002); Wishnie and Meissner, "Policing Immigrants Post-September 11," 23–27; James Jay Carafano, The Heritage Foundation, "No Need for the CLEAR Act: Building Capacity for Immigration Counterterrorism Investigations," Exec. Memorandum No. 925 (Apr. 21, 2004); Margaret D. Stock, "Driver Licenses and National Security: Myths and Reality," *Bender's Immigration Bulletin* 10 (Mar. 1, 2005): 422; Anita Ramasastry, "Why the Real ID Act Is a Real Mess," Findlaw.com, Aug. 10, 2005, http://writ.news.findlaw.com/ramasastry/20050810.html; Michele Waslin, National Council of La Raza, "Safe Roads, Safe Communities: Immigrants and State Driver's License Requirements," Issue Brief, May 2002.

68. See, e.g., Randal C. Archibold, "Immigrants Take to U.S. Streets in Show of Strength," *New York Times,* May 2, 2006, www.nytimes.com/2006/05/02/us/02immig.html.

69. Neuman, "Aliens as Outlaws," 1440.

70. See, e.g., Abigail Eagye, "Immigration Laws Lead to Unintended Housing Problems for Legal Aliens," *Post Independent* (Glenwood Springs, CO), Jan. 4, 2007, www.postindependent.com/article/20070104/VALLEYNEWS/101040031 (discussing complications caused by new Colorado law for lawfully present immigrant seasonal workers seeking housing benefits in Aspen, Colorado).

71. See, e.g., Muzaffar A. Chishti, "The Role of States in U.S. Immigration Policy," *Annual Survey of American Law* 58 (2002): 371, 374 ("Local law enforcement officers, untrained in the complexities of immigration regulations, are more likely to use race or

ethnicity as a substitute for reasonable cause"); Wishnie, "State and Local Police Enforcement of Immigration Laws," 1102 and n.107 (citing statutes prohibiting racial profiling under California, Colorado, Rhode Island, and Texas law).

72. Wishnie, "State and Local Police Enforcement of Immigration Laws," 1104–13.

73. See, e.g., Chishti, "The Role of States in U.S. Immigration Policy," 373; Anita Khashu et al., Vera Institute of Justice, "Building Strong Police-Immigrant Community Relations: Lessons From a New York City Project" (Aug. 2005): 3 ("Immigrant groups often cite fear of deportation [their own or that of family members or friends] as a major barrier to building trust and partnerships with police"), www.vera.org/publication_ pdf/ 300_564.pdf; Nicole J. Henderson et al., Vera Institute of Justice, "Law Enforcement and Arab American Community Relations after September 11, 2001: Engagement in a Time of Uncertainty," (June 2006): 7, 15–16, www.vera.org/publication_pdf/353_ 636.pdf (documenting fears within immigrant communities of immigration enforcement by police and finding that "the threat of detentions and deportations contributed to the underreporting of crimes and exacerbated the general climate of fear and anxiety").

74. See, e.g., Suleman Din, "A Different Tack on Immigration: Edison Balks on Aiding the Feds," *Star-Ledger* (Newark, NJ), Sept. 25, 2006 (quoting Latino community leader who noted reports of "individual officers us[ing] the threat of reporting individuals to immigration as a way of intimidation").

75. Khashu et al., Vera Institute of Justice, "Building Strong Police-Immigrant Community Relations," 3; Henderson et al., Vera Institute of Justice, "Law Enforcement and Arab American Community Relations after September 11, 2001," 13–16; see also National Immigration Forum, "Proposals to Expand the Immigration Authority of State and Local Police: Dangerous Public Policy According to Law Enforcement, Governments, Opinion Leaders, and Communities" (Sept. 18, 2006), www.immigration forum.org/documents/TheDebate/EnforcementLocalPolice/CLEARHSEAQuotes.pdf (compiling statements by state and local police officials across the country opposing expansion of immigration enforcement responsibilities for state and local police); Theresa Vargas, "Wanted: Local Agencies to Enforce Immigration Law," *Washington Post,* Jan. 4, 2007, LZ6, www.washingtonpost.com/wp-dyn/content/article/2007/01/02/ AR2007010201327.html (discussing unwillingness of local police in northern Virginia to engage in immigration enforcement).

76. See Henderson et al., Vera Institute of Justice, "Law Enforcement and Arab American Community Relations after September 11, 2001," 7, 15–16 (noting baseline level of mistrust of law enforcement within Arab American communities and concluding that the decision in one city to enforce immigration laws "appeared to have undermined Arab American trust"); see also Anita Khashu et al., Vera Institute of Justice, "Translating Justice: A Guide for New York City's Justice and Public Safety Agencies to Improve Access for Residents with Limited English Proficiency" (June 2005; updated Apr. 2006), 6 (noting that language barriers interfere with the ability of immigrant victims of crime to seek police assistance).

77. Richman, "The Past, Present, and Future of Violent Crime Federalism," 413–14; Shawn Reese, Congressional Research Service, "State and Local Homeland Security: Unresolved Issues for the 109th Congress" (June 9, 2005), 5.

78. See, e.g., Ferrell, "Immigration Enforcement" (local police should "use the communities' resources to address burglaries, robberies, assaults, rapes, murders, and even

traffic violations occurring in the communities rather than spend those resources addressing the massive national problem of illegal immigration"); Henderson et al., Vera Institute of Justice, "Law Enforcement and Arab American Community Relations after September 11, 2001," 15–16 (documenting objections by some local police to involvement in immigration enforcement and noting refusal by some police to enforce federal immigration laws "because their time and resources were needed for responding to local crime and public safety concerns").

79. See Chishti et al., *America's Challenge*, 148–50.

80. Richman, "The Past, Present, and Future of Violent Crime Federalism," 421; see also Khashu et al., Vera Institute of Justice, "Building Strong Police-Immigrant Community Relations," 3.

81. See Stock, "Driver Licenses and National Security," 424–25.

82. See note 63 above and accompanying text.

83. Indeed, federal authorities relied upon the fact that the September 11 hijackers had driver's license records to identify and investigate the individuals responsible for those attacks (Stock, "Driver Licenses and National Security," 424–25).

84. Stock, "Driver Licenses and National Security," 424. While proponents of driver's license restrictions frequently invoke the driver's licenses obtained by the September 11 hijackers, they often neglect to note that all of the hijackers had foreign passports, which would have permitted them to pass through airport security (Stock, "Driver Licenses and National Security," 425).

85. See, e.g., Wishnie, "Laboratories of Bigotry?" 527–58; compare Spiro, "The States and Immigration in an Era of Demi-Sovereignties," 159–61.

86. See, e.g., Edward L. Rubin and Malcolm Feeley, "Federalism: Some Notes on a National Neurosis," *UCLA Law Review* 41 (1994): 903, 910–26 (discussing distinctions between federalism and decentralization); see also Akhil Reed Amar, "Some New World Lessons for the Old," *University of Chicago Law Review* 58 (1991): 483, 498 ("the best argument for federalism, then, is neither experimentation, nor diversity, nor residential self-selection, but protection against abusive government"); Richard Briffault, "What About the 'Ism'? Normative and Formal Concerns in Contemporary Federalism," *Vanderbilt Law Review* 47 (1994): 1303, 1348–49 and n.161.

87. See, e.g., Ernest A. Young, "Welcome to the Dark Side," *Brooklyn Law Review* 69 (2004): 1277, 1284–90.

88. See, e.g., Amar, "Five Views of Federalism," 1232; William J. Brennan, "The Bill of Rights and the States: The Revival of State Constitutions As Guardians of Individual Rights," *NYU Law Review* 61 (1986): 535; compare Catherine Powell, "Dialogic Federalism: Constitutional Possibilities for Incorporation of Human Rights Law in the United States," *University of Pennsylvania Law Review* 150 (2001): 245 (advocating greater involvement by state and local governments in implementation of international human rights law norms in order to promote democratic deliberation over those norms at multiple levels of government and intergovernmental cooperation and dialogue in their implementation); Eliot Spitzer, Remarks for Law Day, May 1, 2000, www.oag.state.ny.us/press/statements/law_day.html, accessed Aug. 24, 2007 ("As Congress and Courts have succeeded in forging a 'New Federalism,' they have created an opportunity to accomplish things previously thought unsuited to state initiative").

89. See, e.g., *United States v. Morrison*, 529 U.S. 598 (2000); *City of Boerne v. Flores*, 521 U.S. 507 (1997); *United States v. Lopez*, 514 U.S. 549 (1995); see also *Unfunded*

Mandates Reform Act of 1995, Pub. L. 104-4, 109 Stat. 48 (1995) (codified as amended in scattered sections of 2 U.S.C.) (requiring cost-benefit analyses for congressional legislation imposing mandates upon state and local governments and imposing procedural hurdles for enactment of bills imposing mandates greater than $50 million); see, e.g., *Board of Trustees of the University of Alabama v. Garrett,* 531 U.S. 356 (2001); *Kimel v. Florida Board of Regents,* 528 U.S. 62 (2000); *Alden v. Maine,* 527 U.S. 706 (1999); *Florida Prepaid Postsecondary Education Expense Board v. College Savings Bank,* 527 U.S. 627 (1999); *Seminole Tribe v. Florida,* 517 U.S. 44 (1996); see also Pamela S. Karlan, "Disarming the Private Attorney General," *University of Illinois Law Review* (2003):183, 188–95; see, e.g., *Printz v. United States,* 521 U.S. 898 (1997) (holding it unconstitutional for Congress to mandate that state executive officials implement federal policy objectives); *New York v. United States,* 505 U.S. 144 (1992) (holding it unconstitutional for Congress to compel state legislatures or agencies to adopt laws or regulations to advance federal policy objectives); see also Evan H. Camkiner, "State Sovereignty and Subordinancy: May Congress Commandeer State Officers to Implement Federal Laws," *Columbia Law Review* 95 (1995): 1001; see, e.g., PRWORA, Pub. L. No. 104-193, 110 Stat. 2105 (restructuring the federal welfare program as block grants to states); see also Richman, "The Past, Present, and Future of Violent Crime Federalism," 418–21 (discussing possibility that state and local police might exercise power by "exacting a toll from federal authorities," in the form of greater state and local influence over the substance of federal domestic intelligence policies, in exchange for their cooperation and participation in the implementation of those policies).

90. See Briffault, "What About the 'Ism'?" 1335–37 (while independent role of state governments is recognized and protected by federal constitution, "no comparable guarantees" exist for local governments, which are subject to plenary authority of state legislatures). This oversight may be part of a broader lack of consideration of institutional design in immigration law scholarship more generally, as recently noted by Adam Cox and Eric Posner (see their article, "The Second Order Structure of Immigration Law," *Stanford Law Review* 59 [2007]: 809, available at http://ssrn.com/abstract=941730).

91. See, e.g., Spiro, "The States and Immigration in an Era of Demi-Sovereignties," 172–73 (arguing that permitting some states to restrict immigration might permit them "individually to let off their steam, however scalding it may be," so that "the nation need not visit the same sins"); Schuck and Williams, "Removing Criminal Aliens," 460 (advocating a cooperative federalist model in which state and local governments would be "allowed and encouraged to play a greater role in immigration enforcement"); Howard F. Chang, "Public Benefits and Federal Authorization for Alienage Discrimination by the States," *Annual Survey of American Law* 58 (2002): 357 (arguing that Congress may constitutionally delegate the federal government's broad power to discriminate against non-U.S. citizens); see also notes 64 and 65 above.

92. See, e.g., Vicki C. Jackson, "Citizenship and Federalism," in *Citizenship Today: Global Perspectives and Practices,* ed. T. Alexander Aleinikoff and Douglas Klusmeyer (Washington, DC: Carnegie Endowment for International Peace, 2001), 127, 127–29.

93. But see, e.g., Rebecca Smith, Amy Sugimori, and Luna Yasui, "Low Pay, High Risk: State Models for Advancing Immigrant Workers' Rights," *NYU Review of Law & Social Change* 28 (2003–2004): 597; Richman, "The Past, Present, and Future of Violent Crime Federalism," 418–21; Chen, "State Incarceration of Federal Prisoners after September 11."

94. Compare Peter H. Schuck, *Citizens, Strangers, and In-Betweens: Essays on Immigration and Citizenship* (Boulder, CO: Westview Press, 1998), 202 ("to the extent that Congress devolves more immigration policy to the states, *state* citizenship could become more salient than in the past"); Peter J. Spiro, "The Citizenship Dilemma," *Stanford Law Review* 51 (1999): 597, 618–21. European integration may be causing similar developments in Europe. See, e.g., Gerard Delanty, "The Resurgence of the City in Europe? The Spaces of European Citizenship," in *Democracy, Citizenship, and the Global City,* ed. Engin F. Isin (New York: Routledge, 2000), 79 ("with the emergency of a regulatory supranational polity since the 1980s, the sub-national level is now growing in salience; regions and cities are resurfacing and becoming powerful new voices in a world in which sovereignty is shared on many levels").

95. See, e.g., Saskia Sassen, *Territory, Authority, Rights: From Medieval to Global Assemblages* (Princeton, NJ: Princeton University Press, 2006), 291 ("though often talked about as a single concept and experienced as a unitary institution, citizenship actually describes a number of discrete but connected components in the relation between the individual and the polity"); Bosniak, *The Citizen and the Alien,* 3 ("citizenship is not a unitary or monolithic whole: the concept is comprised of distinct discourses designating a range of institutions and experiences and social practices that are overlapping but not always coextensive"); Peter H. Schuck, "Citizenship in Federal Systems," *American Journal of Comparative* Law 48 (spring 2000): 195, 207–208 (discussing and distinguishing among political, legal, psychological, and sociological dimensions of citizenship).

96. Bosniak, *The Citizen and the Alien,* 3, see also 81–82; Jennifer Gordon, *Suburban Sweatshops: The Fight for Immigrant Rights* (Cambridge, MA: Belknap Press of Harvard University Press, 2005), 237–80 (discussing citizenship-like practices of undocumented, non-U.S. citizen workers who organized and advocated for workers' rights legislation during late 1990s in New York).

97. For the recent discussions, see note 95 above. See also Spiro, "The Citizenship Dilemma," 619 n.111; Gerald L. Neuman, "'We Are the People': Alien Suffrage in German and American Perspective," *Michigan Journal of International Law* 13 (1992): 259, 292–93 and n.220 (both discussing potential availability of formal state citizenship to non-U.S. citizens). This may not be true to the same extent of local or regional citizenship, since local governments do not share the same constitutional status as state governments. See Briffault, "What About the 'Ism'?" 1335–37.

98. U.S. Const. amend. XIV.

99. See note 97 above.

100. Schuck, *Citizens, Strangers, and In-Betweens,* 201. These developments parallel experiences in other countries: for example, some observers have suggested that in some countries (including Japan, South Korea, Italy, and Spain) local governments have played a more significant role in facilitating the social integration of immigrants than have national governments (Takeyuki Tsuda, "Localities and the Struggle for Immigrant Rights: The Significance of Local Citizenship in Recent Countries of Immigration," in *Local Citizenship in Recent Countries of Immigration: Japan in Comparative Perspective,* ed. Takeyuki Tsuda (Lanham, MD: Lexington Books, 2006), 6–7 (characterizing immigrants in these countries as "local citizens," given the roles played by local governments in "granting . . . basic sociopolitical rights and services to immigrants as legitimate members of these local communities").

101. FAIR Report 2003, iii.

102. Smith et al., "Low Pay, High Risk," 602; see also Gordon, *Suburban Sweat-shops,* 237 (contrasting policies of the U.S. Department of Labor, which until recently shared information with immigration authorities upon receiving reports of wage law violations, with those of New York State Department of Labor, which "maintained strict confidentiality").

103. Smith et al., "Low Pay, High Risk," 602.

104. Wendy Zimmerman and Karen C. Tumlin, Urban Institute, "Patchwork Policies: State Assistance for Immigrants under Welfare Reform," Occasional Paper No. 24 (1999), 3–4, www.urban.org/publications/309007.html.

105. These laws typically require the students to satisfy certain minimum state residency requirements, have graduated from high schools within the state, and affirm that they are in the process of legalizing their immigration status or will do so as soon as they are able. See, e.g., Ruth Marcus, "Immigration's Scrambled Politics," *Washington Post* (op-ed article), Apr. 4, 2006, A23, www.washingtonpost.com/wp-dyn/content/article/ 2006/04/03/AR2006040301618.html; Raphael Lewis, "In-State Tuition not a Draw for Many Immigrants," *Boston Globe,* Nov. 9, 1995, www.boston.com/news/nation/articles/ 2005/11/09/in_state_tuition_not_a_draw_for_many_immigrants/; see generally Michael A. Olivas, "IIRIRA, the Dream Act, and Undocumented College Student Residency," *Journal of College and University Law* 30 (2004): 435; National Immigration Law Center, "State Proposed or Enacted Legislation Regarding Immigrant Access to Higher Education," www.nilc.org/immlawpolicy/DREAM/DREAM_Bills.pdf (Nov. 13, 2003).

To date, efforts to challenge these laws in court have not succeeded. See *Martinez v. Regents,* No. CV 05–2064 (Calif. Supreme Ct. Oct. 6, 2006) (order); *Day v. Sebelius,* 376 F. Supp. 2d 1022 (D. Kan. 2005), *affirmed sub nom; Day v. Bond,* F.3d, 2007 WL 2452681 (10th Cir. Aug. 30, 2007); see also Josh Bernstein, National Immigration Law Center, "Court Upholds California In-State Tuition Law (AB 540)," Oct. 10, 2006, at www.nilc.org/immlawpolicy/DREAM/Dream006.htm.

106. See Kari Lydersen, "Ill. Governor to Announce New Benefits for Immigrants," *Washington Post,* Dec. 13, 2006, A11, www.washingtonpost.com/wp-dyn/content/ article/2006/12/12/AR2006121201342.html (discussing Illinois's "New Americans" program).

107. See generally Ron Hayduk, *Democracy for All: Restoring Immigrant Voting Rights in the United States* (New York: Routledge, 2006), 87–194 (discussing contemporary instances of local communities granting non-U.S. citizens the right to vote and active campaigns in other states and localities to implement non-U.S. citizen voting rights); see also *Crosse v. Bd. of Supervisors of Elections,* 221 A.2d 431 (Md. 1966) (holding that a non-U.S. citizen satisfies qualifications under the state constitution to hold public office as sheriff).

108. See notes 68–73 above. Jennifer Gordon discusses an earlier example, in which non-U.S. citizen workers "came to act like citizens and won recognition for their basic rights," in the context of the successful campaign in New York to enact the Unpaid Wages Prohibition Act in the mid-1990s (Gordon, *Suburban Sweatshops,* 268–80).

109. See notes 75–80 above and accompanying text.

110. Sassen, *Territory, Authority, Rights,* 305–309; see also Saskia Sassen, *Globalization and Its Discontents: Essays on the New Mobility of People and Money* (New York: New Press, 1998), 12–13, 25.

111. Sassen, *Territory, Authority, Rights,* 314; see also Sassen, *Globalization and Its Discontents,* 11–12.

112. Sassen, *Territory, Authority, Rights,* 320 ("citizenship can undergo significant transformations without needing to be dislodged from its national encasement").

113. I am grateful to Alberta Sbragia for this observation.

114. See Richman, "The Past, Present, and Future of Violent Crime Federalism," 418–21, 427.

Chapter 11: Immigration, Security, and Integration in the European Union

1. United Nations, Population Division, *Replacement Migration: Is It a Solution to Declining and Aging Population?* (New York: United Nations Population Division, ESA/P/WP.160, 2000), 22.

2. Quoted in Robert S. Leiken, "Europe's Angry Muslims," *Foreign Affairs,* July/ Aug. 2005, www.foreignaffairs.org/20050701faessay84409/robert-s-leiken/europe-s-an gry-muslims.html.

3. Speech of July 12, 2005, www.cre.gov.uk.

4. This group included countries with relatively large immigrant populations from their former colonial territories (such as France and the UK), countries that have practiced the recruitment of migrant workers (such as Germany, Austria, Denmark, Luxembourg, and Sweden), and the "new immigration countries" (such as Greece, Spain, Italy, Portugal, Finland, and Ireland).

5. The Race Relations Act of 1976 was completed by the introduction of incitement to racial hatred offenses into the Public Order Act of 1986.

6. According to SOPEMI (Continuous Reporting System on Migration, 2004), 40,000 applications for regularization were lodged in Spain between 1985 and 1987. In Italy, 105,000 migrants regularized their status in 1987–1988.

7. The Schengen Agreements came into force in 1995 and the Dublin Convention, in 1997.

8. Dates when member states joined were as follows: Italy in November 1990, Spain and Portugal in June 1991, Greece in November 1992, Austria in April 1995, and Denmark, Finland, and Sweden in December 1996. In March 1999, the UK asked to take part in some aspects of Schengen (police and legal cooperation in criminal matters, the fight against drugs, and the Schengen Information System [SIS]) (see Decision 2000/365/EC). Ireland did the same in 2000 for the measures concerning SIS II (see Decision 2002/192/EC).

9. Eurobarometer, "Racism and Xenophobia in Europe," Eurobarometer Opinion Poll, no. 47.1, Dec. 1997.

10. Jef Huysmans, "Migrants as a Security Problem: Dangers of 'Securitizing' Societal Issues," in *Migration and European Integration: The Dynamics of Inclusion and Exclusion,* ed. R. Miles and D. Thränhardt (London: Pinter Publishers, 1995), 63.

11. The Council and Commission Action Plan of Dec. 3, 1998, laid down a timetable for measures to be adopted to achieve these objectives by 2004. The UK and the Republic of Ireland opted out of the new measures on the free movement of persons. Denmark, although a signatory of the Schengen Agreements, is reluctant to apply the European Community (EC) method in the area of free movement of persons.

12. The shift to qualified majority voting and codecision took place in May 2000 under article 62 of the EC Treaty (measures setting out the conditions for free circula-

tion of non-member state nationals legally resident on EU territory) and article 63 (for illegal immigration and the repatriation of illegally resident persons).

13. On the inclusive and exclusive aspects of the EU framework, see Council and Commission Action Plan of Dec. 3, 1998.

14. To enable the new member states to use the system, the council adopted a regulation (EC No. 2424/2001) in December 2001, in addition to the Decision 2001/866/JHA based on articles 30(1), 31, and 34 of the Treaty on European Union.

15. See Council Regulation of Nov. 11, 2003, and COM (2003) 687.

16. Council Regulation (EC) No. 574/99, amended by Regulation (EC) No. 539/2001, Regulation (EC) No. 2414/2001, and Regulation (EC) No. 453/2003.

17. See Council Regulation (EC) No. 2252/2004 of Dec. 13, 2004.

18. See Council Directive 2004/83/EC of Apr. 29, 2004.

19. Didier Bigo and Elspeth Guild, "Policing in the Name of Freedom," *Controlling Frontiers: Free Movement into and within Europe,* ed. Bigo and Guild (Burlington, VT: Ashgate, 2005), 1.

20. *Report on the Situation of Fundamental Rights in the EU in 2004,* CFR-CDF.rep.EU.en.2004, 44.

21. Directive 2004/83/EC of Apr. 29, 2004.

22. OJ 1996 C 80/2.

23. See COM (2000) 152 final and COM (2003) 315 final.

24. Directive 2003/9/EC of Jan. 29, 2003; Council Decision 2000/596/EC of Sept. 28, 2000.

25. COM (2001) 386 final and OJ C 332 E of Nov. 27, 2001.

26. Council Directive 2003/109/EC of Nov. 25, 2003.

27. Directive 2004/38/EC of Apr. 29, 2004. The member states were to implement the directive by April 2006.

28. Elspeth Guild, "The Legal Framework: Who Is Entitled to Move?" in *Controlling Frontiers: Free Movement into and within Europe,* ed. Didier Bigo and Elspeth Guild (Burlington, VT: Ashgate, 2005), 26.

29. Council Directive 2000/43/EC of June 29, 2000, implementing the principle of equal treatment between persons irrespective of racial or ethnic origin; Council Directive 2000/78/EC of Nov. 27, 2000, establishing a general framework for equal treatment in employment and occupation. The two directives were to be implemented by December 2003 at the latest.

30. Council Directive 2000/43/EC of June 29, 2000.

31. We must wait for the end of 2007 (the European Year for Equal Opportunities) to determine if this enthusiasm is relevant or not.

32. The EU had to initiate infringement procedures to ensure that transposition would occur (see ECJ ruling in the cases of Germany, Luxembourg, Austria, and Finland in 2005 and 2006).

33. These exceptions include, for instance, the right to treat persons differently on the basis of their religion, and access to family benefits. Furthermore, article 2 (5) of the Employment Equality Directive states that "this directive is without prejudice to measures laid down by national law which are necessary for public security, for the maintenance of public order, and the prevention of criminal offenses." This exception is largely incorporated into the legislation of various EU member states.

34. European Union Monitoring Centre on Racism and Xenophobia (EUMC), *Annual Report on Racism and Xenophobia in the EU Member States* (2005), 102.

35. Ibid., 27.

36. Anna Triandafyllidou, *Immigrants and National Identity in Europe* (London: Routledge, 2001), 73.

37. Resistance to immigrants is defined by the European Social Surveys (ESS) as "the resistance to the influx and admittance of immigrants belonging to a different race or ethnic group than the majority population."

38. The statements included in the survey were: "legally established immigrants from outside the EU should be sent back to their country of origin" and "legally established immigrants from outside the EU should be sent back to their country of origin if they are unemployed."

39. For instance, in the UK (47.8 percent), the Netherlands (36.5 percent), and Belgium (48.4 percent). The Eastern European countries include, e.g., Hungary (47.5 percent) and Slovenia (34.7 percent).

40. This growing preference is measured (ESS 2003) on the basis of responses to two statements: "it is better for a country if almost everyone shares customs and traditions" and "it is better for a country if there is a variety of different religions."

41. This resistance to the idea that diversity has benefits for society is measured (Eurobarometer 2000 and 2003) on the basis of responses to two statements: "it is a good thing for any society to be made up of people from different races, religions or cultures" and "a country's diversity in terms of race, religion, and culture adds to its strengths."

42. EUMC, *Annual Report on Racism and Xenophobia in the EU Member States* (2005), 32.

43. Common Decision (2001/931/CFSP) adopted in December 2001 (redefining terrorism); Council Decision Framework of June 2002 (European arrest warrants). See Council of the EU, "Council Common Position of 27 December 2001 on Combating Terrorism," Dec. 28, 2001; European Council, "A Secure Europe in a Better World—A European Security Strategy," Dec. 2003; Council of the EU, "Report on the Implementation of the Framework Decision 2002/475/JHA of 13 June 2002 on Combating Terrorism," Brussels, Oct. 12, 2004.

44. FRONTEX was used, for instance, in Spain to contain the "threat to security" posed by the flows of illegal immigrants and refugees from Morocco. See chap. 13, by Francisco Javier Moreno Fuentes, in this volume.

45. See for instance, Doron Zimmermann, "The European Union and Post 9/11 Counterterrorism: A Reappraisal," *Studies in Conflict and Terrorism* 29 (2006): 123–45.

46. Amnesty International EU Office, "Human Rights Dissolving at the Borders? Counter-Terrorism and EU Criminal Law," Executive Summary, May 2005, 2.

47. COM (2003) 336 final.

48. COM (2004) 811 final.

49. See Communication on Immigration Policy, COM (2000) 757, Nov. 2000; Communication on Integrating Migration Issues in the EU's Relations with Third Countries, COM (2002) 703, Dec. 2002; Opinion of the Economic and Social Committee on Immigration, Integration, and the Role of Civil Society Organizations, CES 365/2002; Conference on Managing Migration for the Benefit of Europe, Athens Migration Policy Initiative, May 2003; Communication on Immigration, Integration, and Employment, COM (2003) 336, June 2003.

50. COM (2003) 336 final, 25.

51. Examples include the MEDIS project of 2004, the "Green Paper on Equality and Non-Discrimination in an Enlarged EU," published by the Commission in May

2004, the "EU Handbook on Integration" (Nov. 2004), and the "Study on Data Collection to Measure the Extent and Impact of Discrimination in Europe," published by the Working group in December 2004.

52. COM (2004) 811 final, 5.

53. See COM (2005) 184 final.

54. COM (2005) 313 final.

55. EUMC, *Report on Islamophobia,* Vienna, May 2002, 5.

56. Ibid., 36: "The hijab became a visual identifier that not only represented the perpetrators of the attacks on the U.S. but also an embodiment of what is in itself stereotypically Islamophobic, namely the headscarf as a statement that is both anti-feminist and anti-Western."

57. EUMC, *Report on Islamophobia,* 36.

Chapter 12: Muslims and the State in Western Europe

The author is grateful for feedback from workshop participants at the Immigration, Liberty, and Security in Comparative Perspective Conference held at the Institut d'Etudes Politiques de Paris in June 2006 and at the University of Pittsburgh in September 2005, and to the organizers of those conferences: Ariane Chebel d'Appollonia and Simon Reich.

1. Bat Ye'or, *Eurabia: The Euro-Arab Axis* (Madison, NJ: Fairleigh Dickinson University Press, 2005); Niall Fergusson, "Eurabia," *New York Times,* Apr. 4, 2004; Timothy Savage, "Europe and Islam: Crescent Waxing, Cultures Clashing," *Washington Quarterly* 27 (2004): 25–50.

2. René Rémond, *Religion and Society in Modern Europe* (Oxford: Blackwell, 1999); Carolyn Warner and Manfred Wenner, "Religion and the Political Organization of Muslims in Europe," *Perspectives on Politics* 4, no. 3 (2006): 1–67.

3. Joel S. Fetzer and J. Christopher Soper, *Muslims and the State in Britain, France, and Germany* (Cambridge: Cambridge University Press, 2005); Zachary Shore, "Breeding New Bin Ladens: America's New Western Front," *Watch on the West* (Philadelphia, Foreign Policy Research Institute), 5, no. 11 (2004).

4. Yasemin Nuhoğlu Soysal, *Limits of Citizenship: Migrants and Postnational Membership in Europe* (Chicago: University of Chicago Press, 1994); Jytte Klausen, *The Islamic Challenge: Politics and Religion in Western Europe* (New York: Oxford University Press, 2005).

5. Nezar AlSayyad and Manuel Castells, eds., *Muslim Europe or Euro-Islam: Politics, Culture, and Citizenship in the Age of Globalization* (Lanham, MD: Lexington Books, 2004).

6. See, e.g., Felice Dassetto, ed., *Paroles d'islam: individus, sociétés et discours dans l'islam européen contemporain* (Paris: Maisonneuve and Larose, 2000).

7. Ralph Grillo, "Islam and Transnationalism," *Journal of Ethnic and Migration Studies* 30 (2004): 861–78.

8. Steven Krasner, *Sovereignty: Organized Hypocrisy* (Princeton, NJ: Princeton University Press, 1999), 223.

9. Arthur Bentley, *The Process of Government* (Evanston, IL: Principia, 1949); Theda Skocpol, *Bringing the State Back In* (Cambridge: Cambridge University Press, 1985).

10. Alain Gresh and Tariq Ramadan, *L'Islam en questions* (Paris: Sinbad/Actes Sud, 2000).

11. Christopher Caldwell, "Islamic Europe? When Bernard Lewis Speaks," *Weekly Standard* 10, no. 4 (Oct. 4, 2004).

12. Quoted in Lawrence Wright, "The Terror Web," *New Yorker,* July 26, 2004, 52.

13. Eugen Weber, *Peasants into Frenchmen: The Modernization of Rural France, 1870–1914* (Stanford, CA: Stanford University Press, 1976).

14. Gérard Noiriel, *Le creuset français: histoire de l'immigration, XIXe–XXe siècles* (Paris: Seuil, 1988).

15. Don Baker, "World Religions and National States: Competing Claims in East Asia," in *Transnational Religion and Fading States,* ed. Susanne Hoeber Rudolph and James Piscatori (Boulder, CO: Westview Press, 1997).

16. Nancy Rosenblum, ed., *Obligations of Citizenship and Demands of Faith: Religious Accommodation in Pluralist Democracies* (Princeton, NJ: Princeton University Press, 2000), 4; Bhikhu Parekh, *Rethinking Multiculturalism* (Cambridge, MA: Harvard University Press, 2002); Paul Mendes-Flores and Yehuda Reinharz, eds., *The Jew in the Modern World: A Documentary History* (Oxford: Oxford University Press, 1995).

17. Michael W. McConnell, "Believers as Equal Citizens," in *Obligations of Citizenship and Demands of Faith: Religious Accommodation in Pluralist Democracies,* ed. Nancy Rosenblum (Princeton, NJ: Princeton University Press, 2000), 92.

18. Jean-Jacques Rousseau, *On the Social Contract: With Geneva Manuscript and Political Economy,* ed. Roger D. Masters and trans. Judith R. Masters (New York: Bedford/St. Martin's Press, 1978), 126.

19. Patchen Markell, *Bound by Recognition* (Princeton, NJ: Princeton University Press, 2003), 31.

20. Ibid., 141.

21. Michael Minkenberg, "The Policy Impact of Church-State Relations: Family Policy and Abortion in Britain, France, and Germany," *West European Politics* 26, no. 1 (2003): 195ff.; Brigitte Maréchal, "Mosquées, organisations et leadership," in *Convergences musulmanes: aspects contemporains de l'islam dans l'Europe élargie,* ed. Felice Dassetto et al. (Louvain-la-Nueve, Belgium: Bruylant Academia, 2001).

22. Jocelyne Cesari, *Être musulman en France: associations, militants, et mosquées* (Paris: Karthala-Iremam, 1994), 29.

23. Aristide Zolberg and Long Litt Woon, "Why Islam Is like Spanish: Cultural Incorporation in Europe and the United States," *Politics and Society* 27, no. 1 (Mar. 1999): 5–38.

24. Fetzer and Soper, *Muslims and the State in Britain, France and Germany,* 94, 126.

25. See, e.g., Rémond, *Religion and Society in Modern Europe;* Giovanni Sartori, *Pluralismo, multiculturalismo e estranei: saggio sulla società multietnica* (Milan: Rizzoli, 2003).

26. Tariq Modood, "Multiculturalism, Secularism and the State," *Critical Review of International Social and Political Philosophy* 1 (1998): 114.

27. Rémond, *Religion and Society in Modern Europe;* Jonathan Laurence, "(Re)constructing Community: Turks, Jews, and German Responsibility," *German Politics and Society* 19 (summer 2001).

28. Carolyn Warner and Manfred Wenner, "Religion and the Political Organization of Muslims in Europe," *Perspectives on Politics* 4, no. 3 (2006): 461.

29. Sartori, *Pluralismo, multiculturalismo e estranei.*

30. Soysal, *Limits of Citizenship,* 139, 169.

31. Ibid., 87.

32. Olivier Roy, *L'islam mondialisé* (Paris: Seuil, 2002), 19.

33. Shireen Hunter, *The Future of Islam and the West: Clash of Civilizations or Peaceful Coexistence?* (Westport, CT: Praeger, 1998), 158.

34. See Thomas Lemmen, *Islamische Organisationen in Deutschland* (Bonn: Friedrich Ebert Stiftung, 2000).

35. Roy, *L'islam mondialisé,* 29.

36. Quoted in Magdi Allam and Roberto Gritti, *Islam, Italia* (Milan: Guerini, 2001), 54.

37. Dale Eickelman, "Trans-state Islam and Security," in *Transnational Religion and Fading States,* ed. Susanne Hoeber Rudolph and James Piscatori (Boulder, CO: Westview Press, 1997), 37.

38. Roy, *L'islam mondialisé.*

39. Adrian Favell, *Philosophies of Integration: Immigration and the Idea of Citizenship in France and Britain* (Houndsmills, England: Macmillan, 1998); Erik Bleich, "The French Model: Color-Blind Integration," in *Color Lines: Affirmative Action, Immigration, and Civil Rights Options for America,* ed. John David Skrentny (Chicago: University of Chicago Press, 2001).

40. Cesari, *Être musulman en France;* Ruud Koopmans, "Germany and Its Immigrants: An Ambivalent Relationship," *Journal of Ethnic and Migration Studies* 25 (1999): 627–47.

41. Claire de Galembert, "La régulation étatique du religieux à l'épreuve de la globalisation" in *La globalisation du religieux,* ed. Jean-Pierre Bastian et al. (Paris: L'Harmattan, 2001).

42. Confidential interview, June 2002.

43. Susanne Hoeber Rudolph, "Introduction: Religion, States, and Transnational Civil Society," in *Transnational Religion and Fading States*, ed. Susanne Hoeber Rudolph and James Piscatori (Boulder, CO: Westview Press, 1997); Eickelman, "Trans-state Islam and Security."

44. Mustapha Benchenane, *Pour un dialogue euro-arabe* (Paris: Berger-Levrault, 1983).

45. Gilles Kepel, *Les banlieues de l'islam: naissance d'une religion en France* (Paris: Seuil, 1991); Parekh, *Rethinking Multiculturalism.*

46. Hugh Heclo, *Modern Social Politics in Britain and Sweden: From Relief to Income Maintenance* (New Haven, CT: Yale University Press, 1974), 306.

47. Dounia Bouzar, "Etude de 12 associations à référence musulmane: l'islam entre mythe et religion: le nouveau discours religieux dans les associations socio-culturelles musulmanes," *Les Cahiers de la Sécurité Intérieure* (IHESI), 54 (2004); Vincent Geisser and Khadija Finan, *L'islam à l'école* (Paris: IHESI, 2002).

48. Jean-Pierre Chevènement, interview by author, Paris, Nov. 2003.

49. Eickelman, "Trans-state Islam and Security," 31.

50. Laurence, "(Re)constructing Community."

51. Quoted in "La Consulta islamica condanna," *Libertà,* Feb. 10, 2006.

52. Ibid.

53. *Welt am Sonntag*, May 28, 2006.

54. Quoted in Jann Rübel, "Sind die Muslime ein Stück Deutschland, Herr Schäuble?" *Welt am Sonntag*, May 28, 2006.

55. Heidrun Tempel, ministerial advisor on religious communities, Federal Chancellery, interview by author, Berlin, Jan. 12, 2006.

56. Martin Lutz, "Schäuble startet Islam-Konferenz im September," *Die Welt,* May 24, 2006.

57. Wolfgang Schäuble, "Deutsche Islam Konferenz—Perspektiven für eine gemeinsame Zukunft: Regierungserklärung zur DIK am 27. September," Sept. 28, 2006, www.cducsu.de.

58. Quoted in "Kizilkaya will Idomeneo nicht sehen," Sept. 29, 2006, www.stern.de.

59. Quoted in Katharina Schuler, "Der Wohlfühl-Gipfel," *Die Zeit,* Sept. 27, 2006.

Chapter 13: Dissonance between Discourse and Practice in EU Border Control Enforcement

1. Despite the magnitude of those return flows, more than 2 million Spanish nationals were still living abroad at the end of the 1990s.

2. The relatively rapid annual growth in the number of foreign residents of the late 1990s (17.5 percent between 1998 and 1999) accelerated after 2000, with average annual increases of more than 40 percent (Instituto Nacional de Estatistica [INE, Madrid], "Boletín informativo del INE," no. 3, 2006).

3. G. Brochmann, *European Integration and Immigration from Third Countries* (Oslo: Scandinavian University Press, 1996); Z. Layton-Henry, "Citizenship and Migrant Workers in Western Europe," University of Warwick, 1992.

4. In an influential report entitled *Improving Living and Working Conditions: Social Integration of Immigrants from Non-Community Countries* (European Commission, 1994), the Commission had stated the three main lines of policy that should characterize EU immigration policies in the following years: cooperation with sending countries to prevent migratory flows, control of migration flows toward the Union within manageable parameters, and strengthening integration policies for legal immigrants. This document proposed a series of objectives such as the amelioration of the position of third country nationals legally residing within the Union, the improvement of the general conditions for social integration, and the need to combat racism and xenophobia. In 1997, the European Commission presented a new document, *Proposal for a Council Act Establishing the Convention of Rules for the Admission of Third Country Nationals to the Member States* (Brussels, 1997). In it the Commission tried to set out common rules for the admission of third country nationals for the purpose of employment, studying or training, and family reunification. It also attempted to define basic rights for long-term residents, including the possibility of working in another member state besides the one where they acquired their initial residence permits. This proposal failed to receive the necessary support from the Council of Ministers because most member states representatives considered it too liberal (J. Niessen, "EU Policies on Immigration and Integration after the Amsterdam Treaty," Migration Policy Group, 1999, 10).

5. K. Hailbronner, "Third-Country Nationals and EC Law," in *A Citizens' Europe: In Search of a New Order,* ed. A. Roass and E. Antola (London: Sage, 1995), 185; G. Callovi, "Immigration and the European Community," *Contemporary European Affairs* 4 (1991): 25; Christian Joppke, *Immigration and the Nation-State: The United States, Germany, and Great Britain* (Oxford: Oxford University Press, 1999), 36. On specific

philosophies of integration see Adrian Favell, *Philosophies of Integration: Immigration and the Idea of Citizenship in France and Britain* (Houndsmills, England: Macmillan, 1998).

6. See Hailbronner, "Third-Country Nationals and EC Law."

7. P. Weil, "The Transformation of Immigration Policies: Immigration Control and Nationality Laws in Europe: A Comparative Approach," EUI Working Paper 98/5 (Florence, 1998), 22.

8. Those factors in the immigration policy sphere could be classified as conditioned by geopolitical considerations (geographical situation, political culture, historical interactions, and diplomatic interest) and aspects related to the policymaking process proper (degree of politicization of immigration issues, mechanisms of agenda building, and administrative and legal traditions of each specific country).

9. C. Radaelli, "How Does Europeanisation Produce Domestic Policy Change? Corporate Tax Policy in Italy and the United Kingdom," *Comparative Political Studies* 30 (1997): 555.

10. H. Pérés, "L'Europe commence à Gibraltar: le dilemme espagnol face à l'immigration," *Pôle Sud* 11 (1999): 15.

11. That system included building a road around the perimeter of the enclaves and installing a double barbed-wired fence 3.2 meters high, with ditches, turrets, thermal sensors, and infrared cameras to support the patrols of the Guardia Civil (Civil Guard).

12. This change in the visa policy with respect to countries of Latin America was particularly difficult to justify and implement due to the historical connections that link Spain to those countries, to the perception of the existence of a historical debt toward those countries for the role they played as receivers of Spanish emigrants up to the 1950s, and because of the increasing economic interests of Spanish firms in the markets of that area.

13. Public statements by Spanish officials about co-financing border policing efforts have been quite common. See some examples in *El País,* Sept. 4, 1996, Jan. 16, 1998, Aug. 9, 1998, Nov. 14, 1999, and Oct. 21, 2003. The navies of different European countries (Italy, Great Britain, France, and Spain) have been developing closer ties to work together in the patrolling of the Mediterranean Sea to prevent unwanted migratory flows.

14. Africans, those most directly affected by the increased controls on the southern borders, represented roughly 25 percent of the total foreigners legally living in Spain in 2005, but they currently are estimated to constitute only around 10 percent of the total number of undocumented migrants.

15. Hailbronner, "Third-Country Nationals and EC Law," 201. The European Parliament showed a more positive stance toward these kinds of processes, and in April 1997 it advised all member states to regularize the legal status of undocumented immigrants with some period of residence in the host country (Ministerio de Trabajo y Asuntos Sociales [hereafter cited as MTAS], "Informe sobre la Inmigración y el Asilo en España," Foro para la Integración Social de los Inmigrantes, 1998, 27).

16. During the development of the process to legalize undocumented workers, initially designed to last for two months over the summer period, a large number of undocumented immigrants were detained, creating distrust toward the authorities and therefore limiting the efficacy of the regularization process. Together with the strict legislation, the lack of a specialized agency staffed by experienced personnel and supplied with the necessary resources contributed to generating and perpetuating the existence of

a large group of undocumented immigrants. One year after the end of that regularization process, only thirteen thousand of those who had received a permit during the period retained it, due to the strict conditions for renewal of those permits (MTAS, "Informe sobre la Inmigración y el Asilo en España," 33).

17. Bernabé López García, *Immigración magrebí en España: el retorno de los moriscos* (Madrid: MAPFRE, 1993), 66.

18. M. Hernando de Larramendi, "La proyección mediterránea de España: las relaciones con Mazzuecos," in *Murcia, frontera demográfica en el sur de Europa,* ed. J. Vilar (Universidad de Murcia, 1994), 132.

19. Hailbronner, "Third-Country Nationals and EC Law," 203.

20. The granting of those rights to all immigrants may in fact run counter to policy at the EU level, as the strategy paper on immigration and asylum by the Austrian presidency clearly stated: "No European country today would consider going it alone in opening up the right of asylum, making access easier for immigrant workers or increasing social security benefits for immigrants. Such topics do not therefore need to be discussed even at regular intervals" (European Council, 1998, 5, www.proasyl.de/texte/europe/eu-a-o.htm).

21. In 1998 Spain had the lowest fertility rate in the world, with only 1.07 children per woman. Since the beginning of the 1990s, Spain has been at the bottom of the international rankings of fertility rates, together with Italy and Hong Kong. See *El País,* Dec. 22, 1999.

22. In the same report, the UN report estimated that by the year 2025, some 159 million immigrants would be necessary to maintain the current levels of social protection that characterize European welfare states.

23. In the case of labor-intensive agriculture, particularly in the southeastern part of Spain, the possibility of keeping production costs down through the use of low-paid undocumented immigrants allowed many farms to remain competitive in the European markets against imports from other countries such as Morocco, where the same produce is grown at much lower costs.

24. For example, the serious racist incidents in El Ejido in January 2000, when the killing of a Spanish woman by a Moroccan immigrant under psychological treatment was followed by three days of attacks against the immigrant community (houses, shops, and cafés burned, along with the site that was used as a mosque by the Moroccan immigrants), reflected the final explosion of a malaise that had been mounting in the previous years due to the uncontrolled arrival of undocumented immigrants and to the activities of some xenophobic entrepreneurs who capitalized on the tensions generated by that situation.

25. In 2003, both employers and trade unions publicly declared their interest in changing the immigrants' rafts for boat tickets and their shanty towns for decent housing arrangements. They also expressed their intention to negotiate with the Spanish government to set up a new system for the regulation of unskilled labor migration.

26. A Spanish colony until 1975, the Western Sahara was annexed by Morocco after Spain retreated from that territory during a period of internal political instability (just prior to the death of the dictator Franco) and international tension (Moroccan authorities organized the "Green March," mobilizing tens of thousands of Moroccan citizens to claim the territory for Morocco). The final status of that territory remains unresolved after a guerrilla war between the Moroccan state and the Sahrawi Polisario Front ended

in a UN-brokered cease-fire in 1991; a UN-organized referendum has repeatedly been postponed. Although the enclaves of Ceuta and Melilla have been under Spanish control for more than five centuries, Moroccan authorities do not recognize Spanish sovereignty over those cities. The issue has been used by the Moroccan state as a means of pressuring the Spanish governments at critical junctures of the relations between both countries.

27. On joint sea patrols, see *El País,* Sept. 16, 2004.

28. The images of immigrants who drowned while trying to cross the Strait function as a tragic indicator of the importance of rafts as transportation for migrants. According to the ombudsman of Andalucía, more than one thousand immigrants were reported to have died while trying to cross the Strait between 1993 and 1998. For ATIME, an association of Moroccan immigrants in Spain, that figure reflects the deaths for 1998 alone, because most shipwrecks took place near the Moroccan coast or were taken away by the sea's currents and therefore went unnoticed by Spanish authorities (*El País,* Feb. 9, 1998, Aug. 8, 1998).

29. During the 2000–2002 period, relations between both states deteriorated considerably. That period was marked by events such as the nonrenewal of the agreement for the Spanish fleet's access to Moroccan fisheries in December 2000, the increasingly argumentative dialogue that culminated in the withdrawal of ambassadors, and finally the crisis over Perejil/Laila island in July 2002, which ended with the intervention of the Spanish army to establish the *status quo ante* and the United States calling on both parties to stop the escalation of tensions.

30. That strategy was used to bring to Spain some eleven hundred Moroccan workers in 2004, and the agreement was to be expanded to allow entry to some twenty-one hundred workers in 2005 (*El País,* Sept. 16, 2004).

31. E. Gil Calvo, *El miedo es el mensaje: riesgo, incertidumbre y medios de comunicación* (Madrid: Alianza, 2004).

32. The survey of May 2004 elaborated by the *Centro de Investigaciones Sociológicas* (Spanish Center for Sociological Research), largely dedicated to the perceptions of migration, did not include the traditional question on the relative perception of different migrant communities.

33. M. J. Campo Ladero, *Opiniones y actitudes de los españoles ante el fenómeno de la inmigración* (Madrid: Centro de Investigaciones Sociológicas, 2004); Centro de Investigaciones Sociológicas, "Barómetro, mayo 2003," Madrid, 2003; J. Díez Nicolás, *Actitudes hacia los inmigrantes* (Madrid: Ministerio de Trabajo y Asuntos Sociales, 1998).

34. V. Pérez Díaz, B. Álvarez Miranda, and E. Chulea, *La inmigración musulmana en Europa: Turcos en Alemania, argelinos en Francia y marroquíes en España* (Barcelona: Fundación "la Caixa," 2004).

35. M. A. Cea D'Ancona, *La activación de la xenofobia en España: ¿qué miden las encuestas?* (Madrid: Centro de Investigaciones Sociológicas, 2004).

36. L. Cachfin Rodríguez, *Prevenir el racismo en el trabajo en España* (Madrid: Instituto de Migraciones y Servicios Sociales, 1999).

37. Colectivo IOÉ, *Inmigración y trabajo: trabajadores inmigrantes en el sector de la construcción* (Madrid: Imserso, 1998).

38. Article 13 of the Amsterdam Treaty enabled the European Commission to take action to tackle discrimination in a range of areas, including gender, racial or ethnic origin, religion or beliefs, disability, and sexual orientation. Following that mandate, the Commission passed the Racial Equality Directive, requiring EU member states to develop a coherent and integrated approach to fight discrimination.

39. F. J. Moreno Fuentes, "Migration and Spanish Nationality Law," in *Towards a European Nationality: Citizenship, Immigration and Nationality Law in the EU,* ed. Patrick Weil and Randall Hansen (London: Palgrave, 2001)

40. Christian Joppke, ed., *Challenge to the Nation State: Immigration in Western Europe and the United States* (Oxford: Oxford University Press, 1998).

41. E. Malefakis, "Southern Europe in the XIXth and XXth Centuries: An Historical Overview," Working paper, Instituto Juan March de Estudios e Investigaciones, Madrid, 1992.

Chapter 14: The Challenge to Integration in France

1. See Nonna Mayer, *Ces Français qui votent Le Pen* (Paris: Flammarion, 2002).

2. On this debate see Vincent Geisser, *La nouvelle islamophobie* (Paris: La Découverte, 2003) or Thomas Deltombe, *L'Islam imaginaire: la construction médiatique de l'islamophobie en France, 1975–2005* (Paris: La Découverte, 2005).

3. This CEVIPOF survey was conducted with the financial support of the Service d'Information du Gouvernement (SIG or French Government Information Service), the Centre d'Etudes et de Prospectives du Ministère de l'Intérieur (Study and Forecast Center of the French Home Office), the Fonds d'Action et de Soutien pour l'Intégration et la Lutte contre les Discriminations (FASILD or Action and Support Funds for Integration and the Fight against Discrimination), and the Jean Jaurès Foundation.

4. For more information about the INSEE EHF survey, see Michèle Tribalat, "Une estimation des populations d'origine étrangère en France en 1999," *Population* 59 (2004): 51–82.

5. For more information see Jeanne-Hélène Kaltenbach and Michèle Tribalat, *La République et l'Islam: entre crainte et aveuglement* (Paris: Gallimard, 2002).

6. A specific trait of this group is their average age of thirty-nine years, compared to forty-six for republicans and fifty for assimilationists.

7. See Jocelyne Cesari, *When Islam and Democracy Meet: Muslims in Europe and in the United States* (New York: Palgrave Macmillan, 2006), originally published as *L'islam à l'épreuve de l'occident* (Paris: La Découverte, 2004); Rémy Leveau and Gilles Kepel, eds., *Les musulmans dans la société française* (Paris: Presses de Sciences Po, 1988); Nancy Venel, *Musulmans et français* (Paris: PUF, 2004); Sonia Tebbakh, "Identités politiques des Français d'origine maghrébine," Ph.D. thesis, Institut d'Etudes Politiques de Grenoble, Université Pierre-Mendès-France, Dec. 2004; Tebbakh, "L'islam et les Français d'origine maghrébine: incidences du religieux sur le rapport au monde et l'adhésion aux valeurs," in *Religion et valeurs,* ed. C. Dargent, B. Duriez, and R. Liogier (Paris: L'Harmattan, 2006).

8. See Cesari, *L'islam à l'épreuve de l'occident.*

9. See Danièle Hervieu-Leger, *Catholicisme, la fin d'un monde* (Paris: Bayard, 2003); Yves Lambert and Guy Michelat, eds., *Crépuscule des religions chez les jeunes? jeunes et religions en France* (Paris: L'Harmattan, 1992).

10. See Guy Michelat, "L'identité catholiques des Français: I. les dimensions de la religiosité," *Revue Française de Sociologie* 31 (July–Sept. 1990): 355–88; and "L'identité catholiques des Français: II. Appartenance et socialisation religieuse," *Revue Française de Sociologie* 31 (Oct.–Dec. 1990): 609–33.

11. See Sylvain Brouard and Vincent Tiberj, *Français comme les autres?* (Paris: Presses de Sciences Po, 2005).

12. For example, some questions could artificially create an identity clash. Consider, for example, this question: "Do you feel only French, more French than European, equally French and European, more European than French, European only?" Another example is the question asked by the Pew Global Attitudes Project: "What do you consider yourself first? A citizen of your country or a Muslim/Christian?" The wording of these questions places into competition two identities that are not mutually exclusive or even comparable for the respondents.

13. This is the line of questioning that dealt with "proximity": "Would you say that you are very close, close, not close, or not close at all to: the residents of your neighborhood, the French, citizens of other European countries, citizens of the country from which your family emigrated, people your age, people of your social milieu, people who share your religion, immigrants in France?"

Chapter 15: "Weak Immigrants" in Britain and Italy

1. While at the beginning of the 2000s around half a million undocumented immigrants and half a million asylum seekers entered the EU 25 on a yearly basis, these numbers were halved by 2005. For extensive sets of statistics see UNHRC, *Asylum Levels and Trends in Industrialized Countries, 2005* (2006), available online at www.unhcr.org/statis tics/STATISTICS/44153f592.pdf. See also UN Relief and Works Agency (UNRWA) statistics (available online at www.un.org/unrwa/publications/pdf), U.S. Committee for Refugees and Immigrants (USCRI) statistics for the *World Refugee Survey 2005* (available online at www.refugees.org/article.aspx?id=1342), as well as Internally Displaced People (IDP) Project statistics (available online at www.idpproject.org/global_overview.htm).

2. Marco Giugni and Florence Passy (*Political Altruism? Solidarity Movements in International Perspective* [Lanham, MD: Rowman and Littlefield, 2001]) have provided an extensive discussion of political altruism and applications of this concept. See also, by Johanna Simeant, *La cause des sans-papiers* (Paris: Presses de Sciences Po, 1998), and *Le travail humanitaire* (Paris: Presses de Sciences Po, 1998).

3. Andrew Geddes, *Immigration and European Integration: Towards Fortress Europe?* (Manchester, England: Manchester University Press, 2000); Virginie Guiraudon, "Weak Weapons of the Weak? Transnational Mobilization around Migration in the European Union," in *Contentious Europeans: Protest and Politics in an Emerging Polity*, ed. D. Imig and S. Tarrow (Boston: Rowman and Littlefield, 2001), 163–85.

4. Ruud Koopmans and Paul Statham, *Challenging Immigration and Ethnic Relations Politics: Comparative European Perspectives* (Oxford: Oxford University Press, 2000).

5. Giovanna Zincone, "A Model of 'Reasonable Integration': Summary of the First Report on the Integration of Immigrants in Italy," *International Migration Review* 34 (2000): 956–68.

6. Compare UNHCR, *Asylum Levels and Trends in Industrialized Countries, 2005.*

7. R. Kaye, "Redefining the Refugee: The UK Media Portrayal of Asylum Seekers," in *The New Migration in Europe: Social Constructions and Social Realities,* ed. K. Koser and H. Lutz (Basingstoke, England: Macmillan; New York: St. Martin's Press, 1998).

8. For the official estimates, see United Kingdom, Home Office Report 29/05, *Sizing the Unauthorised Migrant Population in the United Kingdom in 2001,* www.home office.gov.uk/rds/pdfs05/rdsolr2905.pdf. For a prompt reaction using this official estimate against asylum seekers, see Migration Watch, *The Illegal Migrant Population in the UK,* www.migrationwatchuk.org/Briefingpapers/migration_trends/illegal_mi grant_pop_ in_uk.asp.

9. See the articles "Labour May Steal Tory Thunder on Migrants Asylum," *Financial Times,* Jan. 25, 2005; and "EU Immigration Deals 'to Stop Asylum Shopping,'" The Press Association, Jan. 25, 2005.

10. Law 28/2/1990 n. 39 (Martelli law); Law 6/3/1998 n. 40 (Turco-Napolitano law); Law 30/7/2002 n. 189 (Bossi-Fini law).

11. It should be noted, however, that specific claims for asylum follow the same pattern in Italy as in Britain. Claims reached a peak of sixteen thousand in 2002, before reaching their lowest level of ninety-five hundred in 2005. Compare UNHCR, *Asylum Levels and Trends in Industrialized Countries, 2005,* and Caritas/Migrantes, *Immigrazione: Dossier Statistico 2004* (Rome: IDOS Centro Studi e Ricerche, 2004), 118–26.

12. See UNHCR, "UNHCR Deeply Concerned over Lampedusa Deportations" (press release), Mar. 18, 2005. Compare the report of the UN Special Rapporteur following her June 2004 visit to "CPTAs" and "identification centers" in Italy (UN Doc No: E/CN.4/2005/85) as well as two reports Amnesty International produced in 2005, namely, *Italy: Temporary Stay—Permanent Rights* (AI Index: EUR 30/004/2005); and *Amnesty International Calls on the European Commission to Take Action against Italy* (AI Index: IOR 61/007/2005).

13. Maria-Teresa Gil-Bazo, "The Practice of Mediterranean States in the Context of the European Union's Justice and Home Affairs External Dimension: The Safe Third Country Concept Revisited," *International Journal of Refugee Law* 18, no. 3–4 (2006): 571–600.

14. Compare the report of Human Rights Watch (HRW), "Stemming the Flow: Abuses against Migrants, Asylum-seekers and Refugees," vol. 18, no. 5(E) (Sept. 2006) (www.libertysecurity.org/IMG/pdf/libya0906web.pdf), which draws on research conducted between April and May 2005. This report states that many of those expelled from Lampedusa have not had access to basic rights. HRW found that Italy has regularly deported undocumented refugees and immigrants to Libya (which in some cases has in turn returned them to their home countries where they are at risk of abuse or persecution) while conducting collective expulsions in violation of Italy's human rights and asylum obligations. The primary problem, it is argued, is that Libya does not have an asylum law and is not a signatory of the UN Convention on Refugees of 1951. See also European Commission, *Technical Mission to Libya on Illegal Immigration, 27 November–6 December, Report,* which presents an analysis of illegal immigration in Libya following a Commission technical mission that was conducted in late 2004.

15. National press, official documents, extracts from research interviews, and Web material of different kinds provide numerous instances of verbal attacks against asylum seekers and undocumented immigrants.

16. For some recent examples of the most rabid attacks in the British tabloids, see the articles "Bombers Are All Sponging Asylum Seekers," *Daily Express,* July 27, 2005; and "This Is Your Mess, Blair," *Sun,* May 4, 2006.

17. On the spread of xenophobic sentiments, see Paul M. Sniderman et al., *The Outsider: Prejudice and Politics in Italy* (Princeton, NJ: Princeton University Press, 2000); Roger Hewitt, *White Backlash and the Politics of Multiculturalism* (Cambridge: Cambridge University Press, 2005).

18. Compare the report of Amnesty International, *Seeking Asylum Is Not a Crime: Detention of People Who Have Sought Asylum* (AI Index: EUR 45/015/2005).

19. See the report of Medici Senza Frontiere (MSF), *Rapporto sui centri di perma-*

nenza temporanei e assistenza, www.medicisenzafrontiere.it/msfinforma/dossier/missione _italia/CPT_FINALE.pdf.

20. See UNHRC, *Asylum Levels and Trends in Industrialized Countries, 2005.* See also Forum Réfugiés (2006), *Rapport annuel sur l'asile en France et en Europe.*

21. At the time of this writing, however, many EU member states (including Britain and Italy) have not made the elements of this directive part of their national legislations, thus delaying the removal of important cross-national disparities on conditions for granting refugee status.

22. See UNHCR, *The European Union, Asylum, and the International Refugee Protection Regime: UNHCR's Recommendation for the New Multi-Annual Programme in the Area of Freedom, Security, and Justice,* Sept. 2004; European Parliament, Sept. 20, 2001, OJ 2002 C 77 E/94.

23. For example, some have gone on hunger strikes or sewn their own lips shut. See the *Guardian,* May 31, 2003; "Da Cpt a centri d'accoglienza," *Il Giornale di Calabria,* Dec. 15, 2006.

24. Meindert Fennema, "The Concept and Measurement of Civic Community," *Journal of Ethnic and Migration Studies* 30, no. 3 (2004): 429–47. See also research that is delivered by LOCALMULTIDEM under the EU Framework Programme 6, available online at www.um.es/localmultidem/index.php.

25. Dirk Jacobs, Karen Phalet, and Marc Swyngedouw, "Associational Membership and Political Involvement among Ethnic Minority Groups in Brussels," *Journal of Ethnic and Migration Studies* 30 (2004): 543–59; Karen Phalet and Marc Swyngedouw, "National Identities and Representations of Citizenship: A Comparison of Turks, Moroccans, and Working-Class Belgians in Brussels," *Ethnicities* 2 (2002): 5–30.

26. B. Rothstein and Dietlind Stolle, "Social Capital, Impartiality, and the Welfare State: An Institutional Approach," in *Generating Social Capital: Civil Society and Institutions in Comparative Perspective,* ed. M. Hooghe and D. Stolle (New York: Palgrave Macmillan, 2003); M. Cinalli and M. Giugni, "Institutional and Discursive Opportunities for the Political Integration of Migrants in European Cities," paper presented at the Conference of the ESA Research Network for the Sociology of Culture, Ghent, Nov. 2006.

27. On resource mobilization theory, see Anthony Obershall, *Social Conflict and Social Movements* (Englewood Cliffs, NJ: Prentice-Hall, 1973); John D. McCarthy and Mayer N. Zald, "Resource Mobilization and Social Movements: A Partial Theory," *American Journal of Sociology* 82 (1977): 1212–41.

28. For the political opportunity structure approach, see Peter K. Eisinger, "The Conditions of Protest Behavior in American Cities," *American Political Science Review* 67 (1973): 11–28; Hans-Peter Kriesi, et al., *New Social Movements in Western Europe: A Comparative Analysis* (Minneapolis: University of Minnesota Press, 1995); Sidney Tarrow, *Power in Movement* (Cambridge: Cambridge University Press, 1998).

29. Available data that are not systematically treated in this chapter refer to exchanges of information, commitment to common projects, participation in the same mobilizations, overlapping memberships, and creation of common organizational structures. All these types of relationships have been taken as ties of cooperation. Regarding disagreements, available data that are not systematically treated refer to ad hoc disputes, latent dissension, and open conflict.

30. For an introductory text on network analysis see John Scott, *Social Network Analysis: A Handbook,* 2nd ed. (London: Sage, 2000), while for a detailed treatment see Stanley Wasserman and Katherine Faust, *Social Network Analysis: Methods and Applications* (Cambridge: Cambridge University Press, 1994). Some scholars have examined network analysis with an emphasis on research methods (David Knoke and James Kuklinsky, *Network Analysis* [London: Sage, 1982]). For the most current treatments, see works by Peter J. Carrington, John Scott, and Stanley Wasserman, eds., *Models and Methods in Social Network Analysis* (Cambridge: Cambridge University Press, 2005), and Wouter de Nooy, Andrej Mrvar, and Vladimir Batagelj, *Exploratory Social Network Analysis with Pajek* (Cambridge: Cambridge University Press, 2005).

31. Density expresses the ratio of the existing ties in the network to the total number of possible ties. Resulting values of density range between 0 and 1, with 1 indicating an ideal field where each actor is tied to any other actor and 0, an ideal field with no ties at all.

32. Larger networks are often characterized by lower density rates because there are only a certain number of exchanges in which actors can realistically engage.

33. The scheme introduced a new system of subsistence benefits for asylum seekers in the restrictive form of vouchers. Furthermore, supermarkets were entitled to keep the change when asylum seekers used their vouchers. Oxfam and the Refugee Council have successfully led the campaign. Among the many protest measures was a supermarket action card, of which more than 100,000 were distributed to groups across the country.

Chapter 16: Immigration

1. See Council of the European Union, Council Directive 2004/83/EC of Apr. 2004, on minimum standards for the qualification and status of third country nationals or stateless persons as refugees; and Council Directive 2005/85/EC of Dec. 2005, on minimum standards on procedures for granting and withdrawing refugee status.

2. According to this article, member states may revoke, end, or refuse to renew the status granted to a refugee by a governmental, administrative, judicial, or quasi-judicial body when there are reasonable grounds for regarding him or her as a danger to the security of the member state in which he or she is present. They may do the same when he or she, having been convicted by a final judgment of a particularly serious crime, constitutes a danger to the community of that member state.

Furthermore, while article 21 reaffirms the obligation of member states to "respect the principle of *non-refoulement* in accordance with their international obligations" (paragraph 1), its second paragraph nevertheless contains an exception to the rule, similar to the one enshrined in paragraph 2 of article 33 of the Geneva Convention: "Where not prohibited by the international obligations mentioned in paragraph 1, Member States may refoule a refugee, whether formally recognized or not, when: (a) there are reasonable grounds for considering him or her as a danger to the security of the Member State in which he or she is present; or (b) he or she, having been convicted by a final judgment of a particularly serious crime, constitutes a danger to the community of that Member State."

3. See European Union Monitoring Centre on Racism and Xenophobia (EUMC), *Annual Report on Racism and Xenophobia in the EU Member States* (2005), 27.

4. In France, the Day-to-Day Security Law (Loi de sécurité quotidienne) was adopt-

ed in October 2001; the German Second Security Package (Sicherheitspaket II) was adopted in December 2001.

5. An ISMI catcher (or GSM interceptor) is a portable electronic device that identifies and registers all mobile phones within a two-hundred-meter radius.

6. See Benjamin J. Muller, "(Dis)Qualified Bodies: Securitization, Citizenship, and 'Identity Management,'" *Citizenship Studies* 8, no. 3 (Sept. 2004): 279–94.

7. Council of Europe, *Impact of Future Demographic Trends in Europe,* DG3/CAPH10 (2005) 6 final, 2005.

8. The old-age dependency ratio (ODR) is the ratio of the size of population aged sixty-five years or more to the size of the population in "productive age" (fifteen to sixty-four years). The ODR in Europe was 22 percent in 2005, and it is expected to reach 45 percent in 2050 (Council of Europe, *Impact of Future Demographic Trends in Europe,* 2005).

9. In order to maintain the unchanged old-age dependency ratio in the twenty-seven European countries included in their study, Bijak et al. estimate that just under 830 million immigrants would be needed in these countries by 2052, well above the absorption capacity of Europe in the coming years. See J. Bijak, D. Kupiszewski, and K. Saczuk, *Impact of International Migration on Population Dynamics and Labor Force Resources in Europe,* CEFMR Working Paper 1/2005 (Warsaw: Central European Forum for Migration Research, 2005).

10. EU Commission, "An EU Approach to Managing Economic Migration" (green paper), COM (2004) 811 final, Brussels, 2005, 5.

11. UN, Population Division, *Replacement Migration: Is It a Solution to Declining and Aging Populations?* (New York: United Nations Population Division, ESA/P/WP.160, 2000), 22.

12. Population change refers to the difference between the actual population change that did occur in a particular period given the presence of both immigration and emigration, and the population change that would have occurred in that time if there had been no immigration or emigration.

13. However, the UN projected that the U.S. fertility rate will fall to 1.91 births per woman in 2015–2020, a rate that is still higher than current European levels.

14. UN, Population Division, *Replacement Migration,* 73.

15. In 2006, the median age was 35.5 in the United States and 37.7 in Europe.

16. According to the UN Population Division, the PSR (potential support ratio) will reach 2.8 in 2050. In the absence of immigration, it would be necessary to raise the retirement age to about seventy-four in order to maintain the same PSR as in 1995. The Center for Retirement Research estimated that men and women between twenty-five and fifty-four years old accounted for 71.7 percent of the labor force in 1998 but expected that their share would fall to 68.1 percent as early as 2006 (Daniel S. Hammermesh, "Older Workers in the Coming Labor 'Shortage': Implications on Labor Demand," Center for Retirement Research, Boston, 2001, www.bc.edu/bc_org/avp/csom/executive/crr/public_spe.shtml).

17. See Scott Lanman and Craig Torres, "Bernanke Warns of Possible 'Crisis' from Budget Gap," Bloomberg News, Jan. 18, 2007, www.bloomberg.com/apps/news?pid=20601087&sid=a_46QcGbvFZk&refer=home.

18. European Social Survey, 2003.

19. See Pew Global Attitudes Project, "Muslims in Europe: Economic Worries Top

Concerns About Religious and Cultural Identity," July 6, 2006, http://pewglobal.org/reports/display.php?ReportID=254.

20. Unemployment rates are consistently higher for immigrants than for the rest of the population. In Europe, the share of unemployed foreigners (relative to their share in the labor force) is highest in the Netherlands, followed by sizable numbers in Denmark and Belgium. It is worth noting that countries that have relatively low aggregate unemployment rates (such as Denmark, the Netherlands, Sweden, and the United Kingdom) also tend to have the highest immigrant unemployment rates. Unemployment rates vary according to the national origin of immigrants. In some states, immigrants from non-Western countries have unemployment rates that are 3 to 4 times higher than the national average (Denmark, Finland, Sweden, the Netherlands); the figure is about double the national average in France and Germany. In France, youth of North African origin (who are mostly French-born) have twice the unemployment rate of "natives." The largest disparity in the UK in 2003, for example, was between Caucasians on the one hand, and Bangladeshis and Pakistanis on the other. While the percentages stood at 5.8 percent for Caucasians, the figures were 13 percent for all ethnic minorities together, and 23 and 20 percent for Bangladeshis and Pakistanis, respectively. See EUMC, *Report on Migrants, Minorities, and Employment* (2003), esp. 31.

21. Eurobarometer 65, "Public Opinion in the European Union," July 2006. Sixty-three percent of the respondents in the former EU 10 expressed this concern, compared to 46 percent in the EU 15. Crime is the second most frequently mentioned concern (24 percent of the respondents in the EU 25).

22. European Social Survey, 2003.

23. Pew Global Attitudes Project, "Muslims in Europe." The German Commission on Immigration estimated that, if Germany maintains a net annual immigration of 200,000 (the average level for the past twenty years), the decline of German population would be limited to 12 million. Without immigration, it will shrink by 23 million between 2000 and 2020 (Rita Süssmuth, *Zuwanderung Gestalten, Integration Förden, Bericht der Unabhängingen Kommission* [Berlin: Zuwanderung, 2001], 67–68).

24. The proportion of youth among the population is already decreasing in the EU 25. In 2004, the population up to fourteen years of age represented 16.5 percent of the total population, compared with 18.8 percent in 1993. The population aged fifteen to twenty-four years had a share of 12.7 percent, as against 14.5 percent in 1993. Meanwhile, the proportion of the age group sixty-five to seventy-nine years rose from 10.9 percent to 12.5 percent (Eurostat, *Europe in Figures: Eurostat Yearbook for 2005,* 64).

25. Pew Research Center, "No Consensus on Immigration Problem and Proposed Fixes: America's Immigration Quandary," Mar. 30, 2006.

26. See, for example, Kristin Wedding, "The Immigration Debate," *Strategy Report* (Center for Strategic and International Studies), 2, no. 7 (Apr. 20, 2006). The Center for Immigration Studies reported 9.6 million to 9.8 million illegal immigrants (on the basis of the March 2005 Current Population Survey [CPS]) while the Pew Hispanic Center estimated that 10.3 million illegals resided in the United States in 2004.

27. Eurostat, "Euro-Indicators" (news release), 143/2006, Nov. 3, 2006.

28. European Commission, report on *Europe's Response to World Aging,* COM (2002) 143 final, Mar. 2002.

29. Jeffrey Passel, "Immigrants and Taxes: A Reappraisal of Huddles's 'The Cost of Immigration,'" The Urban Institute, Washington, DC, Jan. 1994, 51.

30. National Academy of Science, *The New Americans: Economic, Demographic, and Fiscal Effects of Immigration,* Executive Summary, 1997, 6.

31. Patrick J. Buchanan, *The Death of the West: How Dying Populations and Immigrant Invasions Threaten Our Culture and Civilization* (New York: St. Martin's Press, 2002), 12.

32. David A. Coleman, "Immigration and Ethnic Changes in Low-Fertility Countries: A Third Demographic Transition," *Population and Development Review* 32, no. 3 (Sept. 2006):401–46.

33. In the U.S. case see, for example, Diana R. Gordon, *The Return of the Dangerous Classes: Drug Prohibition and Policy Politics* (New York: Norton, 1994). For a broader piece linking waves of migration to ethnic crime waves see James O'Kane, *The Crooked Ladder: Gangsters, Ethnicity, and the American Dream* (New Brunswick, NJ: Transaction Publishers, 1992).

34. A version of this kind of argument is offered by Robert S. Leiken in "Europe's Angry Muslims," *Foreign Affairs,* July/Aug. 2005, www.foreignaffairs.org/20050701faes say84409/robert-s-leiken/europe-s-angry-muslims.html.

35. Ibid.

36. Pew Global Attitudes Project, "Muslims in Europe: Economic Worries Top Concerns about Religious and Cultural Identity," July 6, 2006, http://pewglobal.org/reports/display.php?ReportID=254

37. See Samuel P. Huntington, *Who Are We? America's Great Debate* (New York: Free Press, 2005).

38. "Borderless economy and barricaded border" is from Peter Andreas, *Border Games: Policing the U.S.-Mexico Divide* (Ithaca, NY, and London: Cornell University Press, 2000).

39. Wayne Cornelius, Philip Martin, James Hollifield, eds., *Controlling Immigration: A Global Perspective* (Stanford, CA: Stanford University Press, 1994).

40. Jef Huysmans, "Migrants as a Security Problem: Dangers of 'Securitizing' Societal Issues," in *Migration and European Integration: The Dynamics of Inclusion and Exclusion,* ed. R. Miles and D. Thränhardt (London: Pinter Publishers, 1995), 53.

41. Pew Research Center for the People and the Press/Pew Hispanic Center, Immigration Survey, Feb. 8–Mar. 7, 2006. Only 25 percent approve of President Bush's policy in this field.

42. MORI Social Research Institute, *International Social Trends Monitor,* IPSOS-MORI Survey on Attitudes toward Immigration, Nov. 2006.

43. Eurobarometer, "The Role of the European Union in Justice, Freedom, and Security Areas," EBS 266, Feb. 2007.

44. Wayne Cornelius, "Controlling 'Unwanted' Immigration: Lessons from the United States, 1993–2004," *Journal of Ethnic and Migration Studies* 31, no. 4 (July 2005): 775–94.

45. See EU Commission, COM (2007) 248 final.

Bibliography

Abraham, Spencer. Statements on the "Immigration Control and Financial Responsibility Act of 1996." *Congressional Record–Senate,* Thursday, May 2, 1996, 104th Cong., 2nd sess., 1996. 142 *Cong Rec* S 4592, vol. 142, no. 59. Available at LexisNexis Congressional.

Acer, Eleanor. "Refuge in an Insecure Time: Seeking Asylum in the Post-9/11 United States." *Fordham International Law Journal* 28 (May 2005): 1361–96.

Addi, Lahouari, et al. *Islam et démocratie. Pouvoirs* 104 (special issue). Paris: Seuil, 2003.

Adler, Alexandre. *J'ai vu finir le monde ancien.* Paris: Grasset, 2002.

Afary, Janet, and Kevin Anderson. *Foucault and the Iranian Revolution: Gender and the Seduction of Islamism.* Chicago: University of Chicago Press, 2005.

"After the Defeat." *Economist,* November 12, 2005.

Aguirre, Mariano. "Defense Strategy in the New Bush Epoch: Preventive War and the Empire Ideology." *Revista Internacional de Filosofía Política* 21 (July 2003): 236–42.

Akram, Susan M., and Kevin R. Johnson. "Race, Civil Rights, and Immigration Law after September 11, 2001: The Targeting of Arabs and Muslims." *NYU Annual Survey of American Law* 58 (2002).

Aleinikoff, T. Alexander, and Douglas Klusmeyer, eds. *Citizenship Policies for an Age of Migration.* Washington, DC: Carnegie Endowment for International Peace, 2002.

Aleinikoff, Thomas Alexander, David A. Martin, and Hiroshi Motomura. *Immigration and Citizenship: Process and Policy.* 5th ed. St. Paul, MN: Thomson/West, 2003.

Allam, Magdi, and Roberto Gritti. *Islam, Italia.* Milan: Guerini, 2001.

Allison, Graham. *Nuclear Terrorism: The Ultimate Preventable Catastrophe.* New York: Times Books, 2004.

Almond, Gabriel A., and G. Bingham Powell Jr., eds. *Comparative Politics: System, Process, and Policy.* 2nd ed. Boston and Toronto: Little, Brown, 1978.

———. *Comparative Politics Today: A Worldview.* New York: HarperCollins, 1992.

AlSayyad, Nezar, and Manuel Castells, eds. *Muslim Europe or Euro-Islam: Politics, Culture, and Citizenship in the Age of Globalization.* Lanham, MD: Lexington Books, 2004.

Amar, Akhil Reed. "Five Views of Federalism: 'Converse-1983' in Context." *Vanderbilt Law Review* 47 (1994).

———. "Some New World Lessons for the Old." *University of Chicago Law Review* 58 (1991).

American Immigration Lawyers Association (AILA). "Boiling the Frog Slowly: Executive Branch Actions since September 11, 2001." *Bender's Immigration Bulletin* 7 (October 15, 2002).

———. "The Border Protection, Antiterrorism and Illegal Immigration Control Act of 2005 (H.R. 4437), as Amended and Passed by the House on 12/16/05: Section-by-section analysis" (2005). http://policycouncil.nationaljournal.com/NR/rdonlyres/8B648050-C027–4E13-BB8D-9C9498F8CBF1/35796/Theborderprotection.pdf.

Amis, Martin. "The Age of Horrorism." *Observer,* September 10, 2006.

Amnesty International. *Amnesty International Calls on the European Commission to Take Action against Italy.* AI Index: IOR 61/007/2005.

———. *Italy: Temporary Stay—Permanent Rights.* AI Index: EUR 30/004/2005.

———. "JHA: Closing Eyes to Human Rights Leaves Asylum Seekers and Migrants at Risk." April 10, 2006. www.amnesty-eu.org/.

———. *Seeking Asylum Is Not a Crime: Detention of People Who Have Sought Asylum.* AI Index: EUR 45/015/2005.

———, EU Office. "Human Rights Dissolving at the Borders? Counter-Terrorism and EU Criminal Law." Executive Summary, May 2005.

Anderson, John. *Religious Liberty in Transitional Societies: The Politics of Religion.* Cambridge: Cambridge University Press, 2003.

Andréani, Gilles. "The 'War on Terror': Good Cause, Wrong Concept." *Survival* 46 (winter 2004–2005): 31–50.

Andreas, Peter. *Border Games: Policing the U.S.-Mexico Divide.* Ithaca, NY, and London: Cornell University Press, 2000.

Ansari, Fahad, and Uzma Karim. *Hijab and Democracy.* Wembley, England: Islamic Human Rights Commission, 2004.

Appiah, Kwame Anthony. *Cosmopolitanism: Ethics in a World of Strangers.* New York: Norton, 2006.

Applebaum, Anne. "Think Again, Karen Hughes." *Washington Post,* July 27, 2005.

Archibold, Randal C. "Immigrants Take to U.S. Streets in Show of Strength." *New York Times,* May 2, 2006. www.nytimes.com/2006/05/02/us/02immig.html.

Ash, Timothy Garton. "Anti-Europeanism in America." *New York Review of Books* 50, no. 2 (February 13, 2003). www.nybooks.com/articles/16059.

Associated Press International Affairs Poll, IPOS Public Affairs. Washington, DC, May 2006.

Astier, Henri. "Profile: France's Top Anti-terror Judge." BBC News on Line, January 7, 2003. http://news.bbc.co.uk/2/hi/europe/3031640.stm.

Asylum Procedures Directive, Council Directive 2005/85/EC of December 1, 2005, on minimum standards in procedures in Member States for granting and withdrawing refugee status. *Official Journal of the European Union* L326/13, 13.12.2005.

Badie, Bertrand. *La fin des territoires: essai sur le désordre international et l'utilité sociale du respect.* Paris: Fayard, 1995.

Baker, Don. "World Religions and National States: Competing Claims in East Asia." In *Transnational Religion and Fading States,* edited by Susanne Hoeber Rudolph and James Piscatori. Boulder, CO: Westview Press, 1997.

Baldwin-Edwards, Martin. "Immigration after 1992." *Policy and Politics* 19 (1992): 199–211.

Baldwin-Edwards, Martin, and J. M. Yarango J. *Immigrants and the Informal Economy in Southern Europe.* London and Portland, OR: Frank Cass, 1999.

Barber, Benjamin. *Jihad vs. McWorld.* New York: Ballantine, 1996.

Barker, Geoffrey. *Sexing It Up: Iraq, Intelligence and Australia, Briefings.* Sydney: University of New South Wales, 2003.

Barnaby, Frank. "Weapons of Mass Destruction: A Growing Threat in the 1990s?" *Conflict Studies* 235 (October–November 1990): 1–26.

Barnier, Michel. "A Letter to America." *Wall Street Journal,* November 8, 2004.

Bau, Ignatius. "Cities of Refuge: No Federal Preemption of Ordinances Restricting Local Government Cooperation with the INS." *La Raza Law Journal* 7 (2004).

BBC News. "Africans Die in Spanish Enclaves." September 29, 2005. http://news.bbc .co.uk/2/hi/africa/4292490.stm.

———. "MI5 Chief Reveals Terror Threat." October 17, 2003. http://news.bbc.co.uk/ 2/hi/uk_news/3198828.stm;

———. "MI5 Tracking '30 UK Terror Plots.'" November 10, 2006. http://news.bbc.co .uk/2/hi/uk_news/6134516.stm.

———. "MPs Attack Greer on Circumcision." November 25, 1995.

Beck, Ulrich. "The Terrorist Threat: World Risk Society Revisited." *Theory, Culture, and Society* 19 (2003): 39–56.

Benchenane, Mustapha. *Pour un dialogue euro-arabe.* Paris: Berger-Levrault, 1983.

Bender, Peter. "America: The New Roman Empire?" *Orbis: A Journal of World Affairs* 47 (2003): 145–59.

Benedict XVI. "Europe and Its Discontents." *First Things,* January 2006.

Benesch, Susan, and Devon Chaffee. "The Ever-Expanding Material Support Bar: An Unjust Obstacle for Refugees and Asylum Seekers." *Interpreter Releases* 83, no. 11 (March 13, 2006).

Bentley, Arthur. *The Process of Government.* Evanston, IL: Principia, 1949.

Beres, Louis Rene. *Terrorism and Global Security: The Nuclear Threat.* Boulder, CO: Westview Press, 1979.

Berlin, Isaiah. *Two Concepts of Liberty.* Oxford: Clarendon Press, 1958.

Berman, Paul. *Power and the Idealists: The Passion of Joschka Fischer and Its Aftermath.* New York: Norton, 2003.

———. *A Tale of Two Utopias: The Political Journey of the Generation of 1968.* New York: Norton, 1996.

———. *Terror and Liberalism.* New York: Norton, 2004.

Bernstein, Josh. National Immigration Law Center. "Court Upholds California In-State Tuition Law (AB 540)." October 10, 2006. www.nilc.org/immlawpolicy/DREAM/ Dream006.htm.

Bernstein, Nina. "Invisible to Most, Women Line Up for Day Labor." *New York Times,* August 15, 2005, A1.

———. "U.S. Is Settling Detainee's Suit in 9/11 Sweep." *New York Times,* February 28, 2006, A1.

Bigo, Didier. "From Foreigners to Abnormal Aliens: How the Faces of the Enemy Have Changed Following September the 11th with the Process of Policing beyond Borders." In *International Migration and Security: Opportunities and Challenges,* edited by Elspeth Guild and Joanne van Selm, 64–81. London and New York: Routledge, 2005.

———. "Liberty? Whose Liberty? The Hague Programme and the Conception of Freedom." July 20, 2005. www.libertysecurity.org/article339.html#nb2.

———. *Les nouveaux enjeux de l'(in)sécurité en Europe: terrorisme, guerre, sécurité intérieure, sécurité extérieure.* Paris: L'Harmattan, 2005.

———. "Reassuring and Protecting: Internal Security Implications of French Participation in the Coalition against Terrorism." In *Critical Views of September 11,* edited by Eric Hershberg and Kevin Moore. New York: New Press, 2002.

———. *Sécurité intérieure, implications pour la défense.* Paris: Rapport établi pour la DAS, French Ministry of Defense, 1998.

Bigo, Didier, and Elspeth Guild, eds. *Controlling Frontiers: Free Movement into and within Europe.* Burlington, VT: Ashgate, 2005.

———. "Policing in the Name of Freedom." In *Controlling Frontiers: Free Movement into and within Europe.* Burlington, VT: Ashgate, 2005.

Bigo, Didier, Jean Paul Hanon, and Anastasia Tsoukala. *La participation des militaires à la sécurité intérieure: France, Italie, Allemagne, États-Unis.* Paris: Rapport du Centre d'Études sur les Conflits pour la DAS, 1999.

Bigo, Didier, et al. *Illiberal Practices of Liberal Regimes: The (In)security Games.* Paris: L'Harmattan, 2006.

Bijak, J., D. Kupiszewski, and K. Saczuk. *Impact of International Migration on Population Dynamics and Labor Force Resources in Europe.* CEFMR Working Paper. Warsaw: Central European Forum for Migration Research, 2005.

Blair, Tony. "PM Warns of Continuing Global Terror Threat." March 5, 2004, at Sedgefield. www.pm.gov.uk/output/page5461.asp

"Blair Bashing." *Economist,* November 12, 2005.

Bleich, Erik. "The French Model: Color-Blind Integration." In *Color Lines: Affirmative Action, Immigration, and Civil Rights Options for America,* edited by John David Skrentny. Chicago: University of Chicago Press, 2001.

Bloom, Allan. *The Closing of the American Mind.* New York: Simon & Schuster, 1987.

Bloom, Harold. *The American Religion: The Emergence of the Post-Christian Nation.* New York: Simon & Schuster, 1992.

Body-Gendrot, Sophie. "The USA Patriot Act and the Threat to Civil Liberties." Paper presented at the Center for European Studies, New York University, April 12, 2004.

Body-Gendrot, Sophie, and Catherine Wenden. *Police et discriminations raciales: le tabou français.* Paris: Éditions de l'atelier, 2003.

Boer, Monica Den. *9/11 and the Europeanisation of Anti-Terrorism Policy: A Critical Assessment.* Notre Europe Policy Paper 6. Paris: Notre Europe, 2003.

Boer, Monica Den, and Jorg Monar. "Keynote Article: 11 September and the Challenge of Global Terrorism to the EU as a Security Actor." *Journal of Common Market Studies,* annual review issue (2002): 11–28.

"Bombers Are All Sponging Asylum Seekers." *Daily Express,* July 27, 2005.

Bommes, M., and A. Geddes, eds. *Immigration and Welfare: Challenging the Borders of the Welfare State.* London: Routledge, 2000.

Bommes, Michael, and Jost Halfmann, eds. *Migration in nationalen Wohlfahrtsstaaten: theoretische und vergleichende Untersuchungen.* Osnabrück, Germany: Universitätsverlag Rasch, 1998.

Booth, Ken, and Tim Dunne, eds. *Worlds in Collision: Terror and the Future of Global Order.* New York: Palgrave Macmillan, 2002.

Borrus, Amy, and Dean Foust. "In a World of Trouble, Can He Cope?" *Business Week* 3594 (September 7, 1998): 32–33.

Bosniak, Linda. *The Citizen and the Alien: Dilemmas of Contemporary Membership.* Princeton, NJ: Princeton University Press, 2006.

Boswell, Christina. *European Migration Policies in Flux: Changing Patterns of Inclusion and Exclusion.* Oxford: Blackwell, 2003.

Bouzar, Dounia. "Étude de 12 associations à référence musulmane: l'islam entre mythe et religion: le nouveau discours religieux dans les associations socio-culturelles musulmanes." *Les Cahiers de la Sécurité Intérieure* (IHESI) 54 (2004).

Boyle, Kevin, and Juliet Sheen, eds. *Freedom of Religion and Belief: A World Report.* London and New York: Routledge, 1997.

Brackett, D. W. *Holy Terror: Armageddon in Tokyo.* New York: Weatherhill, 1996.

Brennan, William J. "The Bill of Rights and the States: The Revival of State Constitutions as Guardians of Individual Rights." *NYU Law Review* 61 (1986).

Brettell, C., and J. Hollifield. *Migration Theory: Talking across Disciplines.* New York: Routledge, 2000.

Briffault, Richard "What about the 'Ism'? Normative and Formal Concerns in Contemporary Federalism." *Vanderbilt Law Review* 47 (1994): 1303–53.

Brinker-Gabler, Gisela, and Sidonie Smith. *Writing New Identities: Gender, Nation, and Immigration in Contemporary Europe.* Minneapolis: University of Minnesota Press, 1997.

Brochmann, G. *European Integration and Immigration from Third Countries.* Oslo: Scandinavian University Press, 1996.

Brochmann, Grete, and Tomas Hammar, eds. *Mechanisms of Immigration Control: A Comparative Analysis of European Regulation Policies.* Oxford and New York: Berg, 1999.

Broder, Henryk M. *Hurra, Wir Kapitulieren.* Berlin: Wolf Jobst Siedler Verlag, 2006.

———. "The West and Islam: Hurray! We're Capitulating." *Spiegel Online,* January 25, 2007. www.spiegel.de/international/spiegel/0,1518,462149,00.html.

Brooks, David. "Two Steps Toward a Sensible Immigration Policy. " *New York Times,* August 14, 2005.

Brouard, Sylvain, and Vincent Tiberj. *Français comme les autres?* Paris: Presses de Sciences Po, 2005.

Brubaker, Rogers. *Citizenship and Nationhood in France and Germany.* Cambridge: Cambridge University Press, 1992.

———. *Immigration and the Politics of Citizenship in Europe and North America.* Lanham, MD: University Press of America, 1989.

———. "The Return of Assimilation? Changing Perspectives on Immigration and Its Sequels in France, Germany, and the United States." *Ethnic and Racial Studies* 24, no. 4 (2001): 531–48.

Bruce, Steve. *Fundamentalism.* Oxford: Polity Press, 2000.

———. *God Is Dead: Secularization in the West.* Oxford: Blackwell, 2002.

———. *Religion in the Modern World: From Cathedrals to Cults.* Oxford and New York: Oxford University Press, 1996.

Bruckner, Pascal. "Enlightenment, Fundamentalism or Racism of Anti Racists." *Sign and Sight,* January 24, 2007. www.signandsight.com/features/1146.html.

———. "Europe: Remorse and Exhaustion." *Dissent* (spring 2003). www.dissentmagazine.org/article/?article=499.

———. "The Paradoxes of Anti-Americanism." *Dissent* 53, no. 3 (summer 2006).

Buchanan, Patrick J. *The Death of the West: How Dying Populations and Immigrant Invasions Threaten Our Culture and Civilization.* New York: St. Martin's Press, 2002.

Bunting, Madeleine. "Jack Straw Has Unleashed a Storm of Prejudice and Intensified Division." *Guardian Unlimited,* October 9, 2006. www.guardian.co.uk/commentisfree/story/0,,1890821,00.html.

Bunyan, Tony. *The Political Police in Britain.* London: Quartet, 1977.

Burbach, Roger, and Jim Tarbell. *Imperial Overstretch: George W. Bush and the Hubris of Empire.* New York: Zed Books, 2004.

Bussiere, Robert. "After 11 September: America, Europe, and Global Antiterrorism Strategy." *Commentaire* 25 (2002): 301–309.

Butler Report. "Review of Intelligence on Weapons of Mass Destruction: Report of Privy Counsellors," July 14, 2004, House of Commons, London. www.butlerre view.org.uk/report/report.pdf.

Buzan, Barry. *People, States, and Fear: The National Security Problem in International Relations.* Chapel Hill: University of North Carolina Press, 1983.

Buzan, Barry, Ole Wæver, and Jaap de Wilde. *Security: A New Framework for Analysis.* Boulder, CO, and London: Lynne Rienner, 1998.

Bybee, Jay S., Assistant Attorney General, Office of Legal Counsel. "Non-Preemption of the Authority of State and Local Law Enforcement Officials to Arrest Aliens for Immigration Violations" (April 3, 2002).

Byrd, Robert C. *Losing America: Confronting a Reckless and Arrogant Presidency.* New York: Norton, 2004.

Cachfin Rodríguez, L. *Prevenir el racismo en el trabajo en España.* Madrid: Instituto de Migraciones y Servicios Sociales, 1999.

Caldwell, Christopher. "Islamic Europe? When Bernard Lewis Speaks." *Weekly Standard* 10, no. 4 (October 4, 2004).

Calhoun, Craig J., Paul Price, and Ashley S. Timmer. *Understanding September 11.* New York: New Press, 2002.

Callovi, G. "Immigration and the European Community." *Contemporary European Affairs* 4 (1991).

Camilleri, Joseph A. "Terrorism, Anti-Terrorism and the Globalization of Insecurity." *Arena Journal* 19 (2002): 7–19.

Camkiner, Evan H. "State Sovereignty and Subordinancy: May Congress Commandeer State Officers to Implement Federal Laws." *Columbia Law Review* 95 (1995).

Campo Ladero, M. J. *Opiniones y actitudes de los españoles ante el fenómeno de la inmigración.* Madrid: Centro de Investigaciones Sociológicas, 2004.

Carafano, James Jay. The Heritage Foundation. "No Need for the CLEAR Act: Building Capacity for Immigration Counterterrorism Investigations." Exec. Memorandum No. 925 (April 21, 2004).

Caritas/Migrantes. *Immigrazione: Dossier Statistico 2004.* Rome: IDOS Centro Studi e Ricerche, 2004.

Carrington, Peter J., John Scott, and Stanley Wasserman, eds. *Models and Methods in Social Network Analysis.* Cambridge: Cambridge University Press, 2005.

Casanova, José. *Public Religions in the Modern World.* Chicago and London: University of Chicago Press, 1994.

———. "Religion, European Secular Identities, and European Integration." In *Religion in an Expanding Europe,* edited by Timothy A. Byrnes and Peter J. Katzenstein, 65–92. Cambridge: Cambridge University Press, 2006.

Castle, Stephen. "Nationalists in the European Parliament: Growing in Strength and Numbers." *Independent,* January 17, 2007.

Castles, Francis. *Comparative Public Policy: Patterns of Post-war Transformation.* Cheltenham, England: Edward Elgar, 1998.

———. ed. *Families of Nations: Patterns of Public Policy in Western Democracies.* Aldershot, England: Dartmouth,1993.

Castles, Stephen. *Ethnicity and Globalization: From Migrant Worker to Transnational Citizen.* London: Sage Publications, 2000.

Castles, Stephen, and Mark Miller. *The Age of Migration.* 3rd ed. New York: Palgrave, 2003.

Cea D'Ancona, M. A. *La activación de la xenofobia en España: ¿qué miden las encuestas?* Madrid: Centro de Investigaciones Sociológicas, 2004.

Celaya, C. "La política en la frontera: inmigración y partidos políticos en España durante 1996." *Migraciones* 2 (1997).

Center for Strategic and International Studies. *The Transatlantic Dialogue on Terrorism: Initial Findings.* Washington, DC, August 2004.

Centro de Investigaciones Sociológicas. "Barómetro, mayo 2003." Madrid, 2003.

Cerny, Phil. "The New Security Dilemma: Divisibility, Defection, and Disorder in the Global Era." *Review of International Studies* 26 (2000): 623–46.

Cesari, Jocelyne. *Être musulman en France: associations, militants, et mosquées.* Paris: Karthala-Iremam, 1994.

———. *When Islam and Democracy Meet: Muslims in Europe and in the United States.* New York: Palgrave Macmillan, 2006. Originally published as *L'islam à l'épreuve de l'occident* (Paris: La Découverte, 2004).

Cesarini, David, and Mary Fulbrook, eds. *Citizenship, Nationality, and Migration in Europe.* London: Routledge, 1996.

Chacón, Jennifer M. "Unsecured Borders: Immigration Restrictions, Crime Control and National Security." *Connecticut Law Review* 39 (2007): 1827–91.

Chang, Howard F. "Public Benefits and Federal Authorization for Alienage Discrimination by the States." *Annual Survey of American Law* 58 (2002): 357–70.

Chang, Nancy. Center for Constitutional Rights. *Silencing Political Dissent.* New York: Seven Stories Press, 2002.

Chase, Jefferson. "Europa, Europa. . . ." *Boston Globe,* July 20, 2003.

Chatham House Middle East Programme Report. *Iraq in Transition: Vortex or Catalyst?* London: Royal Institute of International Affairs, 2004.

Chaves, Mark, and David E. Cann. "Regulation, Pluralism, and Religious Market Structure." *Rationality and Society* 4 (1992): 272–90.

Chebel d'Appollonia, Ariane. "Discrimination and Anti-Discrimination in Europe." Paper presented at the Immigration, Integration, and Human Security Issues Post-9/11 in Comparative Perspective Workshop, Paris, June 8–9, 2006.

Chen, Ronald K. "State Incarceration of Federal Prisoners after September 11: Whose Jail Is It Anyway?" *Brooklyn Law Review* 69 (summer 2004): 1335.

Chesterman, Simon. "Bush, the United Nations, and Nation-Building." *Survival* 46 (spring 2004): 101–16.

———. *Just War or Just Peace? Humanitarian Intervention and International Law.* Oxford and New York: Oxford University Press, 2001.

Chin, Gabriel J. "Segregation's Last Stronghold: Race Discrimination and the Constitutional Law of Immigration." *UCLA Law Review* 46 (1998).

Chishti, Muzaffar A. "The Role of States in U.S. Immigration Policy." *Annual Survey of American Law* 58 (2002).

Chishti, Muzaffar A., et al. America's Challenge: Domestic Security, Civil Liberties, and National Unity after September 11. Washington, DC: Migration Policy Institute, 2003.

Cianciarulo, Marisa Silenzi. "Terrorism and Asylum Seekers: Why the REAL ID Act Is a False Promise." *Harvard Journal on Legislation* 43 (winter 2006): 101–38.

CIDOB Foundation. "Anuario internacional CIDOB 2005." Barcelona, 2006.

Cinalli, M., and M. Giugni. "Institutional and Discursive Opportunities for the Political Integration of Migrants in European Cities." Paper presented at the Conference of the ESA Research Network for the Sociology of Culture, "Changing Cultures: European Perspectives," Workshop on Multicultural Democracy in Europe, Ghent, November 15–17, 2006.

Cleveland, Sarah H. "Powers Inherent in Sovereignty: Indians, Aliens, Territories, and the Nineteenth Century Origins of Plenary Power over Foreign Affairs." *Texas Law Review* 81 (2002).

Coker, Christopher. "Globalisation and Insecurity in the Twenty-First Century: NATO and the Management of Risk." *Adelphi Papers* 345 (June 2002): 7–103.

Cole, David. *Enemy Aliens: Double Standards and Constitutional Freedoms in the War on Terrorism.* New York and London: Free Press, 2003.

———. "In Aid of Removal: Due Process Limits on Immigration Detention." *Emory Law Journal* 51 (2002).

———. "Operation Enduring Liberty." *Nation* 274 (June 3, 2002).

Colectivo IOÉ. Inmigración y trabajo: trabajadores inmigrantes en el sector de la construcción. Madrid: Imserso, 1998.

Coleman, David A. "Immigration and Ethnic Changes in Low-Fertility Countries: A Third Demographic Transition." *Population and Development Review* 32, no. 3 (September 2006): 401–46.

Collins, Michael. *The Likes of Us: A Biography of the White Working Class.* London: Granta, 2005.

Collinson, Sarah. *Beyond Borders: West European Migration Policy towards the 21st Century.* London: Royal Institute of International Affairs, 1993.

Colombani, Jean-Marie. "Vivre avec le Terrorisme." *Le Monde,* July 27, 2005.

Commission of the European Communities (CEC). Commission Staff Working Paper, Second Annual Report to the Commission and the European Parliament on the Activities of the EURODAC Central Unit, Brussels 20.6.2005, SEC(2005) 839.

———. Communication from the Commission to the Council and the European Parliament on an Open Method of Co-ordination for the Community Immigration Policy, COM (2001), 387 final.

———. Communication from the Commission to the Council and the Parliament on Strengthened Practical Cooperation, SEC(2006) 189, Brussels 17.2.2006, COM(2006) 67 final. http://eur-lex.europa.eu/LexUriServ/site/en/com/2006/com2006_0067en01.pdf#search=%22communication%20on%20strengthened%20practical%20cooperation%22.

"La Consulta islamica condanna." *Libertà,* February 10, 2006.

Cook, Melissa. "Banished for Minor Crimes: The Aggravated Felony Provision of the Immigration and Nationality Acts as a Human Rights Violation." *Boston College Third World Law Journal* 23 (2003): 293–330.

Cordesman, Anthony H. *Iraq's Evolving Insurgency and the Risk of Civil War.* Washington, DC: CSIS, 2006. www.csis.org/index.php?option=com_csis_pubs&task=view&id=3304.

Cornelius, Wayne. "Controlling 'Unwanted' Immigration: Lessons from the United States, 1993–2004." *Journal of Ethnic and Migration Studies* 31, no. 4 (July 2005): 775–94.

Cornelius, Wayne, Philip Martin, and James Hollifield, eds. *Controlling Immigration: A Global Perspective.* Stanford, CA: Stanford University Press, 1994.

————. "Introduction: The Ambivalent Quest for Immigration Control." In *Controlling Immigration: A Global Perspective,* edited by Wayne Cornelius, Philip Martin, and James Hollifield, 3–42. Stanford, CA: Stanford University Press, 1994.

Council of Europe. Parliamentary Assembly. *Alleged Secret Detentions and Unlawful Inter-State Transfers Involving Council of Europe Member States.* June 7, 2006. www.washingtonpost.com/wp-srv/world/specials/coerenditionreport.pdf.

Council of the European Union (EU). "Conclusions and Plan of Action of the Extraordinary European Council Meeting on 21 September 2001." www.consilium.europa.eu/ueDocs/cms_Data/docs/pressdata/en/ec/140.en.pdf.

————. "Council Common Position of 27 December 2001 on Combating Terrorism," December 28, 2001.

————. Impact of Future Demographic Trends in Europe. DG3/CAPH10 (2005) 6 final, 2005.

————. "Report on the Implementation of the Framework Decision 2002/475/JHA of 13 June 2002 on Combating Terrorism," Brussels, October 12, 2004.

————. "A Secure Europe in a Better World—A European Security Strategy," December 2003.

————. Council Directive 2003/9/EC, January 27, 2003 (Official Journal L 31 of 06.02.03).

————. Council Directive 2004/83/EC, April 2004.

————. Council Directive 2005/85/EC, December 2005.

————. Council Regulation (EC) No. 343/2003, February 18, 2003 (Official Journal L 50 of 25 February 2003).

Coutin, Susan Bibler. "The Oppressed, the Suspect, and the Citizen: Subjectivity in Competing Accounts of Political Violence." *Law and Social Inquiry* 26 (2001): 60–94.

Cox, Adam, and Eric Posner. "The Second Order Structure of Immigration Law." *Stanford Law Review* 59 (forthcoming 2007). http://ssrn.com/abstract=941730.

Cox, Michael. "Beyond the West: Terrors in Transatlantia." *European Journal of International Relations* 11, no. 2 (2005): 203–33.

Crelinsten, Ronald D. "Terrorism and Counter-Terrorism in a Multi-Centric World: Challenges and Opportunities." *Terrorism and Political Violence* 11 (2000):170–96.

Crenshaw, Martha. "The Transatlantic Campaign against Terrorism." Speech delivered to NATO Conference on New Tasks and Responsibilities, July 11, 2005.www.nato.int/docu/speech/2005/s050711h.htm.

Cronin, Audrey Kurth. "Transnational Terrorism and Security." In *Grave New World: Security Challenges in the 21st Century,* edited by Michael E. Brown, 279–304. Washington, DC: Georgetown University Press, 2003.

Crossette, Barbara. "U.N. Warns That Trafficking in Human Beings Is Growing." *New York Times,* June 25, 2000.

CSA. "Les élections legislatives du 25 mai 1997." Sondage sorties des urnes pour France 3, France Info et Le Parisien.

————. "L'élection presidentielle: explication du vote et perspectives politiques." April 2002.

Cumings, Bruce. "Is America an Imperial Power?" *Current History* 102 (2003): 355–60.

Daalder, Ivo H., and James M. Lindsay. *America Unbound: The Bush Revolution in Foreign Policy.* Washington, DC: Brookings Institution, 2003.

"Da Cpt a centri d'accoglienza." *Il Giornale di Calabria,* December 15, 2006.

Dahrendorf, Ralf. "After Assimilation." *Project Syndicate,* September 2004. www.project-syndicate.org/commentary/dahrendorf30/English.

Dalton, Russell J. Citizen Politics: *Public Opinion and Political Parties in Advanced Industrial Democracies.* 2nd ed. Chatham, NJ: Chatham House Publishers, 1996.

Daniels, Ronald J., Patrick Macklem, and Kent Roach, eds. *The Security of Freedom: Essays on Canada's Anti-Terrorism Bill.* Toronto: University of Toronto Press, 2001.

Danner, Mark. "The Secret Way to War." *New York Review of Books,* June 9, 2005.

Danziger, Jeff. "Safeguarding Our Freedoms" (drawing). Tribune Media Services, June 24, 2002.

Dassetto, Felice, ed. *Paroles d'Islam: individus, sociétés et discours dans l'islam européen contemporain.* Paris: Maisonneuve and Larose, 2000.

Davie, Grace. *Religion in Modern Europe: A Memory Mutates.* Oxford: Oxford University Press, 2000.

de Borchgrave, Arnaud. "Transnational Crime: The New Empire of Evil." *Strategy & Leadership* 24 (November–December 1996): 27–31.

de Galembert, Claire. "La régulation étatique du religieux à l'épreuve de la globalisation." In *La globalisation du religieux,* edited by Jean-Pierre Bastian et al. Paris: L'Harmattan, 2001.

Delanty, Gerard. "The Resurgence of the City in Europe? The Spaces of European Citizenship." In *Democracy, Citizenship, and the Global City,* edited by Engin F. Isin. New York: Routledge, 2000.

Deleuze, Gilles. *Foucault: un nouvel archiviste.* Montpellier, France: Fata Morgana, 1972.

Delpech, Thérèse. "One Year After: Four Reactions Regarding September 11." *Internationale Politik* 57 (2002): 39–46.

———. Politique du chaos: l'autre face de la mondialisation. Paris: Seuil, 2002.

Deltombe, Thomas. *L'Islam imaginaire: la construction médiatique de l'islamophobie en France,* 1975–2005. Paris: La Découverte, 2005.

Demleitner, Nora V. "A Vicious Cycle: Resanctioning Offenders." In *Civil Penalties, Social Consequences,* edited by Christopher Mele and Teresa A. Miller, 185–201. New York and London: Routledge, 2005.

Der Derian, James. "Global Events, National Security, and Virtual Theory." *Millennium* 30 (2002): 669–90.

Deschenes, Dany. "French Security Experts and 11 September 2001." *Etudes Internationales* 33 (2002): 763–74.

de Vries, Gijs. Address to the Counter-Terrorism Committee, New York, June 23, 2005. http://ue.eu.int/uedocs/cmsUpload/06_23_final_1373.pdf.

"DHS-ICE Sanctions, Registration." *Migration News* 11, no. 1 (January 2004). http://migration.ucdavis.edu/mn/more.php?id=2968_0_2_0_c, accessed August 24, 2007.

Díez Nicolás, J. *Actitudes hacia los inmigrantes.* Madrid: Ministerio de Trabajo y Asuntos Sociales, 1998.

Dillon, Michael. *Politics of Security: Towards a Political Philosophy of Continental Thought.* London and New York: Routledge, 1996.

Din, Suleman. "A Different Tack on Immigration: Edison Balks on Aiding the Feds." *Star-Ledger* (Newark, NJ), September 25, 2006.

Dixon, David, and Julia Gelatt. "Immigration Facts: Immigration Enforcement Spending since IRCA." Migration Policy Institute, Task Force Fact Sheet No. 10 (November 2005). www.migrationpolicy.org/ITFIAF/FactSheet_Spending.pdf.

Dodge, Toby. "A Sovereign Iraq?" *Survival* 46 (autumn 2004): 39–58.

Dougherty, Mary, Denise Wilson, and Amy Wu. U.S. DHS Management Directorate, Office of Immigration Statistics. *Immigration Enforcement Actions: 2004* (November 2005). www.uscis.gov/graphics/shared/statistics/publications/AnnualReportEnforce ment2004.pdf.

Dow, Mark. *American Gulag: Inside U.S. Immigration Prisons.* Berkeley: University of California Press, 2004.

Drancourt, Michel. "Anti-Americanism French Style: But What Have the Americans Done to the French?" *Futuribles* 280 (November 2002): 51–59.

Dworkin, Ronald. "Political Freedom in Britain." Democratic Findings No. 1, Democratic Audit of the United Kingdom, Human Rights Centre, University of Essex, 1996.

Eagye, Abigail. "Immigration Laws Lead to Unintended Housing Problems for Legal Aliens." *Post Independent* (Glenwood Springs, CO), January 4, 2007. www.postinde pendent.com/article/20070104/VALLEYNEWS/101040031.

Easton, David. *A Systems Analysis of Political Life.* New York, London, and Sydney: John Wiley & Sons, 1965.

Eggan, Dan, and Julie Tate. "U.S. Campaign Produces Few Convictions on Terrorism Charges." *Washington Post,* June 12, 2005.

Eickelman, Dale. "Trans-State Islam and Security." In *Transnational Religion and Fading States,* edited by Susanne Hoeber Rudolph and James Piscatori, 27–46. Boulder, CO: Westview Press, 1997.

Eisenach, Eldon J. *The Next Religious Establishment: National Identity and Political Theology in Post-Protestant America.* Lanham, MD: Rowman and Littlefield, 2000.

Eisendrath, Craig R., and Melvin A. Goodman. *Bush League Diplomacy: How the Neoconservatives Are Putting the World at Risk.* Amherst, NY: Prometheus Books, 2004.

Eisinger, Peter K. "The Conditions of Protest Behaviour in American Cities." *American Political Science Review* 67 (1973): 11–28.

El Battiui, Mohamed, Firouzeh Nahavandi, and Meryem Kanmaz. *Mosquées, imams et professeurs de religion islamique en Belgique: état de la question et enjeux.* Brussels: Fondation Roi Baudouin, 2004.

Endelman, Gary. "After the Fall: Making Sense Out of Sensenbrenner." *Immigration Daily,* January 4, 2006. www.ilw.com/articles/2006,0104-endelman.shtm.

Engene, Jan Oskar. Terrorism in Western Europe: Explaining the Trends Since 1950. London: Edward Elgar, 2003.

Entzinger, Han. "The Dynamics of Integration Policies: A Multidimensional Model." In *Challenging Immigration and Ethic Relations Politics,* edited by Ruud Koopmans and Paul L. Statham, 97–118. Oxford: Oxford University Press, 2000.

Errera, Philippe. "Three Circles of Threat." *Survival* 47, no. 1 (spring 2005): 71–88.

Escudier, Alexandre, ed. *Der Islam in Europa: der Umgang mit dem Islam in Frankreich und Deutschland.* Göttingen, Germany: Wallstein Verlag, 2003.

"EU Immigration Deals 'to Stop Asylum Shopping,'" The Press Association, January 25, 2005.

Eurobarometer. "Public Opinion in the European Union." *Eurobarometer* 65 (July 2006).

———. "Racism and Xenophobia in Europe." Eurobarometer Opinion Poll, no. 47.1, December 1997.

————. "The Role of the European Union in Justice, Freedom and Security Areas." EBS 266, February 2007.

Europa. "02-0-92005—Commission proposes new rules on asylum and immigration." http://europa.eu.int/comm/justice_home/news/intro/news_intro_ ent.htm.

————. "Eurodac: A European Union-wide Electronic System for the Identification of Asylum-Seekers" (press release). MEMO/06/334, Brussels, September 19, 2006. http://europa.eu/rapid/pressReleasesAction.do?reference=MEMO/06/334&format= HTML&aged=0&language=EN&guiLanguage=en.

European Commission. Communication on *Europe's Response to World Aging.* COM (2002) 143 final, March 2002.

————. "An EU Approach to Managing Economic Migration" (green paper). COM (2004) 811 final, Brussels, 2005.

————. "EU Handbook on Integration" (November 2004).

————. "Green Paper on Equality and Non-Discrimination in an Enlarged EU." May 2004.

————. Improving Living and Working Conditions: Social Integration of Immigrants from Non-Community Countries. Brussels, 1994.

————. Proposal for a Council Act Establishing the Convention of Rules for the Admission of Third Country Nationals to the Member States. Brussels, 1997.

————. "Study on Data Collection to Measure the Extent and Impact of Discrimination in Europe."

————. Technical Mission to Libya on Illegal Immigration, 27 November–6 December, Report. www.statewatch.org/news/2005/may/eu-report-libya-ill-imm.pdf.

European Council. "Presidency Conclusions. Tampere European Council." October 15–16, 1999.

————. *A Secure Europe in a Better World: European Security Strategy.* Brussels: EC, December 2003. http://ue.eu.int/uedocs/cmsUpload/78367.pdf.

————. "Strategy Paper on Immigration and Asylum." Austrian Presidency, 1998. www.proasyl.de/texte/europe/eu-a-o.htm.

European Parliament. Report of the Committee of Inquiry on Racism and Xenophobia. Brussels: OOPEC, 1991.

European Social Survey. Attitudes toward Minorities and Migrants in Europe, 2003. www.europeansocialsurvey.org.

————. "Factsheet: The EU and the Fight Against Terrorism" (updated February 2005). http://ue.eu.int/uedocs/cmsUpload/europa.pdf.

European Union. "The Hague Programme: Strengthening Freedom, Security and Justice in the European Union." *Official Journal C 053, 03/03/2005 P. 0001 – 0014,* 52005XG0303(01), (2005/C 53/01). http://europa.eu.int/eur-lex/lex/LexUriServ/ LexUriServ.do?uri=CELEX:52005XG0303(01):EN:HTML.

————. Justice and Home Affairs. "EU Fights against the Scourge of Terrorism." http:// ec.europa.eu/justice_home/fsj/terrorism/fsj_terrorism_intro_en.htm.

European Union Monitoring Centre on Racism and Xenophobia (EUMC). *Annual Report on Racism and Xenophobia in the EU Member States,* 2005.

————. Attitudes towards Minority Groups in the European Union Member States. Vienna, 2003.

————. The Impact of 7 July 2005 London Bomb Attacks on Muslim Communities in the EU. Vienna, 2005.

————. Majorities' Attitudes Towards Minorities: Key Findings from the Eurobarometer and the European Social Survey. March 2005.

————. Manifestations of Antisemitism in the EU (2002–2003). Vienna, 2004.

————. Report on Islamophobia. Vienna, 2002.

————. Report on Migrants, Minorities, and Employment. 2003.

————. Report on Racism and Xenophobia in the EU. Vienna, 2005.

Eurostat. "Euro-Indicators" (news release). 143/2006, November 3, 2006.

————. Europe in Figures: Eurostat Yearbook for 2005.

————. Population in Europe, first results. 15/2005.

EU-U.S. Declaration on Combating Terrorism. http://ue.eu.int/uedocs/cmsUpload/10760EU_US26.06.04.pdf.

Everts, Steven. "Engaging Iran: A Text Case for EU Foreign Policy." CER working paper, March 2004.

Ewing, Walter. *Border Insecurity: U.S. Border-Enforcement Policies and National Security.* Immigration Policy Center Report. Washington, DC, spring 2006.

Faist, Thomas. "Immigration, Integration und Wohlfahrtsstaaten: in Die Bundesrepublik Deutschlnad in vergleichender Perspektive." In *Migration in nationalen Wohlfahrtsstaaten: theoretische und vergleichende Untersuchungen,* edited by Michael Bommes and Jost Halfmann, 147–70. Osnabrück, Germany: Universitätsverlag Rasch, 1998.

Falk, Richard. "Will the Empire Be Fascist?" *Global Dialogue* 5 (2003): 22–31.

Fallaci, Oriana. "Rage and Pride." *Il Corrierre della Sera,* September 29, 2001.

Fanon, Franz. *The Wretched of the Earth.* New York: Grove Press, 1963.

Favell, Adrian. "Integration Policy and Integration Research in Europe." In *Citizenship Today: Global Perspectives and Practices,* edited by T. Alexander Aleinikoff and Douglas Klusmeyer. Washington, DC: Carnegie Endowment for International Peace, 2001.

————. *Philosophies of Integration: Immigration and the Idea of Citizenship in France and Britain.* Houndsmills, England: Macmillan, 1998.

Federal Bureau of Investigation. "An NCIC Milestone" (press release). August 9, 2006. www.fbi.gov/pressrel/pressrel06/ncic080906.htm.

————. "Comparison of H.R. 4437 and S. 2611." July 3, 2006. www.fairus.org/site/DocServer/amnesty_bill_condensed.pdf?docID=1061.

Federation for American Immigration Reform. "Distribution of the Illegal Alien Population." June 2003. www.fairus.org.

————. "National Security Considerations in Asylum Applications: A Case Study of 6 Iraqis." October 8, 1998. www.fairus.org/site/PageServer?pagename=leg_legislation cddf.

————. "State of Insecurity: How State and Local Immigration Policies are Undermining Homeland Security." September 2003.

Fennema, Meindert. "The Concept and Measurement of Civic Community." *Journal of Ethnic and Migration Studies* 30, no. 3 (2004): 429–47.

Ferenczi, Thomas. "L'Union Européenne veut adresser un message positif." *Le Monde,* January 21, 2005.

Fergusson, Niall. "Eurabia." *New York Times,* April 4, 2004.

Ferrari, Silvio, and Anthony Bradney, eds. *Islam and European Legal Systems.* Aldershot, England: Ashgate, 2000.

Ferrell, Craig E., Jr. "Immigration Enforcement: Is It a Local Issue?" *Police Chief* (February 2005).

———. "The War on Terror's 'Absconder Initiative.'" *Police Chief* (October 2002).

Fetzer, Joel S., and J. Christopher Soper. *Muslims and the State in Britain, France, and Germany.* Cambridge: Cambridge University Press, 2005.

Final Report of the National Commission on Terrorist Attacks upon the United States. New York: Norton, 2004.

Finnemore, Margaret, and Kathryn Sikkink. "International Norm Dynamics and Political Change." *International Organization* 52 (1998): 887–917.

Firestone, David, and Christopher Drew. "Al Qada Link Seen in Only a Handful of 1,200 Detainees." *New York Times,* November 29, 2001.

Fischer, Joschka. *Die Ruckkehr der Geschichte* (The Return of History). Cologne, Germany: Kiepenheuer & Witsch, 2005.

Fischer Weltalmanach. *Der Fischer Weltalmanach 2000.* Frankfurt: Fischer Verlag, 1999.

Fitzgerald, Keith. *The Face of the Nation: Immigration, the State, and National Identity.* Stanford, CA: Stanford University Press, 1996.

Flood, Philip. *Report to the Inquiry into the Australian Intelligence Agencies.* Australian government, July 2004. www.globalsecurity.org/intell/library/reports/2004/australia_intell-inquiry_intro.htm.

Fonte, John. "Fracturing of the West?" *Policy* 18, no. 3 (spring 2002): 16–20.

Foran, John. "Confronting an Empire: Sociology and the U.S.-Made World Crisis." *Political Power and Social Theory* 16 (2003): 213–33.

Forcing Our Blues into Gray Areas: Local Police and Federal Immigration Enforcement, A Legal Guide for Advocates. Washington, DC: Appleseed, 2006.

Forsythe, David P. "The United States and International Criminal Justice." *Human Rights Quarterly* 24 (2003): 974–91.

———. "A few observations of the EU Migrant's Forum as regards the draft action plan for Morocco from the high level group 'Asylum and Migration.'" Brussels, 1999.

Forum des Migrants de l'UE. "Immigration under the Watchful Eye of Tampere." Brussels, 2000.

Forum Réfugiés. *Rapport annuel sur l'asile en France et en Europe* (2006).

Fotopoulos, Takis. "The Global 'War' of the Transnational Elite." *Democracy and Nature* 8 (2003): 201–40.

Foucault, Michel. *Abnormal: Lectures at the College de France, 1974–1975.* New York: Picador USA, 2003.

———. *The Order of Things: An Archaeology of the Human Sciences.* New York: Pantheon Books, 1971. Originally published as *Les mots et les choses: une archéologie des sciences humaines* (Paris: Gallimard, 1966).

Fox, Robert. "GWOT Is History: Now for SAVE." *New Statesman,* August 8, 2005.

Franzblau, Kenneth J. "Immigration's Impact on U.S. National Security and Foreign Policy." Research Paper, U.S. Commission on Immigration Reform, October 1997.

Frattini, Franco, vice president of the European Commission Responsible for Justice, Freedom and Security. "Recent Developments of Immigration and Integration in the EU and on Recent Events in the Spanish Enclave in Morocco." Speech delivered at Konrad Adenauer Foundation, Brussels, November 3, 2005. http://europa.eu/rapid/pressReleasesAction.do?reference=SPEECH/05/667&format=HTML&aged=18languageEN&guiLanguage=en.

Freeman, Gary P. "Client Politics or Populism? Immigration Reform in the United States." In *Controlling a New Migration World,* edited by Virginie Guiraudon and Christian Joppke, 65–95. London and New York: Routledge, 2001.

———. "The Decline of Sovereignty? Politics and Immigration Restriction in Liberal States." In *Challenge to the Nation State: Immigration in Western Europe and the United States,* edited by Christian Joppke, 86–108. London: Oxford University Press, 1998.

———. "Migration and the Political Economy of the Welfare State." *Annals of the American Academy of Political and Social Science* 485 (1986): 51–63.

———. "Modes of Immigration Politics in Liberal Democratic States." *International Migration Review* 29 (winter 1995): 881–902.

Freedman, Lawrence. "Prevention, not Preemption." *Washington Quarterly* 26 (spring 2003): 105–14.

———, ed. *Superterrorism: Policy Responses.* Oxford: Blackwell, 2002.

———. "War in Iraq: Selling the Threat." *Survival* 46 (summer 2004): 7–49.

Fukuyama, Francis. *The End of History and the Last Man.* New York: Avon Press, 1992.

———. "Identity and Migration." *Prospect* 131 (February 2007).

———. "The West May Come Apart." *Straits Times,* August 10, 2002.

Fumaroli, Marc. "Les abeilles et les araignées." Preface to *La querelle des anciens et des modernes.* Paris: Gallimard, 2001.

Gallagher, Anna Marie. "The Situation of Undocumented Migrants in the United States." *Immigration Briefings* no. 5–6 (2005).

Gallup Organization. Gallup Surveys, 2001–2005.

Garcia, Michael John. *Criminalizing Unlawful Presence: Selected Issues.* CRS Report for Congress. Washington, DC: Congressional Research Service, May 3, 2006.

Garcia, Michael John, and Larry M. Eig. *Immigration Consequences of Criminal Activity.* CRS Report for Congress. Washington, DC: Congressional Research Service, July 6, 2005.

Garcia, Michael John, Margaret Mikyung Lee, and Todd Tatelman. *Immigration: Analysis of the Major Provisions of H.R. 418, the REAL ID Act of 2005.* CRS Report for Congress. Washington, DC: Congressional Research Service, February 2, 2005.

Garrett, Geoffrey, and George Tsebelis. "The Institutional Foundations of Intergovernmentalism and Supranationalism in the European Union." *International Organization* 55, no. 2 (2001): 357–90.

Garwin, Richard L. "The Technology of Megaterror." *MIT Technology Review,* September 2002.

Gearty, Conor. Review of *The Security of Freedom: Essays on Canada's Anti-Terrorism Bill,* by Ronald J. Daniels, Patrick MacKlem, Kent Roach. *Refuge* 20 (2002): 76–77.

Geddes, Andrew. "The Development of EU Immigration Policy: Supranationalisation and the Politics of Belonging." In *The Politics of Belonging: Migrants and Minorities in Contemporary Europe,* edited by Andrew Geddes and Adrian Favell, 176–91. Aldershot, England: Ashgate, 1999.

Geddes, Andrew. *Immigration and European Integration: Towards Fortress Europe?* Manchester, England: Manchester University Press, 2000.

———. "Lobbying for Migrant Inclusion in the European Union." *Journal of European Public Policy* 7 (2001): 632–49.

———. *The Politics of Migration and Immigration in Europe.* London: Sage, 2002.

Geddes, Andrew, and Adrian Favell, eds. *The Politics of Belonging: Migrants and Minorities in Contemporary Europe.* Aldershot, England: Ashgate, 1999.

Geisser, Vincent. *La nouvelle islamophobie.* Paris: La Découverte, 2003.

Geisser, Vincent, and Khadija Finan. *L'islam à l'école.* Paris: IHESI, 2002.

Geller, William A., and Norval Morris. "Relations Between Federal and Local Police." *Crime & Justice* 15 (1992).

Gibney, Matthew J., and Randall Hansen. "Asylum Policy in the West." Discussion Paper No. 2003/68, World Institute for Development Economics Research, September 2003.

Gil-Bazo, Maria-Teresa. "The Practice of Mediterranean States in the Context of the European Union's Justice and Home Affairs External Dimension: The Safe Third Country Concept Revisited." *International Journal of Refugee Law* 18, no. 3–4 (2006): 571–600.

Gil Calvo, E. *El miedo es el mensaje: riesgo, incertidumbre y medios de comunicación.* Madrid: Alianza, 2004.

Gimpel, James G., and James R. Edwards Jr. *The Congressional Politics of Immigration Reform.* Boston and London: Allyn Bacon, 1999.

Girard, René. *The Scapegoat.* Baltimore, MD: Johns Hopkins University Press, 1986.

———. *Violence and the Sacred.* Baltimore, MD: Johns Hopkins University Press, 1977. Originally published as *La violence et le sacré* (Paris: Grasset, 1972).

———. *Violences d'aujourd'hui, violences de toujours: textes des conférences et des débats.* Lausanne, Switzerland: L'Age d'Homme, 2000.

Giugni, Marco, and Florence Passy, eds. *Political Altruism? Solidarity Movements in International Perspective.* Lanham, MD: Rowman and Littlefield, 2001.

Glazer, Nathan. *We Are All Multiculturalists Now.* Cambridge, MA: Harvard University Press, 1997.

Glazer, Nathan, and Daniel Patrick Moynihan, *Beyond the Melting Pot: The Negroes, Puerto Ricans, Jews, Italians, and Irish of New York City.* Cambridge, MA: Harvard University Press, 1963.

Glucksmann, Andre. "The World of Megaterrorism: Mad Is the European Who Thinks Himself Immune to Terror for Having Opposed Saddam's Overthrow." *Wall Street Journal,* March 21, 2004.

Goetschel, Laurent. "Globalisation and Security: The Challenge of Collective Action in a Politically Fragmented World." *Global Society* 14 (April 2000): 259–77.

Goldberg, Danny, Victor Goldberg, and Robert Greenwald. *It's a Free Country: Personal Freedom in America after September 11.* New York: RDV Books, 2002.

Gonzalez, Daniel. "States Fight Illegal Migration." *Arizona Republic,* August 2, 2006. www.azcentral.com/arizonarepublic/news/articles/0802statelaws.html.

Goode, Erich, and Nachman Ben-Yehuda. "Moral Panics: Culture, Politics, and Social Construction." *Annual Review of Sociology* 20 (1994): 149–71.

Goodhart, David. "Too Diverse?" *Prospect* (February 2004): 30–37.

Gordon, Charles, Stanley Mailman, and Stephen Yale-Loehr. *Immigration Law and Procedure.* Newark, NJ: Matthew Bender, 2004.

Gordon, Diana R. *The Return of the Dangerous Classes: Drug Prohibition and Policy Politics.* New York: Norton, 1994.

Gordon, Jennifer. *Suburban Sweatshops: The Fight for Immigrant Rights.* Cambridge, MA: Belknap Press of Harvard University Press, 2005.

Gordon, Philip H., and Jeremy Shapiro. *Allies at War: America, Europe, and the Crisis over Iraq.* Washington, DC: Brookings, 2004.

Greenberg, Karen. "The Courts and the War on Terror." NYU Center on Law and Security, April 2005.

Greenwood, Christopher. "International Law and the 'War against Terrorism.'" *International Affairs* 78 (April 2002): 301–18.

Gregory, Shaun. "France and the War on Terrorism." *Terrorism and Political Violence* 15 (2003): 124–47.

Greico, Elizabeth M. Report of the Department of Homeland Security Office of Immigration Statistics. *Estimates of the Nonimmigrant Population in the United States: 2004* (June 2006). www.uscis.gov/graphics/shared/statistics/publications/ NIM_2004.pdf; www.uscis.gov/graphics/shared/statistics/index.htm.

Greilsamer, Laurent. "La logique de l'improvisation du Hezbollah." *Le Monde,* January 30, 1990.

Gresh, Alain, and Tariq Ramadan. *L'Islam en questions.* Paris: Sinbad/Actes Sud, 2000.

Griffin, Roger. "Interregnum or Endgame? The Radical Right in the 'Post-fascist' Era." *Journal of Political Ideologies* 5, no. 2 (2000): 163–78.

Griffith, Kati L. "Perfecting Public Immigration Legislation: Private Immigration Bills and Deportable Lawful Permanent Residents." *Georgetown Immigration Law Journal* 18 (2004).

Grillo, Ralph. "Islam and Transnationalism." *Journal of Ethnic and Migration Studies* 30 (2004): 861–78.

Groenendijk, Kees, and Elspeth Guild. "Converging Criteria: Creating an Area of Security of Residence for Europe's Third Country Nationals." *European Journal of Migration and Law* 3 (2001): 37–59.

"Growing European Rejection of Bush's Phony 'Terrorist' Rules: EU Court Scraps Passenger Data Transfers to U.S." TBR News, May 30, 2006. www.tbrnews.org/Archives/a2368.htm.

Guild, Elspeth. "International Terrorism and EU Immigration, Asylum, and Borders Policy: The Unexpected Victims of 11 September 2001." *European Foreign Affairs Review* 8 (2003): 331–46.

———. "The Legal Framework: Who Is Entitled to Move?" In *Controlling Frontiers: Free Movement into and within Europe,* edited by Didier Bigo and Elspeth Guild. Burlington, VT: Ashgate, 2005.

Guiraudon, Virginie. "International Human Rights Norms and Their Incorporation: The Protection of Aliens in Europe." EUI Working Paper No. 98/4, Florence, 1998.

———. "The Marshallian Triptych Re-Ordered: The Role of Courts and Bureaucracies in Furthering Migrant Social Rights." EUI Working Paper No. 99/1, Florence, 1999.

———. "Weak Weapons of the Weak? Transnational Mobilization around Migration in the European Union." In *Contentious Europeans: Protest and Politics in an Emerging Polity,* edited by D. Imig and S. Tarrow, 163–85. Boston: Rowman and Littlefield, 2001.

Guiraudon, Virginie, and Christian Joppke. "Controlling a New Migration World." In *Controlling a New Migration World,* edited by Virginie Guiraudon and Christian Joppke, 1–28. London and New York: Routledge, 2001.

———, eds. *Controlling a New Migration World.* London and New York: Routledge, 2001.

Gunaratna, Rohan. *Inside Al Qaeda.* New York: Columbia University Press, 2002.

Gustafsson, Göran. "Church-State Separation—Swedish Style." In *Church and State in Contemporary Europe: The Chimera of Neutrality,* edited by John Madeley and Zsolt Enyedi, 51–72. Special Issue of *West European Politics.* London: Frank Cass, 2003.

Habermas, Jürgen, Jacques Derrida, and Giovanna Borradori. *Philosophy in a Time of Terror: Dialogues with Jürgen Habermas and Jacques Derrida.* Chicago: University of Chicago Press, 2003.

Hailbronner, K. "Third-Country Nationals and EC Law." In *A Citizens' Europe: In Search of a New Order,* edited by A. Roass and E. Antola. London: Sage, 1995.

Hammar, Tomas. *Democracy and the Nation State: Aliens, Denizens, and Citizens in a World of International Migration.* Aldershot, England: Avebury/Gower, 1990.

———, ed. *European Immigration Policy: A Comparative Study.* Cambridge: Cambridge University Press, 1985.

Hammermesh, Daniel S. "Older Workers in the Coming Labor 'Shortage': Implications on Labor Demand." Center for Retirement Research, Boston, 2001. www.bc.edu/ bc_org/avp/csom/executive/crr/public_spe.shtml.

Hansen, R. "Migration, Citizenship, and Race in Europe: Between Incorporation and Exclusion." *European Journal of Political Research* 35 (1999): 415–44.

Hastings, Max. "Who Do We Think We Are?" *Times* (London), December 17, 2006.

Haubrich, Dirk. "September 11, Anti-Terror Laws, and Civil Liberties: Britain, France, and Germany Compared." *Government and Opposition* 38, no. 1 (January 2003).

Hayduk, Ron. *Democracy for All: Restoring Immigrant Voting Rights in the United States.* New York: Routledge, 2006.

Haynes, Jeff. *Religion in Global Politics.* London and New York: Longman, 1998.

Heclo, Hugh. *Modern Social Politics in Britain and Sweden: From Relief to Income Maintenance.* New Haven, CT: Yale University Press, 1974.

Heisbourg, François. "De l'après-guerre froide à l'hyperterrorisme." *Le Monde,* September 12, 2001.

———. *L'Hyperterrorisme.* Paris: Odile Jacob, 2002.

———. "A Work in Progress: The Bush Doctrine and Its Consequences." *Washington Quarterly* 26 (spring 2003): 75–88.

Heitmeyer, Wilhelm, and Rainer Dollase, eds. *Die bedrängte Toleranz. Ethnisch-kulturelle Konflikte, religiöse Differenzen, und die Gefahren politisierter Gewalt.* Frankfurt: Suhrkamp, 1996.

Henderson, Nicole J., et al. Vera Institute of Justice. "Law Enforcement and Arab American Community Relations after September 11, 2001: Engagement in a Time of Uncertainty." June 2006. www.vera.org/publication_pdf/353_636.pdf.

Henkin, Louis. "The Constitution and United States Sovereignty: A Century of Chinese Exclusion and Its Progeny." *Harvard Law Review* 100 (1987).

Hernando de Larramendi, M. "La proyección mediterránea de España: las relaciones con Mazzuecos." In *Murcia, frontera demográfica en el sur de Europa,* edited by J. Vilar. Universidad de Murcia, 1994.

Hershberg, Eric, and Kevin W. Moore. *Critical Views of September 11: Analyses from around the World.* New York: Norton, 2002.

Hervieu-Léger, Danièle. *Catholicisme, la fin d'un monde.* Paris: Bayard, 2003.

Hewitt, Roger. *White Backlash and the Politics of Multiculturalism.* Cambridge: Cambridge University Press, 2005.

Hiebert, Murray. "The Cost of Security." *Far Eastern Economic Review* 165 (2002): 18–19.

Hing, Bill Ong. *Defining America through Immigration Policy.* Philadelphia: Temple University Press, 2004.

———. "Misusing Immigration Policies in the Name of Homeland Security." *New Centennial Review* 6, no. 1 (spring 2006): 195–224.

Hoffman, Lisa. "U.S. Targets Global Terror Hot Spots." *Washington Times,* December 24, 2001.

Hoffmann, Stanley. "American Exceptionalism: The New Vision." In *American Exceptionalism and Human Rights,* edited by Michael Ignatieff, 225–40. Princeton, NJ: Princeton University Press, 2005.

———. "Clash of Globalizations." *Foreign Affairs* 81 (2002): 104–15.

Hollifield, James F. *L'immigration et l'état nation à la recherche d'un modèle national.* Paris: L'Harmattan, 1997.

———. "Migration, Trade, and the Nation-State: The Myth of Globalization." *UCLA Journal of International Law and Foreign Affairs* 3 (1998): 595–636.

———. "The Politics of International Migration: How Can We 'Bring the State Back In'?" In *Migration Theory: Talking across the Disciplines,* edited by Caroline Brettel and James Hollifield, 137–86. London: Routledge, 2000.

Holusha, John. "In Mexico, Bush Presses Congress on Immigration." *New York Times,* March 31, 2006. www.nytimes.com/2006/03/31/washington/31cnd-immig.html.

"Home-Grown Kamikazes" (editorial). *Le Monde,* July 15, 2005.

Hostettler, John N. Statements on "How Illegal Immigration Impacts Constituencies: Perspectives from members of Congress (Part I)." Hearing before the Subcommittee on Immigration, Border Security and Claims of the Committee on the Judiciary, House of Representatives, 109th Cong., 1st sess., November 10, 2005 (Washington DC; US GPO 2006). http://judiciary.house.gov/media/pdfs/printers/109th/24507.pdf

Houellebecq, Michel. *Elementary Particles.* New York: Vintage International Editions, 2000.

Howard, Michael. "What's in a Name? How to Fight Terrorism." *Foreign Affairs* 81 (January–February 2002): 8–13.

Howorth, Jolyon. "The U.S. National Security Strategy: European Reactions." In *Security Strategy and the Transatlantic Alliance*, edited by Roland Dannreuther and John Peterson, 30–44. London: Routledge, 2006.

———, et al. "L'impact sur les organisations de défense du concept de 'Coalition de Circonstance.'" Paris, IFRI/DAS, 2004.

Hughes, Anwen. "Asylum and Withholding of Removal—A Brief Overview of the Substantive Law." 158 PLI/NY 289 (Practising Law Institute, March 2006).

Human Rights Watch. "Locked Away: Immigration Detainees in Jails in the United States." Report issued September 1998. www.hrw.org/reports98/us-immig/.

———. "Stemming the Flow: Abuses against Migrants, Asylum-seekers and Refugees." Vol. 18, no. 5(E) (September 2006). www.libertysecurity.org/IMG/pdf/libya0906web.pdf.

Hunter, Shireen. *The Future of Islam and the West: Clash of Civilizations or Peaceful Coexistence?* Westport, CT: Praeger, 1998.

Huntington, Samuel P. *The Clash of Civilizations and the Remaking of World Order.* New York: Touchstone, 1996.

———. *Who Are We? America's Great Debate.* New York: Free Press, 2005.

———. *Who Are We? The Challenges to America's National Identity.* New York: Simon & Schuster, 2004.

Huysmans, Jef. "Migrants as a Security Problem: Dangers of 'Securitizing' Societal Issues." In *Migration and European Integration: The Dynamics of Inclusion and Exclusion,* edited by R. Miles and D. Thränhardt. London: Pinter Publishers, 1995.

Immigration and Refugee Clinic and International Human Rights Clinic, Harvard Law School. "Preliminary Findings and Conclusions on the Material Support for Terrorism Bar as Applied to the Overseas Resettlement of Refugees from Burma" (February 2006). www.humanrightsfirst.orgpdf/06619-asy-mat-sup-terr-bar-study.pdf; www.humanrightsfirst.info/pdf/06619-asy-mat-sup-terr-bar-study.pdf, accessed July 22, 2006.

Immigration Law Practitioners Association. "ILPA Response to the Hague Programme: EU Immigration and Asylum Law and Policy." www.libertysecurity.org/article 72.html, posted December 20, 2004.

Inglehart, Ronald. *Modernization and Postmodernization.* Princeton, NJ: Princeton University Press, 1997.

Inglehart, Ronald, and Wayne E. Baker. "Modernization, Cultural Change, and the Persistence of Traditional Values." *American Sociological Review* 65 (2000): 19–51.

Inglehart, Ronald, and Michael Minkenberg. "Die Transformation religiöser Werte in entwickelten Industriegesellschaften." In *Religion und Politik - zwischen Universalismus und Partikularismus,* edited by Heinz-Dieter Meyer, Michael Minkenberg, and Ilona Ostner, 115–30, vol. 2 of the *Jahrbuch für Europa- und Nordamerika-Studien.* Opladen, Germany: Leske+Budrich, 2000.

Instituto Nacional de Estadistica (INE, Madrid). "Nota de prensa, 25 julio 2006."

———. "Boletín informativo del INE." No. 3, 2006.

International Institute for Strategic Studies (IISS). "Cooperative Intelligence: Renewed Momentum?" *Strategic Comments* 12 (May 2006).

———. "The EU's Role in Counter-Terrorism: Coordination and Action." *Strategic Comments* 11 (March 2005).

———. "Islamist Terrorism in London: Unsettling Implications." *Strategic Comments* 11, no. 5 (July 2005).

Ireland, P. "Facing the True 'Fortress Europe': Immigration and Politics in the EC." *Journal of Common Market Studies* 29, no. 5 (1991): 457–80.

"It Isn't Amnesty." *New York Times,* March 29, 2006, A22.

Izquierdo, A. *La inmigración inesperada: la población extranjera en España (1991–1995).* Madrid: Editorial Trotta, 1996.

Jackson, Vicki C. "Citizenship and Federalism." In *Citizenship Today: Global Perspectives and Practices,* edited by T. Alexander Aleinikoff and Douglas Klusmeyer. Washington, DC: Carnegie Endowment for International Peace, 2001.

Jacobs, Dirk, Karen Phalet, and Marc Swyngedouw. "Associational Membership and Political Involvement among Ethnic Minority Groups in Brussels." *Journal of Ethnic and Migration Studies* 30 (2004): 543–59.

Jacobson, Gary C., and Samuel Kernell. *The Logic of American Politics in Wartime: Lessons from the Bush Administration.* Washington, DC: CQ Press, 2004.

Jeffreys, Kelly, and Nancy Rytina. Report of the Department of Homeland Security Office of Immigration Statistics. *U.S. Legal Permanent Residents: 2005* (June 2006). www.uscis.gov/graphics/shared/statistics/publications/USLegalPermEst_5.pdf.

Jenkins, Brian. Quest for Peace Interview. University of California Irvine, 1988. www.lib.uci.edu/quest/index.php?page=jenkins.

———. *Terrorism: Current and Long-Term Threats.* Santa Monica, CA: Rand, 2001.

Jenks, Rosemary. "The USA Patriot Act of 2001." Center for Immigration Studies, December 2001. www.cis.org/articles/2001/back1501.html.

Jensen, Joan M. *Passage from India: Asian Indian Immigrants in North America.* New Haven, CT: Yale University Press, 1988.

Johnson, Dawn Marie. "The AEDPA and IIRIRA: Treating Misdemeanors as Felonies for Immigration Purposes." *Journal of Legislation* 27 (2001).

Johnson, Kevin R. "'Aliens' and the U.S. Immigration Laws: The Social and Legal Construction of the Nonperson." *University of Miami Inter-American Law Review* 28 (1997).

———. "The Antiterrorism Act, the Immigration Reform Act, and Ideological Regulation in the Immigration Laws: Important Lessons for Citizens and Noncitizens." *St. Mary's Law Journal* 28 (1997): 833–36.

———. "Driver's Licenses and Undocumented Immigrants: The Future of Civil Rights Law?" *Nevada Law Journal* 5 (2004): 213

———. *The "Huddled Masses" Myth: Immigration and Civil Rights.* Philadelphia: Temple University Press, 2004.

———. "Racial Profiling after September 11: The Department of Justice's 2003 Guidelines." *Loyola Law* Review 50 (2004).

———. "Why Alienage Jurisdiction? Historical Foundations and Modern Justifications for Federal Jurisdiction Over Disputes Involving Noncitizens," *Yale Journal of International Law* 21 (1996).

Johnson, Paul. "America's New Empire of Liberty." *Hoover Digest,* July 16, 2003.

Johnson, Richard. "Defending Ways of Life: The (Anti-) Terrorist Rhetorics of Bush and Blair." *Theory, Culture, and Society* 19 (2003): 211–32.

Joppke, Christian. "Asylum and State Sovereignty: A Comparison of the United States, Germany, and Britain." *Comparative Political Studies* 30 (June 1997): 259–98.

———, ed. *Challenge to the Nation State: Immigration in Western Europe and the United States.* Oxford: Oxford University Press, 1998.

———. "Europe v. America." *New York Review Books,* February 10, 2005.

———. Immigration and the Nation-State: The United States, Germany, and Great Britain. Oxford: Oxford University Press, 1999.

———. "Why Liberal States Accept Unwanted Immigration." *World Politics* 50 (1998): 266–93.

Judt, Tony. *The Burden of Responsibility: Blum, Camus, Aron, and the French Intellectual Century.* Chicago and London: University of Chicago Press, 1993.

———. "Europe v. America." *New York Review Books* 52, no. 2 (February 10, 2005). www.nybooks.com/articles/17726.

Kagan, Robert. *Of Paradise and Power: America and Europe in the New World Order.* New York: Knopf, 2005.

Kaltenbach, Jeanne-Hélène, and Michèle Tribalat. *La République et l'Islam: entre crainte et aveuglement.* Paris: Gallimard, 2002.

Kanstroom, Daniel. "Deportation, Social Control, and Punishment: Some Thoughts about Why Hard Laws Make Bad Cases." *Harvard Law Review* 113 (2002).

Kaplan, Fred. "Say G-WOT?" *Slate,* July 26, 2005.

Karlan, Pamela S. "Disarming the Private Attorney General." *University of Illinois Law Review* (2003).

Kastoryano, Riva. *Negotiating Identities.* Princeton, NJ: Princeton University Press, 2002.

Kaye, R. "Redefining the Refugee: The UK Media Portrayal of Asylum Seekers." In *The New Migration in Europe: Social Constructions and Social Realities,* edited by K. Koser and H. Lutz. Basingstoke, England: Macmillan; New York: St. Martin's Press, 1998.

Keely, Charles K., and Sharon Stanton Russell. "Response of Industrial Counties to Asylum-Seekers." *Journal of International Affairs* 47 (1994): 461–77.

Kekes, John. *Against Liberalism.* Ithaca, NY: Cornell University Press, 1997.

———. *A Case for Conservatism.* Ithaca, NY: Cornell University Press, 1998.

Kellner, Douglas. *From 9/11 to Terror War: The Dangers of the Bush Legacy.* Lanham, MD: Rowman and Littlefield, 2003.

———. "Theorizing September 11: Social Theory, History, and Globalization." *Social Thought & Research* 25 (2002): 1–50.

Kelly, John D. "U.S. Power, after 9/11 and before It: If Not an Empire, Then What?" *Public Culture* 15 (2003): 347–69.

Keohane, Daniel. *The EU and Counter-Terrorism.* London: Centre for European Reform, 2005.

Keohane, Daniel, and Adam Townsend. "A Joined-Up EU Security Policy." *CER Bulletin* (December 2003–January 2004).

Kepel, Gilles. *Allah in the West: Islamic Movements in America and Europe.* Stanford, CA: Stanford University Press, 1997.

———. *Les banlieues de l' islam: naissance d'une religion en France.* Paris: Seuil, 1991.

Kephart, Janice L. "Immigration and Terrorism: Beyond the 9/11 Report on Terrorist Travel." Center for Immigration Studies Paper 24, September 2005.

Kersbergen, Kees van. *Social Capitalism: A Study of Christian Democracy and the Welfare State.* London and New York: Routledge, 1995.

———. "Translating Justice: A Guide for New York City's Justice and Public Safety Agencies to Improve Access for Residents with Limited English Proficiency." June 2005; updated April 2006. www.vera.org/publication_pdf/300_564.pdf.

Khashu, Anita, et al. Vera Institute of Justice. "Building Strong Police-Immigrant Community Relations: Lessons From a New York City Project." August 2005. www.vera.org/publication_pdf/300_564.pdf.

"The Kindness of Strangers." *Economist,* February 26, 2004.

Kirk, Russell. *America's British Culture.* New Brunswick, NJ, and London: Transaction Books, 1994.

"Kizilkaya will Idomeneo nicht sehen." *Stern,* September 29, 2006. http://www.stern.de.

Klausen, Jytte. *The Islamic Challenge Politics and Religion in Western Europe.* New York: Oxford University Press, 2005.

Kmiec, Douglas W., Assistant Attorney General, Office of Legal Counsel. "Handling of INS Warrants of Deportation in Relation to NCIC Wanted Person File." April 11, 1989.

Knoke, David, and James Kuklinsky. *Network Analysis.* London: Sage, 1982.

———. Center for Immigration Studies. "State and Local Authority to Enforce Immigration Law: A Unified Approach for Stopping Terrorists" (2004).

Kobach, Kris W. "The Quintessential Force Multiplier: The Inherent Authority of Local Police to Make Immigration Arrests." *Albany Law Review* 69 (2005).

Koh, Harold Hongju. "Equality with a Human Face: Justice Blackmun and the Equal Protection of Aliens." *Hamline Law Review* 8 (1985).

Kolodner, Meredith. "County Jails Boost Their Income." *News 21,* Aug. 30, 2006. http://news.yahoo.com/s/news21/20060831/ts_news21/county_jails_boost_their_ income.

Koopmans, Ruud. "Germany and Its Immigrants: An Ambivalent Relationship." *Journal of Ethnic and Migration Studies* 25 (1999): 627–47.

Koopmans, Ruud, and Paul Statham. "Migration and Ethnic Relations as a Field of Political Contention: An Opportunity Structure Approach." In *Challenging Immigration and Ethnic Relations Politics: Comparative European Perspectives,* edited by Ruud Koopmans and Paul L. Statham, 13–56. Oxford: Oxford University Press, 2000.

———, eds. *Challenging Immigration and Ethnic Relations Politics: Comparative European Perspectives.* Oxford: Oxford University Press, 2000.

Koopmans, Ruud, Paul Statham, Marco Giugni, and Florence Passy. *Contested Citizenship: Immigration and Cultural Diversity in Europe.* Minneapolis: University of Minnesota Press, 2005.

Koslowski, Rey. *Migrants and Citizens: Demographic Change in the European State System.* Ithaca, NY, and London: Cornell University Press, 2000.

Kovsky, Steve. "Corporate Terrorism: A New Global Threat." *Management Review* 79 (1990).

Krasner, Steven. *Sovereignty: Organized Hypocrisy.* Princeton, NJ: Princeton University Press, 1999.

Kriesi, Hans-Peter, et al.. *New Social Movements in Western Europe: A Comparative Analysis.* Minneapolis: University of Minnesota Press, 1995.

Krikorian, Mark. "Who Deserves Asylum?" *Commentary* 101 (June 1996).

Kundnani, Hans. "Goodbye to the 68rs." *Prospect,* no. 113 (August 2005). www.prospect magazine.co.uk/article_detailsuphp?id=6969.

Kuntic, Dario. "Terrorism in a Changing World." *Croatian International Relations Review* 9 (2003): 199–204.

Kymlicka, Will, and Wayne Norman, eds. *Citizenship in Diverse Societies.* Oxford: Oxford University Press, 2000.

"Labour May Steal Tory Thunder on Migrants Asylum." *Financial Times,* January 25, 2005.

LaFeber, Walter. "The Post September 11 Debate over Empire, Globalization, and Fragmentation." *Political Science Quarterly* 117 (2002): 1–17.

Lambert, Yves, and Guy Michelat, eds. *Crépuscule des religions chez les jeunes? jeunes et religions en France.* Paris: L'Harmattan, 1992.

Landau, Saul. *The Pre-Emptive Empire: A Guide to Bush's Kingdom.* London and Sterling, VA: Pluto Press, 2003.

Lanman, Scott, and Craig Torres. "Bernanke Warns of Possible 'Crisis' from Budget Gap." January 18, 2007. http://www.bloomberg.com/apps/news?pid=20601087& sid=a_46QcGbvFZk&refer=home.

Lappin, Shalom. "How Class Disappeared from Western Politics." *Dissent* (winter 2006). www.dissentmagazine.org/menutest/articles/wi06/lappin.htm.

Larabee, Ann. "Empire of Fear: Imagined Community and the September 11 Attacks." *Research in Social Problems and Public Policy* 11 (2003): 19–31.

Laufer, Gregory F. "Admission Denied: In Support of a Duress Exception to the Immigration and Nationality Act's 'Material Support for Terrorism' Provision." *Georgetown Immigration Law Journal* 20 (2006): 437–81.

Laurence, Jonathan. "(Re)constructing Community: Turks, Jews, and German Responsibility." *German Politics and Society* 19 (summer 2001).

Lavenex, Sandra, and Emek M. Uçarer, "The External Dimension of Europeanization: The Case of Immigration Policies." *Cooperation and Conflict* 39, no. 4 (2004).

Layton-Henry, Z. "Citizenship and Migrant Workers in Western Europe." University of Warwick, 1992.

———. *The Political Rights of Migrant Workers in Western Europe.* London: Sage, 1990.

Lee, Rensselaer W. *Smuggling Armageddon: The Nuclear Black Market in the Former Soviet Union and Europe.* New York: St. Martin's Press, 1998.

Legomsky, Stephen H. "Deportation and the War on Independence." *Cornell Law Review* 91 (2006).

———. *Immigration and Refugee Law and Policy.* 4th ed. New York: Foundation Press; St. Paul, MN: Thomson/West, 2005.

———. "Immigration Law and the Principle of Plenary Congressional Power." *Supreme Court Review* (1984).

Leiken, Robert S. "Europe's Angry Muslims." *Foreign Affairs* 84 (July–August 2005): 120–35.

Lemmen, Thomas. *Islamische Organisationen in Deutschland.* Bonn: Friedrich Ebert Stiftung, 2000.

Leppard, David, and Nick Fielding. "The Hate." *Sunday Times* (London), July 11, 2001.

Leveau, Rémy, and Gilles Kepel, eds. *Les musulmans dans la société française.* Paris: Presses de Sciences Po, 1988.

Lewis, Jeff, et al. Migration Policy Institute. "Authority of State and Local Officers to Arrest Aliens Suspected of Civil Infractions of Federal Immigration Law." *Bender's Immigration Bulletin* 7 (2003).

Lewis, Raphael. "In-State Tuition not a Draw for Many Immigrants." *Boston Globe,* November 9, 1995. www.boston.com/news/nation/articles/2005/11/09/in_state_tuition_not_a_draw_for_many_immigrants.

Lieven, Anatol. "In the Mirror of Europe: The Perils of American Nationalism." *Current History* 103 (2004): 99–106.

Lijphart, Arend. *Patterns of Democracy: Government Forms and Performance in Thirty-six Countries.* New Haven, CT, and London: Yale University Press, 1999.

Lipschutz, Ronnie D. "The Clash of Governmentalities: The Fall of the UN Republic and America's Reach for Empire." *Contemporary Security Policy* 23 (2002): 214–31.

———. "Imitations of Empire." *Global Environmental Politics* 4 (2004): 20–23.

Liptak, Adam. "Federal Courts Criticize Judges' Handling of Asylum Cases." *New York Times,* December 26, 2005.

"Living Together Apart: British Muslims and the Paradox of Multiculturalism." *Daily Telegraph,* January 29, 2007.

López García, Bernabé. Immigración magrebí en España: el retorno de los moriscos. Madrid: MAPFRE, 1993.

López Garcia, Bernabé, and Ana Planet Contreras. "Islam in Spain." In *Islam, Europe's Second Religion,* edited by Shireen T. Hunter, 156–74. Westport, CT: Praeger, 2002.

Lowe, Peggy. "Deal Guts O.C. Sheriff's Immigration Enforcement Plan." *Orange County Register,* October 6, 2006. www.ocregister.com/ocregister/homepage/abox/article_1299610.php.

Lutz, Martin. "Schäuble startet Islam-Konferenz im September." *Die Welt,* May 24, 2006.

Lydersen, Kari. "Ill. Governor to Announce New Benefits for Immigrants." *Washington Post,* December 13, 2006, A11. www.washingtonpost.com/wp-dyn/content/article/2006/12/12/AR2006121201342.html

Lyotard, Jean François. *The Postmodern Condition: A Report on Knowledge.* Manchester: University of Manchester Press, 1984.

MacDonald, Heather. "ICE, ICE, Baby." *National Review Online,* August 7, 2006. http://article.nationalreview.com/?q=YjRiYzRlYTM4ZjlhOThjYmRlNDUzNjQ3NjRmY2RlZGY=.

Maddox, Marion. *God under Howard: The Rise of the Religious Right in Australian Politics.* Crows Nest, NSW, Australia: Allen & Unwin, 2005.

Madeley, John, and Zsolt Enyedi, eds. *Church and State in Contemporary Europe: The Chimera of Neutrality.* Special issue of West European Politics. London: Frank Cass, 2003.

Makinda, Samuel M. "Global Governance and Terrorism." *Global Change* 15 (February 2003): 43–58.

Malefakis, E. "Southern Europe in the XIXth and XXth Centuries: An Historical Overview." Working paper, Instituto Juan March de Estudios e Investigaciones, Madrid, 1992.

Manne, Robert, ed. *The Howard Years.* Melbourne: BlackInc. Agenda, 2004.

Marcus, Ruth. "Immigration's Scrambled Politics" (op-ed article). *Washington Post,* April 4, 2006, A23. www.washingtonpost.com/wp-dyn/content/article/2006/04/03/AR2006040301618.html.

Marcuse, Herbert. *The One-Dimensional Man: Studies in the Ideology of Advanced Industrial Society.* Boston: Beacon Press, 1964.

Maréchal, Brigitte. "Mosquées, organisations et leadership." In *Convergences musulmanes: aspects contemporains de l'islam dans l'Europe élargie,* edited by Felice Dassetto et al. Louvain-la-Nueve, Belgium: Bruylant Academia, 2001.

Maréchal, Brigitte, and Felice Dassetto. "Introduction: From Past to Present." In *Muslims in the Enlarged Europe: Religion and Society,* edited by Brigitte Maréchal, Stefano Allievi, Felice Dassetto, and Jørgen Nielsen, xvii–xxvii. Leiden and Boston: Brill, 2003.

Markell, Patchen. *Bound by Recognition.* Princeton, NJ: Princeton University Press, 2003.

Markovits, Andrei. "The European and American Left since 1945." *Dissent* (winter 2005).

———. *Uncouth Nation: Why Europe Dislikes America.* Princeton, NJ: Princeton University Press, 2007.

Martin, David. *A General Theory of Secularisation.* London: Blackwell, 1978.

———. "The 1995 Asylum Reforms: A Historic and Global Perspective." *Backgrounder* (Center for Immigration Studies), May 2000.

Martin, Susan. "Politics and Policy Responses to Illegal Migration in the U.S." Working paper, Institute for the Study of International Migration, Georgetown University, Washington, DC, 1998.

———. "The Politics of U.S. Immigration Reform." *Political Quarterly* 74 (August 2003): 132–49.

Marty, Martin E., and R. Scott Appleby, eds. *Fundamentalisms Observed.* Chicago and London: University of Chicago Press, 1991.

Mayer, Nonna. *Ces Français qui votent Le Pen.* Paris: Flammarion, 2002.

McBride, Michael J. "Migrants and Asylum Seekers: Policy Responses in the United States to Immigrants and Refugees from Central America and the Caribbean." *International Migration* 37 (1999): 289–317.

McCarthy, John D., and Mayer N. Zald. "Resource Mobilization and Social Movements: A Partial Theory." *American Journal of Sociology* 82 (1977): 1212–41.

McCollum, William. Statements on the "Criminal Alien Deportation Improvements Act of 1995." *Congressional Record*, House, Friday, February 10, 1995, 104th Cong., 1st sess., 141 *Cong Rec* H 1586, vol. 141, no. 27. Available at LexisNexis Congressional.

McConnell, Michael W. "Believers as Equal Citizens." In *Obligations of Citizenship and Demands of Faith: Religious Accommodation in Pluralist Democracies,* edited by Nancy Rosenblum, 90–110. Princeton, NJ: Princeton University Press, 2000.

———. "Evaluating the Founders' Design." *University of Chicago Law Review* 54 (1987).

McGregor, Andrew. "Jihad and the Rifle Alone: 'Abdullah' Azzam and the Islamist Revolution." *Journal of Conflict Studies* 23 (fall 2003): 92–113.

Mearsheimer, John J., and Stephen M. Walt. "An Unnecessary War." *Foreign Policy* 134 (January–February 2003): 50–59.

"Media Repeated GOP's False Claim That Democrats Are to Blame for Plan to Make Illegal Immigrants Felons." Media Matters for America, April 17, 2006. http://mediamatters.org/items/200604170005.

Medici Senza Frontiere (MSF). *Rapporto sui centri di permanenza temporanei e assistenza.* www.medicisenzafrontiere.it/msfinforma/dossier/missione_italia/CPT_FINALE.pdf.

Megret, Frederic. "Justice in Times of Violence." *European Journal of International Law* 14 (2003): 327–45.

Mele, Christopher, and Teresa A. Miller. "Collateral Civil Penalties as Techniques of Social Policy." In *Civil Penalties, Social Consequences,* edited by Christopher Mele and Teresa A. Miller, 9–26. New York and London: Routledge, 2005.

Melleuish, Gregory. "Globalised Religions for a Globalised World." *Policy* (Australia), winter 2005. www.cis.org.au/policy/winter05/polwin05-3.htm.

Mendes-Flores, Paul, and Yehuda Reinharz, eds. *The Jew in the Modern World: A Documentary History.* Oxford: Oxford University Press, 1995.

Merlini, Cesare. "U.S. Hegemony and the Roman Analogy: A European View." *International Spectator* 37 (2002): 19–30.

Messina, Anthony M., ed. *West European Immigration and Immigrant Policies in the New Century.* Westport, CT: Praeger, 2003.

Meyerstein, Ariel. "Retuning the Harmonization of EU Asylum Law: Exploring the Need for an EU Asylum Appellate Court." *California Law Review* 93 (October 2005): 1509–55.

Michelat, Guy. "L'identité catholique des Français: I. les dimensions de la religiosité." *Revue Française de Sociologie* 31 (July–September 1990): 355–88.

———. "L'identité catholique des Français: II. appartenance et socialisation religieuse." *Revue Française de Sociologie* 31 (October–December 1990): 609–33.

Micklethwait, John, and Adrian Wooldridge. "Faith, Fortune, and the Frontier: The Pillars of America's Unique Conservatism." *National Review Online,* July 14, 2004. www.nationalreview.com/comment/micklethwait_wooldridge200406180914.asp. Accessed September 12, 2007.

Migoya, David. "New Era on Immigration." *Denver Post,* August 1, 2006. www .denverpost.com/search/ci_4813481.

Migration Watch. *The Illegal Migrant Population in the UK.* www.migrationwatchuk .org/Briefingpapers/migration_trends/illegal_migrant_pop_in_uk.asp.

Mikich, Sonia. "What Next, Bearded One?" *Tageszeitung* (Berlin), February 6, 2006.

Miles, Robert, and Dietrich Thränhardt, eds. *Migration and European Integration: The Dynamics of Inclusion and Exclusion.* London: Pinter Publishers, 1995.

Miller, Teresa A. "By Any Means Necessary: Collateral Civil Penalties of Non-U.S. Citizens and the War on Terror." In *Civil Penalties, Social Consequences,* edited by Christopher Mele and Teresa A. Miller, 47–66. New York and London: Routledge, 2005.

Ministerio del Interior. "Anuario de Extranjería." Madrid, 2002.

———. "Anuario Estadístico de Extranjería." Comisión Interministerial de Extranjería, Madrid, 1998.

Ministerio de Trabajo y Asuntos Sociales (MTAS). "Anuario de Migraciones 2004." Dirección General de Migraciones, Madrid, 2004.

———. "Anuario de Migraciones 2005." Dirección General de Migraciones, Madrid, 2005.

———. "Borrador del Plan Estratégico de Ciudadanía e Integración." Madrid, 2006. www.mtas.es/migraciones/Integracion/PlanEstrategico/PlanEstrategico_Indice.htm.

———. "Informe sobre la Inmigración y el Asilo en España." Foro para la Integración Social de los Inmigrantes, 1998.

Minkenberg, Michael. "Mobiliser contre l'Autre: la nouvelle droite radicale et son rôle dans le processus politique." In *Les codes de la différence,* edited by Riva Kastoryano, 263–96. Paris: Presses des la FNSP, 2005.

———. *Neokonservatismus und Neue Rechte in den USA.* Baden-Baden, Germany: Nomos, 1990.

———. "The Policy Impact of Church-State Relations: Family Policy and Abortion in Britain, France, and Germany." *West European Politics* 26, no. 1 (2003): 195ff.

Minkenberg, Michael. "The Policy Impact of Church-State Relations: Family Policy and Abortion in Britain, France and Germany." *Church and State in Contemporary Europe: The Chimera of Neutrality,* edited by John Madeley and Zsolt Enyedi, 195–217. Special issue of *West European Politics.* London: Frank Cass, 2003.

———. "The Politics of Citizenship in the New Republic." *West European Politics* 26 (October 2003): 219–40.

———. "Religion, Immigration and the Politics of Multiculturalism: A Comparative Analysis of Western Democracies." Paper presented at the Immigration Policy Post-9/11 workshop, University of Pittsburgh, September 9–10, 2005.

———. "Religion and Public Policy: Institutional, Cultural, and Political Impact on the Shaping of Abortion Policies in Western Democracies." *Comparative Political Studies* 35 (March 2002): 221–47.

———. "Religious Effects on the Shaping of Immigration Policies in Western Democracies." Paper presented at the ECPR joint sessions workshops, Uppsala, Sweden, April 2004.

———. "Staat und Kirche in westlichen Demokratien." In *Politik und Religion,* edited by Michael Minkenberg and Ulrich Willems, 115–38. Special issue 33/2002 of *Politische Vierteljahresschrift.* Wiesbaden, Germany: Westdeutscher Verlag, 2003.

Minkenberg, Michael, and Ulrich Willems, eds. *Politik und Religion.* Special issue 33/2002 of *Politische Vierteljahresschrift.* Wiesbaden, Germany: Westdeutscher Verlag, 2003.

Mitsilegas, Valsamis, Jorg Monar, and Wyn Rees. *The EU and Internal Security.* New York: Palgrave Macmillan, 2003.

Modood, Tariq, ed. *Church, State, and Religious Minorities.* London: Policy Studies Institute, 1997.

———. "Multiculturalism, Secularism and the State." *Critical Review of International Social and Political Philosophy* 1 (1998): 114ff.

Modood, Tariq, and Pnina Werbner. *The Politics of Multiculturalism in the New Europe: Racism, Identity, and Community.* London: Zed, 1997.

Monod, Jean-Claude. "Destins du paulinisme politique: K. Barth, C. Schmitt, J. Taubes" (Pauline Political Thought and Its Destiny: K. Barth, C. Schmitt, J. Taubes). *Esprit* 292 (February 2003): 113–24.

Monsma, Steven J., and J. Christopher Soper. *The Challenge of Pluralism: Church and State in Five Democracies.* Lanham, MD: Rowman and Littlefield, 1997.

Moore, Laurence. *Selling God: American Religion in the Marketplace of Culture.* New York: Oxford University Press, 1994.

Morawetz, Nancy. "Understanding the Impact of the 1996 Deportation Laws and the Limited Scope of Proposed Reforms." *Harvard Law Review* 113 (2000).

Moreno Fuentes, F. J. "Migration and Spanish Nationality Law." In *Towards a European Nationality: Citizenship, Immigration and Nationality Law in the EU,* edited by Patrick Weil and Randall Hansen. London: Palgrave, 2001.

MORI Political Monitor. "Long-Term Trends: The Most Important Issues Facing Britain Today, 1979–2005." www.mori.com/polls/trends/issues.shtml.

MORI Social Research Institute. *International Social Trends Monitor.* IPSOS-MORI Survey on Attitudes toward Immigration, November 2006.

Motomura, Hiroshi. *Americans in Waiting: The Lost Story of Immigration and Citizenship in the United States.* Oxford: Oxford University Press, 2006.

———. "Immigration Law after a Century of Plenary Power: Phantom Constitutional Norms and Statutory Interpretation." *Yale Law Journal* 100 (1990).

Mousin, Craig B. "A Clear View from the Prairie: Harold Washington and the People of Illinois Respond to Federal Encroachment of Human Rights." *Southern Illinois University Law Journal* 29 (2005).

Mulholland, Hélène. "Muslim Extremists Are a Mirror Image of the BNP, Cameron says." *Guardian,* January 29, 2007.

Muller, Benjamin J. "(Dis)Qualified Bodies: Securitization, Citizenship and 'Identity Management.'" *Citizenship Studies* 8, no. 3 (September 2004): 279–94.

Muller, Harald. *Terrorism, Proliferation: A European Threat Assessment.* Paris: EU-ISS, 2003.

Müller, Jan-Werner. *Memory and Power in Post-War Europe: Studies in the Presence of the Past.* Cambridge: Cambridge University Press, 2002.

Mylroie, Laurie. *Bush vs. the Beltway: How the CIA and the State Department Tried to Stop the War on Terror.* New York: Regan Books, 2003.

Nakash, Yitzhak. *Reaching for Power: The Shi'a in the Modern Arab World.* Princeton, NJ, and London: Princeton University Press, 2006.

National Academy of Science. The New Americans: Economic, Demographic, and Fiscal Effects of Immigration. Executive Summary, 1997.

National Commission on Terrorist Attacks against the United States. *The 9/11 Commission Report.* Washington, DC: Government Printing Office, 2004.

National Commission on Terrorist Attacks upon the United States. Final Report 390 (2004). www.9-11commission.gov/report/911Report.pdf.

National Governors Association, National Conference of State Legislatures, and American Association of Motor Vehicle Administrators. "The Real ID Act: National Impact Analysis" (September 2006). www.ncsl.org/print/statefed/Real_ID_Impact_Report_FINAL_Sept19.pdf.

National Immigration Forum. "Legislation: State and Local Police Enforcement of Immigration Laws." www.immigrationforum.org/DesktopDefault.aspx?tabid=737.

———. "Proposals to Expand the Immigration Authority of State and Local Police: Dangerous Public Policy According to Law Enforcement, Governments, Opinion Leaders, and Communities" (September 18, 2006). www.immigrationforum.org/documents/TheDebate/EnforcementLocalPolice/CLEARHSEAQuotes.pdf.

National Immigration Law Center. "Immigrant Driver's License Proposals and Campaigns: Surprising Progress since 9/11." *Immigration Rights Update* (May 14, 2002). www.nilc.org/immspbs/DLs/DL002.htm.

———. "Most State Proposals to Restrict Drivers' Licenses for Immigrants Have Been Unsuccessful." *Immigration Rights Update* (July 15, 2002). www.nilc.org/immspbs/DLs/DL003.htm

———. "State Proposed or Enacted Legislation Regarding Immigrant Access to Higher Education" (November 13, 2003). www.nilc.org/immlawpolicy/DREAM/DREAM_Bills.pdf.

———. "Twenty-four States Introduce Driver's License Bills." *Immigration Rights Update* (March 23, 2006). www.nilc.org/immspbs/DLs/DL031.htm.

National Intelligence Council. *Mapping the Global Future: Report of the National Intelligence Council's 2020 Project.* Washington, DC, 2005. www.foia.cia.gov/2020/2020.pdf.

Negri, Toni. "Ruptures within Empire, the Power of Exodus: Interview with Toni Negri." *Theory* 19 (August 2002): 187–94.

Neuman, Gerald L. "Aliens as Outlaws: Government Services, Proposition 187, and the Structure of Equal Protection." *UCLA Law Review* 42 (1995).

———. "The Lost Century of American Immigration Law (1776–1875)." *Columbia Law Review* 93, no. 8 (December 1993): 1833–1901.

———. *Strangers to the Constitution: Immigrants, Borders, and Fundamental Law.* Princeton, NJ: Princeton University Press, 1996.

———. "'We Are the People': Alien Suffrage in German and American Perspective." *Michigan Journal of International Law* 13 (1992).

Nevins, Joseph. *Operation Gatekeeper: The Rise of the "Illegal Alien" and the Making of the U.S.-Mexico Boundary.* New York: Routledge, 2002.

Newhouse, John. *Imperial America: The Bush Assault on the World Order.* New York: Knopf, 2003.

"A New, Improved Race Card." *Economist,* April 7, 2005.

Ngai, Mae M. *Impossible Subjects: Illegal Aliens and the Making of Modern America.* Princeton, NJ: Princeton University Press, 2004.

Nielsen, Jørgen S. "Muslims: The State and the Public Domain in Britain." In *Religion und Politik in Deutschland und Großbritannien,* edited by Richard Bonney et al., 145–54. Munich: K. G. Saur, 2001.

———. *Muslims in Western Europe.* 2nd ed. Edinburgh: Edinburgh University Press, 1995.

Niessen, J. "EU Policies on Immigration and Integration after the Amsterdam Treaty." Migration Policy Group, 1999.

Niethammer, Lutz. *PostHistoire: Has History Come to an End?* New York and London: Verso Press, 1992.

Noiriel, Gérard. *Le creuset français: histoire de l'immigration, XIXe–XXe siècles.* Paris: Seuil, 1988.

Noll, Gregor. "Proof and Credibility." The Danish Institute for Human Rights. www.humanrights.dk/departments/research/rrp/repr.doc/proofandcred.doc.

Noll, Mark. "The American Revolution and Protestant Evangelism." *Journal of Interdisciplinary History* 23, no. 3 (winter 1993): 615–38.

———. *The Old Religion in a New World: The History of North American Christianity.* Grand Rapids, MI: Eerdmans, 2002.

Nooy, Wouter de, Andrej Mrvar, and Vladimir Batagelj. *Exploratory Social Network Analysis with Pajek.* Cambridge: Cambridge University Press, 2005.

Nora, Pierre. "The Tidal Wave of Memory." *Project Syndicate,* June 2001. www.project-syndicate.org/commentary/nora1.

Norris, Pippa, and Ronald Inglehart. *Sacred and Secular: Religion and Politics Worldwide.* Cambridge: Cambridge University Press, 2004.

Numbers USA. "Immigration Profile of Rep. James Sensenbrenner." Available at http://profiles.numbersusa.com/improfile.php3?DistSend=WI&VIPID=880.

NYU Center on Law and Security. "Terrorist Trials: A Report Card." February 2005.

Obershall, Anthony. *Social Conflict and Social Movements.* Englewood Cliffs, NJ: Prentice-Hall, 1973.

O'Kane, James. *The Crooked Ladder: Gangsters, Ethnicity, and the American Dream.* New Brunswick, NJ: Transaction Publishers, 1992.

Olivas, Michael A. "IIRIRA, the Dream Act, and Undocumented College Student Residency." *Journal of College and University Law* 30 (2004): 435.

O'Neill, John. "Empire versus Empire: A Post-Communist Manifesto." *Theory* 19 (August 2002): 195–210.

Osuna, Juan P. "The 1996 Immigration Act: Criminal Aliens and Terrorists." *Interpreter Releases: Report and Analysis of Immigration and Nationality Law* 73 (December 16, 1996): 1713–21.

Pabon Lopez, Maria. "More Than a License to Drive: State Restrictions on the Use of Driver's Licenses by Noncitizens." *Southern Illinois University Law Journal* 29 (2004).

Palat, Ravi Arvind, and Mark Selden. "Introduction: 9/11, War without Respite, and the New Face of Empire." *Critical Asian Studies* 35 (2003): 163–74.

Panitch, Leo. "September 11 and the American Empire." *Interventions* 5 (2003): 233–40.

Parekh, Bhikhu. *Rethinking Multiculturalism: Cultural Diversity and Political Theory.* Cambridge, MA: Harvard University Press, 2000.

Parker, Laura. "Court Tests Await Cities' Laws on Immigrants." *USA Today,* October 9, 2006. www.usatoday.com/news/nation/2006–10–08-immigration_x.htm.

Parlement Européen. *Fascist Europe: The Rise of Racism and Xenophobia.* Edited by Glyn Ford. London: Pluto Press, 1992.

Pasquarella, Jennie. "Victims of Terror Stopped at the Gate to Safety: The Impact of the 'Material Support to Terrorism' Bar on Refugees." *Human Rights Brief* 13 (2006): 28–32.

Passel, Jeffrey. "Immigrants and Taxes: A Reappraisal of Huddles's 'The Cost of Immigration.'" The Urban Institute, Washington, DC, January 1994.

———. "Size and Characteristics of the Unauthorized Migrant Population in the U.S." Pew Hispanic Center Report, March 7, 2006. http://pewhispanic.org/reports/report.php?ReportID=61.

Pauw, Robert. "A New Look at Deportation as Punishment: Why at Least Some of the Constitution's Criminal Procedure Protections Must Apply." *Administrative Law Review* 52 (2000).

———. "Plenary Power: An Outmoded Doctrine That Should Not Limit IIRIRA Reform." *Emory Law Journal* 51 (2002).

Peers, Steve. "Building Fortress Europe: The Development of EU Migration Law." *Common Market Law Review* 35 (1998): 1235–72.

"Perdue Signs Georgia Security and Immigration Compliance Act." *Chattanoogan,* April 17, 2006. www.chattanoogan.com/articles/article_83961.asp.

Pérés, H. "L'Europe commence à Gibraltar: le dilemme espagnol face à l'immigration." *Pôle Sud* 11 (1999).

Pérez Díaz, V., B. Álvarez Miranda, and E. Chulea. *La inmigración musulmana en Europa: Turcos en Alemania, argelinos en Francia y marroquíes en España.* Barcelona: Fundación "la Caixa," 2004.

Pérez-Díaz, Víctor, Berta Álvarez-Miranda, and Carmen González-Enríquez. *España ante la inmigración.* Barcelona: Fundación "la Caixa," Colección Estudios Sociales, 2002.

Perrineau, Pascal. "Les etapes d'une implantation électorale (1972–1988)." In *Le Front National à découvert,* edited by Nonna Mayer and Pascal Perrineau. Paris: Presses de la FNSP, 1988.

———. *Le Front National: la force solitaire.* In *Le vote sanction,* edited by Philippe Habert, Pascal Perrineau, and Colette Ysmal. Paris: Presses de la FNSP/Dept. d'Etudes Politiques du Figaro.

Pew Global Attitudes Project. "Muslims in Europe: Economic Worries Top Concerns about Religious and Cultural Identity." July 6, 2006. http://pewglobal.org/reports/display.php?ReportID=254.

Pew Hispanic Center. *America's Immigration Quandary.* March 2006.

Pew Research Center. "No Consensus on Immigration Problem and Proposed Fixes: America's Immigration Quandary." March 30, 2006.

Pew Research Center for the People and the Press/Pew Hispanic Center. Immigration Survey, February 8–March 7, 2006.

Pew Research Center. Pew Global Attitudes Project Survey. Spring 2006.

Phalet, Karen, and Marc Swyngedouw. "National Identities and Representations of Citizenship: A Comparison of Turks, Moroccans, and Working-Class Belgians in Brussels." *Ethnicities* 2 (2002): 5–30.

Piven, Frances Fox. *The War at Home: The Domestic Causes and Consequences of Bush's Militarism.* New York: New Press, 2004.

Piven, Joshua, and David Borgenicht. *The Worst-Case Scenario Survival Handbook: Travel.* San Francisco: Chronicle Books, 2001.

Plesner, Ingvill Thorsen. "State Church and Autonomy in Norway." In *Church Autonomy: A Comparative Survey,* edited by Gerhard Robbers, 467–84. Frankfurt: Peter Lang, 2001.

Potter, Gary W., and Victor E. Kappeler. *Constructing Crime: Perspectives on Making News and Social Problems.* Prospect Heights, IL: Waveland Press, 1998.

Poulain, Michel, and Nicolas Perrin. "Can UN Migration Recommendations Be Met in Europe?" *Migration Information Source,* Migration Policy Institute (MPI), July 2003.

Powell, Catherine. "Dialogic Federalism: Constitutional Possibilities for Incorporation of Human Rights Law in the United States." *University of Pennsylvania Law Review* 150 (2001).

Puar, Jasbir K., and Amit S. Rai. "Monster, Terrorist, Fag: The War on Terrorism and the Production of Docile Patriots." *Social Text* 20, no. 3(72) (2002): 117–48.

Putnam, Robert. "Who Killed Civic America?" *Prospect,* March 1996.

Rabkin, Norman. "Criminal Aliens: INS Efforts to Identify and Remove Imprisoned Aliens Need to Be Improved." Testimony before the Immigration and Claims Subcommittee Committee on the Judiciary House of Representatives, July 15, 1997. United States General Accounting Office. www.gao.gov/archive/1997/gg97154t.pdf.

Radaelli, C. "How Does Europeanisation Produce Domestic Policy Change? Corporate Tax Policy in Italy and the United Kingdom." *Comparative Political Studies* 30 (1997).

Radu, Michel. "London 7/7 and Its Impact." *Watch on the West* (Philadelphia, Foreign Policy Research Institute), 6, no. 5 (July 26, 2005).

Raine, Linnea P., Frank J. Cillufo, and Center for Strategic and International Studies. *Global Organized Crime: The New Empire of Evil.* Washington, DC: Center for Strategic and International Studies, 1994.

Ramasastry, Anita. "Why the Real ID Act Is A Real Mess." Findlaw.com, August 10, 2005. http://writ.news.findlaw.com/ramasastry/20050810.html.

Ramel, Frederic, and Charles-Philippe David. "'Yes But'—The Image of Europe according to the Bush Administration: From Ambivalence to Rigidity." *Etudes Internationales* 33 (2002): 31–55.

Rannik, Julie K. "Comment, 'The Anti-Terrorism and Effective Death Penalty Act of 1996': A Death Sentence for the 212(c) Waiver." *University of Miami Inter-American Law Review* 28 (1996).

Raufer, Xavier. "New World Disorder, New Terrorisms: New Threats for Europe and the Western World." *Terrorism and Political Violence* 11 (2000): 30–51.

Rees, Wyn. "The External Face of Internal Security." In *The International Relations of the European Union,* edited by Christopher Hill and Michael Smith. 4th ed. Oxford: Oxford University Press, 2005.

Reese, Shawn. Congressional Research Service. "State and Local Homeland Security: Unresolved Issues for the 109th Congress" (June 9, 2005).

Reid, Julian. "War, Liberalism, and Modernity: The Biopolitical Provocations of 'Empire.'" *Cambridge Review of International Affairs* 17 (2004): 63–79.

Reid, T. R. *The United States of Europe: The New Superpower and the End of American Supremacy.* New York: Penguin Press, 2005.

Remington, Stella. *Open Secret: The Autobiography of the Former Director-General of MI5.* London: Arrow, 2002.

Rémond, René. *Religion and Society in Modern Europe.* Oxford: Blackwell, 1999.

Reyna Yañez, Linda, and Alfonso Soto. "Local Police Involvement in the Enforcement of Immigration Law." *Hispanic Law Journal* 1 (1994).

Rice, Condoleezza. "Opening remarks to the National Commission on Terrorist Attacks upon the United States." April 8, 2004. www.whitehouse.gov/news/releases/ 2004/ 04/20040408.html.

Richardson, James T., ed. *Regulating Religion: Case Studies from around the Globe.* New York: Kluwer Academic/Plenum Publishers, 2004.

Richman, Daniel. "The Past, Present, and Future of Violent Crime Federalism." *Crime & Justice* 34 (2006).

Rifkin, Jeremy. *The European Dream: How Europe's Vision of the Future Is Quietly Eclipsing the American Dream.* New York: Tarcher Penguin, 2004.

Robbers, Gerhard. "Status und Stellung von Religionsgemeinschaften in der Europäischen Union." In *Politik und Religion,* edited by Michael Minkenberg and Ulrich Willems, 88–112. Special issue 33/2002 of *Politische Vierteljahresschrift.* Wiesbaden, Germany: Westdeutscher Verlag, 2003.

Roberts, Adam. "Law and the Use of Force after Iraq." *Survival* 45 (summer 2003): 31–56.

Robertson, Roland, and William R. Garrett, eds. *Religion and Global Order.* New York: Paragon House, 1991.

———. "Religion und Politik im globalen Kontext der Gegenwart." In *Politik und Religion,* edited by Michael Minkenberg and Ulrich Willems, 581–94. Special issue 33/2002 of *Politische Vierteljahresschrift.* Wiesbaden, Germany: Westdeutscher Verlag, 2003.

Roger, Philippe. *The American Enemy: History of French Anti-Americanism.* Chicago and London: University of Chicago Press, 2005.

Romero, Victor C. *Alienated: Immigrant Rights, the Constitution, and Equality in America.* New York: New York University Press, 2005.

Rosberg, Gerald M. "The Protection of Aliens from Discriminatory Treatment by the National Government." *Supreme Court Review* (1977): 275–339.

Rosenau, James N. *Turbulence in World Politics: A Theory of Change and Continuity.* Princeton, NJ: Princeton University Press, 1990.

Roseneau, William, Kemper Gay, and David Mussington. "Transnational Threats and U.S. National Security." *Low Intensity Conflict and Law Enforcement* 6 (1999): 144–61.

Rosenblum, Nancy, ed. *Obligations of Citizenship and Demands of Faith: Religious Accommodation in Pluralist Democracies.* Princeton, NJ: Princeton University Press, 2000.

Roseborough, Theresa Wynn. Deputy Assistant Attorney General, Office of Legal Counsel. "Assistance by State and Local Police in Apprehending Illegal Aliens." Memorandum Opinion for the U.S. Attorney, Southern District of California, February 5, 1996. www.usdoj.gov/ole/immstopo1a.htm.

Roth, William. Statements on the "Immigration Control and Financial Responsibility Act of 1996." *Congressional Record–Senate,* Thursday, May 2, 1996, 104th Cong., 2nd sess., 142 *Cong Rec* S 4592, vol. 142, no. 59. Available at LexisNexis Congressional.

Rothstein, B., and Dietlind Stolle. "Social Capital, Impartiality, and the Welfare State: An Institutional Approach." In *Generating Social Capital: Civil Society and Institutions in Comparative Perspective,* edited by M. Hooghe and D. Stolle, 191–210. New York: Palgrave Macmillan, 2003.

Rousseau, Jean-Jacques. *On the Social Contract: With Geneva Manuscript and Political Economy,* edited by Roger D. Masters and translated by Judith R. Masters. New York: Bedford/St. Martin's Press, 1978.

Roy, Olivier. "Euro-Muslims in Context." *NYU Review of Law and Security,* summer 2005.

———. *Globalized Islam: The Search for a New Ummah.* New York: Columbia University Press, 2006.

———. *L'islam mondialisé.* Paris: Seuil, 2002.

Rübel, Jann. "Sind die Muslime ein Stück Deutschland, Herr Schäuble?" *Welt am Sonntag,* May 28, 2006.

Rubin, Edward L., and Malcolm Feeley. "Federalism: Some Notes on a National Neurosis." *UCLA Law Review* 41 (1994).

Rubinkam, Michael. "Federal Judge Blocks Town's Crackdown on Illegal Immigrants." Associated Press, November 1, 2006. http://news.findlaw.com/ap/o/51/11–01–2006/2b42000fb270c1a6.html.

Rudolph, Susanne Hoeber. "Introduction: Religion, States, and Transnational Civil Society." In *Transnational Religion and Fading States,* edited by Susanne Hoeber Rudolph and James Piscatori. Boulder, CO: Westview Press, 1997.

Rudolph, Susanne Hoeber, and James Piscatori, eds. *Transnational Religion and Fading States.* Boulder, CO: Westview Press, 1997.

Rumsfeld, Donald. Speech by the Secretary of Defense. Nov. 21, 2003. www.defenselink.mil/transcript/transcript.aspx?transcriptid=2981.

Russell-Einhorn, Malcolm L., U.S. Department of Justice, National Institute of Justice. "Fighting Urban Crime: The Evolution of Federal-Local Collaboration" (December 2003). www.ncjrs.gov/pdffiles1/nij/197040.pdf.

Rustow, Dankwart. "Transitions to Democracy: Toward a Dynamic Model." *Comparative Politics* 2 (April 1970): 337–63.

Ryan, Jason. "Attorney General Chastises Immigration Judges." ABC News, January 11, 2006. abcnews.go.com/US/LegalCenter/story?id=1492671.

Said, Edward W. *Orientalism.* New York: Vintage Books, 1978.

Salter, Mark B. "Passports, Mobility, and Security: How Smart Can the Border Be?" *International Studies Perspectives* 5 (2004): 71–91.

Saltzman, Jonathan. "Governor Rescinds Immigration Order." *Boston Globe,* January 12, 2007. www.boston.com/news/local/massachusetts/articles/2007/01/12/governor_rescinds_immigration_order.

Sanderson, Thomas M. "Transnational Terror and Organized Crime: Blurring the Lines." *SAIS Review* 24 (2004): 49–61.

Sartori, Giovanni. *Pluralismo, multiculturalismo e estranei: saggio sulla società multietnica.* Milan: Rizzoli, 2003.

Sassen, Saskia. *Globalization and Its Discontents: Essays on the New Mobility of People and Money.* New York: New Press, 1998.

———. *Territory, Authority, Rights: From Medieval to Global Assemblages.* Princeton, NJ: Princeton University Press, 2006.

Savage, Timothy. "Europe and Islam: Crescent Waxing, Cultures Clashing." *Washington Quarterly* 27 (2004): 25–50.

Schäuble, Wolfgang. "Deutsche Islam Konferenz—Perspektiven für eine gemeinsame Zukunft: Regierungserklärung zur DIK am 27. September." September 28, 2006. www.cducsu.de.

Scheinberg, Sam. *Survive Bio-Terrorism: A Basic Handbook.* Newport, OR: CYA Publications, 2001.

Schlesinger, Arthur Jr. *The Disuniting of America: Reflections on a Multicultural Society.* Rev. ed. New York: Norton, 1998.

Schmidt, Helmut. "Europe and the Clash of Civilizations." *Globalist,* March 15, 2004.

Schmidt, Manfred G. *Demokratietheorien.* 3rd ed. Opladen, Germany: Leske+Budrich, 2000.

Schmitt, Eric, and Thom Shanker. "New Name for 'War on Terror' Reflects Wider U.S. Campaign." *New York Times,* July 26, 2005.

Schram, Martin, and Ted Turner Documentaries. *Avoiding Armageddon: Our Future, Our Choice.* Companion to the PBS series from Ted Turner Documentaries. New York: Basic Books, 2003.

Schuck, Peter H. "Citizenship in Federal Systems." *American Journal of Comparative Law* 48 (spring 2000).

———. *Citizens, Strangers, and In-Betweens: Essays on Immigration and Citizenship.* Boulder, CO: Westview Press, 1998.

———. "The Message of Proposition 187." *Pacific Law Journal* 26 (1995).

Schuck, Peter H., and John Williams. "Removing Criminal Aliens: The Pitfalls and Promises of Federalism." *Harvard Journal of Law and Public Policy* 22 (1999).

Schuler, Katharina. "Der Wohlfühl-Gipfel." *Die Zeit,* September 27, 2006.

Schulhofer, Stephen J. *Rethinking the Patriot Act: Keeping America Safe and Free.* New York: Century Foundation Press, 2005.

Schulze, Reinhard. *Islamischer Internationalismus im 20. Jahrhundert: Untersuchungen zur Geschichte der Islamischen Weltliga.* Cologne, Germany: Brill, 1990.

Schwartz, Adi. "Between Haidar and a Hard Place." *Haaretz,* August 28, 2005.

Sciortino, Giuseppe. "Towards a Political Sociology of Entry Policies: Conceptual Problems and Theoretical Proposals." *Journal of Ethnic and Migration Studies* 26 (April 2000): 213–28.

Scott, John. *Social Network Analysis: A Handbook.* 2nd ed. London: Sage, 2000.

Seghetti, Lisa M., et al. Congressional Research Service. "Enforcing Immigration Law: The Role of State and Local Law Enforcement" (January 27, 2006).

Sen, Amartya. *Identity and Violence.* New York: Norton, 2006.

Sensenbrenner, James. "Real ID Legislation Introduced in the House" (press release), January 2005. www.house.gov/sensenbrenner/wc20050127.html.

"Sensenbrenner Statement on Border Security and Immigration Reform" (news advisory), March 27, 2006. http://judiciary.house.gov/media/pdfs/immcorrectingrecord 32706.pdf.

Sessions, Jeff, and Cynthia Hayden. "The Growing Role for State and Local Law Enforcement in the Realm of Immigration Law." *Stanford Law and Policy Review* 16 (2005).

Shadid, Anthony. "Remarks by the Pope Prompt Muslim Outrage." *Washington Post,* September 16, 2006.

Shane, Scott, and Adam Liptak. "Le Congrès 'légalise' le programme secret de la CIA." *Le Figaro,* September 23–34, 2006.

———. "Shifting Power to a President." *New York Times,* September 30, 2006.

Shannon, Elaine. *Desperados.* New York: Signet, 1991.

Shapiro, Jeremy, and Bénédicte Suzan. "The French Experience of Counter-Terrorism." *Survival* 45, no. 1 (spring 2003): 67–98.

Shelton, Dinah. "Shifting the Focus of U.S. Law from Liberty to Security." In *September 11th, 2001: A Turning Point in International and Domestic Law?* edited by Paul Eden and Thérèse O'Donnell, 497–532. Ardsley, NY: Transnational Publishers, 2005.

Sheridan, Mary Beth. "Immigration Law as Anti-Terrorism Tool." *Washington Post,* June 13, 2005.

Shore, Zachary. "Breeding New Bin Ladens: America's New Western Front." *Watch on the West* (Philadelphia, Foreign Policy Research Institute), 5, no. 11 (2004).

Sidak, Gregory. "War, Liberty, and Enemy Aliens." *NYU Law Review* 67, no. 6 (December 1992): 1402–31.

Simeant, Johanna. *La cause des sans-papiers.* Paris: Presses de Sciences Po, 1998.

———. *Le travail humanitaire.* Paris: Presses de Sciences Po, 1998.

Simes, Dimitri K. "America's Imperial Dilemma." *Foreign Affairs* 82 (2003): 91–102.

Siskin, Alison. *Immigration-Related Detention: Current Legislative Issues.* CRS Report for Congress. Washington, DC: Congressional Research Service, April 28, 2004. www.fas.org/irp/crs/RL32369.pdf.

Siskin, Alison, et al. *Immigration Enforcement within the United States.* CRS Report for Congress. Washington, DC: Congressional Research Service, April 6, 2006.

Skocpol, Theda. *Bringing the State Back In.* Cambridge: Cambridge University Press, 1985.

Smith, Andrea L. *Europe's Invisible Migrants.* Amsterdam: Amsterdam University Press, 2003.

Smith, Lamar. Statements on the "Criminal Alien Deportation Improvements Act of 1995." *Congressional Record-Extension of Remarks,* Monday, February 13, 1995, 104th Cong., 1st sess., 141 *Cong Rec* E 330, vol. 141, no. 28. Available at LexisNexis Congressional.

———. Statements on "How Illegal Immigration Impacts Constituencies: Perspectives from Members of Congress (Part I)." Hearing before the Subcommittee on Immigration, Border Security and Claims of the Committee on the Judiciary House of Representatives, 109th Cong., 1st sess., November 10, 2005 (Washington DC; US GPO 2006), 30. http://judiciary.house.gov/media/pdfs/printers/109th/24507.pdf.

Smith, Rebecca, Amy Sugimori, and Luna Yasui. "Low Pay, High Risk: State Models for Advancing Immigrant Workers' Rights." *NYU Review of Law & Social Change* 28 (2003–2004).

Sniderman, Paul M., et al. *The Outsider: Prejudice and Politics in Italy.* Princeton, NJ: Princeton University Press, 2000.

Soares Loja, Fernando. "Islam in Portugal." In *Islam, Europe's Second Religion: The New Social, Cultural, and Political Landscape,* edited by Shireen T. Hunter, 191–203. Westport, CT: Praeger, 2002.

SOFRES. État de l'opinion, Clés pour 1987. Paris: Seuil, 1987.

SOFRES/TF1. Exit poll, June 17, 1984. *Le Nouvel Observateur,* June 22, 1984.

Soysal, Yasemin Nuhoğlu. *Limits of Citizenship: Migrants and Postnational Membership in Europe.* Chicago: University of Chicago Press, 1994.

Spiro, Peter J. "The Citizenship Dilemma." *Stanford Law Review* 51 (1999).

———. "The States and Immigration in an Era of Demi-Sovereignties." *Virginia Journal of International Law* 35 (1994).

Spohn, Willfried, and Anna Triandafyllidou. *Europeanisation, National Identities, and Migration: Changes in Boundary Constructions between Western and Eastern Europe.* London: Routledge, 2002.

Stephens, Philip. "An American Map of the Future Bush Cannot Ignore." *Financial Times,* January 21, 2005.

Stevenson, Jonathan. *Counter-terrorism: Containment and Beyond.* IISS Adelphi Paper 367. Oxford: Oxford University Press, 2004.

Stock, Margaret D. "Driver Licenses and National Security: Myths and Reality." *Bender's Immigration Bulletin* 10 (March 1, 2005).

Süssmuth, Rita. *Zuwanderung Gestalten, Integration Förden, Bericht der Unabhängingen Kommission.* Berlin: Zuwanderung, 2001.

Swarns, Rachel L. "Halliburton Subsidiary Gets Contract to Add Temporary Immigration Detention Centers." *New York Times,* February 4, 2006, A7.

———. "Hastert Hints at Compromise." *New York Times,* March 30, 2006, A22. www.nytimes.com/2006/03/30/politics/30immig.html.

Symanska, John, and Nancy Rytina. Report of the Department of Homeland Security Office of Immigration Statistics. *Naturalizations in the United States: 2005* (June 2006). www.uscis.gov/graphics/shared/statistics/publications/ 2005NatzFlow Rpt.pdf.

Tamas, G. M. "On Post-Fascism: How Citizenship Is Becoming an Exclusive Privilege." *Boston Review,* summer 2000, 42–46.

Tamir, Yael. *Liberal Nationalism.* Princeton, NJ: Princeton University Press, 1993.

Tarrow, Sidney. *Power in Movement.* Cambridge: Cambridge University Press, 1998.

Tatelman, Todd B. Congressional Research Service. "Intelligence Reform and Terrorism Prevention Act of 2004: National Standards for Drivers' Licenses, Social Security Cards, and Birth Certificates" (January 6, 2005).

Taylor, Margaret H. "Dangerous by Decree: Detention without Bond in Immigration Proceedings." *Loyola Law Review* 50 (2004).

———. "The 1996 Immigration Act: Detention and Related Issues." *Interpreter Releases* 74, no. 5 (1997).

Tebbakh, Sonia. "Identités politiques des Français d'origine maghrébine" Ph.D. thesis, Institut d'Etudes Politiques de Grenoble, Université Pierre-Mendès-France, December 2004.

———. "L'islam et les Français d'origine maghrébine: incidences du religieux sur le rapport au monde et l'adhésion aux valeurs." In *Religion et valeurs,* edited by C. Dargent, B. Duriez, and R. Liogier. Paris: L'Harmattan, 2006.

Tehranian, Majid. "Global Terrorism: Searching for Appropriate Responses." *Pacifica Review* 14 (2003): 57–65.

"Terrorists or Victims?" (editorial). *New York Times,* April 3, 2006, A16.

"Terrorist Support Exception Made for Karen Refugees." *Interpreter Releases* 83, no. 20 (May 15, 2006).

Terry, Elizabeth, and J. Paul Oxer. *Survival Handbook for Chemical, Biological, and Radiological Terrorism.* Philadelphia: Xlibris, 2003.

"This Is Your Mess, Blair." *Sun,* May 4, 2006.

Thompson, Michael J. "Beyond the Vote: The Crisis of American Liberalism." *Logos* 3–4 (fall 2004).

Thränhardt, Dietrich, ed. *Europe—A New Immigration Continent: Policies and Politics in Comparative Perspective.* Muenster, Germany: LIT Verlag, 1992.

———. "Der Nationalstaat als migrationspolitischer Akteur." In *Migration im Spannungsfeld von Globalisierung und Nationalstaat,* edited by Dietrich Thränhardt and Uwe Hunger, 8–31. Wiesbaden, Germany: Westdeutscher Verlag, 2003.

Thränhardt, Dietrich, and Uwe Hunger, eds. *Migration im Spannungsfeld von Globalisierung und Nationalstaat.* Wiesbaden, Germany: Westdeutscher Verlag, 2003.

Through Our Enemies' Eyes: Osama Bin Laden, Radical Islam, and the Future of America [by Anonymous]. Washington, DC: Brassey's, 2002.

Tismaneanu, Vladimir. *Fantasies of Salvation: Democracy, Nationalism, and Myth in Post-Communist Europe.* Princeton, NJ: Princeton University Press, 1998.

Toffler, Alvin. *The Third Wave.* New York: William Morrow, 1980.

"Tony Blair's Antiterrorism Package" (editorial). *New York Times,* August 19, 2005.

Transactional Records Access Clearinghouse (TRAC), Syracuse University. TRAC Immigration Report, "Immigration Judges." http://trac.syr.edu/immigration/reports/160/.

———. TRAC Immigration Report, "How Often Is the Aggravated Felony Statute Used?" http://trac.syr.edu/immigration/reports/158/, accessed July 22, 2006.

———. TRAC Immigration Report, "Timely New Justice Department Data Show Prosecutions Climb during Bush Years: Immigration and Weapons Enforcement Up, White Collar and Drug Prosecutions Slide" (2005). http://trac.syr.edu/tracreports/crim/136, accessed July 22, 2006.

Triandafyllidou, Anna. *Immigrants and National Identity in Europe.* London: Routledge, 2001.

Triandafyllidou, Anna, and Willfried Spohn, eds. *Europeanisation, National Identities, and Migrations: Changes in Boundaries Constructions between Western and Eastern Europe.* London: Routledge, 2003.

Tribalat, Michèle. "Une estimation des populations d'origine étrangère en France en 1999." *Population* 59 (2004): 51–82.

Tsuda, Takeyuki. "Localities and the Struggle for Immigrant Rights: The Significance of Local Citizenship in Recent Countries of Immigration." In *Local Citizenship in Recent Countries of Immigration: Japan in Comparative Perspective,* ed. Takeyuki Tsuda. Lanham, MD: Lexington Books, 2006.

Turek, Jurgen. "The Global Threat: New Dangers of Terrorism." *Internationale Politik* 56 (2001): 81–82.

Turque, Bill. "Herndon Police May Join Immigration Enforcement." *Washington Post,* September 22, 2006, B1. www.washingtonpost.com/wp-dyn/content/article/2006/09/21/AR2006092101562_pf.html.

United Kingdom. Home Office Report. *Report on the Operation in 2001 of the Terrorism Act 2000,* by Lord Carlile of Berriew QC (2002).

———. Review of the Operation of the Prevention of Terrorism Acts, chap. 12. March 7, 2000.

———. 29/05. Sizing the Unauthorised Migrant Population in the United Kingdom in 2001. www.homeoffice.gov.uk/rds/pdfs05/rdsolr2905.pdf.

United Kingdom. House of Lords European Union Committee. "After Madrid: The EU's Response to Terrorism." March 2005. www.publications.parliament.uk/pa/ld200405/ldselect/ldeucom/53/53.pdf.

United Kingdom. Parliament. House of Commons. Foreign Affairs Committee. *The Decision to Go to War in Iraq: Ninth Report of Session 2002–03.* H.M.S.O. 2003. http://image.guardian.co.uk/sys-files/Politics/documents/2003/07/07/WMD%5Freport.pdf.

United Nations. Population Division. *Replacement Migration: Is It a Solution to Declining and Aging Populations?* New York: United Nations Population Division, ESA/P/WP.160, 2000.

United Nations. Treaty Series. United Nations Protocol Relating to the Status of Refugees, 267, no. 8791, vol. 606.

United Nations. United Nations Recommendations on Statistics of International Migration, ST/ESA/STAT/SER.M/58/Rev.1, 1998.

United Nations High Commissioner for Refugees (UNHCR). "Asylum Levels and Trends in Industrialized Countries, 2005" (2006). www.unhcr.org/statistics/STATISTICS/44153f592.pdf.

———. "Asylum Levels and Trends in Industrialized Countries: First Quarter 2006" (July 2006). www.unhcr.org/statistics/STATISTICS/44d74d9c2.pdf.

———. "Asylum Levels and Trends in Industrialized Countries: Second Quarter 2006" (September 2006). www.unhcr.org/cgi-bin/texis/vtx/statistics/opendoc.pdf?tbl=STATISTICS&id=450fa85d2.

———. "Definitions and Obligations: Basic Definitions." http://www.unhcr.org.au/basicdef.shtml.

———. The European Union, Asylum, and the International Refugee Protection Regime: UNHCR's Recommendation for the New Multi-Annual Programme in the Area of Freedom, Security, and Justice, September 2004.

———. *The State of the World's Refugees 2006.* Oxford: Oxford University Press, 2006. www.unhcr.org/cgi-bin/texis/vtx/template?page=publ&src=static/sowr2006/toceng.htm.

———. "UNHCR Deeply Concerned over Lampedusa Deportations'" (press release), March 18, 2005.

———. "UNHCR Handbook on Procedures and Criteria for Determining Refugee Status under the 1951 Convention and the 1967 Protocol Relating to the Status of Refugees." HCR/IP/4/Eng/REV1, reedited, Geneva, January 1992, UNHCR 1979. www.unhcr.org/cgibin/texis/vtx/home/opendoc.pdf?tbl=PUBL&id= 3d58e13b4.

United Nations Special Rapporteur. UN Doc No: E/CN.4/2005/85.

United States. Congress. House Judiciary Committee. "Majority Staff Description of the Latest Version of the Patriot Act," October 12, 2001. www.cdt.org/security/011012patriotinfo.pdf.

———. House of Representatives. "Border Protection, Antiterrorism and Illegal Immigration Control Act of 2005, Report of the Committee on the Judiciary House of Representatives, to Accompany H.R. 4437, together with Additional and Dissenting Views," December 13, 2005. http://frwebgate.access.gpo.gov/cgibin/getdoc.cgi?dbname=109_cong_reports&docid=f:hr345p1.109.pdf.

———. Senate. Select Committee on Intelligence. Report of the Select Committee on

Intelligence on the U.S. Intelligence Community's Prewar Intelligence Assessments on Iraq Together with Additional Views. Washington, D.C.: GPO, 2004.

United States. Office of the President. *National Strategy for Combating Terrorism*. Washington, DC, February 2003.

———. "President Bush Outlines Iraqi Threat: Remarks by the President on Iraq." Cincinnati, OH, October 7, 2002. www.whitehouse.gov/news/releases/2002/10/20021007-8.html.

United States. Office of the White House Press Secretary. "Address to a Joint Session of Congress and the American People by George Bush" (press release), September 20, 2001.

United States Citizenship and Immigration Service. *2003 Yearbook of Immigration Statistics*. http://uscis.gov/graphics/shared/aboutus/statistics/Asylees.htm.

United States Commission on Immigration Reform. "U.S. Immigration Policy: Restoring Credibility: Executive Summary." 1994. www.utexas.edu/lbj/uscir/exesum94.html.

United States Committee for Refugees and Immigrants (USCRI). Statistics for the *World Refugee Survey 2005*. www.refugees.org/article.aspx?id=1342.

United States Department of Homeland Security. "Department of Homeland Security Launches Operation 'Ice Storm'" (press release), November 10, 2003. www.dhs.gov/dhspublic/display?content=3008.

———. "Department of Homeland Security Unveils Comprehensive Immigration Enforcement Strategy for the Nation's Interior" (press release), April 20, 2006. www.dhs.gov/dhspublic/display?content=5546.

———. "Immigration and Borders." www.dhs.gov/dhspublic/theme_home4.jsp.

———. Office of Immigration Statistics. *2003 Yearbook of Immigration Statistics* (September 2004).

———. *2004 Yearbook of Immigration Statistics* (2005).

———. *Yearbook of Immigration Statistics 2005*. Washington, DC: U.S. Department of Homeland Security, 2006.

———. *Yearbook of Immigration Statistics: 2005* (2006). www.uscis.gov/graphics/shared/statistics/yearbook/LPR05.htm.

———. Office of Inspector General. *Detention and Removal of Illegal Aliens: U.S. Immigration and Customs Enforcement*. Washington, DC: DHS Office of Audits, April 2006.

United States Department of Justice. "Anti-Terrorism Act of 2001: Section by Section Analysis." September 19, 2001. www.epic.org/privacy/terrorism/ATA_analysis.pdf.

———. Bureau of Justice Statistics. *Census of State and Federal Correctional Facilities, 1995*. August 1997. www.ojp.usdoj.gov/bjs/pub/pdf/csfcf95.pdf.

———. *Census of State and Federal Correctional Facilities, 2000*. Revised October 15, 2003. www.ojp.usdoj.gov/bjs/pub/pdf/csfcf00.pdf.

———. Civil Rights Division. "Guidance Regarding the Use of Race by Federal Law Enforcement Agencies" (June 2003). www.usdoj.gov/crt/split/documents/guidance_on_race.htm.

———. Immigration and Naturalization Service. *1997 Statistical Yearbook of the Immigration and Naturalization Service* (October 1999).

———. Office of Inspector General. The September 11 Detainees: A Review of the

Treatment of Aliens Held on Immigration Charges in Connection with the Investigation of the September 11 Attacks. June 2003.www.usdoj.gov/oig/special/0306/index.htm.

United States Immigration and Customs Enforcement. Fact Sheet. Delegation of Immigration Authority, section 287(g), Immigration and Nationality Act (Sept. 24, 2007). www.ice.gov/pi/news/factsheets/factsheet287gprogover.htm.

———. Public Information. "ICE Budget Gains 6.3 Percent in FY 06 DHS Spending Bill." *Inside ICE* 2, no. 23 (2006). www.ice.gov/pi/news/insideice/articles/insideice_111405_Web3.htm.

Vargas, Theresa. "Wanted: Local Agencies to Enforce Immigration Law." *Washington Post*, January 4, 2007, LZ6. www.washingtonpost.com/wp-dyn/content/article/2007/01/02/AR2007010201327.html.

Venel, Nancy. *Musulmans et français*. Paris: PUF, 2004.

Vertovec, Steven, and Ceri Peach, eds. *Islam in Europe: The Politics of Religions and Community in the United States*. 2nd ed. Washington, DC: CQ Press, 1997.

Vries, Gijs de. "The European Union and the Fight against Terrorism." Seminar of the CER, Brussels, January 19, 2006.

Wacquant, L. "Des 'ennemis commodes.'" *Actes de la recherche en sciences sociales* 129 (1999): 63–67.

Wade, Robert Hunter. "The Invisible Hand of the American Empire." *Ethics & International Affairs* 17 (2003): 77–88.

Wald, Kenneth. *Religion and Politics in the United States*. Lanham, MD: Rowman and Littlefield, 2003.

Walker, Martin. "America's Virtual Empire." *World Policy Journal* 19 (2002): 13–20.

Walt, Stephen M. "Beyond bin Laden: Reshaping U.S. Foreign Policy." *International Security* 26 (2002): 56–78.

———. "Hegel on War: Another Look." *History of Political Thought* 10 (1990): 113–24.

———."The Renaissance of Security Studies." *International Studies Quarterly* 35 (1991): 211–39.

Walzer, Michael. "Is There an American Empire?" *Dissent* 50 (2003): 27–31.

Warner, Carolyn, and Manfred Wenner. "Religion and the Political Organization of Muslims in Europe." *Perspectives on Politics* 4, no. 3 (2006): 457–79.

"War on Terrorism: America Takes Action in a Changed World—Pro & Con: Should the Congress Approve Emergency Funding and Military Force in Response to Terrorist Attacks? *Congressional Digest* 80 (November 11, 2001): 257–88.

Waslin, Michele. National Council of La Raza. "Immigration Enforcement by Local Police: The Impact on the Civil Rights of Latinos." Issue Brief, February 2003.

———. "Safe Roads, Safe Communities: Immigrants and State Driver's License Requirements." Issue Brief, May 2002.

Wasserman, Stanley, and Katherine Faust. *Social Network Analysis: Methods and Applications*. Cambridge: Cambridge University Press, 1994.

Watson, Justin. *The Christian Coalition: Dreams of Restoration, Demands for Recognition*. Basingstoke, England: Macmillan, 1997.

Weber, Eugen. *Peasants into Frenchmen: The Modernization of Rural France, 1870–1914*. Stanford, CA: Stanford University Press, 1976.

Wedding, Kristin. "The Immigration Debate." *Strategy Report* (Center for Strategic and International Studies), 2, no. 7 (April 20, 2006).

Weil, P. "The Transformation of Immigration Policies: Immigration Control and Na-
    tionality Laws in Europe: A Comparative Approach." EUI Working Paper 98/5, Flo-
    rence, 1998.
Welch, Michael. *Detained: Immigration Laws and the Expanding I.N.S. Jail Complex.*
    Philadelphia: Temple University Press, 2002.
Whoriskey, Peter. "States, Counties Begin to Enforce Immigration Law." *Washington
    Post,* September 27, 2006, A1. www.washingtonpost.com/wp-dyn/content/article/
    2006/09/26/AR2006092601319_pf.html.
"Why the British Government's Plan for Controlling Immigration Is a Bad Idea." *Econo-
    mist,* February 10, 2005.
Widgren, Jonas, and Philip Martin. "Managing Migration: The Role of Economic In-
    struments." *International Migration* 40, no. 5 (2002): 213–29.
Wiktorowicz, Quintan. "The New Global Threat: Transnational Salafis and Jihad." *Mid-
    dle East Policy* 8 (2001): 18–38.
Wilkinson, Paul. "The Lessons of Lockerbie." *Conflict Studies* 226 (1990): 1–30.
Willems, Ulrich, and Michael Minkenberg. "Politik und Religion im Übergang—Ten-
    denzen und Forschungsfragen am Beginn des 21. Jahrhunderts." In *Politik und Reli-
    gion,* edited by Michael Minkenberg and Ulrich Willems, 13–41. Special issue
    33/2002 of *Politische Vierteljahresschrift.* Wiesbaden, Germany: Westdeutscher Ver-
    lag, 2003.
Wills, Garry. "Fringe Government." *New York Review of Books,* October 6, 2005.
Wilson, Graeme. "Young, British Muslims 'Getting More Radical.' " *Daily Telegraph,*
    January 30, 2007.
Wilson, Wayne, and Jim Whiting. *Tony Blair: A Real-Life Reader Biography.* Bear, Del.:
    Mitchell Lane Publishers, 2003.
Wishnie, Michael J. "Laboratories of Bigotry? Devolution of the Immigration Power,
    Equal Protection, and Federalism." *NYU Law Review* 76 (2001).
————. "State and Local Police Enforcement of Immigration Laws." *University of Penn-
    sylvania Journal of Constitutional Law* 6 (2004).
Wishnie, Michael J., and Doris Meissner. "Policing Immigrants Post-September 11."
    Unpublished manuscript, 2005.
Wolfowitz, Paul. "The Gathering Storm: The Threat of Global Terror and Asia/Pacific
    Security." *Vital Speeches of the Day* 68 (2002): 674–79.
Wolin, Richard. *The Frankfurt School Revisited.* New York and London: Routledge,
    2006.
————. "September 11 and the Self-Castigating Left." *South Central Review* 19, no. 2/3
    (summer/autumn 2002): 39–49.
Woodward, Bob. *Bush at War.* New York: Simon & Schuster, 2002.
————. *Plan of Attack.* New York: Simon & Schuster, 2004.
————. *State of Denial.* New York: Simon & Schuster, 2006.
Wright, Lawrence. "The Terror Web." *New Yorker,* July 26, 2004.
Ye'or, Bat. *Eurabia: The Euro-Arab Axis.* Madison, NJ: Fairleigh Dickinson University
    Press, 2005.
Young, Ernest A. "Welcome to the Dark Side." *Brooklyn Law Review* 69 (2004).
Zagorin, Perez. *How the Idea of Religious Toleration Came to the West.* Princeton, NJ, and
    London: Princeton University Press, 2003.
Zangwill, Israel. *The Melting Pot: A Drama in Four Acts.* New York: Macmillan, 1909.

Zaring, David, and Elena Baylis. "Sending the Bureaucracy to War." *Iowa Law Review* 92, no. 4 (2007).

Zielonka, Jan. *Europe Unbound: Enlarging and Reshaping the Boundaries of the European Union.* London: Routledge, 2002.

Zimmerman, Wendy, and Karen C. Tumlin. Urban Institute. "Patchwork Policies: State Assistance for Immigrants under Welfare Reform." Occasional Paper No. 24 (1999). www.urban.org/publications/309007.html.

Zimmermann, Doron. "The European Union and Post 9/11 Counterterrorism: A Reappraisal." *Studies in Conflict and Terrorism* 29 (2006): 123–45.

Zincone, Giovanna. "A Model of 'Reasonable Integration': Summary of the First Report on the Integration of Immigrants in Italy." *International Migration Review* 34 (2000): 956–68.

Zivier, Ernst R. "Pax Americana—Bellum Americanum: On the Way to a New International Law or to a New International Injustice?" *Recht und Politik* 39 (2003): 194–201.

Zolberg, Aristide R. *A Nation by Design: Immigration Policy in the Fashioning of America.* New York: Sage, and Cambridge, MA: Harvard University Press, 2006.

Zolberg, Aristide R., and Long Litt Woon. "Why Islam Is Like Spanish: Cultural Incorporation in Europe and the United States." *Politics and Society* 27, no.1 (March 1999): 5–38.

Contributors

Elena A. Baylis is an associate professor at the University of Pittsburgh School of Law, where she teaches courses on comparative minority group protections, crimes against humanity, religious and legal frameworks, and the comparative law of new democracies. In addition to her work on political asylum and national security, she is also writing on religious views in the U.S. legal system and conducting research on transitional justice and legal pluralism in Kosovo and in the Democratic Republic of Congo.

Didier Bigo has been professor of international relations at Sciences-Po (maitre de conférences des universités), the Institut d'Etudes Politiques de Paris, since 1988 and is a researcher at CERI/FNSP. He is also the director of the Center for Study of Conflict and the editor of the quarterly journal *Cultures & Conflicts* (published by l'Harmattan and edited once a year in *Alternatives,* published by Lynne Rienner). He is the scientific coordinator of the FR5 program of the EC Commission ELISE (European Liberty and Security) and the 6PCRD (CHALLENGE).

Sylvain Brouard has been senior research fellow FNSP at CEVIPOF (Centre de recherches politiques de Sciences Po) since 2003. He received his Ph.D. in political science from the Institute of Political Studies in Bordeaux in 1999. Brouard studied at the Inter-University Consortium for Political Science Research and at the Oslo Summer School in Comparative Social Sciences. His publications include "The Role of French Governments in Legislative Agenda Setting," in *The Role of Governments in Legislative Agenda Setting,* edited by Bjørn Erik Rasch and George Tsebelis (Oxford: Oxford University Press, forthcoming), and, with Vincent Tiberj, "The French Referendum: The Not So Simple Act of Saying Nay," *PS : Political Science & Politics,* April 2006.

Jennifer Marie Chacón is acting professor of law at the University of California, Davis, School of Law. She received her A.B. with Distinction in international relations from Stanford University and her J.D. from Yale Law School. Professor Chacón's research and teaching interests include criminal law, criminal procedure, immigration law, and international human rights. She has written on human trafficking and smuggling, U.S. deportation policy, and truth commissions in Latin America.

461

Ariane Chebel d'Appollonia is associate senior researcher at the CEVIPOF (Center for Political Research, Sciences-Po) and co-director of the ISI Research Network. She has taught at both the undergraduate and postgraduate levels at universities in France (Sciences-Po, Paris III-Sorbonne, and the Columbia University and University of Chicago Programs in Paris) and in the United States (New York University). She was the Roberta Buffett Visiting Professor at Northwestern University (fall 2005) and the Fulbright Transatlantic Chair to the United States at the University of Pittsburgh in 2006. She specializes in the politics of immigration and anti-discrimination in Europe, racism and xenophobia, extreme right-wing movements, immigrant integration, and urban racism.

Manlio Cinalli is senior research fellow at the CEVIPOF, Centre de Recherches Politiques de Sciences-Po (IEP, Paris). He has been trained as a political scientist at the University of Florence (Italy) and at Queen's University of Belfast (Northern Ireland). He was also research fellow at the University of Leeds (Great Britain) and the Jean Monnet Fellow at the European University Institute (Italy). He is currently director of the French project for LOCALMULTIDEM (European Union's Framework Six Programme).

H. Richard Friman is professor of political science, Eliot Fitch Chair for International Studies, and director of the Institute for Transnational Justice at Marquette University. He is the author of five books and numerous book chapters and articles on transnational justice issues tied to the illicit global economy.

Francisco Javier Moreno Fuentes is a researcher at the Research Unit in Public Policy and Politics of the CSIC in Madrid (Spain). He obtained a master's degree in social sciences from the Juan March Institute in Madrid, and an M.Sc. in social policy and planning from the London School of Economics and Political Science. He has published a book, several chapters in edited volumes, and a number of journal articles on his main areas of interest, which include immigration policies in Western Europe, welfare regimes and their reform, and urban policies.

Jolyon Howorth has taught at universities in England, France, and the United States. He is the Jean Monnet Professor (*ad personam*) of European Politics at the University of Bath and has been a visiting professor of political science at Yale University since 2002. He is a Fellow of the Royal Society for the Arts and of the Institut Français d'Histoire Sociale. He has published extensively in the areas of foreign policy, the European Union, NATO, security, and alliances.

Anil Kalhan was educated at Yale Law School (J.D.), Yale School of Management (M.P.P.M.), and Brown University (A.B.), and he is a visiting assistant professor at Fordham University Law School and a cooperating attorney with the NYU School of Law Immigrant Rights Clinic. From 2004 until 2006, he was an associate in law at Columbia University School of Law, and he previously served as an associate at Cleary, Gottlieb, Steen & Hamilton and as co-coordinator of the firm's immigration and international human rights pro bono practice group.

Jonathan Laurence is assistant professor of political science at Boston College and an affiliated scholar of the Center on the United States and Europe at the Brookings Institution. His areas of research and publication include Islam in France, Germany and Italy, anti-Semitism and postwar Jewish communities, and the politics of postwar immigrant populations in Europe.

Michael Minkenberg has been the chair of Political Sciences/Comparative Analysis of Political Systems, Movement and Cultures at the European University Viadrina Frankfurt (Oder) since 1998. He currently holds the Max Weber Chair at New York University. He has studied and taught at renowned German and U.S. universities, including those at Heidelberg, Berlin, Freiburg, Cologne/Bonn, and Goettingen, as well as Georgetown University, the University of Michigan, and Cornell University.

Ilya Prizel (Ph.D., Johns Hopkins University) is professor of political science and history at the University of Pittsburgh. He is the author of numerous books and articles, including *Latin America through Soviet Eyes* (Cambridge University Press, 1992) and *National Identity and Foreign Policy: Nationalism and Leadership in Poland, Russia, and Ukraine* (Cambridge University Press, 1998), for which he won the Shulman Prize for best book on politics in Eastern Europe and Russia.

Simon Reich is professor at the Graduate School of Public and International Affairs, director of the Ford Institute for Human Security at the University of Pittsburgh, and former director of research and analysis at the Royal Institute for International Affairs at Chatham House in England. Reich is co-director of the ISI Research Network, and he is the author of three books and numerous articles and book chapters.

Martin Schain received his doctorate in government from Cornell University and is currently professor of politics at New York University and visiting scholar at CEVIPOF in Paris. He is the founder and former director of the Center for European Studies at New York University and former chair of the European Union Studies Association. He has written numerous articles on the politics of immigration in Europe, particularly France.

Vincent Tiberj (Ph.D., political science) is senior research fellow at CEVIPOF and lecturer at Sciences-Po in Paris. His main research interests are political sophistication, electoral behavior (France, United States, and Europe), political psychology, and the political sociology of ethnic and social inequalities. He has written several articles on the French party system, ordinary citizens' political reasoning, and the values of immigrant-origin French.

Index

Note: *f* or *t* following a page number indicates a figure or table, respectively.

Abraham, Spencer, 136–37
Absconder Apprehension Initiative, 158
absconders, 189
Acer, Eleanor, 170, 172
Act on the Employment of Foreign Workers (Netherlands, 1978), 208
Action Directe, 116
Action Program (EU), 225
Adenauer, Konrad, 28
advocacy groups. *See* pro-immigrant groups
AEDPA. *See* Anti-Terrorism and Effective Death Penalty Act (AEDPA) (1996)
Afghanistan, 6, 9, 70–72, 77, 245, 353n10
Africa, migration from, 274–75. *See also individual countries*; Maghreb region; North Africans
AFSJ. *See* Area of Freedom, Security, and Justice
Afzalltaq, Nareed, 22
airline bombing plot (2006), 95, 104, 108
Akin, Fatih, 250
Algeria, 239–40, 243–45, 286
Algerian civil war (1992–2000), 117
Ali, Ayaan Hirsi, 32, 231
Alien and Sedition Acts (U.S., 1798), 37, 147
Alien Terrorist Removal Court, 138
alienage-based classifications, 185
"aliens," 373n38
Alleanza Nazionale (Italy), 305
Almond, Gabriel, 50
Amis, Martin, 34
Amnesty International, 177, 224, 279, 305–6, 309
Anarchist Act (U.S., 1918), 150, 151
Andréani, Gilles, 97
Andreotti, Giulio, 244
Ansar, Jose Maria, 36
anthrax, 74, 354n16
Anti-Drug Abuse Act (U.S., 1988), 134
Anti-Terrorism and Effective Death Penalty Act (AEDPA) (U.S., 1996), 135–37, 152–53, 161, 167

Anti-Terrorism, Crime, and Security Emergency Act (Britain, 2001), 115, 224
anti-terrorism policies. *See* counter-terrorism policies
Appiah, Kwame Anthony, *Cosmopolitanism*, 25
Arabs, U.S. targeting of, 157–58
Arafat, Yasser, 343n15
Area of Freedom, Security, and Justice (AFSJ), 18, 206, 213–17, 259
Argentina, 258
arraigo, 270
Ash, Timothy Garton, 4
Ashcroft, John, 120, 157–58, 160, 177, 190
assimilation: in France, 288–91; rejection of, 6. *See also* integration
asylum: attitudes toward, 220, 228; Austria and, 323; Britain and, 211, 228, 301, 303–6, 318, 323; EU and, 173–77, 211–15, 212t, 228, 265t, 306–7, 319–20, 323; France and, 228; Germany and, 211, 323; and immigration policy, 173; international context for, 164–65; international legal obligations concerning, 171–72; Italy and, 301, 303–6, 318; motives for seeking, 170, 177–78; refusal of, 155–56, 179, 323; security and, 15–16, 164–80; after September 11 attacks, 167–71; source countries for seekers of, 165; Spain and, 263, 264t; standards for determining, 168–70, 178–80; state/local policies on, 388n21; U.S. legal structures and processes for, 177–80; U.S. policy on, 155–56, 159, 165–71; U.S. versus international policies on, 16, 171–77; and "weak" immigration status, 300–301
Asylum Act (Austria, 1997), 323
Asylum and Immigration Act (Britain, 2004), 303, 323
Asylum Procedures Directive (EU, 2005), 175, 176, 307

Asylum Rights Campaign (Britain), 311
atheism, 292
Athens Migration Policy Initiative, 225
Atlantic Alliance, 106
Australia: immigrant clashes in, 27; integration policy in, 54, 61; response of, to September 11 attacks, 76–77, 83
Austria: and asylum, 323; identity discourse in, 28; immigration in, 207; integration in, 54, 224
Aziz, Faisal bin Abdul, King of Saudi Arabia, 239

Baker, Don, 233
Al-Banna, Hassan, 241
Barrosso, José, 223
Baudrillard, Jean, 29
Bavaria, 36, 243
Baylis, Elena A., 15–16, 322
Beecher, Lyman, 42
Belgium: integration policy in, 53, 61; and Iraq War, 77; and Islam, 244, 247
Benedict XVI, Pope, 34, 36, 231, 252
Berlin, Isaiah, 38, 345n47
Berlin Tageszeitung (newspaper), 35
Berlusconi, Silvio, 304, 305
Berman, Paul, *Terror and Liberalism*, 35
Bernanke, Ben, 326–27
Bigo, Didier, 6, 11–12, 104, 174, 175, 214
Bin Laden, Osama, 70, 83
Birmann, Wolf, 32
Blair, Tony, 35, 83, 102, 109, 204, 205, 318
Bloom, Allan, *The Closing of the American Mind*, 39
Bloom, Harold, 39
Board of Immigration Appeals (U.S.), 160, 179
Bolivia, 258
border control: Classic security perspective and, 87; disputes about, 84–86; effects of, 337; pre–September 11, 8; Spain and, 262–66, 276, 279–80; U.S. versus EU policy on, ix–x, 7, 85–86, 335. *See also* Schengen Agreement
Border Patrol. *See* U.S. Border Patrol
Border Protection, Antiterrorism and Illegal Immigration Control Bill (H.R. 4437), 141–43
Bosniak, Linda, 198
Bossi-Fini law (Italy, 2002), 304, 305
bracero program, 374n41

Brechon, Pierre, 219
Britain: and asylum, 211, 228, 301, 303–6, 318, 323; counter-terrorism policies of, 13–14, 112–16; detention in, 305–6; domestic terrorism in, 2; immigration in, 31, 115, 124, 126, 129, 207–8, 300–320; integration in, 52, 53, 61, 63, 223; Islam in, 247; left in, 32; multiculturalism in, 31, 32, 204, 223, 301; political issues in, 128*t*; pro-immigrant opportunity networks in, 315–17, 317*f*; pro-immigrant resource networks in, 309–15, 310*f*, 311*f*, 314*f*; religion and politics in, 49, 62; and undocumented immigrants, 303–6; xenophobia in, 227. *See also* London bombings (2005); United Kingdom
British Nationality Act (1981), 207, 208, 210
British National Party (BNP), 305
Broder, Henryk M., *Hurra, Wir Kapitulieren*, 34
Brouard, Sylvain, 7, 20–21
Brubaker, Roger, 45
Bruckner, Pascal, 30
Bruguière, Jean-Louis, 118
Bryan, William Jennings, 39
Buchanan, Pat, 332
Bulgaria, 258
Bush, George W.: and freedom, 323; and immigration, 42, 129, 138, 339; and intelligence sharing, 101; and "Islamic fascists," 2; Modern perspective of, 88; and preemptive war, 106; public opinion on, 338; and terror alert level, 338; and war on terror, 74, 97–98, 104, 106–8, 140
Buzan, Barry, 14
Byatt, A. S., 31

Cachón Rodríguez, Lorenzo, 278
Calvinism, 39–41
Cameron, David, 36
The Camp of the Saints (Raspail), 29
Camus, Albert, 29–30
Canada: immigrant clashes in, 27; integration policy in, 54; response of, to September 11 attacks, 83
Canary Islands, 254, 266
Cann, David E., 57
Caprioni, Valerie, 122
Caritas (Italy), 312, 314, 317
Carr, E. H., 87

Carter, Jimmy, 41, 42
cartoons of Mohammed, 33–34, 231, 249, 252
Casanova, José, 46
Castles, Francis, 54, 60*t*
Catholicism: and church-state relations, 234; in France, 289, 291–93, 292*t*; integration policy and, 55; U.S. evangelicals and, 42
Central Intelligence Agency (CIA): counterterrorism efforts of, 119; and intelligence sharing, 110; reorganization of, after 1993 World Trade Center bombing, 119; secret prisons of, 102
Centro Culturale Islamico d'Italia (CCII), 247–48
Centrumpartij (CP) (Netherlands), 207
Cesari, Jocelyne, 235, 291
Ceuta, 254, 265, 266, 275, 276, 281–82, 408n26
CFCM. *See* Conseil Français du Culte Musulman
Chacón, Jennifer, 6–7, 15, 134, 322, 336
Charter of Fundamental Rights, in EU Constitution, 107
Chaves, Mark, 57
Chebel d'Appollonia, Ariane, 5, 17–18
Chechnya, 78
Chevènement, Jean-Pierre, 246
Chevènement law (France), 211
Children's Society (Britain), 310
Chiles, Lawton, 134
Chinese Exclusion Act (U.S., 1882), 37, 149
Chinese Exclusion Case (1889), 149
Chirac, Jacques, 36, 283
Chomsky, Noam, 33
Christian Democratic parties, 58
Christian Democratic Union Party (Germany), 36
Christianity: in Europe, 10; political role of, 47; third-world evangelism and, 41; in U.S., 11, 26, 38–43. *See also* Catholicism; fundamentalist Christianity; Protestantism
church-state relations, 49, 54–57, 232–38, 252–53
Chy Lung v. Freeman (1875), 185
Cinalli, Manlio, 7, 21
circular migration, 339
citizenship: in Britain, 210–11; in EU, 212, 216, 323–24; in France, 211; in

Netherlands, 211; non-U.S. citizens and, 198–201; postnational, 201, 216; requirements for, 323–24
civil liberties: in Britain, 114, 324; in France, 324; in Germany, 324; of immigrants/asylum seekers, x; restriction of, 112, 324; in U.S., 120. *See also* freedom; human rights; rights protections
civil society, 32
Clarke, Charles, 118
clash of civilizations, 5, 25, 49, 252, 282, 285
Classic perspective on security, 85–93, 357n32, 358n34
The Closing of the American Mind (Bloom), 39
coalitions of the willing, 82–83, 106
Code of Practice for Eliminating Racial Discrimination (UK), 208
Cold War, 23–25
Cole, David, 158
Coleman, David, 332
Collins, Michael, *The Likes of Us*, 32
Colombia, 258, 274
colonialism, 29–30
Comisión Islamica (Spain), 247
Commission for Racial Equality (UK), 208, 304, 310
Community Action Program (EU, 2001–2006), 217
Comprehensive Immigration Reform Act (S. 2611), 141
Computer Assisted Passenger Screening (CAPS) II system, 86
Comunità Religiosa Islamica d'Italia (COREIS), 248
Congressional Record (U.S.), 153
Conseil Français du Culte Musulman (CFCM), 118, 246, 247, 252, 283, 293–94, 297
consensus democracies, 58–60
Conservative Party (Britain), 303–4
Consiglio Islamico d'Italia, 248–49
Consiglio Italiano Rifugiati (CIR), 312, 314, 317
Constitution. *See* U.S. Constitution
Consulta Islamica (Italy), 247–49, 252
Container Security Initiative, 101
Contract with America (1994), 136
Convention against Torture, United Nations, 171
cordon sanitaire, 212

Cornelius, Wayne, 132, 339
Cosmopolitanism (Appiah), 25
Council for Racial Equality (CRE)
    (Britain), 315, 316
Council of Europe, 102, 325; Committee
    for the Prevention of Torture and Other
    Cruel, Inhuman or Degrading Treatment
    or Punishment, 305
counter-terrorism policies: in Britain,
    113–16; in EU, 18, 95–110, 224,
    341n2; in France, 116–18; immigration
    policy and, 111–29; in U.S., 119–24,
    341n2; U.S. versus European, 9, 13–14,
    96–101, 104–12, 128–29. *See also* war
    on terror
Coutin, Susan Bibler, 170
crime: immigrants and, 27–28, 332–33;
    immigration policy and control of,
    133–43, 146–47, 150–54, 162–63; se-
    curitization and, 133–43
Criminal Alien Deportation Improvements
    Bill (H.R. 668), 136
Cuba, 166
cultural pluralism, 53, 55. *See also* multi-
    culturalism
cultural relativism, 31–32
Czech Republic, 323, 328
Czechoslovakia, 25

Dachan, Mohamed Nour, 248
Day-to-Day Security Law (France, 2001),
    224
de Galembert, Claire, 243
de Gaulle, Charles, 28
de Villiers, Philippe, 283
de Vries, Gijs, 99, 100, 102–3, 109
de Wilde, Jaap, 14
Declaration on Combating Terrorism (EU),
    99–101, 360n23
Dekker, Sybilla, 223
DeLay, Tom, 142
democracy: integration policies and,
    58–60, 60t; majoritarian versus consen-
    sual, 58–60; nationalist versus postna-
    tionalist, 35–36; U.S. messianism and,
    41, 42
Denmark: immigration in, 208; integration
    in, 53, 61, 224; Islam in, 252; Mo-
    hammed caricatures published in,
    33–34, 231, 249, 252; xenophobia in,
    227
deportation, in U.S., 148–49, 151–54,
    375n49

Derrida, Jacques, 29, 30, 73
Detainee Treatment Act (U.S., 2006), 112,
    123, 128
detention: in Britain, 113, 115–16, 305–6;
    in France, 117; in Italy, 305–6; in U.S.,
    121, 139, 156, 158–60, 162, 188
Deutsche Islam Konferenz (DIK), 247,
    249–52
development aid, 99–100
Dewinter, Filip, 35
DIK. *See* Deutsche Islam Konferenz
discrimination: EU response to, 208,
    217–22; in Spain, 278. *See also* rights
    protections
dissident Islam. *See* political Islam
Dohm, Christian Wilhelm von, 233–34
domestic terrorism: "enemy inside" and,
    204, 228, 333–34; London bombings
    and, 104, 204, 223, 322; Madrid bomb-
    ings and, 322; prominence of, 2
Dominican Republic, 274
driver's licenses, 191–93, 196–97
drug trade, 133–35
Dublin Convention, 210, 259, 263, 307
due process, 152
Dutch People's Union (NVU) (Nether-
    lands), 207

Eastern Europe: EU enlargement and, 334;
    immigration to Spain from, 256–58,
    280
economics and economy: in EU, 328–30;
    identity and, 24–25; in Spain, 256, 258,
    258t, 272–74, 280–81; in U.S., 329–30
Economist (newspaper), 124
Ecuador, 258, 274
Egypt, 241, 244
8/2000 Law (Spain, 2000), 270
Eisenach, Eldon, 39
Eisenhower, Dwight, 40
El Salvador, 388n21
Electronic Surveillance Modernization Act,
    123
Elmaghraby, Ehab, 159
Employment Equality Directive (EU,
    2000), 217, 320
end of history, 25
enemy: broadening of, 78–82; identifica-
    tion of, 3, 9, 12, 67–68; immigrants
    viewed as, 80–82; inside, 204, 228,
    333–34
enemy combatants, 121, 123
Enhanced Border Security and Visa Entry

Reform Act (EBSVERA) (U.S., 2002), 154–55

Enseignement des Langues et Cultures d'Origine (ELCO), 244

Erbakan, Necmettin, 241

Errera, Philippe, 104

ethnic profiling. *See* racial/ethnic/national profiling

Euro-Arab Dialogue (EAD), 244

Eurobarometer (EB) surveys, 125, 219–20, 279

EURODAC database, 174

Eurodac Regulation (2002), 306

Eurojust, 103

Europe: anti-Americanism in, 30–31; as a civilization, 36; identity discourse in, 10, 24, 28–37; immigrants' importance to, 325–32; immigration in, 26; left in, 28–35; Muslims in, 229–53, 334, 343n21; old versus new, 83, 356n28; population of, 325–26, 332. *See also* Eastern Europe; European Union; European Union (EU) policy; West

Europe Day, 30

European Agency for the Management of Operational Cooperation at the External Borders of the Member States, 101, 214

European Commission, 217–18, 225, 226, 260, 306, 323, 325, 339

European Commission Communication on Strengthened Practical Cooperation, 173

European Common Asylum System, 174, 176

European Convention on Human Rights (ECHR), 109, 115, 237

European Council, 86, 98, 100, 173, 175, 268

European Court of Human Rights, 305

European Court of Justice, 102, 306

European Employment Strategy (EES), 225

European Judicial Network, 214

European Network against Racism (ENAR), 279

European Parliament, 305, 306, 307, 319

European Refugee Fund, 215

European Security and Defence Policy (ESDP), 107

European Security Strategy (EU), 100

European Social Forum (ESF), 225

European Social Surveys (ESS), 219–20

European Union (EU): Action Program, 225; and asylum, 173–77, 211–15, 212*t*, 228, 265*t*, 306–7, 319–20, 323; Asylum Procedures Directive (2005), 175, 176, 307; and border control, 263–66; citizenship in, 212, 216, 323–24; civil liberties in, 324; Constitution of, 107; Counter-Terrorism Group, 103; economy in, 328–30; Employment Equality Directive (2000), 217, 320; enlargement of, 334; immigration and integration in, 203–28, 212*t*, 274–75; Justice and Home Affairs (JHA) Council, 5, 96, 98, 100, 108, 210, 214, 306; Monitoring Centre on Racism and Xenophobia (EUMC), 219, 226–28; net migration in, 212*t*; Network on Independent Experts on Fundamental Rights, 214; population of, by citizenships, 209*t*; public opinion in, 328, 338; Qualification Directive (2004), 307; Racial Equality Directive (2000), 217, 320; Reception Conditions Directive (2003), 307; response of, to September 11 attacks, 98–99; rightist opposition to, 36; Situation Centre, 103; Temporary Protection Directive (2001), 306; Terrorism Working Group, 103; Turkey and, 35, 36, 45, 47; and U.S., after September 11 attacks, 77. *See also* European Union (EU) policy

European Union (EU) policy: on border control, 7, 8; cooperation limitations concerning counter-terrorism in, 102–4; counter-terrorism, 13–14, 18, 95–110, 224, 341n2; enemy as identified by, 3, 9; on immigration, 17–18, 206–16, 259–61, 405n4; on integration, 224–25, 260–61; U.S. policy compared to, ix–x, 3–6

Europol, 103, 210

EU-U.S. Declaration on Combating Terrorism, 101, 360n18

Evrigenis Report (1985), 209

exceptionalism, American, 24, 38, 40

Exécutif Musulman (Belgium), 247

executive powers, 119, 122–23, 128. *See also* war powers

Extradition and Mutual Legal Assistance Agreement, 101

Fallaci, Oriana, 231; "Rage and Pride," 32

family reunification, 208, 215, 267

Fanon, Franz, 30
fear, and terrorism, 73–74, 78
Federal Bureau of Investigation (FBI): and immigration, 158, 189; and subversive organizations, 119
Federal Emergency Management Agency (FEMA), 155
federalism, immigration and, 183, 197–201
Federation for American Immigration Reform, 133
Federation of Evangelic Churches in Italy (FCEI), 312
Federation of Islamic Organisations in Europe (FIOE), 241
Fetzer, Joel, 62, 235, 237; *Muslims and the State in Britain, France, and Germany*, 57
Finkielkraut, Alain, 284
Fischer, Joschka, 35
Fonds d'Action Sociale, 244
Foner, Philip, 24
Fong Yue Ting v. United States (1893), 148, 149
Ford Report (1990), 209
Foreign Intelligence Surveillance Act (U.S., 1978), 120
Foreign Intelligence Surveillance Court, 124
Foreign Relations Authorization Act (U.S., 1988–89), 135
Foreign Terrorist Tracking Task Force (FTTTF), 158
Fortress Europe, 18, 206, 259
Foucault, Michel, 29, 31
4/2000 Law (Spain, 2000), 269–71
Fourteenth Amendment of U.S. Constitution, 199
Fox, Vicente, 42
framing: of immigration policy as security issue, 162–63; of London bombings, 71–72; of Madrid bombings, 71–72; of September 11 attacks, 6, 70–74, 79, 83, 93, 353n8; of terrorist attacks, 70–73
France: Algerian terrorism in, 245; assimilationists in, 288–91; and asylum, 228; Classics versus Moderns in, 357n32; "closed right" in, 284; counter-terrorism policies of, 13–14, 108–9, 112, 116–18; economy in, 329; identity discourse in, 28–29; immigrant clashes in, 27; and immigrant-terrorist conflation, 82; immigration in, 31, 118, 125–26, 129,

207–9, 211; integration in, 20–21, 53, 61–62, 223, 283–99, 287*t*, 288*t*; and Iraq War, 77, 83; Islam in, 241–44, 246–47, 286–87, 289–99; left in, 32–33; multiculturalists in, 289–91; political issues in, 127*t*; population of, 328; public opinion in, 20–21, 284–99, 327; religion in, 62, 291–94, 292*t*, 294*t*; republicans in, 289–91; riots in, 82, 204, 223, 284; and UN, 94
Frank, Anne, 28
Frankfurt School, 29
freedom: definition of, 12; negative, 38, 345n47; security concerns as overriding, 74, 77, 79; state/local role in enhancing, 197–201. *See also* civil liberties
Freeman, Gary, 132
Friman, H. Richard, 14–15, 336
Fromm, Erich, 29
Front National (France), 129, 207, 283
FRONTEX, 224
Fukuyama, Francis, 25
fundamentalist Christianity, 41
fundamentalist Islam: European criticisms of, 35; and superterrorism, 97. *See also* Islamism

G-5, 124
Gambia, 254, 274
Geddes, Andrew, 217
Generation of 1968, 29–35
Geneva Convention, 307, 318, 323, 413n2
Geneva Conventions, 107, 176
Geneva Refugee Convention, 211
Germany: and asylum, 211, 323; counter-terrorism policies of, 116; identity discourse in, 28–29, 33; immigrant clashes in, 27; immigration in, 31, 207–8; integration in, 53, 54, 224; and Iraq War, 77, 83; Islam in, 241, 247, 249–50; left in, 33; population of, 328; public opinion in, 327; religion and politics in, 49, 62; religion in, 47; and UN, 94
Ghana, 274
Gheddafi, Muammar, 304
Giscard-d'Estaing, Valery, 36
Glazer, Nathan, 38
global insecurity: fear and, 73; internal-external security and, 75–76; policy based on, 71; after September 11 attacks, 68–69
global security. *See* security policy

global terrorism, rhetoric of, 69, 71–72, 78, 90
global war on terror. *See* war on terror
globalization: of insecurity, 75; left and, 33
Gonzales, Alberto, 124, 179
Grande Mosquée de Paris (GMP), 240, 241
Grant, Madison, 37, 39
Grass, Günter, 33
Greece, 328
Greer, Germaine, 31
Griffin, Roger, 36
Grotius Program, 210
Guantanamo Bay detention camp, 123
Guatemala, 388n21
guest worker policies, 339
Guevara, Ernesto "Che," 343n15
Guild, Elspeth, 201, 214
Guiraudon, Virginie, 133

Habermas, Jürgen, 29, 30, 32, 35, 216
Haiti, 166, 177
Hamdan v. Rumsfeld (2006), 123
Hamdi v. Rumsfeld (2004), 123
Hamdi, Yasser Esam, 121, 364n28
Hammar, Tomas, 45, 50, 60, 236
Harding, Warren G., 39
hate crimes, 217
Hayden, Michael, 110
head scarves, 235, 237, 245, 295. *See also* veils
Heathrow bombing plot (2006). *See* airline bombing plot (2006)
Heclo, Hugh, 245
Hegel, G. W. F., 23, 25
Helsinki Agreements (1975), 41
High Level Group on Asylum and Migration (EU), 276
Ho Chi Minh, 343n15
Hochhuth, Rolf, 33
Hollifield, James, 132
Holocaust, 33
Homeland Security Act (HSA) (U.S., 2002), 154–55
Hong Kong, 207
honor killings, 33
Horkheimer, Max, 29
Hostettler, John N., 142
Houellebecq, Michel, 34, 231
Howard, Michael, 97
Howorth, Jolyon, 7, 11, 13
Hughes, Anwen, 171, 177–78
Hughes, Karen, 98

human rights: in Britain, 115; EU security policy and, 323; protection of, 109; U.S. disregard for, 107; U.S. foreign policy and, 41. *See also* civil liberties; rights protections
Human Rights Watch, 177
Huntington, Samuel, 25, 37, 38, 46–47, 49, 285
Hurra, Wir Kapitulieren (Broder), 34
Hussein, Saddam, 83, 166, 245
Huysmans, Jef, 213, 338
hyperterrorism, 70–71, 353n7. *See also* superterrorism

identification documents, 191–93, 196–97
identity: French, 297–99, 298t; Muslim, 297–99, 298t. *See also* identity discourse
Identity and Violence (Sen), 25
identity discourse: Cold War and, 23–24; economics and, 24–25; elite versus popular, 32; in Europe, 10, 24, 28–37; immigration and, 31, 37–38; lack of, 23–25, 28; resurgence of, 25; in U.S., 11, 24, 37–43
Idomeneo (Mozart), 231, 250
IGMG. *See* Islamische Gemeinschaft Milli Görüs
IIRIRA. *See* Illegal Immigration Reform and Immigrant Responsibility Act
"illegal alien," 151
"illegal immigrant," 151
Illegal Immigration Reform and Immigrant Responsibility Act (IIRIRA) (U.S., 1996), 135–37, 143, 152–53, 161, 375n49
Illinois, 200
immigrants: advocacy for, 300–320; attitudes of, 27, 195, 285–99; attitudes toward, 20–21, 125–26, 126t, 212, 219–22, 220t, 221t, 227–28, 267, 277–79, 284–99, 327–28; in Britain, 300–320; classification of, 131, 151, 373n38; criminality among, 27–28, 332–33; defined, 341n1; diversity among, 332–36; as enemies, 80–82; importance of, 325–32; in Italy, 300–320; Latino, 42; Muslim, 343n21; paradoxes of, 331; and politics, 27, 327, 331–32, 336; rights-based protections for, 132–33; second- and third-generation, 204, 208, 223, 225–26, 231, 245–46, 327, 333–34; in Spain, 256–58, 257t
Immigration Act (UK, 1971), 208

Immigration Act (U.S., 1882), 149
Immigration Act (U.S., 1917), 151
Immigration Act (U.S., 1924), 151
Immigration Act (U.S., 1990), 135
Immigration and Asylum Act (Britain, 1999), 211, 303, 316
Immigration and Customs Enforcement (ICE), 139, 140, 144, 156, 159, 161, 379n114
Immigration and Nationality Act (INA) (U.S., 1952), 131, 134, 137, 139, 141, 153, 155, 156
Immigration and Nationality Act (INA) (U.S., 1968), 14, 40
Immigration and Nationality Act (INA) (U.S., 1990), 134–35
Immigration and Nationality Technical Corrections Act (U.S., 1994), 135
Immigration and Naturalization Service (INS), 16, 119, 155, 156, 158–60
Immigration and Refugee Control Act (IRCA) (U.S., 1986), 141
immigration enforcement: crime control through, 150, 157–60; and interior enforcement, 181; police involvement in, 188–90, 194–96; state/local involvement in, 181–202
Immigration Law Practitioners Association, 175, 176
immigration policy, 162–63, 327; and asylum, 173; attitudes toward, 125–26, 126t; in Austria, 207; in Britain, 115, 124, 129, 207–8; challenges of, 26–28; civil versus criminal provisions of, 188, 389n28; counter-terrorism policy and, 13–14; crime control and, 133–43, 146–47, 150–54, 162–63; in Denmark, 113, 208; discussion of, as taboo, 30, 31; drug trade and, 133–35; effects of, 336–37; enforcement of, 150, 157–60, 181–202; in EU, 203–28, 206–16, 259–61, 405n4; exclusions in, 150; exclusive/inclusive measures of, 207–8, 214–16; on family reunification, 208, 215, 267; federal-state relations and, 16–17, 183, 194–201; framing of, 162–63; in France, 118, 124–25, 129, 207–8; in Germany, 207–8; history of, 147–48; identity discourse and, 31, 37–38; integration policies and, 53, 53t, 321–25, 338–39; in Italy, 208, 210; in Netherlands, 113, 207; paradoxes of,

203–4; policy areas involved in, 1, 103–4; in Portugal, 208; public opinion on, 113; racial quotas in, 151; reform of, 338–39; religion and, 44–45; rhetoric versus reality of, 160–63; securitization and, 3, 8, 131–44, 206–16, 227, 334–38; security policy and, 14–15, 17–18, 130–63, 167, 187, 321–25; 337–38; after September 11 attacks, 111–30; sovereignty and, 148–49; in Spain, 19–20, 208, 254–82; state/local enforcement and, 194–97; in Sweden, 208; in Switzerland, 113; typology of, 53t; in UK, 210; unintended consequences of, 5–6; in U.S., 37–43, 119, 121–22, 125, 129, 335–36, 345n51; U.S. Congress and, 147–48; U.S. Constitution and, 147–48; U.S. protests against, 194–95
Immigration Reform and Control Act (IRCA) (U.S., 1986), 181
Immigration Restriction Act (U.S., 1924), 37
Improving Living and Working Conditions (European Commission), 405n4
IMSI catcher, 324, 414n5
INA. *See* Immigration and Nationality Act (INA, 1952)
Independent National Bureau against Racist Discrimination (Netherlands), 208
information gathering, 75–76, 78, 79, 81. *See also* surveillance
INS. *See* Immigration and Naturalization Service
insecurity. *See* global insecurity
integration: in Britain, 301; challenges of, 231–32; comparative analysis of, 50–54; components of, 222; cultural group rights and, 51–53, 56t, 59t, 60t, 64, 65t, 66t; "enemy inside" and, 204, 228; EU and, 203–28, 260–61; failures of, 227, 333–34, 337, 339–40; in France, 20–21, 53, 61–62, 223, 283–99, 287t, 288t; immigration policies and, 53, 53t, 321–25, 338–39; individual rights and, 51; in Italy, 301; levels of, in West, 52t; meaning and evaluation of, 226; of Muslims, 231–38, 242–51; nation-state competency and, 222; policy typology for, 53t; political, 58–60, 60t, 231–32; religion and, 11, 55–56, 56t, 58, 59t,

232–38, 242–44, 252–53; scope of, 223; security policy and, 321–25; after September 11 attacks, 60–63; significance of, 204–5, 227–28; Spanish policy on, 261, 267–72, 280–81; terrorism's impact on policies for, 223–27; tests/requirements on, 324; in U.S., 52, 54, 322; U.S. versus European, 7, 21–22; xenophobia and, 219–22. *See also* assimilation; multiculturalism

Intelligence Reform and Terrorism Prevention Act (U.S., 2004), 121, 154, 192–93

intelligence services: cooperation of, 81, 101, 110; debate over, 83; European, 103; in France, 116; and internal threats, 80; preventive capacity of, 77; privileged role given to, 75–76, 79, 91; U.S. Defense Department and, 109–10. *See also* surveillance

International Institute for Strategic Studies (IISS), 110

international law: on asylum, 171–72; U.S. disregard for, 107

Iqbal, Javaid, 159

Iran, 25, 31, 108, 244

Iraq War, 6, 9, 76–78, 97, 105–7, 353n7

Ireland, 328

Irish Republican Army (IRA), 112–14

Islam: attitudes toward, 227–28; European left and, 30, 34–35; European policies/attitudes toward, 18–19, 34, 229–53, 334; in France, 241–44, 246–47, 286–87, 289–99; Islamists versus, 81; *Leitkultur* and, 36–37; nationalization of, 232–38; official, 238–40, 243, 246–47, 251; political, 239–42, 245–46, 248–49, 251; and political integration, 235–36; reformation/counterreformation of, 26; role of, in everyday life, 292–94, 292t, 294t; social-political beliefs and, 296t; transnationalism of, 236–42; West and, 47, 51, 106–7. *See also* fundamentalist Islam; Muslims

Islam Councils, 232–33

Islamic fascists, 2, 3

Islamic Union of Europe, 241

Islamische Gemeinschaft Milli Görüs (IGMG), 240–41, 250

Islamism: Egypt as center of, 241; Islam versus, 81; threats from, 104. *See also* fundamentalist Islam

Islamization of Western societies, 231, 283

Israel, 30, 244

Italy: and asylum, 301, 303–6, 318; detention in, 305–6; immigration in, 208, 210, 300–320; integration policy in, 53, 61, 301; Islam in, 247–49; and migrants/refugees, 177; population of, 328; pro-immigrant opportunity networks in, 315–18, 317f; pro-immigrant resource networks in, 311–14, 312f, 313f, 314f; and undocumented immigrants, 303–6

Ivaldi, Gilles, 219

Ivory Coast, 274

Jackson, Andrew, 39

Jam'at-I Islami party (Pakistan), 241

Jenkins, Brian, 97

Jesuit Refugee Centre (Britain), 310

JHA Council. *See* Justice and Home Affairs (JHA) Council

jihadist terrorism, 2

John Paul II, Pope, 34

Johnson, Paul, 42

Joint Committee for the Welfare of Immigrants (JCWI) (Britain), 309, 314–15

Joppke, Christian, 132, 133

Jospin, Lionel, 33

Judt, Tony, 4

juges d'instruction, 117

Justice and Home Affairs (JHA) Council (EU), 5, 96, 98, 100, 108, 210, 214, 306

Kagan, Robert, 4, 5

Kalhan, Anil, 7, 16–17, 322

Kekes, John, 40

Kelly, David, 355n21

Keohane, Daniel, 102

Kepel, Gilles, 205, 231

Khomeini, Ruhollah, 244–45, 343n15

Khrushchev, Nikita, 30

Khyam, Omar, 333–34

Kissinger, Henry, 40

Klaus, Vaclav, 36

Know-Nothing Party, 37, 39

Koopmans, Ruud, 50–52, 61, 64

Krasner, Steven, 230

Kuwait, 245

labor migration: in Britain, 124; in EU, 328–30; in Spain, 256, 258, 258t, 272–74, 280–81; in U.S., 328–30, 374n41

Labour Party (Britain), 32, 211, 303–4
Lafontaine, Oskar, 34–35
Latin America: immigration to Spain from, 256–58, 264, 265, 280, 406n12; U.S. evangelicalism and immigrants from, 42
Laufer, Gregory, 172, 174–75
Laurence, Jonathan, 7, 18–19
Law on Daily Security (France, 2001), 118
Law on Employment (Czech Republic, 2004), 323
Law on Foreign Workers (Netherlands, 1976), 208
Law Relative to the Struggle against Terrorism (1986), 117
Le Pen, Jean-Marie, 33
left: colonial guilt of, 29–30; compromise position of, 35; and globalization, 33, 34; icons of, 343n15; integration policies and, 58; and Islam, 30, 34–35; metanarratives rejected by, 29; and multiculturalism, 31–32, 34; political collapse of, 32–33; post–World War II mythology of, 28–29; rightist shift by members of, 35; and third world, 30. See also liberalism
Lega Nord (Italy), 305
legitimacy, 338
Leiken, Robert, 333–34
Leitkultur, 36–37
Lenin, Vladimir, 343n15
Levi-Strauss, Claude, 29
Ley de Extranjería (Alien Act) (Spain, 1985), 262–63
liberalism: collapse of, in U.S., 40–41; ethnocratic, 36; nationalism and, 35; Wilsonian internationalism and, 40. See also left
Libya, 176–77, 304, 411n14
Lijphart, Arend, 58–60
The Likes of Us (Collins), 32
Lindh, John Walker, 22, 121
Lipset, Seymour Martin, 38
Literacy Act (1917), 37
Living Together Apart (Mirza), 32
Livingston, Ken, 35
Locke, John, 233
Loescher, Gil, 211–12
London bombings (2005): domestic terrorism and, 104, 204, 223, 322; framing of, 71–72; response to, 3, 69, 108, 112, 173, 227
Luxembourg, 323

Lyotard, Jean François, 29

Maalouf, Amin, 250
Maastricht Treaty (1991), 206, 213, 216, 259
Madrid bombings (2004): domestic terrorism and, 322; framing of, 71–72; response to, 3, 20, 69, 96, 100, 173, 227, 277–78
mafias, 28
Maghreb region, 244, 264, 283
majoritarian democracies, 58–60
Mali, 274
Manningham-Buller, Eliza, 2
Manuel II, Emperor of Byzantium, 34
Mao Tse-tung, 343n15
Marcuse, Herbert, 24, 29
Markell, Patchen, 234
Martelli law (Italy, 1990), 304
Martin, David, 55, 178
Martin, Philip, 132
Marx, Karl, 24
Mauritania, 254
MB. See Muslim Brotherhood
McCarran-Walter Act (1952), 119
McCollum, William, 136
McConnell, Michael, 234
media: and immigrant-terrorist conflation, 81–82; and Modern perspective on security, 91–92
Melilla, 254, 265, 266, 275, 276, 281–82, 408n26
melting pot, 7, 37–38, 335
The Melting Pot (Zangwill), 37
Merkel, Angela, 250
Meyerstein, Ariel, 175
Middle East: immigrants to Europe from, 331; stability of, 106; terrorism rooted in, 105
migration. See immigration; labor migration
military, security role of, 67, 75, 85, 87–88, 90
military tribunals, 123
Minkenberg, Michael, 5, 10, 11
Mirabeau, Honoré-Gabriel Riqueti, Comte de, 233
Mirza, Murina, Living Together Apart, 32
Mitterand, François, 32–33
Modern perspective on security, 85–93, 357n32

Mohammed, cartoon depictions of, 33–34, 231, 249, 252

Le Monde (newspaper), 108

Moore, Laurence, 39

moral relativism, 34

Morawetz, Nancy, 152

Moreno Fuentes, Francisco Javier, 7, 19–20, 334

Morgenthau, Hans, 87

Morocco: and Ceuta and Melilla, 408n26; French survey with ancestors from, 286; immigration to Spain from, 19, 254, 257, 264–66, 268*t*, 274–79; and Islam, 239, 243, 244; and Western Sahara, 407n26

Moussaoui, Zacarias, 121, 333

Mouvement pour la France (MPF), 283

Mozart, Wolfgang Amadeus, *Idomeneo*, 231, 250

multiculturalism: binary structure of, 31; in Britain, 31, 32, 204, 223, 301; in Europe, 29–36; European left and, 29, 31, 33; in France, 289–91; and legal recognition, 29, 38; liberalism and, 35; opposition to, 32–34, 36, 62–63, 62*f*; relativism and, 31; religion and, 45–63; rightist toleration of, 36; after September 11 attacks, 60–63; in U.S., 38, 40. *See also* cultural pluralism; integration

Multi-Ethnic Britain, 31

Muslim Brotherhood (MB), 240–42, 248

Muslim Council of Britain, 247

Muslim World League (MWL), 239, 244, 248–49

Muslims: attitudes toward, 227–28; diversity among, 291–95, 294*t*, 296*t*, 297; in Europe, 229–53, 334, 343n21; organizations of, 238–42; and secularization, 295, 296*t*, 297; social-political beliefs of, 296*t*; U.S. targeting of, 157–58; in Western Europe, 229–53. *See also* Islam

Muslims and the State in Britain, France, and Germany (Fetzer and Soper), 57

MWL. *See* Muslim World League

Myers, Richard, 98

national security. *See* security policy

National Security Agency (NSA), 123

National Security Entry-Exit Registration System (NSEERS), 158, 190, 376n60

National Strategy for Combating Terrorism (U.S.), 99, 101

nationalism: liberalism and, 35; right and, 36

Nationality, Immigration, and Asylum Act (Britain, 2002), 303

nation-state: Classic conception of, 86–89; integration and, 222; Modern conception of, 89–93; and Muslims, in Western Europe, 229–53

Nationwide Crime Information Center (NCIC), 189–90

Nazism, 28

NCIC. *See* Nationwide Crime Information Center

Nederlandse Volks Unie (Dutch People's Union) (NVU) (Netherlands), 207

negative freedom, 38, 345n47

Negroponte, John, 110

Netherlands: identity discourse in, 28; and immigrant-terrorist conflation, 82; immigration in, 207–8, 211; integration policy in, 53, 54, 61; residency requirements in, 324

network analysis, 308–9

Neuman, Gerald L., 147, 185, 195

New York Times (newspaper), 108, 123

New Zealand: integration policy in, 52, 54, 63; response of, to September 11 attacks, 83

Ngai, Mae, 151

9/11 Commission, 119, 192, 194

9/11 terrorist attacks. *See* September 11, 2001 terrorist attacks

1968 youth uprisings, 29. *See also* Generation of 1968

niqabs, 6

Nixon, Richard, 40

non-U.S. citizens: arrests/detention of, 137, 140, 156, 158–60, 162; attitudes of, toward government officials, 195; citizenship-like activities of, 198–201; deportation/exclusion of, 131, 136, 148–54, 156, 159, 161, 184; driver's licenses for, 191–93, 196–97; federal policies on, 120, 121, 123, 146, 183; identification documents for, 191–93, 196–97; monitoring of, 154–55, 157–58; rights of, 143, 162, 183, 185–86, 200; sanctions against employers of, 181; social services for, 186–87; state/local policies on, 182–83, 185, 197–201

Nora, Pierre, 29

North Africans, Spanish attitudes toward, 277–79, 282. *See also* Morocco: immigration to Spain from

North American Free Trade Agreement (NAFTA), 8, 329, 335

North Atlantic Treaty Organization (NATO), 106

North Rhine–Westphalia, 244

Northern Ireland, 98, 113–14

Nouripour, Omid, 251

Office of Immigration (U.S.), 149

Office of the Inspector General (U.S.), 158

official Islam, 238–40, 243, 246–47, 251

Oklahoma City bombing (1995), 167

Operation Predator, 140

Operation Tarmac, 140

Operation TIPS (Terrorism Information and Prevention System), 157

opportunity structures, 235, 237–38, 308

oppression, European identity discourse and, 31

Orban, Victor, 36

Organization of Petroleum Exporting Countries (OPEC), 244

Orientalism, 30

Oxfam, 309

Padilla, Jose, 121, 365n28

Pakistan, 9

Palmer Raids, 151, 373n34

Partido Popular (PP) (Spain), 269–70, 272

Pasqua laws (France), 211

Pasquarella, Jennie, 168

Passel, Jeffrey, 330

passenger name records (PNRs), 82, 101, 102

PATRIOT Act (U.S., 2001), 16, 91, 107, 120–21, 124, 138–39, 143, 154–56, 168, 322

Patten, Chris, 106–7

Perot, Ross, 41

Phillips, Trevor, 205

Philosophy in the Time of Terror (Derrida and Habermas), 30

Pisanu, Giuseppe, 247–49

plenary power doctrine, 147–48, 184

Poland, 274, 278, 329

police: and immigration enforcement, 188–90, 194–96; security role of, 67, 75–76, 87–88, 91

Police Chiefs Task Force, 103

policy: antecedents of, 3, 5, 8, 93, 321; pro-immigrant groups and, 319–20; types of, 50. *See also* asylum policy; counter-terrorism policies; European Union (EU) policy; immigration policy; security policy; United States policy

Policy Dialogue on Border and Transport Security, 101

political Islam, 239–42, 245–46, 248–49, 251

political opportunity structures, 235, 237–38, 308

Portugal: immigration in, 208; integration policy in, 53, 61–62; population of, 328

Posner, Richard A., 179

post-fascism, 36

postnational citizenship, 201, 216

postnationalism, 229, 236–37

Powell, Enoch, 29

Powell, G. Bingham, 50

preemptive war, 106

Prevention of Terrorism Act (Britain, 1974), 113–14

Prevention of Terrorism Act (Britain, 2005), 115

Prevention of Terrorism Act (Britain, 2006), 115

Prizel, Ilya, 6, 10

Prodi, Romano, 223

pro-immigrant groups, 300–320; network analysis of, 308–9, 318–19; opportunity networks of, 302, 308, 315–18; policy role of, 319–20; resource networks of, 302, 308–15

Proposal for a Council Act Establishing the Convention of Rules for the Admission of Third Country Nationals to the Member States (European Commission), 405n4

Proposition 187 (California), 133, 185, 388n23

Protestantism: integration policy and, 55; U.S. identity and, 38–39, 41

public policy. *See* policy

Putnam, Robert, 23, 40

Al Qaeda, 9, 70–72, 78, 98, 104, 105, 333

Quadrennial Defense Review (U.S.), 106

race: in EU, 208–9; immigration policy and, 151

Race Relations Act (UK, 1976), 208

Racial Equality Directive (EU, 2000), 217, 320

racial/ethnic/national profiling, 157–58, 160, 195

racism: anti-French, 284; in Britain, 305; in EU, 212; in Italy, 305; in Spain, 267, 278–79. *See also* discrimination; xenophobia

"Rage and Pride" (Fallaci), 32

RAPFI survey, 285–99

Raspail, Jean, *The Camp of the Saints*, 29

Reagan, Ronald, 40, 134

REAL ID Act (U.S., 2005), 16, 141, 154–55, 168–71, 177, 192–94, 196–97, 381n25

Redeker, Robert, 231

Refa party (Turkey), 241

refoulement, 171, 413n2

Refugee Convention. *See* United Nations: Convention Relating to the Status of Refugees

Refugee Council (RC) (Britain), 309, 311, 314–15, 316

refugees: defined, 165; source countries for, 165. *See also* asylum

Reid, Richard, 121

Reid, T. R., 4

relativism. *See* cultural relativism; moral relativism

religion: citizenship and, 45; in France, 291–94, 292t; immigration policy and, 44–45; integration policies and, 11, 55–56, 56t, 58, 59t, 232–38, 242–44, 252–53; legacies of, 54–57; multiculturalism and, 45–63; political role of, 45–49, 54–60; and religiosity, 55; and secularization, 45–47, 49, 54–55, 295, 296t, 297. *See also* Catholicism; Christianity; Islam; Protestantism

religiosity, 55

rendition, 102

Republican Party (U.S.), 42, 43, 129

republican perspective, in France, 289–91

Republikaners (Germany), 207

resource mobilization theory, 308

Rice, Condoleezza, 97, 105, 108

Richman, Dan, 196

Ridge, Tom, 159

Rifkin, Jeremy, 4

right: "closed right" in France, 284; in Europe, 35–36; former leftists supporting, 35; nativist sector of, 36; post-fascist, 36;

rise of, 35; in U.S., 42–43

rights protections: in Britain, 324; in France, 324; in Germany, 324; in Spain, 267, 271–72, 281; in U.S., 132–33, 136, 138–39, 185–86, 200, 322–23. *See also* civil liberties; discrimination; human rights

rogue states, 72, 97

Romania, 258, 274

Roosevelt, Franklin Delano, 42

Rosenblum, Nancy, 233

Rousseau, Jean-Jacques, 234

Roy, Olivier, 118, 238, 241

Rumsfeld, Donald, 4, 74, 105

Rushdie, Salman, *The Satanic Verses*, 245

Russia: and Chechens as terrorists, 78; and Iraq War, 77; and UN, 94

Rustow, Dankwart, 25

safe countries, 211

safe third countries, 211

Said, Edward, 30

sanctuary doctrine, 116–17

Saramago, Jose, 33

Sarkozy, Nicolas, 82, 108–9, 118, 204, 293

Sartre, Jean-Paul, 30

Sassen, Saskia, 201

The Satanic Verses (Rushdie), 245

Saudi Arabia, 72, 239, 243–46, 353n10

SAVE (Struggle Against Violent Extremism), 98

Scandinavia, 49

Schain, Martin, 5, 13–14, 62, 324

Schäuble, Wolfgang, 249–51

Schengen Acquis, 213

Schengen Agreement, 17, 86, 206, 210, 259–60, 263, 265, 306

Schengen Information System (SIS II), 213

Schlesinger, Arthur, Jr., 38

Schmidt, Helmut, 35

Schopflin, George, 35

Schuck, Peter, 199

Schussel, Wolfgang, 36

Schwarzenegger, Arnold, 42

Seabald, W. G., 33

second- and third-generation immigrants, 204, 208, 223, 225–26, 231, 245–46, 327, 333–34

Second Security Package (Germany, 2001), 224

secularization, 45–47, 49, 54–55, 295, 296t, 297

Securing America's Borders Bill (S. 2454), 141

securitization: and crime, 133–43; definition of, 14, 131; and drug trade, 133–35; effects of, 137–38, 144; and immigration, 3, 8, 131–44, 206–16, 227, 334–38; internal, 324; opposition to, 143; recent legislative efforts concerning, 140–43; after September 11 attacks, 138–40; and terrorism, 135–39

security, defining, 12

security policy: asylum policy and, 15–16; Classic versus Modern, 85–93; consensus on, 68; effectiveness of, 97–98, 137–38, 140, 144, 155, 171, 204, 222, 324, 337–38; and emergency action, 76–78, 91; "experts" and, 89–90; freedom subordinated to, 74, 77, 79; future orientation of, 71, 73–74; global extent of, 79; immigration policy and, 14–15, 17–18, 130–63, 167, 187, 321–25, 337–38; information gathering and, 75–76; integration policies and, 321–25; internal and external, 67–68, 75–76, 86–93; international collaboration and, 82–84, 95–96, 101, 103; international debates over, 84–86; after September 11 attacks, 68–94, 154–56; unintended consequences of, 337–38; U.S. versus European, 13; war on terror and, 69–73

Segi and others v. The Council of the European Union (2004), 214

Sen, Amartya, *Identity and Violence*, 25

Senegal, 243, 254

Seno-ak, Zafer, 251

Sensenbrenner, James, 140, 142, 143

September 11, 2001 terrorist attacks: asylum policy (U.S.) after, 167–71; Classic security perspective and, 87; effects of, 1, 23; framing of, 6, 70–74, 79, 83, 93, 353n8; and global insecurity, 68–69; integration policies after, 60–63; and "mass destruction," 73–74; policies predating, 3, 5, 8; religion after, 46; response to, 42, 69–74, 76–77, 83, 88, 98–99, 120, 138, 145–46; securitization and, 138–40; security policy after, 154–56; security scenario after, 68–94; symbol of, 352n5

September 11 Commission. *See* 9/11 Commission

Shapiro, Jeremy, 117

Shia Islam, 26

Simpson, Alan, 136–37

SIVE system, 266

Slovenia, 328

Smart Borders program, 86

Smith, Adam, 24, 25

Smith, Lamar, 136, 142

Smith, Lawrence, 134

Smith, Rebecca, 199

Social Action Fund (France), 208

Socialist Party (Spain), 270, 271

Solana, Javier, 100

Sontag, Susan, 24

Soper, J. Christopher, 62, 235, 237; *Muslims and the State in Britain, France, and Germany*, 57

SOS Racismo, 279

Soviet Union, 23, 25, 245

Soysal, Yasemin Nuhoğlu, 216, 236–37

Spain: and asylum, 263, 264*t*; border control in, 262–66, 276, 279–80; counterterrorism policies of, 108; economy in, 256, 258, 258*t*, 272–74, 280–81; immigration challenges for, 274–79; immigration in, 256–58, 257*t*, 266–67; immigration policy in, 19–20, 208, 254–82; integration policy in, 261, 267–72, 280–81; Islam in, 247; Moroccan immigration to, 19, 254, 257, 264–66, 268*t*, 274–79; population of, 273, 328; public opinion in, 327; regularization processes in, 267–71, 268*t*; rights of immigrants in, 271–72, 281; in world migration system, 254–59; xenophobia in, 267, 277–79, 278*t*. *See also* Madrid bombings (2004)

St. Patrick's Day, 40, 345n43

Stalin, Joseph, 343n15

Stalinism, 28, 30

state building, 231

State Security Court (France), 117

Statham, Paul, 51

status offenses, 153

Stoiber, Edmund, 36

Straw, Jack, 6, 114

Sugimori, Amy, 199

Sunni Islam, 26

superterrorism, 97. *See also* hyperterrorism

surveillance: cost of, 81; effects of, 82; expansion of, 67–68, 81, 120, 124, 157, 324; government cooperation in, 78; of internal threats, 80; PATRIOT Act and,

120; private industry of, 79, 89; warrant-less, 123. *See also* information gathering
Suzan, Bénédicte, 117
Sweden: identity discourse in, 28; immigration in, 208; integration policy in, 52, 53, 54, 61; population of, 328; religion and politics in, 49
Switzerland, integration policy in, 52, 53, 61

Taft, Robert, 40
Tamas, Gaspar, 36
Tamir, Yael, 35
TCNs. *See* third country nationals
Terror and Liberalism (Berman), 35
terrorism: conditions fostering, 99–100, 224–25; definition of, 155; etymology of, 352n4; fear and, 73–74, 78; framing of, 70–73; global, 69, 71–72, 78, 90; global insecurity and, 68–69; history of, 70–71, 111; hyperterrorism, 70–71, 353n7; jihadist, 2; military versus criminal perspectives on, 71–72; old versus new, 67, 70, 73, 79, 96–98, 105; responses to recent, 69; superterrorism, 97; war on, 69–73, 83, 97, 106–8. *See also* domestic terrorism; September 11, 2001 terrorist attacks
Terrorism Act (Britain, 2000), 114
terrorist organizations, 136, 155–56, 168, 172, 367n21
Thatcher, Margaret, 32
The Hague Programme, 86, 100, 103, 109, 174–76, 226, 307
third country nationals (TCNs), 212, 214–16, 218, 323
third world: EU and, after September 11 attacks, 98–99; European left and, 30; U.S. evangelism and, 41
Tiberj, Vincent, 7, 20–21
Toffler, Alvin, 79, 355n24
Toffler, Heidi, 79
transnational progressivism, 31–32
transversal threats, 90–91
Treaty of Amsterdam (1999), 206, 213, 217, 259–60, 306
Treaty of Nice (2001), 213
Triandafyllidou, Anna, 219
Tunisia, 264, 286
Turco-Napolitano law (Italy, 1998), 304
Turkey: and EU membership, 35, 36, 45,

47; immigration to France from, 286; and Islam, 239–41, 243–45

Ummah phenomenon, 246
undocumented immigrants: in Britain, 303–6; in Italy, 303–6; in Spain, 267–71, 273, 280–81, 300–301; "weak" immigration status of, 300–301
unemployment, 223–24, 328–30
UNHCR. *See* United Nations: High Commissioner for Refugees
unilateralism, 83, 106
Union des Organisations Islamiques de France (UOIF), 241–42, 291, 294
Union of Islamic Organizations of France, 242
Unione delle Comunità ed Organizzazioni Islamiche in Italia (UCOII), 248–49
United Jewish Federation, 22
United Kingdom: counter-terrorism policies of, 102, 108–9; and immigrant-terrorist conflation, 82; immigration in, 210; integration policy in, 61; and Iraq War, 77; Northern Ireland policy of, 98; public opinion in, 327; response of, to September 11 attacks, 76–77, 83; and UN, 94. *See also* Britain
United Nations: Comprehensive Convention against Terrorism, 99; Convention against Torture, 171; Convention Relating to the Status of Refugees, 171, 172, 175, 304; Counter-Terrorism Committee, 99; EU cooperation with, 99; High Commissioner for Refugees (UNHCR), 172, 175, 178, 305, 307; Protocol Relating to the Status of Refugees, 380n1; Refugee Convention, 165; Special Rapporteur for the Human Rights of Migrants, 305; U.S.-led conflict in, 94
United States: and border control, ix–x, 7, 85–86, 335; economy in, 329–30; European identity in opposition to, 30–31; exceptionalism in, 24, 38, 40; identity discourse in, 11, 24, 37–43; immigrants' importance to, 325–32; immigration in, 37–43, 121–22, 125–26, 129, 345n51; nativist populism in, 39–41; political issues in, 128t; population of, 326–27, 332; populist messianism in, 41–43; post–September 11 role of, 82–83, 94; public opinion in, 328–29, 338; re-

sponse of, to September 11 attacks, 42,
    69–74, 76–77, 83, 88, 120, 138, 145–46;
    and UN, 94; unilateralism of, 83, 106;
    Wilsonian internationalism in, 40–41. *See
    also* United States policy; West
United States policy: on border control,
    ix–x, 7, 8; counter-terrorism, 13–14,
    96–101, 104–10, 112, 119–24, 128–29,
    341n2; enemy as identified by, 3, 9; EU
    policy compared to, ix–x, 3–6; federal-
    state relations and, 16–17; on immigra-
    tion, 119, 335–36; on integration, 52,
    54, 322; after September 11 attacks,
    68–94
UOIF. *See* Union des Organisations Is-
    lamiques de France
urban policy, 209
URBAN program (EU), 209
U.S. Border Patrol, 151
U.S. Congress: and driver's licenses,
    191–92; and immigration policy,
    147–48, 184, 186–90
U.S. Constitution: and citizenship, 199;
    and immigration, 147–48, 184–85
U.S. Defense Department, 109–10
U.S. Homeland Security Department: ad-
    ministrative role of, 146, 155; and asy-
    lum, 169, 172; and criminal aliens, 139;
    detentions by, 162; immigration enforce-
    ment/oversight by, 15, 155, 167; INS
    and, 16
U.S. Justice Department, 143, 157–58,
    160, 188–89
U.S. Supreme Court, 123, 148, 149, 152,
    154, 184–85
U.S. Visitor and Immigration Status Indi-
    cation Technology System (US VISIT),
    155
USA PATRIOT Act (2001). *See* PATRIOT
    Act (U.S., 2001)

Van Gogh, Theo, 10, 35, 82, 231
Védrine, Hubert, 97
veils, 6. *See also* head scarves
Visegrad Group, 212
Vlaams Blok, 35
voluntary departure, 162, 379n108

Wæver, Ole, 14
Wallenberg, Raoul, 28
Walser, Martin, 33
Walt, Stephen, 87
war on terror, 69–73, 83, 97, 106–8. *See
    also* counter-terrorism policies
war powers, 112. *See also* executive powers
Warner, Carolyn, 236
Washington Post (newspaper), 140
weak immigrants, 300–320; Britain-Italy
    comparison on, 303–7; defined,
    300–301; opportunity networks of, 302,
    308, 315–18; political issues concerning,
    318–20; resource networks of, 302,
    308–15
weapons of mass destruction (WMD): in
    Iraq, 83, 106, 353n7, 355n21; terrorism
    and, 74, 97, 106, 353n7, 355n21
Weil, Patrick, 261
Wenner, Manfred, 236
West: cultural group rights in, 65t, 66t; in-
    tegration policies in, 50–54; Islam and,
    47, 51, 106–7; religion in, 48t. *See also*
    Europe; United States
Western Europe. *See* Europe
Western Sahara, 254, 275, 407n26
Wong Wing v. United States (1896), 149
Woodward, Bob, 104
Woon, Long Litt, 235
World Trade Center bombing (1993), 119,
    167

xenophobia: in EU, 212, 219–22, 220t,
    221t, 227–28, 327; security policy and,
    322; in Spain, 267, 277–79. *See also* dis-
    crimination; racism
Xhavara and others v. Albania and Italy
    (2001), 214

Yasui, Luna, 199
Yugoslavia, 25

Zangwill, Israel, *The Melting Pot*, 37
Zapatero, José Luis Rodríguez, 81
Zaring, David, 179
Zolberg, Aristide, 235